WITHDRAWN

HD
8073   Mandel   66-3940
G6   Samuel Gompers
M2

JUl   2000
Date Due

JUN	2004	
MAR 7 '68		
MAR 25 '68		
APR 8 '68		
DEC 16 '68	JUN 09 ANS'D	
MAR 10		
	JUL X X 2015	

SAMUEL GOMPERS

By the same author

LABOR, FREE AND SLAVE:
WORKINGMEN AND THE ANTI-SLAVERY MOVEMENT
IN THE UNITED STATES

(1955)

Samuel Gompers

A BIOGRAPHY

by

BERNARD MANDEL

with an introduction
Samuel Gompers: Labor Statesman or Labor Faker?
By LOUIS FILLER

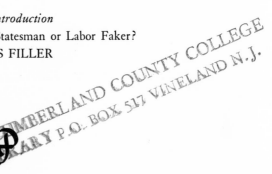

THE ANTIOCH PRESS   •   1963

First Printing December 1963

Second Printing February 1965

Printed in the United States of America
by The Antioch Press, Yellow Springs, Ohio

For

ANITA AND CARLA

CONTENTS

ILLUSTRATIONS

(following page 248)

Sara and Solomon Gompers.
Gompers in the New York A.F. of L. office.
Gompers in the 1880's.
Gompers in 1891.
A labor picnic.
Gompers in 1903.
Sophia Julian Gompers.
The principals in the Buck's Stove and Range case.
The A. F. of L. delegation to the peace conference.
Gompers with La Follette.
Gompers with President Calles of Mexico.
Gompers' favorite cartoon.

ACKNOWLEDGMENTS

The acknowledgment of my debt to those who helped make this work possible is not a mere formality but a sincere pleasure, tempered only by the realization that a few lines of print are entirely inadequate to express my gratitude.

I am indebted to Miss Florence Thorne, former research director of the American Federation of Labor, and Mr. Boris Schishkin, present research director, for permission to use the A.F. of L. archives, which was given without restriction. Mr. Mario Azpeitia, president of the Cigarmakers International Union, also generously gave me access to his office's files of the *Cigar Makers Official Journal*.

Mrs. Eloise Giles, the librarian of the A.F. of L., was unfailingly patient and co-operative with my rummaging through her carefully compiled collection of books, journals, documents, and files. I also received the skillful and willing assistance of the staffs of the Library of Congress, the United States Department of Labor library, the New York and Cleveland public libraries, the libraries of Western Reserve University and Fenn College, the Catholic University of America, which furnished microfilm copies of the Gompers-Powderly correspondence from its archives, and the State Historical Society of Wisconsin, which supplied microfilm copies of the *New York Progress*.

The following people gave liberally of their time to give me their recollections of Mr. Gompers' activities and character: Miss Thorne, Mrs. Giles, Miss Martha Ford, Mr. John Frey, and Mrs. Florence Gompers MacKay, who also gave me access to the documents, clippings, and photographs in her possession.

I wish to record my indebtedness to the many scholars on whose pioneering work I have relied to supplement my own research. Reference to their work in the footnotes of this book is but slight testimonial to their contributions to man's knowledge of man. Of course, none of the people mentioned here is in any way responsible for my interpretations and conclusions or for the defects of this work.

I am obligated to Mrs. Lucy Robins Lang for permission to quote from her book, *Tomorrow is Beautiful* (N.Y., The Macmillan Co., 1955), and to the publishers of the following books for permission to quote from them: Samuel Gompers, *Debate at Carnegie Hall with Henry J. Allen* (1920), *Labor and the Common Welfare* (1919), *Labor and the Employer* (1920), *Out of Their Own Mouths* with William

Walling (1920), and *Seventy Years of Life and Labor* (1925), all by E. P. Dutton and Co., N.Y.; Selig Perlman and Philip Taft, *Labor Movements,* vol. IV of *History of Labour in the United States* by John R. Commons and Associates (N.Y., The Macmillan Co., 1935); Louis Wehle, *Hidden Threads of History* (N.Y., The Macmillan Co., 1953); Benjamin Stolberg, "What Manner of Man was Samuel Gompers," *The Atlantic Monthly,* March 1925; Robert K. Murray, *Red Scare* (Minneapolis, The University of Minnesota Press, 1955); Kenneth Campbell MacKay, *The Progressive Movement of 1924,* vol. 527 of *Columbia University Studies in History, Economics and Public Law* (N.Y., Columbia University Press, 1947); Eric E. Goldman, *Rendezvous with Destiny* (N.Y., Alfred A. Knopf, 1952); Saul Alinsky, *John L. Lewis* (N.Y., G. P. Putnam's Sons, 1949); Louis Adamic, *Dynamite* (N.Y., The Viking Press, 1931); Charles A. Madison, *American Labor Leaders* (N.Y., Harper and Brothers, 1950); Walter Gordon Merritt, *Destination Unknown* (N.Y., Prentice-Hall, Inc., 1951); William D. Haywood, *Bill Haywood's Book* (1929), and William Z. Foster, *From Bryan to Stalin* (1937), both by International Publishers, N.Y.

I am indebted to the many trade union members and officials who helped make possible the publication of this book, and especially Sam Pollock, president of the Meat Cutters Local Union 427 of Cleveland, Ohio. They placed no conditions of any kind on the treatment of the subject, confident that an objective and critical study would be the soundest contribution to the understanding of the labor movement. It is hoped that their farsighted and enlightened encouragement of historical research and writing will become more widespread in the American labor organizations. I also wish to acknowledge the invaluable help of Dr. Louis Filler of Antioch College, who read the entire manuscript and made many thoughtful and helpful suggestions which have improved both the incisiveness and clarity of the book, and of Janet Hanson, who gave so much help with the preparation of the book for publication.

SAMUEL GOMPERS: LABOR STATESMAN OR LABOR FAKER?

Introduction by LOUIS FILLER

THERE WAS A TIME WHEN LABOR WAS NOT MERELY an interest, but a cause. This was true as late as the 1930's, when union partisans made appeals to neighbors and socially conscious sympathizers for aid and support, while they fought bitter battles for union recognition and higher living and working standards. Labor was then not merely labor; it claimed to speak with the voice of Humanity. Strikers at mass-meetings bared their wounds and wants to middle-class audiences, and it was indeed the cynic and egotist who withheld his suffrage, and perhaps his funds, from the embattled martyrs.

Under such conditions, Samuel Gompers in his life-time was a figure of storm and controversy. To upholders of unregulated free enterprise, of the open shop, of unbridled competition, he symbolized curbs on what they grimly saw as the American way —curbs which could only lead to socialism. Indeed, Gompers was, in his youth, all but socialistic in his viewpoint, and though he rapidly moved away from the doctrinaire position until he fiercely opposed it, in the process of change he built a labor organization which was more and more formidable to those who continued to dream of being unchallenged masters in their industrial strongholds. For the most part, and especially in the mass industries, the devout defenders of undiluted capitalism dreamed of quashing once and for all the hopes of labor leaders for acquiring bargaining powers and the hopes of workers for receiving mounting returns for their services.

Among laborers and labor sympathizers, Gompers' reputation varied. Some saw him as the very incarnation of unionism:

saw him as having given dignity and coherence to its irregular components—saw him as having led incomparably its massive drives for the eight-hour day, against the dreaded labor injunction, against government intervention in labor-capital duels on the side of capital. "Conservative" labor certainly saw Gompers in that light. Among many articulate reformers, humanitarians, and radicals, Gompers' reputation was less flattering. They deplored his unwillingness to project long-range social programs, his lack of sympathy for cooperative ideals. Although he voiced and recorded numerous idealistic sentiments, these seemed a species of hypocrisy to critics who noted his firm endorsement of routine labor functionaries—even racketeers—at the expense of ardent organizers, self-sacrificing fighters for the rights of unemployed workers, Chinese workers, Negro workers, and others whose sufferings under industrial exploitation were compounded by their race or other special conditions. Gompers' notorious dictum— that labor had no ultimate goals, except to get more and more of what it had—seemed a model of crassness, of expediency, and of asocial thinking.

A special word needs to be said about Gompers' services to the United States during World War I, because this momentous crisis—from which all our modern problems and attitudes stem— has been persistently avoided by students and theoreticians who presume to tell us who we are and what we ought to think. In the 1920's, there was no problem in coping with World War I. The famous "disillusionment" of the time sank national reputations, sometimes without trace. Newton D. Baker, George Creel, James T. Shotwell—who were they? Students do not always recognize the name of "Black Jack" Pershing, certainly with warmth and affection. The 1930's continued the tradition of scorn and contempt for the Great War as a capitalistic monstrosity. Yet Gompers had believed that his wholehearted effort to hold labor in line for the war effort—abroad, as well as at home, and his ruthless proscription of pacifist labor and anti-capitalist militants, was the crowning triumph of his career. For this, he was not so much remembered by radicals and anti-militarists as he was forgotten. Their main target of criticism continued to be his presumed failures as a labor leader who should have dedicated his abilities to the welfare of all the workers, whether in or out of the American Federation of Labor, whether employed or unemployed, whether organized or unorganized.

Time has passed since the smashing of the great Homestead Strike of 1892, since the pitiful events of Ludlow, Colorado, in 1914, since the cruel failure of the Steel Strike of 1919. The legions of free enterprise found labor irresistible in the 1930's. Against it they vainly raised strikebreakers and company-armed hoodlums, invoked lockouts and evictions, marshalled police and state militia. The economic crisis had simply left the hungry and deprived masses too little to fall back upon, too little to quarrel among themselves about, to permit them to tolerate anything less than an ever-mounting, self-sacrificing, and extraordinary drive toward labor organization. The creation of the C.I.O. and of mass unions in steel, rubber, automobiles, and other giant industries transformed the labor picture. It was completed by World War II which demanded good labor relations on almost any terms, and which ended—thanks to Cold War economics—in nothing less than a social and industrial revolution. With government contracts sparking industrial production, Big Business was now all but matched by Big Labor, which was, much more than after World War I, able to consolidate its war-time gains.

This new labor was formidable to behold. It spawned a race of business agents, union officials, labor lawyers, research experts, and others quick to organize their unions' government, court, and public relations and to further their status and bargaining power. They found it relatively easy to keep their rank and file workers either satisfied or quiescent. Their unions maintained treasuries which would have seemed to labor leaders of the pre-War period out of the dreams of Scheherazade and the Thousand and One Nights. Splendid buildings rose to house labor's elite. Presumably, the rank and file took pride in the affluence of their chiefs; presumably they shared in it. One local branch of a great industrial union was said to have the largest bar in the world.

Some who recalled labor in its heroic decades found much of the above deplorable. Arrogant labor, corrupt labor, labor first concerned for its own security and only secondly for national and social purposes seemed to them a comedown from High Sierras of democratic union achievement. A rank and file largely concerned for pinball machines, bowling, or simple TV did not seem calculated to attract admiration or sympathy. One point was absolutely certain: that such labor had no call whatever to criticize anything Sam Gompers had or had not done, at any time of his life.

The problem, indeed, has not been first to determine whether in fact Gompers had been a labor statesman or a labor betrayer, but *what the uses of Gompers are or can be for us today*. Gompers is not alone in this position. It is startling to realize how little actual light, inspiration, authority, support we are able to derive from figures who once seemed hewn for the ages but whose names are scarcely any longer raised except for trifling or sentimental purposes. Eugene V. Debs, Big Bill Haywood, Henry George, Robert M. La Follette, "Golden Rule" Sam Jones, Lincoln Steffens, Ben Lindsey, Randolph Bourne, E. A. Filene—how do these worthies serve us today? Clarence Darrow has been recalled, by way of the drama, *Inherit the Wind*, as a fighter for free speech. But free speech for what? If we have no social program, it can hardly matter whether we may raise our voices or not. Libertarians without a cause are little more than libertines, in too many cases without even any interesting vices.

And so it has been with Gompers. In a real sense, his record has been lost. He has been seen too often as a group of labor policies, rather than as a man. Worse, it has often been unrealized that Gompers was neither a pillar of principle nor a weathercock. He was a development. Moreover, he developed amid the changing social circumstances and conflicting social philosophies of the entire post-Civil War era, and into the Twentieth Century. It is not possible to assay adequately his role at any period of his career without showing awareness of these attendant factors, without weighing them into the equation.

This Dr. Bernard Mandel has now done. Out of his years of study, in labor as part of the larger American scene, as well as specifically in the detailed records of Gompers and of the American Federation of Labor, he has produced a work which strives powerfully and successfully to present the unadulterated saga of the man who more than anyone else created and molded and became the symbol of the A.F.L. and who lived to see it as inextricably a part of American life as the Presidency of the United States, its Congress and its courts.

In itself, this achievement of Gompers' is so impressive that it merits careful understanding. But, in addition, most of us today realize that labor is under severe public scrutiny, and that ways and means need be found to formulate a useful and accurate measure of its proper role in our affairs. It does not suffice to unearth scoundrels and opportunists among its personnel. Labor hacks and apologists are quick to point to faults and failures among businessmen, and even though the pot calling the kettle black doesn't answer everything, it does take some of the heat off the pot. Moreover, official labor claims to have a social conscience. It popularizes the high cost of living, the need of workers for more money, as for that golden star of our latter-day democracy: higher education for everybody's children. It appeals for Medicare.

Yet public doubts persist, and hurt labor. Unions no longer need the tears and financial assistance of the general public, but can they do without its endorsement? In a large measure, the public has been effectively separated from labor-capital quarrels. The details of their differences are too technical to be commonly handled or appreciated. Questions of shop administration, of seniority rights, of tasks proper to particular labor personnel— who can answer them? How often during a day's work ought a worker to visit the water-cooler, or the restroom? Such matters are matters of experience, of arbitration and conciliation. The public cannot begin to try to judge among them. Thus, the problem has not become whether or not labor was more, or less, right in a particular industrial hassle. The problem has become that there is no genuine rapport between labor and the public, any more, and that the greatest sufferer from this situation has been the public weal. Laborers may be no more responsible for this situation than middle-class elements and the managerial elite, but they are no less responsible for it.

Hence, for all their war-chests and firm status in law, the unions have dwindled in strength, rather than grown. This was the reason for the historic alliance of the A.F.L.-C.I.O. in 1955.

Here was no spontaneous movement for labor unity. It was an effort to consolidate such power as Big Labor still possessed. Big Labor has lost much of its credit with the general public; and no wonder. It has shown no courage whatever in implementing the integration drive in the unions; Negroes must continue their ancient struggle for augmented economic opportunities all but alone. The migrant workers, a sensitive sore not only in American labor, but in American life and ethics and social morale, have been all but ignored by the generalissimos of labor. And so with other needy elements of American society, whose troubles help to compound our social evils and our decay.

The worst failure of all in American labor has been its failure in education. Some sixty million copies of labor newspapers a year are all but unread for lack of impact and penetrating analysis. A few showcase unions conduct intelligent programs of profitable intellectual diversion. A few workers acquire free vacations to attend "institutes" where they can hear a few lectures presumably relevant to labor, or take some more practical work in accounting, labor costs, or whatever. All the unions activate themselves at election time to help elect allegedly pro-labor candidates. The rest is silence. Labor theoreticians shrug their shoulders. What can you do? The rank and file doesn't want education. Perhaps they don't. But all the unions now carry on their payrolls a percentage of intellectuals: college-graduated, and supposedly with labor's cause at heart. What have they to offer society? What interests them? Two years ago, the California State Federation of Teachers, A.F.L.-C.I.O., more or less sponsored an *intellectual* magazine intended to serve national purposes: to offer varied views and information on such subjects as automation, labor goals and experiences, the roles of white-collar and blue-collar personnel in American society, and so on, and so on—there are serious problems in our world which need to be clarified, aren't there? The first issue of the publication included articles by sociologists, economists, culture-bearers, and others, including then-Secretary of Labor Arthur J. Goldberg. The annual subscription was roughly the cost of a bottle of moderately-priced rum. Copies were sent freely to union leaders and headquarters throughout the country for comment and endorsement. So little response was there to all this that no second issue of the magazine was forth-coming.

What *do* the labor-stipendiaries want? Roughly, what Samuel Gompers was so sharply criticized for having demanded: more and more of whatever it is they now enjoy in the way of emolu-ments, gains, bonanzas, benefits. The difficulty with such a pro-gram is that everybody wants the same, and why should people not connected with labor be concerned for *its* wants? Is it con-cerned for theirs? So egocentricity defeats itself. In labor's hours of need, it will be alone.

It is alone already, and in parts as well as altogether. For labor leaders who in the 1930's had been able to muster the courage and energy to defy company agents who sported brass knuckles and revolvers find it hard today to make public declarations against sluggish union policies and corrupt union manipulators. In what are often plush offices with trim secretaries—much like those of the businessmen they often bitterly satirized in their youth—they must persuade themselves that they are holding the fort and doing essen-tially a good work in uninspiring times. As for the ordinary union members, they can drift along with the job, drawing their intel-lectual sustenance from the comic pages. But the day of wrath comes often in our uneasy and automating society. And to whom can an unemployed ex-assemblyline man turn for sympathy who has until last week acted as though the universe has promised him a job and security, expecting nothing from him in return: neither social understanding nor civic responsibility? They drift about the towns looking for work, these formerly well-employed characters, sometimes in very good cars indeed, well filled-out with TV snacks and party delicacies, wondering why the layoff had to happen to them, where another job is to be found—especially one which pays off the way the last one did—and where friends can be found who can talk about something other than baseball. And what is to happen to their unpaid-up homes and accessories?

Samuel Gompers led the A.F.L. at a time when great masses of the workers were in the direst need, and when numerous radicals and reformers dared to dream of millennial times for all mankind. Two of the worst wars and a number of the most terrible tyrannies in history have made us more modest in our expectations. But take a random sample among the shallow and careless-minded citizenry, and discover how many of them are under the impression that times have never been better. The great tensions of international competition have created types of welfare state which have set floors under many of our former problems. Social security and public services may not teach us how to live, but they take care of many aids to living and expeditious dying which formerly required friends, relatives, thrift, and a social conscience. Some of us undoubtedly imagine that times have changed so markedly that Gompers can no longer be considered relevant to our own urgent problems.

When we entertain such fancies, we badly deceive ourselves. We couldn't be more wrong. We have never needed greater instruction in the lessons of the earlier time. *Has* the fact of international danger modified the importance of our domestic problems? If anything, it has magnified their importance. Once, when we were more or less separated from the world, we could struggle along in disunited arrays and let the passage of time give a semblance of order to our affairs. But now? Lack of rapport, lack of direction, lack of intelligent and resourceful build-ups of social groups—all this means that for our multiplying crises we must scrape together hasty and too often specious official policies to try somehow to deal with our situations everywhere in the world.

And *are* the domestic problems which are at the heart of our disunity and ineptness—*are* they so different from what they have been? Is there no poverty in America? We talk proudly of our high "median" income per family, forgetting not only the forty millions of Americans who live in patent squalor, but the fact that much of the allegedly high income comes from the fact that both of the family pillars are working, at nothing but the expense of a stable family situation. A by-product of this is unstable children and a loose societal pattern. In 1906, Upton Sinclair published *The Jungle*, a novel about Chicago. Is it far-fetched to call it a jungle today? Who would care to trust himself to its streets at night, off the main stems?

And the unions—what is their role in this crisis of society? Sometimes they offer helpful plans and services to their members, but so do Rotary and the Lions and other fraternal organizations. The truth is that there was more real activity, group loyalty, and effort intended to teach workers how to cope with their circumstances in Gompers' time than there is today. Then, workers were alert and alive because they had to be to live. They produced realists and idealists who struggled for the suffrage of the rank and file. One way or another, they kept abreast of their predicaments, as individuals and as a class.

I don't for a moment suggest those were the good old days. People have to live within their own times. We must. My point is that we have not been doing a good job at it. We have been drifting; and in a world in which most people are desperately poor—and that is the kind of world we are in—there is only one direction in which we can drift.

Samuel Gompers prided himself on being a realist, and to some extent the labor world we inhabit is molded in his image. He thought the socialists dreamers and fools, but now half the world at least claims to follow socialist principles, and our own welfare state is not wholly disassociated from them. Nobody wants to go back to a time when workers had to appeal to their better-to-do neighbors for nickles and pennies to enable them to carry on heartbreaking strikes. But power creates responsibilities. Unions and unionists have the same duties as other institutions and social groups: to pull their own freight, to contribute to making this a more promising society. This means reading, thinking, and pondering how to improve the institutions with which they are connected.

I take it, then, that there is no simple answer to the question which opened this introduction. Was Gompers a labor statesman or a labor faker? Who is presently in position to say? If one is content with the labor picture, thinks "things are pretty good," and likes to think in a vague way that they will get better, I suppose he will be willing to concede that Gompers was all right, though I doubt that this frame of mind, if one can call it that, would make it urgently necessary to him to look into the details of the question. If one is an idealist who believes that a crusade for universal peace and prosperity must succeed by the end of this year, I imagine he might find himself indignant with Gompers on a number of scores.

But if one is simply a person who is aware of his own falli-
bilities and willing to try to improve, and who has learned some
tolerance of others' human nature, he might prefer to reserve
judgment on Gompers as a whole, and even Gompers in particular
details. He might conclude that this is a time for learning rather
than for peremptory judgment. Gompers lived a long and significant life. The problems with which he boldly dealt were central
to the hopes and necessities of most Americans. If at this late date
we cannot cope with Gompers, we will not be able to cope with
the strange and double-edged dilemmas which push us about
today, and will wait for us tomorrow.

Antioch College

"...I deem that a general diffusion of knowledge of the past struggles of Labor will prove one of the most powerful incentives to stronger efforts in the future to realise [sic] a condition of affairs under which the toilers will no longer be treated with less consideration than beasts of burden."

SAMUEL GOMPERS, in 1889

Part I

THE EVOLUTION OF A TRADE UNIONIST
1850-1886

Chapter One

YOUTH

1. LONDON CHILDHOOD

East of Bishopgate Street and north of the Thames River is a section of London known as Spitalfields. By the middle of the nineteenth century the fields of the ancient priory of St. Mary Spital were wholly covered over with brick and stone, and outside of Victoria Park a tree, a blade of grass, or a flower could scarcely be found. This was the manufacturing center of London, and particularly of the silk industry. In its squalid tenements swarmed the working classes of the great metropolis.

Some five hundred miles of narrow streets cut through the district, and no other place in the world could compare with it for "the unparalleled magnitude of its meanness and monotony." The roads were paved with cobblestones. From the narrow sidewalks rose row after row of dark brick buildings, two to four stories high, flush against each other, making a honeycomb of long enclosed compartments into which little sunlight penetrated through the pall of factory smoke that floated above them. Before day broke over the city, the lanes of Spitalfields became alive with an amazing tumult of people going to work, pushcart dealers with their incessant cries of "Buy, buy, buy," beggars, gamblers, and loafers cluttering the walks, and the unintermitting clatter of carriages, carts, and wagons.[1]

It was in a small apartment in one of these rows of shabby tenements that Samuel Gompers was born on January 27, 1850, the oldest son of Solomon Gompers and Sara Rood. His paternal ancestors, originally Austrian, had long lived in Amsterdam. Although Gompers in later years spoke with pride of his working-class antecedents, it is not likely that membership in the laboring class went back any farther than his own father. His grandfather was a successful businessman, and others among his forebears had been mathematicians, poets, inventors, financiers, composers, philologists, doctors, Biblical commentators, and Talmudic schol-ars.[2] His maternal grandfather was also a well-to-do merchant, descended from a Franco-Dutch union originating with a soldier in Napoleon's army of occupation.

But there is no doubt about the poverty of the London Gompers. Solomon emigrated with his parents in 1844, when he was sixteen years old. Shortly afterward, Solomon's father, who often traveled between London and Amsterdam on business, brought Sara Rood to his home to live, and in about two years she and Solomon married. After Samuel's birth, his parents moved to a three-story brick house at Number 2 Fort Street. They occupied the ground floor, and Solomon's parents lived on the second floor with their other five children. Across the street was a silk factory, and many of the neighbors were silk workers, descendants of French Huguenots. With the invention of machinery, many of them were unemployed, and one of Samuel's early and unfading images was of strong men unable to feed their families, roaming the streets, and struggling against despair.

The young and growing family—there were five children be-fore they left England—occupied an apartment of two rooms. The large front room was a combination sitting room, dining room, kitchen, and bathroom, and the smaller chamber in back was used for storage. But in the summer a little more room and pri-vacy were obtained by having the children sleep in the storage room in bunks built by their father. The front room was periodic-ally converted into a bathroom by the simple device of bringing in a wash tub and filling it with water carried in from a large barrel in the back yard.

The apartment bore the imprint of the Dutch traditions brought over by Mother Gompers. The large fireplace was equipped with a Dutch oven where, with her squat cooking utensils and colorful dishes, she prepared her Dutch-style meals. The children learned a smattering of Dutch from their parents. The floor was covered with sand, and the room was dimly lighted by a rush light or candles, except on Jewish holidays and other festive occasions when the paraffin lamp was pressed into service.

Samuel's boyhood was not unlike that of any other boy of the slums. His playground was on the streets of the neighborhood and in the ruins of a medieval hospital nearby, with an occasional visit to Victoria Park on holidays. His life-long love of music and the theater was developed in these early years by infrequent trips to the concert halls with his grandfather or to the theater with his friends. They sometimes managed to scrape together a few coins for the theater by begging on the streets on Guy Fawkes' Day.

At the age of six, when most of his playmates were being put to work picking and quilling silk, Samuel was sent to the Jewish free school in Bell's Lane near his home. Here, with some 500 other youngsters, mostly from the nearby ghetto, he learned the three R's, geography, and history. He stood third highest in his class, but had to leave after four years to go to work. However, he continued his studies in the free night school, being introduced to the Talmud, Hebrew, French, and music. He was apprenticed to a shoemaker at three pence a week, but he worked only eight weeks, deciding he did not want to continue because of the noise in the shop. Consequently his father offered him the opportunity to learn his own trade, cigarmaking, and he was apprenticed to a cigarmaker on Bishopsgate Street at one shilling a week, to be doubled at the end of one year. The chance to talk to his shopmates while at work was congenial to the boy. However, he disliked the practice of being searched for hidden cigars each night as he left the shop, and his sensitive nature smarted from the indignity.*

One of the chief topics of discussion in the cigarmaker's shop was the American Civil War, which brought great hardships to British workers but inspired them with zeal for the overseas democracy which was waging an epic struggle against slavery. The boy was imbued with the spirit of free America and the opportunities that could be found there. These topics became subjects of animated conversation at home, and with increasing difficulties

---

*It was not an era of promise for British workers. The Era of Reform had passed. The Master and Servant Act of 1867 would outlaw "coercion" and "molestation"—words which, in the hands of prejudiced magistrates, became instruments of oppression. Imprisonment for breach of engagement—for leaving the job—hung over the heads of dissatisfied workers. Peaceful picketing was illegal. Storm and struggle would, by 1875, result in the Employers and Workmen Act which, in law, increased dignity and opportunity for workers. In practice, it offered little more than a verbal occasion to conduct their desperate struggles against tradition and contempt which united to keep them in misery.

due to hard times and a growing family, Solomon Gompers finally decided to emigrate.

The family packed a few belongings and provisions and boarded the *City of London* on June 10, 1863. Mother Gompers had brought salted beef and other preserved meats and fish, dried vegetables, and pickled cabbage, and prepared the family's meals in the galley. It was a rough voyage, lasting seven weeks, and none but Solomon escaped seasickness. The landing at New York's Castle Garden was unpleasant, for it was the time of the draft riots, when anti-Negro prejudice was whipped to a fever pitch; and when Solomon was seen shaking hands with a Negro who had been helpful to him, he narrowly escaped being attacked. But the excitement of promise and wonder in the New World transcended any minor discomforts.[3]

2. YOUNG MANHOOD IN NEW YORK

FROM THE EAST SIDE OF LONDON TO THE EAST SIDE OF New York was, in many respects, a slight change. There was no need to learn a new language or customs, Solomon and Sam continued their work as cigarmakers, living in the same kind of tenements, and remaining in dire poverty. But to Sam, there was something in the air which seemed to make life more exciting, more stimulating: anything could happen in this throbbing city of nearly a million souls.

New York was notorious as a city of extremes, and the Gompers clan found itself very near the lowest extremity. The family settled in the neighborhood east of the Bowery on the lower end of the island, a section known then as Little Germany. "Settled" is not quite the right word, as Gompers moved an average of about once a year during the more than twenty years he lived in that part of the city. This was but a stone's throw from the squalid, crime-infested Five Points district where tens of thousands of immigrants were crowded in the foul, dark, underground lodging houses overrun with vermin. The tenement district in which Gompers lived comprised the next highest level of housing.

Resembling huge barracks, the six-story dwellings huddled together, shutting out the sunlight and air. On a hot day the air was stifling, and on a cloudy day there was hardly enough light in the apartments to see by. But on any day the unventilated rooms were impregnated with a foul stench from the vaults below, which, according to one observer, would poison cattle, and which another could not bear for five minutes. Garbage and refuse were thrown into the rear court, which was never cleaned. The floors and stairs of the dark halls were covered with "unmentionable filth," and the walls dripped with slimy exudations.

The Gompers, soon grown to eleven members, lived in two- or three-room apartments, with few windows, perhaps only one of which opened to daylight. The water hydrant and the toilets in the yard were shared by twenty-five to one hundred or more families in the same building, to say nothing of passersby from the street. To make matters worse, their first home was between a slaughterhouse and a brewery, which filled the whole neighborhood with a sickening odor. Then, to make life almost unbearable, Solomon used the combination kitchen, dining room, and living room as a workshop as well. Here he sat at a table, with Samuel on the other side, and the two rolled cigars, the damp tobacco leaves and scraps covering the floor where the babies played, the air thick with tobacco dust and reeking, shortening their lives with each breath.[4] For a year and a half after his arrival in New York, Samuel continued working in his sweatshop apartment. Then he went out and found a job in a cigar factory.

But squalor and hard work could not repress the amazing energy which possessed the youth, his natural gregariousness, and the thirst for knowledge which he had acquired during his brief schooling. Within a year after his arrival in the United States, he and some friends formed the Arion Base Ball and Social Club, which engaged in athletics, debated public issues, and held a mock court. Sam exhibited natural leadership: he was elected president of the club and here secured his first crude lessons in parliamentary procedure; later these boys joined the Ancient Order of Foresters, and he eventually became Chief Ranger of the Court Empire City of the Order. But he and a few others resented the attempt of the officials in England to dominate them, and established the Independent Order of Foresters. When they were twenty-one, they organized the Rising Star Lodge of the Independent Order of Odd Fellows. Gompers was the first Noble Grand of his lodge and later Deputy Grand Master of the District Order.

In the summer of 1866, one of his companions had to leave the city for a while and asked Samuel to look after his girl friend, Sophia Julian. She worked in the same shop he did, stripping the stems from tobacco leaves, the lowest paid work in the trade. When he looked her up, he was immediately smitten. "She was very pretty," he recollected, "with a clear olive complexion and a glowing color like peach-blow, soft musical voice, and black curls that she arranged most attractively." Like himself, she was a London-born Jew, having come to America as a small child. Sam made the long trip to her home in Brooklyn two or three evenings each week, having to ride the stage coach to the Battery and the ferry across the East River. When he returned late at night, the coach was no longer running, and he arranged to ride with a milk wagon to the Barnum Museum, where he could get a street car. Sometimes he had to walk the five miles from the Battery to his home. But then, as later in his life, sleep meant little to him when he had something to do.

He and Sophia, generally with another couple, enjoyed picnics and parties, the debating club or the theater, dancing and walking. On his seventeenth birthday, they discussed appropriate ways to celebrate the occasion, and someone suggested that he and Sophia get married. They immediately determined to carry out the idea. Since it was too late that night, they went to the City Hall the following morning and were married by the justice of the peace. After celebrating at a restaurant and theater, Samuel took his bride to her home and he went to his. When his family got over the shock, Sophia came to live with them until the couple saved enough money to buy some furniture and establish their own quarters in Hackensack.

Just before the birth of their first child, Gompers took Sophia to his mother's home to be cared for. The boy was named Samuel Julian, and all the other children bore their mother's surname as well as their father's. It was many years before Sophia Gompers would be seen without a baby in her arms or at her feet. She bore twelve or fourteen children, several of whom died in childhood; Gompers himself was uncertain, in later years, exactly how many children they had had.

Working, engaging in fraternal activities, and raising a

family, Gompers still found time to participate in a debating club at Cooper Union and attend its Saturday night lectures quite regularly. For many years he also took classes in history, biography, music, mechanics, elocution, economics, and other assorted subjects. These studies had only a tangential influence on his thought and activities. A major idea that he carried away with him related to religion and the organized churches. Even in childhood he had felt that instinct was a better guide than blind obedience. He later saw himself as by nature a nonconformist, and that was certainly true at least in his youth and young manhood.[5]

His rebellion against the restraints of orthodoxy was greatly influenced by Felix Adler, who founded the Ethical Culture Society in the 1870's. Adler eschewed dogma as both unimportant and unprovable, and in fact harmful, for wrangling over the source of moral law only diverted men from their proper course, which should be to study the nature of moral law and apply it to "the sad realities of the times." Man's duty toward his fellow man was far more important than his so-called duties toward God. Dogma had elevated man's concern with future salvation to unwarranted prominence compared with the interests of the present, and had inflamed man's hatred against his brother. Adler's goal was to refresh the moral sense, to develop a moral ideal that would inspire men "to help in lifting up the fallen, to lend free utterance to the complaints of the oppressed . . . and to push on with whatever power we may have, the progress of our race toward those high and holy goals of which the dreamers dream, the prophets prophesy."

Adler's New Ideal was the Kingdom of Heaven on earth, based on the natural rather than the supernatural, on science rather than on prayer. Its priests were the men of science, dedicated to knowledge; priests of art, dedicated to the service of beauty; "priests of Morality, artists of the Good, sages in the science of Virtue, teachers of the Ideal." It was to be established, not by divine intervention, but by the exertions of men. Its goal would be the establishment of a just social order in which the distribution of wealth would be governed by the sentiment of brotherly love.[6]

Gompers was attracted to Adler's search for a rational standard "that would have meaning in the affairs of everyday life," and he joined the Ethical Culture Society. If he ever had any church affiliation, he dropped it in his youth, and never attended a church or synagogue except to deliver a sermon on the labor movement. He never observed any holidays, and prescribed a secular funeral for himself and his wife.[7]

But in religion, as in other matters, Gompers was much less concerned with its philosophical implications than with its bearing on human welfare. In 1892 he joined Robert Ingersoll, the famed freethinker, Elizabeth Cady Stanton, woman suffrage leader, William E. B. Du Bois, militant spokesman of the Negroes, George Gunton, then with some status as a labor reformer, and others in an effort to establish a Society of Human Progress. They appealed to "liberals, social reformers, and earnest agitators" to assist their plan to educate the masses from a freethought standpoint through Sunday lectures, reading rooms, and conferences. The group protested against superstition and the bigotry of institutional religion, not on theoretical grounds, but because the organized churches were the foremost foes of science and of the search for truth and ethical advance. The church "has ever sided with the wealthy oppressor against his striking employé; with the capitalistic plutocrat in his persecution of the proletariat; with slavery against the claims of liberty. . . ." To remove the shackles of "ancient superstitions and religious puerilities" from the minds of the people, this band of "earnest agitators" demanded the absolute separation of church and state, the abrogation of Sunday and religious laws, the ending of church authority so far as the morals of the individual and society were concerned, the discontinuance of the use of the Bible, prayers, and hymns in the public schools, the taxing of church property, and the repeal of all laws prejudicial to the interests of the working class.[8]

This mingling of freethought and social reform appears in all of Gompers' thoughts on the subject. He could see no purpose in the "cackling" of the priesthood, unless it was to dull the senses of the masses and make them content with their lot in life. The workers would not surrender their right to any happiness a life beyond the grave might hold, but they wanted a better now. "If we are to have such a blissful hereafter, we want to get used to it, so that we will not be shocked at the grandeur of the heavenly world and will be able to appreciate it."[9]

For Gompers, the trade union movement was preferable to the church any way he looked at it. It was more efficacious in the development of social morality and in subordinating man's selfish animal nature to the needs of humanity. It was a more potent instrument for persuading employers to grant fair conditions to the workers. It certainly was a more effective agency than the church for achieving the ideals of the Sermon on the Mount. As he often said, his religion was the brotherhood of man and service in the humanitarian cause of labor.[10]

Of even more concern to Gompers was the hostility of the churches to labor. Most ministers, he told one of them, cared little to have the workers with them except as they might influence them "to bear a yoke of oppression and be the sycophantic slaves of their more favored fellow men." To another he complained that the churches were not in touch with the aspirations of the workers; that they had no sympathy with the causes of their misery; and that they treated the labor movement with contempt.[11]

Gompers' attitude was strengthened by such experiences as the one he had with the Evangelical Publishing Company of Cleveland. In 1890, it was the only printing house in that city that refused to grant the eight-hour day. Gompers appealed to it to reconsider, but the managers replied that they had been antagonized by "infidel movements which fear neither God nor man." Gompers asked them if it was infidelity for working people to forego part of their wages in order to give the unemployed an opportunity to earn wages which would support them "instead of eating the bread of idleness or charity, or possibly something worse . . . [while] you, with a self-satisfied air, deny a concession to the laborer which would have a tendency to raise him not only materially, but morally and socially, to a higher appreciation of his duty as a man. . . ."

These facts convinced Gompers that the churches were "allied to the money interests and basically capitalistic," and that they sought to divert the attention of the laborers from the redress of their present grievances to the "good time to come hereafter." The churches were, in fact, by their indifference or antagonism to the efforts of the workingmen, "criminal parties to the wrongs inflicted upon the oppressed."[12]

Many other labor leaders, as well as some ministers, shared

Gompers' views. Even Terrence V. Powderly, chief of the Knights of Labor, who once referred to Gompers as a "Christ slugger," found that it was the general rule that when men went on strike they were told from the pulpit that they should be content to live in that sphere in life to which it had pleased God to call them.[13]

Desiring passionately to be an American, Gompers did not consider himself a Jew at all. While he made no effort to conceal his religious background, he never mentioned it, and after thirty years of life in the spotlight of publicity, many prominent reporters were still writing that he was not of Jewish birth. He once wrote to a friend, David Lubin, a businessman who initiated the International Institute of Agriculture:

"You say that your chief glory is that you are a Jew. Mine is that I have a heart, a mind and a conscience, that I have struggled with my fellow men, and yearn to struggle on for a better day when the ridiculous divisions, questions which make man an enemy to man instead of his brother, shall be eliminated. . . . Jefferson placed this as a test of Americans: 'Is he honest, is he true, is he faithful to the Constitution?' I am willing that that test be applied to me so far as the labor movement of our country and the struggles of the people are concerned. . . ."[14]

3. A HIDDEN WORLD OF THOUGHT

GOMPERS, IN HIS YOUTHFUL FRATERNAL AND EDUCA-
tional activities, was groping for something that would satisfy his yearning for a more meaningful life, provide gratification for his intense gregariousness, and open a path for achievement. This he was to find at the work bench, for he always learned his main lessons from experience and personal contacts.

Sam and his father took out a card in Cigarmakers Local Union Number 15 shortly after their arrival in New York. For nearly ten years he attended meetings only perfunctorily, being much more interested in fraternal than labor activities. But even then his deep-rooted sense of justice and natural leadership made him the spokesman for his shopmates on several occasions. The first job he had after leaving the bench in his father's tenement was at the Stachelberg shop. Soon the men asked him to represent them in presenting their grievances and demands to the employer.

Stachelberg tried to intimidate him on account of his youth, and, failing, offered him a bribe to sell out. But Gompers was firm and carried the day for his co-workers.

Shortly after his marriage he lost his job, and, the trade in New York being dull, he and some friends found jobs in Hackensack and then in Lambertville, New Jersey. For about a year and a half he lived in boarding houses while his wife remained at his father's house. Returning to New York, he moved from shop to shop, holding jobs for short periods at most of the large cigar factories and many of the smaller ones. These shops were uniformly unpleasant places in which to work, poorly ventilated and heavy with the dust and aroma of tobacco leaves. The toilet facilities were crude and unsanitary and tobacco bagging was used as towels.

Nevertheless, his hours in the factory were among Gompers' most pleasant memories. He took great joy in the comradeship that prevailed among the workers and in their conversation. He took considerable pride in his craftsmanship, becoming highly skilled at rolling the tobacco leaves smoothly over the bunch with a minimum of waste. His employer once pointed him out to visitors with the remark, "He is an agitator, but I don't give a damn, for he makes me good cigars."

His skill as a workman made him independent and self-confident and gave him the respect of his shopmates. His role as unofficial leader and spokesman became more firmly established. On one occasion he admonished his employer when the latter lost his patience and beat a young nephew who was learning the trade in the shop. Gompers told him that this was America and the boy was not his slave. A warning that the men would strike if there was another such beating curbed the man's temper. In another shop at which Gompers worked, one of his fellow workers, a weak man with poor eyesight, was removed to a bench in the dimly lighted rear part of the room, and his position in front given to a young newcomer who had been a strikebreaker. Gompers demanded an explanation from the foreman, and when he received none started gathering up his tools with the remark, "He can have this seat too." The other fifty men began to follow him, but the walkout was averted by the immediate return of the abused man to his former position.[15]

Unionism as yet meant little to the young man. He was, as he wrote later, merely an "onlooker." But the turbulent struggles in New York during the 1870's gave him plenty to look on and ponder. His own union was groping for a solution to post-Civil War problems, and young Gompers was caught up in some of the blind battles that resulted. One day the president of the cigar-makers' union of New York City entered the shop in which he was working and announced that the shop was on strike. Without hesitation the workers laid down their knives and walked out. Gompers might have been impressed by this demonstration of solidarity, but may well have wondered whether his union was organized on the most effective basis.

A more difficult problem was presented by the introduction of the mold into the industry. This was a press for shaping cigars by hand, and was invented in 1867. Until then one man had made the bunch, or filler, and also rolled the wrapper of the cigar. But when the mold was first used in 1870, it divided the trade into two groups, bunch breakers and rollers, and the work of each was made easier and quicker. As a result, women and children were hired in large numbers to replace the men in the trade, and wages suffered a rapid decline. The Cigarmakers International Union immediately began a fight against the new "machine," prohibiting its members from working with bunch breakers, that is, in any shop which employed the mold. The union was too weak to enforce the rule, and it was widely violated. In New York, the cigarmakers had to face the same issue, and at a mass meeting in Turner Hall, Gompers and his friends voted to strike against the mold. The strike was lost, and Gompers received his first lesson—not wholly understood at the time—in the futility of opposing industrial progress.

In 1871 New York was the scene of many militant and color-ful struggles and demonstrations, many of which were organized and led by the International Workingmen's Association, the First International of Marxian socialists. Gompers' "whole being surged with response" to these stirring events. The throb of European struggles for freedom coursed through him as he witnessed the riots between Irish Catholics and Orangemen, the celebrations of the end of the Franco-Prussian War and of Italian unification, the protests against the court-martial of Hungarian revolutionists and the slaughter of the Paris Communards.

But what interested Gompers most was the advance of the eight-hour movement that had begun almost as soon as the last shot was fired in the Civil War. In September 1871, he marched with 25,000 other workers in a great parade over the muddy coblestones of the Bowery to the City Hall, then up Broadway to Cooper Union. The cigarmakers were not strong enough to make a contest for the eight-hour day, but they marched in support of the stonecutters and other trades that were joining the issue. The contingent of the International Workingmen's Association carried the red flag and a banner inscribed with the slogan, "Liberty, Equality and Fraternity." Other banners proclaimed, "Eight Hours For Work, Eight Hours For Rest, Eight Hours For What We Will" and "Peaceably If We Can, Forcibly If We Must." The parade ended with a giant mass meeting in Cooper Union, where it was resolved to continue the eight-hour agitation until success was achieved. The following year there were other great demonstrations, and several trades won the shorter workday.

During the next few years eight-hour meetings gave way to unemployment demonstrations as the workers sought desperately to keep their standards from falling below the starvation level. In New York City about one quarter of the workers were out of work by the end of 1873; by the last year of the depression, 1877 to '78, there would be perhaps three million unemployed workers in the country. Those who had jobs were forced to accept longer hours and drastic wage cuts. Thousands of workers were homeless, and the New York *Tribune* wondered if all the mechanics and laborers would "sink down permanently into tramps and paupers."[16]

Again the I.W.A., with the co-operation of the few remaining trade unions, was the rallying force in organizing the agitation for relief of the unemployed. Leaflets were issued and meetings and demonstrations were conducted during the last months of 1873. The workers demanded employment on public works, immediate relief for families in distress, a moratorium on evictions, and the eight-hour day. This activity culminated in a monster mass meeting at Tompkins Square on January 13, 1874. Permission for the meeting had been granted and Mayor William Frederick Havemeyer promised to address the crowd. At the last minute, however, he decided not to appear, and the police revoked the permit and surrounded the park. But the workers had not been notified, and on the morning of the thirteenth the square and the roads leading to it were packed with the largest labor demonstration in the city's history. Without warning, the police swept down on men, women, and children, trampling them under the horses' hoofs and striking them down indiscriminately with their clubs. Gompers, present only as an observer, was in the crowd on Eighth Street when the police charged, and he narrowly escaped a swinging night stick by jumping down a cellarway. All day the brutal attacks continued on groups of workingmen wherever they were seen. Repressive police action against workers continued and virtually ended the organized movement of the unemployed.[17]

Gompers pondered the meaning of these stirring events. He chanced to get a job, in 1873, with David Hirsch and Company, then the only union shop in the city. Hirsch had been a socialist in Germany and had learned the cigar trade with Ferdinand Laurell, Louis Baer, and a few other socialists who were now employed in his shop in New York. These men discussed social and economic problems while working, and sometimes took turns in reading aloud to the group. They all contributed to a fund for books, magazines, and papers. Gompers drank it all in, and soon began to see a conception of the trade union movement that went far beyond anything he had imagined. He saw a glimpse of the labor movement as an irrepressible force to remake the lives of the workers and in fact to refashion the social order and elevate labor to its rightful position in society.

Gompers was most influenced by Laurell, who had been a sailor before he became a cigarmaker. A leader in the Swedish labor and revolutionary movement, he was elected secretary of the Scandinavian section of the First International. After participating in a demonstration before the royal palace in Copenhagen, he fled to Hamburg and subsequently to New York. Laurell took Gompers under his wing and advised him to go to socialist meetings but not to join the party. He gave the young man a copy of the *Communist Manifesto* in German, which Laurell translated and interpreted for him. This permitted Gompers an "insight into a hidden world of thought," and he was so eager to read more of the German socialist literature, he said, that he determined to study German and read these works for himself.

Gompers was attracted to the principles of the International Workingmen's Association, which appealed to him as "solid and practical." Although he did not join, due to Laurell's influence, his intimate associates continued to be socialists. But he found that while they agreed on goals, they were divided on strategy for the emancipation of labor. The followers of Ferdinand Lassalle maintained that socialism would be achieved through co-operative producers' associations. The chief aim of the workers must therefore be to elect a socialist government, which would provide state aid to establish these co-operatives. Their primary interest was the formation of a labor party, and the organization of trade unions was treated as unimportant. The Lassalleans formed the Labor Party of Illinois and the Social Democratic Party of North America. Adolph Strasser, a member of Gompers' Local 15 of the cigarmakers' union, was head of the S.D.P., and Peter J. McGuire, Hugh McGregor, and J. Speyer were among the other leaders of the party.

Opposed to them were the Marxists, who constituted the majority of the I.W.A. Their ultimate objective was the seizure of the state by the working class through political struggle. However, they recognized that the American labor movement was still too weak to form an effective party. It was necessary to aid in the economic organization and struggles of the workers in order to further their fighting strength, their class consciousness, and their thinking along socialist lines. Electoral defeats and pressure from the rank and file forced the Lassalleans closer to the Marxist position, and in 1876 the two groups united in the Workingmen's party. But the struggle between the "trade union" and "political" factions continued.[18]

Gompers leaned toward the position of the Marxists. He was probably influenced in this view by members of the United Workers of America, which was affiliated with the I.W.A. Its leader, J. P. McDonnell, and a number of other members, including Laurell, were friends of Gompers. Their organization emphasized the building of trade unions and the economic emancipation of the working class; political action could be effective "only by constituting the labor class a separate political party."

But Laurell and others in the "anti-political" wing of the socialist movement soon abandoned the socialist objective altogether. They discarded political struggles and made the labor movement identical with the trade union movement. When Gompers went to Laurell with some new idea, the latter advised him: "Study your union card, Sam, and if the idea doesn't square with that, it ain't true." Gompers accepted this philosophy and crystallized it into the policy which he later dubbed "pure and simple" trade unionism. He subscribed to the view that "Every political movement must be subordinated to the first great social end, viz., the economic emancipation of the working classes. . . ."[19]

In a letter to the president of the Cigarmakers International Union, he asserted that the questions of the day were first, the union of all working people; second, the reduction of the hours of labor; and third, the bringing of the wages of the lowest paid toilers to the standard of the highest. "The fourth," he added cryptically, "will be given at some future time by others if not by me."[20] His association with the socialist movement had given Gompers a facility for using some of their terminology, but he used it in an altogether different sense. The Marxists maintained that the emancipation of labor from capitalist "wage slavery" would be achieved by political struggle, while organizing the workers immediately through economic struggles. Gompers sought the emancipation of labor from grinding poverty and killing exploitation, with any political changes in the system a matter of a distant future which did not concern him.

He began to meet regularly with a small group of Internationalists who were reaching the same conclusions. Among these "Ten Philosophers" were Peter J. McGuire, who had made a complete somersault from his anti-union, politics-only position of a few years previously; J. P. McDonnell, the Irish revolutionist; and Fred Bloete and Louis and Henry Baer, cigarmakers. "From this little group came the purposes and the initiative that finally resulted in the present American labor movement," wrote Gompers. "We did not create the American trade union—that is a product of forces and conditions. But we did create the technique and formulate the fundamentals that guided trade unions to constructive policies and achievements."[21]

Gompers evidently was greatly exhilarated by his contacts with socialist thought and with men who were "genuine revolutionaries," "men who did not hesitate to risk something to accomplish a purpose." He was, with them, seeking for a practical means of raising the working class from economic slavery and of salvaging the labor movement from the ruins in which the depression had cast it. Even the "Ten Philosophers" had not yet found an answer that would satisfy them. For Gompers, the techniques and fundamentals that could create a labor movement as he understood it were to be forged in the struggles of his own trade union, into which he threw all his energy and time, and out of which he emerged as a leader of the "new unionism."

Chapter Two

THE CIGARMAKERS' UNION

1. LOCAL 144

BEFORE THE CIVIL WAR, CIGARMAKERS WERE GENER-
ally independent workmen who sold their own cigars to the consumers. They rarely employed helpers and then only one or two
journeymen. Consequently, unionism was virtually nonexistent
in the trade, the first local being formed in Baltimore in 1851.
During the war, the government imposed an internal revenue tax
on cigars, granting permits to employers and employees and bond-
ing the shops. This drove the industry out of the small shops and
into factories.

With the growth of the factory system, the unionization of
the workers became more widespread, and by 1864 there were
enough locals to establish the National Cigarmakers Union with a
membership of just under 1,000. In 1867, it was renamed the
Cigarmakers International Union. Two years later, the organization had 5,800 members, but then it began to decline, partly because of the introduction of the mold which broke down the
special skill of the cigarmakers, and partly because of the growth
of the tenement system of manufacturing. In 1871 and '72 many
Bohemians emigrated to New York and were employed as unskilled workers under the mold and filler system, working in
tenement houses. The cigarmakers rented the rooms from the
employers, bought their supplies from them, and furnished their
own tools. The whole family was put to work, from early in the
morning until late at night, seven days a week.[1]

Then the disastrous depression of 1873-79 all but wiped out
the trade unions in the United States. The cigar business, as a
luxury trade, was one of the hardest hit. By 1877 there were only
seventeen locals left in the cigarmakers' union, with a membership
of 1,016. The conditions of the workers in the trade sank. In 1869
the average wages of cigarmakers had been $12.35 a week, but in

1878 they were earning only five to ten dollars, if they had steady work. Wages were further reduced by paying the employees in cigars instead of cash, the workers peddling the cigars to saloons at whatever price they could get. Hours of labor in the trade ranged from fifty-four to sixty a week. During the first half of 1878 an average of twenty per cent of the cigarmakers were unemployed, many of them becoming "tramps" roaming the country to look for work.[2]

In danger of extinction, the union was forced to reconsider its policies and organization. At the convention of the Cigarmakers International Union in 1872, President Edwin Johnson pointed out that the union, comprising but a small minority of the workers in the trade, could not effectively combat the evils of the mold. He therefore urged that the constitution be liberalized to make all cigarmakers eligible for admission. The delegates, instead, strengthened the restrictions by forbidding members from even working in the same shops where nonunion mold workers were employed.

The New York cigarmakers decided to act. Their union was in a desperate condition: the English-speaking Local 15, of which Gompers was a member, had dropped to less than fifty members, while the German-speaking local had eighty-five. Under the leadership of Adolph Strasser, who had abandoned socialism and become a pure and simple trade unionist, a plan was worked out for the merger of these two locals with a third organization of Bohemian cigarmakers. The new organization, the United Cigarmakers, opened its doors to the rollers and bunch-breakers and tenement workers who were excluded by the International Union.

The United Cigarmakers began a campaign to legalize its action within the International and to have the latter adopt its principles for the entire organization. In September, New York sent a strong delegation to the International convention to fight for liberal changes in the constitution and the abolition of membership restrictions. They did not succeed completely, but locals were authorized to allow their members to work in shops where bunch-breakers were employed.[3] In 1875 the International amended its constitution to prohibit locals from rejecting applicants for membership on account of sex or "system of work."[4] This was not only a victory for the New York plan, but signalled the adoption of the "new unionism" as the basis for the entire International. The United Cigarmakers applied for a new charter and drafted a constitution which recognized "the solidarity of the whole working class to work harmoniously against their common enemy—the capitalists." Gompers was elected president and Strasser the financial secretary of the new organization. It received its charter in November, being designated Local 144.[5] Gompers remained a member of this local until his death nearly fifty years later. Within twenty years he was the senior member of the International, and his proudest possession was Union Card No. 1 of the Cigarmakers International Union.

The first task of Local 144 was to defend the new policy of the union against the craft exclusiveness which was still strong among the skilled cigarmakers. At a mass meeting called by Local 144, Gompers made one of his first public speeches. He warned that conditions were growing worse every day and that the future was threatening. Wage reductions were almost a daily occurrence because, he said, the capitalists were only interested in profits, "and the time has come when we must assert our rights as workingmen. Every one present has the sad experience, that we are powerless in an isolated condition, while the capitalists are united; therefore it is the duty of every Cigar Maker to join the organization. . . . One of the main objects of the organization," he concluded, "is the elevation of the lowest paid worker to the standard of the highest, and in time we may secure for every person in the trade an existence worthy of human beings."[6]

In the meantime, Local 144 was proceeding with its reorganization, for its policy was based on more than merely the organization of the unskilled. It also involved a more efficient and business-like administration of the union and, above all, the control of strikes; the New York cigarmakers had depleted their resources and nearly wrecked their union by a number of unplanned strikes. In each shop with over seven members, a shop organization was formed, which met weekly. In the other shops, the members were grouped in district organizations of 200 or less. Local authority was vested in these shop and district organizations. Their delegates, together with the officers of the union, constituted a board of administration which met weekly to transact general business. General quarterly meetings of the members discussed union affairs.

Any proposal to strike had to be approved by members of the shop organization by secret ballot. The proposal then went to the Board of Administration. If the Board approved the walkout, it provided assistance and appointed a strike committee to direct the struggle. The workers receiving the lowest wages were to have first claim for the support of the union, because the low-wage factories would not seem inviting to strikebreakers and the other employers would not combine against the union since the low-wage employers were their strongest competitors.[7]

The union obtained a meeting hall over a saloon on the Bowery and proceeded with a campaign of organization. This work fell primarily on Gompers, not only as president of the local, but as organizer for the International, to which position he was appointed in December 1875. He began his organizing campaign with mass meetings, talks, and circulars in English, German, and Bohemian. Gompers was a tireless worker and already exhibited an uncommon ability as an organizer and agitator. By the following March, Local 144 had become the largest in the country, with a membership of 245.[8]

But after two years of effort, the New York cigarmakers were still, as Gompers wrote, "a prey to the avarice of our employers." The depression was still lying over the country like a pall, and the workers, grown desperate and defiant, began to fight back. The Pennsylvania coal miners had organized in a secret terrorist order, the Molly Maguires, in an effort to lift themselves from a state of virtual slavery. In the summer of 1877, the railroad workers, in reply to repeated wage reductions, inaugurated the most widespread strike movement in American history up to that time, but were crushed by state militia, federal troops, and the organized violence of the railroad barons. The workers were deeply stirred by these events. Gompers recalled that "the sky of Pittsburgh reddened by fires started by the company agents and desperate men denied all other recourse, brought us the message that human aspirations had not been killed or cowed." That year, Pinkerton detectives had exposed the Molly Maguire conspiracy, and sent some of its leaders to the gallows. Gompers spoke at mass meetings in New York which endorsed the Mollies and expressed sympathy for the railroad strikers.[9]

The same conditions produced the "great uprising" of the

cigarmakers of New York. In the winter of 1876-77, wages were again reduced, thousands of workers were idle, and the drift of the industry into the tenements continued. In September the workers at DeBarry's factory laid down their tools and demanded a minimum scale of six dollars per thousand cigars. Gompers, serving his third term as president of the union, negotiated with DeBarry, and an agreement was reached by which the workers won their demands. This was the first successful strike in the trade in many years and was the first real achievement of Local 144. Workers in other factories followed it with demands for wage raises, and nearly all won advances of fifty cents to two and a half dollars, an average gain of about fifteen per cent. Gompers' shop, Hirsch and Company, won it without going on strike.[10]

Just as the union felt itself on the way toward real progress, it was faced with an unexpected situation. Encouraged by the victories of the organized workers, the tenement workers went out on strike en masse. This precipitate action, taken without consultation with the union, was a threat to its position. The tenement workers were unorganized and undisciplined, and the union felt unable to cope with a strike of such dimensions. Gompers also resented them because they had remained outside of the union and, with their lower standards, impeded the progress of the more skilled workers. Strasser called them "tenement house scum."[11] The executive committee of the union urged the factory and tenement house workers with relatively good conditions to remain at work and contribute ten per cent of their earnings to support the strikers. But nearly all the workers streamed out of their shops. On October 15 hundreds of other workers were locked out in an effort of the National Cigar Manufacturers' Association to break the union. The executive committee met the challenge by calling a general strike, involving 15,000 workers. The demands were for the recognition of the union, a minimum scale of six dollars per thousand, and a reduction in rent.[12]

The manufacturers' association determined not to yield to the demands of their "late workers" or to reinstate them until they relinquished their membership in the union. They defended "the right of every workman to apply for and to resume work whenever he desires to do so without hindrance from his fellow workmen," and their own "right to operate our factories under such regulations . . . as we may prescribe." They urged the employees to cultivate "a greater degree of confidence and a more perfect spirit of harmony between employers and employed."[13]

The manufacturers soon demonstrated their "spirit of harmony" by evicting hundreds of families from their tenements. Even the sick were moved out on the sidewalks in the dead of winter; this placed a tremendous burden of relief on the strike committee. The union rented over a hundred rooms for them, but could not provide for all. The employers imported strikebreakers wholesale, some 500 being employed at the height of the strike. The police openly sided with the employers, arresting pickets freely without placing charges against them; many were beaten mercilessly by both police and hired thugs. At the end of the strike, the manufacturers' association officially thanked the police commissioner for his assistance.[14]

To meet this concentrated attack, the union needed funds and discipline. The local assessed its members ten per cent of their earnings, and appealed to fellow craftsmen throughout the country for assistance. Mass meetings were held in the large cities of the East and Midwest, in which other trades participated as well, and in two weeks $1,500 was collected and sent to New York. These meetings, and the reports of the strike, also invigorated cigarmakers' locals in those cities. New members were joining the union throughout the country, and a militant spirit was aroused which could strengthen the International in its approaching struggles. The International assessed all its employed members ten per cent of their wages.[15]

A relief committee was set up to investigate cases of need, collect funds in the factories which were operating, and administer relief. A unique feature of the relief program was union operation of a cigar factory. The factory was purchased by the strike committee to provide work for some of the strikers, relieve the burden of relief, increase the income of funds to support the strikers, and, in Gompers' phrase, "to create consternation in the employers association." Gompers was elected superintendent of the factory at twelve dollars a week, quitting his job at Hirsch's at which he had been earning eighteen dollars. About 2,400 workers were employed in the shop, a percentage of their wages being deducted to pay for the factory. Gompers walked two and a half miles each day from his apartment to the factory, often trudging through the snow to save carfare.[16]

In addition to managing the factory, he had a large part of the responsibility for organizing the workers and conducting the strike. Every evening, and often late into the night, he was attending meetings, making speeches at shop meetings and mass meetings, and taking part in conferences, as well as his usual activities as president of the union. He left home early in the morning in order to talk with the pickets on his way to work. A cartoon in *Puck* represented him running to Concordia Hall and answering a man who tried to talk with him: "I can not stop. I am too busy, for I am on strike."[17]

But his energy, the assistance of fellow unionists, and the self-sacrifice of the men and women engaged in the contest were not sufficient to overcome the organized resistance of the manufacturers, the strikebreaking of the police, the lack of resources, and cold and hunger. In January the strike began to crumble, the workers being forced to go back wherever they could find employment and for whatever wages the manufacturers would offer. The strike was officially called off in February, more than four months after the beginning of the struggle. The *Tobacco Leaf*, an employers' organ, gloating over the victory, asserted that the strike was "the most formidable and skillfully managed labor-revolt ever inaugurated in this country."[18]

The strike was not, however, a complete failure. It checked the relentless wage-cutting policy that had been pursued for several years, not only in New York but throughout the country. It was a tremendous stimulus to organization and marked the beginning of rapid increase in membership in the International as well as in Local 144. It brought the issue of tenement-house manufacturing to the attention of the public and prepared the ground for the final struggle against the system.[19] It also increased the prestige of Gompers, establishing his reputation as a leader in the International and making him a well-known figure in union circles in New York. Alexander Schlesinger, a German socialist editor, came to New York in December 1878, when his paper was suppressed by Chancellor Otto von Bismarck. Within an hour of his landing he was brought to the saloon of the anarchist, Justus Schwab, a place frequented by union leaders and radicals, including Gompers. The first question he was asked, and which he heard many times during that day, was, "Have you met Sam Gompers?" "No, who is he?" Schlesinger asked. The uniform reply was, "A cigarmaker, the best trade union orator in town!"[20]

But the immediate future did not look bright for Gompers. He declined an offer to remain as foreman in the union's factory, now restored to private owners, for such a job would be incompatible with his position in the union. His place in Hirsch's shop had been filled, and there was no room for him there. The Cigar Manufacturers' Association had black-listed the strike leaders. Gompers was unable to find work for nearly four months. He had pawned or sold every possession of any value, and his family was desperate. There were five children already, and another was expected momentarily. They subsisted on a diet of soup prepared from water, salt, pepper, and flour, and were often hungry. Sophia suggested that they apply for charity, but Samuel insisted on making his own way. He was saved from the direst necessity by his mother, who often sent food to his house, though she could hardly spare it from her own family.

One day while Gompers was searching for a job, his wife was visited by Jack Pollak, her former suitor. He offered her thirty dollars a week for three months if she would persuade her husband to give up the union and return to work. Sophia indignantly rejected the offer, and Samuel was very proud of her. But their self-respect did not provide for the family; all the children were ill from cold and undernourishment, and Gompers could still find no work.

One day when he returned home from job-hunting, his sister-in-law informed him that the expected child had been born, but there was nobody to help. Gompers rushed to the family doctor. Not finding him in, he went to a doctor on the next block and asked him to attend to his wife and baby. He was refused when he admitted that he had no money.

"I walked up to him," recalled Gompers, "looked him square in the eye and said, 'Yes you will, you will come and see my wife now.' He said, 'Well, I will not.' I put my hand on his coat collar and said, 'You will come now with me or you will never make another move.' He said he wanted me to pay him and I said: 'I have got no money. I have been out of work, but I will promise to pay you everything I can gather tonight, but you will come with me without another minute's hesitation or I will not be responsible for what I will do to you. Come along.' He put on his hat and coat and he went with me." Gompers managed to scrape up two dollars from his family to pay the physician and persuaded the druggist to fill his prescription on credit. The mother and child—Al, "our strike baby"—pulled through.

Laurell finally secured another job for him from an employer who refused to accept the black-listing decree of the employers' association. Gompers was heavily in debt by this time, and practically everything he owned was in the pawn shop. In order to better carry out his family responsibilities, he determined to withdraw from active leadership in the union and moved to the Williamsburgh section of Brooklyn to get away from the union. When his fourth term as president expired in January 1878, he did not stand for re-election. Gompers later described the aftermath: "I stayed away from one meeting of the Board of Administration of the union and perhaps I never passed a more uncomfortable week. The second week I went to the union meeting. I could not go home to supper and so I had to buy some sort of a meal in New York. I went to the meeting, a discussion arose, an important committee was to be appointed and the president appointed me as chairman of the committee. I could not refuse. I reached home about two o'clock in the morning and a few hours later I went to work. In the evening I met with my associates on the committee, had a bite instead of supper, reached home about one o'clock in the morning, and then it was necessary to attend the meeting on the following Monday night and make [a] report. And so it continued until nearly every evening kept me away from home, involving the expense of eating in restaurants and unfitting me for the work in the factory. I saw that the situation was hopeless, went home one Sunday morning and concluded it was no use; we moved back to New York, and if possible, with more zest and energy re-entered the struggle which has continued ever since. That, in my opinion, was the turning point of my life."

From that moment until his death, trade unionism *was* Samuel Gompers' life. It was about this time that he received the first of many offers of political appointment. None other than John Sherman, Secretary of the United States Treasury, proposed that he take a position as statistician in his department, with the assurance that he could devote most of his time to furthering the trade union movement. Although the job carried the "princely" salary of $2,000 a year, Gompers felt obliged to decline. For he had, with the other members of the Economic and Sociological Club, taken a pledge that he would under no circumstance accept public office or become interested in any business venture or accept any preferment outside of the labor movement.[21]

Gompers wrote many years later: "I am not unmindful of the duties one owes to his family and to himself, but there is also a duty which one owes to his fellow workmen and his fellow men." All a trade union official could expect for his services was a "fair livelihood." Beyond this, the practical-minded Gompers, with an eye on the sensation-mongering press, had visions of what its headline-writers could do. When Peter J. McGuire thought of leaving the labor movement, Gompers could see spicy stories with such captions as "McGuire and Gompers Are Out," "The Federation's Split," and "McGuire Deserts the Federation."[22] Gompers would not desert.

2. THE BLACK HOLES OF CALCUTTA

ONE OF THE FIRST THINGS THAT HAPPENED TO Gompers on his return to active union work was his arrest and imprisonment. The cigarmakers at the Kimball factory struck against arbitrary and unjust orders of the foreman. Gompers stopped on his way to work one morning to talk with the pickets. A policeman arrested him and a friend who was with him. They were charged with disorderly conduct and fined ten dollars or ten days in jail. Gompers' defense, that he had a right to walk in front of the building and talk to the men, was disregarded by the judge. But Gompers "would not have paid that fine if my life depended on it," so he was put in the Tombs. "That was one of the most uncomfortable days I ever spent," he recalled, "sitting there in the dirt and filth and vermin surrounded by men of unclean bodies and minds, who used vile language." That evening he was released when some of his union brothers came and paid the fine. It was the only time Gompers was ever in jail, though he narrowly missed a term some thirty years later.[23]

In 1880, Gompers was again elected to the presidency of Local 144. Under his administration, the union entered into an all-out fight to destroy the tenement system of cigar-making, which stood in the way of the further advancement of the organization and the improvement of the conditions of the cigarmakers. The campaign had been initiated in November 1878, when the local held a mass meeting in Germania Hall. "S. Gompertz," as the papers called him, made the main speech. He said that the tenement houses were dens of filth and disease, prisons for small children, and a source of gross immorality and crime. The meeting resolved to call upon Congress and the Commissioner of Internal Revenue to abolish the system, and appointed Gompers to a committee to present the resolution to the Commissioner.[24]

In 1879, the union secured the assistance of the influential New York Congressman Abram Hewitt in introducing an amendment to the federal revenue law which would have placed a prohibitive tax on cigars manufactured in tenement houses. The amendment passed the House of Representatives but was defeated in the Senate. At a great protest meeting in Cooper Union, Gompers asserted that the tenement proprietors had probably carried the day by buying votes. They "worship Mammon," he declared, "and they have called the money god to their aid. . . . Fellow-citizens, we cannot submit to injustice. We are men and women who have rights which must be defended. Oppression such as we experience has in former ages caused rebellion and warfare."[25]

The union then determined to achieve its purpose through state legislation. A bill was introduced providing for the use of the state's police power to regulate the public health. A perpetual lobby was maintained at Albany, sometimes by Strasser, sometimes by Gompers, and sometimes by representatives of the Amalgamated Trades and Labor Unions of New York. Gompers made the trip from New York by boat once or twice a week and presented testimony before the Assembly committee which was considering the bill. He appealed to the local unions of the state to visit candidates for election to the legislature and pledge them to vote for the abolition of tenement cigar factories. This was not party politics, Gompers stated, but "labor politics, pure and simple."[26]

Gompers made a survey of the cigar-shop tenements for the *New Yorker Volkszeitung*, the journal of the Socialist Labor party. He gained access to the apartments by posing as a book salesman. The conditions he found were unpleasantly familiar to him, but the statistical information and the publicity given the horrible details aided in arousing public opinion and influencing the legislators. Gompers found that twenty-seven employers were operating tenement factories housing over 7,000 persons. The employers furnished the tobacco to the operatives, and the entire family, including the children, worked in these dark, filthy, tobacco-laden rooms fourteen to twenty hours a day, their lungs filled with tobacco dust and their nostrils with the foul odors. Nearly three fourths of the young girls working in the tenements became sick after six months' work, and many of the workers continued at their jobs even while suffering from contagious diseases. Gompers was especially impressed by the "little children with their old-young faces and work-weary figures" which "mutely condemned the crime industry was committing against them."[27]

The legislature took no action during the session of 1881, and the union entered into its first political campaign that fall to elect men who sympathized with the prohibition bill and to defeat those who had worked against its passage. The campaign was concentrated on the re-election of Edward Grosse, a former member of the Typographical Union and the International Workingmen's Assocation, who had introduced the tenement-house bill in the legislature. Early in 1882 the state Senate passed the bill almost unanimously. But in the closing hours of the session, when consideration of the bill was called for in the Assembly, it was found that someone had stolen the official copy of the bill and thus prevented action. The notorious corruption that dominated the state legislature at that time explains this "accident."

But the union's campaign was approaching success. In the next session there were three trade unionists in the Assembly, and young Theodore Roosevelt was serving his second term as an Assemblyman. He had little understanding of the movement for social and industrial justice, and was inclined to oppose the bill. But he was appointed to a committee to investigate tenement-house conditions, probably because it was expected that he would report adversely on the need for remedial legislation. Roosevelt told Gompers that if conditions were really as bad as he described them, he would do everything he could to secure the passage of the bill. He accepted Gompers' offer to show him through the tenements, and found that his report was accurate. True to his word, he made a forceful speech in favor of the bill.[28]

The measure was passed by an overwhelming majority and was signed by Governor Grover Cleveland, to become effective October 1. The manufacturers took it to court, challenging its constitutionality. William Evarts, the famous lawyer and Secretary of State, later a Senator, argued that the measure interfered with personal freedom and private property without due process of law; that it was an excessive exercise of the police power of the legislature; and that it contravened the Constitution by impairing the obligation of contracts. Judge Samuel Hand, for the People of New York, contended that the act was within the discretion of the legislature to determine whether tenement manufacturing was prejudicial to the public health, and the prohibition thereof expedient. The Court of Appeals upheld the employers' contention and nullified the law.[29]

The following year a new bill was passed to overcome the court's objections. But many of the manufacturers continued their operations in violation of the law, and a suit was brought against one of them by the name of Peter Jacobs. Evarts again argued the case for the employers, and again the court gave its sanction to the sweatshops. But this time it masked its defense of property rights over human rights by ruling that the law deprived not the employers of their property, but the laborers of the free right to employ their labor to their best interests. The legislature, it ruled, could not deprive the laborers of their right to work and enjoy the fruits of their work in their own residences and in their own way, except for the purposes of police or health regulation. And this, it declared, was not the real purpose of the law, as shown by its discriminatory features. The appellate court upheld this decision, ruling that the act was an unconstitutional and arbitrary interference with liberty and property and the "hallowed" influences of the "home."[30]

This case strengthened Gompers' distrust of political action as a means of improving the conditions of the workers. He saw the state as in the hands of the employers; the workingmen could not hope to beat them at their own game. The cigarmakers turned to their own organization for redress and kept up a steady harassment of the tenement manufacturers by strikes and agitation, until they were forced to the conclusion that it would be cheaper to abandon the tenement system and to carry on the industry in factories. After many years of struggle, the cigarmakers accomplished through economic power what they failed to achieve through legislation.[31]

3. RULE OR RUIN

AN IMPORTANT BY-PRODUCT OF THE CIGARMAKERS' fight against the tenement-house system was that it led to Gompers' first direct conflict with the socialists in the trade union movement. The trouble began when Local 144 decided to endorse legislators who supported the anti-tenement bill. Many of the socialists in the union did not approve of urging workers to vote for representatives of either of the major parties. Such a policy, they believed, was impractical because the "capitalist politicians" could not be trusted to carry out their promises; it was reactionary because it tended to tie the working class to the old parties; and it had the effect of blunting the class consciousness of the workers by leading them to think that they could make progress by cooperating with the employing class instead of fighting it on the political as well as the economic field. There was only one labor party, the Socialist Labor party, and the workers owed allegiance to it just as they did to their trade unions.[32]

A small group seceded from Local 144, but most of the socialists remained in the union, and their disagreement with the union leadership was solely on the tactics to be employed in securing tenement-house legislation. They were not opposed to the tenement act or other labor legislation, but they opposed "lobbyism" as a means of securing it. It was unbecoming, they said, for the workmen to beg their government for legislation, and it was disgraceful to "sneak in lobbies and creep before these governments." Besides, lobbying was conducted by the leaders of the labor organizations, and this gave them the opportunity to make secret deals with the politicians and to sell labor's vote to the highest bidder.

It subordinated the masses to the will of a few leaders and did nothing to develop the political education and organization of the workers. If the workingmen wanted labor legislation, they should form a labor party and elect workers to the legislative bodies to enact it.[33] Gompers later wrote bitterly of the socialists as being willing to see the cigar industry absorbed by tenement-house production unless that fate could be averted by socialism, but even Strasser admitted that they supported the campaign for the passage of the tenement-manufacturing law.[34]

The union divided sharply on the issue, and opposition to the union's policies created opposition to its leaders. The conflict became so intense that scarcely any business could be conducted. To this issue was added another. From the time the union had been established, dues had been ten cents a week. The leaders of Local 144, as well as of the International Union, formed a "twenty-cent party," while their opponents constituted the "fifteen-cent party." At the end of 1881, dues were raised to twenty cents by an amendment to the constitution of the International, and Local 144 voted against the amendment. Thus this question came to a head just as the contest over political action was reaching a crisis. Both sides prepared for a showdown, issuing circulars and using the newspapers to present their positions.[35]

President Strasser informed the International Executive Board of the emergency that had arisen in Local 144 and indicated that the approaching elections in that union might produce serious consequences. Vice-President Fred Blend proposed that Strasser call a special meeting of the Executive Board in New York to supervise the elections and see that no fraud was committed, but Strasser claimed there were no funds to pay the Board's traveling expenses. In reality, Gompers admitted, Strasser was determined to defeat the socialists and would not countenance compromise.[36]

In April 1882, the union elected as its president Samuel Schimkowitz, a socialist. Socialists were also elected to most of the other offices except that of treasurer. Ten members of the union protested the election on the ground that Schimkowitz was an employer and therefore, according to the constitution, not eligible to membership in the union. President Strasser ordered the local to defend its actions and, pending an investigation, suspended

Schimkowitz and fifty-six other members of the local for "conduct unbecoming union-men."[37]

Gompers chaired an investigating committee of the local which reported that Schimkowitz had failed to respond to their invitation to defend himself against the complaint. The committee called eight witnesses, all of whom testified that they had positive information that Schimkowitz was an employer at the time of his election and since. The local board of administration submitted this report to Strasser, who made the suspensions permanent. The expelled members and their supporters defied Strasser and continued to hold their own meetings in the name of Local 144. They also refused to pay their assessment to the International and issued their own stamps and membership cards. Strasser considered these actions as constituting secession from both the local and International Union. There were now practically two unions contending for official status and for possession of the funds.

Schimkowitz presented Blend with a series of charges, stating that Strasser had refused to print his side of the story in the *Official Journal*, that the vote on the twenty-cent dues amendment was illegal, that Strasser intended to destroy Local 144 because of its opposition to the amendment, and that the local was run undemocratically. Blend advised Schimkowitz to appeal Strasser's decision to the Executive Board and agreed that he would then ask Strasser to call a meeting of the Board in New York. If Strasser refused, he promised that the Board would meet anyhow, providing the Schimkowitz faction paid its traveling expenses to New York. This plan was carried out, and on June 2 the Executive Board issued its report.

It found that Schimkowitz had been duly elected and that his suspension was without warrant of law. The Board reversed the decision of the president on condition that Local 144 investigate and enforce the constitution if Schimkowitz were found to be an employer, that all suspended members should be accepted into full membership by the local, and that the Schimkowitz faction turn over its funds to the union treasurer. The Board further recommended that the local hold an election of officers for unexpired terms within thirty days.

The Gompers faction of Local 144 proceeded to conduct another investigation, and again found Schimkowitz to have been an employer and hence illegally elected. The board of administration adopted the report, declared the presidency vacant, and, at a special meeting, elected another president. The Schimkowitz faction then seceded from the Cigarmakers International Union and formed the Cigarmakers Progressive Union.

The last round was fought at the next convention of the International in September 1883, with the socialists absent. Strasser admitted that he had no legal authority to suspend Schimkowitz and the other socialists without their first having been tried by their local union, but asserted that the extraordinary conditions created by the "conspiracy" to capture the union had justified his extraordinary action. Blend, in his report as chairman of the Executive Board, made a devastating attack on the course taken by the Strasser-Gompers group. He accused Strasser of permitting the split to occur by his refusal to take preventive action just before the local election and of using the results of the election to drive his opponents out of the union. He blamed the failure to restore harmony on "unscrupulous leaders," obviously referring to Strasser and Gompers, "who appealed to passion and hatred, whose only ambition was self-aggrandizement, who aspired to both national and local fame, who stooped to every known method of fraud and deception to accomplish their own nefarious ends. . . ." The result, he pointed out, was division in the union, the loss of several thousand members, and the organization of the Progressive Union.

A special committee was elected to investigate the matter. This committee, made up of a majority of Strasser's supporters, conceded that Strasser had acted beyond his constitutional powers in suspending Schimkowitz but supported his action as justified by unusual exigencies. Another special committee reported that the conduct of the "secessionists" was contrary to the principles of unionism and that they were irreconcilable. This report was approved by the convention.

The Strasser-Gompers machine had carried the day, but at a terrible cost to the Cigarmakers International Union. The largest local in the country was disrupted, several other locals seceded and joined the Progressives, a dual union was brought into existence which was considerably larger than the "regular" union, and the two embarked on a fight for control of the cigar factories that enabled the employers to play them against each other to the detriment of both.[38] Gompers thought the policy of the socialists was to rule the union or ruin it, but on this occasion he did not hesitate to disrupt the union himself when he lost control to an opposition which was elected by a majority of the members. Perhaps he felt that the exclusion of the socialists was a necessary part of his program for remodeling the Cigarmakers International Union along lines of "business unionism," a program of which he was the principal architect.[39]

4. BUSINESS UNIONISM

GOMPERS WAS FIRST ELECTED BY LOCAL 144 AS ITS delegate to the Cigarmakers International Union convention in 1877, and he represented his local in every convention but one from that year until his death. His rise as national leader was based on his policy of setting the union on a foundation strong enough to make it a fighting organization, capable of concentrating its forces quickly and at the most strategic point. In the very process of blasting Local 144 into the International, he had won acceptance for the first phase of his program of "new unionism," that is, the recognition of the mold and the opening of the doors of the union to the unskilled workers in the trade. He then set out to carry through the rest of his policy. While this program was not an exclusive invention of Gompers, he played a leading part in evolving it and an even more important part in securing its adoption by the cigarmakers. Later, as president of the American Federation of Labor, he constantly urged the program upon the other affiliated unions as well.

Local 144 had already inaugurated a partial system of benefits. And Gompers was convinced, partly through his study of the British trade unions, that unless such a system of benefits was extended and made universal, the trade union movement had slight chance of permanence. He had seen the depression of the 1870's nearly wipe out the labor unions of the country, and he believed that this was in large measure due to the fact that, when the unions were not able to protect wage standards, their members had no motive to remain in them. The "fraternal system" would provide the incentive to retain membership during a depression, and then, when business revived, the unions could resume the movement for improved conditions. Almost any union, he reasoned, could protect its members during busy seasons; it was far more important to the welfare of the workers to maintain their conditions during hard times. "The very fact that the workers remain organized, ostensibly only for the 'benefits,' is all important, inasmuch as their organization is always a lever to protect them from all the wrong and injustice successfully practiced upon the unorganized."[40]

Gompers' first convention met in Rochester on August 3, 1877. There were only eight delegates present; the other nine locals could not afford to send representatives. Gompers served on several committees, but his principal effort was to secure the adoption of a series of constitutional amendments which he proposed, providing for the support of unemployed, sick, and traveling members of the union. These amendments were defeated, as was his proposal for a revamped revenue system needed to finance this program. Gompers was so disappointed with the work of the convention that he voted against the constitution.[41]

But this defeat did not discourage him. He persisted in his agitation. The following year the International adopted his plan for loans to members who had to move to another city to secure employment. In 1879 he was appointed secretary of the committee on the constitution. It proposed a plan for sick benefits and death benefits for members who had been in good standing during the previous year; this was to keep them "faithful and steady." These proposals were adopted by the convention and ratified by the membership. Gompers believed that the phenomenal increase in the membership of Local 144 was due to the introduction of these benefits. It had less than 300 members at the beginning of 1881 and over 3,000 by September. At the convention that year, the local so far overshadowed the others that Gompers, one of fifty-three delegates, held one third of all the votes.

Local 144 then set out to secure jobless benefits. In 1888 it proposed a constitutional amendment providing that each member in good standing should be entitled to fifty cents for each day of unemployment, up to seventy-two dollars a year. This was to be accompanied by an increase in dues to twenty-five cents a week. The membership defeated these amendments by a narrow margin, but the following year Gompers reintroduced them and this time they were adopted.

The second major phase of Gompers' "new unionism" was a plan for the centralized control of strikes. The cigarmakers laid down their tools recklessly and frequently, often without discussion, and nearly always without adequate preparation. The great majority of their strikes was lost, the treasury of their union was depleted, and members left the organization in disgust or discouragement. It was obvious to Gompers that these practices must be brought under control. Beginning with his own organization, he persuaded the New York cigarmakers to require that when any group of workers went on strike without first having submitted their cause to the organization for consideration and approval, it was the duty of the union to man the shop with other members of the union or even with nonunion men. In 1879, Local 144 proposed an amendment to the constitution of the International Union to guarantee financial support to members on strike at the rate of six dollars per week, providing the strike was approved by the Executive Board. The president would then issue a circular appeal for assistance and a weekly assessment on each local in proportion to its membership, sufficient to secure the necessary funds for strike relief. Every strike involving more than ten members would be submitted to a vote of the locals, and those involving demands for wage increases would have to receive a two-thirds vote to be eligible for assistance. Finally, each local would be required to retain in its treasury a sum of fifteen cents per member to be used as a strike fund.

In a letter to the *Cigar Makers' Official Journal,* Gompers pointed out that the system of sporadic assessments then in use caused sudden strains on almost empty treasuries and pockets, and that it was not always a reliable source of revenue. Furthermore, the periodic publication of the state of the strike fund would have another advantage: members would be more cautious in sanctioning strikes if they knew the fund was low and they themselves might be liable for further assessments. Large numbers of strikers were being forced to return to work due to lack of assistance. In time of peace, he asserted, it was necessary to prepare for war. The amendment was adopted by a two to one vote.[48]

In 1883 President Strasser reported that during the previous two years there had been 218 applications for strikes, nearly all for wage increases; that 194 of them had been approved; and that about three fourths of these had been won. At a cost of $77,000, wage increases of nearly two million dollars had been gained, besides another $500,000 saved by preventing reductions. During the next two years, half of the strikes were successful. This was a fairly remarkable record for those years of depression, but Gompers was not satisfied. In 1885 he was appointed secretary of the committee on strikes at the Cincinnati convention, and in his report he urged the necessity of more stringent regulations:

". . . is it to the best interests of our organization and trade to at all times strike, even when the employer possesses the vantage ground, or is it not better to act like a well-drilled and disciplined army that is directed to reach a certain position, under the very fire of the enemy, with orders *not to shoot*, even amidst the greatest provocation? Certainly some men are shot down and lost; but the ranks are closed up again, and the march is onward until the position is gained, when a volley is fired in return with telling effect. . . . It is not wise nor practical, to *at all times strike, even against a reduction of wages*. The first and main object should be, if a reduction of wages cannot be successfully resisted, accept it; but maintain your organization, for by that means, and that means only, can we at the earliest possible time regain our lost ground, and even something more. . . ."

Gompers recommended that all strikes require a two-thirds vote of approval by the membership of the International before being eligible for assistance, and that after a strike had been in progress for three months, and again every month thereafter, another vote be taken on whether aid should be continued or not. He further suggested that when a strike involving over fifty members had lasted eight weeks, the president should appoint a representative of the International to proceed to the locality of the strike, attend all meetings of the local strike committee, make regular reports to the president, and if necessary examine the books and papers of the union. Most of these proposals were adopted. Thus the Cigarmakers International Union, largely through the prodding of the young delegate from New York, perfected one of the most rigid plans of strike control and strike assistance practiced by any union in the country.

The program of union benefits and strike assistance obviously necessitated a financial system capable of supporting it. While pushing his plan of business unionism through the International, Gompers also succeeded in having the union adopt a uniform initiation fee of one dollar and uniform dues of ten cents a week (increased to two dollars and twenty cents respectively in 1881), and the strike fund and assessment system, with a sinking fund of two dollars per member; Gompers succeeded in getting it raised to five dollars in 1893. He also secured the adoption by the cigarmakers of the equalization system, a plan widely used in British unions but unusual in the United States: if the funds of any local became exhausted through legitimate expenditures, it had access to the funds of the other locals. Thus, the treasuries of the various locals virtually became common property, and every three months they were redistributed on the basis of membership and financial status.

Gompers was a perennial foe of what he called "Cheap John Unionism." "There is not a dollar which the working man and woman pays into an organization of labor," he declared, "which does not come back a hundred fold." Wages are low? True, he answered, but if the unions were not financially sustained, wages could be cut even further, and the "money you refused to pay into your union as dues will go into the coffers of the employers." High dues will keep out new members? When the workers see that the union provides a stone wall of protection for their interests, they will soon come within the wall for protection.[42]

Gompers' conception of the "new unionism" was compounded of several additional ingredients. It included a more efficient plan of local organization. It meant the active support of the official journal as a medium through which grievances and opinions could be exchanged, and, above all, "as a means of promulgating the principles of Trades Unionism and as an agitator for the organization of the working classes. . . ." The new unionism meant the negotiation of trade agreements and their faithful fulfillment. It meant co-operation with other organizations in a national labor federation, and with the cigarmakers' organizations in other countries. It meant whatever was necessary "to develop power adequate to secure better working conditions." It was a "practical" program to secure immediate results through discipline, centralized control, and businesslike methods.[43]

Gompers' efforts in placing the International Union on a sound basis, plus his position as representative of the most powerful local in the country, soon won for him a position of leadership in the organization. In the convention of 1881, he was unanimously elected the union's delegate to the National Labor Congress, out of which grew the American Federation of Labor. He represented the cigarmakers in every convention of the Federation except one until his death. In 1886 the second vice-president of the International Union resigned and Gompers was elected to fill his place, defeating Fred Haller of New York, a socialist. In 1896 he ran for first vice-president and won the position which he retained the rest of his life. In this capacity he had not only the regular duties of a member of the Executive Board—voting on strike applications and appeals from the decisions of the president—but others which took up much of his time. He received an average of twenty appeals a year, each of which required his writing at least four letters and the maintenance of a file on the appeals and votes. In addition there were appeals from the decisions of the Executive Board to the membership, and other matters requiring correspondence. He was allowed up to $250 per year to cover his expenses, but during the first sixteen years of his incumbency he rendered no bill to the union. In 1912 a fixed salary of $150 was made a perquisite of the office, and made retroactive to 1896, so that Gompers received the handy sum of $2,400: a gift, rather than payment for expenses, since Gompers had not actually incurred any considerable expense during that period, conducting most of his business for the union from the offices of the American Federation of Labor.[44]

Solomon Gompers was proud of his son's position in the union, and in his later years referred to him, not as the president of the American Federation of Labor, but as the vice-president of the Cigarmakers International Union. But the greater part of his son's activities was enacted on the wider stage of the national labor movement.

Chapter Three

FEDERATION

1. THE POTTER AND THE POT

EARLY IN HIS CAREER, GOMPERS RECOGNIZED THE importance of federating the trade unions on a local and national scale. He had three objectives: to strengthen the solidarity of labor for mutual self-help; to use the federated bodies as vehicles for the establishment and strengthening of pure and simple trade unionism; and, finally, to create a larger field on which to exercise his talent and ambition and fulfill the mission of his life. His first endeavor was the formation of a new central body of trade unions in New York City.

There were already two central bodies in New York, one consisting of English-speaking workers and the other of German-American unionists. Both of these bodies admitted representatives of socialist organizations as well as trade unions, and they emphasized political agitation and activity as well as economic struggle. Gompers and a group of his friends, mostly ex-socialists like Laurell, Strasser, and McDonnell, determined to establish a central labor union from which socialists would be excluded. They were convinced that the labor movement must consist of trade unionists only and be controlled by them. "We had faith in the democratic theory that wage-earners understood their problems and could deal with them better than outsiders," wrote Gompers. "We preferred to rely upon ourselves, make mistakes perhaps, but we could profit by them and thus advance along the road to knowledge and progress free to follow our best judgment." Consequently, they formed the Amalgamated Trades and Labor Assembly. It was made up only of "bona fide" trade unions, and delegates were required to be wage earners working at their respective vocations.

Gompers and his associates acquired a journal to promote their views of trade unionism: a weekly New York paper, *The*

Socialist, which had been founded by Strasser, McGuire, and McDonnell when they were members of the I.W.A. Aided by Hugh McGregor, its editor, the trade unionists captured the paper, thus securing an established organ for themselves while at the same time striking a blow against the socialist press. The name of the paper was changed to the *Labor Standard,* and McDonnell was made editor. It became the spokesman for the trade union movement and the official journal of the Amalgamated Trades and Labor Assembly.[1]

In the late 1870's, Gompers also conceived the idea of a national federation of trade unions organized on similar principles and with similar objectives. A friend of his recalled that he had met Gompers when the latter got off the train at South Bend, Indiana, where he had come to organize a local of the cigarmakers' union. After discussing the local situation, Gompers told him: "My life work has now begun. As a part of this work I am establishing a union of cigar makers in the principal cities of Indiana. But all this is only incidental to my greater project. I predict that some day I shall be able to form a federation of all the labor organizations of the United States, and that of that federation I shall one day be president."[2]

This was a particularly unfavorable time to attempt the organization of a national labor body, and two such organizations—the National Labor Union and the Industrial Congress—had already gone down in the depression of the 1870's. But Gompers, nothing daunted, kept trying. His efforts were directed through a group known as the Economic and Sociological Club, of which McGregor, McDonnell, Laurell, Berliner, and Edward Grosse, as well as Gompers, were members. This club was organized as an informal group for the purpose of working out a "line" and then boring from within their organizations to secure the acceptance of their program by the labor movement. As Gompers described it, it was "a practical clearing agency in the development of trade union understanding."

They drafted a letter which they sent to the *National Labor Tribune.* It declared "that the present social and political systems are false and require to be changed from their very foundations ... that the present degraded dependence of the working man upon the capitalist for the means of livelihood is the cause of the greater part of the intellectual, moral and economic degradation that afflicts society, that every political movement must be subordinated to the first great social end, viz., the economic emancipation of the working classes."[3] They appealed to workingmen to enter into correspondence with them "so as to effect that unity without which all attempts to achieve social progress by political means must be unsuccessful."[4]

Responses to their appeal were few, and it was not until the clouds of depression were clearing that the successful organization of a national labor body began. In 1878 the Knights of Labor, following some years of development, in the course of which it inherited the organizational remnants of the old National Labor Union, set itself up on a national basis. In the same year the first steps were taken that led to the foundation of the American Federation of Labor. The Amalgamated Association of Iron and Steel Workers entered into correspondence with the other trade unions to arrange for a federation, but there were not sufficient replies to warrant the calling of a convention. In the following two years, the Typographical Union took the leadership in promoting federation, but with little tangible result.[5]

Then an overture came from a new quarter. An invitation was sent out early in 1881 for a conference at Terre Haute on August 2 to effect the organization of an "International Amalgamated Union." The call came from the Knights of Industry, a secret society in Indiana, and the Amalgamated Labor Union, composed of disaffected members of the Knights of Labor. The Cigarmakers International Union resolved to support the conference, and Strasser appointed Gompers to represent the International. But serious illness in his family and the death of one of his children prevented him from going, and the cigarmakers were unofficially represented by W. C. Pollner, the delegate of the Cleveland Trades Assembly. The lake seamen and the typographers were the only other national trade unions to send delegates. The majority of the delegates represented city central bodies and local trade unions, and five represented the Amalgamated Labor Union.

The Amalgamated Labor Union presented a plan of organization which declared against trade unions and expressed the intention of driving them out of existence. The real purpose of the A.L.U. was evidently to establish a secret order to supplant the Knights of Labor and the trade unions, and to dedicate it to the propagation of Greenbackism. The trade unionists proposed that the meeting adjourn until the following day in order to allow time for consideration.[6] They then met in caucus and determined to press for the adjournment of the conference to a later date and to a city where the largest number of trade unions could be represented. They decided on Pittsburgh as the city where they could make the strongest showing. This proposal was presented by McGuire, and during each recess the trade unionists bought drinks for "the boys" and labored to secure their support.[7]

The strategy succeeded, and a call was issued to the trade and labor unions of the United States and Canada, inviting them to send delegates to a National Labor Congress in Pittsburgh on November 15, 1881. The call was written by nine men, one a member of the A.L.U., the others trade unionists. They proposed the organization of a body modeled after the British Trade Union Congress. One hundred and seven delegates, representing about 40,000 union members in thirteen states, attended the Congress. They were fairly evenly divided between trade unionists and Knights of Labor. Thirty trade unions were represented, including the Cigarmakers International, which had unanimously elected Samuel Gompers as its delegate.[8]

Having organized two dual unions already—the United Cigarmakers to force a more liberal constitution on the International, and the Amalgamated Trades and Labor Assembly of New York to wrest local control from the socialists—Gompers now came to Pittsburgh to help launch a new national body in opposition to the Knights of Labor. Gompers' strength as a labor leader rested on the fact that he was a true representative of the organizations he headed, but he first created those organizations in his own image. Omar Khayyam's question might have been asked of Gompers and the trade union movement: "Tell me then, Who is the Potter, pray, and who the Pot?"

2. THE FEDERATION OF TRADES

TURNER HALL IN PITTSBURGH WAS FULL OF RUMORS that the Knights of Labor and the socialists had prepared to capture the National Labor Congress—the former for the purpose of killing it in the bud, the latter for the purpose of committing it to the support of their party. On the evening of November 15, a report leaked out from the committee on organization that it had decided to nominate a well known socialist for president of the Congress. The following morning the *Pittsburgh Commercial-Gazette* appeared with a front page story reporting the prevalent belief that an attempt would be made to capture the organization for Gompers, "the leader of the Socialistic element" and "one of the smartest men present." It added that if this occurred, the Congress would probably be split. Similar accounts were printed in the other dailies. When chairman John Jarrett of the steelworkers called the meeting to order that morning, there was great excitement in the hall. A number of delegates asked for the floor, and Gompers secured it on a question of personal privilege. He asked that the article in the *Gazette* be read to the convention, then made a declaration that he had no sympathy for or affiliation with any organization other than the Cigarmakers International Union, and that his name was considered by the committee without his knowledge or consent. It had been charged, and Gompers believed, that the western delegates had planted the articles in the press in order to discredit Gompers and win the office for Jarrett, but this was denied by one of their spokesmen.

The committee on organization then presented its report, nominating Gompers for the presidency. A minority report recommended Richard Powers of the Lake Seamen's Union. Neither report had recommended for office a representative of the steelworkers, which had the largest number of delegates at the Congress, and consequently both were tabled. Jarrett, Gompers, and Powers were then nominated from the floor. The latter two withdrew in favor of Jarrett in order to preserve unity and prevent dissension from arising over the election of the first president of the organization. Jarrett was elected unanimously, and Gompers and Powers were elected vice-presidents by acclamation.[9]

Gompers was appointed chairman of the committee on organization, and on the third day he presented his report. It proposed that the name of the organization be The Federation of Trades Unions of the United States and Canada. A number of delegates protested that such a narrow designation would exclude the Knights of Labor, local unions not affiliated with a national or international organization, and unskilled workers not belonging to any trade. Although Gompers assured them that there was no intention to exclude any workingman, they were taking no chances, and adopted the name Federation of Organized Trades *and Labor* Unions. However, Gompers' plan of representation virtually assured the domination of the Federation by the trade unions, for it provided representation for national and international unions on the basis of their membership, but only one delegate from each trades assembly. He effectively opposed a substitute resolution which would have given equal representation to all organizations, including locals. He pointed out that this would give greater representation to the smaller unions and that it would practically guarantee control of the convention by the city in which it met. He had in mind his defeat as president of the Congress when he made this point, for the preponderance of Pittsburgh delegates was Jarrett's chief source of strength. As a result of Gompers' plan, few Knights of Labor were present at future conventions of the Federation. The committee's report also provided for a revenue to be derived from a per capita tax of three cents per member annually.[10]

The other sections of the report indicate that Gompers and the rest of the committee looked upon the Federation as primarily a political body. When he arrived in Pittsburgh he gave an interview to the *Commercial-Gazette*, stating that the objective of the convention was to concentrate the forces of labor to gain needed reforms. The principal means would be a Congressional Labor Committee to secure desirable legislation. Gompers referred to the progress being made by the British labor movement by similar means.[11] His committee on organization outlined the objectives of the Federation: to encourage and form trades and labor unions and local trades assemblies, and secure legislation in the interests of the workers. The only officers provided for the Federation were five members of a Legislative Committee, one of whom would be the secretary of the committee and of the Federation, the actual chief executive of the organization. The only remuneration they would receive was three dollars a day for loss of time plus traveling and incidental expenses. These sections of the report were adopted, as was a seventeen-point legislative program.

In the election of the general secretary, Gompers received a plurality on the first two ballots, but when two candidates with-drew, their votes went to W. H. Foster of Cincinnati, and Gompers came out second. He was elected to the Legislative Committee, along with Alex Rankin, Richard Powers, and C. F. Burgman. The committee in turn elected Powers president and Gompers vice-president of the committee for the ensuing year.[12] Gompers was elected president or vice-president of the Legislative Commit-tee each year except 1884, but there was little work or responsibility connected with the office. The committee met only once a year, immediately following the annual session of the Federation, the rest of its duties being performed through a desultory correspond-ence. Gompers was at various times commissioned to represent the Federation in presenting testimony to the New York legisla-ture on the tenement-house bill, to the Senate Committee on Rela-tions Between Capital and Labor, and to a congressional com-mittee in favor of a bill permitting the incorporation of trade unions.

The Legislative Committee met in the St. Clair Hotel on November 19 and 20, 1881, to implement the work of the conven-tion. Other than routine arrangements and the adoption of a seal representing hands clasped across the globe with the motto *Labor Omnia Vincit*, the committee took action on only two matters of importance. Gompers offered a resolution, which was unanimously adopted, that no member of the committee should publicly endorse any political party, although he might advocate the election of a candidate pledged to support labor measures. In addition, Gompers and Rankin prepared an address to the trades and labor unions of North America, reporting on the work of the Congress and appeal-ing to them to ratify its action and to assist the Federation with financial contributions for legislative propaganda. Ten thousand copies of the circular were distributed, but only $300 was con-tributed to finance the work of the Federation. This, together with the lack of a full-time executive, a headquarters, or a journal, greatly limited the work of the committee.[13]

When the second annual session convened in 1882, the leading spirits of the Federation must have questioned whether the organi-zation had not been stillborn. Only nineteen delegates were pres-ent, representing eight national and international unions and ten trades assemblies. Not only had the Knights of Labor been excluded from the session, but many of the unions represented at the founding convention had failed to affiliate with the Federation. Now it was faced with the defection of its largest affiliate. Gompers, as chairman of the committee on platform, recommended repeal of the resolution in favor of a protective tariff which had been adopted the previous year. It was of little or no value to labor, he argued, which needed protection against the importation of cheap labor rather than of cheap goods. It was an issue which would only divide the workingmen. When his recommendation was adopted, the delegates of the Amalgamated Association of Iron and Steel Workers walked out of the convention and the Association later "disaffiliated" itself from the Federation.[14]

A number of steps were taken to pump life into the Federation. The three cents per capita tax, which was not being paid, was reduced to one cent, against the opposition of Gompers. On a motion by Gompers, women's labor organizations were invited to send representatives to future congresses on an equal footing with those of men. But of much greater importance was the tendency to transform the Federation from a legislative body to one which would aid and guide the trade unions in economic struggles. P. J. McGuire, secretary of the newly organized United Brotherhood of Carpenters and Joiners, urged that industrial rather than political unity be the primary objective of the Federation, and that it render pecuniary and moral assistance during strikes and lockouts. He wanted an enactment by the workmen themselves that after a given date eight hours should constitute a day's work, and they themselves should enforce it. He pleaded for harmony on economic questions upon which unionists were agreed and the ignoring of political questions likely to divide them. The convention endorsed these recommendations, thus marking out a new line of development for the Federation.[15]

The implementation of these views was begun at the next annual session, of which Gompers was elected chairman. A resolution was passed recommending that the unions increase their dues so as to accumulate strike funds, that they adopt benefit features to make their organizations more cohesive and permanent, and that the Federation consider a system of mutual strike assistance. Gompers and Fred Blend, co-delegates, took the initiative in following up this resolution in their report to the cigarmakers' convention the following month. They proposed that the International pledge itself to any amount up to ten per cent of its revenue for a Federation strike fund.[16]

Gompers was not able to attend the convention in Chicago in 1884 because of the serious illness of his wife and two of his children, this being the only convention of the Federation he missed in forty-four years. But the action of the cigarmakers' union was reported and approved. The proposal did not receive the necessary number of votes required for ratification, although a majority of the unions were in favor of the idea, and it is evident that at least the leaders of the Federation were coming to regard some system of mutual aid in economic battles as a function which the body must soon adopt.[17]

3. THE EIGHT-HOUR MOVEMENT

THE FINAL EFFORT OF THE FEDERATION TO BE-come a force in the labor movement was the inauguration of the eight-hour movement which culminated in 1886. This was more an unplanned shot in the dark than a well directed campaign. True, most industrial workers desperately needed this reform: they labored under the ten-hour system, or sixty hours a week, and some, like bakers and transportation workers, generally toiled eighty-four to a hundred or more hours a week. But if the depression years of 1883-85 were hardly an opportune time to inaugurate a strike movement for shorter hours, the Federation of Trades, on its last legs, had nothing to lose.[18]

The Cleveland convention of 1882 had adopted Peter Mc-Guire's resolution declaring the supreme importance of the eight-hour workday. It would provide more work, permit the enjoyment of more wealth by those who created it, encourage the intellectual and moral advancement of the masses, and permanently increase wages. It would also strengthen the position of the working class, diminish the power of the rich over the poor, and "gradually merge the wage-system of labor into a system of industrial co-operation in which wages will represent the earnings and not (as now) the necessities of the wage-laborers." Although the resolution was only a declaration of sentiments, Gompers, practical as usual, could not see the value of committing the Federation to a theory, particularly when it included such radical phrases as "lightening the burden of carrying the useless classes," a phrase to which he specifically took exception. Gompers didn't trust theories, even as a guide to action, and much less when they had no immediate relation to any visible consequence. He also believed that the majority of his constituents were not ready for the actual enforcement of the eight-hour day at that time. He therefore opposed the adoption of the resolution. But his suggestion was not heeded, and the resolution was passed.[19]

The following year, Secretary Frank Foster reported that the affiliated organizations wished the Federation to assume the initiative in a national movement for the reduction of hours. There was little doubt, he thought, that a universal, centrally directed movement would prove successful. The convention therefore directed that a vote be taken by the affiliated unions as to the feasibility of a general strike for a working day of eight or nine hours, to take effect not later than May 1, 1886.[20]

The question was submitted to ninety-six unions. Of the seventy-eight which voted, sixty-nine were in the affirmative. However, many of the unions were merely approving the system rather than a general strike, and a number of them doubted the possibility of success on the date indicated. Consequently, the affiliated organizations were asked to report whether they intended to inaugurate the eight-hour day in their trades and what steps they had taken. Before striking, they were to ask their employers to sign an agreement to be prepared by the Legislative Committee of the Federation. If their demands were refused and they called a strike, then the Legislative Committee was to request assistance for them from the organizations that were not ready to make the fight. The preparation of the form agreements and the issuance of the appeal to the trade unions constituted the limits of the Federation's preparation for the inauguration of the movement. Without a treasury or a system of strike benefits, with only seven national affiliated unions, and with the Knights of Labor ignoring their invitation to co-operate, there was little more that it could do. Had it not been for a revival of trade, the growing unrest of the workers, and the spontaneous and rapid expansion of the Knights of Labor in 1885 and '86, the Federation's plan would have been stillborn.[21]

The cigarmakers won the easiest and most complete victory of any union. They decided that after January 2, 1886, they would not work more than nine hours a day, and after May 1 the maximum would be eight hours. This was approved by a two to one vote of the membership and went into effect as scheduled without resistance from the employers.[22] The German printers won a similar victory, but the other trades did not have it so easy. One hundred and ninety thousand workers struck for the shorter workday, and another 150,000 participated in the movement without striking. Although more than half of the strikes were lost, nearly 200,000 workers secured an average reduction of three hours in their work week. However, some of these gains were subsequently lost, and nearly all were accompanied by wage reductions.[23]

One reason for the limited success of the movement was the opposition of the leaders of the Knights of Labor. In 1883 they went on record in favor of the eight-hour day, and the following year adopted a resolution to shorten the hours of labor by a "general refusal to work for more than eight hours." But this was implemented only by agitation, and in 1885 Terence V. Powderly, Grand Master Workman of the Knights, asserted that the eight-hour question was a political rather than an economic one, and that the proposal to inaugurate a general strike on May 1, 1886, should be discountenanced because of lack of preparation and the unreadiness of the workers to carry it through. The following months witnessed an upsurge in the labor movement which tended to focus on the eight-hour movement and May 1. Tens of thousands of workers flocked into the Knights of Labor, often in the belief that the Knights were the sponsors of the movement. Powderly, sensing a "grave danger" in these developments, issued a secret circular on March 13 ordering the assemblies not to strike for the eight-hour system under the impression that they were obeying orders from the organization or that they would receive support from it.[24]

In spite of Powderly, the eight-hour movement provided a tremendous stimulus to the entire labor movement. Secretary Foster of the Federation stated that never before had there been such a general upheaval among the industrial masses in the United States. But the workers, ignoring the organization which had sponsored the movement, swarmed into the Knights of Labor and left the Federation still floundering on its last legs. Gompers was piqued that the Federation went unnoticed while the Knights of Labor was acclaimed as the leader of the American labor movement.[25]

On May 1, Gompers was one of the speakers at a demonstration of nearly 10,000 workers in New York's Union Square. The workers carried banners and torches to the square, where music, fireworks, and electric lights helped to draw 20,000 spectators to the meeting. Union leaders and socialists denounced the reign of terror directed against the rights of the workingmen and declared that May 1 would be forever remembered as a second declaration of independence.[26] In Chicago, a much more fateful meeting was being conducted.

A dispute had arisen between the McCormick Harvester Company and its employees due to the discharge of a number of men engaged in union activity. A lockout and strike resulted in February. The plant was reopened in March with strikebreakers, aided by Pinkerton operatives and the Chicago police. During the following month there were numerous disturbances near the plant, generally resulting from police efforts to break up meetings of the strikers and their sympathizers. This dispute only indirectly related to the eight-hour movement, but both were part of the general labor unrest in Chicago. Both reached a culmination at the same time, and they were closely associated in the public mind as well as in the minds of the union leaders. On May 1, there were parades and demonstrations in the city, and 30,000 workers struck for eight hours, but the day passed peacefully. On May 3, the lumber shovers' union, on strike for shorter hours, arranged a meeting near the McCormick plant. The central labor union sent as a reporter August Spies, an anarchist with influence in the local labor movement, who was a leader of the Eight-Hour League. Asked to address the 6,000 assembled strikers, he spoke only on the shorter hours question and urged the workers to stand together. Before he finished his speech, the strikebreakers began to leave the McCormick plant and about 500 of the men at the meeting went to meet them, although Spies urged them to remain. They attacked the strikebreakers, whereupon the police charged and fired on them, killing or wounding about six men.

The next day the workers were in a bad temper and there

were clashes throughout the day. Arrangements were made by delegates of the unions for a demonstration that evening in Haymarket Square to protest against police brutality. The meeting was addressed by Spies and two other anarchists, Albert R. Parsons and Samuel Fielden. They attacked the tyranny of the police and their capitalistic masters and spoke of the need for changing the existing social system. Mayor Carter Harrison, who was present until ten o'clock and heard all three speakers, found the meeting orderly and left after suggesting to the police inspector that the police be sent home. It began to rain, and most of the audience departed. As the speakers were descending from the wagon, a bomb exploded among the police, killing one of them instantly and wounding almost seventy. The police opened fire on the spectators, killing at least one and wounding numerous others.[27]

It was immediately assumed that the anarchists had perpetrated this outrage, and the press of the country demanded vengeance. Even organized labor joined in the condemnation of radicalism, feeling it necessary to dissociate itself from anarchists. Many unions even abandoned their eight-hour strikes for fear of being identified with anarchism.[28]

Gompers remained silent until after the trial of the eight anarchists charged with being accessories to the murder of the policemen. The trial was marked by Judge Joseph Gary's careless acceptance of obviously prejudiced jurors who were selected to convict the defendants, and by the lack of evidence that any of the defendants threw the bomb or had been involved in a conspiracy to have it thrown. The testimony was contradictory, often false, and in nearly every respect inconclusive. It soon became clear that the defendants were not on trial for the crimes alleged, but for their opinions, and Judge Gary lent his support to this purpose by attempting to sway the jury and by preventing a fair trial.[29] All but one of the defendants were sentenced to death.

The first reaction of the labor movement was again to attempt to dissociate itself from the anarchists. But the labor leaders soon began to realize that the attacks involved labor as well. The labor organizations began a campaign to reverse the process of "judicial murder," and Gompers finally joined the campaign. On September 16, 1887, as the date of execution approached, the Central Labor Union of New York and District Assembly 49 of the

Knights of Labor jointly endorsed a public appeal to the workers to do all in their power to secure a modification of the sentence. Signed by Gompers, James Quinn of D.A. 49, and twelve others, the appeal asserted that "Liberty, free speech and justice impartially and fearlessly meted out to friend and foe, are the only safeguards and the primary conditions of a peaceable social development in this country." Convinced that the condemned men were victims of prejudice and class hatred, and that their execution "would be a disgrace to the honor of our nation, and would strengthen the doctrines that it is ostensibly directed against," it urged all labor organizations to issue a call for a great public demonstration to be held on or about the twentieth of October. Such meetings were held in a number of cities. A crowd of three to four thousand workers packed Cooper Union to hear Gompers, McGuire, Quinn, and Daniel De Leon and to pass resolutions which disavowed sympathy with anarchism but protested against the denial of a fair trial.[30]

Writing to Governor John Oglesby of Illinois four days before the execution date, Gompers emphasized that the Federation was at war with anarchism and that anarchism would be encouraged by the execution of the condemned men. In the name of the Federation he implored the Governor to commute the death sentence.[31] Gompers had another reason for desiring justice for the anarchists, which he only hinted at in his public statements. He felt that the labor movement could not safely abandon its radical wing to the "vengeance of the common enemy." An attack on the rights of one would destroy the rights of all; therefore labor "must do its best to maintain justice for the radicals or find itself denied the rights of free men."

On November 9 he was sitting in his office back of Local 144. Ed King and James Lynch came in and asked him to go to Springfield as the representative of the New York trades assembly on the amnesty committee which had arranged an audience with Governor Oglesby the next day. He left immediately for the train, with nothing but what he was wearing at the time. In a day-long session, Gompers made what the *Chicago Tribune* and the Governor himself considered the most effective appeal for the condemned men. He asserted that while he and the anarchists were "fighting for labor upon different sides of the house," he did not want to see injustice done to anyone, and expressed the belief that the Chicago police were in some measure responsible for the Haymarket incident. "I ask myself what good can come to the people of the State of Illinois; what good can come to the people of our country . . . if these men are executed? . . . Hundreds of thousands of laboring men all over the world would consider that those men had been executed because they were standing up for free speech and free assemblage. We ask you, sir, to interpose your great power and prevent so dire a calamity."[32]

That evening Gompers went to Chicago with some friends. He spent "a night of horror" brooding over the thought of the executions and of the consequences to the labor movement that would follow. They wandered through the streets all the following day, utterly depressed at the tragedy. They learned that their efforts had been only partly successful, resulting in the commutation of the sentences of two of the prisoners who had requested it. Louis Lingg committed suicide in his cell on the eve of the execution date, and on November 11 the other four—Parsons, George Engel, Adolph Fischer, and Spies—went to the gallows, the latter proclaiming that "There will come a time when our silence will be more powerful than the voices you strangle today!" With the election of John Peter Altgeld as Governor of Illinois, the Amnesty Association renewed its activities, and the Federation joined in its plea for the pardon of Oscar W. Neebe, Samuel Fielden, and Michael Schwab. When Altgeld pardoned them, writing a devastating denunciation of the trial proceedings, he received the sincere thanks of Samuel Gompers.[33]

Part II

FOUNDATIONS OF THE
AMERICAN FEDERATION OF LABOR

1886-1892

Chapter Four

GOMPERS AND THE KNIGHTS
OF LABOR

1. AMELIORATION AND EMANCIPATION

WHILE THE FEDERATION OF ORGANIZED TRADES AND Labor Unions was floundering, initiating movements which it could not control, and sinking into oblivion, a conflict was developing between the trade unions and the Knights of Labor which was to bring the unions together in a new national federation on a more solid basis. The antagonism of the Knights of Labor leaders to the eight-hour movement of 1886 was merely a reflection of more deep-rooted conflict between the Order and the trade unions.

The Noble and Holy Order of the Knights of Labor was organized in 1869 by a group of garment cutters in Philadelphia, and in 1878 a national organization, the General Assembly, was effected. Observing the growing power of capital and the consequent danger of the pauperization of the toiling masses, it proposed to check these trends and assure the laborers the fruits of their toil by their thorough unification. It adopted a platform which was similar in many respects to that adopted by the A.F. of L. two years later, with two important exceptions. The K. of L. emphasized producers' and distributors' co-operatives, the reservation of the public land for actual settlers, and the establishment of a national legal tender currency based on the faith and resources of the nation, issues in which the trade unions were not interested. It also deplored strikes and advocated arbitration whenever possible. The constitution of the Order provided for a centralized organization, in which the General Assembly had full and final jurisdiction, with authority to make laws, decide all controversies, issue charters, tax the members, and (later) administer the strike fund. Membership was open to any one except bankers, lawyers, liquor traffickers, professional gamblers, and stockbrokers.[1]

Gompers, reflecting the attitude of most trade unionists, found little in the philosophy of the Knights of Labor he could accept.

Besides, there were temperamental differences between him and Powderly which made it difficult for them to understand each other or to work together. Gompers, the extrovert, the hail-fellow-well-met, militant and aggressive, was almost the direct opposite of Powderly, quiet, cautious, and prim, ever considerate of the "public" attitude toward him. Then again, Powderly was a total abstainer, and had little sympathy or understanding for a man like Gompers, who drank freely and frequented the saloons, which were the workingmen's clubs and meeting places.

More important than personal differences were disagreements over the principles of labor organization. Gompers did not believe in secret organization, or approve of the elaborate ritual which the Knights employed at their meetings. He felt that the workers could not waste time on such nonsense and should be attracted to unionism by an understanding of its principles.

One of the most fundamental differences between Gompers and the Knights of Labor was that the latter was essentially a holdover from the early nineteenth century labor movement. Then class lines had been more fluid than they became later, and the working class had been small, composed largely of artisans rather than proletarians, and constantly renewing itself from other strata of the population. The most articulate sections of the wage-earning class had been more concerned with rising out of the working class than in improving their conditions as workers. There had developed a predominant concern with such issues as land reform and homesteads, prohibition of monopoly, support of public education, and experiments in community living. In the post-Civil War years, the National Labor Union and the K. of L. concerned themselves with monetary nostrums, co-operatives, and the withholding of public lands from speculators and monopolists. Essentially middle-class reforms, their object was to keep open avenues of escape from the wage-earning class or to prevent others being forced into it.

The panacea-venders were many, and some of them were to attract the respect of posterity, as well as of many of their contemporaries. James B. Weaver, of Greenback and Populist fame, Henry George, whose "Single Tax" panacea for social ills went around the world, Edward Bellamy, whose *Looking Backward*, a vision of the future, was not only to attract a million readers, but to inspire some of them to bring the future nearer—these and others were to influence the lives of workers and to inspire legislation in their behalf. Their work did not so much oppose that of Gompers as complement it. But Gompers, fighting to establish labor as a force capable of defending its elemental interests, was in no position to weigh the social contributions of reformers dispassionately.

Such "patent-medicine" panaceas could not cure the ills of our social and economic system, Gompers wrote. They merely tended to put the class struggle out of the workers' minds by spreading the illusion that they could be transformed into farmers, businessmen, or self-employers. "When the Laboring man becomes an investor even in a small way he is less likely to engage in a conflict between labor and capital." He lost his incentive to build stable unions capable of combatting the "avarice of the capitalist classes."[2] Gompers accepted the fact that industrialization was an irreversible process, and that it had created a more or less fixed wage-earning class whose interests were opposed to those of the employers. On the one side, he saw "a class in possession of all the tools and means of labor; on the other, an immense mass begging for the opportunity to labor. In the mansion, the soft notes betokening ease and security; in the tenement the stifled wail of drudgery and poverty. The arrogance of the rich ever mounting in proportion to the debasement of the poor."

The industrial monopoly of the capitalists was the more infamous, Gompers felt, because it was acquired by the abuse of arbitrary power on the part of government which granted "monstrously unjust privileges" in the form of monopoly charters, enabling them to increase the price of their products at will and reduce the wages of labor to a bare subsistence. Gompers was equally scathing in his denunciation of the way in which the capitalists had employed their power, not to organize industry so much as to organize industrial war, and not to produce utilities so much as to extract profits. The result was "a waste of labor appalling in its recklessness and inhumanity, a misuse of capital that is really criminal and a social condition of cheerless drudgery and hopeless poverty, of sickening apprehension and fathomless degradation almost threatening the continuance of civilization."

It was these conditions that produced the labor movement as a permanent feature of modern society, an organized expression of labor's discontent with political, economic, and social misrule. Discontent was the mother of progress, declared Gompers the agitator, and he proudly admitted that he was a fomentor of discontent. When rebellion against wrong and unbearable conditions ceased, the result would be a contentment that meant stagnation and death.[3]

What, then, did Gompers conceive to be the aims of the trade union movement? He often used a phrase, until about 1900, which summed them up: "the amelioration of the conditions of the workers and their final emancipation." What does labor want? he asked, and answered: "It wants the earth and the fulness thereof. There is nothing too precious, there is nothing too beautiful, too lofty, too ennobling, unless it is within the scope and comprehension of labor aspirations and wants."[4]

But no list of specific demands conveyed Gompers' conception of the far-reaching influence of unionism. He agreed with the German poet and rebel, Heinrich Heine, that freedom is bread, and bread, freedom; material improvement in the conditions of the workers was the basis for the exercise and enjoyment of liberty. It made it possible for the working people to live better each day than the day before, "to be happier and think better, larger thoughts, and then to plan greater things for tomorrow's realization." Summing up the human and social meaning of labor's demands, Gompers declared: "We want more school houses and less jails; more books and less arsenals; more learning and less vice; more constant work and less crime; more leisure and less greed; more justice and less revenge; in fact, more of the opportunities to cultivate our better natures, to make manhood more noble, womanhood more beautiful, and childhood more happy and bright."

Gompers emphasized over and over again that there was nothing labor might achieve that could not be secured through the trade union movement. The working people had no need of any other agencies but their unions to secure whatever they wanted—whether it be higher wages, factory inspection laws, or the regeneration of society. The trade union organizes the workers as a class and teaches them the power of combination, he asserted; it imbues them with discipline, self-confidence, and loyalty to each other. "It is practical democracy; it affords within itself daily object lessons in ideal justice. . . . In contending for the political and economic rights of its members, the trade union teaches these rights to the entire working class. And on a knowledge of these rights, society will establish its future development."[5]

But Gompers was always vague about the future development of society and the coming "emancipation of labor." He occasionally asserted that the state belonged, by right, to the workers, and that they would some day come into their own "as the predestined universal element to be in control of society." He also expressed the view, privately, that the trade unions contained the germ of the future state. But what was its nature? Gompers was not sure, although it seems clear that, until the late 1890's, he envisaged the demise of the wage and profit system and the disappearance of classes based on possession of wealth and power.[6]

Gompers never specifically committed himself to a belief in socialism, but he probably came closer to that position in 1894 than at any other time. With hundreds of thousands of workers unemployed during the depression, and with the United States government virtually turned into a police state,[7] using the total executive, judicial, and military power of the nation to break strikes and repress farmers, workers, and unemployed, Gompers reflected the profound and rapid radicalization of the masses that took place in those years. In 1894 the United States strike commission asked him if he did not think the present system was a good one. He replied:

"I think it is the best we have had, but I do not think it is the best we will have.

". . . . I think that scarcely any that could be evolved out of the human mind could be much worse than that which we now have. I do not think the human family will tolerate anything worse than we have. We have grown away from things that have been worse. The question whether the Government employment of all labor— in plainer words, state socialism, is something for the future to decide. . . . I imagine that more than likely it will be necessary for our people to go through that phase. . . ."[8]

The vagueness of Gompers' views regarding his "ultimate aims" was a result of several factors. He did not always believe what he said. His purpose was to fend off criticism that he was confining the labor movement to narrow limits, and to persuade socialists and other radicals to support his immediate objectives. Again, he was constitutionally allergic to speculative thought. Pragmatic, "practical," and opportunistic in his thinking, he eschewed "flights of imagination" which appealed to "the passionate, the nervous, or the sentimental." The trade unions, he said, "are the business organizations of the wage-earners, to attend to the business of the wage-earners; and while the earnest, honest, thinking trade-unionists must necessarily be sentimental, theoretical, self-sacrificing, and brave, these if needs be must sink for a time in order that the best interests of the wage-earners may be advanced."[9]

But if he could not see how socialism would work, he thought he could see how labor's commitment to the theory of socialism would affect the trade union movement. He feared that labor would alienate public opinion if it avowed a socialist program in a nation where the wage-earning class was still a minority. He also feared that the unions, needing unity, would be divided by the question of socialism and distracted from the struggle for more immediate needs. Answering those who regarded the trade union movement as slow and conservative, he warned against hurling it "headlong into a path which, while struggling and hoping for the end, will leave us stranded and losing the practical and beneficial results of our efforts."[10]

Change must come slowly and peacefully, and the agency for effecting it must be the trade union movement. Gompers believed that a radical change in the economy of the nation was inevitable; the only question was when and how it would take place. England had been saved from reaction and slavery by reform, and France by revolution. Modern American society was faced with the same alternatives: "The organized labor movement presents a reasonable and gradual method for the peaceful solution of this great problem, this great question which will not down until it is finally settled by the full installation of man into his natural right. . . ." Gompers did not doubt that "the future will be a brighter, a happier and a nobler one than has yet dawned upon the earth." [11]

But Gompers had been through the mill, and he knew that it would require a long and militant struggle before labor won recognition of its rights. Although he insisted that labor had no desire to make war upon capital as such, but only upon "foolish, greedy, and unreasonable employers," Gompers recognized a fundamental conflict between laborers and employers. For, as he had told the Senate Committee on Capital and Labor, it was not a matter of "feeling" on the part of the employers. As buyers of labor, they wanted wages as low as possible, while the workers, as sellers of the same commodity, wanted it to be as high as possible. This produced an inevitable conflict of interests—a conflict for the largest share of the product of labor—which would last as long as the wage system prevailed. He rejected the charge that the unions were not class conscious:

"Class-conscious! As a matter of fact, there is no other organization of labor in the entire world that is so class-conscious as are the trade unions." The struggle between capital and labor was going on every day, he said, and through it labor would gradually advance toward equality and justice without a "terrible final struggle."[12]

Clearly, Gompers' conception of labor's mission opposed that of the Knights of Labor. He was militant and aggressive where they were conservative and overcautious. He was practical and businesslike, while they were visionary and utopian. He was the worker, and they were middle-class reformers. Gompers could not go along with them in their concern with monetary panaceas, land reforms, and co-operatives, or with their political adventures and their reliance on the state to emancipate the working class.

Gompers could see no sense in the Knights' policy of admitting businessmen, intellectuals, farmers, and professional reformers to their membership. Labor unions must be organizations of the working class, by the working class, and for the working class. Those who would be free, he was fond of saying, must themselves strike the blow. The workers might make mistakes, but it was better to err and learn by experience to avoid those errors in the future, than to have the affairs of the movement directed by those whose interests and understanding were not identical with those of the wageworkers.[13]

Gompers' and Powderly's divergent philosophies were also manifested in their attitude toward strikes. Because of his emphasis on politics to secure improvements for labor, his concentration on middle-class reform panaceas, and his intense conservatism, Powderly was hostile to the use of the strike as a weapon of the labor movement. After the disastrous defeats of the 1870's, he wrote: "I shudder at the thought of the strike. . . . You cannot fight against cold lead and steel with your finger-ends. . . ." Besides, he said, the losses due to strikes could never be replaced by future gains. He condemned strike agitators as firebrands and declared that "the suicidal policy of strikes is a relic of barbarism. . . ." Arbitration was a substitute for strikes, and if employers would not agree to arbitrate he would make it compulsory by law.[14]

Gompers, on the other hand, when asked by the Commissioner of Labor if he had discovered any way to avoid strikes, answered bluntly: "So long as the present industrial and commercial system will last, so long will strikes continue. . . . I believe in diminishing the numbers as much as possible . . . but in the denunciation of strikes I will not join. I regard the strikes as the sign that the people are not yet willing to surrender every spark of their manhood and their honor and their independence. It is the protest of the workers against unjust conditions; and the strike is commanding the attention of the employer class, the capitalist class, and thinkers throughout the world to the problems of labor, who would otherwise not have given the laborer a second's consideration, except as to the amount of labor that he can produce. . . ."[15]

Furthermore, Gompers believed, arbitration was generally not a substitute for strikes, but rather a result of them. For employers usually assumed the attitude that there was nothing to arbitrate, and would concede nothing or listen to no argument until the workers convinced them of their discontent and demonstrated their determination to secure betterment of their conditions by striking. He often told the story of the boy who, seeing a mangy cur whimpering on the street, kicked him and bullied him. But when he saw a bulldog growling and baring his teeth, he was careful to make a wide path around him.

Nor did Gompers, at this stage of his career, agree with Powderly that strikes were too costly a weapon for labor to employ: "When society submits its emotions and aspirations to the cost index it is lost." Who could say to what depths labor would have been degraded if it did not from time to time make a show of grit and protest its grievances in the most effective way it knew? As for the cost to the workers, it was often computed that what strikers lost in wages during a strike took years to recoup. But, Gompers asserted, the time lost in strikes was nearly always made up in greater continuity of production afterward. Workers seldom were employed continually throughout the year, and a strike merely transferred the period of idleness from one advantageous to the employers to another which was to the advantage of the employees. Even defeated strikes were no complete loss, since they demonstrated the spirit and power of organization and would convince employers that they could not attack their employees without a severe contest. Eventually, Gompers maintained with remarkable historical perspective, the "bottled up wrath" of the workers would find a vent, for every demand that the workers had ever made, no matter how often defeated, was eventually gained if they maintained their organizations and persisted in their struggle.[16]

These differences in philosophies, aims, methods, and personalities would have been enough to produce an irreconcilable incompatibility between the Knights of Labor and the trade unions. Sooner or later the former would have to reform itself to meet the needs of labor in modern industrial society or go down before the competition of a more realistic body like the A.F. of L.

The Knights of Labor contained many local trade unions and even a number of national trade unions, but the latter were always precarious and uncomfortable within the Order, accepted only because they were accomplished facts or in order to combat the Federation of Trades. Powderly believed trade districts were a step backward and should be discouraged. The Knights undermined them by permitting their locals to retain a separate existence, by obstructing them, and by failing to give them effective leadership. Even when the trade districts were well represented in the Order, the balance of power was in the hands of the mixed districts, while in the Federation of Trades the trade unions were the basic unit of strength.[17]

The K. of L. was an educational and reform organization of workers, small businessmen, farmers, and professionals, while the trade unions were militant working-class organizations on the economic front. There could have been a role for each if they had retained a division of labor; and they could have co-operated in working for common aims. But they were unable to do so, and in the middle of the 1880's, when the Knights were reaching the height of their phenomenal growth, the two elements locked in a fight to the finish.

2. FORMATION OF THE A.F. OF L.

IN 1881, WHEN THE FEDERATION OF TRADES WAS formed, the Knights of Labor had only 19,000 members. But in the next five years it experienced one of the most rapid increases in American labor history, rising to 111,000 in 1885, and bounding to a membership of between 700,000 and one million the next year. This amazing growth was in itself a major cause of its eventual downfall. It was the result of a spontaneous upheaval among the workers. It brought in its wake a series of strikes which the Knights were incompetent to lead, and which, in fact, they refused to support and sometimes sabotaged. This alarmed the trade unions, for a large part of the increase in membership was due to the affiliation of trade unionists who had rushed into the organization.[18]

The Federation not only invited the Knights to co-operate in the eight-hour movement but even proposed that they discuss possible unification between the two bodies. However, the Executive Board of the Knights aggravated the situation by opposing eight-hour strikes, and conflicts between the trade unions and the local and district assemblies of the Order mounted. K. of L. assemblies did not recognize union cards, they formed caucuses within the unions, accepted scabs expelled from the unions, and boycotted union firms. They were even accused of raiding the membership of the unions and forming dual organizations.[19]

There was scarcely a trade union in the country which did not have a grievance against the Knights of Labor or its assemblies. One of the most acute conflicts was that between the Knights and the Cigarmakers International Union. District Assembly 49 of New York, bent on the destruction of the trade unions, attempted to combine all the labor organizations in and around New York City under its charter.

The situation in the cigar trade was complicated by the continuing discord between the Cigarmakers International Union and the Cigarmakers Progressive Union, which had been formed by the seceding socialists in 1882. Under the vengeful Strasser, the

International had waged continuous warfare against the Progressives. In 1883, Local 144 even joined the cigar manufacturers' association in an effort to destroy the Progressive Union in the New York shops. The Progressives concluded that they must ally with the International, or at least arrange for peaceful coexistence. They appealed to the members of the International to discountenance Strasser's declaration that the two unions "cannot shake hands, there is nothing between them but war to the knife!" They urged unity in the fight against the common enemy. Strasser refused to consider their offer or to allow them to present it to the International convention in 1883.

Greatly outnumbering the International Union in New York, the Progressives secured the support of D.A. 49. In 1884 they struck against a wage cut at the Straiton and Storm factory, and the strike was defeated when members of the International took the places of the strikers. The Progressive Union appointed a committee to meet with the International and Local 144, to discuss amalgamation, and though Strasser expressed himself publicly against it, the New York locals continued to discuss it. At the end of 1884 they effected the first co-operative action between the two unions by agreeing to strike jointly against wage cuts at the Stachelberg factory.[20]

Early the following year, the Progressive Union again invited the International to discuss a merger. At the convention of the International Union in September 1885, Gompers and John Kirchner proposed that a committee be elected to confer with the Progressives, and Gompers was himself elected to the negotiating committee. At the October conference, in Rochester, the International committee was highly conciliatory. The locals in the Progressive Union would be allowed to retain their own declaration of principles and their own name in addition to that of the International and would be granted separate charters; but the funds of the Progressive Union would become part of the general fund of the International. The agreement was ratified by both organizations, and the amalgamation became effective on January 1, 1886.[21]

Although unification was not complete under this arrangement, it was an important step toward harmony, and it came opportunely. On the very next day after its consummation, the United Cigar Manufacturers of New York announced a reduction of wages to compete with the tenement houses. Committees representing the International and Progressive locals conferred about their policy in this situation but reached no general agreement. However, according to Gompers, they did agree that neither would confer with the employers unless representatives of the other unions were present. In any case, both determined to resist the reduction. One International shop and one Progressive shop were struck, whereupon the manufacturers closed down all their factories and locked out their employees.

Early in February the Progressive Union met the manufacturers and agreed on a new price list. The International Union accused the Progressives of breaking faith and accepting a wage scale below that established by the International. The Progressives, they said, had sold out the workers. On February 12 the lockout was called off, but the International's members did not return to work. The Knights of Labor now stepped into the picture. D.A. 49 organized all the workers who had returned to their jobs, including 7,000 Progressives, and granted them a charter as Local Assembly 2814. The District Assembly then made a settlement with the manufacturer's association on the basis of the new price scale, and granted them the use of the white label, against which the International Union promptly instituted a boycott.

Strasser denounced Powderly's "bold and unscrupulous attack" against the cigarmakers and against trade unionism. He charged that the manufacturers' association had admitted to Powderly that the employers would have to surrender unless the Knights saved them from their predicament. Strasser went to Philadelphia several times with Kirchner and Gompers to confer with the Executive Board. They demanded that the K. of L. recognize the International Union's jurisdiction in the cigar trade, denounce D.A. 49, issue no more labels, and expel members taken in after the settlement of the strike. Powderly and three other members of the Executive Board went to New York to investigate the situation, but made no concessions. Instead, they issued a circular charging the International with treachery for boycotting the white label and for accusing the Knights of organizing scabs. The only explanation for such conduct, said Powderly, was that "men who indulge to excess in the use of intoxicants cannot transact business with cool heads. . . . The General Executive

Board has never had the pleasure of meeting with Mr. Gompers when he was sober."

The Executive Board proceeded to expel the Defiance Assembly, but not before Gompers had taken out a traveling card. He, Kirchner, and Fred Haller, vice-presidents of the International, were sent by the union to rouse unionists to the danger from the policies of the Knights and to organize a boycott of the white label. In each town Gompers deposited his card with the local assembly which he addressed. The Executive Board revoked the charters of these assemblies, but Gompers kept one jump ahead of them and preserved his credentials and his good standing until he had completed his task. He then resigned his membership in the Order and surrendered his card. Local 144 also decided to publish a weekly paper to carry on its fight against the Knights. It formed the Picket Publishing Association and made Gompers the editor of the four-page journal entitled *The Picket*. This was Gompers' first job at editing and apparently lasted for only a short time.

D.A. 49, apparently encouraged by the Executive Board, decided to throw aside its Progressive allies and attempt to capture control of the cigar industry. It opened independent negotiations with the manufacturers and offered to fill the shops with workers on condition that the Knights of Labor be given a closed shop. The manufacturers accepted. In July the Knights announced that all cigarmakers who desired to retain their jobs must surrender their Progressive Union cards and take K. of L. cards. The workers rushed from the shops with the cry that they had been sold out. The manufacturers instituted another lockout, this time to enforce the Knights' closed shop. But the Progressives, with the active support and financial assistance of the International Union, took up the challenge and declared a strike. The central labor union also rebelled against the Knights and urged support for the Progressives. The Knights had lost every ally in the labor movement. Practically all the cigarmakers in New York participated in a parade to demonstrate their unity and determination. The manufacturers agreed to the demand of the Progressives that all strikers be reinstated without regard to their membership in the Order and without penalty for having gone on strike. This marked the end of the Knights of Labor in the cigar industry. Three days before this, the Progressives had voted to dissolve their organization and merge completely with the International Union.[22] Similar if less dramatic events had been taking place in other cities, and in October the General Assembly ordered all cigarmakers who belonged to both the K. of L. and the International Union to withdraw from one or the other. The breach was now complete and irreparable.

The conflict between the Knights and the other trade unions had also reached a critical stage. Peter J. McGuire of the Brotherhood of Carpenters called a conference of the national trade unions at Philadelphia on May 17, 1886, to meet the challenge. Twenty unions sent delegates, and twelve others, as well as Secretary William H. Foster of the Federation of Trades, expressed approval of the purposes of the meeting.

The assembled union officials, wearing silk hats and Prince Albert coats, denounced the aggressive acts of the Knights. To end the dissension in the labor movement, the unionists drafted a treaty to be presented to the General Assembly of the Order, which was to meet the following week in Cleveland. The treaty proposed that the K. of L. refrain from organizing dual assemblies and revoke the charters of those already formed. It demanded that the Knights reject members who worked below the union scale or who were convicted of scabbing against any union, and that it refrain from interfering with the trade unions or issuing labels in competition with those of the trade unions. In short, it was to grant the trade unions complete jurisdiction in the economic organization and struggles of the workers, and confine itself to mixed assemblies which would help organize the unorganized workers and conduct educational activities.

A committee of six, headed by McGuire, was appointed to present the treaty to the General Assembly. Also on hand at Cleveland was a special delegation of cigarmakers, including Gompers and Strasser, to present their own grievances. The General Assembly rejected the treaty, taking the view that any difficulties should be negotiated between the Knights and the various unions. Consequently, the trade union committee issued a call for a convention in Columbus, Ohio, on December 8, for the purpose of establishing a national trade union congress.[23]

In these negotiations the Federation of Trades was virtually ignored. It had failed to unite a large number of trade unions or to create an organization with full-time officers and adequate provisions for mutual help and defense. It was committed to relief through legislation rather than through union action. Gompers and the other Federation leaders recognized its inadequacy and conferred with officers of the national trade unions to help arrange the meeting in December. They also changed the date and place of their sixth annual convention so that they could meet concurrently with the trade union conference and effect a united organization.

The Federation convention was called to order on December 8 and immediately instructed the Legislative Committee to discuss amalgamation with the trade union conference. On the second day, the Federation delegates went over in a body as delegates to the trade union conference. The next day, the Legislative Committee reported that the trade union conference had formed the American Federation of Labor and had agreed to accept the old Federation, its funds ($285), papers, and effects. It also took over the Federation's preamble, which declared that "A struggle is going on in all the nations of the civilized world, between the oppressors and the oppressed of all countries, a struggle between the capitalists and the laborers, which grows in intensity from year to year, and will work disastrous results to the toiling millions, if they are not combined for mutual protection and benefit." Gompers was elected president of the new Federation.[24]

3. THE A.F. OF L. VERSUS THE KNIGHTS OF LABOR

GOMPERS SPARED NO EFFORT TO DESTROY THE INFLUence of the Knights of Labor in the trade union movement. The Cigarmakers International Union introduced a resolution in the central labor union of New York City for the endorsement of its blue label, which would mean a boycott of the Knights' white label. The resolution was brought to the floor of the first meeting of the body in 1887, presided over by Gompers. It was endorsed, and the Knights were also denounced for breaking strikes and attempting to divide the central labor union.[25]

At the same time, the issue came to a head in the Workingmen's Assembly of New York State. Gompers, having been elected president the year before, presided over the convention which met in the Albany city hall in January 1887. The trade unions and the Knights each sent the largest delegations they could muster, and rumors were rife that many of the credentials were fictitious. Gompers appointed a credentials committee of four unionists and three Knights, with George Perkins, president of the cigarmakers' union, as chairman. The committee agreed on the seating of 225 delegates but split on the others, the majority contending that they were not entitled to seats and had been sent to the convention to disrupt it. Feeling ran so high that Gompers, fearing a disturbance, ordered the galleries cleared of visitors.[26]

This brought friction to a head. A delegate rushed from the rear of the room, jumped over the bar and onto the platform, and pointed a gun at Gompers' breast. Gompers, without flinching, and smiling all the while, quickly stepped beside the man, threw his arms around him so as to pin his arms to his body, gradually moved his arms down to the gun, put it in his pocket, and said, "Now, beat it, while the going is good."[27]

When the bedlam subsided and Gompers re-established order in the hall, the convention went into executive session to consider the final report of the credentials committee. The convention sustained the trade union majority in refusing to seat the disputed delegates. It was then decided to elect officers and place all the unfinished business of the convention in the hands of a joint committee of three Knights and three unionists, one of them Gompers. Thus the control of District Assembly 49 over the State Workingmen's Assembly was overthrown and a semblance of harmony restored between the trade unionists and those Knights who were least hostile to them. But friction continued, and during the next year the Knights grew stronger. The trade unionists seceded from the Workingmen's Assembly and formed the New York State Branch of the A.F. of L. Gompers issued a charter to this dual organization, whose principal officers for the next twenty-five years were cigarmakers. The split continued for ten years, when the Workingmen's Assembly, then far outnumbered by its rival, agreed to amalgamate and form the Workingmen's Federation of the State of New York.[28]

When Gompers became president of the A.F. of L., the Knights of Labor had already passed the zenith of their power and influence. But that fact was not immediately apparent to either the trade unions or the Knights, and the fight between them remained an important factor in the labor movement for the next decade. At the Federation convention in 1886, Gompers accused the K. of L. Executive Board of selling out the interests of the workers. Reviewing the strikes which had taken place within the Order during that year, Gompers asserted that the Executive Board had consistently acceded to the demands of the employers. Pointing out that the members of the Board were grocers, ex-police chiefs, and others "floating like a scum on the top of a part of the labor movement, continually seeking to divert it to their own personal ends," he denied that they were a legitimate part of the bona fide labor movement.[29]

The impasse between the Knights of Labor and the trade unions did indeed seem unbridgeable. The former would discuss no terms of peace except absorption of the unions into their Order. But Gompers continued to insist that the trade unions must have exclusive control over trade disputes and trade organization, and that the proper role of the Knights was educational and reform activity. The members would eventually realize this and revolt, Gompers believed, and the trade unions should encourage discontent in the ranks.[30]

In 1894, Gompers was approached by Joseph R. Buchanan, a member of the typographical union who had been a labor editor, president of the Denver trades council, an organizer for the Knights of Labor and a member of its Executive Board, and the head of the Rocky Mountain division of the International Workingmen's Association. Buchanan suggested calling a conference of the labor organizations of the country to discuss the labor situation, and Gompers gave him his confidential approval. Buchanan issued the call on March 31, stating that the purpose of the meeting was to make preliminary arrangements "to effect the unity of labor on a common ground of understanding and mutual assistance, on a practical basis of action . . . and to bring about a combination which will present an impregnable front to the enemies of labor. . . ." Gompers, having been in consultation with Buchanan throughout, now submitted the matter to the Executive Council for the first time. They endorsed the purposes of the conference and elected Gompers, James Brettell, and William H. Marden, vice-presidents of the Federation, to represent the Federation.[31]

The conference assembled in Philadelphia, with Buchanan as chairman. Forty-eight delegates were present, representing the Knights of Labor, the American Federation of Labor, twenty-one trade unions, two railroad brotherhoods, and seven district and local assemblies of the K. of L. The leading lights of the labor movement were there, excepting Eugene V. Debs of the American Railway Union, who sent a telegram endorsing the purposes of the meeting. Buchanan began by suggesting that the A.F. of L. be reorganized into a federation which would include the Knights and the railroad brotherhoods. He presented a plan similar to the proposals previously made by the Federation to the Knights of Labor, namely, that the latter abolish their trade assemblies, whose members would join the unions of their trade, the Federation dissolve its federal unions, and the trade unionists join the mixed assemblies to aid the educational work of the Order. J. G. Schonfarber of the Knights would not consider Buchanan's proposition, saying that it meant the disintegration of the Order. He offered nothing but the mutual recognition of working cards. Gompers indicated that he was not willing to go so far as Buchanan suggested, but that if the trade unions were guaranteed full trade autonomy, they would be glad to co-operate with the Knights and the brotherhoods in achieving unity in the labor movement.

It was evident that a detailed, formal plan of unification could not be drawn up at that time, especially since the delegates were not empowered to do more than make recommendations. It was therefore decided merely to agree that a subsequent conference should be held.[32]

It met in St. Louis on June 11. In addition to the A.F. of L. and the K. of L., the "Big Four" railroad brotherhoods and the Farmers' Alliance were represented. Gompers, McGuire, and Foster represented the Federation. John Hayes of the Knights of Labor submitted a series of propositions which would maintain dual organization in the economic field but provide for joint committees to arrange and enforce wage scales and hours of labor, the mutual recognition of working cards, and an arbitration committee to settle disputes between labor organizations. A national congress of labor should meet annually to plan united action on industrial and political questions, including the support of strikes.

Finally, he urged the workers to support the People's party in the approaching congressional elections. Both Federation and brotherhood representatives disapproved the proposals, insisting that the cause of past disputes was dual organization and that no satisfactory results could be expected unless the autonomy of the trade unions in trade affairs was guaranteed. Nor would they commit themselves to support any political party.

A committee of three, consisting of Gompers, M. J. Bishop of the Knights, and Charles Maier of the Brotherhood of Locomotive Firemen, was appointed to draft resolutions which might be acceptable to the conferees. The majority report, presented by Gompers and Maier, proposed semiannual conferences of organized labor to devise plans to protect the workers. There should be no dual organization in any trade, and in matters of trade conflicts, boycotts, and labels the union involved should have absolute authority. These resolutions were approved by a vote of fourteen to four, only the K. of L. and Farmers' Alliance representatives voting against them.[33]

Gompers was convinced that further attempts to conciliate the Knights were useless, not only because of the attitude of their representatives at St. Louis, but because some of them declared after the conference that they would not abide by the resolutions but would deal directly with the national and international trade unions. He summed up his view of the conference in his report to the A.F. of L. later in the year: ". . . the temporary annoyance of obstructionists is preferable to the surrender of any jot or tittle of those principles of economic truth upon which our organizations are based. We believe in harmony; but that harmony, in our judgment, can only be brought about by a firm insistence that the trade union shall be permitted to occupy unmolested its natural and historic field of labor for the benefit and advancement of the wage-earning classes."[34]

The Federation could afford to stand its ground and wait, for the K. of L. was rapidly declining, many of its affiliates going over to the A.F. of L. in a body. Its remaining membership was confined for the most part to the smaller towns, and by 1896 it had become virtually an adjunct of the Populist party. By 1900, the Federation so far overshadowed it that the problem of their relationship disappeared from Gompers' consideration. The shift in their relative strength was reflected in the relations between Gompers and Powderly. When it was announced that President McKinley intended to appoint Powderly as Superintendent of Immigration in 1897, Gompers vigorously protested against it as an insult to the labor movement, but the appointment was nevertheless made. Six years later, Powderly left the Bureau of Immigration and was seeking a position in the Department of Commerce. Reading in the papers that President Roosevelt was going to consult with Gompers, Powderly wrote pleadingly to his old antagonist: "I hope you may see your way clear to say a good word for me. Were the situations reversed I would do it for you."[35] Gompers did not say the word.

Chapter Five

THE CESSPOOL OF CORRUPTION

JUST A FEW DAYS BEFORE THE FORMATION OF THE
American Federation of Labor, Gompers had ended his reluctant
participation in the New York mayoralty campaign. Gompers'
total emphasis was upon the development of an American labor
movement through its trade unions. Only when the workers
were organized and educated, he felt, would they be ready to
enter the political field as a class.

In 1872 the National Labor Union had entered the presidential
contest by setting up the National Labor Reform party. Its platform called for currency reform through a program of inflation,
the eight-hour day, the granting of public land to actual settlers
only, an end to the immigration of forced Chinese labor, and
tariff reduction. The pressure which it exerted upon the major
parties did result in the repeal of the notorious Contract Labor
Law of 1864, which had helped depress wages by bringing in
great numbers of workers from abroad on meager wage scales.
But Gompers did not agree with the National Labor Union's
venture into politics, and besides, he believed that the Republican
party, in carrying out its Reconstruction program, was still fulfilling its antislavery mission. Having become an American citizen
just before the election, he cast his first vote for the re-election of
Ulysses S. Grant.

The outstanding panacea of the reformers in the 1870's was
Greenbackism. About $400 million of the Civil War greenbacks
were still in circulation, and farmers and workingmen demanded
that government bonds, which had been purchased with cheap
greenbacks, should be redeemed in the same currency rather than
in gold specie. Farmers and debtors also insisted that the government continue to issue greenbacks, since they tended to raise
commodity prices and make credit easier. The depression starting
in 1873 gave additional urgency to this inflationary program and

the movement for an independent political party to destroy the "money power." Besides, with the decline of the labor unions, many workers turned to politics for relief. Gompers was inclined to support the greenback movement, especially since the decision of the government to redeem its bonds in gold seemed to indicate that it had "entered into an unholy alliance with the goldbugs, who to us represented the unscrupulous Wall Street exploiters."

In 1876 Gompers voted for Peter Cooper, the presidential candidate of the Greenback party, but the workingmen generally did not respond to the Greenback appeal. The *National Labor Tribune*, which had predicted a revolution in the labor vote, found the results of the election "sickening." After the election, Gompers urged the workers to forget politics for the time and concentrate on the organization of the workers into unions, where they would learn by experience to wean themselves from their enemies, both political and economic.[1]

But the strikes of 1877 and the brutality with which they were crushed produced a determination in the labor movement to elect officials who would defend the workers' rights. Independent workingmen's parties began to spring up in every important city. These parties soon formed an alliance with the Greenbackers, and early in 1878 the National Greenback-Labor party was launched. Blaming the depression on legislative dictation by the moneylenders, bankers, and bondholders, the party's platform emphasized currency reform, but also demanded legislation to reduce the hours of labor, the establishment of state bureaus of labor statistics, the prohibition of convict contract labor, and an end to the importation of "servile labor." The party made considerable gains in the congressional elections of 1878, but the Labor-Greenback alliance already showed signs of falling apart. By 1880, it was almost exclusively an agrarian party, but Gompers voted for its presidential candidate, General James B. Weaver. In 1884 he again cast a protest vote for the Greenback party.[2]

While he was an independent voter himself, he opposed efforts to commit the trade unions to the support of any political party. In 1877, the Cigarmakers International Union narrowly defeated a resolution to support the Workingmen's party, which was tabled on Gompers' motion. But it did endorse the platform of that party, with Gompers casting one of the two negative votes.

Two years later he presented a resolution to the cigarmakers' convention, which was adopted, that declared it "both injudicious and detrimental to the best interests and welfare of the organization for any union as such to contract political affiliations. And for these reasons no union under the jurisdiction of the International Union shall be permitted to aid, co-operate or identify itself with any political party whatsoever."[3]

In the spring of 1886, the Carl Sahm Musical Club placed a boycott on the Theiss dance hall in New York. Several pickets were arrested and sent to prison as felons. One of the men was George Harris, who had worked at the bench with Gompers as a cigarmakers' apprentice in London and later became a vice-president of the A.F. of L. At a conference held on the last day of the trial, delegates from the cigarmakers', bartenders', and waiters' unions, the Carl Sahm Club, and the Socialist Labor party decided to call a protest meeting on July 7 in Cooper Union. John Morrison presided over the meeting, which was addressed by Gompers, George Swinton, and S. E. Schevitsch, editor of the socialist *New Yorker Volkszeitung*. There was strong sentiment for political action to prevent the recurrence of such indictments, which threatened the legality of the trade unions. At the next meeting of the central labor union, a resolution presented by the socialists was passed, calling for a conference on August 5 of all labor and reform organizations.

Four hundred and two delegates representing 165 organizations with 50,000 members attended the conference. The Independent Labor party was established, a platform consisting almost entirely of labor planks was presented, and Henry George was asked to be its candidate for mayor of New York. George was a former seaman, printer, and editor whose experiences and observations in the West had led him to the conclusion that the capitalist class derived its wealth and power and maintained its exploitation of the propertyless classes from its monopoly on land and the unearned increment from it. In his book, *Progress and Poverty*, he described how, with the advance of civilization, the masses were becoming impoverished by the tightening of monopoly control. He offered as a panacea for the ills of society the single tax on land, which would break the monopoly on land-holding and open the doors of economic advancement for all. While his economic analysis may have been faulty and his conclusions inadequate, in terms of his millenial expectations, he opened the eyes of hundreds of thousands to the facts of exploitation and monopoly, and his program appealed to those who looked to political action as the only means of wresting control of the government from the plutocrats.

George did not accept the platform which had been presented at the labor conference, but wrote his own. The labor demands were compressed into one plank, which included the abolition of property qualifications for jurors, stopping police interference with peaceful assembly, enforcement of the laws for safety and the sanitary inspection of buildings, abolition of contract labor on public works, and equal pay for women on such work. Other planks proposed government ownership of the railroads and telegraph and denounced political corruption. The single tax was made the main issue.[4]

Gompers was not enthusiastic about the campaign. He retained his old objections to labor's participation in politics, recalling some of the unsuccessful ventures of the past. Swinton advised him to forget the past: "The world is whirling. . . . Today is not yesterday and tomorrow will be different from both." But Gompers was more inclined to be guided by his experience than by the promises of a better tomorrow. Also, Gompers did not look kindly on the single tax theory, for its acceptance by labor would necessarily imply a lesser need for trade union activity to solve the problems of the workingmen. While the socialists did not agree with the single tax theory either, they considered it a step toward socialism in the thinking of the people, and the George campaign was regarded as a means of uniting labor in an independent political movement which might lead to greater things. The campaign aroused great enthusiasm in the ranks of labor, and Gompers was practically forced to support it. An executive board of trade unionists was appointed to mobilize the support of the labor movement, and on it Gompers was put in charge of the speakers bureau.

Opposing George were Theodore Roosevelt, the young Republican candidate, who told the workers that the solution for their problems lay in individual self-help; and Abram Hewitt, the Democratic candidate, who stated that the issue of the election was the attempt to organize the laboring class against all others.

In September, Gompers went to Syracuse to attend the meeting of the Political Branch of the State Workingmen's Assembly, of which he was also president, as the delegate of the Defiance Assembly. Interest centered around two problems—repeal of that part of the penal code under which the Theiss boycotters had been convicted, and full labor participation in the coming election. Gompers was chairman of the committee on resolutions which reported favorably on both questions. A committee of five, including Gompers, was appointed to call on Governor David B. Hill to pardon the imprisoned boycotters, a mission in which they were successful. The convention also endorsed the candidacy of Henry George and appointed an executive committee—on which Gompers served—to conduct labor's campaign for George and for a pro-labor legislature.

Henry George clubs were organized in every precinct, and all the clubs in a district comprised a Henry George legion to conduct meetings and demonstrations. Gompers was secretary of the city organization of the legions. He spoke to labor meetings daily and sometimes several times a day—at noon shop meetings, after union meetings, and in the evenings. He centered his fire against Hewitt, always emphasizing trade union issues and interests. In a great rally which he organized on the Saturday before election day, he answered Hewitt's charges that the George campaign was a class movement and dangerous to the city, and warned Hewitt that his attacks would merely widen the schism between the classes and drive the workers from constitutional and legal methods to others less constitutional.

The election returns showed 91,000 for Hewitt, 68,000 for George, and 61,000 for Roosevelt. Since the usual Republican vote was 75-80,000, it was apparent that many Republicans had voted for Hewitt in order to secure the defeat of George. It was widely believed that the regular party henchmen had stolen many of his votes, for he had few watchers at the polls and no influence with the police and election officials. One of the local Republican leaders who watched the campaign stated just before he died that he had always felt that George had really won the election.[5]

The results of the election in New York and elsewhere were very encouraging to those who wanted to establish a labor party on a larger scale. The supporters of George called a mass meeting in Cooper Union on November 6, where it was resolved to form a permanent political organization. The central labor union prepared a constitution for the party, named it the Union Labor party, established an organization in each legislative district, and called a county convention. The A.F. of L., meeting a few days later in its founding convention, hailed "the revolution recently witnessed in the election contest," and declared that the time had arrived for the working people to decide on united action at the ballot box. It resolved to urge generous support to the independent political movement of the workingmen.[6]

But Gompers did not give "generous support," or any support at all, to labor's independent political movement. Instead of carrying out the mandate of the Federation, he "stood back and watched" and "did not let the A.F. of L. become entangled in any partisan activity. . . ." He was apprehensive of the intense interest that labor was showing in the new party, and wanted the whole campaign to be turned over to the trade unions, resenting any organization that attempted to advance labor's interests in other ways or through other agencies. In the summer of 1887, he threw cold water on the movement in a letter to the *Leader*. "The labor movement, to succeed politically," he wrote, "must work for present and tangible results. While keeping in view a lofty ideal, we must advance towards it through practical steps, taken with intelligent regard for pressing needs. . . . Mr. George's theory of land taxation does not promise present reform, nor an ultimate solution." When George was nominated for the governorship of New York, Gompers stated that the A.F. of L. was keeping its hands off the fight, that the questions involved were purely political and did not affect labor's interests, and that he personally had nothing to say about the ticket.[7]

As a result of Gompers' opposition, dissension in the party over the issues to be emphasized, and other factors, including improved industrial conditions, the movement began to lose strength, and the election of 1887 was disappointing. George's vote in New York City fell to 37,000, and he polled only 72,000 throughout the state. The election of 1888 was marked by utter confusion so far as labor's participation was concerned, which probably explains why that was the only presidential election in which

Gompers ever failed to vote. The United Labor party movement was ended. In his report to the A.F. of L. convention at the close of the year, Gompers stated that recent experiences showed that independent labor activity would be "in the extreme unwise," and that the unions had all they could do to fight for the eight-hour day. The following year the Federation rejected a resolution to recommend the formation of a labor party, and in 1890 it defeated a motion to maintain a permanent lobby in Washington while Congress was in session. It was at this convention that Gompers coined a famous phrase when he said that "the trade unions pure and simple are the natural organizations of the wage-workers to secure their present and practical improvements and to achieve their final emancipation."[8] The Federation at that time was closer to Gompers' idea of "pure and simple" unionism than at any other time in its history.

Pure and simple unionism did not mean to Gompers, as was often charged, complete abstention from political activities. It meant that the trade unions should be the sole agency of the labor movement, that labor should not form its own political party, that it should not endorse or support any other party, and that its political activity should be confined to agitation for or against particular men and measures in particular elections. His attitude was expressed in a letter to the president of a union that was interested in political action. If the workers would devote their attention to the improvement of their economic conditions, he advised, much more would be accomplished than by "dabbling in that cesspool of corruption commonly known as party politics."[9]

Chapter Six

BUILDING THE A.F. OF L.

1. PUTTING THE WHEELS IN MOTION

GOMPERS WAS JUST UNDER THIRTY-SEVEN YEARS OF age when he was elected to the presidency of the American Federation of Labor. His sturdy frame, mounted on a short pair of legs, held his head only five feet, four inches above the ground. He thought there was an advantage in this: "My legs are so short I never can run away from a fight." His features and bearing tended to draw attention to his elements of strength rather than to his defects. Set on a powerful pair of shoulders was a head that seemed to attest to a bulldog determination. His eyes were long, narrow slits, deeply set in their sockets, appearing to glare out suspiciously at the world. The lower part of his face equally indicated firm resolution. His chin was square and prominent, set with a large dimple in the center. The mouth was a long, narrow crescent, accentuated by a bulging lower lip and a thick black mustache forming an inverted "V" over the outline of his mouth. He was not an unattractive man, and with his shock of black, curly hair might even have been considered handsome.

The presidency of the Federation carried with it a salary of $1,000 a year and expenses. Gompers quit his trade after twenty-six years at the bench. But he never forgot his skill as a craftsman; occasionally he would take a friend or a newspaper reporter to a shop and roll a cigar for him, to show that he retained his touch. He never got very far away from the product of his trade, for he was rarely seen without a cigar in his mouth, a habit resulting from the custom of allowing cigarmakers to have as many cigars for themselves as they could smoke.

Gompers had moved uptown in 1886, but his tenement was hardly an improvement over the squalid apartments in which he had lived on the east side. He still maintained his family—there were six children then—on the ragged edge of poverty. Four years before, Samuel, Junior, had been required to quit school to earn his share of the family's needs. He went to work in a print shop, and his father rarely saw him after that except on Sundays, as he left the house early in the morning. There was seldom a dime to spare for carfare, and he generally walked to work, as did Gompers. Gompers and the children had only one suit of clothes and one pair of shoes each. When they needed repairing, the children stayed home from school, and Gompers made shift with a pair of old slippers while his shoes were being mended. There were times when he had difficulty getting a suit of clothes to wear to a convention, and more often than not he had to borrow money from his friends to get back home. When there was no food in the house, the family was often tided over the emergency by borrowing a few dollars on a token that Gompers was given by the Order of Foresters.

The constitution of the A.F. of L. did not go into effect until March 1, 1887, and, since there was no money in the treasury, Gompers received no pay during the first four months of his tenure of office. He wrote bitterly to the treasurer that "I will have shortly to decide upon giving up the position, take a job at my trade, or starve. If the Unions of the Country don't want a Federation, then they don't, and that settles it. If they do they ought to pay a little for the protection its very existence affords and should not insist upon doing what we protest against employers doing, i.e., exacting work without pay." He did not expect or want a great deal, for he opposed high salaries for union officials as a matter of principle. He thought it a mistake to pay them such high salaries that they would live in a manner far removed from the wage earners. But although his salary was increased to $1,200 the second year and $1,500 in 1889, he still felt that it was an injustice to him, for it was less than he could earn at the cigar trade, and he was still having difficulty making ends meet. He was disappointed at not receiving another increase in 1890, but when the subject came to the floor of the convention, he left the hall, a practice he always followed, so that the delegates could discuss the matter without regard to his feelings.[1]

During the first year of his presidency, Gompers was provided with an office, rent free, by Local 144. It was a small room, about eight by ten feet, with a brick floor, cold in winter and hot in summer. A stove was installed in the fall at a cost of $8.50, and a pine floor was laid. Gompers brought an old kitchen table from home to serve as a desk and used a box for his chair. Later he bought a secondhand desk from Hugh McGregor for two dollars. His time was so largely taken up with trivial things that he secured authorization to hire an errand boy at three dollars a week. He promptly hired his son Henry to work after school and during the summer vacation. Henry set himself up in business by attaching his sister's writing desk to a wall and providing himself with a box for a seat. He secured empty cartons from a neighborhood grocery store and converted them into filing cabinets. He wrapped pamphlets and papers and addressed the wrappers, went to the school to borrow ink, and ran other errands. His father was busy writing letters and laboriously copying them into his copybook, holding conferences, attending meetings, and making speeches, duties which frequently kept him out until midnight.[2]

One of Gompers' big projects during his first year was the editing and publishing of the *Union Advocate*, the official journal of the Federation which had been authorized by the convention in 1886. Gompers was keenly aware of the control of the press by the employing class and of the importance of a labor press to present the workers' side of public questions and especially of industrial disputes. He also appreciated the necessity of a journal to keep alive the flagging interest in the A.F. of L. and to keep its affiliated organizations and members informed of what was happening in the trade union world.[3] The *Union Advocate* was a four-page paper and dealt mainly with news of the national unions, the attacks of the Knights of Labor against them, and the defense of trade union principles. It was written entirely by Gompers, in the heavy-handed and ungrammatical, but earnest and forceful, style which was characteristic of him at that time. As John Swinton said, he seemed to do his editing with an axe.

The leading article in the October issue was typical of his views and style of writing:

"The capitalistic, no less than the aristocratic class, is responsible for the stupid and wicked policy that has turned many of the fairest lands of the world into huge military camps, and has deluged every continent in blood for the aggrandizement of their own countries, and to force upon the conquered people the products which their makers cannot consume in consequence of the lowness of their wages. . . . To the working-people it is of very little consequence whether the United States have a fleet of iron-clads or whether the Republican, Democratic, or any other party are successful in their struggles for offices, loaves and fishes; but it is of very great importance that they have a fair share of the products of their skill, of their brain and muscle; that the neces-saries and comforts of life be within their reach; that they be not herded like brutes in poisonous tenements; that their children be spared the slavery of the coal bunkers and factory, and be per-mitted to acquire the best possible education; that their noble feelings of human dignity be not outraged by the arbitrary regula-tions of an irresponsible and immoral capitalistic class. We, in this generation, by means of our Trade Unions, have challenged the capitalistic policy, and we will not cease our efforts until all workers regardless of creed, color, or nationality, are united in the fraternal bond of one grand federation, making war and robbery forever impossible."

Gompers wrote all the copy in longhand and read the proof himself. Henry addressed the wrappers, and the two, with some help from a few cigarmakers in the office, folded and wrapped the papers, loaded them into sacks, and delivered them to the post office. It was a labor of love, but most trade unionists did not appreciate the importance of an organ of their own, and the second convention of the Federation decided to suspend publication after the appearance of only seven issues. Gompers was deeply dis-tressed; he wrote to the vice-president of the Federation that "the killing of the U.A. [*Union Advocate*] was a calamity, a blunder I was about to say *a crime*. I said 'killing' rather I mean almost suicide or Hari Kari."[4] He did not stop arguing for an official journal until 1894, when the publication of the *American Federa-tionist* was finally authorized.

In 1888 Gompers and his family moved to an apartment on East 91st Street. From 1875 until he left New York in 1895, he moved at least ten times, but this was the only time that it repre-sented a substantial improvement in living conditions, for it was his first home with inside water and a bathroom. The front room had originally been designed as an office, and Gompers set up the A.F. of L. headquarters there. He hired Hugh McGregor as clerk and John McGuire as assistant. Gradually the Federation business encroached on the living space and the privacy of the family, until it "threatened to submerge the whole home." It was soon necessary to find new rooms and the Federation offices were established at 16 Clinton Street, where they remained until 1895. The offices comprised three rooms, rented at sixteen dollars a month. Shortly thereafter, Gompers was permitted to buy a secondhand typewriter for fifty-five dollars, and a stenographer and typist were added to the office force to relieve Gompers of the necessity of writing all his correspondence in longhand.

In addition to his other duties, Gompers had to perform the functions of treasurer, as he was the only full-time official of the Federation. He received all the money and made all the disbursements, kept records of every transaction, no matter how small, made out receipts, and kept the books. He finally demanded that he be relieved of the financial work, which had grown from a matter of dollars and cents to an annual revenue of over $20,000 in 1889. The Federation elected Chris Evans of the United Mine Workers as the first full-time secretary-treasurer of the organization.[5]

In December 1889, Gompers embarked on his first long speaking tour for the A.F. of L. In three months he spoke in fifty cities from New York to Denver. The tour was managed by Emil Applehagen, who was to prepare the itinerary and arrange for each locality to pay its proportionate share of the traveling, hotel, and incidental expenses. But in several places Gompers found that the local unions were without funds or had sent them to Applehagen, who did not give an accounting of the receipts. He came home ninety dollars out of pocket. The following summer he lost another forty-five dollars on an ill-managed speaking trip to New England. He was finally forced to bring this matter to the attention of the Executive Council, and although they had approved the tour only on condition that it entail no expense to the Federation, he asked to be reimbursed for his losses.[6]

Gompers rode on immigrant trains, freight cars, and cheap boats. As a result of these arduous conditions of travel, and speaking almost every evening in the dead of winter, he contracted bronchitis, which gave him no end of trouble for many years to come. In May 1889 he suffered a two weeks' illness. This may have been the reason he asked the Executive Council to accept his resignation as president at that time, or it may have been continuing financial difficulties. However, there is no record of the reply he received, and he never mentioned the matter again.[7]

2. CO-OPERATION, CONTROL, AND AUTONOMY

THIS WAS, INDEED, THE "STARVING TIME" OF THE American Federation of Labor, full of disappointments and defeats for it and its young president. But Gompers did not share the discouragement of many of his colleagues and associates. His confidence was due to his disposition to "look at things as they really are and not as we would have them or wish them to be," and his absolute assurance that the trade union movement was a product of industrial conditions and social forces and was therefore destined to become a powerful force in the life of the country. He was equally convinced that the A.F. of L. was founded on sound principles and required only zealous work to make it the leader of a great working-class movement.

Gompers ceaselessly insisted on the voluntary character of the A.F. of L. and the sovereignty of its affiliates. He emphasized that the Federation had no powers except those which concerned the unions collectively, delegated to it by the organizations that composed it. In matters of local prerogatives and rights, the international unions were sovereign. The Federation had no power of coercion over its affiliates, and could rely solely on moral obligations and the spirit of camaraderie. This was in fact, Gompers asserted, the chief strength of the A.F. of L. Force or compulsion would arouse resentment and repudiation, but a beneficent influence could be exercised by appealing to the better feelings of men and women to do the best they could.[8]

Yet, if the Federation were going to be more than an annual consultative gathering, it had to increase its powers. This meant some increase in its control over the affiliated unions. Gompers believed that one of the principal improvements of the A.F. of L. over the old Federation of Trades was its per capita tax of one half cent per member per year, which enabled it to have a full-time executive, publish a journal, and carry on organizing work. But the International Typographical Union, which had been instrumental in bringing about the formation of the Federation of Trades, at first refused to affiliate with the new Federation because of this provision. It believed that the A.F. of L. should be consultative only, the expenses of its meetings to be paid in equal part by the unions represented. It even objected to applying for a charter, on the ground that "joining" the Federation would acknowledge its supremacy. It finally accepted a "certificate of affiliation."[9]

Gompers sought to have the Federation establish a strike fund, and as in the case of the cigarmakers' union, strike assistance necessarily carried with it the right to approve or disapprove strikes and to require some unions to pay for the support of others. This had been another objection which the typographical union had raised to affiliation. The second convention of the A.F. of L., in 1887, proposed that the Federation support any strike of its affiliated unions when requested, providing they had conformed with the strike laws of their own organizations, and that the Executive Council should levy on each union a weekly assessment of not more than five cents per member, to remain in force until the strike ended. Gompers urged the adoption of this proposition, but it was defeated by a referendum vote; as he said bitterly at the next convention: "It is evident that either the principle of identity of interests of the toiling masses of our country have not been sufficiently recognized, or the unions are acting upon the belief that each should help itself before attempting to aid others."

For the next thirteen years, Gompers repeatedly urged that some means of strike assistance be adopted. The Federation tried various plans, none of them satisfactory to Gompers, and finally repealed them altogether. It stated that the unions must rely on their own efforts and their own funds, and should refrain from striking if they could not carry it through without assistance from the Federation or its affiliates.[10] Gompers accepted this as the final verdict of the Federation and discontinued his efforts to secure a defense fund or any other measure of strike control over the affiliated organizations.

Gompers hoped that the A.F. of L. would create closer relations between the international unions and prevent dissension and conflict, particularly in the form of jurisdictional disputes—conflicting claims between unions for jurisdiction over particular jobs or workers. Such disputes were a constant source of concern to Gompers, as he sought to reconcile them without bringing undue antagonism against himself and the Federation for trespassing on the freedom of action of the affiliated unions. He was often requested to arbitrate them, but always urged the disputants to make every effort to settle them by conciliation and compromise. An arbitrated settlement, he felt, could not satisfy both parties and perhaps neither, and might have the effect of increasing bitterness rather than solving the cause of contention.

The first jurisdictional dispute to come before the A.F. of L. was that between the carpenters and furniture workers in 1889. The number of appeals presented to the Federation increased steadily thereafter, and by 1900 there were twenty-five cases pending. This problem eventually claimed a major part of Gompers' attention through correspondence, Executive Council meetings, and conferences, both at Federation headquarters and in the most distant parts of the country. By 1893, the problem had become sufficiently acute to receive the attention of the Executive Council, and, on its recommendation, the convention empowered it to settle jurisdictional disputes when requested to do so by both parties.[11]

In 1899 Gompers' attention was first called to a disturbing contest which had been going on for several years and which was to continue for many more. This was the controversy between the United Brewery Workers and the trades involved in the brewing industry—coopers, stationary engineers and firemen, and teamsters. The U.B.W. was organized as an industrial union, aiming to organize all the workers in the industry. Each branch of the industry was dependent on the others for success, particularly in case of strikes, said the national secretary, and the motto of the union must be "Solidarity, man for man from roof to cellar, all for each and each for all." Its charter from the A.F. of L. authorized it to organize the industry in accordance with this principle. But in 1896 the engineers, and two years later the firemen, received charters from the Federation, and the teamsters also formed a national union. These craft organizations then called on the U.B.W. to turn over its members employed at those branches of work. The brewers' union refused.[12]

Gompers determined that the time had come to draw a line of demarcation between the jurisdictions of the various trades.

"This constant friction," he declared, ". . . is doing more injury to the interests of the workers, and is a greater hindrance to the progress and success of our movement than all the antagonism of the enemies of our movement. . . ."[13] But he was to find that it was not so easy to draw such jurisdictional lines. In 1899 the Executive Council ordered the brewers to issue no more charters to unions of brewery engineers or firemen and to recognize the cards of those who belonged to their craft organizations. Individual engineers and firemen already belonging to the U.B.W. might retain their membership, and their cards were to be recognized by the unions of the engineers and firemen.[14] But recriminations between the brewers, engineers, and firemen continued, with mutual raiding of membership and imposition of boycotts. Early in 1902, the engineers in the Cincinnati breweries went on strike to force the U.B.W. to relinquish its engineers. Both sides urged Gompers to go there and endeavor to adjust the matter. He accepted, after all parties undertook to abide by the decision he rendered. Gompers spent twenty hours in conference with the brewers, engineers, and firemen. He concluded that the U.B.W.'s claim to the engineers and firemen was unjustified, as the latter were already organized in the unions of their craft. On the other hand, the action of the engineers against the brewers was a gross and indefensible wrong. He ruled that the engineers should withdraw their demands against the brewers. The U.B.W. was to revoke all charters granted to engineers and firemen during the past three months and permit the reinstatement of the engineers and firemen who had been displaced. Engineers and firemen could belong to the U.B.W. only as individuals and by their voluntary action, except in cities where there was no organization of their trades.[15]

This decision meant virtually the transformation of the U.B.W. from an industrial union to a craft union, and the organization protested to the Federation. At the convention of 1902, the committee on the Executive Council's report sustained the protest of the brewers and recommended that Gompers' decision be overruled. A sharp fight ensued, during which Gompers relinquished the chair and entered the fray to oppose the committee's report. The report was defeated, and in its place a substitute was adopted upholding Gompers' decision and further directing that future disputes between the three organizations be settled within sixty days by a joint committee representing those unions and the Executive Council. Only the three large industrial unions in the Federation voted against this resolution.[16]

But the decisions of the convention were of little avail. During the following year, demands were made on the Executive Council for the revocation of the charters of more than a quarter of all its affiliated unions. The brewers' conflict grew more intense, and the Executive Council finally warned the U.B.W. that unless it abided by previous rulings and agreements it would face expulsion from the Federation. Gompers subsequently wrote to Secretary Kemper of the U.B.W. that the A.F. of L. had no power to enforce its decisions, but "if there is any hope entertained for the success and permanency of the trade union movement in our country, it must be by the individual member yielding his judgment to the decision of the local union of his trade; the local union yielding to the international union, and the international union in turn complying with the decision of the highest tribunal of American organized labor—the American Federation of Labor."[17]

Gompers made further efforts to bring the contending unions into agreement, but they failed due to the refusal of the U.B.W. to abandon its industrial form of organization. The Executive Council of the Federation then considered the demands of the engineers and firemen for the revocation of the U.B.W.'s charter. Gompers cast the tie-breaking vote against expulsion. He recognized that the U.B.W. had secured greater benefits for the engineers and firemen than had the organizations of those crafts. But more important was his opposition to the use of compulsion against any affiliated union. He believed that the convention of 1902 had gone beyond its authority in saying that engineers and firemen *must* belong to the unions of their trade. The Federation could make recommendations, but the brewers were correct in protesting the compulsory mandate of the Federation.[18]

Both the engineers and firemen threatened to secede from the A.F. of L. because of its failure to expel the brewers. Gompers appeared before the conventions of both organizations to urge them against such action. What good would it do, he asked them, for the members of their organizations or for the labor movement as a whole? It would not strengthen their power and influence, nor would it secure an increase in wages or a reduction in the hours of labor for their members. It would only encourage other secessions, the labor movement would disintegrate, and each organization would, "like a little grain of sand beaten by wind and storm," be driven from pillar to post by its worst enemies.[19]

Gompers was able to keep these organizations within the fold and, at the Federation convention a few months later, to modify the previous mandate issued to the U.B.W. That union was allowed to retain all brewery employees who desired to remain with it, but it was not in the future, on pain of expulsion, to accept any more engineers, firemen, or teamsters. A deadline of six months was fixed.[20]

Gompers fought off enforcement of the Federation's decision for another year, but the convention of 1906 again demanded the expulsion of the brewers, giving the Executive Council positive instructions to that effect. Still Gompers delayed action, in opposition to the majority of the Council. When the Council finally voted to carry out its instructions, Gompers entered an emphatic protest in the minutes. He was badly shaken by this step. He had placed himself on record as against the instructions of the "highest tribunal of the American labor movement." Then he was in the position of having to carry out a policy "with which I am in essential variance and against the enforcement of which my judgment revolts." He debated for some time what course he should take. He even thought of resigning his office, but decided that this would only accentuate the difficulties and strengthen the contention of the U.B.W. and the advocates of industrial unionism. "I am not only heart-sore, I am astounded," he wrote of the Council's action to John B. Lennon, Secretary of the Journeyman Tailors' Union and treasurer of the Federation.[21]

At the convention of the Federation the following December, Gompers fought to permit the Council to revoke charters of affiliated unions only when it had been ordered by a two-thirds majority of the convention. This amendment was adopted. When the U.B.W. conflict came up for discussion, Gompers took the floor and urged that its charter be restored, but without altering previous decisions in regard to the jurisdictional claims of the engineers, firemen, and teamsters; that within ninety days a conference should be held between the unions involved and the

Executive Council to effect an agreement; and that the Council be empowered to impose such disciplinary punishment as it might direct upon the organization responsible for the failure to reach an agreement.[22] His proposal was accepted, but conferences and correspondence failed to produce a settlement. The Council did not fix the blame for this but restored the brewery workers' charter on the basis of the jurisdictional limitations imposed by previous conventions of the Federation.

During the following A.F. of L. convention, an agreement was reached between the engineers and brewers which was endorsed by the Federation. It provided that engineers belonging to the International Union of Steam Engineers should continue with it, those belonging to the U.B.W. should retain membership in that union temporarily, their permanent affiliation to be determined by a referendum vote. In locals where the engineers had jurisdiction, joint conference boards might be created for collective bargaining, and all contracts governing the two unions should be made so as to expire simultaneously. The referendum subsequently held among the engineers resulted in a vote of seven to one in favor of remaining in the U.B.W. The following year a similar agreement was reached between the brewers and the firemen and teamsters.[23] The controversy of a decade was finally ended, at least in its acute stages, vindicating Gompers' faith in voluntary methods—in patience and flexibility—as the best means of resolving conflicts.

3. THE GOMPERS MACHINE

To EXERCISE ANY DEGREE OF CONTROL AND INFLUENCE over the A.F. of L., Gompers had to rely largely on his powers of persuasion and his ability to command the personal allegiance of his followers. Over a period of years, the "Gompers machine" was built up and strengthened, and Gompers was transformed from the labor agitator to the labor boss, or as the press was fond of calling him, "the little Napoleon of the labor movement." Gompers had a natural temperamental advantage as the leader of such a loosely knit organization as the A.F. of L.—a rope of sand, he called it. He loved to meet new people, to talk with them and drink with them. He was "one of the boys," and many difficult situations were ironed out in a saloon that might have ripened into open conflict in the charged atmosphere of a formal meeting in a union hall.

Gompers recognized the importance of personal contacts and as a result did an immense amount of traveling. He spent about a third of his time on the road, averaging 30,000 miles a year. On his first organizing trip in 1888, his main purpose was to get acquainted with the active labor men. "I wanted to establish sources of information," he wrote, "and to get acquainted with those upon whom I could rely to stand staunchly for trade unionism." In his travels he "came to know men from coast to coast, knew them by name and with the knowledge that comes from fighting shoulder to shoulder for a common cause. In each industrial center there naturally drifted together a group of tried-and-true trade unionists. These men constituted the local shock troops of trade unionism. They were the group with whom I corresponded and upon whom I depended for loyal support. This was a sort of subconscious inner organization devoted to trade unionism. For example, in Chicago in the early 'nineties there was a wonderful group of good fellows. . . ."[24]

Gompers manifested a strength of conviction, a whole-souled devotion to the cause of the A.F. of L., and a sense of optimism that captured the loyalty of throngs of workers and sympathizers. Many a person who detested Gompers for his policies came to admire him when he knew him personally. He was also a very effective lecturer, able to make an appeal that went straight to the hearts of his listeners. In his earlier years Gompers made up in blunt force for the lack of polish in his speaking and writing, but by the 1890's he had become a better than average speaker and writer. He could even be eloquent, and often was, but he usually spoke calmly and reasonably rather than emotionally.

Gompers' position as president of the Federation gave him a great advantage in welding together a group of loyal supporters whom he could always count on to stand with him against his opponents. He had his organizers, labor men whom he selected and commissioned as official representatives of the A.F. of L. in various localities throughout the country. In 1888 he issued about eighty commissions, and before long he had several thousand organizers, a few of whom were employed on a full-time basis with regional offices. Their chief function was to organize workers into unions, but they also served as Gompers' informants on local conditions and as his agents in helping to settle disputes, to advise the local unions, and to carry out his policies. They were responsible to no one but Gompers, and their jobs depended on their performing in a manner satisfactory to him.

Furthermore, Gompers was editor of the *American Federationist*. At first he was inclined to use the *Federationist* as a forum for the free discussion of all phases of the labor problem, but he soon made it an organ for promulgating his own concept of unionism. He wrote all of the several pages of editorials himself, and very often the leading article as well, and generally published excerpts from his addresses besides. The other articles were usually written upon his invitation, often with suggestions as to how they should be written. Thus, he once asked his close friend, John O'Sullivan, an A.F. of L. organizer, to write a report of the typographical union's convention. He instructed him not to mention the actions of the convention with regard to union finances and political matters, but to comment on those things "which are commendable . . . and try and cover up those which will have a tendency to discourage or mislead."[25]

Gompers always insisted that the idea of entering a caucus was repugnant to him and that he had never participated in one. But the Economic and Sociological Club of which he was a leading spirit served for a while very much in the nature of a caucus. As Gompers wrote, "Each of us had his group of personal friends in which he wielded influence so that the Club served as a practical clearing agency in the development of trade union understanding. . . . The so-called 'progressives' of New York City recognized in the 'No. 10 Stanton Street group' an indomitable foe to their proposals. . . ."[26]

One of Gompers' closest cronies on the Executive Council later admitted that Gompers had a powerful machine which could exert tremendous influence on the election of Federation officers and the determining of policy and was rarely defeated.[27] His control of the conventions was strengthened by his prerogative of appointing committees, for which he always selected a majority of his friends, with members of the Executive Council generally receiving the appointment as chairmen of the most important committees. On some occasions, Gompers increased the representation of his supporters by paying the delinquent dues of their unions from A.F. of L. funds, thus entitling them to send delegates to the convention, although this procedure was an evasion of the spirit if not the letter of the A.F. of L. constitution. He could also influence the outcome of deliberations by his rulings as chairman of the convention. For example, the constitution clearly provided that no claim for extension of jurisdiction could be considered by the convention until the parties interested had tried to resolve their differences, but in 1909 Gompers overruled the constitution and stated that the convention should decide the matter. In another case, however, when the convention gave the Executive Council instructions to revoke the charter of a union, he insisted that since the constitution gave this prerogative to the Council, it could not be bound by instructions from the convention, and he refused to abide by the decision.

Gompers often avoided the necessity of carrying out convention decisions or constitutional provisions by ignoring them, as in the case of the United Labor party.*

On another occasion, one of Gompers' associates was hampered in his plans by a regulation of the constitution. He wrote to Gompers to ask what he could do about it, and received the following reply:

"Dear Sir and Brother:

"At a railroad station a young man was about to enter a car on the train. Seeing the conductor, he asked him whether he could

---

*Again, in 1895, the Federation directed Secretary August McCraith to codify and publish all resolutions passed by the A.F. of L. until that time. Upon examination of these resolutions, Gompers found that many of them were in conflict with each other and that others, adopted in the early, militant period of the Federation's history, "now would scarcely look good in print." He therefore suggested to McGuire that "the matter might well be dropped or deferred until some more opportune time, when trade union opponents will not be so ready to take advantage of every little inconsistency or impracticable resolution. I suppose no one will really call for it so that the matter might be easily dropped, providing you give your consent to it. You know our friend McCraith is a conscientious officer and desires to carry out any instructions from the convention, and a statement from you in line with my thought would be the only one which would justify him in letting the matter lay in abeyance where it is. . . ."[28]

smoke his cigar in that car. The conductor peremptorily said, 'No,'
when the young man retorted:
    " 'Why, I saw a man coming out of that car smoking a dirty
old pipe.' The conductor replied: 'Well, he did not ask me.'
    "Your letter of the 7th to hand, and I make this private reply.
Fraternally yours,
Samuel Gompers."[29]

    As the A.F. of L. grew in numbers and influence, Gompers
was increasingly potent in making recommendations for public
office. This provided another means of keeping ambitious unionists "in line," for he made such recommendations only for "true
trade unionists." In order to avoid refusing such favors when he
did not want to make recommendations, he made a "rule" that
neither he nor the Executive Council would endorse any person
for any public office, either elective or appointive. Gompers claimed
that he had never recommended any person for a government
position, but that was simply not the truth. When he so desired, he
merely ignored his "rule" or evaded it by writing a personal letter
to the aspirant for office, with the authority to use the letter as he
saw fit.[30]
    The transition of Gompers from a labor agitator to a labor boss
is indicated by the shift in his attitude toward leadership and rank-
and-file control of the unions. As early as 1881 he had proposed
the election of officers in the Cigarmakers International Union by
a popular vote of the membership. He continued to urge this
measure until its adoption ten years later. In 1897 he recommended
that the A.F. of L. officers should also be elected by referendum,
as a means of placing more responsibility upon all the workers
and of furthering the achievement of a labor movement of the
workers, for the workers, and by the workers. Within three years,
however, when Max Hayes, the delegate of the Cleveland Federation of Labor, introduced a resolution to that effect, Gompers
opposed it, and helped secure its defeat.[31]
    The fact that Hayes was a socialist is significant, for at least
part of the explanation for Gompers' about-face on this issue was
that the socialists were becoming stronger in the labor movement
and the opposition to Gompers was largely organized by them.
Gompers had also begun to adopt the attitude that opposition to

his policies was equivalent to antagonism to the trade union movement, and that those unionists who disagreed with his views were
enemies of the A.F. of L. So, when the International Association
of Machinists instructed its delegates to oppose the re-election of
Gompers as president of the Federation in 1903, he protested that
men who had never seen him or heard or read a word from him
were not competent to judge his qualifications for office. Thereafter, in order to allay the sentiment in favor of the initiative and
referendum for the A.F. of L., he took the position that he supported it in principle, but that no practical machinery had been
devised to carry it out.[32]

In 1905, a concerted effort was made in the Cigarmakers
International Union to elect its delegates to the A.F. of L. by
referendum vote, similar to the manner in which it elected its
officers. Resolutions to this effect were presented by four locals,
including Milwaukee, which had a socialist majority. Since there
had been no convention of the International since 1896, Gompers,
Thomas Tracy, and J. Mahlon Barnes were perennial delegates to
the Federation's conventions, their election in that year remaining
in effect until another convention of the cigarmakers would be
held or a new method of electing delegates adopted. In addition
to those who were simply "getting tired of having these men hold
over forever," and who favored a more democratic process of
elections, there were many who hoped to unseat Gompers as a
delegate and thereby secure his defeat as president of the A.F. of L.

Faced with the certainty that some such plan would be
adopted, and being unwilling to openly oppose a popular and
democratic innovation, Gompers decided to support the amendment proposed by the Westfield local for elections every five years
rather than the Milwaukee plan for biennial elections. The former
plan also had the advantage, from his point of view, of specifically
stating that a candidate for office in the union might at the same
time be a candidate for convention delegate, whereas the Milwaukee amendment might be interpreted to mean that Gompers
would have to take his choice between running for vice-president
of the International or delegate to the A.F. of L. He therefore
issued a circular to all the locals urging the adoption of the Westfield amendment and the defeat of the Milwaukee proposal. On
whose authority or at whose expense this circular was printed and

circulated is not known, but it certainly was not authorized by the cigarmakers' union. The result of the balloting was that the Milwaukee amendment was defeated by a narrow margin. The Westfield amendment was subsequently adopted.[33]

Gompers was beginning to think that the International should hold more frequent conventions instead of relying so much on referendums. In 1901 he had questioned whether another convention need ever be held, as the International was self-operating through the initiative, referendum, and popular election of officers, and the money spent on conventions could be better devoted to organization and the promotion of the interests of the members. But now he was finding that it was much easier to control the organization in a convention, where through personal contact and exchange of opinions the officers could exercise greater influence on the delegates. Of course, Gompers' argument that full and free discussion of union affairs was impossible under the initiative and referendum was a subterfuge, for it was precisely that full discussion in the locals that he desired to circumvent and replace with decisions by the "leaders." As he admitted, by 1912 he had lost confidence in the initiative and referendum.[34]

This attitude reflected an increasing loss of confidence in the wisdom of the rank and file to control their affairs in a labor movement "of the workers, for the workers, and by the workers." In 1888, he warned the A.F. of L. against entrusting great power to the executive officers of the labor movement, particularly in the matter of strikes, and urged that the power of initiation and rejection should be vested in the masses, who must learn to govern themselves in labor organizations as well as in the state. But ten years later he was urging that the question of strikes and boycotts should be determined by "the calm judgment of experienced officers" rather than by the membership, which was "prone to do many things, under the influence of enthusiasm." And he thought it very "peculiar" when, in 1903, the machinists' union conducted a referendum vote on the issues of socialism and industrial unionism. Gompers thought that after nine or ten hours of labor, the workers had neither the time nor the inclination to make a study of these questions which would qualify them to pass an intelligent judgment. He said that their vote in favor of these two propositions was a great mistake, and that such questions should not be decided by the rank and file. Apparently he had forgotten his words of advice fifteen years earlier: "Mistakes may be made by the masses, but they learn to do better by reason of their mistakes. The individual, on the contrary, when having absolute power, rarely makes mistakes, rather commits crimes. The man who would arrogate to himself in the labor movement absolute and autocratic power would be a tyrant under other circumstances and has no place in the labor movement."[35]

Chapter Seven

EIGHT HOURS AND THE WORLD LABOR MOVEMENT

1. THE EIGHT-HOUR STRUGGLE RESUMED

GOMPERS CONTINUED TO REGARD THE SHORTER WORK-
day as the most important objective of labor, the principal reformatory effort of modern times. The eight-hour struggle, he stated,
"has clearly revealed the power of the working people to realize
an improved industrial system and raise the hopes that we may
yet be able to stem the tide of economic, social and moral degradation, robbing those who work of four-fifths of their natural wages
and keeping the whole of society within a few months of
destitution."

Two and a half years after the Haymarket bombing, Gompers
decided that it was time to resume the fight for eight hours. In his
address to the A.F. of L. convention in 1888, he recommended
that a date be fixed not later than 1890 when the workers of the
entire country should be called on to simultaneously demand the
enforcement of the eight-hour day. The convention agreed and
fixed May 1, 1890, as the date for the inauguration of the eight-
hour day.[1]

But many of the international unions, including some of the
biggest and most decisive, were not prepared to enforce the demand at that time. Of course, the Federation could not force any
union to go on strike, resolution or no resolution, and Gompers
soon had to repudiate the idea that they were all bound to strike
on the assigned date. But he urged all unions to make the effort if
possible, and if they could not they should lend all their resources
to aid those who did, for the success of some would make it easier
for the others to win the demand later. He entered energetically
into the campaign of agitation and education, urging preparations
for mass meetings, making suggestions, and prodding the unions
into action. In New York City, the central labor union failed to

take the initiative in organizing a meeting for Washington's birthday, so Gompers did it himself. He was one of the speakers at that meeting, at which he impressed the workers with the importance of the eight-hour campaign as a means of rousing the labor movement from its lethargy, for it was an issue upon which all workers could unite.

Gompers was pleased with the enthusiasm with which the workingmen were taking hold of the eight-hour movement, and he intensified his efforts to perfect the campaign. He arranged for the writing and publishing of three comprehensive pamphlets on the subject, 60,000 of which were issued. He sent out over 250,000 circulars, calling on the local and international unions to keep the agitation continually in the foreground, to arrange shop meetings of the unorganized workers, to form central labor unions and eight-hour leagues, to build up funds in preparation for May 1, and to "arouse *en masse*" for the demonstrations of July 4 and Labor Day, 1889, and February 22, 1890. He wrote letters to several hundred men in public, professional, and business life to gain their sympathy for the movement and sent several special organizers through the country to agitate the question.[2]

As in 1886, Gompers again appealed to the Knights of Labor for co-operation. He and Powderly met twice in 1889 to discuss the question, and Gompers sent an appeal to the General Assembly in November. But Powderly declared his preference for gradual reduction of the hours of labor and refused to endorse "any foolhardy or unwise methods" of hastening it. Shortly after, Powderly wrote to a friend, with an obvious reference to Gompers: "We are more sincerely desirous of aiding the movement than a lot of damn gin guzzling, pot bellied, red nosed, scab faced, dirty shirted, unwashed, leather assed, empty headed, two faced, rattle headed, itch palmed scavengers in the field of labor reform."[3]

At the Federation convention the following month, Gompers suggested that one or two trades be selected to inaugurate the eight-hour day on May 1, with the assistance of the entire labor movement. The agitation and mass meetings should continue, and after the first organization won, another would be chosen to make the fight. The convention approved these recommendations and directed the Executive Council to levy a strike assessment of two cents per member.[4]

The United Brotherhood of Carpenters and Joiners was selected to make the demand first, and the whole machinery of the Federation was put into motion to secure victory. On the eve of May Day, Gompers sent a final word to "the toilers of America." He viewed the impending contest as a critical phase of the world-wide conflict between the lovers of progress and the "Emperors, Kings, autocrats and all other enemies to the cause of labor." He warned the workers that the combined power of position and wealth would be concentrated not only to antagonize the movement but to provoke them into a breach of the peace, and he urged them to refrain from violence. He also advised them not to go out on sympathetic strikes, but to turn out in monster demonstrations in support of the carpenters. Over 70,000 carpenters in 150 cities walked out on May 1. About 50,000 won a reduction in hours. Nearly 100,000 workers in other trades also gained shorter hours, almost always without a decrease in wages, and the movement had the general effect of infusing new strength and enthusiasm into the labor movement.[5]

The Executive Council selected the miners to follow the carpenters in the contest for the eight-hour day on May 1, 1891. It received assurances that the United Mine Wokers, some of whose locals still belonged to the Knights of Labor, would receive the co-operation and assistance of that body. Gompers issued circulars to the workers appealing to them to support the miners and to build up an assistance fund. He made a ten-week trip, his first to the west coast, making some sixty speeches in support of the eight-hour movement and addressing some of the largest meetings ever held in many cities. The U.M.W. convention in April reaffirmed the demand. It appeared that the earnestness of the miners and the response of the working class portended another success for the eight-hour movement.

But in the meantime a strike had broken out in the Connels-ville coke region. The operators presented a three-year contract calling for the nine-hour day and a substantial reduction in wages. Secretary Chris Evans of the Federation was informed by the union that the eight-hour struggle had been forced upon it and that unless it was met and won, the larger movement of May 1 would be doomed to failure. The Executive Council of the A.F. of L. and the Executive Board of the K. of L. were asked to meet with the miners' officials in Pittsburgh on March 31. Gompers was in Duluth at the time, and Evans did not notify him of these developments, but other members of the Council went to Pittsburgh. The Knights of Labor did not appear. The miners requested the Federation to endorse their appeal to the labor movement for the financial support of the 14,000 coke miners, declaring that the eight-hour fight was on. Vice-President McGuire was reluctant to endorse the circular, fearing that an attempt was being made by the K. of L. to force upon the Federation the expense of supporting an ordinary trade dispute. He stated that the vote of the Council would have to be taken by mail.[6]

Evans then sent a report of these developments to Gompers, who was startled and infuriated by the proceedings. ". . . for the first time in the history of the Federation," he wrote to Evans, "the president was not only not in attendance at a Council meeting, but was not consulted in reference to holding one & not even invited or requested to be present. . . . That an action of this kind is a slight to an Executive Officer is beyond doubt. I can bear the taunts, insults and bitter opposition of our enemies but the tacit action which declares louder than words that my presence is not necessary at, or my views consulted in reference to the holding of a meeting of the Ex. Council of the A.F. of L. while holding the office of president, is humiliating in the extreme. I am free to say that if the president of the A.F. of L. is of such little consequence, if the position is but the fifth wheel to the wagon, more ornamental than useful I don't want to occupy it; and shall willingly lay it down, yes place it in the hands of the E.C. to fill the position with one who is inclined to play the part of a figurehead. Had I been notified that a meeting of the E.C. was necessary and in view of the importance of the subject I would have cancelled every other engagement and come right to the seat of the trouble. . . ."[7]

But Gompers and the rest of the Council did vote their endorsement of the miners' appeal, although with considerable reluctance. However, on April 27, the officials of the union decided to call off the May 1 movement because some miners were opposed to the strike, the unorganized miners might not join it, and in one instance the miners had already entered into an agreement for more than eight hours. Besides, the U.M.W.'s funds for the May 1 movement had been severely depleted by aiding the Connelsville coke workers.

The defection of the miners was a serious blow to the eight-hour movement, and not only for that year, for their action demoralized the whole Federation campaign. The conventions of 1891 and 1892 refused to endorse any union's effort to enforce the eight-hour day, and the Executive Council decided that the time was not opportune to begin another struggle. Then the depression of 1893 threw the entire labor movement on the defensive. However, Gompers felt that the great extent of unemployment merely strengthened the need for the eight-hour day, and at the convention of 1895 he introduced a resolution to revive the machinery and agitation that had been commenced in 1888, to levy a ten-cent assessment on every member of the A.F. of L., and to select another trade to contest for the eight-hour day on May 1, 1896. The convention approved his proposal.[8]

During the following year, the horseshoers' and carpenters' unions struck for eight hours, but they did not need the financial assistance of the Federation, and the Executive Council did little to further the organization of the movement. At the 1896 convention, Gompers recommended that a permanent advisory board be established at Federation headquarters, comprising representatives of every national union in the A.F. of L., to plan a campaign for the general enforcement of the eight-hour day on May 1, 1898. The Federation approved these recommendations and voted a one-cent assessment to carry them out.[9]

Once again the Federation receded from its ambitious program for a universal eight-hour movement, instructing the Executive Council to select one or more unions which were prepared to make a struggle in 1898. The International Association of Machinists was chosen, but when its membership voted on the proposition, it was defeated. The Federation concluded that despite organized labor's theoretical belief in shorter hours, "Selfishness and the fear of recurring depressions, with their suffering and poverty, combine to make men eager to work to the limit of endurance when opportunity affords." This ended the Federation's effort to direct the shorter-hours movement of American labor, except by general agitation and occasional assistance to organizations which went on strike to enforce the demand. When Gompers in 1907 again urged the Federation to concentrate its efforts to secure the eight-hour workday, his suggestion was repudiated by the A.F. of L., and he never raised the question again.[10]

2. THE SOCIALISTS AND THE INTERNATIONAL LABOR MOVEMENT

ONE RESULT OF THE EIGHT-HOUR FIGHT WAS THE establishment of May Day as the workers' holiday and day of demonstration of their strength and solidarity. The Federation had been invited to co-operate with the International Socialist Congress, which met in Paris on July 14, 1889. Gompers decided to try to strengthen the relations between the organized workers of America and Europe by appealing to the Congress to support the carpenters' eight-hour movement. He sent Hugh McGregor as a special courier to deliver his message. The Congress decided that the international labor movement was not yet strong enough to call a universal eight-hour strike, but it called for an international demonstration in support of the American movement on May 1. Such meetings were held in many European countries, nearly half a million workers demonstrating in London alone. Gompers wrote excitedly:

"Think, my friend, what this portends for the future. Yes, the time when imaginary lines that have so long and often divided the 'hewers of wood and drawers of water' is about coming to an end and the solidarity and identity of interests of the toiling masses of the world are becoming more closely recognized every day[,] in the end tending to the establishment of those fraternal relations when 'man's injustice to man' will be a thing of the past, only to be remembered with other incidents of an inhuman and unnatural condition of affairs." Four years later he hailed May Day as "a day resplendent with a brighter hope of the good time to come."[11]

He had hopes that the A.F. of L. would collaborate with the European movement, and that an international labor organization would result, modeled along the lines of the A.F. of L. In 1887 the Trade Union Congress of Great Britain resolved to bring about united action by means of an international congress, and Gompers recommended that the Federation send a representative. But the convention voted down his suggestion. The following year Wilhelm Liebknecht of the German Social Democratic party asked Gompers to append his name to a call for an International Congress of Workingmen to be held in Switzerland. Gompers would have liked to accept the honor, but since the Federation had voted against participating in international congresses for the time being, he was constrained to decline the request. He wrote that the A.F. of L. took the view that the American labor movement had not yet sufficiently developed to permit its participation in an international congress. But in his report to the A.F. of L. convention, in calling attention to the coming congress, he stated his belief that the A.F. of L. would have to wait until the *European* trade unions had more opportunity to develop before harmony or successful results might be expected from such a meeting.[12]

Gompers was already distinguishing between an international labor organization and an international trade union federation. While he strongly favored the latter, he was less than anxious to co-operate with the socialist movement. He wanted an international movement based on pure and simple unionism and not on "pseudo-philosophical vagaries."[13]

Since the initiative for such a movement apparently would not be forthcoming from Europe, Gompers conceived the idea of sponsoring an international congress himself. An international exposition was being planned for Chicago in 1893 to celebrate the four hundredth anniversary of the discovery of America, and Gompers received from the Federation authority to call an international labor congress at the same time and place. The response to his invitation was rather discouraging, and Gompers thought that it would be necessary for the Federation to be represented at the International Socialist Congress in Brussels the following summer, the first session of the Second International.[14] The Federation did not approve his suggestion, but it took another action that virtually sealed the doom of the American-sponsored labor congress.

In February 1889, the Central Labor Federation of New York City had been organized and received a charter from the A.F. of L. The charter was allowed to lapse, and subsequently application was made for a new one. This time Gompers refused to grant it, on the ground that the New York section of the Socialist Labor party was affiliated with it. Gompers' ruling was based on two considerations: there was no provision in the constitution of the A.F. of L. for the affiliation of a political party; and he believed that no political party had a place in a strictly trade union organization, especially since there were non-wage earners in the party and A.F. of L. membership was confined to wage earners.

The socialists were surprised at Gompers' action, because they considered it natural to be affiliated with the local central body, and had been for twenty years. Sixteen other city centrals also recognized delegates from the local branches of the Socialist Labor party. The Central Labor Federation therefore refused to expel the socialists and appealed Gompers' decision to the convention of the A.F. of L. It elected Lucien Sanial, the S.L.P. delegate to the Central Labor Federation, as its delegate to the A.F. of L. convention in Detroit in 1890. Sanial's credentials were challenged, and he was given the privilege of the floor to explain his case. He stated that the S.L.P. was not a political party "as understood by workingmen," because its primary functions were organizational and educational rather than electoral; that it was engaged in the organization of trade unions; that it was a bona fide labor organization; and that its purpose was co-operation with the A.F. of L., not disruption.[15]

Sanial's credentials were referred to a special committee, which recommended that Gompers' action be affirmed and Sanial's credentials refused. The better part of a day was spent in debating this report, with Gompers and Thomas Morgan of Chicago carrying the burden of the argument for and against it. Morgan asserted that the S.L.P. was not asking for admission into the Federation, but only for recognition of its legitimate role in the labor movement as a member of the Central Labor Federation. Gompers replied that a socialist might be a member of a union and a delegate to the A.F. of L., but only as a union man and not as a party man. He added:

"Now I maintain that we do not antagonize the Socialist Labor Party. . . . but we ask that the trade unions be let alone. We ask that we may be enabled to work as trade unionists.

"I say to you, friends and delegates, that the man who would accuse me or charge me of being an anti-socialist simply says what he does not know anything about, he does not know Sam Gompers. I say here broadly and openly that there is not a noble hope that a Socialist may have that I do not hold as my ideal. . . . But our methods are different; inherently do they differ in their methods."

The committee's report was upheld by a vote of 1,574 to 496. Because of Gompers' attitude, the socialists ran Morgan in opposition to him for the presidency of the A.F. of L. The first time he was not elected unanimously, Gompers received 1,716 votes from 31 delegates, to Morgan's 194 from 36 delegates.[16]

All socialists did not agree with the policy of the New York S.L.P. leaders, and Gompers was anxious to secure their approval of his course. He wrote a long letter to Frederick Engels recounting the history of the incident and asking for an expression of his opinion. Engels did not reply, for he did not want to inject himself as the "arbitrator" of the dispute, but he did write to Hermann Schluter, one of the leading socialists in the United States. Engels would not say that the A.F. of L. had taken the proper action, but he agreed that, since it was an association of trade unions and nothing but trade unions, it had "the *formal right* to reject anyone coming as the representative of a labor organization that is *not* a trade-union, or to reject delegates of an association to which such organizations are admitted. . . . [The rejection] had to come, and I, for one, cannot blame Gompers for it." Whether the S.L.P. ought to be represented in the A.F. of L. or not, he thought the socialists had made a tactical blunder in exposing themselves to the inevitable rejection and in antagonizing Gompers, "who has more workers behind him, at any rate, than the S.L.P." This was especially so in view of the approaching international congress in Brussels, for Engels thought that the fight with the socialists in the Federation had been principally responsible for its failure to elect delegates to the congress, where "They would see many things . . . that will disconcert them in their narrow-minded trade-union standpoint. . . ."[17]

The A.F. of L. did not send a representative to the Brussels congress, but the Central Labor Federation of New York did—it sent Lucien Sanial. The Knights of Labor also sent a representative. Gompers was not especially interested in having a delegate at the congress for its own sake, but he thought it necessary to his plans for an American labor congress in 1893. Besides, the previous international congress had chosen him as its secretary for the United States to conduct international correspondence. This was a position he did not particularly relish, for it was "nothing but work and an empty honor," but he fully expected that an S.L.P. or K. of L. representative would now get the job, and the A.F. of L. would be "frozen out," with its prestige in the international movement further diminished.[18]

But he sent greetings to the Brussels congress in a letter which illustrated his method of appealing to his particular audience, going as far as he could in agreeing with their views, even admitting to things he did not really believe, but at the same time carefully advancing his own ideas:

"COMRADES—Though oceans divide us, the same spirit and purpose prompts us to seek in organization the amelioration in the condition and final emancipation of the Proletariat of the world. . . .

"It appears to us that notwithstanding the differences in the character of the Labor Movement in our respective countries, caused by conditions possibly beyond our past control, we should yet endeavor to inculcate the knowledge and the recognition by our fellow-toilers of the interdependence, internationality and identity of the interests of the wage-earning masses.

"Of course, it is difficult to judge as to the form that the labor organizations should assume in other countries than those we respectively inhabit, but I trust I do not trespass in propriety when I suggest the thought of the importance of the organization of Trade Unions for all wage-workers, and, at least for a time, concentrating all efforts to the economic aspect of the Movement. . . .

"There can scarcely be a division of opinion that when the economic movement has sufficiently developed so as to produce a unity of thought on all essentials, that a political labor movement may be the result. . . .

"It is true that our Movement is a Trade Union Movement, and in connection with this I beg to assure you that we base our Trade Unionism upon the broad field of labor, giving every shade of thought, opinion and expression full play, where every member or Union enjoys the utmost freedom of expression, whether of the most radical or conservative character. . . ."

Repeating his appeal to support the congress in Chicago in 1893, he signed the letter, "Your Comrade in the Holy Cause of Labor, Samuel Gompers."[19]

But his effort was without avail, for, as he expected, Sanial's presence was more potent than Gompers' words. The congress declined his invitation and decided to hold its own session in 1893 in Switzerland. Declaring the congress to be sour grapes, Gompers said he didn't want its collaboration anyhow, for it was not really a "purely working-class" organization but a socialist political body. He wrote to the British Trade Union Congress meeting a few weeks later, "Under these circumstances we deem it the duty of trade-unionists to clasp hands more determinedly than ever in order that the beneficent influences of our Unions may be extended and emulated. We pledge to you our sacred word of honor that our International Labor Congress at Chicago in 1893 will be strictly a *bona fide* representative body. . . ."[20]

The British trade unions accepted his invitation, but no one else did, and the A.F. of L. was compelled to call off its project. All that came of Gompers' efforts was a "General Labor Congress" officially sponsored by the Columbian Exposition, at which Gompers and a few others read addresses on the labor movement. Thus, as a result of Gompers' tilt with the socialists, the A.F. of L. declined to participate in the International Labor Congress and the socialists refused to co-operate with his projected congress. The cause of world labor fraternity suffered a severe blow.

Part III

STRUGGLE AND COMPROMISE
1892-1897

Chapter Eight

FIGHTING HARD TIMES

1. DEPRESSION

WHEN GOMPERS ENTERED THE CITY HALL OF Chicago during the A.F. of L. convention in December 1893, he had to step carefully over the bodies of unemployed and homeless workers who were huddled together on the steps and in the corridors. These were but a handful of the 100,000 Chicago workers who could not find jobs during that first winter of the terrible depression of the 1890's. Gompers was incensed at this aspect of misery, and his indignation grew as unemployment mounted to over two million, perhaps three million, during the next two years. After three years of hard times, Gompers wrote:

"The world is filled with the cry that there is nothing wrong at the foundation of society. . . . nature is generous in her bountiful gifts, man is a willing worker, genius has made it possible to make the laborer's productivity manifoldly greater than his progenitor's. . . . Yet . . . misery, heart-rending misery, abounds.

". . . . there are myriads of our fellow-workers who walk our cities and stalk like spectres throughout our country, vainly pleading for an opportunity to earn their bread by the sweat of their brows. Those employed, overworked and underpaid, while the rest—the 'superfluous' balance—may, through lack of opportunity to find work at all, go down step by step to the verge and abyss of misery, demoralization and despair. Modern society answers these conditions with erecting more jails and alms-houses, the police club or the military force. . . .

"The workers are organizing. . . . No! It will not ever be thus."[1]

Gompers was outraged not only by the conditions he saw but by society's lack of responsibility for the effects of its own disorder. The only provisions for relief were those made by private charitable organizations—wayfarers' lodges, woodyards and laundries for employment, bread funds, and clothing funds. Gompers insisted that the unemployed should have work, not charity. Charity was not only humiliating, but it made the recipients mere consumers, while employment on public works would make them producers as well as consumers of wealth.[2]

In the summer of 1893, Joseph Barondess of the Jewish Clothing Workers' Union urged Gompers to call a demonstration of the unemployed to bring pressure upon the public officials for relief. Gompers, however, was opposed to the suggestion and instead called a conference of trade unionists. The conference met on August 20 with Gompers as chairman. He placed the blame for the crisis on the "wealthy possessors of our country," and asserted that since they were apparently willing to let the unemployed starve, it was the duty of government to relieve them. He called on the cities, states, and federal government to inaugurate public works. The conference endorsed Gompers' recommendations and decided that he should write to Governor Roswell P. Flower, urging him to call a special session of the legislature to provide relief through a program of public works. Flower rejected the demand with the statement that "In America the people support the government; it is not the province of the government to support the people."[3]

Gompers and other labor leaders began to organize a campaign to force action. Gompers instructed his organizers to arrange meetings of the unemployed. A committee on unemployment, composed of representatives of the trade unions, Knights of Labor, and the Socialist Labor party, arranged a demonstration in Madison Square Garden. An immense crowd packed the hall and listened to speeches by Seth Low, Daniel De Leon, Henry Weissman of the Bakery Workers Union, Felix Adler, Abe Cahan of the Yiddish-language *Forward*, and Gompers. When Gompers mounted the platform, he was received coolly by the radical-minded, angry workers. But silence and hisses soon changed to unreserved enthusiasm and applause as Gompers flayed the capitalists in a manner that won the favor of the socialists. His speech, working on the misery of the unemployed workers in the audience, brought them to their feet cheering and shouting, aroused and ready for action. Gompers drew back with a start; he had gone farther than he intended. He wrote later, "The responsibility of my utterance haunted me not only that night but for many a day after." He was more careful thereafter with his thoughts and words.[4]

The most ambitious plan for a federal program of public work relief was that devised and organized by Jacob Coxey, of Ohio. He proposed that the national government issue $500 million in legal tender notes, to be expended over a period of two years on a road-building program, and that the government loan additional notes to the states to be used for public improvements. In 1893, Coxey met some of the leaders of the unemployed workers in California who were planning a march to Washington, and it was decided to combine the two plans. The march of the "industrial armies" would be a petition in boots for Coxey's bills. The endorsement of Coxey's "Good Roads" bills was secured from the A.F. of L. in December, the plan was announced in January, Senator William A. Peffer of Kansas introduced the bills the next month, and the march began in April. Some 500 workers arrived in Washington on April 31.[5]

Gompers went to Washington to help Coxey get a hearing for his project. He spoke personally to many congressmen and urged that Coxey's army be permitted to petition for redress of their grievances. Congress refused to extend the right of free speech and assembly to the Capitol grounds, and when Coxey led a parade toward the Capitol he and two of his lieutenants were arrested and jailed for twenty days for walking on the grass, and his crowd of followers was charged by policemen swinging clubs, beating and trampling fifty or more. Before leaving the capital, Gompers addressed several divisions of the army camped outside of Washington. At one meeting, a collection was taken to relieve the urgent needs of the marchers, and Gompers emptied his pockets. He had to walk back to town, where he was fed and lodged by his son, and the next morning he borrowed enough money to return to New York.

He went to his office and wrote a vigorous editorial protesting the brutal assault on the industrial army and the outrageous sentence imposed on its leaders. If they had been bankers or monopolists, arriving in palace cars to lobby with their millions, they would have been given a respectful hearing, Gompers wrote. But because they came as plain citizens to plead for the "poor, outraged, robbed, idle millions," the whole power of government was brought to bear to crush out their constitutional rights. But, Gompers warned, history demonstrated that bludgeons and prisons had never yet prevented the truth from becoming accepted.[6]

During the depression of the 1890's, Gompers began to develop his economic theory, if theory it can be called; he never worked out a thoroughly articulated system. As need for action arose, he selected ideas which seemed to provide a basis for it. He intuitively rejected those ideas which did not square with the few underlying conceptions of the labor movement as he understood it. Consequently, his economic philosophy was not consistent, for it was constantly undergoing revision as a result of his experiences, and reflected the general shift in his attitude toward labor's role in industrial society. But his thinking started from one premise, namely, that the so-called "natural laws" of political economy were inventions of apologists for the ruling classes. The political economists were the "priests of Mammon," he declared. "The words of the song they sing are stolen from the vocabulary of science, but the chant itself is the old barbaric lay. It tells us that the present absolute domination of wealth is the result of material and invariable laws and counsels the laborers, whom they regard as ignorant and misguided, to patiently submit to the natural operations of the immutable law of 'supply and demand.' The laborers reply. They say that the political economists never learned sufficient science to know the difference between the operations of a natural law and the law on petty larceny. The day is past when the laborers could be cajoled or humbugged by the sacred chickens of the augers or by the bogus laws of the political economists."[7]

Gompers was willing to concede that there was a conspiracy against the wealth producers on the part of the bondholders and bankers. But he rejected the views that had previously been dominant in the labor movement, that the "money power" was at the root of the nation's economic troubles, and that the solution lay in banking reform and currency tinkering. He found the source of the maladjustment lying deeper in the technological developments of industry and the social arrangements of industrial control. He pointed to the vastly improved machinery and methods of production that had been rapidly introduced after the panic of the 1870's, and the general application of steam and electric power that resulted in a stupendous augmentation of the productive forces. The capitalist class had no other impulse but to produce more and faster and gave no thought to the workers who comprised the great body of consumers. As a result, labor was displaced, wages remained low, and the storehouses were glutted. Thus, "the ownership and control of the wealth, of the means of production, by private corporations which have no human sympathies or apparent responsibility, is the cause of the ills and wrongs borne by the human family. . . ." The only solution was to reduce the hours of labor commensurate with the introduction of machinery, so as to spread out the work and at the same time increase the consuming power of the workers. This would eventually relegate to the barbarism of the past a society based upon injustice. This was the mission of organized labor.

Although Gompers regarded the question of wages as secondary to that of hours, he recognized that if wages could be maintained it would help relieve the burden of the depression on the workers and hasten a revival by sustaining their purchasing power. Gompers optimistically asserted that the trade unions had largely prevented a reduction in wages and thus made the panic less acute than it otherwise would have been. Actually, he knew the unions were not strong enough to withstand the attacks on the living standards of the workers. He received constant appeals for assistance from affiliated organizations which were on strike or contemplating a strike during the depression years, and his consistent reply was that the Federation was not only unable to render support, but that strikes were unwise in view of the industrial stagnation. Labor must retrench rather than become involved in contests which might destroy the unions.[8] Gompers noted that the depression was the first one in American history which did not wipe out the trade union movement. Maintenance of the unions provided the basis for the growth of the Federation during the years that followed.

2. NEITHER WINCHESTERS NOR KNIVES

THE 1890'S WERE A PERIOD OF INTENSE INDUSTRIAL struggles and involved widespread strikes against the growing monopolies in many basic industries. The period was characterized

by a well-organized attack by employers against the labor movement; they used violence without restraint and the power of the
government to suppress labor. When Gompers arrived in the
Connelsville coke region during the strike against wage cuts and
for the eight-hour day in 1891, he found that several miners had
been shot by the police. In a bitter speech to the strikers he
denounced the coke barons and warned them to be careful: "Do
not turn your backs on labor or you will widen chasms still more.
Everything may change. Our Bible lessons even may be changed,
and your God may not be our God. Do not turn your Winchesters
on our hearts and heads, for, by the blood of the martyrs, there
will be a day of reckoning. The spirit of '76, of '61, of Washington,
of Lincoln, is marching on, and you must not forget it. Labor is
going to obtain more of the wealth it produces, and neither Winchesters nor the knives of deputy sheriffs will prevent it."[9]

In the following year occurred one of the most dramatic and
significant strikes in American history, one which demonstrated
the perfection of the strikebreaking technique that had been used
in 1877 and would become a pattern for the new industrial giants.
The only important steel mill then unionized was Andrew
Carnegie's Homestead works at Pittsburgh, which was organized
by the Amalgamated Association of Iron and Steel Workers, the
largest union in the country. Carnegie and his lieutenant, Henry C.
Frick, determined to destroy the union, and "King Andrew" went
to Europe, leaving Frick with a free hand to do the job as he saw
fit. He decided to provoke a strike by announcing wage cuts,
amounting in some instances to nearly forty per cent. He had
prepared for the strike by converting the plant into an armed
fortress, recruiting a strikebreaking force in other parts of the
country and in Europe, and hiring an army of 300 Pinkerton
agents to guard their entry into the mill. Early in the morning of
July 6, the Pinkerton "detectives" were towed up the Monongahela
and Ohio Rivers on barges. The strikers met them on the banks
and in the ensuing fight, which lasted all day, three Pinkertons
and seven union men were killed and over sixty wounded before
the Pinkertons were called off.

A week before the strike began, Gompers had instructed his
organizers to prevent the company from hiring strikebreakers,
and he had dispatched others to various cities to picket the employ-

ment agencies and ships coming from Europe with strikebreakers. He also urged the Secretary of the Treasury to increase his forces at the ports of entry to enforce the Alien Contract Labor Law. He urged the New York central labor union to organize a protest against the "monstrous avaricious corporation trying to pauperize their employes by carnage and bloodshed" and to express their support for "the noble and manly defense of their lives and families by the striking iron and steel workers." At the same time he offered his services to the union in any way it desired to command them.[10]

A few days after the battle at the plant gates, Frick wired the governor, who sent 8,000 state troops into Homestead to protect strikebreakers. The same governor had refused the request of the sheriff of Homestead to send troops the previous week, when the danger of armed conflict was impending. A week later, some 200 strikers were arrested and indicted for murder, riot, conspiracy, and treason. They were eventually cleared of every one of the charges, but they were kept away from the strike until it suffered defeat. This outcome was aided by the attempt of Alexander Berkman, a young anarchist, to assassinate Frick; a deed which had nothing to do with the strike, but which the company used as propaganda in order to discredit it.

In August, Gompers went to Homestead to confer with the strikers. He assured them of his sympathy and told them that he was a man of peace, "but I am like that great man Patrick Henry, I stand as an American citizen and, 'give me liberty or give me death.'" Gompers returned to New York and issued an appeal for financial aid for the strikers. Later, at the request of the Amalgamated Association, he called a meeting of the Executive Council at Pittsburgh, after which he issued other appeals for money for the strikers and to defend the arrested strike leaders. But by November the strike was over, the union smashed. The strongest craft union in America could not stand before the power of a modern trust. Many of the strikers believed that the Executive Council did not perform its full duty, failing to act decisively until it was too late to influence the outcome of the strike.[11]

The pattern of Homestead was repeated in many other conflicts during the next two years. Gompers was convinced that the capitalist class had entered into a conspiracy with the government to strike down organized labor. Hence, "if we cringe before the corporations," he predicted, "and are afraid to meet the issue, without doubt it will be some years before labor's voice can dare to be heard or we may be in a position to raise our heads. I believe we should not be cowed by demonstrations to thwart our people and to deprive us of our rights. On the contrary, now more than ever does it become our duty to face the conditions presented, and by our pertinacity bring dismay to our enemies. . . ."[12]

Soon Gompers had another opportunity to confront corporate aggression, but he met it with something less than pertinacity.

On May 11, 1894, the employees of the Pullman Palace Car Company went on strike in Pullman, a little suburb of Chicago, against layoffs, wage cuts, and feudal despotism. In this "model community," owned lock, stock, and barrel by George Pullman, "the most consummate type of avaracious wealth absorber, tyrant and hypocrite" of the age, Gompers found families who had for years eked out existence in one room and been left destitute and in debt when the head of the family died. When a committee of workers called on Pullman to ask for a restoration of the wage scale or a reduction of rent in the company houses, they were dismissed and discharged, and the company refused to arbitrate their grievances. Theirs was a strike of desperation.[13]

The Pullman employees were members of the American Railway Union, a federation of all crafts of railroad workers, recently organized by Eugene Victor Debs. Debs, the secretary-treasurer of the Brotherhood of Locomotive Firemen and editor of its journal, had become disillusioned with the narrow craft exclusiveness of the railroad brotherhoods. These organizations, led by the most conservative men in the labor movement, did not even regard themselves as labor unions, opposed strikes, remained aloof from the A.F. of L., and even refused to aid each other. They commonly scabbed on their fellow employees on the railroads.

While Gompers was in Kansas City in 1891, George W. Howard, head of the Brotherhood of Conductors, came to see him. He told Gompers of his plan to bring all railroad workers into one organization and asked him to take the initiative in launching the new union and to become its president. Gompers admitted that the railroad men were not well organized, that the brotherhoods had developed no plan for concerted action, and that their policy did not facilitate the organization of the mass of the workers. But he told Howard that his plan was not practical and could not succeed, and that it would be wrong to undermine the brotherhoods, which should be allowed to correct their own mistakes. "Well, then, I shall have to go to 'Gene Debs," said Howard. Gompers replied that he did not believe Debs would have anything to do with it. He wrote later that he was shocked when he learned that Debs had indeed accepted the presidency of the American Railway Union. "I never could quite forgive him for his action and particularly for retaining the position of editor of the official magazine of the Brotherhood of Locomotive Firemen while undertaking to establish a rival organization which aimed for the disintegration and destruction of the brotherhoods, his own included." In another place, he charged that while Debs was a high official in the Brotherhood of Firemen, he had never attempted to persuade that organization to join the A.F. of L.[14]

None of these charges was accurate, and Gompers knew it. While plans for forming the A.R.U. developed, Gompers was in constant touch with Howard, who specifically told him that Debs was coming into the new organization but refused to have anything to do with it until after the expiration of his term as editor of the journal. The American Railway Union was not launched until six months after Debs had retired as secretary of the brotherhood. When Debs announced that he was going to retire, at the convention of the brotherhood in 1892, the delegates refused to accept his resignation, in spite of his unqualified attack on the craft narrowness of the organization. They finally agreed to accept his resignation as secretary-treasurer only on condition that he would continue to edit the union's journal, with a clear mandate to write anything he pleased. Even after he had helped to organize the A.R.U., he continued to advise all firemen to join the brotherhood. Even when the brotherhood worked actively against the new union, he refrained from attacking its leaders. Debs assured Gompers, several months after the formation of the Railway Union, that it had no purpose to antagonize existing organizations.[15]

Gompers' second charge, that Debs did not attempt to bring the B. of L.F. into the Federation, was also spurious. As Gompers himself admitted, Debs was one of the brotherhood officials who "heartily favored affiliation with the A.F. of L." In 1890, Debs sent fraternal greetings to the A.F. of L. convention, asserting that the interests of all labor were confided to that organization. "The principle of federation," he concluded, "which your great Order so splendidly champions is everywhere gaining ground, and no longer opposed by workingmen of intelligence. . . ." Debs printed Gompers' proclamations announcing the Federation conventions, prefacing one of them with a commendatory note that the A.F. of L. "has accomplished splendid results" and that Gompers "is eminently the right man in the right place." He published two articles by Gompers on the need for federation, and in turn wrote an article for the *American Federationist*. Gompers was sufficiently impressed with Debs' sympathetic attitude to invite him to address the convention of the Federation in 1892, which Debs was prevented from accepting only because of illness.[16]

The real sin which Debs had committed, as Gompers understood sin, was the organization of a dual union. Although Gompers himself had four dual unions to his credit, that fact did not interfere with his upholding the principle of "legitimacy." Gompers assumed that any organization affiliated with the A.F. of L. was such a union. He included the railroad brotherhoods in that category because they were first in the field, and because he was making efforts to secure their affiliation. Gompers had urged Debs to remain in the brotherhood, and the latter's great respect for Gompers' judgment had made him pause and reconsider his course. He remained in the brotherhood until after it had refused to aid the switchmen in their Buffalo strike, then resigned to launch the A.R.U. Gompers complained to Tom Mann, great English labor leader and socialist, that the A.R.U. was instituted "not for the purpose of consolidating the existing railroad organizations, but to supplant them."[17]

Worse, the American Railway Union was an industrial type of organization. Just before the fateful Pullman strike began, Gompers wrote to one of his organizers: "I see you have the proper appreciation of the makeup of the A.R.U. It is indeed a second edition of the K. of L. except that they propose to confine themselves to the railroad men." Consequently, when the organization entered into a fight for its life, Gompers was not anxious to help it, and may even have been willing to see it meet destruction.[18]

One month after the Pullman strike began, the first convention of the A.R.U. met in Chicago. After hearing a report from a committee of the strikers and from delegates who had made an inspection trip to the company town, the convention determined to help the strikers by declaring a boycott against all Pullman cars. Debs tried to prevent headstrong action and finally persuaded them to send a committee to the company to propose arbitration. After being rebuffed twice by the company, which would not discuss the dispute with "outsiders," the A.R.U. voted that if the company did not agree to arbitrate by June 26, its members would not handle sleeping cars and would ask other workmen to do likewise.[19]

Debs tried to restrain the railroad men. There were too many unemployed workers ready to take their jobs, and the railroad brotherhoods would certainly fight the movement. The General Managers' Association would undoubtedly throw its support to the Pullman Company. Court injunctions and military suppression were probable if not inevitable. The A.R.U. was too inexperienced and too inadequately prepared to cope with a strike of such magnitude. Gompers would have agreed with Debs as to the wisdom of the movement. He also would have agreed that the boycott was completely justified. It was enough for him that the railroad men were "expressing the inarticulate protest of the masses against wrongs."[20]

But Debs, as the servant of the A.R.U. members, was obliged to make every effort to carry the struggle to victory. Gompers felt no such responsibility. In his eyes, it was not only a contest between the railroad workers and the Pullman Company, but also between the A.R.U. and the railroad brotherhoods. At first, his sympathies were on the side of the strikers. Later, he was against them; at least, he would not actively help them while waiting to see what developed.

On the day before the boycott was declared, Debs sent a telegram to Gompers, as well as to the brotherhoods, asking for assistance. Gompers wired Debs to verify the telegram by letter and to give full particulars, which Debs did not have time to send. Gompers used this as an excuse to contend that the Federation was not yet officially concerned with the boycott and was therefore justified in watchful waiting.[21]

By July 1 the strike was on the road to victory, but the General Managers' Association and the United States Attorney General, Richard Olney, were preparing its defeat. The managers suggested that Olney appoint Edward Walker, a railroad attorney and a member of the managers' association, as special federal attorney to handle the strike situation. Olney complied immediately. Then, on the dubious assumption that the boycott was essentially illegal and violent, he determined to break the strike with the use of the United States Army. He wired Walker that "the true way of dealing with the matter is by a force which is overwhelming and prevents any attempt at resistance." In order to prod President Cleveland into sending the army to Chicago, he decided to secure an injunction against the strike, and then use the military to enforce the court order.

On July 2, in the federal circuit court in Chicago, a sweeping injunction was issued against the A.R.U. leaders by Judge William Woods, who had received important favors from the railroads, and Judge Peter Grosscup, who had recently declared that the growth of labor organizations must be checked by law. The injunction, for which Walker had applied, used the Sherman Antitrust Act to enjoin the strike leaders from aiding the boycott by answering questions, sending telegrams, urging men to join the boycott, or in any other way. Gompers characterized this injunction as a perversion of the Sherman Act from its intended purpose to protect the people against the railroads into an instrument to oppress workingmen attempting to redress their grievances. He protested against its virtual outlawing of the strike and the union, as a blow to workers' constitutional rights.[22]

The A.R.U. decided to ignore the injunction as illegal, and because obedience to it would crush the strike, destroy the union, and open an employer attack against the entire labor movement. The following day Judge Grosscup and Walker sent a misleading telegram to Olney, stating that violence had occurred, that the workers of Chicago were preparing to join a general strike, and that the mails could not be moved without the support of the army. On July 4, President Cleveland ordered the command at Fort Sheridan into Chicago to protect federal property, prevent obstruction of the mails and interference with interstate commerce,

and enforce the decrees of the court. Not only Debs, but Governor
Altgeld of Illinois, protested that there was no need for federal
troops, and the arrival of the military was "the signal for civil
war." Gompers protested to Cleveland against the "base action"
of the judiciary and the "improper use" of the military. He declared later that Cleveland had violated the Constitution and
invaded the sovereign rights of the states, not for the purposes he
announced, but to overawe the strikers.[23]

But still he would not act, although he was being importuned
by many unionists, including John Lennon, treasurer of the A.F.
of L. On July 3 Lennon wrote to him: "The news from the great
R.R. Strike appears to me to be of such a serious character by the
interference of the State and Nation that at any moment it may
be necessary for the A.F. of L. to take a determined stand, and if
we must be Slaves let us fight first." Several leading unionists in
Chicago, notably Thomas Kidd of the woodworkers, had proposed
calling a meeting of the trade unions to devise means of aiding
the strikers. At a preliminary meeting it was agreed to set a meeting for the following Sunday, July 8, and to invite all other organizations. Debs invited the officers of the railroad brotherhoods,
Gompers, James Sovereign of the Knights of Labor, and others to
come to Chicago. All the brotherhoods ignored the invitation
except the firemen. Sovereign went to Chicago, but Gompers
refused.[24]

At the meeting in Uhlich's Hall, all the locals in Chicago and
the heads of seven national unions were represented. They appointed a committee to request Pullman to arbitrate, threatening a
general strike if he refused. They also telegraphed Gompers, not
only inviting him but demanding that he call a special session of
the Executive Council in Chicago. Gompers could no longer resist
the pressure. He called a meeting of the Council for July 12, and
also invited the presidents of a number of affiliated unions, as well
as of the railroad brotherhoods, which had been freely strikebreaking against the A.R.U. His telegram read: "A crisis in the industrial situation of the country is at hand. It behooves us to endeavor
to bring order out of what threatens to become chaos." It may be
surmised that he called the meeting not so much to aid the boycott
as to find ways of stopping the rising sentiment for a general

strike. A rumor, when he left for Chicago, had him saying that he was going to attend a funeral, that of the American Railway Union. Gompers, of course, denied the statement.[25]

Two days before the conference opened, a federal grand jury indicted Debs and three others for conspiring to interfere with interstate commerce. When the Executive Council met at the Briggs House on the twelfth, the strike was virtually lost. Gompers had done nothing to arouse public support for the boycott, to aid the strikers in any way, or to give leadership to the Chicago labor movement. Only drastic action now could save the strike and the A.R.U. from utter defeat, and it is clear that Gompers did not go to Chicago with drastic action in mind, or any action at all for that matter.

Gompers called the meeting to order. Trade unionists had insisted that it was his duty to be there, he said, as if to emphasize that the meeting was not his doing. A committee of the Chicago cigarmakers appeared before the Council to say that the A.F. of L. could settle the strike by calling for a universal walkout, but that if it decided against such a move it would be responsible for the defeat of the strike. The local cigarmakers had already gone out on a sympathy strike. Telegrams were also received from the city centrals of St. Louis, Milwaukee, and Pueblo, stating that they would strike to a man if the conference so declared.

That evening, Debs appeared and made an unimpassioned statement of the cause of the strike and the situation as it then stood. He proposed that the strikers return to work at once, provided they were restored to their former positions without prejudice. He asked Gompers to submit this proposition to the General Managers' Association. Gompers feared that this would involve the Federation in the dispute. What if the managers refused the request? he asked Debs. ". . . do what you believe you should do under the circumstances," replied Debs. Gompers asked him what he would do if he were in his place. Debs answered: "Now understand me, I am speaking for no one but myself, but I would make an injury to one in the cause of labor the concern of all. My theory has always been and is now that labor ought to stand by labor, and if I were you, in your place and you in mine, I would muster all the forces of labor in a peaceable effort to secure a satisfactory adjustment of our grievances, even if we had to involve all the . . . industries of the country."[26]

Near midnight, Debs retired, and the other labor leaders discussed his proposition for another two hours. They decided that Gompers should not present the A.R.U.'s proposal to the managers because it was a virtual confession that the strike had failed and would only implicate the Federation in a lost cause. But they agreed that Gompers and anyone else Debs might select would accompany Debs in presenting the document to the employers. Debs declined the offer, knowing that the managers would not receive him. The Executive Council quickly disposed of the request to call a general strike. Gompers admitted that such a call would have been honored by organized labor, and that it would have been justified if it had a chance of success, but he was sure it hadn't. The strike was practically lost already, and the general trade union movement would have gone down with the A.R.U.[27]

Gompers was probably right. He had already let slip his opportunities to help the strikers. Debs undoubtedly allowed his bitterness to color his thoughts when he declared, twenty years later, that "Gompers did everything he could to break the strike. . . . Mr. Gompers' attitude was identical with that of the grand chiefs of the railroad brotherhoods. He was an apt scholar of P. M. Arthur, grand chief of the Brotherhood of Locomotive Engineers, who was cheek by jowl with the Railroad Managers' Association." But Gompers was not unhappy to see the A.R.U. smashed. As he admitted in his autobiography, "The course pursued by the Federation was the biggest service that could have been performed to maintain the integrity of the Railroad Brotherhoods. Large numbers of their members had left their organizations and joined the A.R.U. It meant, if not disruption, weakening to a very serious extent."[28]

The Executive Council reconvened on July 13 and appointed Gompers chairman of a committee to draft a statement. All those already on strike were urged to return to work and devote themselves to developing a stronger organization and unification of forces, "to educate and prepare ourselves to protect our interests, and that we may go to the ballot box and cast our votes as American free men united and determined to redeem this country from its present political and industrial misrule."[29]

Accordingly, the Chicago building trades called off their sympathy strike. The Chicago *Tribune* announced:

DEBS' STRIKE DEAD
It is Dealt Two Mortal Blows by Labor
Federation Hits First
Trades Council Follows with a Crusher

The day that Gompers returned to New York, Debs and the other leaders were again arrested on a contempt charge for violating the injunction of July 2. They refused bail and were imprisoned. Gompers issued an appeal for contributions to Debs' legal defense fund: "The corporations now have their claws ready to fasten them upon the body of Debs, not simply to try and crush him, but they hope to awe the men of labor into silence and slavish submission. That purpose cannot, dare not and will not succeed. Debs must be defended and ably defended. In his person at this time he represents the rights of Labor before the law to organize, to quit work in defense, protection and advancement of its interests." Only $240 was raised through this appeal, and $500 was donated by the A.F. of L.[30]

Chapter Nine

THE TRUSTS

1. RIGHT AND INEVITABLE

THE DEFEAT OF THE BUFFALO SWITCHMEN, THE Homestead workers, the Coeur d'Alene miners, and the A.R.U brought Gompers and the labor movement face to face with the seemingly invincible power of the industrial monopolies. In 1894 the United States was the leading industrial country in the world. The value of manufactured goods had increased tenfold since the Civil War, and the number of wage earners in industry more than tripled, reaching nearly five million. While the workers were producing 130% more per capita in 1900 than they had half a century earlier, their wages had risen only 77%, and their share of the national wealth decreased from 62% to 15%. At the same time, 9% of the people owned 75% of the nation's wealth. Industry was being consolidated into monopolies of various forms—pools, trusts, and mergers. By the end of the century there were 440 large industrial, franchise, and transportation trusts, with a total capital of over $20 billion, and soon after the first billion-dollar corporation, United States Steel, was created.[1]

The rise of the "trusts," as all monopolies were popularly called, to a position of dominance in the American economy was profoundly disturbing to many people. Not the workers alone, but small businessmen as well were squeezed to the wall. Farmers felt the scissors closing in on them as monopoly prices for manufactured goods and freight rates soared, while the prices of their own products sank. And social reformers viewed with alarm the growing corporation control of national, state, and municipal governments, portending the demise of democracy. Demands were raised on all sides to regulate the trusts, to bust them, or to nationalize them, and to curb their power and influence in government. In 1890 the Sherman Antitrust Law was enacted, declaring illegal any combination in restraint of trade.

But Gompers opposed the passage of the Sherman Act, for

two reasons. He feared that labor unions would be construed by the courts as combinations in restraint of trade. When the bill was before the Senate, he insisted that an amendment be added specifically exempting organizations of workers and farmers from the application of the law, and Senator John Sherman sponsored such an amendment. It was later suppressed in committee. Gompers and others protested, but acquiesced when assurances were given that labor unions and farmers' organizations were not intended to be covered by the act.[2] Then came Pullman. By 1897, Gompers was saying flatly that the so-called antitrust laws were, in their purpose and effect, a means of robbing labor of the legal right to organize.

His second reason for opposing antitrust laws was that he did not share the general clamor against monopolies. For a short while, he was inclined to wonder whether there was any inherent good in the trusts and whether they ought not to be "smashed into their individual parts," but by 1899, he wrote that the trusts were a more scientific organization of industry and were intrinsically no more inimical to the interests of labor than was new machinery, providing the workers organized and secured the benefits which accrued from them. Within a few years, he was defending monopolies as a positive good. In an address before the Chicago Conference on Trusts in 1907, he depicted the trust as a natural result of the growth of industry, machinery and corporate capital. It made production more economical and efficient, and had to be accepted as a condition of the existence and progress of modern industry. In any case, Gompers contended, trust-busting was impossible, a mere tilting at windmills. The graveyards were well populated with the skeletons of forgotten laws and lawmakers, he pointed out, but the trusts were greater than ever, because they were economically right and inevitable.[3]

Gompers conceded that the concentration of wealth tremendously increased the power of the capitalist class to corrupt the political affairs of the country. But, he added, "the state has always been the representative of the wealth possessors," so the workers would have to endure that evil at least until they were organized and educated to realize that "the state is by right theirs, and finally and justly come to their own. . . ."[4] Later, he modified this view.

He thought the trusts might be reformed by creating a public opinion which expressed the will of the people. The trusts would then be brought to an awareness of their social responsibility.

A second danger in the trusts was that they made capital more powerful in its efforts to suppress labor. The remedy for these evils was not more laws but more unionism. The growing power and concentration of capital would be met by the increasing power and concentration of labor.[5]

Gompers was compelled to consider two special problems of organization that were forced upon labor by the concentrated power of monopoly. The first was the necessity of organizing the masses of unorganized workers, largely unskilled, in the basic industries, such as steel, textiles and railroads. The second was the question of new forms of labor organization for coping with new forms of industry: craft versus industrial unionism.

2. ORGANIZATION OF THE UNORGANIZED

The American Federation of Labor was composed primarily of unions of skilled workers who were employed in small establishments, such as cigar, printing, tailor, and barber shops. The unions in several mass production industries—steel, textiles, glass, and shoes—consisted almost entirely of the skilled crafts in those industries. The so-called "common and general laborers," such as the men who built the roads and railroads, lumberjacks, foundry laborers, and stevedores, were largely unorganized, as were the migratory and agricultural workers.

One of the primary purposes of the A.F. of L. was supposedly the organization of new unions, but it was limited in the extent to which it could realize that objective. The first limitation imposed upon it was the paucity of funds available for that purpose. Gompers never ceased his agitation for higher dues in the affiliated organizations and larger per capita payments to the Federation, at least partly to enable it to enlarge the scope of its work in this field. But he never achieved the results he asked for in that respect.

Another reason for the Federation's failure to organize unskilled workers in the basic industries was the inherent caution of Gompers and other A. F. of L. officials. Gompers felt that a rapid growth in the membership of the trade unions was unhealthy and would usually end with a reaction or complete collapse, which would be more dangerous than a slow and steady growth and development.[6] Gompers realized that the backbone of the A. F. of L. was the international unions of skilled workers who supported him. The large industrial unions containing masses of unskilled workers were generally more radical and formed the core of opposition to Gompers and "Gompersism" in the Federation. The significance of the fact that his only defeat as president of the Federation was at the hands of John McBride of the United Mine Workers was not lost upon him. Of the four largest unions in the basic industries—the miners, brewers, carriage workers, and woodworkers—the first three had a socialist majority during part or all of the years before the First World War and consistently voted against Gompers' policies and often against his re-election as president. The organization of the mass of industrial workers would shift the balance and alter the entire character of the A. F. of L. and thus jeopardize the position of those who had a vested interest in maintaining its traditional composition.

The Federation also reflected the narrow outlook of its affiliated organizations. Gompers was more farsighted than the officials of many of the craft unions in this respect and made occasional efforts to overcome their aristocratic exclusiveness. This policy, he said, had no place in the trade union movement, which should be based on the principle of solidarity and identity of interests of the wage earners. In 1899 the secretary of the tin plate workers' union told Gompers that his union did not want the unskilled workers in the industry; they should be allowed to organize as local unions directly affiliated with the A. F. of L. or remain unorganized. Gompers warned him that this would create a division in the ranks and that the unorganized workers, resenting neglect, could be utilized as strikebreakers by the employers: "The effort of organized labor is to protect and advance the interests of every wage earner, and to secure justice for all; and experience has demonstrated that these can be best attained by a broad and comprehensive organization of the workers of all branches, in any given industry, under one jurisdiction. . . ."[7] But Gompers' advice was not heeded, and under the Federation rule of craft autonomy, which Gompers made the heart of his creed, there was nothing else he could do but advise the international unions.

The successful organization of the workers required that special attention be given to immigrants, women, and Negroes. The A. F. of L. was a notorious failure with respect to their organization. There were serious problems in connection with this task: language barriers, cultural differences, and lack of understanding. Immigrant workers also tended to form separate organizations, primarily because of their common language, and partly because of their exclusion from the established unions or their hostility to the conservative policies of those unions. This was especially the case among the Jewish and German workers.

Gompers was strongly opposed to the separate Jewish unions and to the United Hebrew Trades, partly because of their socialist views, partly because they were outside the Federation and he feared that the tendency to form separate unions would cause schisms. He yielded only because opposition was fruitless, and accepted the United Hebrew Trades as a means of introducing Jewish immigrants to the American labor movement. Typically, he justified this policy as "theoretically bad but practically necessary" and ended up by claiming credit for having helped organize the U.H.T.[8]

He took the same attitude toward separate unions of German, Italian, or other foreign-born workers. His policy did not extend, however, to Oriental workers. Gompers shared the blindest prejudices of the American workers toward the Chinese and Japanese, an attitude strengthened by the conflict between the white and Chinese cigarmakers in the 1880's. The Cigarmakers International Union excluded Chinese from membership. The A. F. of L. had no such exclusion in its constitution. Nevertheless, said Gompers, for "obvious" reasons, it was against the entire policy of the Federation to admit to membership in its affiliated organizations either Chinese or Japanese workmen. He not only refused them union charters; he went beyond his authority in denying to central bodies the right to accord them representation. His growing administrative conservatism was shown in his explanation of his course: since the A.F. of L. had set its face against Orientals coming to the United States, it could not consistently unionize them, and to do so would create a "rumpus."[9]

Gompers showed an early interest in the problems of working women and their relationship to the general labor movement. The Legislative Committee of the Federation of Trades appealed to working women to form labor unions and promised them assistance. It declared its creed to be the unity of men and women workers and equal pay for equal work. In the early 1900's, Gompers appointed several women organizers. He urged the labor movement to recognize the identity of interests of men and women, and advised them to organize in common unions rather than form separate women's organizations. Gompers refused to sanction a union's effort to force women out of employment and warned against employers using women workers to divide the employees and cut wages.[10]

The constitution of the A. F. of L. was silent with regard to the organization of Negro workers, but the Federation inherited the attitude of the Knights of Labor and in 1894 reaffirmed the principle that "the working people must unite and organize, irrespective of creed, color, sex, nationality, or politics."[11] But the A. F. of L. consisted primarily of craft unions of skilled workers, and as a result it gradually retreated to a policy of discrimination and segregation. It was an even greater retreat for President Gompers, who had a more advanced point of view in the early days of his career than most of the other trade union leaders.

The question first came to the attention of the Federation in 1888 in connection with the National Association of Machinists, which was primarily a Southern organization. Except for the railroad brotherhoods, the machinists' union was almost the only national union that excluded Negroes from membership by constitutional provision. Gompers believed that this would doom the union to failure. "Wage-workers," he wrote, "like many others may not care to socially meet colored people, but as working men we are not justified in refusing them the right of the opportunity to organize for their common protection. . . . we will only make enemies of them, and of necessity they will be antagonistic to our interests." Gompers ruled that machinists' locals which were excluded from the national union, or which refused to join it until its color line was removed, might become directly affiliated to the A.F. of L. as federal trade unions.[12]

In 1890, the Federation urged the National Association of Machinists to remove discriminatory conditions from its constitution. Gompers visited the convention of the N.A.M. in Pittsburgh and underscored this request, but it declined to comply. He then called a convention of all independent machinists' unions, and the International Machinists Union was organized and affiliated with the A. F. of L. It pledged that, if the N.A.M. eliminated the color line, it would amalgamate with that organization.[13]

The A.F. of L. did not receive the report of these developments with the satisfaction that might have been expected. It "deplored" the formation of the I.M.U. as "premature." Owen Miller of the musicians' union asked Gompers if the A.F. of L. dictated to affiliated organizations as to qualifications for membership. Gompers admitted that it did not, and stated that the N.A.M. would receive a charter from the Federation if the color line was withdrawn. The implication was that the Federation could not openly recognize discrimination in its affiliated unions, but that it would not interfere with their policies so long as they did not proclaim them in their constitutions.

This was plainly hinted by Gompers in his letter to the next convention of the N.A.M. He emphasized that "under the banner of the American Federation of Labor there is no right that any trade union possesses which it would surrender by becoming affiliated with us," and that the word "white" in the constitution, while being of no advantage to the organization, was costing it the good will and co-operation of the labor movement. Finally, in 1895, the year that Gompers was on "leave" from the Federation, the N.A.M., renamed the International Association of Machinists, dropped the color line from its constitution and received a charter from the A.F. of L. The I.M.U. was then asked to endorse this action and to merge with the I.A.M.[14]

But the I.A.M. eliminated the color line in name only. The restriction on membership was kept in the ritual of the organization for half a century afterward. The secretary of the Washington lodge wrote frankly to W.E.B. Du Bois that "the Negro is not admitted to the International Association of Machinists," and the secretary of the international refused to answer questions as to the eligibility of Negroes. Even Gompers admitted that the constitutional amendment had not interfered with the "autonomy" of the organization.[15]

The course of the A.F. of L. in chartering the I.A.M. was not in accord with the original understanding that a merger between the two machinists' organizations would be effected prior to affiliation. It also violated a principle of craft autonomy: when a union of one trade was already affiliated with the Federation, it must give its consent before another union of the same trade could receive a charter. The I.M.U. attempted to effect an amalgamation with the older body after the latter had amended its constitution, but the I.A.M. refused to co-operate. It would not accept the I.M.U. as a body, but required the members to apply as individuals for membership. The Negro members were not admitted, and many of the white machinists also had difficulty in gaining acceptance. These facts were pointed out to Gompers, who ignored complaints. He unceremoniously informed the I.M.U. that its charter was revoked and that he assumed this met with its approval. Secretary Thomas Morgan assured him that his assumption was erroneous.[16]

The International Brotherhood of Blacksmiths also drew the color line, and in 1893 a number of locals urged Gompers to call a convention to form a new union without discrimination. Gompers, recalling the 1891 convention's criticism of his "premature" organization of the machinists' union, would not support the movement on the grounds that it constituted dual unionism. But he agreed with the position of the dissident locals and, though he wanted the affiliation of the blacksmiths, he used his influence to prevent it as long as its constitution prohibited Negro membership.[17] Four years later, the brotherhood changed its constitution and was admitted to the Federation.

Of course, there was a great deal of prejudice among many white workers, especially in the South, against Negroes belonging to their locals. Recognizing this, Gompers was willing to leave the question of integrated unions to local option, but at the same time he tried to persuade them to take the farsighted course and eliminate the color line. When he heard that a local teamsters' union was discriminating against Negroes, he informed it that "the American Federation of Labor positively places its stamp of disapproval upon such an attempt" and advised it to accept Negroes and accord them every benefit that membership entitled them to. In St. Louis, the hod carriers' union refused to accept Negro workers, and Gompers told them that if they did not admit Negroes, he would issue a charter to the Negro workers as a separate local, with the requirement that they adopt the same working rules and rates of wages.[18]

Gompers hoped and expected that these arrangements would be only temporary and that they would lead to more satisfactory relations. He wrote to a local union that the organization of both white and Negro workers was the best way to overcome and eliminate prejudice.

"Inasmuch, however, as that prejudice still exists, and that many white workmen will not belong to the same local organization with black men, and will not meet with them as members of the same local union, it might be more advantageous to go to work gradually to accomplish the desired end. In other words, have the Union of white men organize, and have the Union of colored men organize also, both unions to work in unison and harmony to accomplish the desired end. . . ."[19]

It seems evident that Gompers sincerely believed in the complete organization of the working class, and that he understood the necessity for unity between skilled and unskilled, men and women, Negroes and whites. But his understanding was tempered by the caution that marked the entrenched administrator, and his determination to organize the masses was weakened by the exclusiveness of the trade union officialdom, to which he was always inclined to yield even when he disagreed with it. Any serious effort to organize the basic industries was doomed to failure until the Federation was willing to go beyond its narrow craft organization which by its very nature virtually excluded the millions of unskilled workers.

3. INDUSTRIAL UNIONISM AND
CRAFT AUTONOMY

IN THE COURSE OF THEIR FIGHT WITH THE KNIGHTS
of Labor, the craft unions made a fetish of trade autonomy, which
became a brake on the progress of the labor movement. The
local union had been the natural form of organization in the
early days of industrial development, when artisans were often
manufacturers, workers, and merchants all in one, producing for
the local market. The national trade union was the logical form
of organization when industry and the market became nation-
alized, machinery was still rudimentary, and distinct crafts
were key factors in the labor force. With the further development of mechanization, the blurring of craft lines, and the
entrance of unskilled workers into gigantic corporations and
trusts, the craft union in its turn became obsolete. It proved
virtually impossible effectively to organize the mass production
industries through craft unions.

Intelligent union leaders became aware of the need for a
closer alliance between the trades, particularly after the strike
defeats of 1892-94. The concentration of industry, wealth, and
power by capital called for a corresponding concentration of
power by labor. The increasing frequency of jurisdictional
disputes made the problem even more urgent, as union was
set against union and brother scabbed against brother. Gompers,
aware of these problems, favored closer co-operation between
the trades. Besides, some of the strongest unions in the Federation were industrial organizations or claimed jurisdictions which
would make them such. But most of the affiliated organizations
were craft unions, jealous of their rights, and Gompers could
not set his face against them without jeopardizing his job. His
policy, therefore, was a wavering one: he tended toward
sympathy with industrialism, but when the chips were down
he stuck with the autonomists.

As president of the A.F. of L., Gompers could not contend
for industrial organization among the affiliated unions as he had
in the cigarmakers' union; this was an internal matter over which
he had no control. But he did urge a closer working relationship
or amalgamation between existing organizations as a step in the
direction of industrialism. In 1888 he recommended that in the

near future the Federation remodel its structure by having the various industries classified by divisions. For example, the metal industry might have a convention of representatives of all the trade unions in that industry, the building trades in theirs, and the railroad employees in theirs, each legislating on subjects affecting their general interests. These industrial divisions in turn would be represented by their proportionate number of delegates in the conventions of the A.F. of L., and each would have a representative on the Executive Council. The A.F. of L. would thus become a federation of industrial federations rather than of trade unions.[20]

Gompers sometimes made an effort to win others over to his viewpoint before compromising his position. But in this case, he must have heard a loud squeal, for he immediately went to the opposite extreme and became the bulwark of craft unionism, or trade autonomy as he preferred to call it. This capitulation, made early in the history of the A.F. of L., was crucial in his development, for in making it he allied himself with forces and principles that demanded further retreats on other key issues.[21]

The events of 1892 stimulated the movement toward industrial unionism, but Gompers held the line against any innovation in the Federation's policy. The next year, with the depression adding to the discontent of the workers, Gompers had rough sailing. The convention adopted a resolution declaring that it would be to the best interest of the Federation that the various building trades unions form a council and that similar councils be organized in all other industries having more than one craft. Gompers met the first serious opposition to his re-election. John McBride of the United Mine Workers was pitted against him, and Gompers squeaked through by the narrow margin of 1314 to 1222, being saved by the votes of the socialist delegates.[22]

Gompers, however, did nothing to implement the resolution to form industrial departments. When a National Building Trades Council was actually formed in 1897, he and the Federation looked upon it with disfavor, because it was not formed under the auspices of the A.F. of L. and smacked of dual unionism. Gompers was not opposed to the formation of such councils if they were kept within the control of the Federation. In 1900 he took the initiative in arranging a conference of the metal trades unions so that they could meet the employers' association and establish standard working conditions throughout the country. At the Federation convention later in the year, he arranged another conference at which the Metal Trades Council was formed.[23]

In the meantime, with Gompers' approval, the Federation took another step in the direction of industrialism. In 1899 it instructed the Executive Council to assist in the amalgamation of five craft unions in the textile industry, to form an organization of all mineral mine workers, and to amalgamate the painters and paperhangers. It also recommended the amalgamation of the coopers' and cooper machine workers' unions and of the stogie makers and cigarmakers. At the same time, it reaffirmed its adherence to the principle that each affiliated union had complete jurisdiction over the workers in its craft irrespective of where they might be employed.[24] Gompers attempted to carry out these instructions, but in some cases, he met resistance from the unions. He did effect the healing of the long schism between the two rival organizations of painters and made a start toward bringing unity into the textile industry. In 1901, a joint convention of the unions in the industry was held and they amalgamated as the United Textile Workers of America. This marked the end of Gompers' willingness to compromise with the principle of craft unionism.

Chapter Ten

LABOR POLITICS AND UNION POLITICS

1. POPULISM AND THE POLITICAL PROGRAMME

THE 1890's WITNESSED A GREAT UPRISING AMONG THE American people against the two major political parties. It began as an agrarian crusade and remained primarily a farmers' movement, but there were also strong trends in the labor movement toward independent political action and the development of an alliance with the farmers to overthrow the domination of the trusts. The independent political movements of the farmers and workers were merged in the early 1890's in the formation of the People's, or Populist party.

The spirit of Populism was expressed at the 1890 convention of the party by the Kansas firebrand, Mary Ellen Lease. The country had been subverted from its popular origin, she declared, into "government of Wall Street, by Wall Street and for Wall Street. The great common people of this country are slaves, and monopoly is the master. . . . Our laws are the output of a system which clothes rascals in robes and honesty in rags. . . . The people are at bay, let the bloodhounds of money who have dogged us thus far beware." In 1892 the party met in Omaha to draft a platform and organize for the election. Its great tribune, Ignatius Donnelly, pointed to a corrupt political system, a subsidized press, business prostrated, homes covered with mortgages, and the land concentrated in the hands of the capitalists. "The urban workmen are denied the right of organizing for self protection; imported pauperized labor beats down their wages; a hireling standing army, unrecognized by our laws, is established to shoot them down, and they are rapidly degenerating into European conditions. The fruits of the toil of millions are boldly stolen to build up colossal fortunes for the few, unprecedented in the history of mankind; and the possessors of these, in turn, despise the republic and endanger liberty. . . ."

To remedy these conditions, the Populists demanded a national currency issued by the government only, a subtreasury plan of warehouse loans, the free and unlimited coinage of silver at a ratio of sixteen to one, an increase in the circulating medium, a graduated income tax, a postal savings bank, government ownership of the telegraph and telephone systems, abolition of land monopoly and alien land ownership, the Australian secret ballot, restriction of undesirable immigration, strict enforcement of the federal eight-hour law and support of labor's effort to shorten the hours of labor, the abolition of the Pinkerton private armies, the initiative and referendum, the direct election of Senators, and opposition to subsidies for private corporations.[1] General James B. Weaver, Iowa statesman, was nominated for the presidency of the United States.

Gompers at first looked on the formation of the party as a healthy development. It might shake up the old parties and force them to make concessions, and several of its planks were very desirable. But his early sympathy for the party quickly turned to cold aloofness. Besides being opposed to labor's involvement in independent political movements, he was distrustful of the farmers, mostly self-employed and often employers of farm labor, who formed the backbone of the party. He observed that the Farmer's Alliance had opposed every effort of the farm laborers to organize unions. The Populists simply did not understand the trade union movement, and were a middle-class movement doomed to impotence.[2]

Gompers either failed to appreciate the possibilities of developing a mass movement of workers as well as farmers around the Populist party, or discountenanced it for that very reason. During the 1892 election campaign, in an article for the *North American Review*, he held that regardless of which party was elected, it would not affect the conditions of the workers. The Populist party was, at best, the lesser evil. The American Federation of Labor would maintain its nonpartisan policy, look with equanimity upon the campaign, and concentrate on the economic struggle. And "when the blare of trumpets has died away, and the 'spell-binders' have received their rewards, the American

Federation of Labor will still be found plodding along, doing noble battle in the struggle for the uplifting of the toiling masses."[3]

This article aroused discussion among Populists, labor leaders, and reformers. Some accused Gompers of presenting specious arguments against the party in order to prevent the workers from taking political action. Several A.F. of L. organizers feared Gompers' attitude would antagonize local unions which were co-operating with the Populists, and throw them into the arms of the Knights of Labor. They felt that his position was too negative; the issue was political co-operation, not economic alliance. They pointed to enthusiastic Populist support for many recent strikes and for its campaign against the use of Pinkertons, convicts, and contract labor in breaking strikes. Henry Demarest Lloyd informed Gompers that he had read his article with considerable agreement. But he believed it the duty of organized labor, which was ahead of the farmers in comprehending social and economic developments, to help guide the movement against monopoly capital.[4]

Gompers himself voted for Weaver, the "lesser evil," as a protest against existing conditions and the negative platforms of Harrison and Cleveland. He even sought to credit the trade unionists with the dramatic gains of the Populists in the election. But at the Federation convention the next month, he repeated that there was no need to change labor's tactics, and sought to thwart the growing sentiment for a positive political program. The trade unions, he insisted, were capable of coping with the power of wealth, and any attempt to "artificially and prematurely" expand their scope to include political activity would disrupt them.

But the action of the convention foreshadowed a shift from the pure and simple policy of the past few years. It endorsed the initiative and referendum and government ownership of the telegraph and telephone systems, two of the leading Populist planks, and it instructed the Executive Council to carry on a campaign of education which would increase the political action of the trade unions.[5] Gompers ignored these instructions, but the onset of depression and the repeal of the Sherman Silver Purchase Act the next year gave impetus to the demand for independent political action by labor.

At the convention of the Federation in December 1893, sentiment for independent political action, Populism, and socialism
was at a high pitch. The delegates declared in favor of the free
coinage of silver and instructed the Executive Council to bring
about an alliance with the farmers' organizations: many, like
McGuire, wanted to form an alliance with the Populist party.
Finally, Thomas Morgan, the Chicago socialist, introduced the
"Political Programme" for the approval of the Federation. It
declared that the British trade unionists had adopted the principle
of independent labor politics as an auxiliary to their economic
action, with "most gratifying success." Morgan proposed that
the A.F. of L. endorse their action and submit their program to
organized labor in the United States.* The resolution was adopted
by an overwhelming vote, thus committing the A.F. of L. to
independent politics and alliance with the farmers, and leaving to
the members the decision about the platform, particularly the
socialist Plank 10.[6]

Gompers did not approve of the action taken but felt he had
to swim with the current. As he wrote to Walter MacArthur,
leader of the Seamen's Union on the West Coast, shortly after
the convention, "We must hold on to every inch we've got till
matters resolve themselves into a condition of stability. In revolutionary times it is little use to preach conservatism—better go
out of the way than try to stem the torrent." So he told the press
that he approved "nearly everything" in the Political Programme
and that he believed "the time has come for independent action
on the part of organized labor."[7]

For a year this question formed a leading topic of discussion in
the unions and the labor press, and the *American Federationist*
was made a forum for debate on political action and socialism,

---

*The Programme, as amended, contained eleven planks: compulsory educa-
tion, direct legislation, a legal eight-hour workday, sanitary inspection of
workshops, mines, and homes, liability of employers for injury to health,
body, or life, abolition of the contract system in public work, abolition
of sweatshops, municipal ownership of street cars and gas and electric
plants, the nationalization of the telegraph and telephone systems, railroads,
and mines, the collective ownership by the people of all means of production and distribution (Plank 10), and the principle of referendum in all
legislation.

participated in by Morgan, Powderly, Frank Foster, Joseph Labadie, Joseph Buchanan, and Tom Mann of the British Trade Union Congress. Gompers' only contribution to the discussion was a guarded endorsement of the program without committing himself on Plank 10, but he resisted the movement for a labor-Populist alliance, which was being pressed forward on many fronts. In the spring, the People's party of New York asked him to appoint a committee to confer on co-operative action with representatives of other organizations. Gompers refused, claiming that he had no such authority.[8] He did, however, find authority to appoint a representative to the meeting of the Bi-Metallic League; the latter was not a partisan organization.

At the labor unity conference called in July by Joseph Buchanan, Gompers was compelled to make another gesture for independent political action. The Knights of Labor had proposed outright endorsement of the People's party. Gompers and the representatives of the Knights and the locomotive firemen, chosen to draft a program on which all could agree, brought out a compromise which recognized that the money classes were dictating the policies of government. It urged the workers to throw off the yoke of political partisanship and vote independently in order to gain full representation in the government. Subsequently, Gompers, along with Powderly, Debs, and others, went into New Jersey to support Buchanan's unsuccessful campaign for Congress on the Populist ticket.[9]

Elsewhere, the labor-Populist alliance was being forged. In Ohio, John McBride of the miners called a state convention of organized labor, which adopted a platform acceptable to the Populists. Organized labor in the Western mining states was lining up solidly behind Populism. In Illinois, an industrial conference was called by the state federation of labor to consider the Political Programme and to concert measures for independent political action. It endorsed the Omaha platform of the Populists as well as the Political Programme of the A.F. of L., except for Plank 10, which was modified to approve collective ownership of all such means of production and distribution as the people would elect to operate.

The distress of unemployment, the breaking of the miners' strike, and the Pullman boycott gave an even greater impetus to the Populist-labor coalition. The United Mine Workers and Debs' American Railway Union endorsed the party, and the Knights of Labor, socialists, single taxers, the Chicago trades assembly, and many local unions entered actively into preparations for the campaign. Henry Demarest Lloyd, popular reformer and leading spirit in this movement, besought Gompers to help extend the labor-Populist alliance and urged him to convene a national convention of unionists, single taxers, socialists and Populists. But Gompers withheld support for this proposal. His hostile attitude was revealed in a letter to Joseph Labadie, in which he prophesied that the venture of trade unionists into independent politics would prove "not an unmixed evil." First-hand experience with the disruptive effects of politics, he said, would lead them to re-examine the desirability of an independent national party, and they would send delegates to the coming convention of the Federation who would "save the general movement" from involvement in partisan politics.[10]

Seventy-seven delegates appeared at the A.F. of L. convention in December to vote on the Political Programme. Most of them had instructions from their organizations. Seventeen of the thirty national unions had endorsed the Programme unconditionally, and three approved all but Plank 10. The Cigarmakers International Union supported the whole Programme, with over seventy-five per cent endorsing Plank 10. Only the bakers rejected the Programme entirely. Practically all the state federations and a large number of city centrals had approved it. A large majority of the organized workers favored the Programme as a whole, although perhaps they were not in favor of the tenth plank.

But Gompers and his lieutenants were not ready to accept their verdict. He launched into an attack on the Programme in his report. He agreed that independent voting and political action by union workmen were desirable, but only to the extent of voting for their friends and against their enemies, regardless of party affiliation. If the Federation were to attempt to extend this movement nationally, the results would be "too portentious to contemplate." It was a course "strewn with shattered hopes and unions destroyed. . . . A national labor movement cannot and will not succeed upon the ruins of the trade unions." As for Plank 10, it was "not only controversial, but decidedly theoretical, . . . and so remote as to place ourselves and our movement in an unenviable light before our fellow-workers, and which if our organization is committed to it, will unquestionably prevent many sterling national trade unions from joining our ranks to do battle with us to attain first things first."[11]

Two days of the convention were given over to a debate on the Programme. In the vote on the Programme, Gompers executed the *coup de grace*. The convention of 1893 had adopted the preamble and resolution, declaring for independent political action, and had submitted to the membership only the platform which should be the basis for such action. Most of the unions had accordingly voted on the eleven planks only, assuming that this was the only question at issue. But Gompers submitted the entire Programme for another vote. The preamble was stricken out by a vote of 1345 to 861. Gompers voted with the majority, in spite of the cigarmakers' endorsement, justifying his action by stating that his union had instructed him only with regard to the platform. Then the eleven planks were voted on separately. All but number 10 were adopted, with slight modification. When Plank 10 came up, all sorts of substitutes were offered, and one was finally adopted calling for the abolition of monopoly landholding and the substitution of a title of occupancy only. After adopting the planks separately, the delegates voted against the Programme as a whole and against the endorsement of independent labor politics by a vote of 1,173 to 735.[12] There was difference of opinion as to the interpretation of the Federation's action. It was decided in 1895 that the final vote was determining, and that the Federation had no political program. However, the separate planks were retained as the legislative program of the A.F. of L.

2. "SABBATICAL LEAVE"

In the discussion on the Political Programme, Gompers stated that the time had come for a parting of the ways with the socialists. They evidently agreed with him, for the votes they had cast for him the year before to save him from defeat now went to his opponent, John McBride, and he lost his office—the only time in thirty-nine years. There were other reasons for his dethronement in that year. A principal one was the dissatisfaction of the Western unionists with the Federation. They had long felt neglected, and with the growth of the labor movement west of the Alleghanies, they thought the East had been represented in the president's office long enough. Besides, the Westerners were the strongest Populists and silverites in the labor movement, and McBride was more acceptable to them because of his more forthright position on those questions. This sentiment was reflected in the decision to move the Federation headquarters from New York to Indianapolis.

Gompers returned to New York to attend the convention of the State Federation of Labor, where he led a successful fight against a resolution for political action and socialism. "After killing me and nicely laying me away," he told the socialists, "you find I still live. . . . I shall meet you and yours in the days to come and then and there when the labor movement is antagonized by your organization or any one else you will find me in evidence."[13]

He then prepared to turn over his files and unfinished business to the new officers of the A.F. of L. August McCraith, the new secretary, came to the office to receive the properties and ship them to Indianapolis. Gompers had been very careful to compile and preserve the Federation's archives as well as pamphlets, documents, and other publications on the labor movement. He recalled: "McCraith declared there was no use of paying freight on all that stuff and began to discard what he did not consider valuable. I stood there and watched him go through my precious files and throw out what he did not consider worth keeping. There were two big heaps on the floor over six feet high when he had finished. I rescued some of the more important papers and carried them home. Next morning I returned with two suitcases intending to salvage more, but the janitor had cleaned the rooms over night and disposed of my papers."[14]

It was necessary for Gompers to earn a living, and he had no savings. He thought of accepting a political appointment, but probably ruled that out as a bar to his return to the presidency of the A.F. of L. Six months before, he had received a tempting business offer, which was still open. The president of a Mexican land company offered him a position at $50,000 a year for five years, and if he would go to Mexico and examine the project, he would receive $25,000 even if he turned down the offer. But he declined the proposition as inconsistent with both his sense of honor and his duty to the workingmen. He was wedded to the movement, he said, and to "lay down the duties devolving upon me in the present industrial and commercial crisis would be an act of treachery and cowardice against which my whole soul revolts. . . ."[15]

He also thought of returning to the cigarmaker's bench, but apparently not for long. He had many requests for lectures and articles, which provided him a greater income than he had received as president of the Federation and more than he could earn at his trade. So he decided to combine this with organizing work. The United Garment Workers asked him to make an organizing tour in the South, which he started at the beginning of April. He visited all the principal cities of the South and Southwest, and made about sixty speeches on labor problems in general as well as on the organization of the garment workers and the promotion of the union's boycotts. His salary was thirty dollars a week and expenses.[16]

On his return to New York, he began making arrangements for a trip to Europe. The A.F. of L., as a consolation prize, had elected him, along with McGuire, as the first fraternal delegates of the Federation to the British Trade Union Congress. He and McGuire sailed in the middle of August. They went first to London, where Gompers visited his childhood home and his relatives who still lived there. They then traveled to Manchester, Liverpool, and Dublin, meeting the labor leaders and addressing meetings in each city. On September 2 they presented their credentials to the Trade Union Congress at Cardiff, Wales. They made brief reports on the aims of the American labor movement, received medallions as tokens of fraternal good wishes, then sat back and observed the proceedings, noting anything that would justify their position on the A.F. of L.'s Political Programme. Gompers witnessed the defeat of a proposal for the nationalization of land and the means of production. He spelled out this decision in his report to the A.F. of L., and explained that the Congress' endorsement of socialism the previous year had been

a mistake, implying that he had saved the Federation from a
a similar blunder. He also noted with satisfaction the nonpartisan
policy of the British and Irish trade unionists.

Gompers and McGuire could not secure return passage until
three weeks after the conclusion of the Congress, so they decided
to extend their tour. They went to Paris together, after which
McGuire returned to Ireland and Gompers went to Cologne,
Bremen, Hamburg, and Amsterdam, consulting with labor
leaders in these cities and addressing the local trades councils.
While in Amsterdam, Gompers met his mother's sister, whom he
had never seen before. He had a strong family feeling, and
derived a great pleasure from meeting relatives.[17]

Gompers did more writing, lecturing, and organizing after
his return to the United States. Soon it was time to prepare for
the A.F. of L. convention. Although he was doubtful that he
would be returned to office, he determined to make the effort.
He always claimed that he never solicited votes or tried to influence Federation elections, but that was definitely not the case
in 1895. George Perkins, president of the cigarmakers' union,
particularly was busy lining up votes for him. Gompers wrote to
him: "I am frank to say to you that I should esteem it a pleasure
to be again the president of the Federation. . . . The movement as
I have often said has become part of my very self[,] my yearnings,
hopes—everything. . . . I fall entirely into your way of thinking
on this matter. . . . If you can show to a number of delegates
that in the interest of our cause they ought to vote for me I am
sure that you will do so and I shall appreciate your action beyond
measure. Heretofore I even forbade that but in so far I now
can see my error, more especially in view of what I am reliably
informed McB. is doing." He went on to discuss the convention
delegates: the dependable ones, and those from whom support
could be solicited.[18]

If Gompers' friends secured the votes of one delegate for
him—one delegate representing eighteen votes—it was enough,
for he was elected again by the narrowest margin in the history
of the Federation, 1,041 to 1,023. Gompers could not feel that
his future tenure was very secure. Therefore, when he was nominated the next month as first vice-president of the Cigarmakers
International Union, he accepted because, he said, one year hence,

"in the varying processes going on in the labor movement, your humble servant may again be a high private in the rear ranks. . . ." Although he was re-elected in 1896 without opposition, he continued to express doubts about re-election. In 1897, he was opposed by Ernest Kreft of the Philadelphia United Labor League, who secured just over one quarter of the votes. Gompers expected stiffer opposition from the socialists and industrial unionists the following year, and made up his mind that if he were defeated then or any other time in the future he would never again be a candidate for the office. But there was no opposition to his re-election, and from that time on he appeared quite confident that he could hold the position as long as he wanted it, and came to regard it as virtually belonging to him.

3. GOMPERS AND BRYAN

WITH HIS RETURN TO OFFICE, GOMPERS HAD TO move to Indianapolis. Raised on the sidewalks of London and New York, he felt that being sent to the backwoods of the West was virtual exile. Besides, he had lifelong friends and a large and closely knit family in New York, and dreaded the thought of leaving them. But he left his family at home, not knowing whether the next year headquarters might be moved again or he restored to the "rear ranks."

Hardly had he arrived in Indianapolis when he was stricken with a severe case of gastritis, later complicated with rheumatism and eczema. He was confined to bed for several weeks, and then for a few more could go to his office only a few hours a day. "Mamma" Gompers came out to look after him until he recovered. For over a month he suffered extreme pain, weakness, and sleeplessness He lost fifty pounds and for some time his life was in the balance. According to his doctor, only his "bull dog tenacity" pulled him through. His illness also put him into debt over $300, and with the added expense of maintaining his home in New York as well as his own quarters in Indianapolis, he was in serious financial straits. His son Abe was working in a clothing factory, and Gompers wrote to the president of the United Garment Workers to see if he could not get a promotion for him so that he could contribute to the family's support.[19]

By the time Gompers recovered fully, the presidential election campaign of 1896 was getting into high gear. The national leaders of the Populist party retreated from the collectivist program of the Omaha platform to a single-minded championship of the free coinage of silver. They hoped by this action to win the silver Republicans and Democrats of the West while appeasing the antimonopoly Populists with the prospect of smashing Wall Street's "money power," and at the same time stop the growth of radicalism in the party.

When the Republicans nominated William McKinley on a gold standard platform, it was evident that the Democrats could win the election only by espousing the cause of free silver, and the silver Democrats, led by William Jennings Bryan and Altgeld, had been waiting and planning for the opportunity to capture the party. Amid scenes of frenzy and religious fervor, Bryan captured the Democratic convention with his "Cross of Gold" speech and was nominated as the party's standard bearer on a platform of free silver and opposition to national banks, high tariffs, and government by injunction. The conflict within the Populist party came to a head when its nominating convention met and had to decide whether to maintain its independence or offer itself on the altar of Democracy and free silver. The conservatives won, and Bryan was endorsed as the candidate of the People's party.

Many A.F. of L. unions, as well as the Knights of Labor and the A.R.U., endorsed Bryan. The A.F. of L., though officially neutral in the campaign, stood for practically everything Bryan and the Populists advocated. However, Gompers pointed out, this did not mean that the Federation supported the Populist party or Bryan, explicitly or implicitly. "I will endeavor to the very best of my ability to keep out of the maelstrom of partisan politics," he wrote. Besides, the money question was greatly overestimated by both sides. Free coinage would prevent a few people from controlling the nation's currency, but the cause of the country's ills lay deeper than the question of gold and silver. This was a middle-class issue, he thought; it merely diverted attention from labor's real interests.[20]

In July, Gompers issued a circular to the affiliated unions, warning that their passions would be aroused by "the partisan zealot, the political montebank, . . . the effervescent, bucolic political party, cure-all sophist and fakir," and that labor organizations in the past had gone to extinction by following the siren call of politics. Whatever labor had secured was due to the efforts of the trade unions, and they should not expose themselves to the virus of political partisanship which carried the malignant disease of division and disruption.[21]

Many unions ignored Gompers' warnings or condemned them as a violation of local autonomy, and Gompers was told to mind his own business. The reaction to his circular was so hostile that he issued another in August, claiming he had been misunderstood. He insisted that he had not intended to deny the right of workers to take such political action as they pleased or that he had even advised against political action by the unions. But his critics were not satisfied, because he failed to endorse Bryan. Local unions charged that he was inconsistent in endorsing free silver but opposing affiliation with the party that championed it. Hundreds of letters and telegrams urged him to "get off the fence." But he would not budge, agreeing with McGuire that an endorsement would enable the socialists to reopen their political agitation in the A.F. of L.[22]

Gompers personally hoped for the election of Bryan, and voted for him, and it was reported that Bryan had announced his intention of appointing him to the cabinet if he were elected. But Gompers was very careful to keep his private views and actions from public notice. He wrote confidentially to one of Bryan's managers that he would like to meet Bryan and "talk over matters of interest," but did not see how it could be arranged. He did meeet Bryan once or twice during the campaign, apparently by accident, announcing on one occasion that he hoped Bryan would be elected but that he would accept no office under any circumstances.[23]

Gompers was less disturbed over the defeat of Bryan than he was gratified over the fact that the election was over. The unions had "weathered the storm successfully and will now have a clear field to work upon." They could now go on with the work of organization, having learned to avoid the rocks of political partisanship on which they had split during the campaign.[24]

Part IV

THE MIDDLE AGES

1897-1906

Chapter Eleven

THE LOBBYIST

1. AT THE CAPITAL

In 1896, the A.F. of L. decided to give up its
isolated headquarters in Indianapolis and move to the District
of Columbia, where the officers could give more direct attention
to their legislative program. Gompers packed up again and went
to the nation's capital, then a small provincial city with a distinct
Southern flavor. He rented a home on H Street, N.E.—a two-story
brick home in a row-building, its narrow front facing directly on
the sidewalk—and brought his family down from New York.
But for a number of years he regarded his residence in Washington as temporary, maintaining his legal address in New York
and going back each year to vote. Since Washingtonians were
disfranchised, Gompers felt that to make the capital his legal
residence would be an act of expatriation. Besides, he was fond of
the metropolis: "too good a place to 'swear off.'"

In the next few years, a series of misfortunes struck Gompers'
family. In 1898, while he was in Omaha for a Labor Day address,
his mother died. She had become quite helpless in her old age,
and lived in Samuel's apartment in New York. Since it was not
possible for him to return to New York in time for the funeral,
his family did not notify him of her death until his return.
Gompers' father, Solomon, then came to Washington to stay
with him, along with three of Samuel's still unmarried children.
A few months later, Gompers was again in the far West, attending
a labor rally in Des Moines. He was introduced by the chairman
of the board of public works in place of the mayor, who was
unable to be present because of the death of his daughter the day
before. Gompers prefaced his speech with a few words of condo-
lence to the mayor and his family. He then proceeded with

his address, in the course of which a messenger came on the platform and placed a telegram on the table next to him.

Gompers concluded his point, picked up the telegram, tossed it aside, then picked it up again and opened it. Before reading it, he started to speak again: "Wages, after all, find their own level—." There was silence in the theatre as he read the message, tried to resume his spech, but was unable to pick up the thread of his argument. He asked the audience to excuse him for a few moments. The chairman addressed the audience for a few minutes, and then determined to dismiss the meeting. Gompers returned to the stage and explained:

"I exceedingly regret that I should thus disappoint this audience. Never before in my work have I disappointed my audience in failing to complete my address. The telegram which was dropped upon the table tells me to come at once, as my eldest daughter is very low. It means more than that to me, for I know that my family, desiring to encourage my work as much as possible, would not wire me unless the very worst had occurred. It means that I have no hope. I trust you will excuse me, and that some time I may again visit your city and speak to the people."[1]

When Gompers got home, Rose was dead. He brought her two children home to live with him and Sophia. A year later his son Abe contracted tuberculosis and had to go West to try to recover his health. He was able to work for a while, but soon became too weak to continue. It was necessary to give him greater care and more expensive treatment, and Gompers was without funds. Max Morris, the president of the retail clerks' union, who was living in Denver, arranged to take care of the boy and to foot the bills until Gompers was able to repay him. Abe died after two years' illness. Gompers owed Morris about $2,000 and in order to pay the debt, he contracted for a series of ten lectures on the Chautauqua circuit.[2]

In 1902, Gompers' son Al married and it was planned to have him and his wife live at his home, so more room was needed. Gompers bought a house on First Street, N. W., for $5,700: a large, six-room, stone-front building. The living room was small, with a few old-fashioned chairs covered with linen, a piano for Sadie, a bust of Gompers, four or five paintings on the walls, and some bric-a-brac distributed over the room. There was an artificial fireplace on one wall, and the room was heated with a parlor stove. The third floor was fitted up as a workroom and library, where Gompers often worked until three in the morning; his granddaughter Florence studied typing and stenography so she could help.

The Gompers household was a constellation which revolved entirely around the "old man," as Sam was already known by his friends. "Mamma" lived only to make him happy, and she catered to his every whim. Short, plump, and motherly, her world was encompassed in her home, her family, and her husband. While Gompers had educated himself, Sophia remained the simple housewife, who knew, however, what unionism meant to a worker and understood that her husband had a big job in the labor movement. She had endured years of poverty and loneliness, but never complained: helping Sam, she was content.

Gompers' youngest daughter, Sadie, was the apple of his eye. When there were guests, she was the hostess, as she had an urbanity and brightness that were lacking in Mamma. Her father had great hopes of an operatic career for her. She had been encouraged by her music teacher in school, and Gompers provided singing lessons for her for seven years. In 1906, she went on a vaudeville tour for the Keith circuit. Mamma always accompanied her, either because she did not want to travel alone, as Gompers wrote, or because he insisted on it, as his grand-daughter says. Sadie decided to give up her career so that her mother could stay at home and be with Sam. It is doubtful if the sacrifice was a great one, for her talents were over-rated, and a large part of her audiences was made up of people who were curious to see Gompers' daughter on the stage and workers who were urged to go to the theatre to give their chief's daughter a break.[3]

When Gompers was in the city, there was often company at his home. Many times he would bring associates home for din-ner, so that they could discuss labor matters, and often they would come even for breakfast to get an early start on the day's work. James O'Connell, the president of the International Association of Machinists and a vice-president of the Federation, was a neighbor and frequent visitor. Tom Tracy, a cigarmaker and later an organizer and member of the legislative committee in Washington, was another close friend who often came to his home. Others for whom Gompers had a particular attachment were George Perkins, president of the cigarmakers' union, and John O'Sullivan, whom the Gomperses called their "son." But they were only occasional visitors, as they did not live in Washington. Besides his family and friends in the labor movement, there were many others whom Gompers entertained at home. There were convivial gatherings with his Elks brothers, visits by politicians, clergymen, and industrialists, and many parties for actors who were playing in Washington. Gompers became acquainted with many actors, singers, and chorus girls, as he often went to the same restaurants and bars after meetings, when they were coming from the theater. He also met some through his cousin, Sam Collins, who was a well-known comedian.

When Gompers was at home, Sunday was always open house. He expected every member of the family who was in the city to visit him, and friends were always there too. They would talk, play penny ante, or listen to music. Gompers was very fond of music, and had one of the first Victor machines and a fine collection of records. At these gatherings, Gompers always insisted on occupying the center of the stage. If some one else seemed to be attracting the attention of the group, he would step in and steal the show. These were his parties, it was his home, and he wanted to be the "big man."

When he could not go home to dinner because of evening work at his office or elsewhere, Gompers generally dined at Perreard's, a French theatrical boarding house and restaurant. The proprietor, known as "The Count," and his wife presided over the festivities, introducing the guests to each other as "Citizen So-and-so," and often entertaining by singing. The restaurant was frequented by French citizens, ambassadors, and reporters, actors and actresses, and intellectuals and *bon vivants* from all countries. On Bastille Day each year, the regular patrons, known as the "reptiles," were invited to a special ceremony, with Gompers as guest of honor. In the small back court, covered with latticework and vines, the birthday of the French Republic was celebrated with more than the usual quantities of "red ink."

For all his family spirit and his devotion to his brothers and children, Gompers consistently refused to use his influence to help them. When he first came to Washington, both of his unmarried sons were unemployed. Henry was a stone mason and Al a painter whose hands were weakened by disease. Yet Gompers would not give them work in the Federation mailing room. Years later, Al besought him for an appointment from Herman Robinson, Gompers' former organizer in New York who was then New York commissioner of licenses. Gompers would not make the request. He felt that if he were to have any influence with men in public office, he had to remain absolutely independent of any obligations to them. He also had to avoid anything that might be interpreted as misuse of his office. One day he came to his office and found that his granddaughter Florence had secured a job there as a stenographer. He immediately ordered her discharge.[4]

By the turn of the century, Gompers' physical appearance had changed markedly since his advent to the presidency of the American Federation of Labor a decade and a half earlier. His intemperate eating and drinking showed itself in stoutness to such an extent that vaudeville comedians drew laughs by patting their bellies and referring to them as their "Sam Gompers." Following the national trend in styles, he had shaved his walrus mustache and goatee, revealing the very wide mouth with its turned-down corners and prominent lower lip. As a result of the attack of eczema which he suffered in 1896, his large face was pock-marked and his graying hair had begun to fall out in patches. Mark Sullivan observed that his hair looked "like a piece of worn-out buffalo robe which has lain in the garret and been chewed by the moths since 1890, and then been thrown out in the rain and laid in the gutter for a year or two, and been dragged back by a puppy dog to cut his teeth on."[5] In order to hide this condition, Gompers (like John D. Rockefeller) took to wearing a black skullcap, or *yamelka*. He almost invariably wore it in his office, and when he went out he put it in his pocket for later use. Occasionally he wore it even at public appearances when addressing meetings or testifying before legislative committees. His weakening eyes caused him to begin wearing glasses about this time, which added to his middle-aged appearance.

Gompers' appearance seemed to depend largely on the

observer's attitude toward him. Walter Gordon Merritt, a writer for an antiunion employers' association, saw him for the first time about 1902 and was impressed with the qualities which he thought would "inspire a small-town boy with fear and admiration. Wholly un-American in appearance; short; with large eyes, dark complexion, heavy-lined face, and hair slightly curly but looking moth-eaten—he was impressive. As I sat in the audience . . . I wrote the name 'Marat' on a slip of paper and handed it to my companion. He nodded."[6]

To those who were more sympathetic, the same features gave evidence of different qualities. All agreed that he gave an impression of great power and determination. Benjamin Stolberg saw in him "a touch of anthropoid strength," and noted that his head was like an animated boulder, and his face, granite-complexioned, had an Oriental cast which gave him a fascinating "noble freakishness." There was also agreement on the intensely mobile face which constantly reflected his emotions. "All his vital expressions rose and fell together as though controlled by some inner mechanism," wrote Stolberg. "One moment, the mobile mask would be cunningly furtive and quizzical, then intimately and wistfully kind; then again it would glow with a self-righteous passion that in retrospect seemed grotesque. It was a congenitally histrionic face, and its outlay in spiritual energy bespoke an enormous vitality."[7] The key words are passion and histrionics, for Gompers was a man of deep emotions but he had learned to control them and to display himself with the utmost dramatic effect.

As the influence of the A.F. of L. grew, Gompers became a prominent figure in the public eye, the object of frequent comment and cartoons in the press, a speaker at important meetings, a witness before congressional committees, a friend of politicians, industrialists, and social leaders. He became more self-conscious and self-impressed. He began to dress more carefully than he had in his youth, even nattily, with a diamond pin in his cravat. His bearing was one of great dignity—some thought he was cocky and a show-off. Among his friends he was Sam Gompers the cigarmaker, one of the boys, a hail-fellow-well-met, bubbling over with fun and affability, a good story teller, and a congenial companion. But when he appeared as Samuel Gompers, president of the American Federation of Labor, he was a different man—"calm, dignified, and unapproachable, jealously resenting anything and everything that would detract from the dignity of the position he holds."[8]

On one occasion he called at the White House to express to Theodore Roosevelt his displeasure at a public statement made by the latter. He spoke so vigorously that Roosevelt, showing irritation, hit the desk with his fist and said, "Mr. Gompers, I want you to understand, sir, that I am the President of the United States." Gompers faced him with blazing eyes, and hitting the desk with equal emphasis, shot back, "Mr. President, I want you to understand that I am the president of the American Federation of Labor."[9]

While he was becoming middle-aged, dignified, and respectable, he did not slow down. His energy was tireless, and his constitution apparently impervious to abuse. He took a Rabelaisian joy in the pleasures of life, and his work was one of those pleasures. He became more intemperate in his drinking, and sometimes became drunk even in public. After dinner or an evening meeting, he often went out to "take a walk" which invariably brought him to a saloon. At conventions, he would get roaring drunk nearly every night after the session was adjourned, but the next morning he appeared on the platform fit, clear, and ready for business. John Frey once reproved him for drinking too much, and Gompers said, "Well, John, we're all different in our make-up. When I have to think a great deal I become tense, and the only way I can relax is to take a few drinks." He was equally regardless of the rules of common sense in matters of diet, sleep, pleasure and work. Even his relaxation, which he often took in one of the cheap burlesque houses on Pennsylvania Avenue, was of the same pattern.[10]

His schedule of work was onerous. He seldom traveled less than 10,000 miles a year, sometimes 25,000, making as many as 150 addresses in the course of a year and appearing at twenty-five to fifty hearings before congressional, state, and municipal committees. He held hundreds of conferences yearly with labor men, representatives of other organizations, employers, and congressmen. His activities during one month were typical. The Federation convention in New Orleans adjourned at three in the

morning on November 23, 1902. The same day he held a con-
ference with representatives of various labor organizations and
a meeting with the Executive Council. Two days later he was
in Birmingham to address a mass meeting. He returned to
Washington on the 28th, and four days later went to Hartford,
Connecticut, to attempt to adjust a dispute between the Horse
Nail Makers Union and the Capewell Horse Nail Company.
The following day he was in Boston, where on successive evenings he lectured at Faneuil Hall and debated with Louis D.
Brandeis on the incorporation of unions. Stopping at New York
to address the National Civic Federation, he returned to the capital
to make two appearances before a Senate committee considering
the eight-hour bill. He went back to New York the next day to
lecture on strikes to the League for Political Education, returned
to Washington, and stayed only a few hours, when he was called
to Scranton to testify before the Anthracite Coal Strike Commission. He returned to his office on December 18. During that
month he sent out some 5,000 letters, of which he probably dictated
500 personally.

Gompers tried to instill into his associates the same enthusiasm
and crusading spirit that he had for the labor movement. In 1899
one of his organizers wrote him about the lack of interest the
workers displayed toward their union and asked if he could be
blamed for becoming discouraged. "Blame you?" Gompers ex-
postulated. "Of course, I do. You have no right to become discouraged. Men are not angels, and all men are not heroes. You
must take them as they are, and try by every means in your power
to mold them into better and sterner stuff. Do you think that
every cause was brought to victory by the active men themselves
becoming discouraged? . . . [The things we strive for] are not
secured in a month, or a year, yes, in even a century. We have
done much; by continually applying ourselves to the work, we
shall secure more, and work right along without swerving from
the path of duty, enlisting the cooperation of the now listless and
apathetic, who will perform a greater share of the duties in furtherance of the holy cause in which we are engaged. . . ."[11]

Gompers established the headquarters of the Federation in
three rooms of a building on 14th Street, N.W. One room was the
president's office, and in the others the four employees of the

Federation handled the paper work of the organization. After one year, they moved to new quarters in the Typographical Building on G Street. As the membership of the Federation entered a period of rapid growth, from 278,000 in 1898 to 1,500,000 five years later, activities at the central office expanded, and the president became an administrator as well as organizer, a manager as well as executive, and an employer as well as a leader of the employed. Fortunately, there came into Gompers' life at this time a young woman who was admirably equipped to assist him.

Miss Rosa Lee Guard was a frail and delicate girl who had been told that she could expect to live but a few years more. Her melancholy was augmented by disappointment in love. She decided to cast aside the traditions and prejudices in which she had been reared and to seek a career in a man's world. With no knowledge of the struggles of labor for a better life, but with a deep understanding of human nature and an intense longing to identify herself with something larger than her own narrow life, she applied to Gompers for a job as a typist and was hired at ten dollars a week. She sought in his work a mental absorption that would leave her no time to think of herself and her problems. She found what she was seeking, becoming a devoted assistant and friend to Gompers. She recovered her health and outlived the man in whose service she had come to die.

Miss Guard was quickly promoted to chief clerk over the growing headquarters staff, and then to Gompers' private secretary. She handled his correspondence, ran the office, and even looked after his personal financial affairs. Gompers spent his money recklessly. If Miss Guard had not withheld enough to make the payments on his house before she gave him his pay check, he probably would not have been able to meet them. She was "a combination of private secretary, confidential right-hand man, trained nurse, something of a grandmother, and acting president of the American Federation of Labor." She was completely devoted to Gompers and his cause, regarding him as an "unselfish soul and big, warm heart, filled to overflowing with sympathy and tenderness, for all mankind, yet controlled by a clear, sanely-thinking brain. . . . [H]e stands apart from his fellows," she wrote, "a myriad-sided nature; a creature of poetry and practical action; a dreamer, yet a doer of the world's work; a soul of storm while

diffusing sunshine—a combination of wholly opposing character-
istics. . . . I love him next to my mother."[12]

2. LABOR LEGISLATION

WITH THE TRANSFER OF THE AMERICAN FEDERATION
of Labor to Washington, Gompers entered a new phase of activity.
Labor legislation now became a major goal in his work. During
these years Gompers defined more clearly his attitude on the role
of the state in effecting labor reform. He believed the government
should do nothing for labor that labor could do for itself through
its trade unions. The government ought, however, to regulate
directly the wages, hours, and working conditions of its own
employees and those employed on government contracts. It ought
to regulate the standards of women and children, whose defense-
lessness endangered the standards of adult male workers. It ought
also to protect the rights of workers to organize and strike. Finally,
it should protect labor when legislation alone could do so, as with
immigration restriction and the regulation of convict labor.

Trade unionism was self-help, Gompers declared, and, left
free and untrammeled, the unions would achieve better conditions
by their own efforts.[13] There were various reasons for Gompers'
apprehensions about unbridled legislation. He feared the growing
power of the state, controlled, as he thought, by the wealthy classes.
Experience had demonstrated to him that increase in governmental powers invariably resulted in the greater oppression of
labor, as in the use of the Sherman Antitrust Law. Gompers also
regarded reliance on government for regulating contracts in industry as violating his sacred principle of voluntarism. The spirit that
made America great and the American labor movement the best
in the world, he asserted, was the rugged spirit of red-blooded men
and women who dared to conquer the wilderness and to fight for
right, justice, and equality. Unions which let go ultimate control
over industrial welfare stultified initiative and weakened their
own fighting force.

Reliance on political struggles would weaken the workers'
attachment to trade unions and strip them bare of defenses. Besides, legislation by itself could not bring about permanent progress, which must come from within men. Even if desirable laws

were enacted, there was constant danger that they would be repealed by a swing of the political pendulum. The workers must keep control over economic functions in their own hands, and so ensure the enforcement of those laws that were adopted.[14]

The growing importance of the labor movement as a political force was reflected in an incident which occurred shortly after the Federation's move to Washington. Just one week before the opening of the Detroit convention, Gompers left his home on his bicycle to go to his office. Before he had gone ten yards he was struck by a street car running at full speed and was thrown twenty feet. He fell on one of the spokes which pierced his right lung, his ribs were crushed, ligaments were torn from both knees, his head, chest, and legs were cut, and his left knee was dislocated. He could not breathe or speak without agony, and morphine was administered, rendering him unconscious until the evening. When the convention opened, Gompers was still in bed with a cast on his leg.

Shortly before his accident, a representative of the shipping interests had endeavored to argue and cajole him into throwing the support of the Federation behind a ship subsidy bill. A group of lobbyists offered him any sum to support the bill, as well as $10,000 for a list of delegates to the convention. Gompers knew that the lobby would be active at Detroit and would undoubtedly attempt to bribe the delegates to vote for their bill. He apprised Vice-President McGuire of the situation and was confident that he would be able to handle it. But when he heard that McGuire was indisposed and that the lobby was pressing its measure at the convention, he determined to go to Detroit himself, in spite of his doctor's orders to remain in bed. He was carried to the depot, put on the train, and on the fifth day of the convention he assumed the chair. He entered the debate on the ship subsidy, told the story of the attempts to bribe him, and asserted that the measure was a scheme to loot the public treasury for a project that was not in labor's interest. The convention, except for the representative of the boilermakers, voted unanimously against the subsidy.[15]

Gompers was confined to his hotel during the remaining sessions. The convention voted him a thirty-day leave of absence, but the Executive Council, he said, gave him sixty days' work to do in that time. He went to Chicago to deal with some trade disputes, and from there went to Indianapolis to address the United Mine Workers' convention. He suffered a relapse and was ordered by his physicians to take a vacation. He decided to go to Cuba to recuperate, leaving Washington on January 31 for a three weeks' trip.

Gompers' legislative activity did not often involve such dramatic incidents. Most of it was an endless—and often futile—round of conferences with presidents and congressmen, meetings with labor legislative committees, arguments before congressional and state legislative committees, and routine paper work and correspondence. Measures of greatest importance to the Federation in the early years of the twentieth century were those concerning hours and wages, child labor, workmen's compensation, immigration, convict labor, and the right to strike.

Gompers continued to place the eight-hour day at the top of his program, and the adoption of improved eight-hour laws for government employees was one of his major projects. The first federal eight-hour law was passed in 1868, but this law was either ignored by executive officials or put into effect with a reduction in wages. The Workingmen's Union of New York and the New England Eight-Hour League sent Gompers to urge President Grant to enforce the law without wage reductions. Grant twice issued proclamations that the law be enforced by all departments without wage cuts, but the law was emasculated by a ruling of the Attorney General that it applied only to workers directly employed by the government, and by a decision by the United States Supreme Court that even in those cases the application of the law was not obligatory.[16]

In 1897, the House committee on labor introduced the Phillips Bill to extend the eight-hour law to contractors and subcontractors with government agreements. Gompers appeared at committee hearings several times, and the bill was favorably reported to the House. Thomas Phillips' term expired with that Congress, and at the request of Gompers and the Federation's legislative committee, John J. Gardner was appointed to the chairmanship of the committee on labor. In collaboration with the Federation committee, he worked out a perfected bill. It passed through the House by an almost unanimous vote, but was prevented from coming to a vote in the Senate. Year after year this process was repeated, opponents of the measure using tactics of delay, procrastination, and extended hearings to prevent action by the Senate, acting in the interests of the National Association of Manufacturers and other business organizations.

For a short time, Gompers was an advocate of a universal eight-hour law for all workers. But by 1888 he had assumed the position that, except for state or federal employees, women, and children, the workers should not invoke government interference in the matter. He maintained that principle throughout his life, in spite of repeated declarations by the A.F. of L. in favor of eight-hour laws for all workers.[17]

Gompers' arguments against eight-hour laws for workers in private industry were varied and often disingenuous. Thus, he once stated that men did not need hours legislation because they were part of and had a voice in government, and could secure shorter hours through their own initiative and action, whereas women and children were to some extent wards of the nation, without the elective franchise. He failed to explain the connection between the right to vote and the right or ability to improve status through trade union action. Nor did it occur to him that the same reasoning justified an eight-hour law for disfranchised Negroes and immigrants.

Gompers also argued that government-established minimum wage or maximum hours laws probably would compel men to work at those standards: "When that time comes, when by statutory enactments wages are set, it will only be another step to force working men to work at the behest of their employers, or at the behest of the State, which will be equivalent to, and will be, slavery." This view contradicted an earlier one favoring a constitutional amendment which empowered Congress to fix wages. At that time he had asserted that the history of industrial legislation made it inconceivable that the government would use its power to the detriment of the workers. In any case, Gompers insisted that a law was not effective unless enforced by a strong organization, and that the movement to secure laws would weaken the trade unions so that they would not have the militancy necessary to enforce them. Gompers cited union experiences in Colorado, but the same experiences could have been used to demonstrate the falsity of his claim, for the most militant struggles of the decade were fought there to enforce the eight-hour law.[18]

Within the A.F. of L., sentiment for eight-hour laws gathered strength during the early years of the twentieth century. The issue came to a head in 1913-1915. At its Seattle convention in 1913, the Federation resolved that renewed efforts be made to secure a more general eight-hour workday. In pursuance of this resolution, the federations of the three Pacific Coast states initiated universal eight-hour laws for submission to popular referendum. Manufacturers' associations circulated literature and posters stating that Gompers opposed such legislation. The trade unionists urged him to make a statement to the contrary, but he refused to do more than declare that the Federation had taken no position on the matter. Subsequently he explained that the Seattle resolution referred only to eight-hour legislation for government employees, and, while not denying the right of workers to strive for general eight-hour laws, he stated that he did not agree with them and would not give his sanction to their "riveting chains on their wrists."[19]

At the Federation convention the following year, the California Federation of Labor introduced a resolution attacking Gompers for contributing to the defeat of the referendums in the Western states and calling for the reaffirmation of the Seattle declaration. Gompers went before the resolutions committee and secured a substitute resolution putting the Federation on record as opposed to eight-hour legislation for adult male workers. This opened an all-day debate on the subject. J. A. Taylor of the machinists' union denied that the Washington eight-hour law for women had weakened the desire of the workers for organization; on the contrary, it strengthened the unions because the women workers came to them for help when the law was violated. Besides, some employers had discharged their employees and substituted men who were not limited to eight hours a day. He appealed for the Federation's support in the effort to secure the eight-hour law for all workers two years hence. "If you don't," he added, "we will pass it anyway, and the American Federation of Labor goes on record that it does not believe in getting anything when we can go straight across and get it; but we must walk around and around in a circle. . . ."

J. G. Brown of the timber workers asked why there was any more danger of state tyranny under eight-hour laws for men than under similar ones for women. He thought it alarmist to fear that these laws would open the gates to the evils which existed in the fifteenth century. His own union had spent considerable time and money in an unsuccessful attempt to organize the nonunion timber workers who were laboring twelve and a half hours a day, and this was preventing other workers from reducing their hours of labor. Paul Scharrenberg of the California Federation rebuked Gompers for arbitrarily upsetting the declared policy of the A.F. of L. by his "interpretation" of its meaning.

Gompers retorted that after the Seattle convention he had come to have a better understanding of the meaning of the words employed in the resolution, and it was not fair to call him a pettifogging lawyer for applying a more discriminating interpretation to their meaning. He emphasized that the labor movement was in its infancy and just beginning to shake off the grip of tyrannical government. If the courts were given jurisdiction over industrial matters, he warned, they would leave no stone unturned to exercise it to the detriment of labor. Gompers dramatically appealed for "industrial, humanitarian statesmanship" to keep the labor movement going forward in a logical and natural order on the basis of self-help and mutual help.

By a vote of 11,000 to 8,000, the Federation reversed its position and for the first time endorsed Gompers' views on eight-hour legislation. This ended the movement for such laws within Gompers' lifetime: in one interpretation, a victory for the strong skilled trades, which feared that if their gains were universalized by law, their unions would be weakened by workers who would fail to see the need for unionism.[20]

Gompers underwent a similar change on wage and hour laws for women. In the 1890's he fully supported them; by 1912 he doubted that such measures were defensible. In the earlier period of industrial development, he maintained, women were a minor element in the labor force; they were denied all rights, being "wards of the State, dependents upon father, husband, or relative, to be petted, supported, commanded, but never given the right of individual freedom." Custom and law enforced on them a parasitic life. Under those conditions, Gompers recognized the need for legislation to secure for them what men had got for themselves through organization and collective action. But with the growth of women's educational, legal, and economic freedom, with their entrance into industry on a large scale and on a permanent basis, with the beginning of their organization and the development of their struggle for better conditions, the situation changed in Gompers' view.

"This woman movement," he wrote, "is a movement for liberty, freedom of action and thought, tending toward a condition when women shall be accorded equal independence and responsibility with men, equal freedom of work and self-expression, equal legal protection and rights." Women, like men, had to solve their problems by the development of individual responsibility and initiative, not by setting up government agencies that would fetter them.[21]

Gompers was fighting against the tide, for the movement for wage and hour legistration for women was an integral part of the progressive movement of the period. From 1909 to 1917, nineteen states passed maximum hours laws and twenty others improved previous statutes; and between 1912 and 1923, fifteen states enacted minimum wage laws for women. Organized labor generally gave only nominal support to the movement, and sometimes actively opposed it. Gompers' own opposition was partly responsible for its lack of greater success and for the recession of the movement after 1913.

In the 1880's, only one state in the Union prohibited the employment of minors, although most of the Northern and Western states limited the hours of labor or the type of industrial establishments in which children could be employed. This was a subject about which Gompers felt very keenly. Child labor was, of course, a menace to the workingmen, for it degraded their standards by a competition of the worst sort. In addition, Gompers said, it was an expression of the most inhumane exploitative character of capitalism. The exploitation of child labor he found repulsive to every instinct of humanity.

At the first session of the Federation of Trades in 1881, a delegate opposed a resolution against child labor on the ground that its enforcement would interfere with individual rights. Gompers recounted a recent experience in investigating the tenement cigar shops. "I saw there on that visit," he said, "scenes that sickened me. I saw little children, six and seven and eight years of age, seated in the middle of a room on the floor, in all the dirt and dust, stripping tobacco. Little pale-faced children, with a look of care upon their faces, toiling with their tiny hands from dawn till dark; aye, and late into the night, to help to keep the wolf from the door. . . . Often they would be overcome with weariness and want of sleep, and fall over upon the tobacco heap. Shame upon such crimes; shame upon us if we do not raise our voices against it."[22] The resolution was passed unanimously, and Gompers never ceased his efforts to abolish child labor.

When the state of New York was preparing to hold a constitutional convention in 1894, Gompers submitted four proposals to be incorporated in the new charter. They provided that the state maintain free industrial schools at which children over thirteen might be educated in the agricultural and industrial arts; that the employment of minors for more than eight hours a day be prohibited; that the labor of children under fourteen be completely abolished; and that the employment of children in tenement houses be prohibited.[23] In 1894, too, Gompers began publication of the *American Federationist*, where he constantly exposed the horrors of child labor and agitated for its abolition. Many noted reformers, such as Florence Kelley, were invited to write on the subject for the journal.

Gompers particularly attacked the problem in the Southern states, where the exploitation of children was worst. In 1891, he wrote in his usual vein of sincerely-felt rhetoric to the secretary of the Birmingham Trades and Labor Assembly, urging his organization to take action to secure the enforcement of the ten-hour law for children: "The cruel and iniquitous employers and companies who think more of dividends than of human hearts and bodies and souls, should be taught a lesson that organized labor will not stand idly by in having the blood of defenseless women and innocent children being used as the lubricating oil for the machines that grind their very bones into cash to gratify the wishes of the insatiable monsters whose only deity is the almighty dollar."[24]

In 1900, Gompers commissioned Mrs. Irene McFadden Ashby, a wealthy socialist reformer, to go South to aid in the fight against child labor, particularly in Alabama. Bills were presented to several of the state legislatures, but Tennessee was the only state which adopted a law. Mrs. Ashby established permanent committees in all the large cities to continue the campaign. As a result of their agitation, Kentucky was added to the list of states limiting child labor, and a strong sentiment developed throughout the South in support of the movement.[25]

The first decade and a half of the twentieth century was the heyday of child labor legislation. The National Child Labor Committee carried its message to a sympathetic public. During those years every state passed new laws or strengthened old ones. Still the standards were pitifully low. Ten states had no laws requiring school attendance during the full term; two states had no minimum age for employment, and in all but five the minimum was only twelve or fourteen years; only nineteen states restricted the hours of labor for children to eight per day; many did not prohibit night work; and many of the laws were weakened by inadequate enforcement provisions. In 1914, Gompers was still appealing for an end to the disgrace of child labor.[26]

Another field of labor legislation with which Gompers was actively concerned was employers' liability and workmen's compensation. The United States had the highest industrial accident and mortality rate in the world, about a half million workers being injured and 30,000 killed every year. The coal mines alone took more lives in preventable accidents than had all the wars of the United States. The disregard of employers for their workers' safety was due to the fact that they were practically immune from liability. The American courts accepted the common law doctrine that an injured worker could not claim damages if contributory negligence of his own led to the injury; if the negligence of a "fellow-servant" contributed to the injury; or if the worker could be expected to know of the dangers involved in the job and therefore to have "assumed the risk" as a condition of employment.

Gompers pointed out the injustice of requiring the injured workers or their widows and orphans to bear the burden of suffering due to industrial accidents and deaths. The "effete decisions of courts, coined centuries ago under comparatively primitive conditions, should have no application in our modern industrial era," he asserted. This burden should be assumed either by society, through automatic compensation laws, or by the employers, by repealing the common law doctrine of liability. He himself preferred the former, because it made unnecessary the prolonged and uncertain litigation which workers could ill afford and would not disturb the relations between the injured workman and his employer. But because of constitutional objections that had been raised by many courts, it was necessary to work for improved liability laws, at least as a step toward creating a healthier public opinion on the problem.

Gompers, with his own "constitutional objections" to government's doing for the workers what they could do for themselves, proposed that the Federation work only for state laws amending the rules for employers' liability, and for federal laws providing compensation to several categories of government employees.[27] But the organized labor movement in the states paid little attention to him on the issue. It worked actively not only for modifying the liability laws, but also for state compulsory compensation for all injured workers. As a result, thirty-nine states passed workmen's compensation laws between 1911 and 1919.

While Gompers' support of workmen's compensation was limited, his opposition to other forms of social insurance was positive and persistent. The Federation first took a stand against old-age pensions in 1899. In 1902 Victor Berger, the socialist leader representing the Milwaukee trades council, introduced a resolution declaring that labor created all values but was unable to protect itself against want and the indignity of capitalist charity in old age. He proposed that the Federation work for a federal law providing a pension of at least twelve dollars a month at the age of sixty. His resolution was defeated by a vote of ninety to eighty-five. Gompers explained that this action was due to the fact that the unions desired to develop their own systems of protection against all the vicissitudes of life as a means of gaining recruits. Social security would deprive them of that function.[28]

Berger presented his resolution again in 1904 and 1907. By then, the idea had gathered sufficient support so that the Federation endorsed the principle of old-age pensions and instructed the Executive Council to investigate the methods by which they could be attained. The Council turned the matter over to Gompers. He pointed out that the federal government could only provide pensions for its own employees or for workers engaged in interstate commerce. The states would have to provide for other workers, and Gompers was sure that it would take many years of effort to even get serious consideration of the subject. There would also be constitutional questions regarding the power of taxation, and the whole matter would raise many new and complex issues that would be difficult to solve. The committee on resolutions was not so pessimistic—or indifferent—as Gompers and stated that justice and humanity to the producers of wealth required a system of government pensions. The Federation agreed and directed the Executive Council to draft a suitable bill for federal old-age pensions.[29] Gompers did not thereafter express his opposition to old-age pensions, but he did nothing to implement the decision of the Federation.

The question of unemployment compensation came to the fore during the depression of 1914. Gompers rejected this as a "utopian dream" and advocated instead that the employed workers should resist reductions in wages, enforce the eight-hour day in order to spread the work, and under no circumstances work overtime.

In 1916, legislation for the establishment of compulsory health insurance was introduced in many states. Gompers was in the fore again, opposing such measures and stating that the consequence would be the establishment of a bureaucracy that would have some degree of control over all the workers. State sickness insurance, he wrote, was based on the theory that the workers could not look after their own interests and the state must therefore interpose its authority and assume the relation of guardian. This suggestion was "repugnant to a free born citizen . . . at variance with our concepts of voluntary institutions and of freedom for individuals."[30]

Meyer London, the New York socialist congressman, introduced a joint resolution for the appointment of a commission to prepare a plan for the establishment of a national insurance fund for the mitigation of sickness, disability, and unemployment. In testifying on this resolution before a congressional committee, Gompers declared: "As I live, upon the honor of a man, and realizing the responsibility of my words, I would rather help in the inauguration of a revolution against compulsory insurance and the regulation than submit. . . . I am heart-sore, ill and sad when any, the least of my fellows, is hurt in any way. And sore and saddened as I am by the illness, the killing and maiming of so many of my fellow-workers, I would rather see that go on for years and years, minimized and mitigated by the organized labor movement, than give up one jot of the freedom of the workers to strive and struggle for their own emancipation through their own efforts." He would not see the masses of labor crushed under the juggernaut of government.[31]

One of the Federation's major legislative efforts was the campaign for immigration restriction. Many middle-class reformers looked upon restriction as a means of alleviating the problems of poverty and political corruption. Many had lost faith in the capacity of America to absorb limitless numbers of immigrants. And it was during this period that the great "new immigration" was beginning. The number of immigrants in the 1880's was almost double that of each of the two previous decades. The percentage from Eastern and Southern Europe more than doubled and after 1890 became a majority of the total.

Gompers' first reference to the general immigration question appeared in his report to the Federation convention in 1891. He referred to the situation as "appalling"; the time had passed when the United States could be a haven for the oppressed of all nations. Previously, America's industry was in its infancy, her lands were undeveloped, and her resources apparently unlimited. People who came here did so voluntarily and harmonized and blended with native Americans. But the development of industry and the closing of the frontier created a native labor surplus, and the European masses, starved by artificial famines caused by the monopolistic landholding system, were being dumped on American shores. They were aided by American steamship companies which stimulated unhealthy immigration, and by corporations which violated the contract labor law to bring servile labor to compete with American workers. Gompers proposed that, without bigotry or narrowness, these wrongs should be remedied by legislation to restrain such immigration and to strictly enforce the contract labor law.[32]

Gompers welcomed "every man and woman who comes here of his or her own volition. We want that energy and zeal infused in the blood of the people of our nation which prompt those leaving home, kindred and fond ties behind to battle along with those in (to them) a new country for improved conditions." He was, after all, an immigrant himself: a fact which distinguished him from followers of the sharply reactionary, anti-immigration American Protective Association. But Gompers' generous views were strictly limited. He always favored the prohibition of Chinese immigration, whether it was voluntary or not. He supported the Exclusion Act of 1882 and stated bluntly that "the immigration of Chinese into this country is undesirable and should be prohibited. . . ."[33]

The Act was due to expire in 1902, and the year before Gompers warned that, next to the concentration of wealth in the hands of a few, "the menace of a possible overwhelming of our people by hordes of Asiatics" was the most serious problem facing the workers of America. He called for an energetic and ceaseless campaign against Chinese immigration, and himself attempted to persuade Congress and the public, as well as the workers, of the "Yellow Peril." In speeches, articles, and congressional committee hearings, he developed the baldest racist arguments, completely in the spirit of the bigotry he had deplored a decade earlier, and with little regard to his old view that the interests of the workers of all countries were identical.

His chief contribution to the anti-Chinese campaign was a pamphlet which he prepared in collaboration with his old friend, Herman Gutstadt of Local 144, then in the labor movement on the West coast. Reprinted as a Senate document early in 1902, it was entitled "Meat vs. Rice: American Manhood Against Asiatic Coolieism—Which Shall Survive?" Gompers had it that many Chinese immigrants had been brought by the mysterious Tongs, which bound their victims in exchange for contracts which virtually enslaved them. They invaded one industry after another, he went on, displacing thousands of American workers, who found it impossible to compete with their low wage standards.

The menace of the Chinese, in Gompers' view, lay in their innate racial inferiority, which made their Americanization impossible. They could not even live side by side with Caucasians except at the peril of destroying the civilization of the latter. As Gompers explained later, his policy was based on the principle that "maintenance of the nation depended upon the maintenance of racial purity and strength." The Chinese were unfit to live in the United States because they were incapable of self-government or economic improvement. Gompers described their living conditions and habits in lurid terms. Their wages averaged $260 a year, they lived in overcrowded, unsanitary hovels, and were badly fed and clothed, living like "the rats of the waterfront." Their ability to subsist and thrive under conditions which would mean starvation and suicide for even the cheapest laborers of Europe gave them an impossible advantage over the workers pitted in competition with them. This was not due to their exploitation by the employers, or the fact that they were discriminated against, boycotted by Americans, and excluded from the trade unions. It was their congenital love for filthy surroundings, their preference for damp cellars, vermin, open cesspools, and stinking toilets. It was the instinct of the Chinese race to enjoy vice, filth, and horror. What made the menace even greater, according to Gompers, was the complete lack of moral standards: widespread gambling, cheating, murdering, promiscuous sex habits, few families living as such with legitimate children, the women in a state of concubinage or prostitution, girls sold into concubinage, addiction to the daily use of opium.

Gompers reported to the Federation, on the eve of the exclusion law's expiration, that the Chinese were entirely at variance with Americans in political, social, and moral conceptions, absolutely incapable of adaptation to the "Caucasian ideals of civilization." They were unassimilable in the melting pot, and their presence was "ruinous to our general prosperity, blighting to our every prospect," and destructive to American institutions. "The hearthstone of every American citizen is in danger."[34]

Even with regard to Europeans, Gompers was inaccurate in stating that he did not oppose voluntary immigration. He distinguished Northern and Western Europe immigrants from Southern and Eastern Europeans who began to enter the United States in large numbers in the 1880's and 1890's. The former he did not regard as "foreigners" because, like himself, they were quickly Americanized and joined the trade unions. But the latter

were really foreigners: unskilled workers with low wage standards
and no understanding of unionism. Many were illiterate, they
did not speak English, their customs were different, and they
came too fast to be assimilated. Gompers regarded them as unde-
sirables and concluded that "some way must be found to safeguard
America."[35]

As early as 1893 he proposed that illiterates be excluded from
entering the United States. This would have restricted the immigration of unskilled workers from Italy, Russia, Poland, Hungary,
and Greece. The depression that set in that year brought many
American workingmen to agree with his idea. In 1896 Gompers
wrote to the secretary of the *Camera del Lavoro* of Italy that with
widespread unemployment in the United States, the immigration
of large numbers of workers could only have a harmful influence.
The American people, he said, were swayed by the sentiment that
the United States should be an open and free asylum to the
oppressed of the world. "But, counter to this feeling and this sentiment, is presented the fact that we have a hard and bitter struggle
to maintain or to make any progress in our standard of life, and
that, what with the inventions and introduction of machinery, and
the application of new forces to industry, on the one hand, and the
wholesale immigration of low-paid workers from other countries,
on the other hand, we have a conflict that increases in intensity
and bitterness with each recurring day. . . . At a convention of the
American Federation of Labor, held a few years ago [1891], a
resolution was adopted declaring that a further restriction of the
immigration laws was not necessary, but if I read the temper of
our people aright, I am inclined to the belief that they will soon
make another declaration, and of a different character."[36]

At that moment he was himself preparing a report to the
next convention, in which he proposed the endorsement of Senator
Henry Cabot Lodge's bill for a literacy test as a qualification for
immigration to the United States. But the measure encountered
strong opposition. Even the resolutions committee, which supported the bill, acknowledged that the immigration question was
often used as a pretext to gloss over social wrongs, and that the
United States could readily support many times the existing population but for the practices of the "greedy interests of speculators
and monopolists." The convention decided to postpone action

until the following year, to give the unions time to discuss the question and instruct their delegates.[37]

The Lodge bill was passed by Congress, but President Grover Cleveland vetoed it. The Federation in 1897 endorsed the literacy test by a large majority, but three years later, after the depression had passed, it reversed itself and again opposed further restriction of immigration. Gompers chose to accept the earlier declaration as the policy of the Federation, and in 1902 he attempted to secure the passage of a literacy law. This provision, he explained, would exclude practically none from the British Isles, Germany, France, or Scandinavia, but would shut out a considerable number of Italians, Slavs, and "others equally or more undesirable and injurious. . . . A provision of this kind will be beneficial to the more desirable classes of immigrants, as well as to ourselves. It is good for them, no less than for us, to diminish the number of that class which by reason of its lack of intelligence, is slowest to appreciate the value of organization, and furnishes the easiest victims of the padrones and the unscrupulous employer. . . ."[38] From that time on, the A.F. of L. consistently supported the literacy test as the most practical means of effecting immigration restriction.

3. THE RIGHT TO STRIKE

To GOMPERS, THE MOST IMPORTANT LEGISLATIVE aim of labor was relief from government strikebreaking. The workers were faced with attacks on their very existence by all branches of the federal and state governments. Legislatures were considering laws for the compulsory arbitration of labor disputes, executives were employing the military forces to break strikes, and courts were outlawing union activities by the use of injunctions. The labor movement had to overcome all these obstacles if it were to have any security during its normal activities.

Until 1894, Gompers supported compulsory arbitration laws, for he felt that the unions would be strengthened by the government's compelling employers to recognize them and negotiate with them. But by 1894 he had come to recognize such laws as designed to deprive labor of its most potent weapon, the strike. Several state and federal laws previously enacted provided for arbitration, but without compulsory enforcement of mediation

board decisions. Gompers saw such boards as dangerous mon-
strosities. His guiding thought was that arbitration must be free
and voluntary. A wage earner differed from a serf in his ability to
make a free contract. Compulsory arbitration would push him
back toward that status from which he had been emancipating
himself for six centuries. Only strong unions would enable the
workers to make free contracts with the possessors of concentrated
wealth; unions would also insure the workers' abiding by the
decisions of the arbitrators. Gompers warned that the workers
would not yield to arbitrary decisions of the courts. And if the
decisions were enforced by the government? "The striped suit,
the lock-step, the prison cell by night and convict State employment by day. What then? The secret meeting, the plot and
counter-plot, the midnight outrage . . . the death scaffold and the
legacy of revenge."[39]

Gompers' apprehensions were confirmed when the Erdman
Arbitration Bill was introduced in Congress in 1896. It provided
for the compulsory arbitration of labor disputes on railroads and
ships engaged in interstate and foreign commerce, and originally
contained provisions for imprisonment of those who refused to
abide by the awards of the arbitration board. To Gompers, it
re-established the system of involuntary servitude which had been
abolished by the Thirteenth Amendment to the Constitution. But
the railroad brotherhoods endorsed the bill and came to the
Executive Council of the A.F. of L. to secure its support. The
Council permitted the head of the Order of Railroad Conductors
to present his arguments before the Federation convention.

The convention reaffirmed its protest against any legislation
that would make it a legal offense for a worker to quit his employment at any time or for any reason. But the railroad brotherhoods
maintained their stand, and Gompers was in the uncomfortable
position of having to exert his influence against them. The bill was
defeated in the Senate after having passed the House of Representatives, but Gompers' hopes of securing the affiliation of the
brotherhoods to the A.F. of L. were not enhanced. To propitiate
them, he proposed to the convention that if the railroad employees
desired a compulsory arbitration law, applying only to disputes
between them and the railroad companies, the Federation should
interpose no objection. But the Federation would not yield this

principle for the sake of "craft autonomy" and reiterated without qualification its opposition to compulsory arbitration.[40]

Closely connected with compulsory arbitration was the idea of incorporating trade unions so as to make them "legally responsible." Gompers and the labor movement had once also been in favor of this policy; in the early 1880's permission to incorporate had been among their chief legislative demands. As with compulsory arbitration, they had regarded this as a means of securing recognition and legal standing. They soon learned better.

Gompers told the United States Industrial Commission he feared incorporation would be the means by which the unions' treasuries might be mulcted by antagonistic courts. Why did labor unions not assume pecuniary responsibility for keeping their contracts, as employers did? Gompers answered that employers had many ways of breaking their contracts, such as by announcing "reorganizations" which were really lockouts, or by surreptitiously nibbling away at the terms of a contract. Labor unions, by virtue of their numbers and character, he thought, could have no such recourse; by their nature their actions were virtually public and, as such, known to the employers. Incorporated unions would be subject to interminable judicial proceedings, which would in no way force compliance with contracts on the employers. Then how could union responsibility be secured? Only by organizing the workers. Organized workmen were more likely to keep an agreement than unorganized workers. The real problem was to get the employers to negotiate with the unions.[41]

Three years later Gompers debated the question of incorporation with Louis D. Brandeis before the Economic Club of Boston and countered the arguments of that eminent attorney. Brandeis believed the acts of the unions were not amenable to the law, and that they must be made so. Amenable for what? asked Gompers. For any crime? "If any crime has been committed by any man or set of men, there is an ample remedy at law, and if there be no crime in the doings of organized labor . . . I protest against the attempt to invent new laws so as to create a new crime to apply to organized labor alone. . . . No, I am neither vain enough nor poor enough to imagine that I know much about the law, but I do know—perhaps instinctively feel, if I lack the comprehension to understand—when an effort is made to put the clutches upon the trade unions and prevent their development and growth."[42]

The problem of the judiciary was in many respects more serious than that of the legislature and executive. The courts did not need laws to issue crippling injunctions or damage suits against the unions, and it was these injunctions that generally provided the excuse for calling out the armed forces. Just before the Pullman boycott, Judge Jenkins of the United States Circuit Court had granted the request of the receivers of the Northern Pacific Railroad to reduce the wages of its employees and issued an injunction restraining the employees from quitting work. Gompers wondered what would happen if the workers refused to accept the reduction and sought employment elsewhere. Would the judge have issued an order to bring them back to work or send them to prison for contempt of court? "Are we to have more Dredd-Scott [sic] decisions? Are workingmen of America to be brought back like the slaves in ante-bellum days? Is there to be a fugitive slave law for working men, working women and working children? Will there yet be a decision rendered that 'Labor has no rights which the corporations are bound to respect?'"[43]

Gompers worked out a two-pronged attack against judicial usurpation of power to prevent workers from exercising their rights. Such orders as that of Judge Jenkins he recommended treating "with the contempt which they deserve." His consistent advice was to ignore them. He personally defied an injunction against speaking to the West Virginia miners during the coal strike of 1897. Three years later, the employees of the Kerbs cigar factory in New York went on strike against wage reductions, and the Cigar Manufacturers' Association instituted a sympathetic lockout against their employees. One of these manufacturers, Levy Brothers, obtained a sweeping injunction from Judge Freedman which forbade the strikers from picketing in front of their factory or in the streets adjacent to it. The union was also prohibited from giving financial assistance to the strikers, thus encouraging them to continue the strike. Gompers, as first vice-president of the International Union, was one of those specifically enjoined by the order, and he decided to openly defy it.

The alternative, he said, was to obey the injunction, lose the strike, and have the workers "starved into submission, and then without courage enough or manhood enough left among them to call their souls their own." It was necessary to resist this court-made law, even at the risk of imprisonment. "Men long ago—men whose memories are revered—preferred death to slavery," Gompers reminded them. "Liberty is a misnomer when men can not associate for the purpose of lawful redress of grievances, and to secure amelioration in their condition, relief from the burdens which wear them down."[44]

Gompers publicly contributed five dollars to the strikers for the express purpose of continuing the strike, and on May 7 he went to New York and spoke to the strikers. He advised them to follow his policy of disregarding the injunction and to "Go right on with your strike." That evening he informed the Central Federated Union that he was there especially to violate the injunction: "I have done so before, at a distance. Now I want to 'face the music,' if there is any." There was none at that time, for the New York Supreme Court dissolved the injunction, asserting that the laws recognized the right of men and women to work or not to work, and to advance their purpose by striving to win others to their support by reason and argument.[45]

Gompers spent the last twenty-five years of his life working for legislative relief from the abuse of the injunctive writ. He conceded that it had a legitimate role in the legal structure, but he claimed that its application to labor disputes involved abuses of the judicial process in five ways. It caused irreparable damage. When an injunction was issued during a strike to prevent men from aiding each other, the effect was to cripple their efforts. No suit could thereafter remedy the wrong. The purpose of the injunction had been served, even if it was afterward found to be invalid.[46]

Another way in which the injunctive process was abused was by depriving strikers of rights which were conceded to others and even to themselves under other conditions. This was done by resurrecting in a new form the old doctrine of conspiracy and making an act which was perfectly legal for one person, illegal if done in combination with others. This doctrine was invoked particularly against picketing, generally on the ground that the mere presence of numbers constituted intimidation or the threat of violence.[47]

Gompers also objected to the injunction in labor disputes because the courts tended to regard labor as a species of property

For example, the superior court of Cincinnati granted an injunction against the molders' union because it had induced strike-breakers to quit their jobs and join the union, the union paying their initiation fees. This, said the court, was not "persuasion" but "seduction" of the employees for the purpose of aiding the strike and unlawfully interfering with the company's business. Since the strikebreakers had the lawful right to quit, Gompers could see no rational logic behind the decision except the assumption that an employer had a property right in the services of his employees. "The monstrous medieval character of such an assumption is manifest," Gompers roared.

"NO MAN CAN HAVE A PROPERTY RIGHT IN THE SERVICES OF A FREE WORKMAN. . . .

"Employers have clamored for the absolute right to discharge men at the advice and suggestion of fellow-employers, and the courts have never shown the least inclination to oppose that claim, but the prejudiced 'class' judges are seeking to revive antiquated and revolting doctrines implying the subordination of 'men to masters,' and reintroducing distinctions and inequalities that have no place in modern industrial relations."[48]

In this way, Gompers observed as his fourth argument, the injunction substituted judge-made laws for statute laws and even constitutional rights. There was no law against strikes in any part of the United States, and in some states, such as New York, the right to strike was specifically recognized by law. Yet when the typographical union in that state threatened to strike if a nonunion worker employed by a newspaper were not discharged, the courts declared this action an illegal conspiracy. The judge agreed that the workers had a right to "withdraw" if a man obnoxious to them were employed, but ruled that they had no right to force the man out of his position. "What kind of logic is it," Gompers wanted to know, "that says a union has a right to strike when an obnoxious man is employed, but has no right to get rid of the obnoxious man by threatening to strike? Was such self-contradiction ever heard outside of bedlam?" The only possible alternative, he pointed out, was for the union to go on strike without giving any reason for its action. But if the employer then requested an explanation, and the union gave it, it would be guilty of illegally "forcing" the man from his position![49]

Finally, Gompers maintained, not only did the courts create offenses unknown to the law, but when workers violated the injunctions, they were arrested, brought before the court, and charged, not with committing any crime, but with having violated the injunction. They were not confronted with anyone who alleged a crime, there was no jury of their peers to hear and determine guilt or innocence. They were tried and sentenced by the very judge who had issued the order in the first place. Thus the judge turned the criminal system into a personal and arbitrary process, with the defendants denied the constitutional safeguards of a fair trial.[50]

Gompers demanded the absolute prohibition of injunctive writs in labor disputes. There was no need for them, he contended, for if an offense was committed, the worker was amenable to the law the same as if there were no dispute. A number of anti-injunction bills were introduced into Congress, providing that in labor disputes no injunction should be issued except upon due notice to the opposing party and after a hearing on the merits of the application. Gompers opposed such legislation vigorously, even though it would eliminate some of the current abuses. He asserted that there was not on the statute books of the federal government a single line that could be construed as a warrant for the issuance of such injunctions. The enactment of a bill regulating their use would simply put in the law books what was now only judicial usurpation.

Gompers, in the name of organized labor, demanded equality before the law. He demanded government by law and of law: the rights and the liberty which the Constitution guaranteed.[51] But he did not get what he demanded. Labor only got more injunctions. And one of them was marked, "The United States *vs.* Gompers."

4. LOBBYING VS. A LABOR PARTY

THE GENERAL FAILURE OF THE A.F. OF L. TO SECURE its legislative goals, as well as its opposition to the eight-hour law for all workers and a social insurance program, increased left-wing enthusiasm within the A.F. of L. for political action. Although Gompers' faction defeated the Political Programme of 1894 and the labor-Populist alliance of 1896, their proponents were still strong. In 1897 Peter McGuire introduced a resolution at the Federation's convention, which it adopted, calling unequivocally for the independent use of the ballot by trade unionists and workingmen.[52]

The following year Gompers sought to scotch the movement for a labor party. His annual report declared that "each ism has stood but as an evanescent and iridescent dream of poor humanity groping blindly in the dark for its ideal; and it has caused many a heart-wrench to relegate some idealism to movements which do not move, to the dead ashes of blasted hopes and promises." But through it all the trade unionists had kept plodding along in a practical fashion toward better conditions of life. Gompers did not advise the workers to abstain from using their political rights but insisted on the folly of trying to form a labor party, which would turn the trade unions into partisan ward clubs.[53]

Many delegates did not agree with him. They believed that labor must develop political power by political means. A rash of resolutions called for independent political action on a purely labor or socialist platform. Delegates favoring the resolutions called attention to the folly of workers' acting concertedly throughout the year in their economic struggles, and then going to the polls once a year disunited and split, or worse, voting into office the representatives of those they had been fighting on the other 364 days.

After some six hours of debate, Gompers entered the fray to tell the Federation that it must declare for trade unionism pure and simple, "without frills or feathers," or confess that the trade union movement was wrong. He did not argue the principles of the question but accused the socialists of seeking to disrupt the labor movement and make it a tail to their kite. "The men who did not grope, but have fought in the struggle and have never shirked their duty nor their responsibilities, the trade unionists, have met the problems as they arise, and are willing, not simply to indulge in what is known as radical talk, but enter right into the midst of the battle and take the responsibilities, no matter what the results might be to them." The convention upheld Gompers by a vote of 1,971 to 493.[54]

The following year Gompers refused to represent Local 144

in the convention of the New York State Workingmen's Federation because it instructed its delegates to support the organization of an independent labor party. He attributed this action to the fact that he had been away from New York and the socialists had been able to gain dominance under the leadership of secretary Morris Brown. Gompers longed to get back in the thick of the fight to bring his union "back to its old moorings."[55]

The debate on socialism, lobbying, and a labor party became a regular feature of the annual conventions of the Federation. In 1899 the previous position was not only reaffirmed, but the Federation even refused to endorse candidates for election who supported its legislative program. The discussion of independent labor politics reached a climax in 1904, when J. Mahlon Barnes, the national secretary of the Socialist party and a delegate of the Cigarmakers International Union, proposed an amendment to the Federation constitution prohibiting the maintenance of a lobbying committee. "All methods of lobbying," he asserted, "are bowing the head and presenting ourselves in an undignified attitude, and the results obtained so far have not been commensurate with the efforts put forth or the funds expended in that direction." Both the major parties were tools of the capitalist class and vied with each other in beating down the legislation requested by labor. They would respect labor only when the latter ceased to beg for its rights and stood up and organized politically to fight for them.

Gompers, in reply, denied that he or the members of the legislative committee had been "wearing out their knee pads" begging for legislation. He challenged his critics to point to any remark in their testimony before congressional committees which was not a bold assertion of labor's rights or which indicated a demeaning of the character, the dignity, the strength, or the honor of the labor movement. He admitted that the Federation had not yet secured all that it demanded, that it had suffered setbacks. But he pointed to the achievements secured by nonpartisan legislative methods: the abolition of slavery in Hawaii, the Chinese exclusion act, wage lien laws, the ventilation of mines, safety appliances in shops and on railroads, and child labor laws. The legislative committee had also successfully prevented passage of much hostile legislation, such as the compulsory arbitration bill. "We move on and on. Sometimes we are forced back, or cannot proceed further, but those who have the grit, the intelligence and the courage to fight and use every legal and moral weapon at their command are the men that make up a movement that . . . though defeated now and then . . . cannot and will not be conquered."[56] Gompers won out again, but within two years he had to admit the necessity of adopting new methods if labor were going to achieve satisfactory political results.

But Gompers had another alternative for a labor party—direct government. In 1894 he wrote in support of the movement for the initiative and referendum as the best means of accomplishing government by the consent of the governed. Thereafter he gave continuous support to those measures, as well as the recall, including the recall of judges and judicial decisions, the curbing of the power of judicial review, the direct election of Senators, and suffrage for the District of Columbia. These devices, he believed, were in accord with the spirit and principles of democratic institutions. Opponents emphasized the alleged unreasoning impulses of the voters, as tending to government by the mob. The logic of this argument, Gompers asserted, was to abolish elections and majority rule altogether.[57]

Gompers was oversanguine in his judgment of the results of direct government. Certainly he exaggerated in estimating that the A.F. of L.'s efforts for those measures had in a decade enabled the people to permanently break the power of the political bosses and obviated the necessity for a third party.[58] As usual, Gompers was overanxious to claim every step forward as the harbinger of a new era in social relations. Or perhaps he was just trying to make out a case for the success of pure and simple unionism.

Chapter Twelve

IMPERIALISM AND WAR

1. THE VORTEX OF IMPERIALISM

IN THE 1890'S, AS A RESULT OF ITS ADVANCED INDUS-
trial economy, the United States entered fully upon imperialism.
Two decades earlier, the nation had achieved a favorable balance
of trade, and the list of exports contained increasingly larger
amounts of textiles, machines, railroad equipment, and other
manufactured goods. As settlement of the country's continental
limits was completed, foreign exports became important to absorb
the growing production of American factories. Shipowners saw
an opportunity to revive the faltering American merchant marine.
Investors and promotors looked for new investments for their
capital—railroads and bananas in Central America, copper and
silver mines in Canada, Mexico, and South America, sugar in
Hawaii and Cuba. Impetus to expansionism was given by missionaries who established outposts of American trade and influence;
by navalists like Theodore Roosevelt and Captain Alfred Mahan
who flexed the muscles of the rising republic; and by politicians
who employed jingoism for party purposes and to divert the public
mind from internal discontent.[1]

As early as 1886, Gompers perceived the economic aspects of
imperialism and its effect on workers. He wrote then that the
capitalists had turned their nations into huge military camps and
deluged every continent with blood to force on the conquered
people the products which their makers could not purchase because of their low wages. Eight years later, he warned that expansionism was a form of devilry which could bring only disaster to
the American workingmen. The capitalists wanted to invest their
profits in colonial countries where the cheap labor of women and
children would be employed to compete with the labor of Ameri-

can workmen at home. Gompers urged protest against government plans for building a large navy, for annexing Hawaii, for
pushing missionaries into China: "The call for the unity of the
working class to stamp out forever this diabolical capitalistic policy,
should strike like a trumpet's blast on the ear of every toiler in
America, and stir him to energy like a battle cry."[2]

By the 1890's, the United States had already acquired colonial
outposts—Alaska, Midway, the Howland and Baker guano islands,
and Samoa—and a naval base and economic domination in
Hawaii. American business interests in Hawaii organized a rebellion in 1893 and set up a "republic" headed by Sanford Dole.
They petitioned for annexation to the United States, and a treaty
was sent to the Senate. But President Cleveland withdrew the
treaty, stating that the provisional government was established by
the armed invasion of the United States and that the entire transaction was characterized by fraud and violence.

Two years later, however, Cleveland assumed an imperialistic
posture when a boundary dispute developed between Great Britain
and Venezuela. His Secretary of State, Richard Olney, addressed
a belligerent note to England and declared that the United States
exercised supreme sovereignty in the Western Hemisphere.
Gompers voiced labor's opposition to war against Britain in an
address to the New York central labor union. "The working
people know no country," he declared. "They are citizens of the
world, and their religion is to do what is right, what is just, what
is grand and glorious and valorous and chivalrous. The battle for
the cause of labor, from times of remotest antiquity, has been for
peace and good-will among men."[3]

Efforts to annex Hawaii were renewed by President William
McKinley in 1897, and Gompers blasted the scheme in the *American Federationist*. The business interests would not benefit, because they already owned the resources of the islands, and the
United States already had a dominant influence in the islands.
Their domination of the Hawaiian government was secure as long
as "wealth shall hold sway in the councils of nations." He admitted
that the islands would prove a good coaling station for the navy,
but this would justify annexation only if the United States ought to
enter into the struggle for the acquisition of territory. He denied it
should and called, instead, for a halt to the spirit of jingoism.[4]

When the joint resolution for the annexation of Hawaii was being debated in Congress the following summer, Gompers registered his opposition with the Speaker of the House, Thomas B. Reed. He emphasized labor's fear of Hawaiian contract labor and Oriental immigration: about half of Hawaii's population of 100,- 000 were contract laborers, and eighty per cent of those were Japanese and Chinese. The contract labor system was based on terms of service of seven years, during which time the laborers could not leave their employer. The annexation of the islands would mean the admission of a slave state. In addition, annexation would obliterate the result of twenty years of agitation for Chinese exclusion, for the inhabitants of Hawaii would be free to migrate to the United States.[5]

By this time the country was engaged in war with Spain, the fever of expansionism was at high tide, and protests were unheeded. Cuba provided a convenient pretext for American imperialists to launch their program at the expense of the decadent Spanish empire. Spanish oppression and exploitation and the prostration of the sugar and tobacco industries brought about the renewal of the Cuban revolutionary movement for independence in 1895. A Cuban junta was active in New York, and Gompers had earlier attended some of its meetings on the invitation of a Cuban shopmate. There he met many of the revolutionary leaders, including Estrada de Palma, the first president of Cuba. The sympathy of the American people for the insurrectionists and a series of incidents between the United States and Spain produced a widespread demand for intervention. Cleveland resisted it but early in 1896 went so far as to recognize the existence of a state of rebellion. Gompers congratulated the Cuban revolutionary party on this act, which he hoped would be the first step leading to recognition of the belligerent rights and finally the independence of Cuba Libre.[6]

At the Federation convention later in the year, Gompers and ten other delegates introduced a resolution tendering the sympathy of the A.F. of L. to the revolutionists and calling on the United States government to recognize their belligerent rights. Gompers called the independence of Cuba the indispensable basis for the economic organization of the Cuban workers. Workers and capitalists in Cuba had to co-operate to achieve freedom before the

workers could commence the struggle for their own emancipation. The United States must stop the butchery of Cubans to
establish peace in Cuba; and he was ready to fight for peace if
necessary. Andrew Furuseth of the seamen's union warned that
war with Spain would merely change one set of robbers for another and would establish militarism in the United States, but
Gompers' resolution was overwhelmingly endorsed.[7]

McKinley was elected on a platform calling for Cuban independence, but expressed himself against jingoism or acquisition
of territory. Early the following year, the battleship *Maine* was
blown up in Havana harbor by causes unknown, and the jingoists
seized the opportunity to inflame the public against Spain.
Gompers was alarmed, for he knew that in the event of war calm
thought and discussion of labor legislation would be deferred
indefinitely. He praised McKinley for resisting the popular clamor
for war; Gompers would advocate war if the national honor
required it, but he still hoped for a peaceable settlement.[8] But,
although Spain acceded to every American demand, on April 11
McKinley asked for and got a declaration of war. The crusade was
on to establish United States domination in Central America, and
others kept the Pacific in view as well.

Gompers accepted the declaration of war as signalling a holy
concern for Cuba's freedom. He was probably influenced in his
view by labor leaders who believed labor had to emphasize its
unstinted patriotism to forestall efforts to utilize war hysteria in
order to attack labor organizations as un-American. But in just a
month Gompers was becoming alarmed by the jingoist spirit that
was beginning to dominate the country. The demonstration of
American power might lead to an aggressive attitude by the
government and a departure from the traditional policy of avoiding entangling alliances. "It seems to me," he wrote his vice-president, "that there is an effort being made to have our country enter
into the struggle of European and Asiatic nations for conquest."[9]

Gompers' worst fears were quickly justified. Theodore Roosevelt and other jingoes acted to capture the Philippine Islands,
where the insurgents had been on the verge of liberating themselves from Spanish rule, and McKinley had a nocturnal vision
that told him the United States had to keep the Philippines in
order to civilize and Christianize the natives who had long been

Catholics. He also kept Puerto Rico, established a protectorate over Cuba, and snatched up Hawaii. Gompers' first reaction was to give his consent. Speaking to the central labor union of New York on July 31, he warned against efforts which were then in the making to strengthen the contract labor system in Hawaii, and added: "The Government may annex any old thing, and I shall be content, so long as the laws relating to labor are observed. The war is a glorious and righteous one as far as the United States is concerned."[10] Gompers' opposition to expansionism stood revealed as not fundamentally anti-imperialist, but as based on opportunistic fears of threats to economic status, and as founded on a sense of racial superiority to conquered peoples.

At a national conference on the foreign policy of the United States arranged by the National Civic Federation at Saratoga, New York, on August 20, Gompers delivered a panegyric on the spirit of liberty which led the United States to enter the war. He then turned to the question of annexation. He repeated what he had written a year before about contract labor in Hawaii. As for the Philippines, they had seven or eight million inhabitants "of a semi-barbaric population almost primitive in their habits and customs, as unlike the people of the United States in thought, sentiment, education, morals, hopes, aspirations, or governmental forms as night is to day." The acquisition of this territory would be inimical to liberty in the United States, for no government could be truly free, prosperous, or progressive when slave labor in any form existed within its domains. It was vitally important to save American labor from the evil and degrading influence of close competition with the half-civilized people of Asia. Moreover, "How long will it be . . . before the dominant classes in this country will look to the use of force rather than the will of the majority for support in furthering their plans? Will it not be easy to pass from contemptuous indifference to the natural rights and wishes of the dark-skinned wage-earners of the Philippines to a similar attitude toward manual toilers of our own blood and country?"

Gompers saw no contradiction between his praise of the recent war and his denunciation of imperialism as pointing "to large armaments and more frequent wars,"[11] and neither, apparently, did his auditors. Gompers was elected vice-president of the con-

ference on foreign policy, which was made permanent. In the
resolutions which it adopted for presentation to Congress and the
President, Gompers insisted on and secured the inclusion of one
which demanded the abolition of involuntary servitude, by contract or otherwise, in any territory over which the United States
had or might have jurisdiction. The conference distributed copies
of his address to the members of Congress.

Two months later, the Republicans and expansionists promoted a great "peace jubilee" in Chicago. President McKinley
reviewed a parade, and several meetings were held all over the
city with prominent speakers, nearly all of whom favored keeping
the former Spanish colonies. Gompers spoke in the afternoon at
the Second Regiment Armory and denounced the "heartless enthusiasts, grab-all monopolists, and imperialists" who would sacrifice liberty for the sake of the profits they hoped to gain from the
domination of Cuba, Hawaii, Puerto Rico, and the Philippines.
What happened to the paeans of praise for the brave Cubans, he
wondered. What of the declarations pledging the country against
conquest and acquisition of territory? Now the moneymakers
were insisting that those promises be forgotten. The nature of the
territorial rule they anticipated was already foreshadowed by
events in the Philippines, where they were finding it necessary
to subdue a people who had been on the way to winning their
own freedom and independence: "There is an universality of the
law of right, and its transgression brings the penalty and certain
punishment in its wake," Gompers concluded. "America and
particularly American institutions are not only worthy of our
love and veneration because they give us greater freedom than
those of any other nation, but the institutions of the United States
represent a principle—the great principle of self-government. . . .
This principle we shall only prove ourselves worthy of representing . . . by manifesting restraint upon ourselves or upon those
who would thrust us out of our physical, moral, progressive and
powerful sphere into the vortex of imperialism, with all the evils
which that term implies. . . ."

Gompers was on the unpopular side. During his address, he
was frequently interrupted by hisses, and protest was so loud at
the close of his talk that the chairman of the meeting suggested
that it might be a good time for the band to play "America" or

"The Star Spangled Banner." The band played both. Newspapers charged Gompers with "treasonable hostility" to the government of the United States, and even in the A.F. of L. there was much criticism of his position. He confessed that the approval of his fellow workers and fellow citizens would be gratifying, but if they did not always approve, that was not his fault. His duty was to be right and try to do as nearly right as he knew how, trusting to the judgment and conscience of the workers now or later when their minds would not be clouded or benumbed by the propaganda of the capitalists. In the meantime, "all we can do is to abide our time, and while the question is seething, endeavor to perform our duty so it shall not militate too severely against the interests of the working people and the citizens of our country and our Republic as such."[12]

At the convention of the A.F. of L. in December, Gompers made a strong plea for the support of his position. There was little opposition, as socialists and nonsocialists joined in condemning imperialism. However, no plan of concerted action was devised, action being left to the local unions and individual workers.[13]

At the end of 1898 Gompers joined a galaxy of distinguished Americans in forming the Anti-Imperialist League, of which he was elected one of the vice-presidents. With him in this organization were such well known reformers as Carl Schurz and Jane Addams, single taxers, pacifists, abolitionists and their sons, clergymen, former Presidents Cleveland and Benjamin Harrison, prominent educators like William Graham Sumner, William James, and Felix Adler, writers including Mark Twain and William Dean Howells, and a few businessmen like Andrew Carnegie. Gompers was the only important labor leader who showed much interest in the movement.

When the peace treaty was under consideration in the Senate, some of the anti-imperialists, led by William Jennings Bryan, favored ratification because they thought the war should be ended and the question of the former Spanish possessions disposed of later. They believed the issue should be decided by the people in the coming presidential election and they could consider it more rationally if the country were at peace. Gompers pointed out that the country was already at peace and there was no possibility of Spain's resuming the conflict. After the treaty was ratified, it was declared that the islands had come to the United States "by solemn treaty" and that she was therefore bound to take possession of them. Gompers reported this development to the Federation convention with bitter disappointment.[14]

But he would give no support to political action by labor for the defeat of pro-imperialist candidates, holding that the A.F. of L. was prohibited from meddling in party politics. When a number of Federation officials in Minnesota organized a committee to mobilize labor for an anti-trust and anti-imperialist campaign, Gompers refused to endorse their activities. He mixed praise with opposition to a similar plan in Ohio and was responsible for its abandonment. The *Cleveland Citizen* criticized Gompers' policy, asking what value there was in his declarations against imperialism if he refused to supplement them with organized political power to defeat imperialism.[15]

After the conclusion of the treaty, Gompers turned his major attention to the question of contract labor in Hawaii. A bill providing a code for the government of the islands, including a provision for the perpetuation of involuntary servitude, passed the House of Representatives and was reported favorably by the Senate committee. Gompers and the A.F. of L. legislative committee were able to secure important amendments to the bill. One substantially made illegal suits to enforce contracts for labor or service, the other rendered null and void all contracts made since American occupation.[16]

Gompers had accomplished his main purpose, and the rest of his anti-imperialist slogans were forgotten. He reverted to the position he had taken two years earlier that the United States could annex "any old thing" as long as satisfactory labor laws were enforced. He was silent when Roosevelt "took the Panama Canal," when he established a protectorate over Santo Domingo and proclaimed his imperialistic corollary to the Monroe Doctrine. Gompers voiced no protest against Taft's "Dollar Diplomacy" in the Far East or his intervention in the affairs of Santo Domingo, Haiti, and Nicaragua. He accepted imperialism as part of the American fabric, working only to improve the conditions of labor within that framework. Thus he extended pure and simple trade unionism from the United States to her colonial possessions.

2. THE AMERICAN EMPIRE

GOMPERS' FIRST DIRECT CONTACT WITH THE NEW American empire came as a result of his vacation trip to Cuba in February 1900. He used the opportunity to investigate labor conditions, the labor movement, the rule of the military, and a recent proclamation by General William Ludlow, the governor-general of Havana, by which a general strike for the eight-hour day was broken. He addressed several meetings of workers, urging the need for organization along the lines of the American Federation of Labor. He also had interviews with Governor-General Leonard Wood and other American authorities for the purpose of protesting the action of General Ludlow and discussing Cuba's political status. After this visit, Gompers paid little more attention to Cuba. He also showed little interest in Hawaii and the Philippines, except to send a special commissioner to those countries in 1903 to investigate labor conditions and to encourage the organization of unions on the principles of the American Federation of Labor, which was also encouraged by the Philippine governor-general, William Howard Taft, in preference to the old unions, which had been outlawed because of their advocacy of independence.[17]

With Puerto Rico, Gompers had a much closer relationship, because of the island's proximity to the United States and because it already had a well-developed labor movement. No sooner had Puerto Rico become a possession of the United States than its authorities committed a series of acts that called forth Gompers' angry protest. At the time of annexation, the people of Puerto Rico were suffering from unemployment and the ravages of storms and hurricanes. President McKinley urged Congress to suspend the tariff on imports to Puerto Rico as a means of providing relief. But Congress, in what Gompers called an act of infamy, proposed a duty of twenty-five per cent on all goods entering that country. He accused the tobacco trust, the sugar trust, and other monopolistic interests of having put pressure on Congress to impose the tariff and of having threatened to withhold contributions to the "corruption fund" for the presidential election campaign unless it was adopted. The opposition was strong enough to reduce the duty, but not strong enough to prevent the passage of an act providing for a fifteen per cent duty. McKinley now shifted his stance and asked Congress to pass the act. Gompers regarded the whole proceeding as indicative of the workings of imperialism, which bent President and Congress to its will in violation of the Constitution, and which could destroy democracy at home and in the colonies.[18]

On July 8, 1900, the day when the exchange of Spanish for American money was to take place, the Free Federation of Workmen of Puerto Rico drew up a wage scale that would not be based on depreciated currency, and demanded weekly pay and the eight-hour day. The demands were rejected by the employers, who refused to deal with the unions' arbitration committee, and a strike of all the trades was called. About thirty trade union officials were arrested, including Santiago Iglesias, the president of the Free Federation. The strike ended with moderate wage increases, but a number of men were kept in jail and the others subject to re-arrest. They were charged with the crime of conspiring to raise the price of labor, which was an offense under the Spanish penal code still in force on the island.[19]

Blacklisted and unable to find work, Iglesias left Puerto Rico and went to work as a carpenter in Brooklyn. A socialist and a nationalist revolutionary, he got in touch with radicals in New York, who advised him to make contact with Gompers in Louisville, where the A.F. of L. was in convention. There, the Federation pledged its assistance in securing the right of fair trial and the freedom of assembly, speech, and press for the workers of Puerto Rico. The Executive Council engaged Iglesias to return to Puerto Rico as an organizer for the A.F. of L. Gompers took him to see President Roosevelt, whom he assured that Iglesias would work purely on trade union lines and would not engage in revolutionary political activity. Roosevelt thereupon directed Governor William H. Hunt not to interfere with him so long as he conformed to the laws of Puerto Rico and the United States. So Iglesias returned to Puerto Rico, but when he stepped ashore at San Juan he was arrested on the charges pending against him, as well as for failing to appear in court, a summons having been allegedly sent to him while he was in New York.[20]

Gompers immediately went back to Roosevelt to protest the arrest and to find out the charges against Iglesias. Roosevelt, after inquiry, informed him that Iglesias had broken his parole by leaving Puerto Rico without notifying the court. Iglesias assured Gompers that he had not received any summons to appear in court since his arrival in New York. Gompers felt that Iglesias' arrest for breaking his parole was justified, but he wanted to challenge the conspiracy law which was the basis for the original charge against him. He therefore posted $500 bail to secure Iglesias' release. He advised Iglesias to stand trial and to plead justification against the charge of conspiracy.

In a brief trial, Iglesias was found guilty and sentenced to three years and four months in prison. The Free Federation was declared illegal and dissolved. Gompers, in a letter to Governor Hunt, protested both the conviction and the sentence. The law under which Iglesias was convicted, Gompers asserted, was a relic of medievalism, depriving men of their liberty to exercise their natural right to improve their conditions. He urged Hunt to pardon Iglesias and to call a special session of the General Assembly to revise the law code and the judicial system of Puerto Rico.[21] Hunt did not pardon Iglesias, and although he did ask the Assembly to amend the laws to provide freedom of association and peaceful labor organization and activities, this was not done. However, in the spring of 1902, the Supreme Court of Puerto Rico reversed the decision of the lower court, ruled that with the assumption of American sovereignty the constitutional rights of free assembly and organization obtained in Puerto Rico, and acquitted Iglesias of all charges against him.

By this time, Gompers had come to accept United States possession of Puerto Rico as permanent. The Free Federation, again legal, had affiliated with the A.F. of L., and Iglesias had been converted to pure and simple unionism, working for improved conditions within the framework of colonialism and abjuring socialist and revolutionary propaganda. The A.F. of L. undertook, in Gompers' words, to "spread the gospel of Americanism among the people of the Island,"[22] as well as to extend the influence of the A.F. of L. in Puerto Rico.

In February 1904, Gompers made his first visit to the island, visiting nearly every city and important town. What he saw was not a testimonial to the benefits of United States rule. He saw men working in the sugar refineries fifteen and sixteen hours a day for thirty-five or forty cents; women working in coffee houses ten and twelve hours for fifteen to twenty cents; myriads of workless men; the small dark rooms of their homes, often housing eight or more persons, without facilities to let in air or light except through the open door. He saw workmen paid in tokens that had to be redeemed at company stores, where prices were twenty to thirty per cent higher than on the open market for inferior goods, resulting in indebtedness and peonage: "I have seen more ragged men and women and children in Porto Rico [sic] than I have ever seen in my whole life; I have seen more squalor, more degradation, and more poverty, hunger and misery stamped upon the faces of men and women and children in Porto Rico than I have ever seen in my whole life, and I pray and hope that I may never see the like again."

In a farewell address in San Juan, Gompers urged the Puerto Rican workers to take intelligent and practical action to bring about a change in these conditions. This meant their organization in unions affiliated with the A.F. of L., which he pledged would help in every way. He promised that if they followed the policy of the Federation, and avoided political dissension, "surprising" economic and material improvements would surely result. He pleaded for patience with Puerto Rico's colonial status: ". . . I want you to bear in mind that the people of the United States are a just and generous people, I want you to understand that the Government of the United States is founded upon the everlasting principles of justice and fair dealing among men. The Declaration of Independence and the Constitution of the United States still live in the hearts and in the minds of my countrymen, and you may rest assured that . . . the time will soon come when you will no longer be regarded as stepchildren, but that you will be recognized as members with full rights in the family of the great American Republic."[23]

When Gompers returned to the United States, he made a number of public talks in which he presented the conditions that he had discovered in Puerto Rico. He declared that the time had come for the United States to admit Puerto Rico to "full fellowship in the family of the American republic" with a full share of home rule.[24]

Shortly after, an incident occurred which illustrated his attitude toward the policies and methods of the Puerto Rican labor movement. On the Fourth of July a parade was held in San Juan, and it was reviewed by the island's new governor, Beekman Winthrop. Iglesias sent him a cordial letter of greeting, but during the parade a banner was planted in front of the reviewing stand, demanding "Give us work, and hunger and anemia will cease." Gompers commended Iglesias for the spirit of co-operation displayed in his letter, but regarded the message on the banner as unjustified and in bad taste. He thought Winthrop had displayed a kindly and sympathetic attitude toward the Puerto Ricans, and expressed the belief that if the workingmen would reciprocate, a more cordial feeling between Puerto Rico and the United States would develop. Later in the year, he urged Iglesias not to oppose the establishment of a United States naval station at San Juan. Gompers himself urged its desirability on Governor Winthrop. It would furnish employment and train mechanics in Puerto Rico; and it would be advantageous to the United States to have a naval base in its own territory.[25]

In the spring of 1905, the agricultural laborers in the southern provinces of Puerto Rico determined to seek improvements in their conditions and appealed to the Free Federation for assistance. The Federation agreed and presented demands for seventy-five cents for a nine-hour day and the abolition of child labor. Most of the planters refused to acknowledge the demands or to submit them to arbitration, and 14,000 workers went out on strike. After three weeks, the police began a crusade against the strikers. On one occasion Governor Winthrop, at the behest of the sugar companies, sent the police to disperse a meeting, and thirty workers were wounded. On April 5 the police rushed upon a peaceful meeting in the public plaza of Ponce, fired into the crowd, and swung clubs and sabres indiscriminately at the panic-stricken crowd. Several of the labor men were arrested.[26]

Gompers protested to Governor Winthrop. He called Winthrop's attention to the declaration he himself had made previously, ordering the police to protect the people in their right of peaceable assembly. "Surely it is the hope of us all," he wrote, "that American ideas and American ideals shall be instilled into the hearts and minds of the people of Porto Rico, and I submit that nothing can be accomplished, nor can their affections for the institutions and the flag of our country be encouraged and maintained unless they learn by experience that American rights and American guarantees mean more than mere declarations on each recurring Fourth of July."[27] Two weeks later the strike was ended, the workers securing a nine-hour day and twenty to thirty per cent increase in wages. But Puerto Rico was still, Gompers noted, "a great factory exploiting cheap labor for the benefit of large corporations in the United States."

3. THE BROTHERHOOD OF MAN

APART FROM THE QUESTION OF EXPANSIONISM AND the Spanish-American War, Gompers was a firm advocate of the peaceful settlement of international disputes. In 1887 he welcomed to the convention of the A.F. of L. William R. Cremer, a labor member of the British Parliament who was working for an arbitration treaty with the United States. Gompers remained an enthusiastic supporter of arbitration, although he did not regard it as a probable means of ending wars in the immediate future. When the Anglo-American arbitration treaty was before the Senate in 1897, Gompers urged its ratification, stating that war was "at best brutal and an arbitrament by force of arms ever unsatisfactory." The workers always bore the brunt of war in money and lives, and progress was always set back by war.[28] Gompers continued his support for arbitration by participating in national and international peace congresses which were working for the extension of arbitration treaties between all countries.

Gompers opposed militarism and war preparations, not only because of their effect in contributing to war, but because of their possible use in repressing the workers. When an appropriation for increasing the size of the army and navy was before the Senate in 1896, Gompers wrote to Vice-President Adlai E. Stevenson that the bill was a covert attempt of corporate power to overawe the masses and a danger to free institutions. In other countries, he observed, the workers were crushed under the burden of enormous taxes to support the military and naval establishments, which in turn were used to crush out the spirit of liberty and justice. There was no danger from which the people could not fully defend themselves, for in time of need all citizens would be soldiers. "It is the conscious fear of monopoly and capitalism of their wrong doing which makes such asinine or brutal exhibitions and propositions possible."[29]

Gompers' anti-militarism reached its apex immediately after the Spanish-American War, when American military power was being employed to crush the independence of the Filipinos and the freedom of the mine workers in Colorado. In a speech to the Peace Society in Boston, he declared that if the authorities could not secure peace, then the organized workers must do so by refusing to make and transport implements to be used to destroy their fellow men. Six years later he presented a watered-down version of the same proposal to the A.F. of L.[30] But he put more faith in the possibility of labor's influence for peace through less direct action. In 1894 the custom of exchanging fraternal delegates at the conventions of the American Federation of Labor and the British Trade Union Congress was inaugurated. In introducing the British delegates, David Holmes and John Burns, Gompers declared that their presence was a demonstration that "though men may be proud of country, humanity has a higher consideration than nationality." Five years later he commended the practice of exchanging delegates as contributing to a recognition of the identity of interests of the workers of the world. While alliances might be broken and treaties trampled under foot, he declared, "if the workers of our country, as well as the workers of the civilized world be organized in trade unions and will it so, no power evolved out of the brain of the cunning or avaricious can involve us in bloody strife."[31]

But Gompers and the Federation remained aloof from the international labor movement. In 1895 the International Congress of Socialist Workers invited the A.F. of L. to send delegates to its congress in London the following year. The British Trade Union Congress decided to participate after it changed its name to the International Socialist and Trade Union Congress, but the A.F. of L. refused, on the ground that it would involve the acceptance of socialism and political action. Gompers declared that these congresses of "conglomerate bodies of labor, middle class men and party politicians" had failed, and he again decided to attempt the formation of a purely trade union congress. He cabled Strasser and Sullivan, the Federation's fraternal delegates at the British Trade

Union Congress in Edinburgh, to urge that body to take the initiative in organizing such an international congress.[32] The British failed to act on the suggestion, but in 1901, on the initiative of the Danish Federation of Trade Unions, a conference was held of the trade union officials of the Northern and Western European countries. It was decided to hold periodic conferences of the secretaries of the national trade union centers, and in 1903 a formal organization was set up called the International Secretariat of National Trade Union Centers. Gompers took no steps to secure the Federation's affiliation with the Secretariat until 1909. It would seem that he was less concerned with international organization as a means of strengthening labor solidarity and world peace than as a means of establishing the A.F. of L.'s influence in the labor movement of the world.

What did Gompers mean by all his declarations for peace, arbitration, anti-militarism, and disarmament? After twenty years of such talk, and only a few years following war with Spain, he praised the peace among nations as "greater and longer than has been the case for many centuries past," and derogated "hysterical and vain striving after peace through the medium of resolutions and rant." Nations, he observed, were "on a far better war footing than at any time in the history of the world"; and this was good, since "each nation has bent every energy to making war as terrible and destructive as possible. . . . Peace comes from conscious intelligence and power, and not from hysterical, effeminate supplications for an ideal state. . . ."[33]

Chapter Thirteen

LABOR UNDER FIRE

1. MACHINES, WORK, AND WAGES

IN THE 1870's, GOMPERS HAD SUPPORTED THE CIGAR-makers' opposition to the mold. Although he favored the organization of the mold workers, he still hoped to protect the position of the skilled hand workers by resisting the introduction of machinery. In 1887 he supported Strasser's recommendation that the union deny the use of the union label to manufacturers using machines. However, some time during the next decade he became converted to the view that labor could not prevent the introduction of machines and should devote its efforts to securing union wages for those employed on them.

The question was first presented to him as president of the A.F. of L. in 1899. The coopers' union went on strike and levied a boycott against the Pabst Brewing Company in Milwaukee when the latter introduced barrel-making machinery. The company bought none but union-made barrels but could not get enough for its needs, and in making its own barrels it offered to employ only union men at the union scale of wages and hours. The union refused its permission, stating that it would prefer the company to buy nonunion barrels rather than to make its own by machine. The company threatened to lock out all the coopers and cancel all contracts with labor organizations unless the boycott was withdrawn. Gompers agreed that the company was blameless and that its efforts to adjust the difficulty had failed because of the irrational attitude of the union. In the face of this opposition, the union submitted and withdrew its boycott. Gompers then went to Milwaukee to help effect a permanent settlement of the dispute. He secured an agreement by the union to recognize the machine, and in return the brewers' association granted recognition to the union, the eight-hour day, the regulation of apprentices, and a substantial increase in wages. Gompers was convinced that this action, although violating the letter of the coopers' union constitution, was justified because the alternative would have been the loss of the strike and the eventual destruction of the union.[1]

Gompers maintained that it was futile for organized labor to attempt to prevent the use of machinery which proved itself successful. The intelligent course for labor to follow was to accept industrial progress but insist that the machine work be given to union members at union standards and that the machine workers be brought into the union so as to protect those standards against unfair competition. Besides, the introduction of improved machinery and the greater division of labor resulting from it made for greater production of wealth, lowered the cost of production and the price of goods, and tended to raise the standard of living of all the people, providing it was accompanied by shorter hours of labor to prevent permanent displacement of workers.[2]

Gompers was instrumental in securing the adoption of this policy by the capmakers and printers as well as the coopers. His greatest difficulty was in convincing his own organization of its wisdom. For nearly fifty years he urged the International to abolish its membership restrictions against machine workers. The folly of its long and futile fight against machinery was finally recognized, and the union removed all obstacles in the constitution and regulations which interfered with the thorough organization of every worker in the industry.[3]

Gompers' slogan was, "Let the unions control the machines, rather than the machines controlling the workers." He had to combat the economic theory of the business classes which tried to tie the laborer and his wages to the machine and its output. Among the academic economists this was known as the productivity theory of wages. In the popular press it took the form of an attack on the unions for their alleged efforts to limit output. Gompers always denied that the unions deliberately attempted to restrict production and he energetically defended the capacities of American workers: "Work hard! Work harder, my Heavens! . . . [it seems] some men believed they were put on earth not only to work but to be worked, and inasmuch as they were but a very short time on earth, for Heaven's sake work them harder; you don't know when they are going to drop off. The idea of suggesting that American men work harder!"[4]

Gompers devoted considerable attention to the productivity theory of wages, which was as old as classical economics but refurbished in modern, "scientific" form by a number of contemporary economists, whom Gompers preferred to call special pleaders of the capitalist class. Professor J. Lawrence Laughlin wrote an indictment of labor unions in the *Journal of Political Economy* and suggested that the alternative to unionism was greater productivity by the workers, which would bring them higher wages. Gompers pointed out that this was based on the assumption that the workers were already getting fair wages for what they produced. But since this was rarely the case, it was more logical for the workers to demand an increase which was already their due for their work and to quit if they did not obtain it. Unionism had secured wage raises in that way, proving that increased output was not always necessary to enable employers to pay higher wages. Besides, increased productivity did not automatically bring about higher wages. It would still be necessary to form unions and to strike or be ready to strike. He noted the piecework system and the common employers' practice of reducing the rate when their employees "worked too much." In those cases, increased productivity resulted in less rather than more pay. Unions did not generally limit output, he concluded, but they tried to check practices to which greedy employers resorted to get an unconscionable amount of work out of their employees. They objected to the "pace that kills," driving labor at a rate that resulted in mental and physical collapse at the age of forty or forty-five.[5]

Furthermore, Gompers argued, the productivity theory was false because it was practically impossible to fix wages rationally to the actual production of each individual worker. Nor were wages determined by such "natural laws" as the law of supply and demand. Employers offered as little as they could induce workers to accept, and the latter demanded as much as they could persuade the former to grant. Wage rates resulted from collective bargaining and were determined by the relative bargaining strength of the opposing parties. In the course of years, labor's productivity had increased faster than real wages; the goal of collective bargaining was to bring wages up to a fair level. The problem of the labor movement was not primarily one of production, but of more equitable distribution. For the wage theories of the professors, Gompers would substitute the claim of organized labor to a return "commensurate with the standard of life demanded by the progress and degree of civilization of the community in which [the worker] lives."[6]

It was not only a theory that Gompers had to contend with in securing union control over machines. "Scientific management" was introduced in industry in the early twentieth century. Frederick W. Taylor, in an address to the American Society of Mechanical Engineers in 1895, had proposed a scientific determination of work standards by time studies and rate fixing, and a differential rate system of piecework to reconcile the apparently irreconcilable wage and production aims of capital and labor. He later elaborated on this with a complex and rigid set of rules to govern the tasks, procedures, conditions, time, and payment for each job. This was done by selecting a first-class workman, fixing his maximum production as the standard, and then paying bonuses for work above that standard and applying penalties for failure to meet it. The system was based on the theory that the interests of employers and employees were mutual, that they depended on high production, that the workers should be dealt with as individuals rather than collectively, that they should have no voice in fixing standards, and that slow or recalcitrant workers should be replaced by "co-operative and loyal" workers who would act as pacemakers. It not only left no room for unionism and collective bargaining, but regarded them as a handicap if not a downright evil. For organization and co-operation it would substitute an appeal to the self-interest of each worker, playing them off against each other in the scramble for higher production and greater rewards. As for the labor leaders, Taylor regarded them all as misleaders, and of course Gompers was the greatest misleader of the lot, a "blatant demagog."[7]

Gompers set his face against Taylorism as a hoax with the single purpose of speeding up the workers to fantastic lengths. Until then, he wrote, it was thought that the workman's reputation as a man, his pride in his work, his necessity to make good, his fear of losing his job, even the pangs of hunger, were sufficient incentive for him to "get a move on." But now these were deemed inadequate goads. "He must further be taken in hand and taught the most economical lifts, pushes, jumps, steps, stoops and bends, the quickest looks and thinks, the most dexterous fingering, the most supple wrist-play, the finest elbow work, and the most powerful full-arm swings, throws, blows and jerks. Withal, dangling before him are to be rewards, hanging over him are to be penalties. Then let him go it! He'll do his twentieth century best."[8]

Taylor set a goal of forty-seven tons a day in the handling of pig iron, but admitted that only one man in eight was physically capable of that load. Gompers denounced the effort to have men turn themselves into high-speed automatic machines and increase their output 400 per cent in order to get an increase in wages of forty per cent. The experiment to ascertain the breaking point of seven out of eight laborers, he said, "presents novelty only in its cold bloodedness and its endeavor to transfer material observations of the strength of metals to those of the strength of men's muscles and spirit."[9]

In 1911 Gompers testified before a congressional committee considering a bill to prohibit the Taylor system in government work. He emphasized the folly and the wrong of sacrificing men to the single-minded goal of more and more production. "I wish to say this for the men of labor . . . that there are some limits beyond which we will not allow you to go with your domination as captains of industry. You are our employers, but you are not our masters. Under the system of government we have in the United States we are your equals, and we contribute as much, if not more, to the success of industry than do the employers. We are not bent serfs nor docile workers. . . . We propose to have our voices heard in any discussion of the conditions under which we shall labor. Nor are we going to permit, without a protest, the introduction of a system that places a premium upon a man's mere vitality, to be exhausted to the fullest, to the neglect of his own well-being in all respects."[10]

There was another reason for Gompers' hostility to scientific management. He recognized that the fight against Taylorism was a struggle for the preservation of unionism. "There is not one of the advocates of this scheme except Mr. Brandeis," he wrote, incorrectly, "who does not predicate it upon the destruction, the elimination, the abandonment of organized labor."[11] There were, in fact, reformers who were enthusiasts of efficiency, and believed it would minimize the differences between capital and labor. Thus, Morris L. Cooke, reformer, in that era, of municipal services, was an admirer of Taylor. Also meriting notice is the fact that the principles of Taylorization eventually triumphed; the need for efficiency became a recognized principle of industry, accepted by labor and capitalist alike. Nevertheless, it was true that this condition did not come about automatically. Such labor leaders as Gompers were required to fight to prevent the use of Taylor's program from becoming an anti-labor weapon.

2. THE OPEN SHOP CAMPAIGN

AS THE LONG DEPRESSION OF THE 1890's CAME TO A close, the A.F. of L. counted a quarter of a million members. It then entered a period of rapid growth, passing the half million mark in 1900, reaching one million in 1902, and shooting to over one and a half million in 1904. At the same time, the trust movement was blossoming to maturity, following the rigid pattern of antiunionism set by the United States Steel Corporation. The conjunction of these two developments led (in the midst of a great reform period) to a mass crusade of the employers to crush the trade union movement throughout the United States. The first attempt to form a general antiunion association was made in Dayton, Ohio, in 1900, when thirty-eight firms combined propaganda, pressure on manufacturers and bankers to co-operate, and mutual assistance in strikes and lockouts to establish the open shop throughout the city in two years. Similar movements were organized in other cities, and at the same time national trade associations were founded for similar purposes. They boycotted union goods and concerns, gave financial aid to employers contending for the open shop, furnished strikebreakers, boycotted unfriendly newspapers, bribed union officials, black-listed union workers, employed labor spies, used the police, militia, and courts to break strikes and cripple unions, and organized powerful lobbies against labor legislation.[12]

National leadership and organization in the campaign were supplied in 1903 by the National Association of Manufacturers and its militant president, David M. Parry. In his circulars to the members of the association he warned against "turning over the United States to trade-union domination" and "agitators." In the same year he launched a Citizens' Industrial Association, comprising 124 employers' organizations, to co-ordinate the fight for "those fundamental principles of American government guaranteeing free competitive conditions."

Day in and day out, year after year, through every medium that was open to him, Gompers countered the propaganda campaign for the open shop. The favorite argument of the manufacturers' association was that organized labor, by insisting on the exclusive employment of union workmen, was depriving nonunion men of their liberty and their right to earn a livelihood. But, Gompers pointed out, the employers' interpretation of freedom of contract was based on the conception that the workman was a servant who did not have the same right of contract. The law gave the employer the right to hire any labor he could get, Gompers admitted, but not the right to impress workmen, to drag them into his factory on any terms he chose to grant them. On the other hand, every man had the right to sell his labor as he saw fit and the same right not to sell it to the employer who wanted an open shop. He had the right to say he would not work for an employer unless he made a contract with the union and agreed to employ none but members of that union. Any other conclusion was equivalent to saying that he could sell his labor only on the terms fixed by the employer.[13]

The defenders of the open shop also based their position on the moral right of the individual workers to control their own labor independent of the union. Their morality was as antiquated as their economics and jurisprudence, Gompers contended. He refused to grant the strikebreaker an equal moral right with the union man pursuing a lawful course in furthering the interests of his union and his fellows. The strikebreaker, by aiding the employer in defeating a union that protected the workers from deprivation and misery, was destructive to the welfare of his class. "This he has no moral right to do. Nor, under the principle of group-justice has he the right to take the place of the union man who is striving to maintain the objects of trade-unionism—the welfare of the group."[14]

Another aspect of the antiunion offensive was the development of welfare capitalism, particularly in the form of profit shar-
ing. This scheme was designed primarily to secure the "loyalty
and co-operation," that is, the unstinted effort, of the employees
by making them feel that they were partners in the business, to
reduce labor turnover, and to discourage unionism. Gompers told
the industrial commission in 1899 that this was a utopian—even a
ridiculous—attempt of individual concerns to solve the social problem for themselves. Even with the best of motives, and even when
successful, they contributed nothing to the movement for general
social improvement.

Gompers found altruism generally a cloak for the promotion
of "loyalty" and "efficiency." He thought the worker should be
first of all loyal to himself rather than to his employer. Efficiency
was just another word for push, grind, and hurry. And as for the
profits shared, they were generally nothing but the withholding
of part of the employees' wages, returned at the end of the year. If
the employers wanted to demonstrate their altruism, Gompers
suggested, let them start out by granting the union scale of wages
and hours and then confer with the union about the granting of
any additional benefits. He observed that profit-sharing schemes
were advanced only when organized labor became strong enough
to command the employers' attention to the rights of labor. It
was an attempt to accomplish by wile what could not be accomplished by bitter and cruel opposition—the destruction of the
trade union movement.[16]

Above all, welfare programs in industry expressed the paternalistic philosophy of employers who would like to have their
workmen "perform like cows that resignedly chew their cud and
submissively give sweet milk." But much of the welfare endeavor
was doomed to failure precisely because men were not cows.

"The paternalistic idea is the child of autocracy. It is not a
democratic institution. The best American citizenship is not
developed through coddling, through consistent applications of
charity and through impositions of social welfare programs
founded on the 'contented cow' theory.

"[The A.F. of L.] contends that welfare work should be
developed so far as necessary through government organizations
controlled by the people and should not be dressed up as benevo-

lences of employers who are seeking to perpetuate the process of milking contented cows. . . ."[17]

3. THE STEEL STRIKE

DAVID M. PARRY OF THE NATIONAL ASSOCIATION OF Manufacturers was quoted as saying that "organized labor never intends to stop until . . . every employer in this country [is] placed at the mercy of the agitators who hold for the employing class nothing but envy and hatred." Gompers not only denied that this was labor's aim but that there was an "employing class." The employers were not homogeneous but divided into two groups. One was the Parry type—bigoted, stupid, and incompetent, waging war on organized labor in order to establish absolute domination. But there was also another group of employers—willing to be on good terms with labor, seeking to insure peace and harmony in the industrial world.[18]

The second group was represented by the National Civic Federation. It was in this organization that Gompers found the expression of the new views and attitudes that he developed during the 1890's. Until then he had been a class-conscious, militant, sometimes radical agitator and organizer. But in that decade he underwent a slow and subtle change. In 1893 he had pointed to the "impassable chasm" that separated rich and poor, capitalists and workers. In 1901 he observed that, despite occasional conflicts, "there is a substantial trend toward agreement between the laborers and capitalists, employed and employer, for the uninterrupted production and distribution of wealth, and, too, with ethical consideration for the *common interests* of all the people."[19] Before, he had referred to the victories of organized labor, the securing of recognition and better conditions, as milestones on the road to emancipation. Now he regarded these victories themselves as the emancipation of labor. When he was asked how the industrial struggle would end, he replied, "I believe it will end in better relations between organized employers and organized employees. Trade agreements will be the rule." But was not a trade agreement merely a truce in the struggle? No, he said, it was "a treaty between powers which recognize each other. As nations emerge from barbarism and become more enlightened and more powerful, they make treaties. So with labor and capital in America. Before, labor was a slave. Today labor is being disenthralled."[20]

In his colloquy with the socialist Morris Hillquit before the commission on industrial relations, Gompers refused to say that labor's struggle was directed against the employing class as a whole, but insisted that it was directed only against those employers with narrow social vision, and that group was becoming smaller and smaller. The others had learned—and more were learning all the time—that it was more costly to enter into prolonged strikes or lockouts than to concede labor's demands; their attitude toward the workmen changed so that their "sentiments and views are often in entire accord with the organization of the working people."[21]

The expression of this changed sentiment which reconciled the interests of workers and employers, at least temporarily, was the trade agreement, the formal recognition of standard conditions arrived at through collective bargaining between the union and the company. When that was accomplished, Gompers said, the necessity for militancy on the part of labor passed; "constructive service" followed, based on the rule of reason. Instead of isolation, mutual suspicion, and antagonism, in which class conflict had its roots, there would be face-to-face discussions between employers and wage earners and mutual respect, making for orderly and peaceful industrial progress. Gompers' trade union policy for the twentieth century marked the end of the A.F. of L.'s youthful militancy and the beginning of its conservative middle age. Gompers regarded the National Civic Federation as a principal agency in bringing together individuals committed to recognizing organized labor and arranging contacts and conferences between employers and labor representatives.[22]

Gompers' new attitude toward labor-capital relations was produced by the same factors that had brought about his acceptance of the trusts as right and inevitable, his abandoning of the organization of the unorganized, his concession to craft unionism, his yielding to Jim Crow, his abdication of leadership in the eight-hour movement, and his shift from sympathy to hostility to socialism. Most important, perhaps, was his recognition that big business was not only inevitable but practically invincible. The

Homestead, Coeur d'Alene, and Pullman strikes had convinced him that unionism could exist in the trustified industries only by the sufferance of the employers, and that they would tolerate it only if it confined itself to the skilled trades, maintained a sacred compliance with contracts, repressed militancy and radicalism in the labor movement, and was generally "reasonable."

This industrial policy was made possible by the rapid growth of industry and its tremendous strength. Business could afford to pay higher wages to a small number of skilled workers so long as the great body of unskilled workers was unorganized. In no other country in the world was there such a large gap between the wages of skilled and unskilled labor, and the gap was constantly widening. From 1850 to 1910 some of the skilled trades increased their wages threefold while reducing their hours from ten to eight, while common labor advanced its wages only fifty to a hundred per cent without a reduction in hours. Capital was thus able and willing to share some of its profits with skilled labor in order to eliminate guerilla warfare and violence, while the conservative labor leaders would co-operate to combat radicalism and keep the masses of workers unorganized. In some cases this agreement was explicit, in others it was tacit, and in still others it was induced by bribery, corruption, and open collaboration. Gompers was personally incorruptible, but he closed his eyes to such policies when they were cloaked under the name of the American Federation of Labor.[23]

There was an alternative to these policies: organization of the mass production industries on the basis of industrial unionism. But that was just what Gompers had turned his back on, and it was just what he could not do and continue to be tolerated as president of the A.F. of L. by the skilled trade unions which formed its backbone. He was the head of the bureaucracy of business unionism; to be more exact, he was its servant. And business unionism had a different meaning in 1900 than it did in 1875. Gompers had established business unionism in the cigar industry primarily as a means of bringing order and regularity into the union. It was a means of strengthening the union in its battles with the employers; it was a disciplined solidarity. But in the twentieth century, his conception of business unionism was that of unions run by their leaders—machine rule by the "experienced officers"—engaged in the business of supplying labor to employers at prices fixed by contractual arrangements.

The Civic Federation was formed in Chicago in 1893 by Ralph M. Easley and a group of businessmen and professionals; in 1900 it changed its name to the National Civic Federation. In December 1900, the N.C.F. held a national conference, urged voluntary conciliation based on the trade agreement as the means of settling industrial disputes, and appointed a committee on conciliation and arbitration. Included on this committee were Gompers, three vice-presidents of the A.F. of L., three large employers, and Bishop Henry C. Potter. When the anthracite coal miners voted to strike in April 1901, the committee called on Mark Hanna, industrial magnate and boss of the Republican party, and he succeeded in arranging a conference of mine workers and operators which averted a strike for another year. As a result, Hanna became convinced that the Civic Federation was working along fruitful lines, which moreover fitted into the methods of personal intercourse that he had himself used as an employer.

He had other reasons for supporting the work of conciliation. He had become convinced that the constant warfare between capital and labor constituted a threat to political security, and he believed class conflict could be averted by mutual efforts to eliminate suspicion. He frankly admitted that the Republican party and he personally represented the interests of big business, and if his political system was to prevail, the ultimate identity of interests between capital and labor must be made more immediate, particularly by the avoidance of serious labor disputes. He found the N.C.F. an instrument to give systematic practical expression to this objective.[24]

In May its committee on conciliation and arbitration met in New York. Gompers presided over the meeting and opened it with an expression of hope that a new epoch had come in the relations of labor and capital, based on mutual respect and avoiding strife through conciliation. The others spoke in the same spirit. The committee drew up a statement which announced its purpose of preventing strikes and lockouts. This was to be accomplished by educating public opinion to expect full and frank conferences between employers and employees, and by establishing a board of employers and employees which would be available when required.[25] During the next months the committee participated in efforts to settle a number of strikes, the most important of which was the steel strike.

In 1900, after the United States Steel Corporation had been formed, the Amalgamated Association of Iron, Steel, and Tin Workers decided that if a strike occurred in one mill, the workers in all the other mills should also cease work until the grievance was settled. The corporation was willing to avoid a fight for the time being by retaining the status quo in the constituent companies that had merged into the trust, but would not permit the unionization of mills then unorganized. Early in 1901, the union determined to demand the union scale for all the mills of the corporation, whether organized or not. The union failed to reach an agreement with the American Sheet Steel and the American Steel Hoop Companies for the union scale and recognition of the union, and on July 1 it issued a strike order against the twenty-three mills of those two subsidiary companies. Thirty-eight thousand workers downed tools. On July 10, in a conference with the union, the companies offered to sign the scale for all the tin mills except one, all the sheet mills except five (giving the union recognition in six new mills), and for the hoop mills that had been unionized the previous year. The union refused this offer; hundreds of men had gone on strike at the hoop mills not embraced by the proposal who could not be deserted without provoking indignation in the ranks of the union. Accordingly, a strike was called against the American Tin Plate Company on July 15, involving about 22,000 workers.[26]

From the beginning, Gompers was doubtful about the wisdom of the strike and suspicious of the leadership of the Amalgamated Association, particularly President T. J. Shaffer. Two months before the demands were made on the Sheet Steel Company, Shaffer wrote Gompers that the company's McKeesport mill was discharging men for joining the union and that a strike was probable, which might involve the entire steel corporation. He asked Gompers to instruct his organizers to keep men from going to McKeesport. Receiving no reply, Shaffer wrote again two weeks later, repeating his request and suggesting that if the expected strike came in July, the A.F. of L. call out all other trades employed in the steel industry to support the Amalgamated. Gompers finally wrote Shaffer that the workers would not support a call for a general sympathetic strike in the steel industry, and that they would be right. Obviously, he himself would not approve or support the Amalgamated's strike, to say nothing of a sympathetic strike. Furthermore, Gompers suspected (with some justice) that Shaffer favored the formation of an industrial union comprising all steel workers, presumably outside of the A.F. of L. He was not appeased by Shaffer's assurances that he desired to work only through the Federation.[27] Gompers also believed the union was not strong enough to take up the gage of battle with the largest aggregation of wealth in the world and that it should accept what it could get rather than hazard all in a contest which was almost certain to be lost. In his view, the union had made a terrible blunder in not accepting the terms offered on July 10.[28]

After the strike began, Gompers got involved in one of the bitterest inter-Federation rows of his career. It began with a letter from Henry White, president of the United Garment Workers and now a member of the arbitration committee of the National Civic Federation. White wrote that the strike could probably be settled if recognition of the union were waived (although union recognition was the real point at issue). Ralph Easley, secretary of the Civic Federation, was in contact with men "very close to the management of the corporation" and with M. M. Garland, former president of the Amalgamated Association and now a Republican officeholder. White suggested that Gompers see Easley, while he would see Shaffer.

About the same time, the editor of *Harper's* arranged a conference between the union leaders and J. P. Morgan, Elbert H. Gary and Charles M. Schwab of United States Steel. The latter proposed to concede the unionization of additional mills, but not all. The union refused the offer, asserting that the workers would not approve such a settlement. When, finally, the corporation refused to bargain further, the union determined to make an all-out fight for recognition. On August 6 it issued an order for a general strike in all mills of the corporation, effective the tenth. At the same time, Shaffer asked Gompers and Frank Morrison to come to Pittsburgh for a conference.[29]

Gompers and Morrison arrived in Pittsburgh on the eighth.

Shaffer urged them to make the steel strike the central fight for unionism and to call a conference of the leaders of the international unions in Pittsburgh. Gompers refused, and refused also to call a meeting of the Executive Council. But he did promise to attempt negotiations with the corporation and meanwhile to place twenty organizers at the disposal of the union and to issue a public declaration in support of the strike. He was to meet J. P. Morgan in New York the following day to propose arbitration of all matters in dispute but, for reasons never satisfactorily explained, called off the meeting. "We felt convinced," Shaffer reported, "that the A.A. need not look for help from the A.F. of L."[30]

Sixteen thousand men answered the second strike call on the tenth, bringing the total to 62,000. The United Mine Workers met in Indianapolis, endorsed the strike, and called on Gompers to call a meeting of the officers of all international unions to devise plans to aid the strikers. But Vice-President Tom Lewis gave contractual obligations as the reason why the miners would not strike in sympathy with the steel workers.[31]

Within another week several of the mills had been reopened, and prospects in the others looked bad. Steel workers were scabbing in large numbers, and the union was running out of money. On August 23, President Mitchell of the United Mine Workers, Easley, White, and Professor Jeremiah Jenks of Cornell University called at the office of the Amalgamated Association. After a discussion of the strike situation, they asked for authority to submit a proposition to the steel corporation. It provided that the scale be signed for the mills which were signed the previous year, that union wages be paid in those mills then on strike, and that no worker should lose his job because of membership in the union. According to Shaffer, Mitchell assured him that if the corporation rejected this offer, the miners would go on strike in sympathy with the steel workers. The union agreed to the plan of the committee, and September 4 they went to New York, accompanied by Gompers and Frank Sargent of the railroad trainmen, to present their proposition to the company. Its officials offered instead to sign the agreement for all the mills which were union the previous year except nine, which were to become nonunion. No worker would be discriminated against for participating in the strike or for union membership. The committee urged Shaffer to accept the proposal. One historian has Gompers accepting the corporation's proposition in return for a promise that Schwab and Cory of United States Steel would support the eight-hour bill then pending before Congress. The union's executive board rejected the counterproposal, and the strike continued, waiting for Mitchell to call out the miners. But the miners were not called out, and the strike was crumbling. On the fourteenth Shaffer was forced to come to terms. The scale was signed for twenty mills, a loss of seven for the union. The company agreed not to discriminate against workers for union membership, and the union agreed to accept the nonunion mills with no further attempt to organize them.[32]

On September 21, Shaffer issued a circular to the members of the union. He criticized Gompers for failing to keep his appointment with Morgan on August 9, for refusing to call a meeting of the labor leaders or of the Executive Council to aid the strike, for failing to give any financial assistance, and for accepting the counteroffer of Cory and Schwab. Mitchell's sin was the failure to carry out his alleged promise to call a sympathetic strike. This circular appearing in the newspapers, Gompers and Mitchell immediately demanded an investigation of the charges. They proposed that a committee of three be selected by Shaffer from a list of union officials nominated by Gompers and Mitchell. If the committee found them guilty of the charges, Gompers would resign as president of the A.F. of L. and vice-president of the Cigarmakers International Union, and Mitchell would resign from the presidency of the United Mine Workers and the vice-presidency of the A.F. of L. Shaffer turned down this challenge, feeling that all the persons nominated were friendly to Gompers. In turn he proposed a committee to be composed of one person named by himself, one by Gompers and Mitchell, and one by the other two. Gompers and Mitchell declined this offer.[33]

Gompers committed no fewer than fifteen pages of the *American Federationist* to his defense. The A.F. of L. had given no financial assistance to the strikers because the Amalgamated had never officially applied for it, nor had it requested the Federation's endorsement of its appeal for funds. He had failed to keep his appointment with Morgan because John Stevenson, an independent steel manufacturer, had said he would undertake the mission. Feeling that Stevenson could be more influential than he, Gompers had called off his meeting. (However, he soon learned that Stevenson was not going through with his trip; Gompers did not trouble to explain why he had not carried out his original plan.) Finally, he asserted that his presentation of the corporation's counteroffer on September 4 was in the best interests of the union and the workers, and a better settlement than Shaffer secured ten days later. What other officer in the American labor movement, he asked, would sign an agreement guaranteeing that for three years no attempt would be made to organize and that no charters would even be issued to men who might want to organize of their own volition? As for Mitchell's alleged promise to call out the miners, Gompers had assurances from Mitchell that there was no foundation for the statement. Gompers concluded by accusing Shaffer of rebuffing the kindly assurances of Morgan that the steel corporation might recognize the union in a few years if the union would not now "attempt to drive him further than it was possible for him to go."[34]

Thus the controversy ended, at least as far as the public was concerned, although Gompers and Shaffer continued it in private, calling each other liars in general and in particular. There is little doubt that both were at least partly correct in these accusations. There is also little doubt that Gompers' position was based on several underlying considerations that he did not bring into the open during the controversy: his fear of the steel trust and his readiness, if not eagerness, to accept the professions of the officials of the corporation at face value. Gompers and Mitchell, it has been noted, "prizing union recognition by the leaders of finance and business as their greatest possible achievement, were anxious for a speedy ending of a situation that put labor in an unfavorable light on the all-important issue of honoring its contractual obligations. Gompers was even impressed by J. P. Morgan's avowal of friendship for organized labor. Ten years later, the investigation of the Stanley Congressional Committee showed the true value of that 'friendship,' when it published the text of a resolution ... adopted by the Board of Directors of the United States Steel Corporation in one of its sessions early in 1901 and prior to the strike. It read: 'We are unalterably opposed to any extension of labor organization and advise subsidiaries to take firm positions when these questions come up and say that they are not going to recognize it,

232 THE MIDDLE AGES, 1897-1906

that is, any extension of unions in mills where they do not now exist.' . . . In the light of this resolution, the position of the Amalgamated in demanding complete unionization was justified. . . ."[35]

Following the defeat of the strike, the Amalgamated made an effort to cultivate what its new president, Michael Tighe, called a "business relationship" with the steel corporation. That meant, he explained, "giving way to every request that was made by the subsidiary companies when they insisted upon it," and agreeing not to extend the unionization of the industry.[36] Many of the other craft unions entered into a similar tacit agreement with the corporations, refraining from organizing the unskilled workers and sacrificing their interests in order to hold on to a minimum of union security for themselves and a relatively high wage differential for the skilled craftsmen. Although Gompers had criticized Shaffer for signing such an agreement, his own failure to appreciate the significance of the steel strike and his failure to back it up energetically were partly responsible for the conditions that led the union to follow that policy.

Chapter Fourteen

"A COMMUNITY OF INTERESTS"

1. CLOSING THE DOORS

After 1901, Gompers reversed his attitude toward the organization of unskilled workers and adopted the exclusionist policy against which he had formerly contended. From 1901 to 1905 several attempts were made to form a national union of unskilled laborers. Gompers consistently repressed these efforts, stating that such a union would include all workers except those organized in the unions of skilled workers and would "practically encompass the whole labor movement." But it was clear that he did not want such a union under any circumstances, for he adamantly rejected a proposal to grant it a charter with jurisdiction only over general laborers who were not eligible in any union affiliated with the A.F. of L.[1]

In 1905 Gompers stated publicly that the masses of the unskilled were probably unorganizable, blaming it on their lack of intelligence. Later he also imputed to them lack of courage, persistence, and vision.[2]

While he continued to urge the organization of women workers and the principle of equal wages, he turned to the view that women should not be wage earners, that their place was in the home. In 1905 he was asked by the *Woman's Home Companion* to answer the question, Should the wife contribute to the support of her family by working for wages? His answer was, "positively and absolutely, 'No.'" He was not opposed, he said, to the full and free opportunity of women to work whenever necessity required it, but "In our time, and at least in our country, generally speaking, there is no necessity for the wife contributing to the support of the family by working. . . . the wife as a wage-earner is a disadvantage economically considered, and socially is unnecessary."[3]

Gompers had clearly veered to the position that women ought

to be excluded from industrial employment as much as possible. He thought that industrial labor was almost universally objection- able, and that the only acceptable occupations for women were certain types of outdoor work such as gardening. In direct contrast to his position two decades earlier, Gompers gave his unqualified approval and support to the effort of a union in Massachusetts to force women out of the coremaking trade, asserting that their employment at that work was a degradation of womanhood in the name of liberty.[4]

In 1897 Booker T. Washington, the famous Negro spokesman and educator, stated that the trade unions were hindering the advancement of the Negroes by failing to organize them. The A.F. of L. denounced this statement as untrue, and reaffirmed its policy of welcoming all labor, without regard to creed, color, sex, race, or nationality, and of encouraging the organization of those most needing its protection. Gompers supported this resolution, and while some of the Southern delegates were on their feet clamoring for the floor to oppose it, Gompers put it to a vote and declared it adopted.[5]

But resolutions were not actions. In fact, they were often a substitute for action. Most of the A.F. of L. affiliates at that time did actually bar Negroes from membership, and some of their delegates, including James O'Connell of the machinists, were most vociferous in advocating the passage of this resolution. Gompers had often stated that the lack of organization among the Negro workers and their employment as strikebreakers were caused by the prejudice of white workers who refused to make common cause with them in the labor movement. But he had already begun to shift the blame to the Negroes themselves.

When asked why there were not more skilled Negro workers, he assigned two reasons for it. First, he said, Negro workers did not possess the required skill. (He did not mention the fact that most of the trade unions prevented them from acquiring that skill by refusing to accept them as apprentices.) The second reason was that in many cases, when white workers were on strike, Negroes took their places. While he had previously argued that this was the inevitable result of the white workers' ignoring the organiza- tion of the Negroes, he now stated: "If workers will not organize to protect their own interests and the interests of their fellow workers, or if workmen are so lost to their own self respect and interests as to turn the weight of their influence on the side of the capitalists as against that of the workers, these men are the enemies of progress, regardless of whether they be white or black, Caucasian or Mongolian." In the *American Federationist* he gave space to an article which referred to Negroes who had been brought to Chicago in 1904 to replace the striking stockyard workers as "hordes of ignorant blacks," "possessing but few of those attributes we have learned to revere and love," "huge strapping fellows, ignorant and vicious, whose predominating trait was animalism."[6]

Just one month after the close of the convention in which the Federation declared for the organization and unity of all workers, Gompers published an article by Will Winn, the A.F. of L. organizer in Georgia. Gompers thought that this article, entitled "The Negro: His Relation to Southern Industry," was a fair presentation of the subject.[7] Winn wrote that even if the Federation threw all its forces into a campaign to unionize Southern Negro workers, little success could be expected for many years because they did not possess "those peculiarities of temperament such as patriotism, sympathy, sacrifice, etc., which are peculiar to most of the Caucasian race. . . ." Since, in his opinion, the Negro workers could not be organized and constituted a growing menace to the status of the white workers, Winn proposed as the best solution of the problem the colonization of the Negroes in Liberia or Cuba.

Early in 1899, the Executive Council decided to launch a Southern "organizing campaign." It appointed two organizers for one month, and another, Will Winn, for three months. In view of the number of organizers, the short time allotted, and the defeatist attitude of Gompers and Winn, it is apparent that this drive was undertaken not so much to organize the workers as to enable the Council to claim that it was not neglecting this field of organization. None of the organizers was a Negro, and Gompers read with agreement and amusement a report from one of them that he, "a full-blooded Irishman," was "up against a hard proposition" in trying to organize "Jews and niggers." One year later Gompers told his New Orleans organizer that "while it is desirable to organize them . . . yet the organization of the white workmen is of paramount importance, and should not be hazarded." When a reporter asked Gompers why the South had not been effectually organized, he assigned three reasons, the first of which was "the fault of the Negroes."[8]

Thus, by the end of the nineteenth century, Gompers was in full retreat from the position he had earlier espoused with regard to the place of Negro labor in the A.F. of L. Gompers told the United States Industrial Commission in 1899 that if organized labor discriminated against Negroes, it was not because of prejudice against their color, but because they had "so conducted themselves as to be a continuous convenient whip placed in the hands of the employers to cow the white men and to compel them to accept abject conditions of labor." In explaining the Federation's attitude toward Negro workers in the *American Federationist*, Gompers devoted most of his attention to rebuking them for being "cheap workers," for demanding "special privileges," and for being suspicious of white workers.[9]

In the 1890's Gompers had refused to permit segregation by central labor unions and revoked the charters of several which refused to accept delegates from Negro unions. But in 1900 he urged the A.F. of L. not to insist on this policy and to allow the formation of separate trades councils for unions of colored workers. The Federation endorsed his suggestion, and also authorized the policy which Gompers had already initiated of organizing Negroes into separate federal labor unions.[10]

Gompers and the Federation settled into a fixed policy of Jim Crow unionism. He no longer viewed the formation of separate locals and central labor unions as a temporary if undesirable expedient but accepted it as the final and best solution to the problem. He abandoned the earlier requirement that Negro as well as white workers should desire separate organizations before their formation would be permitted. He no longer urged white unions to accept Negro workers before yielding to the establishment of separate unions. He even specifically refused to make such a request of a central labor union, deciding in advance that, because of existing prejudice in the South, it was best for both the Negro and white workers that they be segregated to avoid "arousing bitterness." Finally, he refused to grant charters as federal locals to Negro unions when affiliated unions or the railroad brotherhoods would neither accept them themselves nor surrender jurisdiction over them.[11]

The only place Gompers drew the line was in refusing to allow the Federation's directly affiliated locals to prohibit their members from working with Negroes on the same jobs. At the same time Gompers was still arguing with President W. S. Carter of the locomotive firemen the desirability of organizing Negroes.[12] He did not change his private opinion, but he had completely surrendered his official policy to the local and craft prejudices of the organizations affiliated with the A.F. of L. As in other areas, he sacrificed principle to the "practical" end of making the Federation "work" smoothly and without friction.

In 1902, William E. B. Du Bois was making a study at Atlanta University of the Negro in the trade unions. He showed that forty-three national organizations had no Negro members, and that in sixteen of them this was due to discriminatory policies. Twenty-seven others had very few Negro members, partly due to the failure of the unions to train Negro apprentices. Du Bois then prepared a fairly accurate summary of the evolution of the Federation's policy with regard to Negro workers. He added that some broad-minded leaders like Gompers had striven to maintain high and just ideals, but because of the prejudices and greed with which they had to contend, the policy of the Federation had retrogressed. He sent this study to Gompers before publishing it, with a request that he make any comment that he desired. Gompers found Du Bois' statement "neither fair nor accurate. . . . you are inclined, not only to be pessimistic upon the subject, but you are even unwilling to give credit where credit is due. Let me say further, that I have more important work to attend to than correct 'copy' for your paper."[13]

The Atlanta Conference on Negro Artisans, for which this report was prepared, recommended that Negroes should support the labor movement where it pursued a fair policy, but denounced the unjust proscription of Negroes practiced by some unions. The National Association for the Advancement of Colored People made similar criticisms of the A.F. of L.'s policy. Gompers took little cognizance of them. While in St. Louis in 1910 for the convention of the A.F. of L., he addressed the local trades council. One of the local newspapers the next morning stated that he had "read the Negro out of the labor movement." This was reported throughout the country, and resulted in a flood of protests from Negro spokesmen, including Booker T. Washington. Gompers stated that he had been misquoted and that the alleged remark in no way represented his attitude toward the Negroes. What he did say, he explained, was that it was difficult to organize Negro workers because they did not have the same conception of their rights and duties as did the white workers and were unprepared to fully exercise and enjoy the possibilities existing in trade unionism.[14]

Gompers continued to ignore protests, and he continued to ignore the Negro workers. Shortly before he died, the National Association for the Advancement of Colored People addressed an open letter to the A.F. of L. It stated that the interests of white and Negro labor were identical and that the latter had been demanding admission into the unions for many years, but they were still outside the ranks of organized labor because the unions discriminated against them and because "black labor has ceased to beg admission to union ranks." It proposed that the N.A.A.C.P., the A.F. of L., and the railroad brotherhoods form an interracial labor commission. The appeal fell on deaf ears. Gompers had little sympathy with the militant policies of the N.A.A.C.P. Although he had once criticized Washington for recommending that Negroes rely on the good will of their employers to improve their status, he was later reconciled to his conservative policy of achieving freedom "by the slow process of education and development" and by "rendering service to society that would assure their value and independence."[15]

Gompers never registered any protest against any of the conditions or events which concerned the Negro people. He was silent about the disfranchisement of the Southern Negroes, about lynchings, exclusion of Negroes from jury service, inferior and segregated accommodations in the public schools and colleges, railroads, and other public places, about chain gangs or involuntary servitude through debt peonage. Even when the A.F. of L. denounced restrictions on the suffrage and directed the Executive Council to help thwart the disfranchisement movement, Gompers did nothing to carry out the instructions. In an address at Jacksonville, Florida, he expressed his unwillingness to interfere with the "internal affairs" of the South. But such scruples did not prevent him from publicly defending the policy of San Francisco in segregating Japanese students in the public schools.[16]

Gompers had begun with a relatively advanced attitude toward Negro workers, but one based on a narrow trade union desire to keep the Negroes from competing with white labor and neglecting the broader vision of labor solidarity which marked the policy of the Knights of Labor. With the positive aspects of his policy had been mixed a considerable amount of racial prejudice. So it was easy for him to retreat into Jim Crowism when his principles were attacked by trade union leaders bent on excluding Negroes from industrial life altogether.

The greatest impediment to the organization of the unskilled, including immigrants, women, and Negroes, was the craft policy of the A.F. of L. Until 1900 Gompers had been its reluctant supporter. He recognized the need for greater unification among the workers to meet the increased power of aggregated wealth. But he would not countenance the formation of industrial unions which might swallow up the trade unions and strengthen those elements in the Federation that were more militant and socialistic than the leaders of the craft unions. The growth of industrialism in the Federation would mean the loss of all their jobs.

Gompers constantly insisted that the members of the trade union movement could have any form of organization they wanted. The A.F. of L. was flexible and allowed complete freedom of action to its affiliates. If they wanted industrial unionism, all they had to do was decide upon it and act. If the Federation was not progressing as fast as some desired, it was only because the members were not prepared to go further. But he determined that, if he could help it, they would not go any further than they already had. The action of the Federation in 1900 was the limit. In that year the convention acquiesced in industrial unionism for the miners and brewers, with Gompers voting against it.[17]

He made up his mind that it was time to call a halt. At the convention in Scranton the following year, he appointed a special committee on trade autonomy and appointed himself as chairman. The committee submitted the famous Scranton declaration, which Gompers had himself carefully prepared in advance. It conceded that jurisdiction in the mining and brewing industries by the paramount organization would best serve the interests of the workers, at least until the separate trades had grown larger, and it approved trade councils among closely allied crafts. But it insisted that the success of the Federation and the trade unions depended on the recognition of the principle of craft autonomy. Finally, it declared that the A.F. of L. should not adopt measures offensive to established trade unions.[18]

The Scranton declaration caused as much dissatisfaction among the industrial union advocates in the Federation as the brewery decision did among the autonomists. Discontent was aggravated when Gompers, in arbitrating the brewers' and engineers' dispute, arbitrarily reversed the decision of the 1900 convention and directed the brewers to turn over all engineers' and firemen's locals to those organizations. He deliberately took that action as a test case. Rumors were rife in the Federation that the coming convention would bring a showdown battle. The miners, carpenters, and brewers, and possibly the United Garment Workers and the Typographical Union, were expected to join in an attempt to dethrone Gompers. Vice-Presidents John Mitchell of the miners and James Duncan of the granite cutters were mentioned as possible successors to the presidency. Gompers was prepared to meet the challenge. "I have felt the necessity growing," he wrote to a friend, "for strong and determined action being taken to maintain true trade union autonomy, and on several occasions, particularly during this past year, I have not hesitated to make a stand. It is for that reason that this opposition has been aroused against me by those who are suffering from this expansion malady . . . and it is equally true that they may bring about my defeat at the New Orleans Convention. That, however, is their perfect right. . . . but in the language of one of America's famous statesmen, 'I would rather be right than be President' even of the A.F. of L. . . ."[19] In his annual report, he attacked the "tidal wave of expansion madness" and virtually demanded a vote of confidence on his decision in the brewery case. After a bitter fight, Gompers was upheld, and when the time came for the nomination of officers, the opposition disintegrated, as usual.

Year after year resolutions for industrial unionism were introduced at the Federation conventions, generally by the socialists. Just as regularly, Gompers and the assembled trade union officialdom beat them down. But Gompers in the meantime worked at his "counter-reformation," the "natural, orderly and well-defined course" of promoting co-operation while respecting trade autonomy. He forced a number of amalgamations upon weak unions in the 1900's: the metal mechanics with the machinists, the coremakers with the molders, the lasters with the shoemakers, and the car workers with the railway carmen. The method by which the last two amalgamations were brought about indicates that trade autonomy was not so sacred that it might not be sacrificed to satisfy the demands of a powerful union in the Federation or to gain the adherence of a large organization, in violation of the Scranton declaration as well as of the Federation constitution.

Finally, two decades after Gompers had first proposed it, the A.F. of L. inaugurated the formation of industrial departments. In 1907, it was decided to charter a Building Trades Department, to be composed of the building trades organizations affiliated with the A.F. of L. In the next three years, departments were also formed among the metal trades, railroad employees, and mine workers. This action, said Gompers, "will prove conclusively that the carping critics of our movement who charge, or insinuate, that the trade union movement does not progress, advance or develop, is baseless and mischievous untruth."[20] But these departments far from met the demands of those favoring industrial unionism. They did not affect the essential character of the A.F. of L., which kept action by the departments at a minimum. While they tended to reduce jurisdictional disputes, they did not carry on true collective bargaining. Professor John R. Commons aptly characterized the departments as "industrial unionism of the upper stratum" of the labor movement, and an official of the automobile workers' union commented that "they were nothing less than a confession that greater unity is needed, but those in control of the old machinery of the Labor Movement are reluctant to give way to the new order of things. They would patch up the old vehicle; they would put a motor in the old wagon and thus make an up to date automobile of it, but would decline to accept the modern vehicle, because it means a new deal in the Labor Movement and they are afraid they would be lost in the shuffle."[21]

2. THE NATIONAL CIVIC FEDERATION

IN DECEMBER 1901, THE COMMITTEE ON CONCILIA-
tion and arbitration of the N.C.F. changed its name to the Industrial Department. An executive committee was appointed, with Hanna as chairman and Easley as secretary. Gompers, as first vice-president, addressed the new Department:

"There is in our time, if not a harmony of interests . . . yet certainly a community of interests, to the end that industrial peace shall be maintained. . . .

"I want to see the organization of the wage-earners and the organization of the employers, through their respective representatives, meet around the table . . . there to discuss the questions of wages and hours of labor and conditions of employment and all things consistent with the industrial and commercial success of our country, that shall tend to the uplifting of the human family. . . .

"We want better relations with the employing class. We are contributing our quota toward that desirable end. But we claim, even if it be not generally recognized, that there is no factor in our behalf so potent to secure consideration at the hands of our employers, or fair agreements from them, or a faithful adherence to the terms of the contracts or agreements, as a well organized body of wage-earners in the unions of their trades. . . ."[22]

Gompers' part in the formation of the Industrial Department and his activities in the National Civic Federation aroused a storm of criticism from socialist and nonsocialist radicals and militants, in the A.F. of L. as well as outside of it. Some merely felt it improper for the leader of the American labor movement to hobnob with such financial tycoons as Hanna, Schwab, August Belmont, financier and traction magnate, and Morgan. Others did not trust him to associate with them without being contaminated or "bought." Still others regarded the whole movement as one designed to mislead the workers into a false notion of their common interests with capital, to chloroform them into relying on the good will of their employers rather than on their own strength. It substituted class collaboration for class struggle.

Gompers defended the formation of the Industrial Department as a victory for labor. Employers had generally refused to meet and confer with organized labor to adjust grievances, he asserted, while labor had always striven for such conferences. The Department was proof that labor had won over a large number of capitalists to its point of view and had neutralized their hostility. Many improvements had been won through negotiation which otherwise might not have been secured, at least without bitter and costly struggle. Above all, the Department provided an opportunity for workers and employers to meet face to face, to learn what was in each other's hearts and minds, and to bring about the recognition of mutual respect to which each was entitled. In this way, they could "go along hand in hand in the production and distribution of the great wealth of our country." On the other hand, if the unions indulged in "wholesale and unnecessary denunciation" of the employers, they would be less willing to deal with the unions, and the effectiveness of negotiations for trade agreements would be weakened.[23]

During the next few years, Gompers was deeply involved in two strikes with which the N.C.F. was not directly connected, but the employer in each case was serving as chairman of its Industrial Department and the critics of the Civic Federation were treated to the spectacle of Gompers supporting the position of the employer against the union in both cases. In June 1903, an agreement was reached between the Buffalo Union Furnace Company, which was owned by Mark Hanna, and the local of the blast furnace workers, which was an industrial union comprising all the workers in the plant. The contract provided for a scale of wages, a twelve-hour day, and a preferential union shop. It was further agreed that in case of any difference, the dispute should be settled by the superintendent and a committee representing the workers. If they were unable to arrive at a settlement, the case would be submitted to an arbitration committee. The decision of the committee was to be final and binding, and the men were to continue work pending a settlement.[24]

Three weeks later, Gompers received a telegram from Hanna, stating that the workers had violated the agreement by going on strike, and advising him to send representatives "to see if agreements can be flatly broken in this manner." Without knowing any more about the situation, Gompers ordered his organizer, Thomas Flynn, to go to Buffalo and help adjust the matter in order to maintain the interests and good name of the A.F. of L. At the same time he wired James McMahon, the president of the National Association of Blast Furnace Workers, with a similar request.[25]

On July 27, Flynn and McMahon arrived in Buffalo and went into conference with mill and union officials. It appeared that the superintendent had removed a man as foreman of the blacksmith shop and downgraded him because he had refused to withdraw from the union. The president of the local had given the superintendent five and a half hours to reconsider the matter and to consult with the Hanna Company. The superintendent had replied, "You have my final answer now." Only after the men had walked out had the superintendent asked if the contract provision calling for arbitration had not been violated, and the president had replied that it was still not too late to discuss the matter. The general manager of the Hanna Company had asserted that it was not only too late to arbitrate, but that the contract was nullified by the union's action. "It is our business," he had declared, "and we are going to run it. . . . We are going to hire and discharge foremen as we see fit, and from now on, we are going to hire and discharge men as we see fit . . . and it is not going to be a cause for arbitration." Flynn closed the conference by asking if the company would arbitrate the question of the foreman's reduction, and the general manager replied: "Not now. We have been damaged by the men going on strike without notice. . . . It is up to organized labor to do something now."[26]

When Gompers received the report of this conference, he asked Hanna if he would not advise his Buffalo representative to arbitrate. Hanna replied that the union had abrogated the contract by striking "without cause and without notice to our company leaving three furnaces standing under full burden, which in blast furnace practice is considered a criminal offense. . . . We will have nothing to do in the future with officers or committees of Unions that are liable to act in this way. . . . We will start this plant in our own way. . . ." Specifically, the company proposed to reopen the plant on a nonunion basis and would give the workers ninety days in which to reorganize on a craft union basis, after which the company would recognize the union if it were "controlled" by the A.F. of L. Gompers told Flynn to keep the union intact if possible, but that it would probably be necessary to accede to the company's demands. In any case, he was to settle the strike and try to have the union "emerge from this most unpleasant situation with the least possible discredit." The most important thing was to save organized labor's reputation for living up to its agreements.[27]

Flynn agreed that the strike should be called off on the company's terms, but he did not have the authority to do so, and McMahon went to Cleveland to see Hanna. The men would not accept a settlement without the reinstatement of the foreman, and the company insisted on the right to choose its own foreman. On August 3, after refusing McMahon's offer to arbitrate and to reorganize the union, Hanna told Gompers that he should call the strike off at once and allow the "better men" to return to work, otherwise the company would have no dealings with the union in the future. But Gompers replied he had no authority to order strikes off, that the company was equally at fault with the men, and that the trouble could be adjusted if a conciliatory spirit was manifested. Hanna asserted that the men were solely responsible for the situation, and that the company's last offer was an ultimatum. "If you are powerless to interfere [I] will not trouble you further about the matter."

McMahon finally returned to Buffalo, on Gompers' insistence, where he was informed that the company insisted on firing twenty-two of the best men in the plant for some minor offenses before it would make any settlement. He would not stand for that, but he offered to drop three of the men who were clearly guilty of offenses, to call off the strike, and to arbitrate all other differences. "If Hanna is as friendly to labor as he says, it is time for him to interfere. I don't think we can hold the men much longer." Hanna did not interfere, McMahon did not hold the men, and on the twenty-eighth the union surrendered and called off the strike. Four days later the convention of the Blast Furnace Workers' Association met. Gompers urged Flynn and the secretary of the Association to see that the convention took some positive action to prevent the recurrence of "such an outrageous breaking of agreements with employers." The convention revoked the charter of the Buffalo local and issued a new one to the blast furnace workers exclusively. Gompers noted in a private memorandum that had such a union been in existence at the beginning, there would have been no strike, and that under the new organization "there is a greater future than ever in store for the blast furnace workers."[28]

In 1904, Mark Hanna died and was replaced as chairman of the Industrial Department of the N.C.F. by August Belmont. In September, Belmont's Interborough Rapid Transit Company took over the Manhattan Elevated Company and announced that it would train men to operate the new subway and that they would work at longer hours and lower wages than those that prevailed for the elevated workers. The three unions represented on the elevated—the Brotherhood of Locomotive Firemen, the Brotherhood of Locomotive Engineers, and the Amalgamated Association of Street Railway Employees—objected and demanded that preferential employment and seniority privileges be given to their members, that the medical examination of applicants be made less severe, and that the subway workers be granted the same wages and hours as the elevated employees, which was $3.50 for a nine-hour day. The company rejected the wage and hour demands. The three unions voted overwhelmingly for a strike, and the company began recruiting strikebreakers. The N.C.F. proposed arbitration, and Belmont agreed to meet the union representatives. He offered three dollars for a ten-hour day, to be increased to $3.50 after one year. The unions accepted the offer, and the B. of L.E. signed a three-year contract.

Belmont was anxious to avoid a strike at that time because of the impending presidential election. But when that was over, he resumed preparations against a strike, if he did not actually undertake to provoke one. Dissatisfaction soon arose over alleged violations of the agreement by the company. In the meantime, the Amalgamated Association had begun an organizing campaign, which had to be done secretly because of the company's antagonism. The union organized eighty per cent of the employees eligible for membership and was preparing to make further demands.[29]

At this time, Belmont's re-election as chairman of the Industrial Department was due. He told the labor members, "It will be a mistake for me to be re-elected because we may have a strike and it would embarrass you, the National Civic Federation, and the Interborough." Gompers and the others, including William Mahon, president of the Amalgamated, and Warren Stone, Grand

Chief of the B. of L.E., assured him that they wanted him for another year, and Stone promised him that there would be no strike. If any disagreement arose, he stated, it would be referred to him and Belmont, and if they could not agree, they would select a committee to arbitrate it. Belmont was unanimously re-elected and left at once for his vacation in Italy. He had no sooner arrived there than the whole Interborough system was tied up by a strike.[30]

In February, Gompers' representative in New York warned the officers of the Amalgamated local that reports of strike preparations were hurting their organization, that their alliance with the engineers' local did not have the authorization of the international union, and that it would prove detrimental in case of a strike. On March 4 Secretary Andrew B. Madden of the local wrote to Mahon urging him to come to New York, as the situation was critical. Mahon arrived two days later and was shown a copy of the union's demands: a nine-hour day with a maximum run of 100 miles and a ten per cent wage raise. Mahon urged the union not to strike for these demands because they included those of the motormen, for whom the B. of L.E. had signed a three-year agreement; and because the constitution of the Amalgamated required that controversies should be submitted to the international before a local went on strike. He said that if the matter were referred to him he did not doubt that he could arrange a conference and secure their demands. The joint union committee nevertheless decided to present the demands to the company. They were rejected as a violation of the agreement, and on March 7 the men struck.[31]

Mahon went into conference with his executive board, some of whom disagreed with his insistence on the absolute maintenance of agreements and believed that since the men were being mistreated they should be supported. Besides, the Amalgamated's agreement had expired; if any contract was violated it was that of the engineers, and the most that the Amalgamated could be accused of was supporting the engineers in violation of their agreement. Mahon went to Gompers, who was staying in the same hotel in New York. Gompers urged upon him the absolute necessity of maintaining agreements, for any other course would discourage other companies from making agreements with the unions. Besides, the workers should not strike when the employers were trying to provoke them, for the circumstances themselves proved that the company would be prepared for the strike just then. Gompers and Mahon jointly drafted a message to the union expressing sympathy with its just cause but advising it that the strike was impractical, dangerous, and illegal under the rules of the Amalgamated. The men were ordered to return to work on penalty of having their charter revoked. Mahon went back to the executive board with the draft telegram and secured unanimous approval to send it out.[32] In the meantime, Grand Chief Stone had also arrived in New York, made an investigation, denounced the strike, ordered the men back to work, and withdrew the charter of the engineers' local. Thus was the promise to Belmont fulfilled.

This action, together with the invasion of a thousand strike-breakers that the company had been recruiting for some time, broke the strike. In four days the workers were forced to return, or at least those whom the company would take back, and the union was destroyed, as the company insisted on establishing an open shop both on the subway and elevated trains.

It was widely believed that Belmont had deliberately provoked the strike. George Perkins, president of the Cigarmakers International Union, rebuked the men for striking without exhausting conciliatory means, but nevertheless asserted that they had been goaded to desperation by the despicable nagging and persecution of the employers, who tried to force the men into a hasty strike for which they were not prepared. Mahon and Gompers intimated that the strike had been provoked by the company for the purpose of eliminating the union. Nevertheless, in a public meeting shortly after the end of the strike, Gompers had nothing to offer but denunciation for the strikers. "I think that their strike was unjustified," he declared, "for the simple reason that the employees violated their agreement and verbal contract. The most important object in the labor organizations today is the honor of agreements between employee and employer. The violation of agreements was the main cause of the strike. . . . It was a simple case of the members of the union flying off half-cocked and not taking the advice of the men who have made the labor organizations in the United States what they are today."[33]

The Central Federated Union of New York sent a committee

Sara and Solomon Gompers, Samuel's parents.

Gompers and his secretary in the New York A.F. of L. office, about 1890.

A labor picnic about the turn of the century. Gompers is in the center, under the sign.

Gompers in "a speaking pose," in the 1880's.

Gompers in 1891.

Gompers in 1903.

Sophia Julian Gompers.

John Mitchell, Frank Morrison, and Gompers at the time of the Buck's Stove and Range case.

The A.F. of L. delegation to the peace conference: Third Vice-President Frank Duffy, First Vice-President James Duncan, Fourth Vice-President William Green, Former Third Vice-President John R. Alpine, President Samuel Gompers.

With candidate Robert M. La Folle during the 1924 Presidential campai

With President Calles of Mexico. One of the last photographs of Gompers.

Gompers' favorite cartoon: "No Longer the Man With the Hoe" by J. M. Baer.

to Belmont to ask for the reinstatement of the strikers. When they were rebuffed, the body ordered any of its members or members of affiliated unions who belonged to the Civic Federation to resign from it. Later another resolution was introduced denouncing the N.C.F. and the labor leaders who participated in its activities. A committee was appointed to investigate and Gompers went to New York to defend his activities. He insisted that the N.C.F. had been helpful to many unions in accomplishing their purposes with the least possible friction or strife. The committee recommended that the N.C.F. should be endorsed as conducive to peaceful settlement of disputes and its report was defeated by a large majority. However, a few weeks later it unanimously adopted a resolution introduced by Local 144, expressing implicit confidence in the honesty and integrity of Gompers and asserting that wherever his assistance had been requested to adjust labor disputes he had always acted faithfully in the interests of labor.[34]

Encouraged by the action of the New York body, Victor Berger, Milwaukee socialist, introduced a resolution at the next convention of the A.F. of L. It denounced the "hypocritical attempt of the Civic Federation plutocrats to convince organized laboring men that the interests of capital and labor are identical" and the "close intimacy and harmonious relations established between Samuel Gompers and other labor leaders with the great capitalists and plutocratic politicians. . . ." His resolution was unanimously defeated.[35]

3. THE LEFT WING

UNTIL THE 1890's GOMPERS ALWAYS INSISTED THAT he was not anti-socialist, that he shared the goals of the socialists, and that he could work with them as long as they did not attack the trade unions. It was only in methods that they differed. But it was becoming increasingly clear that the difference in "methods" was a result of a fundamental difference in philosophy and objectives, as Gompers and the socialists found themselves on opposite sides of every major issue that faced the labor movement. The radicals in the Federation opposed Gompers' views on industrial unionism, on nonpartisan politics, lobbying, and a labor party, on social security, on his conservative and cautious strike policies, and on his participation in the National Civic Federation, as well as on the question of socialism itself. As a result of such clashes, as well as Gompers' growing conservatism in general outlook, he began to cultivate a bitter hatred of radicals, and especially socialists, and to attack not only the latter but socialism itself.

References to "wage slavery" and the "emancipation of labor" dropped out of Gompers' vocabulary. He no longer gave even lip service to the notion that labor would some day come into its own as the controlling element in society. There was no more talk about subordinating the final emancipation of labor to the attainment of immediate goals. Amelioration became synonymous with emancipation.[36]

At the 1903 convention of the Federation, during the debate on a labor party, Gompers announced his first clear-cut expression of opposition to socialism in a declaration that was carefully prepared for its dramatic effect. At the close of his speech, he gave vent to the statement that was intended to be the last word on the subject:

"I want to tell you, Socialists, that I have studied your philosophy; read your works upon economics, and not the meanest of them; studied your standard works, both in English and German—have not only read, but studied them. I have heard your orators and watched the work of your movement the world over. I have kept close watch upon your doctrines for thirty years; have been closely associated with many of you, and know how you think and what you propose. I know, too, what you have up your sleeve. And I want to say that I am entirely at variance with your philosophy. I declare it to you, I am not only at variance with your doctrines, but with your philosophy. Economically, you are unsound; socially, you are wrong; industrially, you are an impossibility."[37]

As a result of Gompers' onslaught, he was hailed by the press as a hero. The National Civic Federation printed a picture of him on the front page of its journal with the caption, "Socialism's Ablest Foe." This pleased Gompers, for he wrote to a friend that his renunciation of socialism "largely disarmed our opponents and clarified the air of the prejudice of public opinion which was leveled against us last year, and it will undoubtedly take away much of the sting of antagonism directed against our movement

by Mr. Parry and those who follow him." Gompers misjudged
Parry; for the N.A.M. president was soon to declare: "The A.F.
of L. voted down the socialism that aims for peace through means
of the ballot, but it did not vote down the socialism that President
Gompers stands for—mob force socialism. It is this mob force
socialism that we have to combat as much as the other."[38]

Gompers made little if any distinction between the different
varieties of socialists, although they followed different trade union
policies. In 1901, the Social Democratic party merged with a faction of the Socialist Labor party that had become fed up with the
doctrinaire and autocratic leadership of De Leon and his dual
unionism, to form the Socialist party. The new party declared that
both economic and political action were necessary to bring about
socialism and that the formation of trade unions would strengthen
the power of the working class for the eventual struggle for socialism. Its goal was to convert trade unionists to socialism and induce
them to affiliate with the party. But this resolution concealed basic
differences between the right-wing and left-wing socialists. The
former, led by Hillquit, leaned toward collaboration with
Gompers. Their purpose was to strengthen their influence in the
A.F. of L. by refraining from attacking its leaders and by remaining neutral on industrial unionism. By aiding the unions in their
economic struggles, they hoped to win their support for the party
in its political struggles. The left wing, headed by Debs, believed
socialists could not be neutral on vital questions. They denounced
the Federation leaders for their stand on industrial unionism and
for participating in the National Civic Federation, and held that
socialists must fight to establish a revolutionary labor movement
based on class-conscious struggle. Some proposed to make this
fight within the A.F. of L., but most favored the organization of
dual unions.[39]

Since most of the left-wing socialists wanted nothing to do
with the A.F. of L., Gompers faced little real opposition from
them. While the "pro-Federation" socialists opposed him on some
issues, they gradually soft-pedalled their agitation for industrial
unionism and a labor party. Nor did they make any serious effort
to depose Gompers from the leadership of the Federation. From
1898 to 1902 he was re-elected without opposition. In 1903 he was
opposed by Ernest Kreft of the United Labor League of Phila-

delphia but won by a ten to one majority. The following year Max Hayes stated that it did not matter much who was chosen to transact the Federation's business, and that it was pointless to fight its leadership. The socialists put up no opposition candidate from 1904 to 1912.

It was the left-wing, dual-union socialists who were Gompers' bitterest opponents. The stronghold of this group was the Western Federation of Miners, led by Ed Boyce and "Big Bill" Haywood. Haywood's attitude toward the A.F. of L. was evidenced in his remark that its 28,000 locals were 28,000 agencies of the capitalist class and that he would rather cut off his right arm than join it. In 1902 the Executive Council threatened to destroy the Western Federation of Miners if it did not immediately affiliate with the A.F. of L. The W.F. of M. replied by forming the American Labor Union, claiming jurisdiction throughout the United States, declaring for political action and industrial unionism, and adopting the platform of the Socialist party.[40]

The following year class warfare erupted in Colorado on a mass scale. This was caused by two events: a concerted effort by the employers' associations and "Citizens' Alliances" to destroy unionism in the state, and the failure of the legislature to implement, and the refusal of the employers to enforce, an eight-hour amendment to the constitution which had been passed in a popular referendum in 1902. The Western Federation of Miners struck early in 1903 for the eight-hour day, and also for recognition of the union, wage raises, and reinstatement of the workers who had been fired for joining the union.

Some mills granted the union's demands, but the Standard Mill, at Cripple Creek, Colorado, refused to accede, and the union placed a boycott on the mill and struck the mines which refused to stop shipping ore to the mill. The governor sent in 1,000 soldiers, and a number of mines resumed operations with nonunion men.

Then began one of the most flagrantly brutal instances of military rule and vigilantism in American history. The Citizens' Protective League deported eighteen miners who had been seized in their homes, although no charges were placed against them. Arrests of strike leaders began on grounds of "military necessity." The union instituted *habeas corpus* proceedings, and when the case came before the court a cordon of cavalrymen was formed around the court house and the petitioners were escorted by a company of infantry with fixed bayonets and guarded by armed soldiers while in court. The judged ordered the men released, but General John Chase leaped to his feet, announced that he was acting on orders of the governor, and refused to honor the court's order. The men were taken to a bull pen, or concentration camp, where they were joined by the staff of the *Victor Record* and other union men seized by the military. The attitude of the military was expressed by General Thomas McClellan, who stated, "To Hell with the Constitution. We are not going by the Constitution, we are following the orders of Governor Peabody."[41]

At the time of the Federation's 1903 convention, nearly a year after the beginning of the Cripple Creek strike, Gompers had taken no notice of the affairs in Colorado. A resolution was introduced in the convention to extend sympathy to the Western Federation of Miners in its fight and to donate $1,000 to aid it. Gompers opposed the donation on the ground that the W.F. of M. was a dual union, but the delegates passed it over his objection.[42]

The following June, the railroad depot at Cripple Creek was blown up, killing thirteen and wounding sixteen men. The W.F. of M. disclaimed any connection. A mob organized by the Citizens' Alliance forced the sheriff to resign, and the local militia attacked the miners' halls, destroyed the furnishings in them, rounded up union men, and threatened deportation or death to any man who belonged to the union. The state militia returned and took command. General Sherman Bell arrested over 1,000 and deported over a hundred men. The *Victor Record* was again invaded, the presses destroyed, and the staff put in the bull pen. Mobs invaded the homes of "suspects," terrorized the occupants, and deported them.[43]

The Chicago Federation of Labor requested Gompers to call a conference of delegates of all central bodies in the United States to consider the situation in Colorado. A few other central bodies and international union leaders endorsed the plan, but Gompers refused to call such a meeting. Under pressure to do something for the miners, he issued an appeal for financial assistance. All semblance of civilized law and constitutional rights in Colorado were being trampled under foot, he wrote, and being replaced by the rule of gun and bayonet in the service of the mine owners. Gompers repudiated any crime committed by either side, and hinted that the W.F. of M. had committed its share. But they were still entitled to the same rule of law and justice as the mine owners and antiunion mobs.[44]

The Chicago Federation of Labor was not satisfied that this was sufficient to meet the situation and determined to call the conference of central bodies itself, to meet in Victor, Colorado, on August 25. Secretary Ed Nockels handed the call to Gompers and asked him to endorse it. Gompers refused; he could not sanction a meeting which might commit the labor movement to some declaration by men "who can not represent the rank and file of the bona fide labor movement of the country." Yet it was precisely to secure the expression of the rank and file that the conference was called. The city centrals were closer to the ranks than were the leaders of the international unions or even the conventions of the A.F. of L.[45]

Early in August, Gompers addressed the Baltimore Federation of Labor. He felt impelled to notice the charge that he lacked sympathy for the striking miners in Colorado. He denied this and affirmed that their cause was just, but went on to say that they had made many mistakes. Although no evidence had been presented connecting the union with any violence, and the arrested strikers had not yet been brought to trial, Gompers denounced the Western Federation of Miners for not adhering to law and order.[46] In November, the cases against the forty-two men indicted for murder as a result of the Victor riots were dismissed, and two months later the cases against the officers of the W.F. of M. for the railroad station explosion were also dismissed for lack of evidence. But by this time the strike had been broken.

At the end of 1904, the W.F. of M. invited about thirty people to a secret conference in Chicago on January 2, 1905, to consider the formation of a labor organization that would unite the entire working class in industrial departments which could take over and administer industry whenever the people voted for a socialist government. Among those present were Bill Haywood and President Charles Moyer of the W.F. of M., President Dan McDonald of the American Labor Union, Eugene Debs and Algie Simons of the Socialist party, William Trautmann of the Brewery Workers

Union, Charles Sherman of the United Metal Workers, George
Estes of the United Railway Workers, "Mother" Jones, fiery
United Mine Workers organizer, and "Father" Thomas J. Hag-
erty, an unfrocked priest of militant propensities. Some 50,000
workers were represented. A manifesto was adopted declaring
that modern industry had destroyed craft lines and skills, sinking
all workers into a uniform mass of wage slaves. The A.F. of L.,
based on the worn-out and corrupt system of craft divisions, shattered the working class into fragments, rendering it helpless on
the industrial battlefield. It offered only a perpetual struggle for
slight relief, but hindered the growth of class consciousness and
was blind to the possibility of establishing a democracy in which
industry would be owned by the workers. A call was issued for a
convention in Chicago on June 27 to form a revolutionary industrial union movement to supplant the A.F. of L.[47]

The Executive Council met following the publication of this
manifesto and call and declared that the Western Federation of
Miners was repaying the A.F. of L.'s assistance in its eight-hour
strike by further efforts to divide the labor movement. It therefore called on its affiliated unions to make no further donations to
the legal defense fund of the W.F. of M. Gompers further demanded that the W.F. of M. give an accounting of the use of all
contributions it had received. He was deluged with protests from
city centrals and from local unions of many affiliated international
organizations. The Haverhill central labor union declared that
Gompers had overreached himself by misusing his power and
forsaking the miners in their hour of need. While Moyer was in
the bull pen, it asserted, Gompers was "reveling in aristocratic
dissipation" with Belmont and other antiunion employers at the
National Civic Federation. The union determined to give all the
aid it could to the W.F. of M. The Salt Lake local of the bridge
and structural iron workers stated that Gompers' spiteful action
would bring discord into the labor movement, and added that the
W.F. of M. commanded the respect and admiration of the world
for its heroic struggle for industrial freedom.[48]

On June 27, over 200 delegates attended the convention in
Chicago to form a new labor organization. Gompers was very
much concerned about the new rival, particularly because a number of A.F. of L. locals were represented at the founding conven-

tion, as well as the Illinois District of the U.M.W., Trautmann of the brewery workers, the president of the American Flint Glass Workers, and the United Metal Workers, which had recently withdrawn from the A.F. of L. The W.F. of M., with its 27,000 members, was the dominant group, and Haywood was elected president of the convention. The Socialist Trades and Labor Alliance, represented by De Leon, and the American Labor Union were other important groups in the conclave.

Haywood called the meeting to order and took note of the accusation that the convention intended to compete with the A.F. of L.: "That is a mistake. We are here for the purpose of organizing a labor organization. . . . The aims and objects of this organization should be to put the working class in possession of the economic power, the means of life, in control of the machinery of production and distribution, without regard to capitalist masters. . . . this is a revolutionary movement and the capitalists are not the only foes that you are to fight, but the most ardent enemies have been the pure and simple trade unionist." Other speeches were in the same vein, and the convention wound up by launching the Industrial Workers of the World.[49]

Even before the I.W.W. was formed, Gompers denounced the plans for its organization. He denied industrial unionism was the real purpose of its promoters: the A.F. of L. itself allowed for industrial unions wherever they were advisable or desired by the workers. The real purpose was to divide, disrupt, and destroy the trade union movement in order to promote socialism. After the organization was launched, Gompers' apprehensions were somewhat relieved, for he felt that it was not so strong as he had feared. But he was still concerned, and in a circular to the labor movement he tried to cover the I.W.W. with ridicule: "The mountain labored and brought forth a mouse." He listed the thirteen industrial divisions of the I.W.W. and commented that in such an organization "the tinker, the tailor, and the candlestick maker would legislate upon every minute detail affecting the interests of the workers. . . . The whole scheme died aborning and went up on thin air. . . . [The future] will record the Chicago meeting as the most vapid and ridiculous in the annals of those who presume to speak in the name of labor and the participants in the gathering as the most stupendous impossibles the world had yet seen."[50] But the I.W.W. could not be laughed out of existence, and Gompers had not seen the last of it.

On December 30, 1905, ex-Governor Frank Steunenberg of Idaho was killed by a bomb while opening the gate to his home. Harry Orchard, a member of the W.F. of M., was arrested on suspicion. In a confession to the Pinkerton Agency, he claimed that Secretary Haywood, President Moyer, and executive board member Pettibone had hired him to commit the crime, allegedly to get revenge for Steunenberg's use of the military against the Coeur d'Alene strikers in 1899. A secret complaint was filed against them, the governor of Colorado secretly signed extradition papers, and on the night of February 17 the three accused men were seized in their homes, conveyed to a special train, whisked away to the penitentiary in Boise, and indicted for murder.

The unionists of Idaho charged that the proceedings were the result of a conspiracy between state officials and the mine owners to punish innocent men and destroy the W.F. of M. Gompers agreed that the kidnapping of the defendants and their illegal extradition justified the suspicion of a frame-up. He wrote later in his memoirs that the labor movement "could not abandon the labor men helplessly to the vengeance of employers who were in control of the machinery of the state." They were at least entitled to a fair trial, which they could not get without the financial assistance of the labor movement.[51]

At the Federation convention at the end of the year, Gompers denounced the outrage against constitutional rights but made no recommendations for financial aid or a campaign to secure justice for the victims of the frame-up. Meanwhile, they were still languishing in prison awaiting their trial. The conservative press had already found them guilty in lurid headlines and baseless stories, but the great muckraking periodicals of the time were holding popular judgment in suspension while they unfolded the details of industrial strife in the West and humanized the miners. The W.F. of M., the I.W.W., the Socialist party, and nearly the entire trade union movement had rallied to the cause of the defendants. As the date for the trial approached, protest parades were held in every major city. Fifty thousand men marched through the streets of Boston chanting, "If Moyer and Haywood die, twenty million workingmen will know the reason why." Socialists and unionists contributed over $60,000 to fight the case.[52] And they wanted to know what Gompers was going to do.

In December 1906, the executive committee of the Socialist party asked Gompers to call a national conference of labor organizations, under the auspices of the A.F. of L., to provide means of protection, methods of defense, and channels of publicity in behalf of the defendants. The request was accompanied by supporting petitions from leading officials of seventeen national unions. Gompers opposed the requested action, explaining that he doubted if such a conference would accomplish any good results for the defendants, and might even react to their detriment. Any action "should take the form that will have at least some assurance that it will be of a practical and tangible character. Agitation is one thing; tangible and practical results are another."[53] The labor movement waited for Gompers to propose some more "practical and tangible" action.

A month later the New York Central Federated Union held a mass meeting. Its representative said that Gompers and the Federation had still done nothing for the defendants and declared that unless they soon "show their colors in this fight, I will be compelled to share the views of many of my friends that Gompers is too closely allied with the employers of the country." On the motion of the secretary of Local 144 of the cigarmakers' union, the C.F.U. called on the Executive Council to convene a national conference of labor unions to urge that Roosevelt use his influence to obtain a fair trial.

Gompers hastened to New York to defend himself at the next meeting of the Central Federated Union. "How have I been lukewarm?" he asked. "Is it because I haven't stood upon a soapbox on the street corner and howled?" He pointed to his editorial in the *Federationist* and his report to the A.F. of L. convention as evidence of his attitude on the case, and added that he wanted it distinctly understood that "goading and baiting are not the way in which the officers of the A.F. of L. may be influenced."[54] The Denver *Miners' Magazine* commented that Gompers was "peddling hot air" as a substitute for "tangible action." During February and March, Gompers received scores of letters asking him what he would do to strengthen the defense campaign. Gompers replied to all of them with a form letter which stated that "It is the determination of the Executive Council to do anything and everything that it can to be helpful to Messrs. Moyer, Haywood and Pettibone." Again, as proof that he had not been inactive in the case, he referred to his editorial and convention report. It seemed evident to his critics that his statements were intended to thwart criticism while substituting expressions of sympathy for effective action in the case.

On March 18 the A.F. of L. Executive Council met. The pressure of the rank and file impelled them to make a statement, and they adopted a resolution demanding an impartial jury and an unbiased judge, expressed their confidence in the innocence of the defendants, and assured them of "every assistance within our power to the demonstration of their innocence before the world."[55]

On the eve of the trial, President Roosevelt stated in a press conference that Moyer and Haywood were "undesirable citizens." Debs accused him of improper action and charged him with conniving at the legal murder of the two labor leaders. When a reporter asked Gompers about the President's remarks, he said, "I would rather say nothing of that matter. I do think, however, that it would have been better if President Roosevelt had been more discreet." Shortly after, Roosevelt repeated and defended his remark and accused the Moyer-Haywood defense committee of desiring to coerce the court or jury because their slogan was "Death cannot, will not, and shall not claim our brothers." After reading this letter, Gompers commented: "It is a remarkable letter. . . . I do not feel in a position to make any statement just at present, while the discussion is at its heat. This letter will undoubtedly cause a great deal of comment and further discussion, and I must decline to be drawn into it."[56]

The trial of Haywood began on May 9, and for three months the defense campaign mounted in vigor and scope. But Gompers remained silent. On July 23, when he was in St. Louis, a reporter asked him his opinion. "They are not under our jurisdiction," he said. "It would, therefore, be indelicate to say anything about their cases until the courts have passed upon them." In a passionate closing address to the jury, Clarence Darrow warned that the feelings and hopes of the workers could not be crushed out, the Western Federation of Miners could not be strangled by tying a rope around Haywood's neck. If he were killed, a million men would take up the banner of labor at the open grave where he laid it down. If he were martyred, the vultures of Wall Street would send up paeans of praise, but the poor and weak and suffering of the world implored the jury to save his life. On July 28, the jury returned a verdict of not guilty. Pettibone's trial was a mere formality, and the case against Moyer was dismissed.[57]

Gompers congratulated the jury and the American people for maintaining justice. Although he could claim little credit for having helped to achieve it, Gompers had more reason than he knew to be pleased with this victory, for he had already been chosen as the next victim of the National Association of Manufacturers. Within a month he would be called before the bar of justice to defend himself against the charge of criminal contempt.

Part V

PRE-WAR YEARS

1906-1914

Chapter Fifteen

"THE WORLD WOULD BE
A NARROW CAGE"

J. W. Van Cleave, president of the National Association of Manufacturers, continued the aggressive antiunion warfare inaugurated by his predecessor, David Parry. The Stove Founders' National Defense Association, of which he was a member, had a detailed plan of mutual assistance to drive unionism out of the industry. In his own company, the Buck's Stove and Range Company of St. Louis, he determined to establish an open shop. He placed spies in his shop, refused to confer with representatives of the union, and plotted to substitute nonunion for union men. He hoped to provoke the union into an overt act which would excuse cancelling existing contracts between the Founders' Association and the Iron Molders' and Metal Polishers' Union—"those obnoxious agreements that they tried to put upon us."[1] He finally ordered the discontinuance of the nine-hour day in the polishing department. On August 29, 1906, the polishers went on strike to enforce the nine-hour day.

The union declared a boycott against the company, and, following the usual course of inquiry, the Executive Council of the A.F. of L. found that Van Cleave would not consider an adjustment of the dispute. The Council therefore endorsed the boycott and published the name of the company on the "We Don't Patronize" list of the *American Federationist*. The company claimed the boycott was unlawful and calculated to injure its business and that the local unions of St. Louis had declared secondary boycotts against retailers of the company's products. It applied to the Supreme Court of the District of Columbia for an injunction against the A.F. of L., the members of the Executive Council, and the unions involved, to prohibit them from carrying on the "conspiracy" to boycott. The Federation had been looking for an injunction case on which it could make a clear test of the fundamental constitutional questions involved. The Executive Council decided that this was it and determined not to ask for modification of the injunction but to meet it by defending the justification of its actions. The very right to issue injunctions was to be challenged.

Gompers was authorized to represent all the defendants, and on August 29, 1907, he appeared before the court to reply to the bill of complaint. He denied that a company's business was property or a property right, and he therefore had a right to stop any citizen from trading with a given firm, providing he used no illegal means. The constitutional guarantees of free speech and free press precluded any effort to prevent him from inducing others to withhold their patronage. Finally, he urged that if there were to be any limitation or regulation of the right to boycott, that was a legislative function. Until some law was violated, there was nothing upon which a court could pass judgment. "The spirit of self-assertion and resentment of wrongs, real or imaginary, is too generally prevalent in a self-governing people to be subdued or controlled even by police power much less by the courts."

Eight years earlier, in testimony before the United States Industrial Commission, Gompers had presented a thorough exposition of his views on the legality of the boycott. He based his position on the definition of boycotts in Anderson's Law Dictionary: "A combination between persons to suspend or discontinue dealings or patronage with another person or persons because of a refusal to comply with a request of him or them." Gompers pointed to the fact that such a practice was not illegal under the criminal laws of the United States or any of the states. The courts had generally upheld the legality of the primary boycott on the ground that no firm had a vested right or claim to the patronage of its employees. But many courts had held illegal a secondary boycott, that is, a withdrawal of patronage by persons not directly involved in a dispute. Gompers asserted the right of boycotters not only to resort to moral suasion to enlist the aid of others, but the right of outsiders to heed their appeal and, of their own free will, suspend dealings with persons who had incurred the displeasure of their friends. Gompers admitted that it would be illegal to force third parties into a boycott by threatening illegal action but insisted that if a third party refused to join the boycott, the boycotters could suspend dealings with him and transfer their patronage to those who sympathized with them. Since they had a right to suspend dealings, they had a right to threaten it. The principle was the same whether one man acted alone or a vast combination of men acted together. "It is quite possible that this is a crime under the old common law," Gompers concluded. "An agreement to strike for higher wages was a crime in the early days of our Government, under the common law. The common law was vague, obscure, and, as interpreted in less enlightened days, tyrannical. The common law as to strikes has been abandoned, and it will have to be abandoned as to the boycott."[2]

The A.F. of L. denied any conspiracy to boycott or injure the Buck's Stove Company's business or to restrain the sale of its products, or that its "We Don't Patronize" list prohibited any constituent organization or its members from dealing with any person who handled its products. Furthermore, the Federation was a voluntary unincorporated organization and therefore not suable, nor could the individuals named in the complaint be sued as representatives of the Federation. It therefore asked that the case be dismissed.

Judge Ashley M. Gould granted all the company asked and more. He issued a temporary injunction, effective December 23, 1907, restraining the defendants from conspiring, agreeing, or combining in any manner to restrain or destroy the business of the company, from interfering with the sale of its products, from boycotting the company or its agents, from publishing the company's name in the "We Don't Patronize" or "Unfair" list, or from calling attention to the existence of a boycott. He admitted that there was no logical answer to the defendants' claim that people could do in combination what one could do legally, except that the proposition was firmly engrafted upon the traditional practice of the courts. To the defense of freedom of the press, the judge replied that this right did not justify the publication of the "Unfair" list as part of a conspiracy to unlawfully interfere with the company's freedom to trade.[3]

When the injunction was issued, the Federation's attorneys advised Gompers to comply with it because violation would prejudice the case against the defendants in the higher courts. But Gompers contended that if he continued to perform those acts which he had a lawful right to do, even though enjoined from doing them, he would rivet public attention on the injunction procedure and do more than anything else to secure either a favorable decision from the courts or relief from Congress. He would not humiliate himself by "purging himself of contempt," that is by complying with an illegal injunction.[4]

In the October issue of the *American Federationist*, Gompers predicted that long after the National Association of Manufacturers had gone out of existence, the labor movement would still give its patronage to its friends and withhold it from its enemies. "So long as the right of free speech and free press obtains, we shall publish the truth in regard to all matters. . . . If for any reason, at any time, the name of the Buck's Stove and Range Company does not appear upon the 'We Don't Patronize' list . . . all will understand that the right of free speech and free press are denied us; but even this will in no way deprive us . . . from exercising [our] lawful right and privilege of withholding [our] patronage from the Van Cleave company. . . . Until a law is passed making it compulsory upon labor men to buy Van Cleave's stoves we need not buy them, we won't buy them, and we will persuade other fair-minded, sympathetic friends to co-operate with us and leave the blamed things alone. Go to —— with your injunctions."

In a Labor Day speech at the Jamestown Exposition, he declared to the world that when any court undertook, without warrant of law, to deprive him of his constitutional liberties, he would have no hesitancy in asserting and exercising those rights, "all the contesting money power to contrary notwithstanding." John Mitchell, one of Gompers' co-defendants, objected to his statements. He suggested many modifications in his language and lectured him that dignity and restraint were as essential as courage and candor. But Gompers thought the "virile militancy" of labor was more important than dignity.[5]

While Gompers awaited the date when the injunction would go into effect, Miss Guard bought him a small brown rabbit with cork legs. The injunction case reminded her of the stories of Bre'r Rabbit and the repeated efforts to pin him in some inescapable corner. She thought it looked like Gompers because it seemed so wise and canny, had such a glint of knowingness in its eyes and such an all-pervading air of good will and absence of malice. This rabbit became Gompers' mascot; he kept it on his desk and always took it along to the Federation's conventions. In the meantime, he was preparing the January issue of the *Federationist*. Instead of issuing it at the very end of the preceding month, as was his custom, he rushed its publication in order to get it out before the 23rd—this was the last opportunity to publish the Buck's Stove Company on the "We Don't Patronize" list.

On December 23 the temporary injunction went into effect. On the same day Gompers moved the court to amend and correct the order. He claimed that it was erroneous in enjoining the defendants from agreeing not to patronize the company's products and in abridging their freedom of speech and press. While this motion was pending, Gompers went ahead with his decision to assert and exercise his lawful rights. He continued to send out copies of the January *Federationist*, as well as earlier issues, and of the convention proceedings, specifically calling attention to the "We Don't Patronize" list and the name of the Buck's Stove Company. He pointed out that there was no law or court decision compelling people to buy Buck's stoves, adding: "In any event I am not going to buy them and take it for granted that you and our other friends will act likewise."[6]

In the February issue of the magazine he printed the text of the injunction. He prefaced it with a note observing that the N.A.M.'s counsel had declared that punishment for violation of the injunction applied particularly to those in the District of Columbia, and that those who violated it in any other part of the United States could be punished only if they thereafter came to Washington. In an editorial he declared:

"With all due respect to the court *it is impossible for us to see how we can comply with all the terms of this injunction*. A great principle is at stake. Our forefathers sacrificed even life in order that these fundamental constitutional rights of free speech and free press might be forever guaranteed to our people. We would be recreant to our duty did we not do all in our power to point out to the people the serious invasion of their liberties which has taken place. That this has been done by judge-made injunction and not by statute law makes the menace all the greater. . . .

"Justice Gould seems to base this injunction on the *assumption* that there has been a combination of numbers of wage-earners

'conspiring' to commit unlawful acts. *Such is not the fact.*"
Gompers challenged anyone to prove that the defendants had
used coercion to prevent others from purchasing Buck's stoves.
They had simply performed a public service by informing their
fellow workers of the fact that certain employers refused to recognize the associated efforts of the workers; the workers were free
to use their own judgment, to patronize those employers or not.
Gould admitted that workers had the right individually or collectively to decline to buy the company's stoves or to traffic with
dealers who handled them. But this, asserted Gompers, was the
whole case of the A.F. of L.; that was all the defendants had done.[7]

On January 30, Gompers appeared in court to give testimony
on making the injunction permanent. But it was evident that the
attorneys for the Buck's Stove and Range Company were more
interested in proving that Gompers had violated the injunction
than in showing why it should be extended. Daniel Davenport,
attorney for the Anti-Boycott Association which supported the
Buck's Stove Company in this case, called attention to Gompers'
assertions that the company would continue to be regarded as
unfair whether or not its name appeared on the "We Don't
Patronize" list. Gompers explained that this was merely an editorial expression of opinion and not an official notice and did not
conflict with his statement that no notice referring to the company
as "unfair" had appeared in the *American Federationist* since
May 1907. Davenport asked him if he had sent out copies of the
December issue or of the convention proceedings after the date
the injunction became effective. Gompers admitted that he had,
but did not know if any had been distributed in the District of
Columbia. Davenport retorted that he had a copy of it in his files.

"Mr. Davenport," Gompers replied with an injured expression, "you asked me to send you the *American Federationist* and I
did you the courtesy of sending it to you gratuitously."

Davenport jumped to his feet: "That I move to strike out as
utterly irresponsive to any question that has been propounded to
you by myself."

"Well, it is a fact," Gompers shot back scornfully. "You ought
not to induce me to violate the terms of the injunction."

Davenport asked him about his report to the 1897 convention
of the Federation, in which he had suggested that in case any

boycott was restrained, the unions should announce that "We have been enjoined by the courts from boycotting this concern." Gompers declared that he had never withdrawn that suggestion and would affirm it again now. Davenport then asked him if the company was published on the "We Don't Patronize" list in the January issue.

"A. Yes, sir.

"Q. In the February number would it have been published, except for the injunction?

"A. I do not know. That is a question depending—it is hypothetization.

"Q. I wish you would search your conscience on this, Mr. Gompers.

"A. My dear brother, I would say that, in reference to my conscience, I think it will bear as close scrutiny as yours.

"Q. Oh, that is immaterial.

"A. So is your question."[8]

On March 23, 1908, the injunction was made permanent, and Gompers filed an appeal in the Court of Appeals of the District. He claimed that the lower court had erred in two principal respects. First, Judge Gould had assumed the existence of malice, but the motives of the defendants were immaterial as long as they acted within their rights, as they had. Second, the court erred in finding certain acts unlawful, such as boycotting and engaging in unlawful combination, publication of the company as unfair, coercing or threatening persons not to buy the company's product, and impeding the company's business. In addition, the decree had infringed upon the constitutional guarantees of free speech and free press. Finally, the court had committed a legal error, for the A.F. of L., as an unincorporated body, had no legal entity and could not be sued.[9]

Four months later, the Buck's Stove Company petitioned the Supreme Court of the District of Columbia to judge Gompers, Mitchell, and Morrison in contempt of court, alleging that they had continued the boycott and conspiracy in violation of the injunction. The court ordered them to show cause why they should not be so adjudged. Gompers admitted that he had discussed orally and editorially both the suit and the principles involved in the injunction. But he could not conceive that any injunction could prohibit the free discussion of fundamental questions involving such basic issues as constitutional rights. He had removed the company's name from the "We Don't Patronize" list. What else would the court have him do? he asked. Could he be prohibited from publishing the news of the day and commenting on it simply because he was concerned as an interested party? "What hope can our people entertain for reform at the hands of the law-making bodies for any evils unless the freedom of the press and of speech be maintained at all hazards?"[10] Besides, he could not restrain himself from discussing the case even if he wanted to. On September 29, he told an audience in Indianapolis:

". . . . I want to say this to you, and to all that it may concern, that so long as I retain my health and my sanity, I am going to speak upon any subject on God's green earth. . . . I have not yet surrendered, and I am not likely to surrender, the fight of the freedom of speech and the freedom of the press, and let the consequences be what they may, before I get through this evening . . . I shall discuss the merits of the Buck's Stove and Range Company injunction. . . .

". . . . if the injunction is strictly construed and enforced, I am in contempt of court again for telling you that, but I propose to discuss this thing. . . . I can't help it. I must discuss it. I will explode if I don't, and I don't want to go to jail, but I prefer that to exploding. . . ."[11]

Gompers again tangled with Davenport when the latter examined him before the bench. Davenport asked him if he furnished any copies of the January issue of the *Federationist* to the Washington News Company, which distributed it. Gompers replied in the affirmative, but repeated several times that he did not know how many.

"Q. Is your mind blank on that point?

"A. I resent the insinuation, that you are speaking of my mind as being a blank.

"Q. I do not think that is very serious.

"A. It doesn't make a particle of difference. I want you to address me in a respectful manner.

"Q. I will ask the question, is your mind a blank on that subject?

"A. That is an impertinent question."

Gompers finally answered that he did not recall giving any direction for the number of copies to be furnished to the news agency. Davenport then called attention to several instances in which Gompers had referred to the Buck's Stove Company as being on the "Unfair" list. Gompers asserted that the use of that term was a mistake; he really meant to say that it was on the "We Don't Patronize" list, which was simply a statement of fact and did not urge or request anyone to do anything at all. Davenport then turned to another matter:

"Q. Was [Mitchell] not here in Washington on the day that the subpoena was served upon you?

"A. I have already said that if you will let me ascertain, I can do so in a moment and tell you.

"Q. If it is necessary in order to ascertain such a simple fact as that, do so, and do it now.

"A. I protest against the language you use. . . .

"Q. Mr. Gompers, I don't want to have you lumber up this record with all such irrelevant matter.

"A. You want to do it all yourself, do you?"

Davenport tried to find out exactly how many copies of the January issue were printed, to whom they were sent, and when. Gompers was not very co-operative in supplying this information but admitted that he had made no effort to recall from the post-office or the news agency any copies that had not been sent out when the injunction became effective, nor did he give specific directions that no more copies should be sent. Davenport asked him about the statement with which he prefaced the publication of the injunction in the February issue. Gompers denied that his intention was to encourage violation of the order; it was merely to give information and was based on an opinion by Davenport himself. "Your opinions are always so very valuable to me that I thought they would be valuable to the working people of the country." When questioned about the editorial in which he wrote, "Go to —— with your injunctions," Gompers explained that this was simply the use of the classical phrase, "Go to," meaning "Oh pshaw." Davenport called attention to numerous statements in various labor papers which stated:

IT IS UNLAWFUL TO

BOYCOTT THE BUCK'S STOVE AND RANGE CO.

He tried to show that these notices were published in accordance with the suggestion made by Gompers in his report to the convention of 1897. He also noted Gompers' report to the Executive Council in January, in which he reported on the issuance of his circular to organized labor and stated that the Council had been kept advised of all steps that had been taken with regard to the matter. This was intended to demonstrate that Gompers was continuing the conspiracy to carry out the boycott.

One month after these hearings Gompers made an address at Baltimore. He declared: ". . . . I am enjoined from telling you I won't buy a Buck's Stove or range. But I won't buy one just the same. I am enjoined from telling you there is no law compelling you to buy one; but there isn't such a law.

"Because of this case I am on trial, and may have to go to jail. There is no fun in going to jail, and I don't want to go, for no man would feel more keenly the sting of having his liberty restrained. But the whole world would be a narrow cage were I denied the freedom of speech. . . . jail or no jail, I'm going to discuss the principles of it."[12]

On December 23, 1908, Gompers, Mitchell, and Morrison appeared in court to hear Justice Daniel Thew Wright's decision on the contempt charge. Gompers described the dramatic scene: ". . . . Justice Wright directed that three seats be placed side by side and directly facing him. The 'culprits' were ordered to occupy them. It was at once apparent to all in the crowded court room, including the defendants, who were so deeply interested, that the flashing eyes, the twitching lips, and the contemptuous frown of Justice Wright but poorly concealed a volcano of surging, relentless hatred. The judge sat in silent attitude for fully a minute, riveting his fierce gaze upon the defendants. It was quite evident that the judge intended to make them quake or quail and to work himself up to the pitch to sound the defendants' condemnation. At last he found his voice. It came in low, quivering, yet incisive tones. As he progressed with the delivery of his decision his voice rose and fell. At times it was pitched to a high key, at others it was scarcely more than the moving of his lips with teeth set fast, hissing his bitter invective."[13]

Wright upheld all the contentions of the company's attorneys. He maintained that the A.F. of L. coerced union members and dealers into supporting the boycott in order to destroy the business of the company and that the defendants had unlawfully combined to restrain trade and commerce among the states. They had set in motion the machinery to continue the boycott before the injunction was issued, and continued the conspiracy afterward. "[T]he position of the respondents involves questions vital to the preservation of social order," he declared, "questions which smite the foundations of civil government, and upon which the supremacy of law over anarchy and riot verily depend. . . . Are decrees of courts to look for their execution to the supremacy of law, or tumble in the wake of unsuccessful suitors who overset them and lay about the matter with their own hands, in turbulence proportioned to the frenzy of their disappointment?" Even if the injunction were erroneous, Wright contended, "yet it must have been obeyed." The issue involved, he concluded, was "between the supremacy of law over the rabble or its prostration under the feet of the disordered throng. . . . There is a studied, determined, defiant conflict precipitated in the light of open day, between the decrees of a tribunal ordained by the Government of the Federal Union, and of the tribunals of another federation, grown up in the land; one or the other must succumb, for those who would unlaw the land are public enemies. . . ."[14]

While Wright was reading his opinion, Mitchell and Morrison listened with self-possession, apparently indifferent, and a trace of scorn on their lips. But Gompers, always emotional, seemed to be cut by every statement uttered by the youthful judge. Astonishment and grief were visible on his face; he turned pale and red by turns, constantly shifting his position, and his lips worked involuntarily, as though constantly suppressing his urge to protest the unfair declarations from the bench. After reading his decision, Wright asked if the defendants had anything to say why judgment should not be passed. Gompers rose and addressed the bench in a soft voice:

"Yes, sir. Your honor, I am not conscious at any time during my life of having violated any law of the country or of the District in which I live. I would not consciously violate a law now or at any time during my whole life. . . . the freedom of speech and the freedom of the press has not been granted to the people in order that they may say the things which please, and which are based upon accepted thought, *but the right to say the things which displease*, the right to say the things which may convey the new and yet unaccepted thoughts, the right to say things, even though they do a wrong, for one can not be guilty of giving utterance to any expression which may do a wrong if he is by an injunction enjoined from so saying. It then will devolve upon a judge upon the bench to determine in advance a man's right to express his opinion in speech and in print. . . .

"I may say, your honor, that this is a struggle of the working people of our country, a struggle for rights. . . . it is a struggle of the ages, a struggle of the men of labor to throw off some of the burdens which have been heaped upon them, to abolish some of the wrongs which they have too long borne and to secure some of the rights too long denied.

"If men must suffer because they dare speak for the masses of our country . . . then they must bear the consequences. . . .

"I say this to you, your honor, I would not have you to believe me to be a man of defiant character, in disposition, in conduct. Those who know me, and know me best, know that that is not my makeup; but in the pursuit of honest conviction, conscious of having violated no law, and in furtherance of the common interests of my fellow-men, I shall not only have to but be willing to submit to whatever sentence your honor may impose."[15]

After hearing this statement, Judge Wright proceeded to pass sentence, which was unprecedented both as to the nature of the acts which were held as contemptuous and as to the length of the sentence. Morrison was sentenced to six months in the United States jail in the District of Columbia, Mitchell to nine months, and Gompers to twelve months. They appealed to the Court of Appeals and were released on bail of $3,000, $4,000, and $5,000, respectively. Although he had no doubt of what was coming, Gompers seemed almost dazed when the vindictive words were actually uttered, and tears flowed down his cheeks. The idea that he, who had striven so hard to make himself and the labor movement conform to the highest ideals of Americanism and to win the favor of the American public by a conservative policy, should be convicted and sent to jail as a law breaker was a blow to his ego, his ambitions, and the goal of his life. But he quickly got over the hurt as he prepared to fight the verdict. "If we must go to jail we shall," he told a Lincoln's Birthday rally in Lincoln, Nebraska. "Better men than we have gone to jail. If they must have their pound of flesh they may have it, but they won't find any yellow streaks in it."

This issue solidified Gompers' leadership in the labor movement as did no other in his entire career. He received hundreds of letters and telegrams pledging support in his fight for his own liberty, the rights of labor, and the freedom of speech of the American people. Many of these came from socialists, including some of his bitterest antagonists. J. Mahlon Barnes, the national secretary of the Socialist party and a co-delegate of the Cigarmakers International Union, praised his determined course of opposition to the injunction infamy, stating that public contempt for autocracy would insure free speech and a free press. Gompers was grateful for his expression and hoped the injunction fight might help to unite the labor movement in the struggle for human liberty.[16]

In writing an editorial comment on his sentence, Gompers realized that he might be held in additional contempt but declared, more unequivocally than he had previously, that it might be necessary to disobey a judge in order to preserve freedom of the press. "Judges sometimes usurp power and become tyrants. Disobedience to a tyrant is obedience to law." He insisted that if anything he wrote or said was unlawful, libelous, or damaging, the only legal punishment lay in a suit for damages and a trial by jury, in which not only the fact of the spoken or written words would be passed upon, but also the truth and justification of those words. This was the only process authorized by the Constitution of the United States. What had started out as a labor dispute had been transformed into the much broader question of whether the traditions and guarantees of American liberties would be destroyed.[17]

In March 1909, the appeal from the injunction reached the Court of Appeals. Justice Robb, delivering the opinion of that court, found no room for doubt that the boycott was inaugurated and pursued in accordance with the policy of the A.F. of L., and the defendants were therefore clearly responsible for the unlawful coercion of the firm. As for the claim that the injunction infringed upon constitutional rights of free speech and press, Robb held that the restraint of acts in furtherance of the unlawful boycott did not constitute such abridgment. However, he continued, the decree went too far when it enjoined the publication and distribution of any reference to the company, its business, or product. The court properly enjoined publication of the "Unfair" list but had no control over other matter. When the conspiracy was ended by the cessation of the "Unfair" list, the Federation had the same right as any other organization or individual to comment upon the relations of the company with its employees. The court therefore affirmed so much of the original injunction as related to the boycott, but voided those portions relating to the subject of writing, speaking, and printing.

Justice Josiah A. Van Orsdel wrote a separate opinion concurring with Robb but going much further in his criticism of the lower court. He asserted that the injunction was a means to protect rights and restrain wrongs where there was no remedy at law. But it could never be used as an instrument of oppression, as a short cut to escape the inconvenience of a suit at law, to avoid a jury trial, or above all as a means to nullify constitutional guarantees. As far as the boycott was concerned, Van Orsdel ruled, it was just as legal as the strike, and the exercise of that right, though causing injury to others, could not be prevented by the law. The property right of a man in his business was no more sacred than the right of a man or a number of men not to patronize a certain firm, to agree together not to do so, and to advise others to do likewise. The sustaining of the decree, he concluded, would mark the beginning of an era of judicial tyranny. ". . . it would be difficult to conceive of a more effective method of establishing a government censorship than through the writ of injunction. . . ." Chief Justice Shepard wrote a dissenting opinion which completely sustained the arguments which Gompers had made concerning the legality of the boycott and the abuse of the injunction.[18] Both sides appealed from this ruling, the company petitioning for a restoration of the original terms of the injunction, and Gompers appealing for its complete nullification.

Gompers' case in the contempt proceedings was strengthened by the modification of the injunction. His attorneys, in appealing against the sentence, pointed to the established principle that part of a decree could be voided and the remainder allowed to survive only when the valid provisions formed a perfect and complete whole. But in this case the various acts were so interwoven that they could not be separated. The purpose of the order was not solely to restrain the publication of the "We Don't Patronize" list. It was interpreted to mean that the mere publication of the injunction was a violation of the decree. And Gompers' editorials, aimed entirely against the attempt to restrain free speech and not at all against the boycotting provisions of the injunction, were taken by Judge Wright as conclusive evidence of a violation of the order. Since the sentences were based on violations of the void provisions of the injunction as well as the valid portions, they could not be affirmed.[19]

But Justices Van Orsdel and Robb brushed these arguments aside by ruling that the valid part of the injunction, that is, the order against continuing the boycott, had been violated. The only question, therefore, was whether those actions constituted contempt of court. They proceeded to rule in the affirmative on that question, not because of any actions in furtherance of the boycott, but because the defendants criticized the injunction! The sentence was justified because the defendants had made remarks which tended to "inflame their followers into a feeling of resentment to the decree of the court and lead to disobedience of its commands. . . . If a citizen, though he may honestly believe that his rights have been invaded, may elect when, and to what extent, he will obey the mandates of the court and the requirements of the law as interpreted by the court, instead of pursuing the orderly course of appeal, not only the courts, but government itself, would become powerless, and society would soon be reduced to a state of anarchy." Chief Justice Shepard again dissented, pointing out that there was no allegation in the petition that the defendants had, after the date the injunction became effective, committed any act enforcing the boycott, which was the only valid portion of the injunction. All the defendants had done was to state that the injunction did not compel anyone to purchase the goods of the company, and that was a true statement of a fact. The severity of the sentences indicated that the lower court had based its judgment on other charges than those actually in violation of the injunction, on acts committed before the order became effective and those in violation of the parts of the injunction later eliminated. Therefore, in his opinion, the injunction, which was rendered in excess of the power of the court, was absolutely void and the sentences based on it should be reversed.[20]

Shortly after the Court of Appeals upheld the sentences against Gompers, Morrison, and Mitchell, the A.F. of L. met in its annual convention. Gompers reported the verdict that he was compelled to obey the court's decree whether it was right or wrong, valid or invalid. He repeated that when a judge invaded constitutional rights, it was the duty of the citizen to refuse obedience and to take whatever consequences may ensue. "We have come too far in the march of human progress for any set of influences to drive us back into slavery."[21] The convention unanimously upheld Gompers' course.

When his name was put in nomination for re-election to the presidency, pandemonium broke loose for five minutes. The delegates yelled themselves hoarse with cries of "Gompers! Gompers!" Then the unanimous vote of the convention was cast for the Chief, and for fifteen minutes more men cheered and shouted and cried, and a parade started marching around the hall. Finally the "old man" himself came forward and raised his hand for silence. With hand still uplifted he stood still and his lips moved, but there came no sound as tears streamed down his cheeks. Twice he tried to speak and finally articulated: "I can't—I can't." He buried his face in his hands and retreated from view. Mamma Gompers, sitting near the stage, sobbed like a child at this demonstration of loyalty and commendation. Mrs. Gompers' emotional upset also reflected the severe anxiety induced by her apprehension regarding the outcome of the case. She became obsessed by fears for her husband's safety and scarcely talked about anything else. Finally she became seriously ill and suffered a nervous collapse, was confined to bed with excruciating pain, was delirious much of the time, and had continual fears for her husband.[22]

Nearly a year later, while the cases were still pending before the Supreme Court, a new development arose. Van Cleave died and was replaced as president of the Buck's Stove and Range Company by Frederick Gardner. The new management of the company declared its desire to treat with organized labor on a friendly basis and authorized the Stove Founders' Defense Association to negotiate for the company. Gompers, representatives of the company, and the four unions involved in the dispute agreed to

settle wages, hours, and conditions of employment, based on conditions existing in competing firms operating union shops. The
labor organizations promised to call off the boycott, and the company agreed to withdraw its attorneys from all cases pending
in the courts.[23]

This did not close those cases, but Gompers feared that the
Supreme Court might be led to dismiss the appeals without passing
on the principles for which he was contending. In order to avoid
that, he persuaded the company to withdraw that clause in the
agreement withdrawing its attorneys. Gompers stated later that if
he had suspected that the agreement with the company would
interfere with the court's passing on the principles involved in the
injunction and contempt cases he would never have consented to
the agreement until after the cases had been decided. The Federation's attorneys urged Gompers to request the Supreme Court to
dismiss the cases, since it would probably not be willing to rule
on the injunction but might nevertheless uphold the sentences for
contempt. But Gompers, Mitchell, and Morrison rejected the
suggestion and insisted that the case be fought through to the end.
"It is farthest from our minds to attempt the role of martyrs,"
they told their attorneys, "but there are other considerations
equally important, and one is that we shall not carry to our graves
the consciousness of cowardice and poltroonery."[24]

Gompers' fears were justified, for when the Supreme Court
considered the validity of the injunction, it ruled that the questions
involved had become moot and dismissed the appeals.[25] On February 20, 1911, that court refused to disturb the terms of the injunction as modified by the Court of Appeals. There remained for
consideration only the appeal from the sentences for contempt of
court. Davenport pleaded for justice for the Buck's Stove and
Range Company—"this poor company, this unfortunate company, this victim of this outrageous conspiracy"—although the
company no longer had any grievance, Davenport's services being
paid for by the Anti-Boycott Association. "A more infamous
combination to violate every law of God and man was never
attempted or consummated," he thundered. Gompers' main contention was that the injunction, being a violation of the constitutional guarantee of free speech and free press, was invalid, and
consequently no sentence on charges of violating that injunction

could be upheld. He insisted that no evidence had been produced to show that he and his co-defendants had continued a boycott after December 23, 1908, at least not a secondary boycott.[26]

Justice Joseph R. Lamar, delivering the opinion of the Supreme Court, declined to consider the constitutional questions of free speech and free press because, he stated, the injunction did not restrain any form of publication. The only question involved was the power of a court of equity to enjoin a boycott which caused or threatened irreparable damage. He admitted that the courts of the United States differed as to what constituted a boycott that could be enjoined. But if a boycott was enjoinable, then any means used to continue the boycott, including the publication of any printed matter, constituted a violation of the injunction. Constitutional guarantees could not protect the use of words when they were employed as instrumentalities for effecting an illegal purpose. Otherwise the law would be rendered impotent. Lamar therefore accepted the findings of the lower court that property was unlawfully damaged by the boycott and upheld the injunction.

Turning to the question as to whether the defendants disobeyed the injunction and were therefore in contempt of court, Justice Lamar found it necessary to determine whether the proceedings were for civil or criminal contempt. The lower court ruled that it was a case of criminal contempt, requiring a punitive sentence. But the Supreme Court could not concur in that judgment, finding nothing in the record to indicate that the case involved the government on one side and the defendants on the other. On the contrary, the contempt proceedings were instituted, tried, and treated as part of the original cause in equity. The Buck's Stove and Range Company was the only party in opposition to the defendants, and remained so in the present hearings before the Supreme Court. The civil nature of the case was further indicated by the fact that the company petitioned for relief, not for punishment. The only relief it could have had was a fine payable to the company. But instead of providing remedial relief for the company, the lower court had imposed a punitive sentence appropriate only to a proceeding for criminal contempt. This was beyond the court's power, for since the original cause of equity had been settled, every proceeding which was dependent on it was also settled. Therefore, the sentences were reversed and the lower court ordered to dismiss the contempt proceedings instituted by the Buck's Stove Company. However, Lamar pointed out, this did not prejudice the right or duty of the court to itself institute criminal contempt proceedings for violation of its injunction.[27]

Thus the original injunction and the civil contempt case arising out of it came to an end. Gompers was greatly disappointed with the decision. He would have preferred to have the court affirm the jail sentences rather than to free him and his colleagues on a technicality. The defendants would now have to go through the whole proceeding again, with all the expenditures of time, energy, and money, with an almost certain verdict of guilty, and with little possibility that they could urge the principles for which they had made this a test case.

This was exactly what "Gompers et al." had in store for them, for the Supreme Court of the District of Columbia immediately acted upon the suggestion of Justice Lamar to institute criminal contempt proceedings against them. On the very next day after the Supreme Court decision, Judge Wright ordered an inquiry to be made by J. J. Darlington, Daniel Davenport, and James Beck. The first two were the original prosecutors in the injunction and contempt proceedings, in the employ of the American Anti-Boycott Association, and Beck was counsel for the National Association of Manufacturers. On June 26, 1911, this committee reported to the court that it had found sufficient evidence to warrant prosecution of the three men for contempt. Justice Wright then appointed the same three men to serve as prosecutors.

After presenting its charges, the prosecuting committee suggested that Gompers might now be prepared to purge himself of contempt by making "such due acknowledgment, apology and assurance of further submission to the court as may sufficiently answer the necessary purpose of vindicating its authority, and that of the law." Gompers rejected this offer as "an effort to humiliate me and break my heart and break my spirit." Repeatedly pressed to buy his immunity with an apology, Gompers sturdily refused. He commented later that he did not refuse submission to lawful orders, nor did he contemptuously defy lawful and constitutional authority. "Quite the contrary, our publicly avowed and most earnest purpose has ever been to uphold and strengthen lawful and constitutional authority, to protect it against any invasion, yea, even against the courts themselves or the resentment of private vengeance. We would make law supreme. We would protect it against the abuses of discretionary power. We have asked for no mercy, only justice—justice for ourselves, for the toilers, for all humanity. . . . We have nothing to modify, nothing to retract, nothing for which to make an explanation, much less an apology. We stood and stand for free speech and free press, be the consequences what they may."[28]

After hearing testimony and arguments which went over the same ground as in the first proceeding, Justice Wright delivered an opinion which was even more biased and vindictive than before. The young judge apparently felt that he had to send Gompers, Mitchell, and Morrison to jail not only to vindicate the authority of the court but to assert his own authority over rebellion. He cited numerous acts, speeches, and publications, many of which had been made years before the issuance of the injunction and some of which were done by people other than the defendants themselves, and found that they constituted an expression of hostility and defiance to the courts and a "revolutionary determination" to thwart the purposes of justice. He asserted that the powers and processes of the court were "over, above, and beyond the law," and that the "defiant, unsubmissive attitude of the defendants to that power and those processes continues at this moment as militant as before." Wright proceeded to order "that the said Samuel Gompers be confined in the prison of the Washington Asylum and Jail for and during the period of twelve months. . . ." Morrison was sentenced to six months and Mitchell to three months.[29]

In an editorial review of the case, Gompers compared Wright's doctrine to that of the divine right of kings.[30] But by now, he, Mitchell, and Morrison had had their bellies full of the injunction and contempt cases. They now came around to the opinion of their attorneys and agreed to seek dismissal of the proceedings. They appealed Wright's decision to the Court of Appeals, not on grounds of the right to boycott or the right to exercise free speech and press without the interference of injunctions, but mainly on technicalities. The most important of these were the claims that the statute of limitations barred any further prosecution of the alleged acts of contempt and that the punishments meted out were cruel and unusual.

Justice Van Orsdel of the Court of Appeals ruled that the statue of limitations did not apply to contempt proceedings, which were neither civil nor criminal in character, but in a class by themselves! He concurred with Wright's findings that Gompers, Mitchell, and Morrison had violated the injunction, and held that they were in contempt for violating not only the valid portions of the injunction, but even for violating those parts of it which Van Orsdel himself had declared to be beyond the power of the court, the matters pertaining to speaking and writing. The only sane feature in this Alice-in-Wonderland scene was the court's conclusion that the punishment was unusual and excessive, because after the settlement of the original dispute a severe sentence was not necessary to secure compliance with the orders of the court. It therefore reversed Wright's judgment and instructed him to impose sentences of thirty days for Gompers and $500 each for Mitchell and Morrison.[31]

Justice Wright then took another unprecedented step. He filed a petition in the Supreme Court of the United States, asking it to review the decision of the Court of Appeals. Gompers also petitioned for the issuance of a writ of certiorari to the Supreme Court. Just one year later, Justice Oliver Wendell Holmes read the opinion of the Supreme Court. He "assumed" that the evidence required a finding that the defendants were guilty of at least some of the violations of the injunction that were charged against them, and stated that their only real defense was the statute of limitations. He ruled that the contempt charges were criminal offenses and were therefore covered by that statute. Since all charges against the defendants were more than three years old, the judgment was reversed.[32]

Thus, after seven years of litigation, the Buck's Stove and Range case wound to a dull finish. As Gompers commented, "the judiciary has refused to pass upon the great human issues involved in the case. The principles of justice have been lost in the maze of legalism. Instead of clearing aside everything that would in any way interfere with justice, technicalities and legal quibbles were allowed to obscure the great things and were used to avoid deciding the big issues. Since reform of the abuses of the injunctive process can not be secured by a legal decision ... the workers must rely upon other methods. These reforms must be secured by an act of legislation."[33]

Chapter Sixteen

"REWARD YOUR FRIENDS"

1. LABOR'S GRIEVANCES AND PROTEST

FOR TWO DECADES GOMPERS HAD BEEN ABLE TO KEEP the A.F. of L. to the pure and simple path of "no politics in the unions and no unions in politics," confining its political activities to lobbying for labor legislation. But this nonpolitical, or "nonpartisan," policy was a failure. Labor got nothing but the runaround, as Gompers told the House Committee on Labor in 1900. "There is not anywhere that we can go for the purpose of trying to bring about some remedy, some change, some improvement but we are met by the same position . . . prompted by the same motive, and that is to leave the workmen helpless to the mercy of the employing class. I think, though, I may say that that time has gone by. The workingmen of our country have learned somewhat of their rights, and they propose to stand by them, and they have the courage to do so, too."[1]

The Federation was being forced by its failures into a more positive political policy, and being encouraged to do so by the spirit of the times. Even though middle-class reformers had only a moderate interest in union aspirations—and laborers shared their middle-class aspirations—they all gained from the great reform wave a keener sense of their constitutional rights and legitimate human expectations. And with the popular magazines vibrant with criticisms of municipal, state, and national legislators, and reporting the deeds of political reformers, from Joseph W. Folk in St. Louis to Robert M. La Follette in Wisconsin, it was not surprising that the Federation developed a more aggressive sense of their need to influence congressmen and others in high office. At the 1905 convention, Gompers again reported the failure of Congress to enact measures desired by labor and declared that he held the Republican party, as the majority party, responsible for ignoring labor's demands. This was a step in advance, for he had previously held only individual congressmen responsible. But he urged only a continuation and extension of the system of questioning candidates, opposing the enemies of labor, and electing those who were friendly to labor legislation.[2] However, he soon decided that other measures were necessary. The composition of the new Congress and Roosevelt's message gave little hope that any labor measures would be enacted. Another barren year was in sight.

Gompers called a conference of the Executive Council and the presidents of all affiliated international unions to meet in Washington on March 21, 1906. The labor leaders adopted a Bill of Grievances drawn up by Gompers. They protested that the eight-hour law was ineffective, was being grievously and frequently violated, and was not applied to the work on the Panama Canal. They complained that labor had urged in vain the enactment of laws to safeguard it from the competition of convict labor and from induced and "undesirable" immigration, that the Chinese exclusion act was being flagrantly violated and now threatened with invalidation, that the seamen were denied their freedom, and a disposition was shown to extend compulsory labor to other workers. The antitrust laws, the protest continued, had been perverted to invade the personal liberty of the workers; the abuse of injunctions continued; and government employees had been forbidden to petition Congress for redress of grievances.

"We present these grievances to your attention," the labor leaders told Congress and the President, "because we have long, patiently, and in vain waited for redress. . . . Labor now appeals to you, and we trust that it may not be in vain. But if, perchance, you may not heed us, we shall appeal to the conscience and the support of our fellow citizens."[3]

Gompers sent a copy of the Bill of Grievances to each member of Congress and to the President, who promised only to enforce the eight-hour law. A week later Gompers led a delegation to see Roosevelt personally. The President received them in his usual belligerent manner and rejected their demands as either unnecessary or impossible.[4] The Speaker of the House, Joseph Cannon, was even more patronizing and antagonistic when the Bill of Grievances was presented to him. He insisted that the composition of the committees was fair and impartial, although it was well known that his appointment of reactionaries to committee posts was one of the principal means by which he dominated the House and kept the lid on all progressive and labor legislation. When Gompers pointed out this fact, Cannon shouted: "You are not the whole thing. You are not the only pebbles on the beach." Gompers replied: "We are just a few pebbles whom you ought to consider and whether we are small or large, influential or impotent, at least our earnest requests ought to be given favorable consideration." Cannon abruptly ended the interview with some rather "lurid" language.[5] "Czar" Cannon had little idea of the day of wrath which was being prepared for him by Progressive statesmen and also by the labor leaders whom he presumed to despise.

Reactionary politicians and press denounced Gompers and the Federation for their intrusion into politics. The Los Angeles Times, for example, stated that Gompers proposed to establish "government by intimidation" in place of government by injunction. The Cincinnati Commercial Tribune accused him of desiring a "class Congress and a class judiciary," legislating and construing laws on his dictation.[6] These accusations infuriated Gompers. He gave vent to his feelings before the House Committee on Labor:

"Some men have said that we are indulging in threats, because we have expressed our dissatisfaction . . . because we dared to say that our patience has been tested to the limit. . . . For Heaven's sake, when has it become a crime or an offense for an American citizen to express his preference for one Congressman or another? I imagine that it is not so grave an offense for the workingmen to exercise their sovereign political power accorded to them equally with all other citizens, in furtherance of their interests or in furtherance of the principles in which they believe.

". . . . we find that Congress has turned a deaf ear to our complaint. . . . What shall we do—continue to come here year after year and year after year and decade after decade, and still go back reporting to the men who selected us to come here and present their claims: 'Defeat! Defeat! Nothing accomplished.'?"[7]

Some unionists likewise took an exaggerated view of what Gompers was actually doing. The organ of the Texas Federation of Labor, for instance, saw in the Federation's political campaign the beginning of the end of pure and simple unionism. "Pres. Gompers," it asserted, "has at last realized that to be successful, the unions must have the government with them, and to have the government they must elect members of their class. . . . But the new unionism involves another idea. It involves the idea of 'class struggle'. . . . Gompers has been forced to see the class struggle."[8]

But Gompers made it quite clear that his plans were strictly limited. "I don't look for the millenium through the ballot box," he said. "What we want to accomplish in politics is to take the hand of the oppressor of organized labor from our throats," and leave the workers free to fight out their economic problems in the economic field. Nor did he want the political campaign to overshadow the economic activities of the trade union movement. He asserted that he would rather have the campaign doomed to absolute failure than to see it develop into an all-pervading movement to the neglect of the economic effort; for whatever success labor had achieved, including its political activity, was due primarily to trade unionism pure and simple.[9]

On July 22, the Executive Council issued its official statement on the coming political campaign, pointing up the need of working people to maintain and advance their position by organizing for the exercise of their political as well as their economic functions. Congress and the administration had turned a deaf ear to labor's demands, and, true to the promise of the Bill of Grievances, the Federation was appealing to the American people to supplant aristocracy with democracy, to elect men more honest, faithful, and progressive than those then in power. "Labor demands a distinctive and larger share in the governmental affairs of our country; it demands justice; it will be satisfied with nothing less." The circular outlined the plan worked out by the Council: actually a series of recommendations to be carried out by central bodies and local unions. They were urged to endorse candidates who would support labor and progressive measures, and above all to defeat those who had been hostile or indifferent to them. If both parties ignored labor's legislative demands, a straight labor candidate should be nominated. But this must be only a last resort, Gompers emphasized. To co-ordinate the work of the local unions, question candidates on their program, publish their records, and furnish campaign literature, a Labor Representation Committee was established, consisting of Gompers, James O'Connell, and Frank Morrison.[10]

Gompers decided personally to help defeat Congressman Charles Littlefield of Maine, an antilabor partisan who had been conspicuous during the defeat of labor's bill to exempt the unions from the Sherman Antitrust Act. Overbearing and rude in his attitude toward labor's spokesmen, he had had several run-ins with Gompers. Since the Maine election was earlier than others and regarded as a political barometer, his defeat could have significance in the campaign in other parts of the country. In July Gompers sent organizers to prepare for the campaign, and the next month he delivered thirteen speeches in different Maine cities during a three-week period.

Gompers' campaign in the Littlefield contest alarmed such organs as the New York *Journal of Commerce*; if Littlefield were defeated, practically any representative could be "coerced" into submitting to labor's wishes. "This would mean that an almost intolerable state of affairs would grow up, and that the tyranny of labor interests would be as intense in the House as that of the capitalistic forces in the Senate." The Republican party anxiously sent its big guns into the district to bolster Littlefield. Secretary of War Taft, Senator Lodge, Speaker Cannon, and others, including Senator Albert J. Beveridge (a striking compound of Progressivism and party loyalty), sought to discredit the labor fight. Lodge, though a Republican stalwart, wrote Roosevelt that the question of whether a Republican or Democrat was elected was insignificant compared to the question "whether Gompers shall dictate the choice of Congressmen." Roosevelt himself said in a letter to Maine that Littlefield's defeat would be a national calamity. He also issued an order in the midst of the Maine campaign that the eight-hour law be applied to contract work for the government. The Boston *Herald* interpreted this action as a bow to labor's strength, commenting that "Gompers seems to have got the administration on the run." The National Association of Manufacturers gave strong financial backing to the Republican campaign fund, as did the commercial, railroad, and shipping trusts.[11]

While the Republicans denounced Gompers' campaign as a step toward labor dictation of American political life, the socialists attacked it because of its halfway measures. Shortly after the adoption of the Bill of Grievances, Gompers was invited back to his cigarmakers' union, Local 144, to debate the subject "Can Trade Unions Longer Keep Out of Politics?" with Morris Brown, the union's socialist secretary. Brown insisted that the "nonpartisan" policy was doomed to failure because it kept the workers within the confines of the two-party system, both of which represented capitalistic interests. Labor must organize its own party or support the Socialist party. "There are some men," Gompers replied, "who can never understand political action unless there is a party. As a matter of fact, there is no worse party-ridden people in the whole world than are the people of the United States. It is nothing but party, party, your party and my party. It is the abomination of American politics."[12]

Littlefield was re-elected, but his plurality of 5,400 in 1904 was cut down to less than 1,000. Gompers regarded this as a sufficient victory to convince labor's enemies that the warning contained in the Bill of Grievances was not a bluff. The Federation, he explained, had inaugurated an educational campaign that would not cease until labor's demands were met. It had secured the election of several trade unionists to Congress, around whom would gather others pledged to labor's program. The majorities of many legislators hostile to labor had been cut. Gompers confidently expected a fairer temper toward labor's demands in the ensuing session of Congress.[13] But he was to be disappointed in the new Congress, dominated as it was by Speaker Cannon and Senator Aldrich, as well as in the Roosevelt administration.

Labor was soon presented with the ruling in the Danbury hatters' case: not only a devastating blow against the boycott but a threat virtually to outlaw normal labor union activity. In 1901, the United Hatters of North America, determined to organize the shop of Dietrich E. Loewe in Danbury, Connecticut, had called a strike and declared a boycott. Loewe's fight against the union was financed by a group of hat manufacturers, and the Anti-Boycott Association agreed to help finance a test case of the boycott.

He filed suit against the union for common law conspiracy, claiming $100,000 damages, and another in the United States Circuit Court for violation of the Sherman Act, claiming $240,000. Simultaneously, the homes and bank accounts of 248 members of the union were attached. On February 3, 1908, the United States Supreme Court ruled that the Sherman Act was applicable because it forbade *any* combination to obstruct the free flow of commerce or restrict the liberty of a trader to engage in business. Innocent acts were unconstitutional when they formed part of a plot, in this case one to compel third parties not to engage in trade with the firm until it agreed to the union's demands.[14]

Gompers wrote confidentially to the Executive Council: "I read [the decision] not less than half a dozen times and the more thought I gave it, the broader its scope and character appeared in its inimical attitude toward even the most innocent and theretofore lawful action of the trade unions." He called in the resident members of the Council, along with their attorneys, and after discussing the situation for over four hours they decided to discontinue the publication of the "We Don't Patronize" list. Otherwise the Federation, its affiliated organizations, their officers and members, as well as the Executive Council, could not only be proceeded against under the penalty of a possible one year's imprisonment, $5,000 fine, or both, but all the firms carried on the list could sue for threefold damages of what they claimed they lost by reason of the boycotts.

Gompers called the decision the most drastic and far-reaching ever handed down by the Supreme Court. "The language of the Hatters' decision," he asserted, "makes it clear that the Supreme Court has not informed itself on modern economics. In its opinion the rights of hats seem to be greater than the rights of man. . . . No effort, however, is made to protect the right of man to a fair return for his labor, and the opportunity to labor under the prevailing conditions. In fact this decision goes to an unheard of length in punishing the workers for the exercise of their rights."[15]

Gompers received a large number of communications and resolutions from various unions demanding that the Executive Council take some more positive action to meet the danger presented to the labor movement. Many of them demanded the creation of an independent political party, others a mass convention to consider the situation. To head off the movement for independent politics, Gompers called a special meeting of the Council on March 16 to outline a course of action, and invited the executive officers of the international trade unions to join it two days later to ratify its decisions.[16]

On March 19 representatives of the trade unions, as well as

organizations of farmers and the railroad brotherhoods, endorsed the statement drawn up by Gompers and issued "Labor's Protest to Congress." They demanded immediate relief from what they called the gravest situation that had ever faced the working people, resulting from the courts' invasion of legislative and executive prerogatives. They asked for laws to restrict the jurisdiction of the courts of equity to property rights and which would define them so as to respect labor. They demanded exemption from the application of the Sherman Antitrust Act and protection of their freedom of speech and press. "Only by such action will a crisis be averted," the Protest continued. ". . . . we aver that the party in power must and will by labor and its sympathizers be held primarily responsible for the failure to give the prompt, full and effective Congressional relief we know to be within its power."[17]

In two trials of the Danbury hatters, extending from 1909 to 1911, the jury found the boycotters guilty of forming a conspiracy in restraint of trade and awarded the Loewe Company $80,000 damages, which was trebled under the Sherman Act. The decision was upheld by the Supreme Court in 1915. The company began to foreclose the homes of the 186 surviving workers. In order to save them, the A.F. of L. asked all its members to contribute an hour's pay, and the workingmen of the country paid the damages to Loewe.

In the summer of 1908, Gompers appeared at the convention of the Republican party in Chicago to present labor's program to the platform committee. He was allowed only ten minutes to present his position, and then only to a subcommittee. His arguments were given no consideration, Taft was nominated for the presidency, and Gompers was told to "Go to Denver," where the Democratic convention was held. Taft himself wrote the injunction plank, which proposed to give enjoined persons the right to a notice and hearing before the issuance of injunctions, but he insisted that he would rather cut off his hand than take from the courts their power to protect property. Nor was any relief promised from prosecution of unions under the Sherman Act. Gompers saw labor as "thrown down, repudiated and relegated to the discard."[18]

Gompers proceeded to Denver, where he presented the identical propositions that had been presented to the Republican convention. He was given a much more sympathetic hearing by the platform committee. The Democratic party adopted a labor plank which accorded substantially all that the A.F. of L. asked. William Jennings Bryan was again nominated as the party's standard bearer. Gompers and several other members of the Executive Council stopped at Bryan's home on their way east and conferred on the campaign which was about to get under way.

The Council did not officially endorse Bryan, and some members retained their Republican affiliation. But Gompers entered actively into the campaign to defeat Taft and the Old Guard Republicans. He publicly announced that the Democratic party had made labor's fight its fight, and that it was labor's duty to stand by it and see that it won. On August 26 he conferred with Norman Mack, chairman of the Democratic national committee, who agreed to print and distribute the campaign literature of the Federation; Gompers in turn assigned organizers to Democratic headquarters to work for the party. The Republican party, attacking Gompers for his "promise to deliver the labor vote to Bryan," established a labor bureau to start "brush fires" behind him and to organize a revolt against his leadership in the A.F. of L.[19]

Gompers centered his attack on Taft, whom he labeled the "injunction judge." Taft defended his action when, as a federal judge in Cincinnati during the Pullman boycott, he had issued an injunction against a strike on a railroad which was in the hands of a receiver appointed by him. Taft had sentenced one of the American Railway Union leaders to six months in jail for contempt of court. Gompers attacked Taft for failing to submit evidence of the strike leader's guilt to a grand jury for indictment instead of acting as prosecutor, judge, jury, and executioner himself, and all because the man had persuaded the railroad workers to quit their employment. Gompers held that Taft's position on the injunction issue was designed to perpetuate the injunction abuse rather than remedy it. Taft was compelled to devote an entire campaign meeting to his view that the "insidious attack on the courts" by Gompers and Bryan was the most important issue in the election.[20]

Gompers also electioneered against Republican standpat congressmen in Pennsylvania, Michigan, Ohio, Indiana, Illinois, and New York, campaigning particularly against the re-election of "Uncle Joe" Cannon to the House. He went into Cannon's home district for the highlight of labor's campaign, the Labor Day meeting. In the evening he went to Chicago to confer again with Bryan, who was making an address there.

The Federation's political campaign drew wails of anguish from employers' spokesmen, who saw "malign labor leaders" demanding "the most destructive and subversive kind of class legislation" in the form of immunity from prosecution for conspiring to prevent men from working without belonging to unions and to ruin the business of those who employed them. President Roosevelt publicly defended the party platform and sweepingly attacked Gompers for entering into collusion with Bryan to deceive labor. Gompers retorted with a restatement of labor's position on injunctions and non-partisan political activity.[21]

Although the Republicans took the election, Gompers was convinced that labor and the progressive forces had won a moral victory and that a more respectful hearing would have to be given its demands in the future. His own efforts during the campaign— he had also been giving testimony in the Buck's Stove case—had been intense. He had a few recurrences of an earlier neuralgia. Miss Guard did her best to induce him to spare himself, but found that an impossible task. He began to have dizzy spells, he would not rest, and his restoration evidently proved that his was not ordinary flesh and blood. As he often said, the Gompers clan were sturdy as oaks.[22]

In spite of the Republican victory in 1908, the liberal revolt known as the progressive movement was making large strides in the land. One manifestation of the insurgent movement was the campaign to overthrow "Cannonism," the dictatorial rule of the House of Representatives by its Speaker. As Gompers pointed out, Cannon was the instrument of big business in thwarting even the consideration of labor and other progressive legislation by his arbitrary rules and committee appointments. "For sake of party," Gompers stated, "of party harmony; for patronage or its possible loss; for the sake of a re-election, the members have sat idly by, closed their eyes, refused to listen to the voice of duty, until such weakness has culminated in establishing the custom by Representatives of 'holding their tongues' for fear they might lose caste with the Speaker whom they periodically and mechanically elected as their servant, yet to whom they have submitted as their master. . . .

while this un-American attitude prevails the privileges, the dignity, the unquestioned prerogatives of legislation . . . are being gradually alienated from the House of Representatives by the courts and by the President. . . ."[23]

Gompers played some part in the dethroning of Cannon and the abolition of the rules that permitted him to exercise his power. In 1906 Congressman Albert S. Burleson of Texas asked Gompers if he would co-operate in the effort to change the rules. Gompers agreed, and a group of insurgent congressmen came to his office to discuss their plans. They believed Gompers could speak for a large part of the population and thus help instill confidence in Representatives that there was sufficient public support to justify their effort to overthrow Cannon. A number of other conferences was held, and a public meeting, during which the incipient progressive movement in the Republican party began to crystallize. In 1908 the Executive Council and several other men conferred with President Roosevelt and Cannon. Gompers accused Cannon of packing the committees with reactionaries and preventing the calling up of reform legislation, thus stifling progressive measures and preventing even a fair consideration of them. During the four-hour conference, members of the House swarmed into the chamber and Gompers' protest helped to stimulate the sentiment for a revision of the rules.

In 1909 about twenty of the leading insurgents met in Gompers' office and there agreed upon the changes in the rules that they would press in the special session of Congress. The principal provision was that any member of the House might move to discharge a committee from further consideration of a bill, that recognition of such motions must be made in the order in which they were entered, and that they could be adopted by majority vote. The effort was defeated at that time, but the following year the rule was adopted along with another giving the House greater control over the appointment of committees and the assignment of bills. Then, in the 1910 elections—thanks to the dramatic impact of the famous Ballinger affair, which cast doubt on the good faith of President Taft and his Secretary of Interior in administering the public lands—the Democratic party secured a majority in the House and Champ Clark was elected Speaker. Thus Cannonism was overthrown. When the House convened,

Gompers was on the floor and was greeted by many of the Democratic members. So was William Jennings Bryan. This led one of the leading Republican members to call Gompers, Bryan, and Clark "the triumvirate behind the organization of the House of Representatives."[24]

The Federation's new political démarche led it to seek means of co-operating with the organized farmers of the country for the achievement of common legislative interests. In 1905 and 1906 the Farmers Educational and Cooperative Union and the A.F. of L. exchanged fraternal delegates and agreed to aid each other in the recognition and support of union labels. The Federation also instructed the Executive Council to seek co-operation with the farmers on defensive and offensive lines. Similar action was taken by the Federation and the American Society of Equity, which Gompers hoped would eventuate in a concert of action to advance the common interests of farmers and workers.[25]

In 1910 Gompers attended the joint convention of the two farm organizations in St. Louis, where they merged to form the Farmers National Union. Gompers told it that his objective was to cement the bonds of unity between agrarian and industrial wealth producers, and that he hoped eventually to see them united in one federation. He recommended the Federation's nonpartisan policy for electing farmers and workingmen to Congress. The convention appointed a committee to confer with Gompers and drafted a document, unanimously adopted, which, among other things, recognized the common aims and aspirations of all producers and pledged the Farmers Union to co-operate with the officers and legislative committee of the Federation in securing reformatory legislation.[26]

Gompers' activities in this era signalled the merging of labor's political program with the progressive movement. To him, the most promising aspect of progressivism was the establishment of true representative democracy through the initiative, referendum, and recall, the elimination (he thought) of political bosses and machine rule, and the enlightened, nonpartisan use of the ballot. Thus government would be transferred from the corporations to the people and labor could secure the relief it had long demanded. Gompers insisted that the progressive movement was forming in both major political parties and must be promoted through both parties by a nonpartisan policy. But actually he had given up all hope that the Republican party as such could be the instrument of reform—depite the presence in it of such figures as La Follette and the great conservationist, Gifford Pinchot—and felt it was destined to remain the representative of big business. His concern was for the Democratic party, which would either compete with the Republicans for the favor of the corporations or take up the cause of the masses. If it did the former, it would eventually be replaced by a radical labor party, but if it followed the latter policy it would become the agency for achieving real democracy. By 1912, Gompers was convinced that this was the path American history would follow.[27]

In the summer of 1912, Gompers again went to the party conventions to present labor's program. The Republican convention was dominated by the Old Guard, which renominated Taft and rejected all of labor's demands except those concerning immigration, workmen's compensation, and seamen's rights. Gompers then presented his demands to the Democratic convention. The Democrats endorsed labor's principal demands, but were silent on the question of convict labor, immigration, and woman's suffrage. It nominated Governor Woodrow Wilson of New Jersey as its candidate for President. The Progressive Republicans bolted their party's convention and, augmented by notorious non-Progressives like the publisher Frank Munsey, formed the Progressive party, with Theodore Roosevelt as their candidate. Gompers did not attend this convention, but it adopted a labor plank which endorsed most of the Federation's demands and went even further in some respects, especially in advocating the prohibition of child labor, minimum wages for women, and other legislation to raise the standards of the wage earners.

Gompers saw the Republican party as in every respect a failure, hopelessly antagonistic to the interests of labor and progressive reform. As between the Democrats and "Bull Moose" Progressives, he pronounced their platforms equally favorable to labor and their candidates equally outspoken in favor of labor's principal demands. Gompers did not trust Roosevelt as a true Progressive, however, remembering especially the fact that as President six years earlier he had turned a deaf ear to labor's Bill of Grievances. He was also disappointed in the nomination of

Wilson, who until two years before had been frankly hostile to unionism. Gompers was apparently not convinced that his recent conversion was genuine or very profound.[28]

Gompers centered his attack on Taft, and as between the other two candidates favored Wilson, probably because he considered his chances for election best. He commended the Progressive platform in general terms, but praised the Democratic party's record during its two-year majority in the House of Representatives. The House had passed an injunction limitation bill, a contempt bill, a convict labor bill, a Department of Labor bill, an eight-hour bill, the income tax amendment, the seamen's bill, federal workmen's compensation, and others.

Gompers clearly regarded the Democratic victory in 1912 as a culmination of labor's political campaign inaugurated six years before. The election of sixteen union members to the House and one to the Senate was also considered an important indication of political progress.[29]

2. THE CHARTER OF FREEDOM

WOODROW WILSON'S ATTACHMENT TO PROGRESSIVE principles was tenuous. He had been selected as candidate for President by the Democratic managers to thwart the more radical Western wing of the party under Bryan's leadership, and his essential conservatism was manifest. During his first administration, tariff reduction, banking reform, and strengthening of the antitrust laws constituted the basis of his program, designed to restore free competition in business. But with the exception of the Seamen's Act, he was cool or hostile to most of the legislation being pushed by the Progressive social reformers—child labor legislation, woman's suffrage, rural credits, and immigration restriction. On the issue which concerned labor above all others, exemption from antitrust prosecution, he was squarely in opposition.

The Federation's efforts to secure legislation to this effect had never gotten out of committee. The first opportunity for a test vote on the issue came in the closing hours of the Sixty-First Congress, in 1910. A bill providing appropriations for the Department of Justice to be used in prosecuting antitrust cases had been under consideration. An amendment was introduced on the suggestion

of the A.F. of L. legislative committee prohibiting the expenditure
of this money for the prosecution of organizations or individuals
entering into combinations to increase wages, shorten hours, or
otherwise lawfully to improve the conditions of labor. The measure was passed by the House but defeated in the Senate. The
following year it was passed by both houses of Congress, but Taft
vetoed it on the last day of his administration, calling it "class
legislation of the most vicious sort." When the same measure came
up in the special session of Congress in 1913, Wilson intimated he
would not oppose it. But under pressure he weakened and reversed
his position. The rider was passed by Congress, and Wilson signed
it only because he could not reject the appropriation for numerous
government agencies. At the same time he explained that he considered it merely an expression of congressional opinion and that
he would find money in the general funds of the Justice Department for the prosecution of any groups that violated the antitrust
laws.[30]

To secure the principle established in the rider, it had to be
enacted into substantive law, as pledged by the Democratic platform. The Federation at first sponsored its own bill for that purpose, but later decided to go along with the antitrust measure
being sponsored by Congressman Henry De Lamar Clayton with
administration backing. Gompers worked closely with the union
"card members" of Congress and others who were sympathetic
with labor's objectives. When the bill had been reported from the
judiciary committee to the Senate, Gompers suggested to Senator
Albert B. Cummins that the labor section would be strengthened
by a statement of the underlying principle that "The labor of a
human being is not a commodity or article of commerce." Cummins proposed this phrase as an amendment to Section 6. Gompers
was dissatisfied with the wording of the rest of the section, which
provided that the antitrust laws should not be construed to forbid
the existence and operation of unions and farm organizations or
to restrain individual members from lawfully carrying out the
legitimate objects of unionism, nor should such organizations or
their members be held to be illegal combinations in restraint of
trade. This clause did not squarely meet the threat posed by the
Supreme Court in the hatters' case, for it still left room for prosecution of unions if they engaged in activities which the courts could

construe to have an "unlawful purpose." Consequently, Gompers urged an amendment declaring that "nothing contained in the antitrust laws shall be construed to apply to labor organizations." This would cover all possible contingencies, but Gompers did not insist on its adoption. Apparently he was willing to compromise on this vital point in return for the acceptance of his beloved phrase, "labor is not a commodity," a vague declaration of principle that accomplished nothing. As later court decisions were to prove, this section gave little relief to beleaguered unions. Section 20 aimed to prohibit the federal courts from issuing injunctions in labor disputes unless necessary to prevent irreparable injury to property or property rights, or in any case to restrain striking, peaceful picketing and assemblage, and boycotting. This also proved to be ineffective. Another section of the act even worsened labor's position, for it permitted private parties as well as the government to obtain injunctions under the antitrust laws.[31]

The weakness of the Clayton Act was partly due to subsequent emasculation by courts, but even at the time of its passage its serious defects were evident. The United States Commission on Industrial Relations pointed out that the effect of the law was uncertain and must be until tested in the courts, but legal authorities had already expressed doubts that it would accomplish the desired results, and it was clear that the act did not remove the root of existing injustice, even within the limited field of federal jurisdiction. It did not prevent damage suits or clearly forbid injunctions against picketing and boycotts. The law actually returned the unions to their status under the common law before the passage of the Sherman Act of 1890.[32] Even Gompers must have recognized the act's limitations, for he did not resume the publication of the "Unfair" list which had been abandoned as a result of the hatters' decision.

But Gompers resented any suggestion that the act "will not accomplish everything the legislators intended." He ignored the fact that many of the legislators, as well as President Wilson, refused to admit that the intention of the act was to exempt labor from the Sherman Act, or even to limit the power of the courts to grant injunctions. Their view was that the act merely codified existing law and made unions indissoluble as combinations in restraint of trade. Senator Knute Nelson, a conservative Republi-

can, went so far as to say that it was a "sop" to make labor believe
it was getting something when it wasn't.[33] But Gompers sat in the
Senate galleries overcome with emotion when the act "foreshadow-
ing a new order of human relations in industry" was passed, and
he received with great pride the pen with which Wilson signed it.
He hailed the law as "the industrial Magna Carta upon which the
working people will rear their structure of industrial freedom,"
"the most comprehensive and most fundamental legislation in
behalf of human liberty that has been enacted anywhere in the
world."[34]

The 1914 elections considerably reduced the Democratic
majority in Congress. It became clear that the Democratic party
could win again in 1916 only by gaining the support of a large
number of former Progressives, and that only by convincing them
that it had repudiated laissez-faire and state rights and supported
the Progressive program of domestic social reform. Wilson therefore abandoned his earlier opposition to the rural credits bill, which
was passed in May. Under administration pressure, Congress also
passed a model workmen's compensation act for federal employees
and the Keating-Owens child labor law.[35]

This record was deemed by Gompers sufficient reason to support Wilson's re-election, although the Democratic platform promised little more reform than the Republican party. Wilson was a
man of "clear vision and courageous heart and mind," dedicated
to a policy of progress, justice, freedom, and humanity, while
Charles Evans Hughes was "the reactionary candidate of predatory
wealth." Gompers wrote a statement for the Democratic campaign
committee, which used it in a pamphlet addressed to workers. It
informed them that in his forty years of experience with Congress,
Gompers had not seen anything like the fine spirit toward labor
pervading the Wilson administration. Labor had been recognized
neither in the spirit of deference nor patronage, but by being made
part of the nation's councils (William Wilson of the United Mine
Workers was appointed first Secretary of Labor) and by being
given a "paramount voice" in legislation directly affecting its own
rights. "Because of that spirit and its results in definite laws and
policies, how can liberty-loving Americans loyal to the Republic
and its ideals fail to sustain an Executive who has done so much
for their realization?"[36]

After the election, Gompers was called on the phone by the secretary of the Democratic campaign manager, who told him that Wilson's victory was due to him more than to any other one man. The following year saw the enactment of the eight-hour law for railroad workers, civil government for Puerto Rico, and the literacy test for immigrants, which was passed over Wilson's veto. Thus, in eleven years, every measure demanded in Labor's Bill of Grievances had been enacted except the exclusion of the products of convict labor from interstate commerce.

Chapter Seventeen

LABOR STRUGGLES AND VIOLENCE

1. THE HEAVY HAND

THE DECADE BEFORE WORLD WAR I WAS A PERIOD OF unprecedented prosperity for the American economy, and it was widely proclaimed that times were never better for the working-men. To Gompers, such glittering optimism was merely a "stereotyped Christmas text for Big Business." Citing official and unofficial sources, he showed that the conditions of the workers were in fact a mockery of the vaunted "American standard of living." Millions of workingmen were still employed on the twelve-hour system, seven days a week, deprived of any life other than that devoted to earning their bread and butter, driven to exhaustion, alcoholism, and premature breakdown. Hundreds of thousands of children labored long hours for a pittance in mines, factories, and farm enterprises. The sweatshop evil continued.[1]

Such conditions produced widespread discontent, rising to revolt in the case of the sweated garment workers and violent class warfare in the case of the West Virginia and Colorado miners. But in the steel industry a powerful trust, an inept union leadership, and an abject mass of workers combined to produce nothing more than the tragic defeat of a defensive holding action.

In June 1909, the United States Steel Corporation announced that all its plants would henceforth be operated as open shops, with wage reductions ordered of about three per cent. The steel workers' and tin plate workers' unions called a strike to maintain what was left of unionism in the steel industry. The A.F. of L. convention in November called a conference of the officers of all affiliated national unions to meet in Pittsburgh and plan action.

Nearly fifty of the eighty-seven unions were represented at the December 13 meeting under the chairmanship of Gompers. They decided that all the national unions should be asked to furnish at least one organizer each to the Amalgamated Association of Iron and Steel Workers, that the Federation should place as many of its organizers as possible in the field, and that in every city where steel mills were located the central labor unions should appoint special organizing committees. They also planned to appeal for financial assistance to the strikers, to distribute a series of educational circulars, and to popularize a statement of grievances against the corporation. They urged the steel workers and tin plate workers to amalgamate into one union. In January, Gompers called on every union to donate at least ten cents per member to support the strike. A committee headed by Gompers presented labor's grievances against the corporation to the President and Congress and urged an investigation.[2]

After one month, only five international unions had complied with their promise to send organizers, and Gompers urged them again to fulfill their obligations. Little more response resulted. Three weeks later, President P. J. McArdle of the Amalgamated Association wrote Gompers that he was going to discontinue the campaign to organize the employees of the corporation. Gompers immediately telephoned to dissuade him from that course but learned to his disgust that the ten or eleven organizers placed at his disposal had already been dispersed. A fighter like Gompers used up the most meagre resources and hoped for the best: "Any moment might have developed into the psychological time when the interest, the intelligence, the hearts and conscience of the workers of the corporation themselves might have been reached, and an organization which had dwindled could have been revivified. . . . I can't escape the conviction that an opportunity which might have proven of the most intense interest and advantage to the cause has been thrown away. . . ."[3] The strike dragged on until August, when it ended in dismal failure, and the last vestige of unionism in the steel industry was eliminated.

The garment industry differed from the steel industry in every important respect except the long hours, low wages, and the attempted suppression of all unionism. But in place of a trust-dominated industry, the garment industry was fiercely competitive, conducted in innumerable small shops and tenement work-shops as well as a few large factories. Its working force was made up of a very large percentage of women, whose plight and struggles helped to arouse public sympathy. It was centered in the large industrial cities rather than in company-dominated towns. And a large number of the workers were intelligent, educated, socialistic workers, many of them veterans and refugees of the Russian revolution of 1905.

In the summer of 1909 there were some scattered strikes among the shirt-waist workers of New York, followed by dis-criminatory discharges. Local 25 of the International Ladies Garment Workers Union, one of the striking unions which was down to its last resources, began to think in terms of a general strike. A meeting was called to discuss the question in Cooper Union on November 22. The speakers included Gompers and other labor leaders, who spoke in a moderate vein, being unwilling to assume the responsibility for radical action and probably believ-ing it unwise. The workers were cautioned to use deliberation, to be sober in their decision, but if they did strike to stand by the union until they won. Then a young girl arose and proposed that a general strike be declared immediately. The crowd was on its feet immediately, shouting its approval, and before the leaders knew what was happening, the proposal was put to a vote and adopted by wild acclamation.

Within a few days, the "Uprising of the 20,000" was electrify-ing the city. Without preparation or finances, girls walked the picket line through the rain and snow, remaining solid and loyal in spite of beatings, arrests, fines, and jailings. After nearly three months, the vast majority of the workers won a fifty-two hour week, paid holidays, and improvements in working conditions and methods of settling wages. It was a tremendous inspiration to the workers in the other branches of the industry, supplying the initial impulse which led to the "Great Revolt" of the cloakmakers.[4]

The general strike of 60,000 cloakmakers was a revolt against the sweating and subcontracting systems at their worst. Men worked nine to sixteen hours in the shops, at ten o'clock each night left the factories with great bundles of clothing on their heads, and until two o'clock in the morning worked in the crowded tenements with their wives and children so that they might report at six o'clock in the morning with their tasks completed. Wages averaged fourteen to eighteen dollars a week.

In June, the convention of the I.L.G.W.U. empowered its executive board to call a general strike, and preparations were begun. A committee went to Washington and secured from Gompers the assurance of assistance by the A.F. of L. A mass meeting was called in Madison Square Garden on June 28. There was an overflow crowd of enthusiastic workers, addressed by Gompers and leaders of the union. A few days later, the workers voted almost unanimously for a general strike, which had more of the appearance of a "gigantic uprising of a whole people against their oppressors." The union demanded increased wages, the forty-eight hour week, abolition of subcontracting, and the closed shop. The union negotiators agreed to compromise the closed shop issue, but the strikers denounced and rejected the proposed settlement. The union president, acting alone and in secrecy, submitted a new compromise. Some members of the strike committee refused to take part in further conferences on these conditions. To avoid a split in the strike committee and a complete breakdown in negotiations, the union wired to Gompers. He immediately came to New York and assisted in securing a compromise on the basis of the preferential union shop. The employers agreed, but there were strong demonstrations against it by the strikers, who called it "the open shop with honey." After considerable maneuvering, the negotiators came to an agreement with the employers, hurriedly called a meeting of the shop chairmen, and on September 2 secured authorization to settle the strike on the basis of the "Protocol of Peace."

Gompers later expressed his attitude toward these negotiations and the dissatisfaction of the strikers: "Strong, resourceful leaders were instilling into these mutinous, undisciplined minds the fundamental theories of unionism. They were held steadily in line, taught to curb their fighting spirit that terms of agreement might be devised; taught that unreasoning resistance to the finish is vain bravado without profit; taught that negotiation is not a sign of weakness, but is the most potent means by which permanent gains can be secured; taught the lesson of self-restraint; taught that carefully-planned policies are of infinitely greater value than irresponsible, revolutionary uprisings—in a word the cloakmakers were taught unionism."[5]

The Protocol of Peace abolished subcontracting, established the preferential union shop, and provided for the settlement of disputes by a grievance committee and a board of arbitration. The workers also won the fifty-hour week, wage increases, double pay for overtime, ten paid holidays, and other concessions. In addition, a joint board of sanitary control was set up to wipe out the sweatshop and maintain decent conditions of hygiene and safety.

Addressing the Maryland Federation of Labor a week later, Gompers spoke of the uprising with tears trickling down his cheeks, his voice trembling with emotion. He declared that the strike was the greatest triumph for labor in the history of the world; he was particularly pleased with the Protocol of Peace, which was based on the principle that all disputes could be peacefully adjusted by impartial arbitrators. Assuming a community of interests between employers and employees, it abandoned the strike in favor of a complicated system of arbitration and conciliation. The unions relied on the machinery of the Protocol and the good will of the employers to establish permanent industrial peace; consequently, they failed to build a strong organization, and the terms of the Protocol were freely violated and evaded by the employers. But the I.L.G.W.U. leadership opposed the demands of the rank and file for greater union control over working conditions. It believed in "going easy" on the employers; and when strikes were called against violations of the Protocol, it broke them by issuing union cards to strikebreakers.[6]

In the United Garment Workers there was a similar disparity between the views of the leadership and the rank and file. The leaders represented the skilled workers to whom the manufacturers granted concessions in order to preserve industrial peace, and who preferred to rely on the union label and the co-operation of the employers rather than organizing drives and a militant strike policy. The less skilled workers and the progressive tailors, discontented with their officials' inclination to settle disputes on any terms and without resistance, demanded a more militant policy and the right to strike without interference by the national officers. In 1910, a spontaneous general strike among the men's clothing workers in Chicago was sold out by President Thomas A.

Rickert. They repudiated Rickert and his settlement and continued the strike, but three weeks later he called it off without consulting them.

Resentment against the United Garment Workers leaders was rife throughout the country, and the New York tailors initiated a movement for a general strike in that city. The national officers refused to have anything to do with it. The organizing campaign brought thousands of workers into the union, and in 1912 they voted for a general strike. Sixty thousand workers responded, and when they were winning in shop after shop, the U.G.W. officials made another agreement behind their backs. The strikers nevertheless continued the strike until their major demands were won. The tailors, representing one-half to two-thirds of the national membership, now determined to oust their treacherous officials at the convention in 1914. Rickert and his lieutenants used every means to retain their control of the organization, even refusing to seat 105 delegates representing the majority of the members. These, joined by a few from the convention, withdrew to another hall, declared themselves the bona fide convention of the U.G.W., and elected Sidney Hillman president.[7]

At the A.F. of L. convention in November, delegates appeared from both factions of the U.G.W. The credentials committee seated the Rickert group as having been regularly elected. The I.L.G.W.U. delegates made a motion to give the insurgent leaders a hearing, but Gompers rejected this on the ground that they were seceders from an affiliated union and entitled to no recognition and rejected, too, a proposal to investigate their claim to recognition. "Right or wrong," Gompers declared, "no act of secession will be tolerated." While the convention was in session, Gompers circularized the locals of the U.G.W., informing them that Rickert was the president of the union, that it was the bona fide A.F. of L. organization, and that all communications and remittances should be sent to it.[8]

The following month, the insurgents formed the Amalgamated Clothing Workers of America, with over 40,000 members. It immediately launched a vigorous drive to reconstruct the labor relations of an industry notorious for its low wages and abominable working standards. In this effort it had to face the opposition of not only the employers but of the U.G.W. and the A.F. of L., which branded it a dual union and sought to destroy it. Gompers brought pressure on the journeymen tailors' union, which had taken steps to join the new organization, and it reluctantly withdrew from the proposed alliance. In a series of strikes in the large clothing centers during the next two years, the Federation openly championed the cause of the manufacturers against the union, even going so far as to support legal prosecutions against strikers. During a strike in Philadelphia in 1916, the U.G.W. offered to break the strike, and Gompers sent a telegram to the employers urging them to make no concessions to the A.C.W.[9]

In his campaign to isolate and annihilate the new organization, Gompers found a strong obstacle in the United Hebrew Trades. This federation recognized the A.C.W. locals. The Executive Council of the A.F. of L. ordered it to expel those unions and seat the locals of the U.G.W. Gompers himself appeared before a crowded meeting of the United Hebrew Trades in May 1916 to prevail on it to carry out the order. Wearing his Prince Albert coat and a *yamelka*, he exhorted it to break with the A.C.W. He stormed back and forth on the platform, dramatically beating one hand against the other, and thundering against the "secessionists." His pleas for "unity," often ringing with pathos, left the delegates unmoved. They could not agree that organizational discipline was above elementary democracy. When the rules of a union and the tactics of the officers prevented the expression of the will of the majority, they asked, how else could they change policies and personnel except by withdrawing? If the Federation did not exert its disciplinary powers to insure honesty and democracy in its component unions, secession was made necessary.

When the A.C.W. went on strike in Chicago the next year, Gompers effectively prevented the Chicago Federation of Labor from aiding the strikers. The *New Republic* commented: "So heavily lies the hand of Gompers on the trade union world of Chicago." And from Ellen Gates Starr, an associate of Jane Addams who had helped the Chicago clothing workers: "The hand which should have been the strongest and readiest to aid those brave and oppressed people was the one which shut off from them the most powerful sources of aid. . . . And why? Because a spirited body of people, unable to rid themselves, otherwise, of corrupt officials, had dared to secede in overwhelming majority and form a new and clean organization under honest and able leadership." Referring to Miss Starr as a "so-called uplifter" who was trying to interfere with trade union democracy and dominate the labor movement by "benevolent officiousness," Gompers explained why he would not help the Chicago strikers. The power and effectiveness of the labor movement, he stated, depended upon its solid and united action. But the labor movement was a voluntary association, and therefore its solidarity must be maintained by self-discipline; its members must stand together and fight out their differences within the organization. By seceding, they incur all the dangers and consequences of that action, bringing upon themselves all the evils which ensue, and they could not expect protection from the organization from which they seceded. "It was not 'the heavy hand of Mr. Gompers,' that shut off sources of aid from the striking garment workers of Chicago, but it was their own voluntary act in dissociating themselves from the labor movement as well as the necessity and the duty of those who are in the labor movement to defend its existence from menace and attack both from without and within."[10]

2. THE McNAMARA CASE

GOMPERS WAS UNALTERABLY OPPOSED TO THE USE of violence in industrial contests but, taking the long view of history, found nothing greatly alarming about occasional incidents of violence in the struggles of labor. For every movement of the people that had made for human progress, including the American Revolution, had "some little element of roughness connected with it." But, he concluded, "In the great struggles for human freedom, and for justice and a higher civilization, thank God men forget in the ennoblement of these great struggles . . . the incident of roughness connected with it." In 1911 the labor movement was rocked by one of these "incidents of roughness."[11]

Five years earlier, the National Erectors' Association had declared war on the International Association of Bridge and Structural Iron Workers. It declared for the open shop, broke off all relations with the union, and sent spies into it. In 1910, the metal trades workers of Los Angeles went on strike for the eight-hour day and a minimum wage. The Founders and Employers'

Association refused to meet with the unions or communicate with them, and by June every metal trade plant in the city was involved in a strike or lockout, affecting 12,000 men. The city passed an antipicketing ordinance in July, and soon nearly 500 strikers were arrested for its violation. The employers refused to arbitrate, and the strike dragged out into the winter. "The union was faced by a stone wall," writes one historian of the labor movement. "In its despair it turned to terrorism and the dynamiting of non-union erecting jobs."[12]

At the same time, a determined campaign of extinction was being waged against the labor movement in Los Angeles, led by Harrison Gray Otis, the publisher of the Los Angeles *Times*. At one o'clock in the morning on October 1, 1910, an explosion in the *Times* building caused the death of twenty people and injured seventeen others. The next morning the *Times*, printed in an auxiliary plant, flashed the headline: UNIONIST BOMBS WRECK THE TIMES. Unexploded bombs were discovered near the homes of Otis and F. J. Zeehandelaar, leader of the Los Angeles manufacturers' association.

The municipal authorities employed William J. Burns, a nationally known antilabor detective, to investigate the case. The manufacturers' association and the Chamber of Commerce hired hundreds of other detectives, and Los Angeles was placed under a virtual reign of terror as the employers sought to utilize the hysteria to exterminate the organized labor movement. The city passed ordinances denying men the right to walk peaceably on the streets and talk with friends. Hundreds of union men were arrested, prosecuted, and tortured in an effort to fasten the crime on the labor movement. The state's governor stated publicly that "Whether guilty or not the unionists will have to be blamed for the crime until it is shown they are not guilty."[13] Otis editorialized in his paper: "O you anarchic scum, you cowardly murderers, you leeches upon honest labor, you midnight assassins. . . ." And *American Industries*, the organ of the N.A.M., immediately tried to implicate Gompers and other A.F. of L. officials, implying that there was a murderous motive behind the Federation's decision in 1909 to raise a "war fund" to combat the antiunion campaign of the Los Angeles *Times*.

On April 12, 1911, Ortie McManigal and J. B. McNamara,

two officials of the Bridge and Structural Iron Workers Union, were arrested in Detroit. Dynamite, percussion caps, and alarm clocks were found in their valises. McManigal confessed to participation in the crime and implicated the officials of the union. Eleven days later, John J. McNamara, secretary-treasurer of the union and J.B.'s brother, was arrested without a warrant by policemen who had no jurisdiction, in the union headquarters in Indianapolis while meeting with the executive board. He was taken to the police station, manacled, and taken to Los Angeles to stand trial on charges of blowing up the *Times* building. Gompers denounced this as an outrageous violation of constitutional guarantees and joined in the demand that Congress make a special investigation and frame the necessary laws to prevent a repetition of such a travesty of justice.[14]

Two weeks after the unlawful extradition of McNamara, Gompers went to Indianapolis and conferred with Secretary William J. Spencer of the Building Trades Department and Attorney Frank Mulholland. The information he received confirmed his belief that the accusations against McNamara constituted a conspiracy to crush the iron workers' union. He agreed to have the Executive Council receive and disburse all defense funds and to serve as a central agency for co-ordinating the defense campaign. He led a delegation to Clarence Darrow, who had defended Haywood, Moyer, and Pettibone, and persuaded him to undertake the defense of the accused men.[15]

William J. Burns inadvertently revealed that the arrest of the McNamaras was part of a plot to discredit the entire labor movement when he declared to the press that Gompers was a party to the crime and demanded that he and the other "higher ups" be removed from their positions. Gompers stated that Burns was lying, as he had lied about everything else connected with the case. "I have investigated the entire case," he declared, "and I am more convinced than ever that there is a 'frame-up' and a plot behind their arrests." He became angrier as he spoke, and added: "The interests of corporate wealth are always trying to crush the labor movement, and they use the best way to strike at the men having the confidence of the working people. . . . I admit that we can't compete with the capitalists in questions of litigation. But we will meet them this time on their ground and fight them in their own way, but it is the last time we will do it. There may come a time when we can't meet them that way any more, and when they hang a few of us we will show them a new way to meet an issue."[16]

Gompers repeatedly expressed his abhorrence of the *Times* dynamiting and of any other violence committed by anyone, in the labor movement or not. But these expressions were suppressed by the majority of the newspapers of the country, which not only tried to give the impression that he and other labor leaders condoned the crime, but implied that they were directly implicated in it. Seth Low, the president of the National Civic Federation, demanded that Gompers not only repudiate the crime, but that he offer every facility at the command of the A.F. of L. to run down the criminals. To this suggestion, Gompers replied that the Federation was not a detective agency: "We harbor no criminals nor criminality. . . . Anyone who may be guilty of crime must suffer the consequences of his conduct, but I take it that our movement will, and at least I shall continue to, presume that Mr. McNamara is innocent of any crime, at least, until he is proven guilty after a fair trial by a jury of his peers." He offered to resign from the National Civic Federation if his membership was embarrassing to Low, and temporarily suspended official activity in the organization.[17]

Later in the summer, Gompers made a trip to the West Coast and went to visit the McNamara brothers in the county jail, where they were photographed together for the press. J.J. said to him over and over again, "I want to assure you that we are innocent of the crime with which we are charged. It's all right; you can rely on us." When Gompers left him the last time, McNamara took his hand and looked him in the eye and declared: "Sam, I want to send a message by you to organized labor and all you may meet. Tell them we're innocent—that we are the victims of an outrageous plot." Gompers believed him.[18]

As the summer passed and fall came, the reactionary press continued to use the *Times* bombing and the assumed guilt of the defendants as a means of discrediting the labor movement. A concerted effort was made to prove that violence was an essential and approved element in the struggles of organized labor. In order to counteract this propaganda, Gompers called attention to the acts of violence on the part of employers, including a recent one in which the vice-president and four members of the machinists' union were arrested on dynamiting charges; during their trial it was established that they had been framed by detectives in the employ of the large corporations. In view of such facts, Gompers asked, why was it unthinkable that the McNamara case was another frame-up? "Remember that not one single dynamite explosion has ever been traced to organized labor. . . . Remember that with every union honeycombed with detectives, it would be impossible for an organization to enter into such a conspiracy without the immediate knowledge of detective agencies. Remember that the income of each one of these detectives, and of the agencies behind them, depends upon the ability to discover or create crime within the unions."[19]

J. B. McNamara was brought to trial in October, and as the proceedings went on it became clear that an acquittal could not be secured. Darrow pointed out that there were twenty-one separate indictments against the brothers. "The situation looked hopeless to me, for even though we might get a disagreement, or 'Not guilty' in the first case, there were all the others, which would make endless trials possible. . . . I knew that the State would never submit to defeat so long as there was any hope for them to win." Darrow's main concern was to save the lives of his clients, particularly since he was convinced that they had not intended to destroy the *Times* building or to take any lives, even if they had planted the dynamite. He believed J.B.'s statement that he had merely wanted to set off a small explosion in the alley next to the building to scare Otis, and that the explosion had ignited the ink barrels and the gas in the building. Darrow therefore effected a secret settlement with the prosecution. They persuaded the McNamaras to change their pleas to guilty, with the understanding that J.B. would receive a life sentence and J.J. ten years. On December 1, they made their confession to the court. The trial was then brought to a quick conclusion in accordance with the agreement, except that the judge insisted on giving John fifteen years.[20]

The country was electrified by the McNamaras' confession, and the labor movement was rocked back on its heels. Gompers was returning from the A.F. of L. convention in Atlanta when he heard the news. He seemed dazed, and then as the full import of the situation came to him the tears welled from his eyes. "I have been grossly imposed upon!" he choked. "It won't do the labor movement any good!" When he arrived in New York, he was interviewed by the press.

"Can you explain how it happens that you were kept in ignorance?" he was asked.

"Explain? Kept in ignorance? Why, we want to know that ourselves. We, who were willing to give our encouragement, our pennies, our faith, why were we not told the truth from the beginning? We had a right to know."

"... what would have been your advice if they had sought it?"

"I would have told them to plead guilty, sir. If they were guilty, if they did this thing, and if they had told me so, I would have said to them to plead guilty. I believe in truth. . . . I do not believe in violence. Labor does not need violence." But later he added that "If John McNamara had told me in confidence that he was guilty, I don't believe I would have betrayed him. I am willing to stand by it—I don't believe I would have betrayed him. But I certainly would not have declared my confidence in him. I certainly would not have raised money for his defense."[21]

Burns was also interviewed. The press wanted to know his opinion of Gompers. "Why, boys," he replied in his best theatrical manner, "what I think of that man is unfit to print. Had Gompers been honest, he would have demonstrated it by apologizing, not to me—but to organized labor and the American people generally for his abuse and villification of me when I arrested the McNamaras."[22]

After pondering the matter for a week, Gompers issued a statement for the McNamara defense committee. He expressed labor's satisfaction that justice had been maintained and the culprits punished for their crime. Yet, he remarked, it was an awful commentary upon existing conditions which brought a man to the frame of mind that the only means to secure justice for labor was in violence and murder. But most important to Gompers was the protection of the good name of organized labor, which should not be held legally or morally responsible for the crime of an individual member. He told the Federation convention the following year: "We are hurt and humiliated to think that any man connected with the labor movement should have been guilty. . . . The lesson this grave crime teaches will, however, have its salutary effect. It will demonstrate now more than ever, the inhumanity, as well as the futility, of resorting to violence in the effort to right wrongs, or to attain rights."[23]

The socialists drew a different conclusion from the McNamara incident and its denouement. They declared that acts of individual violence by unionists were a product of desperation and hopelessness, and that these were the results not only of capital's merciless and brutal assaults on the workers, but also of the A.F. of L.'s ineffectiveness, its antiquated craft union organization, its refusal to endorse independent labor politics, and its preaching of class harmony. John Spargo, a member of the national executive committee of the Socialist party, and himself a bitter critic of labor violence, denounced Gompers and his supporters as "men whose teachings inevitably lead to the kind of thing to which the McNamaras have confessed, however clean their own hands may be from crime." As Louis Adamic wrote long after, the dynamiting policy was "pure and simple unionism in action."[24]

As soon as the trial was over, the effort to implicate the entire trade union movement in the dynamite conspiracy was stepped up. The Los Angeles *Times* called for the formation of vigilance committees to "remove" the labor leaders. Burns stated that the case was ended only so far as the McNamaras were concerned and hinted that others might be arrested any day. "Gompers?" he was asked, and he shrugged his shoulders meaningfully. He intimated on several occasions that Gompers knew all along that the McNamaras were guilty, that he was concealing "other McNamaras" in the labor movement, that he was indifferent to the dynamite inquiry, and that he was one of the "higher ups" who were master-minding the whole dynamite conspiracy. The *Wall Street Journal* declared that no one in Gompers' position who was not a congenital idiot could have ascribed the dynamiting to anything but the deliberate policy of violence pursued by the iron workers' union, "and we do not believe for a moment that Mr. Gompers is a fool, whatever else he may be."[25]

Shortly after the end of the McNamara trial, Darrow was indicted on charges of attempting to bribe the jury. Throughout Darrow's trial repeated efforts were made to drag in Gompers' name, attempting to show that the money used in the alleged bribery had come directly from him. No evidence was produced, nor could it be, as Gompers never handled the funds of either the Federation or the McNamara defense campaign. During the trial, Darrow was hopefully, if foolishly, offered immunity from prosecution if he would furnish evidence against Gompers.[26]

Meanwhile, a second "dynamite conspiracy" investigation was begun by federal authorities in Indianapolis—the heralded plan to "get the higher-ups." A United States attorney declared that Gompers was "unsafe" and should be retired from office, and Burns was telling the nation in carefully planned press releases that Gompers was deceiving the workingmen and should be "dropped." Burns concocted a story that the former mayor of Indianapolis had been induced not to prosecute McNamara for criminal activities in return for a position with a printing company in which Gompers was allegedly interested. A searching examination of the Federation's books and records failed to unearth any evidence that the A.F. of L. or any of its officials had any connection with the crime. Olaf Tveitmoe, secretary-treasurer of the California Building Trades Council and one of the defendants, charged that he and the other defendants had been promised their freedom if they would state that Gompers knew that the McNamaras were guilty before they entered their plea on December 1. These facts, Gompers observed, brought out "the real meaning of the trial—the well-known struggle waged against organized labor by militant, hostile forces, behind whom stand the relentlessly antagonistic erectors and other employers' associations."[27]

Fifty-four officers and members of trade unions were indicted. Forty of them were brought to trial and thirty-eight were convicted, including President Frank M. Ryan and Tveitmoe, receiving sentences ranging from one to seven years. Burns regarded Tveitmoe's conviction the most important because he was a friend of Gompers.

The New York *Tribune*, like hundreds of other papers, asked, "What will Mr. Gompers do about it?" Mr. Gompers gave his answer to a special convention of the iron workers' union in Indianapolis on February 27, 1913: "I am not unmindful of the incidental errors and mistakes, and even those wrongs, which may be done in the name of organized labor ... but what I think is one of the greatest wrongs that can be perpetrated upon the Bridge and Structural Iron Workers of America is, if your own men are not true to each other and true to the international organization. . . .

"Now, one thing you should bear in mind. I am not your accuser. I am the accuser of no man. I am not a detective and I am not a police officer, nor am I a prosecuting officer. For those are the duties of the government and not of the man in the ranks of labor who tries to serve his fellows. . . .

"[I cannot] say that these men are innocent, and I am not going to say that they are guilty; but there is one thing which was evident to every fair-minded observer, and that is that the entire case was conducted with a prejudice and bitter partiality against the men, that it raises the question of an honest doubt in the minds of honest men. . . .

"The mistakes which have been made in the past must be corrected. The policy of true trades unionism must be impregnated upon the men of your craft. You must rely upon your own manhood and your own character. . . . Do that. Meet the situation as it confronts you men and you will come out of this crisis chastened, improved, stronger, more influential and powerful than ever before. . . .

". . . a few months ago, one of the attorneys for the Manufacturers' Association taunted me before the Senate Judiciary Committee and asked me whether, now, I would repudiate the Bridge and Structural Iron Workers International Union, and my answer was 'No! Now, more than ever, they need friends, and he isn't a friend who deserts those who need his assistance.'. . ."[28]

In 1921, John McNamara was released from prison and appeared at the A.F. of L. convention in Denver. When Gompers met him he said, "I can only repeat what I stated after your confession. If you had told me in confidence that you were guilty, I would not have betrayed you, and you know it. But you should not have risked the prestige of the entire labor movement." "That is past," McNamara replied. "All we ask now, my brother and I, is that we do not stand condemned in the eyes of labor forver." He offered his hand, but Gompers refused to shake it. "The last time I took your hand, you assured me of your innocence. After that, you betrayed yourself and labor. I can only say this: I will not attack you and your brother."[29]

3. THERE ARE STRIKES, AND THERE
ARE STRIKES

GOMPERS' CONTENTION THAT INDUSTRIAL VIOLENCE
was generally perpetrated by the employers was amply illustrated
by the strike history of 1912-1914, beginning with the Lawrence,
Massachusetts, textile strike. Most of the workers in the Lawrence
mills were unskilled, immigrant workers, whose wages averaged
from five to seven and a half dollars a week; nearly one-third of
the employees were minors earning less than three dollars a week.
Many of them lived in company-owned tenements marked by
overcrowding and filth, resulting in a death rate among the children under one of over seventeen per cent. In January 1912, a state
law went into effect reducing the hours of women and children
from fifty-six to fifty-four. The corporations reduced wages pro-
portionately and speeded up the machines to get the same labor as
before. When the first pay envelopes were received on January 11,
the cry of "short pay" went through the mills, and tens of thousands of unorganized workers spontaneously rushed out of the
mills and into the streets.

The strike committee called in Joseph Ettor, an I.W.W. organizer in New York, to take command. Demands were formulated
for a fifteen per cent wage raise, overtime pay, abolition of the
bonus and premium system, and no discrimination against the
strikers. Arturo Giovannitti, New York labor editor and poet, also
came to Lawrence and threw himself into the strike, in charge of
relief work. The strike was marked by savage official repression.
Police and militia attempted to break up picket lines, and, as a
result of clashes, the commissioner of public safety announced that
"there will be no more toying with these lawless strikers. . . . The
soldiers . . . will shoot to kill." Strikers were arrested, given no
access to counsel, and kept in jail for weeks. Dynamite was discovered in the homes of strikers, later revealed as having been
planted by conspiracy of mill executives, including the president
of the American Woolen Company; more arrests were made to
break up the "dynamite conspiracy." On January 29, a riot resulted
from police interference with picketing, and a young girl striker
was shot dead. Ettor and Giovannitti were arrested on charges of
inciting murder in pursuit of an unlawful conspiracy and held as

accessories before the fact. Bill Haywood then came in and took charge of the strike.[30]

The strikers decided to send their children to stay with friends and relatives outside of Lawrence for the duration of the strike in order to lessen the burden of relief. On February 24, about forty children were brought to the railroad station by their mothers. Some thirty policemen and some militia were present, and the marshal ordered the mothers not to place the children on the train. When they started to do so, the officers stood at the door of the station with drawn bayonets and did not permit them to leave. Many of the mothers and children were pushed, beaten, choked, and clubbed, and some were stabbed in the back while running away. They were dragged along the platform and thrust into patrol wagons and taken to the police station.[31]

This incident caused the Rules Committee of the House of Representatives to hold hearings to determine if there was need for official investigation of the strike. John Golden, President of the United Textile Workers, testifying, admitted that before the strike only 208 skilled mule spinners were members of his union. He denied the charges of the I.W.W. that his union had failed to organize the unskilled workers and had blocked efforts to do so. He agreed the strike was justified, but condemned the manner in which the strike was brought about—"This is a revolution, not a strike"—and the manner in which it was led by the "anarchistic" I.W.W. He also opposed sending the children away because he believed the real motive was to "keep up the agitation and further the propaganda of the I.W.W. . . . which means the destruction of our movement . . . and the destroying of industrial peace of a former peaceful community."

When Gompers took the stand, he recognized that Golden had made a bad impression with his hostile remarks and extenuated them by explaining that Golden had been through a great deal of stress and was under pressure of time. But he defended Golden as self-sacrificing, honest, and altruistic; the failure to organize the textile workers in the U.T.W. was due to the tyranny of the mill owners and the "perversion of the trades-union men and their organizations" by the I.W.W. However, he defended the strike, even if it was a revolution: "Sometimes a protest in the form of a revolt against tyranny and injustice is justified by every law of self-defense and common humanity." He even defended the lawful right of the I.W.W. to work for industrial revolution, although he disagreed with that purpose. He also defended the right of the strikers to send their children out of the city as a means of aiding their struggle.

A week after these hearings took place, the Lawrence strike ended with a great victory: the strikers won wage increases of five to twenty per cent, time and a quarter for overtime, the readjustment of the premium system, and the reinstatement of the strikers without discrimination. Some months later, Ettor and Giovannitti were brought to trial and acquitted.

Gompers, unlike Golden, would not lend himself to crude red-baiting during the strike, but he was equally hostile to the I.W.W. Writing in the *American Federationist* after the strike was over, he derogated the vision of the world's workers banded together against the rest of society as "too chimerical to be entertained by an intelligent man or woman confronted with the practical problem of securing a better home, better food and clothing, and a better life." Practical men wanted an organization that would benefit them now.

Gompers' chief objection to the I.W.W. was not its utopian theory but its program of violent class warfare, inflicting needless suffering on the workers and society, sacrificing present individual welfare for the ultimate good of all. Besides, the I.W.W. disseminated impracticable ideals which "inflame the imagination by the hallucination that in yet a little while the workers shall inherit the whole earth and all its riches." Unorganized and exploited workers were misled into chasing a will-of-the-wisp, only to come to a realization of the futility of their visions, of blasted hopes, and wasted opportunities.[32]

However, it was the policy of Gompers, Golden, and the rest of the A.F. of L. hierarchy that made possible the limited successes of the I.W.W. The A.F. of L. made slight effort to organize the unorganized, especially the mass of unskilled workers, and did not even recognize the opportunity for expansion provided by such spontaneous movements as the Lawrence strike. On the contrary, they viewed such manifestations with alarm: they neither understood nor wanted the mass of immigrant workers and even looked upon them with a degree of contempt. These "neglected and despised workers found in the [I.W.W.] a champion which saw in their very degradation and weakness a justification for its intervention."[33]

Gompers had some "labor troubles" of his own during this period. In 1909, the Federation headquarters were moved from the Typographical Building to larger quarters in the Ouray Building three blocks away on G Street. Here a large staff of stenographers, clerks, and other employees worked under Gompers, an employer whose salary had increased in the past ten years from $1,800 to $5,000. In 1910, the stenographers' union at Federation headquarters submitted a new agreement to Gompers, asking for four weeks vacation instead of two, higher wages, two weeks dismissal notice, notification in writing of the cause for dismissal, time and a half for overtime, and other improvements. Gompers replied that these demands were unreasonable, mainly on the ground that the Federation was being asked to grant more liberal conditions than those provided in the agreement with the machinists' union, to say nothing of commercial employers. As for overtime, he thought that since the Federation worked for the betterment of all labor, its employees should not object to helping when necessary by working after hours, without pay.

The union reminded him that one of the objectives of the A.F. of L. was to do away with overtime work; if overtime were necessary, even for the betterment of the labor movement, it should be paid for rather than the demand for payment be construed as disloyalty to labor. The union women pointed out that the wage scale of the A.F. of L. and the machinists' union were practically identical, but those receiving the same pay from the Federation had been working much longer than those working for the machinists. They defended four weeks vacation, since they got no sick leave or Saturday half-holiday, but withdrew it and substituted a request for a thirty-nine hour week instead of forty-two.

Gompers thought this request even more unreasonable than the original, for three hours a week came to 150 hours a year, equivalent to nearly four weeks in addition to the two weeks vacation. "When the entire effort of organized labor has for years been concentrated upon the endeavor to secure an eight-hour work-day without vacation, which is not by any means fully achieved, the members of the Executive Council would be recreant to the trust reposed in them by the masses of labor did they consent to a week's work of less than 42 hours . . . with two weeks' vacation with pay. . . ." So the stenographers learned that they could not get what the A.F. of L. advocated for the working class until the rest of them had gained it, and that they were fortunate to be giving their services, overtime and all, to an organization that was striving for their uplift.[34]

Chapter Eighteen

GOMPERS, THE SOCIALISTS, AND INTERNATIONAL LABOR

1. SHOWDOWN ON SOCIALISM

DURING THE FIRST DECADE OF THE TWENTIETH CEN-
tury, the Socialist party was becoming a radical middle-class reform party. This tendency was reflected in its trade union policy,
which was based on co-operation with the A.F. of L. and the craft
unions. The socialists agreed that Gompers' opposition to their
party had been justified, agreed they had been wrong to believe
that trade union success retarded the coming of socialism by making the workers contented with their lot, and repudiated the dual
union tactics of De Leon, Haywood, Debs, and other left-wing
leaders. They hoped now to win the good will of Gompers and
other labor leaders by supporting them and claimed that the
electoral aims of the party and the economic aims of the unions
were not antagonistic.

The Socialist party made two major compromises in its program in order to cater to the Federation leaders and win their
support. It abandoned its internationalist position on the immigration question and adopted an exclusion policy. It also abandoned
the fight for industrial unionism, conceding that the party had no
right to interfere in union controversies over organization or
tactics proper to industrial struggle. The party emphasized that it
no longer sought endorsement by the A.F. of L.[1]

Whatever criticism the socialists may have planned to present
to the A.F. of L. in 1907 was withheld when Gompers revealed the
attempt of the N.A.M. to bribe him. The following year, socialist
activity at the Federation convention was limited to criticism of its
support of the Democratic party and to an attempt to force an in-

vestigation of Gompers' charge that Debs' famous "Red Special" campaign train was financed by big business. In 1909 and 1910 they decided not to introduce motions for independent political action and government ownership of industry, in the interest of a united front in the face of the Buck's Stove case crisis, and because, in view of the increasing socialist vote, they did not want to encourage further debate in the Federation on the question of forming a labor party.

But in 1911 the party evidently decided that Debs was at least partly right in noting the tendency in the party to weaken its principles and to cater to "Gompersism"; if the party compromised its revolutionary character and purposes, he asserted, it had better cease to exist. Without changing its fundamental trade union policy, it determined that its old fight to liberalize and revitalize the Federation must be resumed. Some of the party members were tired of seeing Gompers get up year after year at conventions, assuming the martyr's role and pleading for unity with tears in his eyes. Some of them suspected he might have been putting on an act in order to disarm criticism and opposition.[2]

The party outlined a program to advance at the Federation convention in 1911: the election of officers by referendum; financial assistance for the McNamaras; denunciation of the National Civic Federation; a propaganda campaign for industrial unionism; and placing a socialist candidate against Gompers for the presidency of the A.F. of L. About forty socialist delegates attended. At the last minute they abandoned their plan to oppose Gompers, and they got nowhere with their referendum and industrial union planks. There was no difficulty in getting support for the McNamaras. The big fight arose over the National Civic Federation.

Socialist resolutions declared that the N.C.F. had been organized by the employers to blind the workers to their true conditions, condemned it as hostile to workers' interests, and called upon organized labor to sever its connections with it. The resolutions committee recommended nonconcurrence. It held that the N.C.F. was organized to further the adjustment of disputes through friendly conferences and the consummation of joint agreements. It did not assume the interests of capital and labor to be identical. It had never been unfriendly to organized labor and had often persuaded reluctant employers to undertake negotiations which led to satisfactory adjustment of disputes.

Gompers denounced the campaign against the Civic Federation as entirely a scheme of the socialists, its only purpose being to traduce and antagonize the trade union movement. He rebuked his foes for suggesting that he or other officers of the A.F. of L. could be "chloroformed" or "hypnotized" by the enemies of labor simply by meeting and conferring with them. He described himself as more radical and persistent in his utterances before the N.C.F. than in speaking to union meetings and challenged any man in the convention to point to one utterance of his in the Civic Federation that could be questioned as to its accuracy and its insistence on the trade union position. "When we meet these people we endeavor to drive home the claims of labor. They do not often get this otherwise, and now the proposition is that they shall not get it at all!"

He agreed that the mere cultivation of friendly relations between employers and representatives of the workers should be avoided. He had often been invited to the social functions of businessmen and government officials but invariably declined. "Personally I have no relations with those people, but as a trades unionist and an officer of the American labor movement it is my duty to defend and protect and advocate the cause of labor wherever and whenever I can." After some irrelevant rambling, Gompers concluded:

"I want to say to you candidly this: I am going to stick to the trade union movement, no matter what you do. It is dearer to me than any other institution on earth. I owe it so much, the opportunities it has given me, the opportunities to be helpful to others. To have witnessed the gleam of light and life that has come into the homes of our working people where gloom and misery obtained before, is no mean thing to surrender. . . .

"It is true I am sixty-one years old. I think that if I only took a little bit of care of myself I will outlive lots of fellows, and I am not going to let up. I am not going to quit, I am going to stick to the union. It is too late for me to change my whole mind and life, it is too late for me to learn new tricks. The labor movement is ingrained in my very being. The cause of labor, the cause of humanity, the cause of justice, the cause of freedom, have too deep a rooting in my make-up for me to give up this movement in which I see the future hope for liberty and justice and humanity. I want to be of service. I have tried to be of service. I propose to be of service. I think there would be no greater mistake made in the labor movement of our country than to attempt to cripple or limit the service that the men of labor propose and are anxious to give to the cause of organized labor and humanity."

The report of the resolutions committee was upheld by a vote of 12,000 to 5,000.[3]

The large vote against the N.C.F. encouraged the socialists in the belief that they could make an effective fight against pure and simple unionism and the Gompers leadership. Socialism seemed to be sweeping the trade union movement. International unions with nearly half a million members, as well as scores of state and city federations, had endorsed the socialist program. There were also large socialist minorities in a number of other unions. A striking fact was that the treasurer of the A.F. of L. (John B. Lennon of the tailors' union) and two of its vice-presidents (O'Connell of the machinists and Mitchell of the miners) had become "ministers without portfolio," having lost the basis of their influence as a result of socialist victories which put them out of office in their own organizations. Even Gompers was fearful of the imminent danger that the socialists would win the support of the majority of the cigarmakers, and suggested that the initiative and referendum might have to be abandoned as one means of checking their growing strength.[4]

The socialists went to the 1912 convention of the Federation determined to make a militant fight against the old guard. There were a hundred socialist delegates, the largest contingent in the history of the Federation. Their program was confined to a resolution on the election of officers by referendum and another for industrial unionism. Both were defeated by two-to-one votes. Then, for the first time in a decade, an opposition slate was put up. Max Hayes, head of the Cleveland Federation of Labor and editor of the Cleveland *Citizen*, was nominated for president against Gompers. Gompers was re-elected by a vote of 12,000 to 5,000.

Gompers had often attacked the socialists' tactics and methods and occasionally their principles as well, but he had rarely attempted theoretical criticism of the socialist philosophy. In fact, he ridiculed them as theorists rather than practical men. From 1910 to 1914, however, their growing influence among workers impelled him to undertake such a critique. In a 1910 article in the *American Federationist*, he showed that he either did not understand Marxism or was distorting it in order to flail a straw man. The fundamental error of socialist theory, he contended, was the doctrine of surplus value, which meant to him that the workers could never secure more than enough to keep them alive. Gompers argued that the working class, at least in the United States, was constantly improving its conditions and status. The error in the doctrine of surplus value, according to him, was the foundation for other errors, particularly the notion that increasing misery and exploitation would produce a social revolution and the establishment of a co-operative commonwealth. "As many a thousand soapboxer has voiced this pivotal point: 'Things must be worse before they can be better.' This idea is at once the kernel, crux, and culmination of Marxism." Gomper's answer to this supposed Marxist doctrine was the constantly increasing wages of the workers, shorter hours, elimination of child labor, improvements in education, increase of home ownership, and a higher level of comfort. The ownership of industry was becoming more extended through widespread stock ownership and the bank deposits of wage earners. Finally, increased government regulation of public utilities was undermining the exploitative powers of capital. "Capitalism as a surviving form of feudalism—the power to deprive the laborer of his product—gives signs of expiring, to leave the laborer the possessor of his just share of capital as one person living under a state exerting a minimum of interference with the citizen while giving full recognition to the present fundamental institutions of government, liberty and property."[5]

Gompers contrasted socialism and trade unionism as opposed in their expectations of a reconstituted economic system. The former enlisted the support of dreamers who believed that the co-operative commonwealth would replace the competitive regime by sweeping changes effected by legislatures. Unionists rejected the dogma of "an automatic progress towards a general social catastrophe. . . . instead of trying to keep the eyes of mankind upon a remote and problematical end to what evils affect our present society, [unionism] directed attention to the correction of the remedial evils closest at hand. These attended to, . . . others lying next behind them could be grappled with in their order, and at last, if man is capable of clarifying his purposes and ideals with social advance, the goal of economic justice would be attained."[6]

The socialist path was futile, Gompers maintained, for it meant simply waiting for the cataclysm, or at best voting the socialist ticket year after year until it secured a majority of the electorate. But in the meantime, it offered no practical, constructive program for improving the workers' conditions. It diverted the attention of the workers from here-and-now problems. Gompers' primary interest in combatting socialism was to advise trade unionists "not to lose their time in fruitlessly going on excursions to the end of the rainbow while their efforts might be placed to practical advantage in trade union matters immediately within their reach."[7]

Thus, by 1915, Gompers had come full circle. Beginning his labor career as a socialist sympathizer, a believer in the class struggle, and an admirer of Karl Marx, in the 1890's he insisted that he was not antagonistic to socialism but only attacked socialists who were hostile to the trade union movement or who antagonized it by forming dual unions. In the next decade he dropped his belief in the class struggle, and in 1913 he specifically committed himself to the acceptance of capitalism. He told the House lobby investigating committee that he had come to the conclusion that "it is our duty to live our lives as workers in the society in which we live and not to work for the downfall or the destruction or the overthrow of that society, but for its fuller development and evolution. . . ." Two years later he wrote, "It is not against Socialists as individuals that I contend. . . . What I oppose is the system, the fundamental principles which underlie socialist theory."[8]

After 1912, the Socialist party abandoned virtually all opposition to the leadership and policies of the A.F. of L. There were no more of the great debates that had marked Federation conventions for the past two decades. But in 1914, a unique debate took place outside the A.F. of L. The United States Commission on Industrial Relations offered Morris Hillquit and Gompers the opportunity to question each other publicly on the policies, methods, and aims of the A.F. of L. and the Socialist party, and for three days these spokesmen for socialism and trade unionism exchanged views, baited each other, and threw lances for their respective philosophies. Hillquit was only incidentally interested in demonstrating the superiority of socialism; his primary aim was to show Gompers that the socialists and unionists had much in common, that the socialists were not antagonistic to unionism, and that there was a field for effective co-operation between them. But Gompers was unwilling to recognize this proposition and was constantly on guard lest Hillquit "trap him" into admitting that he agreed with much of the socialist program. Consequently, he sparred warily and was on the defensive most of the time, refusing to recognize any distinction between socialists who wanted to supplant the A.F. of L. or transform it into a revolutionary body and those who wanted to work in it and with its leadership. Gompers kept on quoting Debs, and Hillquit kept repeating that Debs' views did not represent the official doctrines of the Socialist party. Nor would Gompers recognize any difference between antagonism to the A.F. of L. and criticism of some of its policies or leadership; anyone who did not agree with his conception of trade union policies was a "wrecker," "smasher," or "borer."

Hillquit questioned Gompers about a whole series of social, political, and economic reforms which Gompers supported except for a legal maximum workday and minimum wages. Yet Gompers refused to accept this as evidence that the A.F. of L. and Socialist party had similar programs. The Socialist party didn't really believe in these reforms, he asserted, but "purloined" them from the Federation's program merely to catch votes.

Later, Gompers tried to establish that, apart from the goal of a co-operative commonwealth, the purposes of the socialist movement did not practically differ from those of the A.F. of L.; apparently he thought to show that the Socialist party was superfluous in the reform movement. But Hillquit quickly agreed with Gompers, emphasizing that the political and economic movements went hand in hand, and that, as such, socialists were a critical but real part of the labor movement.

He got Gompers to agree that the workers did not receive the whole product of their labor and that it was the function of the unions to constantly increase their share. Would they ever stop in their demands for more before they received the full product of their labor? "Not if I know anything about human nature,"

Gompers replied. "They are working towards the highest and best ideals of justice."

"MR. HILLQUIT: Now, 'the highest and best ideals of social justice,' as applied to distribution of wealth, wouldn't that be a system under which all the workers . . . would together get the sum total of all the products of their toil?

"MR. GOMPERS: Really, a fish is caught by tempting bait; a mouse or rat is caught in a trap by tempting bait. The intelligent, commonsense workmen prefer to deal with the problems of to-day . . . rather than to deal with a picture and a dream which has never had, and I am sure never will have, any reality in the actual affairs of humanity. . . .

"MR. HILLQUIT: Mr. Gompers, I would like to get an answer. . . . can you locate a point at which the labor movement will stop and rest contented so long as the workers will receive less than the full product of their work?

"MR. GOMPERS: I say that the workers . . . will never stop at any point in the effort to secure greater improvements in their conditions. . . . And wherever that may lead and whatever that may be in my time and at my age, I decline to permit my mind or my activities to be labeled by any particular ism."

Hillquit asked whether the A.F. of L., in working for improved conditions, had a general social philosophy, or worked "blindly from day to day." Gompers flared up at what he regarded as an insulting question, and refused to answer it. Hillquit rephrased the question, and Gompers replied that the Federation was guided by the history of the past. "It works along the line of least resistance, and endeavors to accomplish the best results in improving the condition of the working people, men, women, and children, today and tomorrow—and tomorrow's tomorrow and each day, making it a better day than the one that had gone before."[9]

Hillquit did not succeed in bringing Gompers closer to an understanding of socialism or into a more friendly relationship with the socialists, and three years later, the war was to fix their hostility in implacable and rancorous enmity.

2. THE I.F.T.U.

AT THE A.F. OF L. CONVENTION IN 1908, THE fraternal delegates from the British Trade Union Congress invited Gompers to attend their congress the following year. The Federation agreed to send him as a special representative. He was also instructed to attend the International Federation of the Secretariats of the National Trade Union Centers (International Secretariat) and to visit such other countries as the Executive Council should determine. The International Secretariat was scheduled to meet in Stockholm in 1910, but changed its meeting to Paris in 1909 in order to make Gompers' attendance possible.

He left New York on June 19, 1909, with his wife and daughter, arriving in Liverpool a week later. On July 1 and 2, he attended the meeting of the General Federation (executive council) of the British trade unions at Blackpool. He then visited Dublin, Manchester, and London, where meetings and conferences were arranged for him. Then he went on a two-month tour of the continent, taking in the large cities of Germany, Austria-Hungary, Italy, Switzerland, and Holland. In many cities he met with labor leaders and central labor committees, and in some places spoke at mass meetings. Everywhere he carried the gospel of pure and simple unionism. "And so the light is spread!" Gompers exclaimed.[10]

Gompers' tour confirmed his belief in the superiority of American over European society and the essential correctness of the principles and practices of the American trade union movement. In Hungary he found a working class steeped in misery and an extremely weak labor movement, which he ascribed primarily to the hostility of the government. Furthermore, eighty per cent of the workers were disfranchised, there was an established church and compulsory military service, and the government was ruled by the landed aristocracy. Gompers was shown a penitentiary in which, he was told, were confined robbers, murderers, and socialists. "Well," he commented, "what American animated by the spirit of '76 would not qualify himself quickly for prison in such a country as Hungary—and do it under the name of Socialist if necessary?" But in America he would be a trade unionist because of the democratic rights of the workers and the possibility of peaceful progress.[11]

On August 30, Gompers attended the conference of the International Secretariat at Paris. He was not an official delegate, as the A.F. of L. had not decided on affiliation. Because he did not commit the Federation to joining at that time, he was attacked by the Austrian representative, A. Hueber, a leader of the socialist faction, to whom it appeared that Gompers had come to give advice but not to participate. Gompers retorted that the chief obstacle to American participation in the world trade union movement was the attitude of the socialists who believed that they should dominate trade union affairs. He explained further that he could not make the decision on affiliation by himself, but promised to do his best to bring it about, and believed it would come in time. Hueber found Gompers' explanations unpleasing. "We thank you for your opinions," he declared brusquely, "but we do not need them. Your policies may not permit you to come to us, but one day, American workmen, you will realize that your policies are erroneous, and you will see the necessity of joining the international confederation." Gompers explained that the A.F. of L. was willing to join only an international movement whose objectives were limited to strictly trade union matters but not an organization dedicated to the discussion of social problems. After a two hour discussion, Gompers was seated as a guest with a right to speak. "This was my initiation into the active work of organized international labor," he later sourly commented.

Gompers submitted two resolutions which had been prepared by his own Executive Council. The first suggested that an International Federation of Labor be established with regularly elected delegates and with the autonomy of the trade union movement of each country guaranteed. The purpose of the federation should be to protect and advance the rights of wage earners everywhere and establish international solidarity. The second resolution urged the labor movements of all countries to endeavor to prevent workers from one country being induced to emigrate to other countries during periods of depression or when trade disputes existed or were being contemplated, and that the existence of such situations should be reported by the international secretary to the trade unions of all countries. Since these matters were not on the agenda, and were not presented as formal resolutions by an accredited delegate, no vote could be taken on them, but it was decided to place them on the agenda of the next conference to be held in 1911. Gompers was assured that labor in every country must be free to decide its own policies and methods, and to further satisfy his fears it was ruled that all decisions of the International Secretariat must be unanimous in order to be binding.[12]

Following the international conference, Gompers went to Ipswich to attend the British Trade Union Congress. He made a brief speech transmitting the greetings of the American workers, and he, his wife, and his daughter were given a case of cutlery as tokens of friendship. He sailed for the United States on September 29.

In November, at the Toronto convention of the A.F. of L., he reported on his trip to Europe and particularly on the meeting of the International Secretariat. The conference, he thought, had helped clear the field for a possible deliberative international body, democratically organized, leaving to the labor movement of each country its autonomous rights, and excluding political questions. He recommended "without hesitation" that, though the Secretariat left much to be desired, the best interests of the American workers would be served by the affiliation of the A.F. of L. with it. The "substantial benefits," he admitted, would be meager, but the spirit of international fraternity it would foster would be measurable and would hasten the establishment of an International Federation of Labor. The convention voted unanimously to affiliate.[13]

The next meeting of the Secretariat was held in Budapest in 1911, and Vice-President James Duncan was elected as the A.F. of L. representative. The resolution on migration of workers during depressions and strikes was adopted, and the resolution for an International Federation of Labor was recommended to the affiliated labor centers for further discussion. In 1913, George Perkins, of the Cigarmakers International Union, represented the United States at the meeting of the Secretariat in Zurich. The conference accepted his invitation to meet in San Francisco in 1915 and also adopted the plan of reorganization submitted by the A.F. of L. The name of the world body was changed to the International Federation of Trade Unions, and a commission was appointed to draft a plan, constitution, and by-laws.[14]

3. PUERTO RICO

THE FEDERATION WAS ALSO DEVELOPING GREATER
concern for the problems of labor in Latin America, especially in
Puerto Rico and Mexico. In 1907, the A.F. of L. made its first
formal demand for self-government for Puerto Rico through the
establishment of a territorial form of government. It also called
for increased school appropriations, the enforcement of the eight-
hour and employers' liability laws, abolition of convict labor, and
increases in the wages of government employees. It urged restrictions on landholding, improvement of sanitary conditions in
homes and shops, an end of strikebreaking by the insular police,
and the abolition of child labor. All these demands came from the
Puerto Rican delegates to the A.F. of L., with the exception of the
proposal for self-government, which they did not want at that time
because they thought this would result in political domination by
the sugar and tobacco trusts. They asked, rather, for American
citizenship and protection of their rights by the United States
government.[15]

The A.F. of L. later acceded to the Puerto Ricans' demand for
American citizenship, and Gompers worked closely with the labor
members of Congress to secure it, as well as the labor demands of
the Free Federation of Workmen of Puerto Rico. Gompers even
turned against "home rule" or independence for the island, because the agitation for it was an obstacle to the work of the
A.F. of L. organizers. Those who favored national independence,
"a considerable part of the population," according to Gompers,
expressed dissatisfaction with American rule by refusing to give
assistance to United States organizations or institutions, including
the A.F. of L., which they regarded as designed to "keep the
island in the position of a great factory, exploiting cheap labor for
the benefit of large corporations in the United States."[16]

In 1914, Gompers visited Puerto Rico for the second time and
found that conditions were no better than they had been a decade
earlier, except for the industrial workers in the cities. The agricultural workers, particularly in the sugar fields, who formed the
bulk of the population, were if anything worse off than ever. Their
appalling circumstances, to Gompers, were "a stigma upon the
record, the history, and the honor of our country." Furthermore,

the Puerto Ricans had less political and commercial freedom under American rule than they had possessed as Spanish territory.[17]

After Gompers' visit, a depression on the island made conditions even worse. Unemployment and wage reductions were widespread. Early in 1915, there was a general strike of agricultural workers. Strikers were placed on trial for alleged acts of violence, and many union officials, including Iglesias, were indicted for "inciting to riot." Gompers urged Wilson to have an investigation made of conditions in Puerto Rico, violations of the Constitution and laws, and denial of the freedom of organization by the workers. It was deplorable, he thought, "that the burden bearers of an Island under our protection and for which we are responsible, should have the conception that the government of Puerto Rico is under the control of the 'interests' and is concerned solely with property and rights arising from ownership."[18]

Gompers also demanded a new organic law for Puerto Rico which would assure the people a measure of self-government and justice. Testifying on the Jones bill to provide civil government for Puerto Rico, Gompers told the Senate Committee: "There is scarcely within my range of reading and observation an instance of darker pages of tragedy and wrong doing and injustice and brutality than the pages of the history of the people of Porto Rico since they have become part of the United States. I mean this both economically, industrially, socially, judicially, and politically. The rights to which they were entitled and which they exercised under Spanish domination have been denied them by the Government of the United States." Gompers appealed for an organic act which would grant American citizenship to the people of Puerto Rico, incorporate a bill of rights, establish a maximum eight-hour day for government employees, and provide universal manhood suffrage.[19]

In 1917, the Jones bill was passed by the House of Representatives, granting American citizenship but only minor increases in self-government. It took away the right of franchise and eligibility to membership in the insular legislature from those who did not have certain property and educational qualifications. Gompers, following events closely, asserted this would force upon Puerto Rico "a feudal government dominated by political and financial pirates." It would disfranchise 160,000 of the 205,000 voters and intrench the power of the American trusts. He urged that we keep faith with Puerto Rico. As a result of protests from the A.F. of L., the Free Federation of Puerto Rico, and others, this provision was removed from the bill, and on March 2 the organic act was passed. By this act, Gompers believed, the United States had redeemed its pledge to the people of Puerto Rico, "the inhabitants of that island were given a country." The main struggle for political freedom was over, he thought; it only remained for the workers, through their trade unions, to continue the struggle to destroy privilege and establish equality of opportunity.[20]

4. THE MEXICAN REVOLUTION

GOMPERS' INTEREST IN MEXICAN AFFAIRS, AS IN other international labor relations, was motivated by two considerations. By helping the workers of other countries to raise their standard of living, there would be less danger of their undermining American standards. Also, the co-operation of the workers of the world would help to establish brotherhood and peace and strengthen democracy everywhere, including the United States.

In 1911, Diaz resigned as the result of a revolutionary movement he could no longer suppress. He had ruled for thirty-five years in the interests of the landed aristocracy and foreign capitalists. The revolution was led by the middle class under Francisco Madero and supported by the peons in the hope of recovering their lands and liberties.

American business interests with Mexican investments, led by William Randolph Hearst, immediately began to press Taft to intervene against the revolutionists and protect their property holdings. Taft resisted this pressure, but thousands of American soldiers were sent to the Mexican border for "maneuvers," actually to prevent international complications that would stimulate pressure for intervention. The Mexicans were alarmed, fearing that these troops were to be used to stamp out the revolution. R. Flores Magon, one of the revolutionary leaders, wrote to Gompers, urging him to speak out promptly and decisively against intervention. He stated that the Mexican people were fighting to throw off the chains of the same monopolistic Wall Street autocracy against which the American workers were contending, and they were therefore united in a common cause.[21]

Gompers replied that it was not known what the purpose of the military maneuvers was, but he hoped that Magon's apprehensions were unfounded, not only because the Mexican people had the right to govern their own affairs, but because intervention would be a blow to the integrity of the United States and the liberty of the American people. But Gompers wanted more specific information as to the principles and purposes of the Mexican revolution: "If the present regime is to be supplanted by another, the present revolutionary party, without fundamentally changing conditions which shall make for the improvement of the workers' opportunities, and a greater regard for their rights and their interests, then the American labor movement can look upon such a change with entire indifference."[22]

Magon replied that the revolution was an economic war, the purpose of which was to secure to the workers the full product of their toil through the possession of land by the peasants, the reduction of hours and increased wages for the laborers, and liberty for all. He argued that American capitalists were looking to cheap Mexican labor to break the back of organized labor in the United States, both by importing Mexican workers and by transferring capital to Mexico. "If our people can win for themselves industrial liberty they will work out their own salvation. But if American labor stands idly by, and permits them to be crushed by militarism, at the behest of the money power, they will drag with them, to the lowest depths, their immediate neighbors—the American workingmen."[23]

Gompers transmitted this correspondence to his Executive Council and asked whether the requested protest against intervention should be made, reminding his colleagues that the A.F. of L. had gone on record in favor of arbitration of international disputes. Only Mitchell was in favor of the action, as the miners faced the competition of Mexican workers more than any other group of organized labor; other labor leaders preferred to wait and see what developed. Not until a year and a half later, at the convention of 1912, did the A.F. of L. express its sympathy with the Mexican revolution and state its opposition to any intervention by the United States government.[24]

The inauguration of Wilson changed the situation. Whereas Taft had pursued a consistent policy of nonintervention, Wilson desired to shape the Mexican revolution into a constitutional and moral pattern of his own making and to establish a constitutional government responsive to the needs of the people (as he saw them) and amenable to his direction. The situation was complicated by a counterrevolution, supported by the landowners and foreign investors, in which Victoriana Huerta was installed as president. Although pressed by powerful financial interests, Wilson refused to recognize a "government of butchers" which had overthrown a constitutional government by military usurpation; besides, the Constitutionalist revolutionary movement under Venustiano Carranza indicated that Huerta's claim to having pacified Mexico was false. However, Wilson was convinced that unless a stable constitutional government was elected, full-scale American intervention was inevitable. He declared that if Huerta would give assurances of a free election in which he would not be a candidate, the United States would attempt to bring the warring factions together in a common program and government. But his intervention was resented by all factions in Mexico, and his proposals were indignantly rejected. Wilson then adopted the policy of "watchful waiting," urging American citizens to withdraw from Mexico, and forbade the export of arms and munitions to either side in the civil war.

In October, Huerta, with the support of British oil interests, inaugurated a military dictatorship. Wilson then adopted a new course: he announced that the United States would employ such means as necessary to secure Huerta's "retirement." He sought to isolate him diplomatically, urging all nations to withhold recognition from his government, and to encourage the Constitutionalists. Wilson's only interest in Carranza was whether he could control Mexico and whether Wilson could control him in the establishment of a government in which foreign property and contracts would be safe. He offered to co-operate with Carranza on certain conditions, but Carranza made it plain he did not want the advice and support of the United States and would resist the entry of American troops into Mexico.[25]

At the A.F. of L. convention in November 1913, a resolution was introduced sharply opposing armed intervention by the United States in Mexico and urging President Wilson to continue his efforts to effect a peaceful adjustment of the Mexican conflict.

Gompers opposed the first part of this resolution. Madero, he asserted, had represented the best interests and aspirations of the Mexican people and had been overthrown in a blood bath for the purpose of restoring the old regime. If the Huerta regime was permitted too long to strengthen its hold on Mexico, it would take at least another generation before the people could inaugurate another revolution. For Gompers, the Monroe Doctrine, the purpose of which was to make the American continent secure in order to work out its own salvation through self-government, could only be maintained if the American nations gave reasonable protection to foreign investments. Otherwise, despite protests from the United States, foreign governments would interfere and the Monroe Doctrine would be destroyed. Gompers was, in essence, upholding the Roosevelt corollary to the Monroe Doctrine and endorsing Wilson's effort to guide and control the Mexican revolution and to "teach the South American republics to elect good men." The A.F. of L. should strengthen Wilson's hand in trying to find a peaceful solution of the problem; "but I do not believe we should resolve under any and all circumstances to denounce intervention and thus bring comfort and hope into the heart of Huerta. I do not think we ought to encourage him to say that the labor movement of America . . . will not permit intervention and he may go on carrying out his bloody record." That clause of the resolution was thereupon withdrawn and the remainder adopted unanimously.[26]

American financial interests were pressing for intervention in order to establish "order" in Mexico, and in April 1914 an excuse was provided: the crew of an American naval ship was arrested in Tampico for allegedly violating martial law. The Mexican authorities soon released the men and apologized for the act, but the commander of the American fleet demanded a formal apology, punishment of the guilty officer, and a twenty-one-gun salute to the American flag. Appealing to national dignity and honor, Wilson asked for and received authority from Congress to intervene in Mexico with armed force. The next day, a German merchantman was about to land a cargo of arms at Vera Cruz, and to prevent them from getting into Huerta's hands, Wilson ordered American forces to bombard and capture Vera Cruz. Both Huerta and Carranza protested against this invasion of Mexican sov-

ereignty. War was averted by a mediation conference sponsored
by Argentina, Brazil, and Chile—the ABC powers—but Huerta
was unable to resist Wilson's further pressure and abdicated in
July, to be succeeded by Carranza. Wilson had achieved his purpose, but he had failed to secure control of the revolution and
threw his support to Pancho Villa, one of Carranza's chieftains
who had manifested a willingness to follow Wilson's advice.[27]

The A.F. of L. Executive Council expressed its gratification
at the victory of the Constitutionalists. It urged Carranza to reconsider his declaration that draconian punishment and retribution
would be meted out to the Huertists. A more humanitarian course
would have a tranquillizing effect and tend to unite the people of
Mexico in support of an orderly government. It was also suggested
that a definite declaration be made that the Constitutionalists
would effect a just division of the lands of Mexico for the working
people, which would do more than anything else to bring peace,
unity, and progress to the people, and stability to the government
of Mexico.[28]

When it became apparent that Villa's chances of success were
hopeless, and that Carranza had the backing of the people for his
land and labor reforms, Wilson dropped his support of Villa and
shifted to a policy of neutrality. But powerful forces were again
pressing for intervention; these included Hearst, Theodore Roosevelt, and the Catholic Church. Receiving reports that Mexico was
ruined and devastated, the people near starvation, and anarchy
imminent, Wilson determined to establish a government capable
of restoring order. On June 2, he warned the Mexican leaders to
stop fighting or face American intervention. But Carranza denied
the right of the United States to interfere, and the House of the
World's Workers (Casa del Obrero Mundial) sent Gompers an
energetic protest, asking that no action be taken to prevent the
fulfillment of the revolution. Gompers transmitted this protest to
Wilson, along with the information that Carranza had guaranteed
freedom of speech, assembly, and association for the Mexican
workers.[29]

Although Wilson continued his efforts to drive Carranza
from power and refused to recognize his government, Gompers
told the Mexicans that Wilson was trying to deal with the situation
with "earnestness, intelligence, and sense" and that he would not

feel obliged to interfere with the internal affairs of Mexico "except in an advisory and friendly capacity." Also, it was the duty of the Mexicans to bring their revolutions to an end, for the United States had a responsibility to help maintain the integrity of the governments of the Latin American countries against interference or invasion by other nations. However, in September, the A.F. of L.'s Executive Council urged Wilson to recognize Carranza, stating that nations had the right to their freedom "without unwarranted outside interference even from those who seek their welfare." Gompers now put it that Carranza was the recognized leader of the Mexican people and had proved himself the friend of the working people. They were supporting him against Villa and others who were pressing their own personal interests.[30]

Three weeks later, Wilson finally recognized Carranza when it became clear that he was firmly established in power. Then Villa turned on the United States, began a campaign to exterminate Americans in the northern states of Mexico, and conducted a series of raids across the United States border, killing a number of Americans in New Mexico. Demands for intervention again arose, this time louder than ever, and Wilson sent a punitive expedition under General John J. Pershing to capture Villa. As the American forces grew in size and penetrated deeply into Mexico, they showed no signs of stopping and began to assume the appearance of an army of occupation. Carranza demanded their withdrawal. Wilson refused, and preparations for war were put in motion. At this moment of crisis, on May 23, Gompers wrote to the House of the World's Workers, calling attention to the necessity of a closer understanding between the workers of the two countries. He proposed that the Mexican labor organizations meet in conference with representatives of the A.F. of L. to discuss matters for the mutual welfare and co-operation of the workers of the sister republics.[31]

A week later, Gompers received an appeal from the leaders of twelve Mexican labor unions. Two armies were facing each other on the border awaiting the signal to throw themselves into a war that could only bring evil to both countries and crush the Mexican revolution. They appealed to the workers of the United States to "raise a formidable agitation against imperialism, agitation against a war between two brother countries, the consequences of which we, the workers on both sides of the frontier, alone would suffer; because the instigators, the jingoes, those of the holy alliance—composed of exiled Mexicans, reactionaries, land owners, Wall Street grafters, and clerical magnates—would remain in their homes, quietly waiting the moment for the distribution of the booty."[32]

Gompers saw great hope in the coming conference between American and Mexican labor representatives. If it checked the forces clamoring for intervention, the world would be given a note of inspiration that would somewhat compensate for the failure of labor to prevent the outbreak of the World War. Gompers urged the American workers and the people generally to be patient with the mistakes of those who were learning how to be free. The workers had a concern in the success of the Mexican revolution, for there was no boundary line between the industrial problems of the workers of the two countries: "The labor movement of Mexico has dared to assert that there is something infinitely higher than property rights and the mere forms of established law and order. They have proclaimed to the world that they wish to establish a government in which human rights shall be paramount and land and property shall be made to serve mankind." The American workers could not but do all in their power to help such a struggle in the spirit of fraternity and co-operation.[33]

In response to Gompers' invitation of May 23, a delegation of Mexican labor representatives was chosen to meet with the Executive Council. While they were en route to Washington, a clash occurred between American and Constitutionalist soldiers at Carrizel and several American soldiers were taken prisoner. Wilson presented an ultimatum to Carranza that the American soldiers be released and prepared to ask Congress for authority to use armed forces to clear the northern states of "bandits." Gompers was advised that the Mexican ambassador in Washington was convinced that the only hope that Carranza would release the prisoners was through an appeal made by Gompers. Thereupon Gompers immediately wired to Carranza: "In the name of common justice and humanity, in the interests of a better understanding between the peoples and the governments of the United States and Mexico, for the purpose of giving the opportunity to maintain peace and avoid the horrors of war, upon the grounds of the highest patriotism and love, I appeal to you to release the American soldiers held by your officers in Chihuahua." On the same evening Carranza issued an order to release the soldiers, and Gompers expressed his appreciation for an act which would clear the way for a mutually honorable settlement of the difficulties between the two countries.[34]

On July 1, the Mexican labor mission appeared at the Executive Council meeting, representing the Mexican Department of Labor, the House of the World's Workers, the Mexican Federation of Labor, the Federation of Workers' Syndicates, and several other trade and regional organizations. Gompers stated that an effort was in progress to import Mexican workers to the United States as strikebreakers and to undermine work standards. The purpose of the conference between the United States and Mexican labor representatives was to counteract this movement, as well as to consider economic relations between the workers of the two countries and the political crisis between the two governments.

The Mexican mission agreed with Gompers' views, stressing that the most important objective now was to prevent war. The labor movement and the revolutionary movement led by Carranza were one and the same, they asserted; land was being distributed to the peons, an eight-hour law was in effect, and labor was being recognized. If intervention succeeded in overthrowing the Constitutionalist government, the labor movement and its gains would also be crushed.

A joint statement was adopted by the Executive Council and the Mexican labor spokesmen. It expressed the hope that their conference had laid the basis for better understanding and collaboration between the workers of the two countries and that it would lead to better relations between the two nations. It agreed that another conference should be held, in which the workers would be more generally represented, to establish a federation of the labor movements of all the nations of the Western Hemisphere. The relations between Mexico and the United States must be based upon the will of the masses of the people and the labor movements were their best instrumentalities. The declaration called upon the governments to adjust their differences without war and to establish conditions conducive to permanent peace with justice. Finally, it urged the governments to appoint commissions to consider the differences that had brought them to the brink of war and to make recommendations for adjustment of those differences.[35]

The action of the Mexican and American workers' representatives was an important force in the flood of protests to Wilson against war, and a more rational attitude returned immediately in the administration and in Congress. In July, an agreement was signed providing for a joint commission to investigate the relations between the two countries and to make recommendations for their adjustment. When the announcement was made of the agreement for a mediation conference, Edmundo Martinez, Mexican labor leader, wrote to Gompers: "We all probably will never fully realize the great consequences of your wonderful work for the welfare of the working masses and incidentally for the happiness of the people of the great American continent. . . . It seems to me like a dream to have been aligned against the most powerful interests of the world, and have won. God grant that the working people of our two countries may realize their great power and work hand in hand for our general emancipation. . . ."[36]

Gompers asked Wilson to appoint a representative of the labor movement to the commission, but, since this was not done, he had to work behind the scenes in an effort to influence its work. The conferences were bogging down over Mexican demands for the withdrawal of the Pershing expedition and American insistence on discussing Mexican taxes on American property, internal conditions in northern Mexico, and the protection of British and American oil properties. Franklin K. Lane, chairman of the American commissioners, wrote to Gompers stating that the situation was not hopeful and intimating that he would like to talk to Gompers. Gompers went to Atlantic City, where the joint commission was meeting, and conferred with Lane for two hours. It is not known what Gompers said to Lane, but evidently Lane asked him to use his influence with the Mexican commissioners to drop their demands for withdrawal of the punitive expedition. Gompers then secured a meeting with the Mexican commissioners.

He admitted that their demand was well founded on the grounds of international law and the sovereignty of Mexico as a nation, and he believed Wilson would really like to withdraw the troops. But he also believed that if they were withdrawn without any safeguard being provided for life and property in the United

States, and if another attack was made on American soil by Mexicans, the American people would become so inflamed that nothing could prevent war between the two countries. Therefore he urged the Mexican commissioners not to demand withdrawal, as the presence of American troops was really in Mexico's interest. Wilson and the American commissioners had a high-minded attitude and were disposed to be fair. Gompers went on to remind them that an election was impending, and that in view of Hughes' statements on the Mexican situation and the known interests that were supporting his candidacy, if he were elected "nothing but darkness [would be] before us all." Failure to reach a settlement would injure Wilson's chances for re-election.

Gompers then raised another matter which was even more important to him. On August 1, Carranza had issued a decree providing the death penalty for striking or inciting strikes in enterprises devoted to the public service. Gompers protested to the commissioners against this decree on the ground that it was a violation of the agreement between the government and the labor movement of Mexico and that it was brutal and contrary to justice. He warned that the American labor movement would not co-operate with a government which depended for its existence on carrying out such a decree.

The meeting of the A.F. of L. convention in November brought the matter to a critical stage, for Gompers was convinced that unless the decree were repealed, the Federation would express its deep indignation, and if labor withdrew its support from Carranza his government would fall, since it depended for favor-able publicity in the United States primarily on the A.F. of L., the socialist *Call*, and a few other publications. Gompers believed that he, in co-operation with Carranza's opponents in the United States, could instigate a publicity campaign that would "tear up all Mexico." "If all other means failed, we knew that we could use this threat to secure the repeal of the Carranza decree." The Mexican commissioners subsequently assured Gompers that the decree would be withdrawn as soon as the situation permitted. This information was received in time to present it to the Federa-tion convention in the report of the committee on international relations, with which Gompers had been in constant consultation.[37]

Shortly afterwards, a protocol was signed by the commissioners, providing for the withdrawal of the American expedition within forty days if conditions in the northern states warranted it. But Carranza rejected this agreement and the commission broke up. However, it had served to preserve the peace and helped Wilson win the election. The United States then had to withdraw or else break off relations with Mexico and attempt to occupy the northern states. With impending war against Germany staring him in the face, Wilson could do nothing but withdraw. In the meantime, the Mexican people had elected a constituent assembly which adopted a new constitution. In March, a Constitutionalist government was elected, with Carranza as president, which was recognized by the United States two days later.[38]

Part VI

THE WAR
1914-1919

Chapter Nineteen

NEUTRALITY AND
INTERVENTION

For a generation, the great powers of Europe had scrambled for markets and raw materials, for control of trade routes and strategic bases, for railroad and mining franchises in the "backward" areas of the world, for domination of peoples and the wealth of their lands. By 1914 most of the available world had been grabbed up, and as their rivalry grew more intense, the powers embarked on unprecedented programs of militarization and naval construction in preparation for the showdown.

On June 28, 1914, the Crown Prince of the Austro-Hungarian empire was assassinated in Serbia, Austria-Hungary mobilized its forces and presented ultimatums, and Russia mobilized to thwart her rival for domination of the Balkan peninsula. On July 28, Austria declared war on Serbia, a chain of alliances was set into motion, and by August 4 all the great powers of Europe were at each other's throats.

The day after Austria's declaration of war against Serbia, Gompers condemned her for launching a slaughter "for the glory and aggrandizement of an effete royalty." All over Europe, he said, the masses were struggling for economic, political, and social improvement; now the monarchs were inaugurating war to divert people's attention from their own ills and their own struggles. "There is no telling yet what course the masses of the people of Europe are going to pursue in regard to this unnatural, unjustified and unholy war. These men do not lack patriotism . . . but the people can no longer ruthlessly . . . sacrifice their lives and their beings. . . ."[1]

After the European powers had exchanged militant declarations, Gompers declared that the war was condemnable "from every viewpoint," and that he would associate himself with any movement to end it and to work for permanent international peace and democracy.[2] But he did not hold the Allies equally responsible with the Central Powers for the outbreak of war. Fundamentally, he asserted, the war was caused by two conditions. One was the wielding of autocratic power by irresponsible monarchies, by which he plainly meant Germany and Austria. The war was planned and precipitated by autocrats who saw the forces of democracy constantly displacing the institutions of reaction. Gompers saw evidence of the growth of democracy in the campaign of the German workers for free speech and libertarian principles, in the agitation of the Austrian workers for freedom of association and improved conditions, in the discontent and strikes of the Russian workers, and *in the granting of social security and Irish home rule by the British government*. Thus he contrasted growing British democracy with the struggles of continental masses against German and Austrian autocracy.

The second cause of the war, according to Gompers, was the competitive arms race among the nations. This was made possible by the existence of autocratic governments which were not responsible to their peoples. He saw it as significant that England and France, the two most democratic European countries, were the most unwilling to be drawn into the war. It was England which had proposed a naval holiday in 1913 and the "war lords" who refused to accept the proposal. Gompers passed over the fact that the Central Powers were behind in the naval race and the acceptance of a construction holiday would have meant accepting and freezing British naval superiority; the United States also rejected the proposed holiday.[3]

Gompers did not have to wait long to find out what course the masses in Europe would take. The Second International had repeatedly declared in its congresses that the socialist parties would not only agitate against the war, but would vote against furnishing men and money for it and would utilize the political and economic crisis caused by the war to rouse the people and thereby hasten the abolition of capitalism. But when war came, most of the socialist parties ignored their pledges, accepted the "defense of the fatherland" slogans, and followed their governments into war.

Gompers rebuked "the absolute treachery of the socialist

movement in Europe to the ideals and aspirations of international solidarity and human brotherhood." A year later he spoke of the failure of the socialist movement as weakness rather than treachery. In the hour of crisis, he stated, the pledges of the workingmen were shattered by the outbreak of war. "Secret diplomacy and arbitrary autocracy lifted the battle standards, raised the cry that the integrity of the fatherland was at stake, and placed the working men of all nations in a position where adherence to their pledges and to the larger interests of humanity would have branded them as traitors." In this situation, instinct prevailed over reason and the workers rushed into the path that had been marked out by the ruling classes.[4]

But whether due to treachery or weakness, the policy of the European socialists and trade union leaders was exactly the policy followed by Gompers, who supported the pro-Allies "neutrality" policy of the Wilson administration, endorsed the "preparedness" program, shed his "pacifism," and, when the time came, supported United States intervention in the war—in fact, helped to lead the country into the war. As Gompers became a "belligerent," he discovered that the European abandonment of the antiwar position was neither treachery nor weakness, but that the position itself had been a mistake. In a speech in 1916, he stated that pacifism was a beautiful theory but was based on wishes rather than on reality. "No one can hear of the atrocities of the terrible carnage of the present war, of the destruction on the battlefields and on the high seas without a feeling of horror that civilized men can plan such methods, can use the skill of their minds and bodies and the wisdom of past generations to such terrible purpose. But what if these horrors done to the bodies of men shall prevent great horrors to the minds—the souls of men? The pacifists . . . have failed as I had failed to understand and to evaluate that quality in the human race which makes men willing to risk their all for an ideal. . . . Resistance to injustice and tyranny and low ideals is inseparable from a virile fighting quality that has given purpose and force to ennobling causes to all nations."[5]

When the United States itself became an official belligerent, Gompers went to the last extreme in denouncing his former "pacifism." Now it was not only a mistake but a gigantic hoax perpetrated by the Kaiser. He revealed that the Carnegie Peace

Association had arranged with him before the war to publish a compilation of his antiwar utterances. While the manuscript was at the printer's, war broke out. "I had been befuddled and fooled by a schemer and deviser unparalleled in the history of the world," he declared, and rushed to the printer to get hold of "that damn-fool stuff" he had written and stopped the publication. Gompers now realized, he stated, that the "bunk" about international peace had been foisted upon the labor movement of the world by the German socialists who were acting as agents of the Kaiser to lull the world into a fancied security while they were preparing to dominate the world.[6]

On September 4, 1914, President Wilson issued a proclamation of neutrality, and Gompers endorsed it, but neither was really neutral. The government could not have entered the war in 1914 even if it had wanted to, for the majority of Americans saw no reason for involvement in a senseless holocaust. Also, by remaining neutral, the United States could act as mediator and thus either bring the war to an end, as some hoped, or influence the outcome of the war in a manner favorable to the United States, as others expected. Finally, by remaining a non-belligerent, the United States could profit from the neutral munitions trade and shipping, and later through financial loans.

But the "neutrality" policy, or more correctly nonbelligerent status, of the United States obviously served the British from the beginning. Partly this was because British naval supremacy made America's neutral trade almost exclusively a trade with the Allies, partly because German military and economic aggrandizement was held by powerful American interests to be more dangerous to their interests than a victory of the Allies, and partly because British traditions, culture and political ideas and forms were more in harmony with those of influential American groups than were Germany's. American policy, which was acquiescence in England's violation of American neutral rights, forced Germany to resort to submarine warfare. Then the United States held Germany "strictly accountable" for the interference with American commerce and the destruction of American property and lives.

As early as February 1915, Robert Lansing, then a counsellor in the State Department and soon to become Secretary of State when Bryan resigned in protest against the government's unneutral policy, saw that the situation and the policy of the United States would lead the country into war. For, he believed, since the United States was rapidly becoming a cobelligerent, Germany had much to gain and little to lose by hostilities with the United States; war could not harm Germany's commercial fortunes while it would make possible the disruption of the American-Allies trade. In addition, he considered that the American navy would add little to the potential of the Allies, and that it would never be possible to send large armies to Europe. By the sumer of 1915, the policy of the United States was clearly and definitely established: protect American economic and business activities within the framework of a pro-Allies "neutrality"; attempt to influence the outcome of the war by acting as mediator; maintain an attitude of "strict accountability" toward Germany; and prepare public opinion for eventual entry into the war if that should become necessary to prevent a German victory.[7]

Gompers' "war policy" was almost identical with that of the government. He was in general agreement with the reasons which underlay the government's policy, and besides, his ties with the Wilson administration and the Democratic party strengthened his inclination to support their position. His own English background might well have contributed to his attitude. But, in addition, Gompers had objectives in the labor movement that were remarkably parallel to those of the government in the political field. He too found it necessary to maintain a pretense of neutrality while striving to lead the labor movement into a prowar position. Gompers was not only pro-Ally from the beginning, but was actually in favor of entering the war at that time. As Florence Thorne, who probably knew the working of Gompers' mind better than anyone else, put it, he "went to war in 1914," discarding all of his previous antiwar declarations as "childish nonsense." But he could not say so publicly at that time, because the American workers were strongly in favor of staying out of the war. Furthermore, a partisan attitude toward the war might have disrupted the A.F. of L., with the multitude of nationalities among its members.[8]

Just as the government hoped to use its neutral position to mediate between the belligerents, thus securing an influence in the war's settlement and in world councils afterwards, so Gompers expected that labor's neutrality would permit it to help end the war, influence the settlement in ways favorable to its interests, and establish its leadership in the international trade union movement. Just as business would profit by carrying on "neutral" trade, so labor would, in expanding war production industries, find fuller employment, higher wages, and recovery from the depression that began in 1914.

In addition, Gompers hoped that by supporting the administration in its foreign policy and eventually in war, the trade unions could secure recognition from the government, a greater voice in the councils of the nation, and many concessions in the way of union standards in war work. Furthermore, by proving its loyalty and patriotism, Gompers expected to win respectability for organized labor: the support of public opinion and a degree of friendliness from employers and government. At the same time, he could personally demonstrate his passionate devotion to "Americanism," convince the public that he was not an "agitator" and a "demagogue," to say nothing of a lawbreaker, and attain recognition as a "statesman of labor."

For a while, Gompers hoped that the United States might act as a mediator between the warring nations, and that the A.F. of L. might play a prominent part in such action. But he soon gave up the idea, not only because it was impractical, but because he was quickly moving toward a position of unneutrality. Easley had advised him to leave all peace moves up to the President, and Gompers was also receiving advice from British labor emissaries and information on the "true history" of the war from Sir Gilbert Parker, later official secret head of British propaganda in the United States.[9] During the first year of the war, Gompers corresponded with Karl Legien, president of the International Federation of Trade Unions and leader of the German trade union movement, and with W. A. Appleton, secretary of the General Federation of Trade Unions of England. Legien warned Gompers not to be deceived by the lies about Germany that were being broadcast in the United States due to the cutting of the transatlantic cable and the British monopoly on propaganda emanating from Europe. But Appleton poured into Gompers' ears stories of the uncivilized methods of warfare being employed by Germany. He believed—and Gompers substantially agreed—it would take many years to restore fraternal relations between the British and

German workers and therefore suggested the importance of maintaining and developing amicable relations between the English-speaking workers.[10]

Gompers was inaugurating his own campaign against neutrality and peace. In June 1915, he declined an invitation to speak at a peace meeting in Carnegie Hall. He explained that he had come to the conclusion that there were some things even more abhorrent than war, namely to be deprived of freedom, justice, and security. Against any attempt to undermine or destroy these fundamentals of human existence and development, "I would not only fight to defeat it, but prevail upon every red blooded, liberty and humanity loving man to resist to the last degree." If the United States were dragged into the war to defend its freedom and safety, he added, the labor movement could take only one position, and that was to support the war.[11]

This meeting was part of a campaign by the American League to Limit Armaments and the American Neutrality League, which had succeeded in enlisting the support of a number of labor men. After the sinking of the *Lusitania*, a sizable labor opinion against war came to the fore, particularly in the Midwest and on the Pacific Coast. The international unions with headquarters in Indianapolis (miners, carpenters, barbers, teamsters, bookbinders, stonecutters, iron workers, and printers) held a conference of officers on May 27 to discuss the situation. Daniel Tobin, the chairman of the meeting, wrote to Gompers that it had decided to suggest that a general trade union conference be called by Gompers in case the situation reached a dangerous point. Gompers received similar communications from several other affiliated organizations. He told them all that he would consider the proposal, but set himself to the task of discrediting the peace movement and retrieving from it the labor men who had been "caught in the net." He eventually secured the withdrawal of practically every one of these men from the peace movement.[12]

By July 1 he not only abandoned the hope that the United States might mediate in the war but positively opposed the idea. He indicated that he could not support a demand that the Allies end the war, because they were fighting for their freedom and must continue to fight until it was won and justice established.[13]

By this time Gompers had got himself into a frame of mind

in which all peace propaganda or advocacy of strict neutrality appeared to him as German propaganda. "I was convinced," he wrote later, "that the real issues of the War concerned those who believed in democratic institutions and that the time had come when the world could not longer exist part democratic and part autocratic. It was an issue upon which there could be no real neutrality, and therefore propaganda for neutrality was propaganda to maintain autocracy." Every strike among the seamen, longshoremen, and munitions workers he believed or suspected to be the work of the Kaiser's agents, every peace meeting a secret plot to commit the United States to pro-German policies.[14]

During 1916 the chief domestic issue connected with the war was "preparedness." The demand for an accelerated armament program came primarily from business and industrial interests and from those who favored intervention in the war. Partly because of their pressure in an election year, and partly because Wilson and others believed the nation must be prepared for any eventuality, Gompers gave his support to a series of measures for strengthening the military and naval forces. He fully supported the preparedness program but insisted that it be carried out without establishing militarism or losing its democratic character and control.

As early as April 1915, Gompers told the *Army and Navy Journal* that "The power to enforce the right is a tremendous element in establishing justice. . . . Anti-militarism does not mean to give up the right of national defense." With the growth of the United States and its increasing interest in the world, a larger military establishment was necessary to keep peace, but this could be done without creating militarism, for control of the army and navy and the state militias was in the hands of elected civilian officials. Gompers also favored a general military training program to create a reserve army, providing it did not become an agency for inculcating militaristic ideas. Advocates of preparedness did not take seriously his remarks about militarism and democratic control; the president of the Army League, one of the leading jingo organizations in the country, expressed admiration for Gompers' patriotic stand for the "correct solution" of the national defense problem. He was gratified "that such a distinguished labor leader entertains the same general ideas on the question of national defense as the advocates of military preparedness both in civilian life and in the army."[15]

Gompers presented a comprehensive statement of his views on preparedness at the meeting of the National Civic Federation in Washington in January 1916, and his speech was printed as a government document. Asserting that most people wanted preparedness, he asked what policies should be adopted to meet the need. Gompers believed that the nation must not only consider armaments but must also give consideration to the development, health, and conservation of the people. He would have had the physical training of the citizens directed by the public schools, and seen it furthering broad, general usefulness and ideals rather than narrowly specialized or military purposes. There must also be a spirit among the people that would make them loyal to their country and willing to give themselves to its protection. That spirit could not exist unless they felt that the nation would assure equal opportunities and justice to all. The organizations of the workers must therefore be recognized not only in determining industrial policies, but in directing the political and military agencies that controlled the preparedness program.[16]

In advancing this program, which he hammered away at throughout the year, Gompers had two main objectives. Since there was going to be some kind of preparedness, he wanted to use the opportunity to secure recognition for organized labor and a voice enabling it to minimize militaristic tendencies and gain concessions for itself. But also, he sought to persuade the workers to support the preparedness program by convincing them that it was strictly for defense. As he told the Council of National Defense a year later, England had experienced trouble early in the war in attempts to enlist the services of the workers, and the lack of unity between the government and labor could be duplicated in the United States if the situation were not taken in hand early: "I want the workingmen to do their part if war comes to America."[17]

At the end of 1916, Gompers came out flatly in support of the Allies. In a carefully prepared article for the press, he affirmed that the war had been begun by Germany, and that the governments of England and France had had no intention or desire to make war. The war was clearly a struggle between militaristic

domination and "the fundamental principles of right government." The mission of the world was to destroy Prussian militarism. And, he added, "if I could stop the present conflict by the
raising of a finger I would not raise the finger, because I feel that
something must be determined by this war; that is whether the
rule of the future is to be of autocracy and militarism or of
democracy, liberty and humanity."[18]

In January 1917, the German government decided to resume
unrestricted submarine warfare. The United States had refused to
make any effort to force England to abide by international law,
and U-boat warfare was regarded as the only means of breaking
the blockade and bringing England to consider peace negotiations.
As far as the United States was concerned, Germany determined
that her passage from secret war to open hostilities could have
little effect. Gompers called Germany's policy a warning of "ruthless destruction" of the life and property of any people who might
come within a zone where they had a perfect, lawful right to go:
". . . I could not blind myself to the altered situation in the world's
affairs; that the gauntlet had been thrown down to democracy
and that unless the challenge was accepted autocracy would run
rough-shod over the peoples of the whole world; and from pacifist
came my evolution into a fighting man."[19]

On February 3 the United States broke off diplomatic relations with Germany, and the next day Gompers cabled Legien in
Berlin, with the approval of President Wilson, asking if he could
not prevail on the German government to avoid a break with the
United States and prevent extension of the war. Legien replied
that the resumption of submarine warfare was provoked by the
Allies' rejection of immediate peace negotiations and the continuation of "starvation war" on women and children. No intervention
on his part with the government would have any success unless
the United States prevailed on England to abide by international
law. "I appeal to American labor not to allow themselves to be
made catspaws of warmonger[s] by sailing war zone and thus
contribute extending conflict. International labor must unflinch-
ingly work for immediate peace."[20]

Immediate peace was just what Gompers did not want; he
wanted immediate war. As he put it, a few months later: "To me
it seemed that the entrance of our Republic into this conflict had

been too long delayed, but as a loyal citizen I yielded to the judgment of the Commander-in-Chief of the army and navy of the United States. I felt that the time was near at hand when the outrages would increase in such numbers and in such horror that in self-respect we would take advantage of the current as it served or we would lose our ventures."[21]

At a meeting of the Advisory Commission of the Council of National Defense, Gompers asked for the privilege of making a personal statement. Dr. Franklin H. Martin, another member of the Commission, wrote that Gompers controlled his emotions with difficulty as he began to speak in a low tone: "Providence and opportunity have made me a leader of men who work with their hands. . . . They have accepted me as their teacher. . . . Ten million of these honest men are now looking to me for guidance and leadership in this menace to their principles, to their country, and to their homes. All around us aggression is in the air. Another great President [Wilson] is struggling to find another way out. You, my associates in the Commission and in the Council, no longer believe that peaceful methods will prevail." Then he buried his face in his hands and burst into tears. Suddenly he threw his head back and broke forth: "By God's help I can no longer stand it! I must yield. War to suppress crime is justifiable; and with all my energy and influence I will induce my boys, many of them already straining at the leash, to follow me."[22]

On February 26 Wilson took the last step toward war and the neutralists made their last stand against it. The President appeared before a joint session of Congress and asked for authority to arm merchant ships and to employ any other methods that might be necessary to protect American ships and citizens "in their legitimate and peaceful pursuits on the sea." Senator La Follette, the leader of the Progressives, was convinced that this meant war and furthermore put the power to make war entirely at the President's discretion. Besides, the destruction of armed Allied merchantmen demonstrated that guns did not afford protection against submarines; it would therefore be criminal to arm American ships and lure them to embark on a voyage fraught with peril in the belief that they might resist attack. Supporters of the administration admitted that the effect of the bill would be to take the United States into the war. La Follette and other Progressives prevented the measure from coming to a vote before the adjournment of Congress, but a week later Wilson, declaring that the government had been rendered helpless by "a little group of willful men," accomplished his purpose by Executive Order.[23]

Meanwhile, Gompers had been endeavoring to educate "his boys" to meet the approaching crisis, and late in February decided that it was time for "the teacher of the workers" to line them up for war. On February 27 a meeting of the Railway Employees Department of the A.F. of L. was being held in Washington. Gompers asked them to meet with him that evening for a special conference. He told them that war was probably imminent, and that the labor movement could not wait until it happened before formulating a definite policy and deciding on the part labor must take. In England the workers had not taken the war seriously when it began, or had been hostile to the war and the government. Consequently, the government, without the co-operation or consultation of organized labor, had introduced compulsion in industry and in military service, and the workers had had to submit or be regarded as traitors to their country. "I am unwilling to contribute to that attitude on the part of the American labor movement," Gompers declared. The alternative he proposed was for labor to take its place in the war effort, perform its patriotic duty, and at the same time see to it that its rights were protected during the war. Labor had to choose between casting its lot with the government and "help guide it aright" or withhold its co-operation and be whipped into line.

The union leaders present agreed with Gompers and it was decided that a conference of all union representatives should be called to declare labor's position on the war. Two reasons for the action were expressed. A movement was developing to undermine existing trade agreements, and in case of war the effort would undoubtedly be stepped up. A labor conference could place labor on the right side of public opinion and the government and help to give it influence in government agencies to stop the antilabor movement. Also, such a conference would head off the peace movement, which seemed to be growing day by day, particularly in the labor movement.[24]

The Executive Council met on March 9 and approved a declaration that had been drawn up by Gompers. Three days later it was presented to the full conference of officers of the A.F. of L.'s affiliated unions and adopted without amendment. "American Labor's Position in Peace or in War" declared that the masses, who represented the ideals and institutions of democracy, must determine the course they would pursue if a crisis arose necessitating the protection of the country. Labor had reached an understanding of its rights and power obliging it to make constructive proposals for the nation's problems.

War did not stop the necessity for struggle to establish and maintain industrial rights. Workers in wartime had to keep one eye on the exploiters at home and the other upon the enemy, thus making full mobilization for defense impossible. Now, as a fundamental step in preparedness, the nation must establish justice in social and economic relations. Instead of finding in war new opportunities for exploitation under the guise of national necessity, the rights of the workers must be recognized and protected so that they might give wholehearted service to the country. They must have a voice in the councils that dealt with the conduct of war and the conditions under which the workers gave service.

Labor, the manifesto continued, recognized its obligation to serve in defense of the country, whether in the military or industrial force. But the conditions of work and pay should conform to principles of human welfare, and the government which demanded that men and women give their labor power or their lives to the country should also demand the service of property, the profits of which should be limited to fixed percentages. Labor further demanded that the mobilization of industry be left in the hands of industry and organized labor in co-operation with the government. Work in government and private establishments should conform to trade union standards, and when women were employed they should receive equal pay for equal work.

The labor leaders concluded by eloquently "pledging ourselves in peace or in war, in stress or in storm, to stand unreservedly by the standard of liberty and the safety and preservation of the institutions and ideals of our Republic. . . ."

The conference adopted their declaration unanimously, although Tobin of the teamsters gave his approval reluctantly, resenting the manner in which Gompers tried to ram it down the throats of the delegates, who were "not allowed to change a word."

When the declaration had been adopted, Andrew Furuseth came up to Gompers and said, "That sounds the death-knell of the American Federation of Labor, and your forty years of work for labor you have destroyed today." The officials of the United Mine Workers, International Typographical Union, Western Federation of Miners, Ladies Garment Workers Union, and the Journeymen Barbers had refused to attend the conference, feeling that labor should attempt to halt the drive to war instead of encourage it by giving prior endorsement. As John P. White, president of the miners' union, wrote to Gompers, "I see no humanitarian issues in the present war. In my broad travels, I find little sentiment among the working people in favor of this terrible war." Within the trade unions, the declaration met with lukewarm endorsement or unorganized opposition. Even those who accepted it generally did so because of its demands for union standards and recognition rather than its pledge of support for the war. Few labor bodies were given an opportunity to express themselves on the declaration, and its acceptance was therefore largely passive. But it was interpreted by the country as an active endorsement of America's participation in the war and as a pledge of labor's loyalty.[25]

This was also Gompers' interpretation of the proclamation. In reporting it to the Council of National Defense, he did not even bother to refer to the demands for recognition, protection of rights, and equality of sacrifice, but spoke only of the "comprehensive declaration of loyalty" which the conference had produced. And Gompers proudly boasted that the declaration smoothed the way for America's entrance into the war. He stated later that the only thing standing in the way of a declaration of war at that time was that the President and Congress were not sure of the position that would be taken by the masses of the working people, and that labor's proclamation of united support gave them the necessary assurance and encouragement and helped to prepare public opinion for the declaration of war.[26]

On March 14, Germany's threatened submarine warfare was resumed, and five American merchantmen were attacked in the next five days. About the same time, Ambassador Walter Hines Page was writing Wilson from London that England would be unable longer to continue her large purchases of war supplies from the United States without a large credit from the United

States government. This would cause almost a complete cessation of the war trade and produce a panic in the United States. The only way to avoid this, he advised, was by declaring war on Germany, which would enable the United States to grant the necessary credit. On April 2, President Wilson came before Congress and stated that neutrality was no longer desirable when the peace of the world and the freedom of the people were menaced by autocratic powers. He asked Congress to declare war on Germany "for the ultimate peace of the world and for the liberation of its people. . . . The world must be made safe for democracy." Brushing aside a last plea from La Follette to let the people vote on the question, Congress passed a joint resolution on April 6 declaring war on the German Empire.

Chapter Twenty

IN THE SERVICE OF
HIS COUNTRY

1. THE COUNCIL OF NATIONAL DEFENSE

As PART OF THE PREPAREDNESS PROGRAM, CONGRESS created a Council of National Defense in August 1916. The Council was charged with co-ordinating industries and resources for national security and preparing for their immediate concentration and utilization in time of war. It consisted of the Secretaries of War, Navy, Interior, Agriculture, Commerce, and Labor and was to be aided by an Advisory Commission of seven persons to serve without compensation. Gompers was appointed to the Advisory Commission.

The Council of National Defense and the Advisory Commission held their first meeting jointly at the Willard Hotel in Washington on December 6. The members were invited by Julius Rosenwald, a member of the Commission, to dine at his home the preceding evening. Most of the men there met Gompers for the first time and, according to Dr. Frank Martin, were surprised to find that this "foreign agitator" spoke quietly, in correct English, and had a courteous and genial manner which immediately won their sympathy and even admiration. Martin remarked that the "personal charm of Samuel Gompers, one of the secrets of his leadership and influence, had been borne in upon us."

When the Commission met, it discussed at length the formulation of rules and regulations and proposals for action. The discussion continued the next day, each member having a different point of view on how to prepare the nation for war. They continued until about 5:00 p.m., making apparently little progress, and all being quite weary. Then Gompers said he believed he might be able to dictate a plan of organization that would crystallize the consensus of opinion. The other members welcomed the suggestion, and a stenographer was called. To their surprise, Gompers did not retire from the room, but called the stenographer in. "With resignation we sat back to watch this test," Dr. Martin wrote. "His ever-present solace, a big cigar, held between his lips with two fingers, his large shaggy head resting on the back of his capacious chair, his eyes turned ceilingward, our brilliant associate began slowly to speak. Without hesitating, he dictated within the next 15 minutes an orderly outline of a plan of organization for the conduct of the routine business of the Advisory Commission and of joint service with the Council of National Defense. . . . The result was almost a miracle of perfection. . . . As the reading ceased, his six tired conferees broke forth in applause and voiced their appreciation and approval."

Gompers modestly stated that he had done nothing unusual, for he had been formulating organizational documents for the past forty years. "Some people say," he remarked, "that I have a genius for organization, and some philosopher has said that a successful organizer requires the lowest type of intellectuality." The plan which Gompers had dictated became the fundamental scheme of organization which guided the work of the Advisory Commission during the next two years.

Between December 6 and the time when the United States entered the war, the work of the Council and the Advisory Commission consisted principally of planning, making preliminary investigations, outlining policies, lining up necessary personnel, and generally preparing for the real work that would come with war. Gompers was assigned the task of preparing a plan to enroll skilled labor in industrial reserves and, with Howard Coffin, a business executive and a member of the Labor Commission of the War Labor Board, undertook to draft rules and policies pertaining to the exemption of labor from military service.[1]

The objects of the Labor Committee formed by Gompers were to advise on the welfare of workers in industry and to make recommendations as to means of adjusting employment problems without interrupting war work. He called a meeting to organize the committee on April 2, the day that Wilson read his war message to Congress. He invited the presidents of all international unions to the meeting, but twenty-eight declined to accept membership on the committee. Their motives varied, but Tobin, for one, stated that he was too busy trying to improve the conditions of the teamsters. Besides, recalling the labor conference of March 12, he had no confidence in a committee run by Gompers, because "things will have to run as you want them to run or they can not run at all."[2]

More than 150 persons attended the organization meeting at A.F. of L. headquarters, including representatives of most of the international unions and the railroad brotherhoods, employers, welfare experts, and representatives of commercial, transportation, financial, and civic interests. An executive committee was formed with Gompers as chairman and Ralph Easley and James W. Sullivan, an initiative and referendum reformer, as his assistants. In addition to the executive committee, a number of national subcommittees were formed, including ones on wages and hours, mediation and conciliation, welfare work, women in industry, information and statistics, publicity, and cost of living. Since Congress did not provide appropriations for the work of these committees, the Labor Committee and others were financed by contributions from wealthy individuals.[3]

At the conclusion of the meeting, which lasted from 11:00 a.m. to 11:00 p.m., Gompers informed the members that they were to serve without compensation and added that that was the only condition upon which he could accept appointment on the Commission. "This is to be a work of love and duty, and I have never yet found in the world such services performed as the service which is given without pay. . . . it cannot be bought and it cannot be paid for. Our work in the time of this crucial hour must be first for defense and the mobilization of good will among the people of this country. . . . Practically tonight the die is cast. The President . . . has declared that a state of war exists. . . . Let us men and women of America make up our minds that come what may we will stand loyally, unitedly in defense of the ideals of the Republic of the United States of America."[4]

On April 5 the executive committee of the Committee on Labor met to consider the problem of labor standards during the war. A resolution was prepared by William B. Wilson, Elisha Lee of the Pennsylvania Railroad, and Louis Schram of the N.C.F., and adopted. It recommended that the Council of National

Defense issue a statement to the employers and employees advising that neither side endeavor to take advantage of the country's necessity to change existing standards, except when required by emergency and approved by the Council. The Council should urge upon the state legislatures and administrative agencies the duty of rigidly maintaining existing safeguards for the health and welfare of workers, and no departure from existing standards should be made except on certification by the Council that it was essential for national defense. Finally, the Council should urge the legislatures to delegate to the governors of their respective states the power to suspend or modify restrictions in their labor laws when such action was requested by the federal government.

This resolution was approved by the Advisory Commission and the Council of National Defense and published the following day. Immediately there was a roar of criticism and condemnation from the labor movement. Unions wanted to know why they should not attempt to improve existing standards and safeguards or why they should submit to those standards being suspended by executive order. It seemed to them that the Council was simply using the war situation to freeze labor conditions, if not to undermine them, while no provision was made to prevent profiteering by the employers or to control the cost of living. Gompers was widely criticized for allegedly promising that there would be no strikes during the war. Gompers insisted that he had neither made nor intended such a pledge, although he hoped that all citizens would give patriotic regard to the need for industrial peace. But each trade union was to be its own judge of the policies to follow.[5]

To further clarify the meaning of the declaration on standards, the Committee on Labor explained that it advised against any changes by employers, employees, and governments in hours of labor, safety and sanitary regulations, maximum hours of labor for women, and child labor laws. The Council believed that no "arbitrary" changes in wages should be sought by either employers or employees through strikes or lockouts without at least giving the established mediation and conciliation agencies an opportunity to adjust the difficulties.[6]

Gompers constantly insisted that he had not pledged that there would be no strikes. Statements that he had "bound the working people of the country hand and foot to the capitalist class and to the Government," he said, emanated from "so-called organized pacifists [who were] against our movement and our country." True, the declaration of April 6 did not contain such a pledge, but only the expression of a hope. Gompers did not have the authority or power to prevent strikes. But he was in favor of prohibiting strikes in war industries. As he wrote later, "When the world was aflame, men could not stand on ceremony or precedent. Those who knew what ought to be done owed it to civilization to see that machinery was set in motion. Many decisions were a complete reversal of prevailing thought and practice. Many of us who had been most resolute in advocacy of voluntary principles found it necessary to assume responsibility for initiating policies which placed control in the hands of the government."[7]

This attitude was revealed in a plan for industrial peace which Gompers presented to the Council of National Defense on April 28. He suggested that a National Board of Labor Adjustment be established, consisting of seven members, two of whom should be trade unionists, two manufacturers, and three representatives of the public. The Board would establish minimum standards, including the eight-hour day and prevailing union wages, and enforce them in all government contracts. When grievances could not be settled in any plant, the Board would make a final and binding decision.[8]

This plan was not enacted into law, and in August the representatives of the manufacturers urged the Council to create a federal board to fix standards that would be binding on employers and employees and to prohibit strikes. On September 6, the Council decided to call a conference of employers and labor leaders to find out, as Taft put it, "whether we can arrange a truce between labor and capital in this country." Secretary Wilson appointed a conference board consisting of co-chairmen Taft and Frank P. Walsh, five members nominated by the National Industrial Conference Board, and five by Gompers. On March 29, this commission recommended to the President the establishment of a War Labor Board to bring about a settlement, by mediation and conciliation, of every labor dispute affecting war production and if necessary to appoint an arbitrator to decide the controversy.*

---

*The Board was to be controlled by the following principles: (1) There

On April 8 President Wilson issued a proclamation establishing the War Labor Board.[9]

While the War Labor Board proclamation did not positively prohibit strikes, the Board consistently refused to hear any complaint until the men returned to work, thus practically requiring the workers to waive the right to strike. Gompers not only approved of the principles on which the War Labor Board was established, but asserted his influence to make the no-strike provision stick. He repeatedly warned unions that if they went on strike to enforce their demands, Congress would unquestionably pass a law for compulsory labor and compulsory arbitration. He appealed to labor to avert such a necessity by voluntarily pursuing a no-strike policy and submitting all disputes to the war production agencies. "If we voluntarily waive our rights to strike in this hour of dire necessity," he stated, "there will be no opportunity to stigmatize our movement as unresponsive in the hour of need, and our appeal for justice will take on redoubled force when this terrific conflict shall have been brought to a close."[10]

While the War Labor Board was being created, a bill was introduced in Congress making it unlawful for any workman to strike during the war. Gompers warned that while the workers aimed to work without interruption, nothing would do more to create resentment than making it illegal for men to stop work. So far labor leaders had been effective in preventing serious interruptions in industry or transportation. But "once take away the

---

should be no strikes or lockouts during the war. (2) The right of workers to organize in unions and to bargain collectively through chosen representatives was recognized and was not to be denied or interfered with by the employers, and the workers were not to use coercion to induce persons to join their organizations or to induce employers to bargain with them. (3) In establishments where the union shop existed it was to continue and union standards as to wages and other conditions were to be maintained; but in nonunion or open shops the continuance of that status was not to be deemed a grievance, although the workers in such shops could freely join or form unions. (4) Women were to receive equal pay for equal work. (5) The question of hours of labor, other than where covered by existing law, was to be settled in line with government necessities and the welfare and health of the workers. (6) In fixing wages, hours, and conditions of labor, regard was to be given to the prevailing standards in the localities affected. (7) The right of all workers to a living wage was recognized.

voluntary influence which we may be able to exert, and say that we
have no power, no influence of a voluntary character, and you
have taken away every instrument which we have been enabled
to employ in order to gain the good will and the voluntary, continued service of the workers of America."[11]

Gompers' abandonment of "voluntarism" during the war
involved the question of conscription as well as compulsory labor.
On March 23, 1917, the subject of universal military service was
discussed in the Advisory Commission. All the other members had
expressed their support, and Gompers was pressed to declare himself. He stated that he favored the draft, but could not announce
his support at that time because of the widespread opposition in
the A.F. of L., and a premature endorsement might set back its
approval by the Federation. One month later, its Executive Council considered a conscription bill pending in Congress and decided
to register opposition. In a letter to Champ Clark, Speaker of the
House, the Council declared that the American people were patriotic and intelligent freemen, and that compulsory service imposed
upon them would imply lack of freedom or of willingness to serve
voluntarily in the national defense. Conscription must be regarded
as repugnant to the Constitution, at least until proved necessary.[12]

But this protest was evidently for "domestic consumption."
For Gompers, at least, the die had been cast. Labor's traditional
opposition to compulsory service, he wrote later, had derived from
conditions different from those facing it in the war, which made
it necessary for the government to utilize natural resources for the
defense of the country. "The most important natural resources
were the citizens of the country. The most essentially democratic
method of mobilizing human resources was universal draft.
Viewed in this light, I knew that this draft was in harmony with
the principles of organized labor and that organized labor, after
it had had the opportunity to consider the new situation would
approve the policy. *I therefore assumed responsibility* as representative of labor on the Advisory Commission of co-operating in the
development of plans for the draft."[13] When the conscription law
was passed, Gompers interpreted the labor declaration of March
12 as his authorization to accept the action of Congress. He made
no criticism of the act and refused to support efforts to secure
its repeal.

As part of his campaign to educate "his boys" for support of the war and conscription, Gompers asked the Council of National Defense to invite the British government to send a labor delegation to the United States to give the benefit of their experiences and to travel over the country and address labor gatherings and "lead them to an understanding of English labor's surrender to the support of war." The Council agreed, and on April 12 Gompers cabled the invitation to Prime Minister Lloyd George. George acted at once. On May 15 the Council held a special meeting to hear C. W. Bowerman, secretary of the British Trade Union Congress and a privy councillor, and James H. Thomas, secretary of the railwaymen's union and a Member of Parliament, explain why they had abandoned antiwar sentiments to give full support to their government. It was possible, they thought, to accept compulsory military and industrial service without sacrificing ability to protect workers' standards. They appealed to American labor to enter war service with their own spirit of enthusiasm and sacrifice.[14]

Other work of the Labor Committee was carried out by the various subcommittees, but under the direction of the executive committee. It included such matters as training skilled laborers, providing housing for war workers, securing information concerning the employment of women and making suggestions for their protection, making reports on industrial fatigue, sanitation, lighting, heating and ventilation, safety, and fire prevention. Gompers' guiding thought in these activities was that workers must be assured satisfactory working conditions, for discontented workers would not yield maximum service. "The great task undertaken by my associates and me . . . was to adjust these matters in the interest of a contented, cheerful, willing body of workers yielding up every day their maximum physical and mental energy to help in the winning of the war."[15]

For these services, Gompers won the unstinted praise of the nation's leaders. Secretary of the Navy Josephus Daniels stated that the workers in the navy yards had remained loyal and refused to leave their vital work for more lucrative jobs elsewhere, and that their devotion to duty in securing maximum production of war materials had a great effect in preventing labor disputes from disrupting production. Much of this devotion, he said, was due to the loyal co-operation of Samuel Gompers, "whose wise and patriotic councils have done much to keep such yard workmen as were members of labor organizations keenly alive to a sense of their duty as American citizens." Senator John S. Williams of Mississippi stated in the Senate that, after the President of the United States, to Gompers was due the chief credit "for harmonizing our national purposes and for unifying our national effort." Even Taft extolled him. ". . . when you consider the currents that were strong in many directions, and when you consider what he had to meet and oppose in that regard, I think no one who understands it could possibly withhold from him the need of praise to which he is entitled." The United States government regarded Gompers as sufficiently important to assign a Department of Justice agent to guard him during the period of the war.[16]

2. THE OWLISH WINK

GOMPERS STATED DURING THE WAR THAT HE COULD not tell where his duties as chairman of the Labor Committee ended and his duties as president of the American Federation of Labor began. In truth, there was little distinction in his mind between his efforts to serve the government and his efforts in behalf of labor. He regarded the winning of the war as a necessary condition for the preservation and advancement of labor's gains, and he considered the defense of labor's position as essential for victory in war. He realized that a discontented working class would not and could not give its enthusiastic service to the war effort. Regarding the war as a crusade for democracy, he could see no point in fighting such a war if it entailed the destruction of labor's rights and the gains it had secured in a generation of struggle. In addition, Gompers had to mix his pleas for self-sacrifice with others calculated to strengthen labor's position in order to retain the confidence of the workers.

For the preparedness program, in 1916, Gompers had demanded labor participation in government agencies established for preparedness and war. Later he expanded this demand to include representation on all government commissions. His appeal fell on deaf ears. Although labor was given representation on various boards dealing with labor disputes, the Council of National Defense and the War Industries Board, whose committees doled out the profitable war contracts, ignored labor. This made it impossible for the labor unions to influence the placing of contracts with unionized firms, a policy demanded by William Hutcheson of the carpenters' union. Such a policy would give recognition to and encourage unionism and collective bargaining, Hutcheson explained; it would also enable workers to use their organizations to speed up production and prevent strikes. It would incidentally "restore the injured prestige of Mr. Gompers."[17]

The first major labor dispute to affect the preparedness program was the demand of the railroad brotherhoods for the eight-hour day, and with it was involved the issue of compulsory arbitration and the right to strike in war-time. In the spring of 1916, the four brotherhoods presented demands for the eight-hour day with no wage reduction. They refused to compromise or to submit this issue to arbitration, and in June negotiations were broken off. A strike call, backed by over ninety per cent of the employees, was issued for September 4, bringing the country face to face with a strike when war seemed imminent.

Wilson then went before Congress and asked for the enactment of the eight-hour day for railroad workers and the prohibition of strikes pending government investigation of the issues involved. Gompers was opposed to both suggestions, for the fixing of work standards by the government in private employment and compulsory investigation of disputes was a "revolutionary proposition totally out of harmony with our prevailing institutions and out of harmony with our philosophy of government." It was an embarrassing situation for Gompers. He did not want to "jeopardize the nation" at a time when war was imminent; he did not want to appear in the position of thwarting the securing of the eight-hour day by the railroad workers; and he did not want to oppose the administration on a major issue, especially when Wilson had made a strong endorsement of the principle of the eight-hour day. The brotherhoods appealed to the Executive Council for support of the Adamson Bill, which embodied Wilson's recommendations. The Council refused, but Gompers agreed to appear with them before the Senate Committee on Interstate Commerce, where he remained silent while the brotherhoods appealed for passage of the eight-hour provision and joined them in urging defeat of the compulsory investigation feature.

"The only protection that wage-earners have," Gompers declared, "is the right to withhold their labor power—the right to
strike. To deprive them of this protection in the name of industrial
peace would only result in increasing their feeling of injustice and
in converting governmental agencies and institutions into agencies
that bind them powerless against employers, however rapacious
and inhumane." The compulsory investigation provision was dropped, and the eight-hour day was passed the day before the strike
was to begin. The law was to become effective January 1, 1917.[18]

In November the railroad executives challenged the constitutionality of the Adamson Act and secured an injunction preventing it from becoming operative. The trainmen threatened to strike
on January 1 if the eight-hour day was not instituted, but backed
down. Gompers regarded that as a mistake, as he felt that was the
psychological time to press the demand, with the law on the side
of the workers. However, in March, the brotherhoods determined
to force the issue before the country went to war, and announced
that every railroad in the country would be struck on March 17.
The brotherhoods and the managers immediately entered into
conference, and on March 16 Secretary Baker appointed Secretary
Lane, Secretary Wilson, Daniel Willard, and Gompers as a commission to meet with the conferees and bring about an adjustment.
Gompers was in Atlantic City for the weekend, and in order to
insure a complete rest had not given his address to his secretary.
When the announcement of the commission was made, Gompers
could not be found, and the newspapers carried the story that he
was hiding to avoid serving on the commission. He did not learn
of his appointment until the following day, when he immediately
left for New York. He joined the conference on the eighteenth
and participated in the closing session which lasted throughout the
day and the following night. He pressed upon the unions and the
managers the grave peril to the nation involved in the impending
strike and urged them to adjust their differences in order to avert
a strike during the emergency. The managers agreed to grant the
eight-hour day, and the next day the Supreme Court upheld the
constitutionality of the Adamson Act.[19]

Gompers bitterly criticized the Supreme Court decision. He
held that the eight-hour day had not been won by enactment of
the Adamson Act or by the Court's ruling, but by the voluntary

agreement of the managers and the brotherhoods. Consequently, if the Court had held the act unconstitutional, the eight-hour day would have gone into effect anyhow, and the precedent for government regulation of work standards would have been averted. Gompers was displeased that the Court had based its decision on the right of the government compulsorily to arbitrate labor disputes and had declared that the right to strike was surrendered when workers were engaged in public service. Gompers declared that the Court had paved the way for "the establishment of industrial slavery and a fugitive slave law, and if followed . . . the working people of the United States may be compelled to work at the command of their employers or go to prison."[20]

When the United States entered the war, a major task was the construction of training camps. The letting of contracts to construction companies was put in the hands of Louis B. Wehle. He recognized that provision had to be made for the adjustment of labor disputes, and suggested to Secretary Baker that all disputes be submitted for decision to an adjustment board representing the army, labor, and the public. Although he had never met Gompers, he believed that the latter would be willing to have labor controlled by such a board and would concede the open shop in construction work in exchange for an agreement that the board could use union scales of hours and wages, modified by changes in costs of living, as a basis for contract agreements. Baker approved, but doubted that Gompers would agree. Wehle drafted a memorandum and took it to Gompers' office.

Wehle found Gompers to be a man of deep feeling, readily expressed, but in full command of himself in controversy and with a ready fund of telling and tactful humor: "There was something inherently formidable about him." Wehle had a "long and lively" discussion with him about the memorandum, but finally got his signature on the famous Baker-Gompers agreement. It provided that the labor aspects of cantonment construction would be governed by a commission of three appointed by the Secretary of War and representing the army, public, and labor, the last to be nominated by Gompers. The commission was to use the union scale of wages, hours, and conditions in force in each locality, giving consideration to subsequent changes in the cost of living. Standards fixed by the board were to be binding on all parties.

According to Wehle, Gompers agreed orally to the open shop, but it was not written into the agreement because Gompers had to proceed cautiously on that point, especially since in signing the memorandum he was assuming authority possessed only by the presidents of the building trades unions. "Yet we realized," he wrote, "that it was clearly impracticable for me to enter into protracted negotiations with them over a point so loaded with dynamite." The day after the memorandum was signed, Gompers went to New York. Frank Morrison was unwilling to take the responsibility of giving written confirmation of the understanding on the open shop, so Wehle wrote Gompers that the government could not commit itself to the closed shop in any labor adjustment machinery and that the clause pertaining to prevailing conditions did not include any provisions with reference to the employment of nonunion labor. Two days later, Wehle phoned Gompers in New York and told him that he must have immediate confirmation of this understanding or the Baker-Gompers agreement would be torn up. Gompers wired: "Your understanding of the memorandum signed by Secretary Baker and me is right. It had reference to union hours and wages. The question of union shop was not included." The unwritten understanding was not publicized to the general public or to the labor movement.[21]

The Baker-Gompers agreement was later extended to naval construction by agreement of Gompers and the Secretary of Navy. These agreements amounted to a bargain for union wages and hours in return for the open shop. Many labor unions chafed under this policy, as "Gompers' loyalty program was starting to look suspiciously like a sellout." He received numerous complaints from union presidents, particularly in the building trades. But most of them were afraid to face public censure by opposing Gompers openly. Besides, many of them were held in line by Gompers' occasional militant calls for the recognition of organized labor as the spokesman and agent for all workers, calls which were issued largely for that purpose.[22] William Hutcheson of the carpenters was the only labor leader who spoke out against the agreement and pressed for coequal representation, participation, and responsibility of labor and for government recognition of the union shop. His objection to the Baker-Gompers policy statement and similar set-ups in other agencies was that they did not give unions first chance to supply needed workers and that they did not guarantee the closed shop in areas where it had been a long-standing and hard-won tradition. He refused to recognize the agreement or to serve on any of the tripartite boards. He accused the War Department of circulating an interpretation of the Baker-Gompers agreement which had Gompers agreeing that union workers would work with nonunion men.[23]

In August, Wehle was asked by President Wilson to organize similar labor adjustment machinery for shipbuilding. Wehle proposed to Gompers that when there was a dispute in a plant, standards that had been in force in that plant, whether union or nonunion, should apply. Gompers insisted that the basic standards should be the union standards in force in the district where the plant was located; this meant that if a plant were located in a union district, it would be transformed from an open to a union shop. Wehle would not negotiate on such terms, as it amounted to profiteering on the emergency by labor. He would go, instead, to the metal trades unions to secure an agreement, and when he had signed up two or three of them, he would come back to Gompers and expect him to back it up and enlist the other necessary signatures. As Wehle told it: "Our words had been sharp. As I reached the door, I turned and saw Gompers still seated. He met my eye with a solemn owlish wink." Wehle secured the reluctant agreement of James O'Connell and A. J. Berres, president and secretary of the Metal Trades Department, and two other labor leaders, and it was approved by the Navy Department. The following Sunday Gompers came to Wehle's apartment for breakfast and subscribed the agreement. True to his tacit understanding with Wehle, he called a number of union presidents on the phone and secured their approval. Only Hutcheson refused to sign or approve the document.[24]

With the coming of war there was a determined effort by interested elements to break down established standards of labor. A provision in the naval appropriation bill of 1917 sought to repeal the eight-hour law. Gompers pointed out to Congress that this was not necessary, as the law provided that the eight-hour day might be suspended in case of extraordinary emergency. If Congress repealed the eight-hour law, then after the war all the work would have to be gone over again to secure the enactment of another.[25] Not only was the repeal clause dropped from the bill, but a provision was added that when the eight-hour day was suspended, wages would be computed on a basic day rate of eight hours with time and a half for overtime. This provision was written into all war and navy contracts.

Gompers urged that the eight-hour day be extended by administrative authority to all private concerns as a war measure. The failure of all industry to adopt the eight-hour system caused more industrial discontent and unrest than any other one condition, he argued, and created disturbances that interfered with war production. Such a measure would do more than anything else "to hearten the entire nation, to put courage into those upon the firing line, and to demonstrate beyond a shadow of a doubt the honesty of purpose and the idealism of our government in the fight it is making for better standards of life and for humanity as a whole."[26] Gompers did not attempt to explain in what way such a measure would constitute less involuntary servitude than the enactment of the eight-hour law for railroad workers.

Gompers took a similar position on efforts which were made by both employers and politicians to suspend child labor laws, to relax the standards of women's work, or otherwise to lower established standards. At a meeting of the Labor Committee of the Council of National Defense, Gompers warned the employers that labor was not going to give up its liberty and its rights. The United States could not endure, he declared, by following the German policy of autocracy. "What matters it to the men of labor if, in the struggle for the freedom and democracy of the United States, while that struggle is going on, chains in the guise of slavery are fastened upon them?"[27]

One of the most blatant attempts to utilize war hysteria to suppress labor was the Mooney case. In the spring of 1916, Tom Mooney and his wife led a bitter and unsuccessful fight to organize the carmen of San Francisco. As President Wilson's Mediation Commission later reported, the utilities determined to "get" Mooney, and they were joined by the employers of San Francisco who were determined to maintain the open shop. A private detective was hired to direct the effort, and the opportunity came during a Preparedness Day parade on July 22. A bomb was thrown into the ranks of the marchers, killing nine and wounding forty. Without even attempting to find the guilty, a corporation-associated District Attorney, Charles Fickert, arrested Mooney and Warren Billings, another young labor leader, fastened the crime on them through perjured and bought testimony, and had Mooney sentenced to death and Billings to life imprisonment.

Organized labor saw that the case was a colossal frame-up. The A.F. of L. demanded a new trial, and mass protest meetings were held not only in the United States but in Europe. Gompers received a large number of letters and telegrams from various unions demanding vigorous action to save Mooney's life, including a suggestion that he inaugurate a general strike throughout the country if Mooney should be executed. Gompers was apprehensive of what might happen if the execution were carried out. He advised the unions which had written to him to exercise self-control but to continue their persistent efforts to secure a new trial, and promised his full support. But he did not want any great public demonstrations, partly because he did not want radical sentiments stirred up during the war, or anything that would embarrass the administration, and partly because he remembered the McNamara incident and feared Mooney might be really guilty.

On March 20, Gompers went to the White House, where he expressed his apprehensions to the President. Wilson told him that he had no power to act but was doing what he could to persuade Governor William D. Stephens of California to commute the death sentence. Ten days later, Gompers was called to a conference by Secretary of State Lansing. Gompers submitted the facts in the case, which indicated a miscarriage of justice, and reported the strong feeling among the workers of the United States and the Allied nations against the frame-up. Lansing stated that Wilson had sent a telegram to Governor Stephens and was doing his best to save Mooney's life. "I stated to the Secretary," Gompers wrote in a memorandum, "that the question had passed the stage of judicial processes—that it was one of industrial and political importance—that I hoped action would be taken to save Mooney's life before the feeling became still more acute." A week later,

Gompers called on Attorney General Thomas W. Gregory and submitted information which seemed to exculpate Mooney. Gregory did not think this material was of sufficient value to warrant a protest to Governor Stephens, but Gompers called his attention to the need for some action because Mooney was regarded in the United States and in Europe as a martyr to "capitalistic interests and designs."[28] President Wilson's Mediation Commission investigated the case and recommended a new trial in order to remove the widespread belief that the convictions had been secured through perjured testimony. Wilson twice requested Stephens to pardon Mooney.

On April 22, Gompers issued a public statement to head off the growing demand for a general strike. He stated that the A.F. of L. had done and would do everything possible to secure justice for Mooney, and a strike would violate both the laws of the labor movement and the interests of the workers. Such a strike would be dangerously prejudicial to war production and would only react against Mooney.[29]

One of the leaders in the effort to secure a new trial was Lucy Robins, a libertarian long interested in left-wing causes and propaganda; she and her first husband had traveled about the country doing semi-skilled work and publishing material with their own small printing press which they carried along. She had fought to free Big Bill Haywood from prison, and the McNamaras, and she was now absorbed in Mooney's cause. Though no longer the anarchist she had been, she was still a bitter opponent of Gompers' conservative brand of trade unionism. In the summer of 1918, she went to the A.F. of L. headquarters to try to enlist his support in her efforts. She was met by Miss Guard, who listened to her story with strict impersonality and told her the Chief was too busy. Three times she tried to see him, but without success. She went to the telegraph office and wrote a message to Gompers which ended with the words: "I now understand why the great masses of workers despise you, curse you, and eagerly await your death."

When Gompers received the telegram he immediately sent for Miss Robins. This time she was ushered in by Miss Guard. Gompers rose from his seat behind the desk and peered at her over his spectacles. "So everyone loathes me," he chuckled. "All people despise me and await my death. Are you among them?" As Miss

Robins stumbled in embarrassment, he went on, "Suppose I should die, what would you do? If you have any good ideas, I might be willing to co-operate." Two girls filing papers in the office began to giggle, and soon Gompers and Miss Robins were laughing together without restraint. The air was cleared, and Miss Robins began to speak her piece. She told him what she knew about the Mooney case and finally asked him why he had done nothing to help him. "We hate you," she said frankly, "but we know you have power."

Gompers sat with his head back on the chair, his eyes closed, while she talked. When she finished, he opened his eyes and ordered one of the clerks to bring in the folder on the Mooney case. She read the memoranda of Gompers' interviews with Wilson, Lansing, and Gregory and realized that while she and others had been organizing mass meetings in protest, he had been silently trying to pull strings behind the scenes, and had secured a presidential investigation into the case. He had written to the Governor and Attorney General of California and had stirred up a movement to impeach District Attorney Fickert. More embarrassed than ever, Miss Robins asked why the labor movement had not been allowed to know of these things. Gompers gently took her hand and explained that his experience in the McNamara case had taught him that he must operate without publicity in such matters. "We must help our people, but we must not endanger the labor movement." Miss Robins suggested that all the agitation had been futile, but Gompers replied that the public opinion aroused by the campaign was helping him in his efforts. "Besides," he added, "we need indignation like yours. It shows a healthy social conscience." He assured her that the movement to save Mooney's life would not fail. Gompers arranged for Wilson to receive a delegation, and continued his quiet efforts to save Mooney's life and his public efforts to quell a militant protest movement.[30]

In June, the A.F. of L. convention demanded that Governor Stephens grant a pardon and urged the President to exert his power to prevent the execution. In the fall, Mooney's sentence was commuted to life imprisonment, but this did not end the growing demand for a new trial. On the contrary, it accelerated it, for it was a virtual admission that the conviction as well as the sentence was unjust. At the A.F. of L. convention in 1919, resolutions were introduced demanding a new trial or Mooney's release, and demanding that the A.F. of L. devise definite plans to secure that purpose. A second resolution called for a referendum vote of the affiliated unions on a 24-hour general strike if a new trial was not granted by Labor Day. The first resolution was adopted, but the second was defeated, as the resolutions committee asserted that it would be contrary to the rule of autonomy and the strike movement was being instigated by an organization that was trying to interfere with and wreck the trade union movement. Besides, a general strike would only injure the effort for a new trial.[31] Gompers did not follow up the instructions of the convention, virtually washing his hands of the whole matter, and Mooney languished in prison for twenty more years until, a dying man, he was pardoned by the New Deal governor.

One of the most difficult war labor situations concerned the Northwest lumber camps, where industrial strife was hampering the aircraft production program. Prior to the war, the timber industry of the Northwest was rent with labor difficulties, and the I.W.W. was particularly strong among the workers in the lumber camps. Wages had not kept pace with rising living costs, and the ten-hour day prevailed. Living conditions in the camps were crude and unsanitary, and the workers suffered severe hardships. When the war broke out, as Gompers said, "the employers in the timber industry seemed to regard it as their patriotic duty to refuse all wage increases and improved working conditions while at the same time insisting on the most liberal compensation from the Government for their services."

The timber workers' union, the principal A.F. of L. organization involved, demanded the eight-hour day, wage increases, and other improvements, but the employers refused to negotiate. The State Council of National Defense finally arranged a conference, and the union agreed to waive all other demands if the employers would grant the eight-hour day. The employers rejected this settlement, claiming this would constitute a change in working conditions and thus be contrary to the wartime policy of the Labor Committee of the Council of National Defense. The president of the union, J. G. Brown, and the president of the Washington State Federation of Labor wired to Gompers, stating that the conference was breaking down. Unless the eight-hour day and at least partial recognition of the union were granted, lumber operations would be disrupted and the I.W.W. would be strengthened.[32]

Gompers replied that the eight-hour day was not only the recognized normal workday but had been established as law by the Washington legislature, and its enforcement would not be regarded by the government as a change in standards. A longer day should be permitted only under extraordinary conditions, and then overtime should be paid. He urged a settlement on that basis so that the necessary materials might be supplied. Three days later the conference broke up over the refusal of the operators to concede the eight-hour day, and a general strike in the lumber camps and shipyards threatened. Brown asked Gompers if the government could not establish the eight-hour day through its contracts for lumber. Gompers emphasized to Secretary Baker that the attitude of the employers was "giving aid and comfort to that organization [the I.W.W.] which has for its purpose the disruption of the trade union movement." The government must take action to remedy fundamental wrongs: ". . . the American Federation of Labor has neither sympathy nor approval for the methods of the Industrial Workers of the World, but on the other hand, we hold that there are constitutional fundamental rights that can not be denied any citizens or group of citizens under a free government by law." The employers of Washington, as in other states, were forming "Loyal Leagues" and "Patriotic Leagues," the sole purpose of which was to use the war as a cloak for schemes to deny the masses political and economic freedom and "to fasten upon them the most pernicious of all despotisms founded upon economic disorganization and helplessness." They were sowing the seeds of anarchy in order to increase their profits. Gompers recommended that the government provide agencies for adjusting the dispute, based on the eight-hour day and the right to organize.[33]

Nevertheless, the government did nothing for nearly two months other than appoint the Mediation Commission to investigate. In October, Gompers conferred with Howard Coffin of the Defense Council's aircraft board. Coffin decided to send Col. Brice Disque of the Signal Corps to attempt mediation. Disque generally agreed with Gompers, and when he got to Portland he said he would try to persuade the employers to accept the eight-hour day but that the government could not wait for that. He proposed to send 9,000 soldiers into the camps and mills in order to insure production. He insisted that he had no intention of trying to break the strike but must get increased production regardless of the dispute.

The A.F. of L. organizer opposed this plan, believing that if the eight-hour day were granted, the striking workers would return and meet the production needs of the army. Gompers saw eye to eye with Disque, and secured an agreement with him and the Department of Labor that the soldiers would receive the prevailing wages less their army pay and would be employed only to the extent that civilian labor was unavailable. Gompers also told his organizers that the federal eight-hour law would be enforced in the camps, but there was no such agreement. Gompers' desire to smooth the way for Disque with Northwest labor may have been influenced by Disque's promise to him that he would secure the immediate appointment of Private First Class Samuel Gompers, grandson of the labor chief, to the rank of Second Lieutenant.[34]

Disque returned to the Pacific Coast, not with the possession of "much sympathy" for the workers, as Gompers reported, but with the conviction that it was his mission to stabilize timber production by supplanting unionism with military organization and his own brand of Loyal League. He organized what he called the "Loyal Legion of Loggers and Lumbermen," making the workers sign a pledge of support to the government and of their best efforts to work every day possible in the production of lumber. The Loyal Legion was nothing more than a militarized company union. Membership was compulsory, and spying on suspected union members and radicals was rewarded. The dues, if any, were very small, but the benefits to anyone but the employers were nonexistent.

It seems to have been Disque's view that the Loyal Legion made unionism unnecessary in the camps and mills, and Loyal Legion "organizers" agitated against unions and the eight-hour day. When an organizer of the carpenters' union came to the Northwest to organize the lumbermen, a member of Disque's staff appeared and demanded in the name of the United States army that he disband his union. He also demanded his records and papers. Disque avoided meeting with the union representatives except to criticize them for not boosting his Loyal Legion and to complain that production was not increasing, but he was in constant touch with the operators. The unionists were convinced that Disque's policies were encouraging the employers to stand firm in their refusal to grant the eight-hour day, which was the only way to get the mills back to work.[35]

Stimulated by the President's Mediation Commission, negotiations were resumed between the employers, unions, and Col. Disque, and in January 1918, it was finally agreed to establish the basic eight-hour day, with time and a half for overtime, as well as improved sanitary and living conditions, in all the mills and camps in Washington and Oregon. On March 1 the agreement went into effect by executive order of President Wilson. At the same time, Disque, without consulting the unions, established a complete scale of minimum *and maximum* wages for all classes of workers in the camps and mills, a scale the unionists claimed was a reduction in the existing rates. Disque denied that wages had been reduced, but he did protest publicly and in letters to Gompers about the unionization efforts of the timber workers' and shingle weavers' unions. He asserted that it was a "fatal error" to take "unfair advantage" of the employers to unionize the workers, and that the attempt would cause "greater damage to the country than the presence of a similar number of enemy spies in our midst, and will not be tolerated." The workers should show their patriotism by leaving their interests in the hands of Col. Disque and the Loyal Legion. He went on to warn the workers that unless they "speed up in efficiency" he would reduce wages. He urged them to co-operate with the employers through the Loyal Legion, that the unions stop agitating and stirring up discontent (he threatened to suspend publication of their journals), and that they emulate the co-operative, patriotic, and reasonable attitude of Gompers. He wanted Gompers to influence the unions to discontinue their organizing efforts.[36]

Gompers informed Disque that he mistook his "reasonable attitude" for surrender of unionism. There could be no serious objections to the efforts of the unions to extend their membership, he argued, particularly when the unions were pledged to support Disque's production program and were co-operating with him and the Loyal Legion. But when the war was over there would be great industrial problems, and there would then be a need for a strong organization to meet them. Disque disagreed. The Loyal Legion would teach workers and employers the need for collective bargaining and mutual understanding, and at the end of the war the union would convince the employers that it was the logical heir of the Loyal Legion, "providing it is represented by the proper kind of leadership." Shortly afterward, the timber workers' union notified Gompers that Disque had broken up a meeting of the union in Sandpoint, Idaho, and was trying to disband another local. "Is there anything you can do to put a stop to this high handed proceeding?" There is no record that Gompers ever replied to this letter or protested against Disque's antiunion activities. A couple of days later he reported to the A.F. of L. convention that Disque had provided for such organization of workers as was necessary to mobilize the needed labor power.[37]

Gompers was not particularly interested in extending organization during the war. It presented unusual opportunities for unionization, but Gompers never prepared any plan for a comprehensive organizing campaign. He rarely mentioned the subject, and when such campaigns were undertaken as the stockyards organization drive initiated by the Chicago Federation of Labor, he gave it no encouragement or support. Indeed, his commitments led him to oppose mass organizing campaigns even after the war had ended. At the 1919 convention of the Federation, John L. Lewis, then acting president of the United Mine Workers, demanded a resolution calling for a vigorous organizing campaign. He believed that there was a perfect opportunity for a successful drive to build the ranks of organized labor. But Gompers told him that his own agreement with Wilson forbade any disturbance such as a union organizing drive might create. The fact that the state of war had not been officially declared over seemed important to him. Lewis related that when Gompers told him that, "it chilled the very marrow of my bones; and I decided right then and there that I would never permit a union or myself to get so involved in and so dependent upon a federal administration that in times of crisis the ties of loyalty and agreement and obligation to that administration would paralyze me from acting in the interests of labor as it did with Gompers in 1919. The favorable opportunities for labor to organize are precious few and they cannot be waived at the whim of a president."[38]

Gompers' infatuation with officialdom was exemplified in the matter of the Lever Act. The 1916 convention of the Federation had directed that the Executive Council make an effort to secure the passage of legislation which would insure relief from the high cost of living. Gompers brought the matter up with the Advisory Commission, which urged Congress to enact such a law. A bill was introduced in Congress, known as the Food Control Bill, or the Lever Bill, empowering the President to oversee the production and distribution of food and fuel and to prohibit profiteering, among other things. Gompers gave his full support to the measure, but was leery about one section which provided severe penalties for conspiracy to limit the facilities for producing, transporting, or dealing in necessities, for restricting their supply, and for preventing or lessening their manufacture in order to enhance prices. He proposed an amendment expressly stating that nothing in the law should be construed to repeal or modify the labor sections of the Clayton Act.

The amendment was defeated, and Gompers had to decide whether to accept or oppose the bill. He decided to accept it, feeling that adequate assurance was given that it would not be used against labor. In due course, he had sadly to write: "I, as a citizen, as a man, and as president of the American Federation of Labor and a member of the Council of National Defense, issued a circular to all labor in the United States, begging and pleading with them to urge their respective United States Senators and Representatives to vote for the Lever bill. I think it is not unfair for me to say that as much as I wanted the greatest success, and did what I could for our armies in the war, I do not think that I would have advocated the passage of the bill as a great emergency if I had not the assurance that it would not be used as against men who labor, to enslave them, and to compel them to do the things that they had a perfect lawful right not to do." Gompers admitted that he had closed his eyes to the dangers, clearly pointed out in the Senate debates, that the courts could interpret the law against labor, assurances from the President or not. But, he said, he was "delirious with patriotic feeling during the war.... A great transformation came over me."[39] Labor would pay for Gompers' delirium in days to come.

3. THE ALLIANCE FOR LABOR
AND DEMOCRACY

PRESIDENT WILSON ADMITTED, AFTER THE WAR WAS
over, that Germany's submarine warfare was not the cause of
America's entrance into the war. The real cause of the war was
commercial and industrial rivalry, and the United States hoped to
secure international financial leadership, industrial supremacy,
and political direction as a result of the war. But Gompers never
deviated from his view that the war meant the establishment of a
higher conception of justice for all time to come, a crusade for
freedom. In his eyes, opposition to the war or advocacy of a negotiated peace was a pro-German plot, "a movement of the military
juggernaut to crush the spirit of the men of the world."[40]

The peace movement was composed of diverse elements based
on different philosophies and with differing objectives. There were
religious and pacifist groups who believed that no war was ever
justified. There were progressives who viewed it as an unnecessary
war to enrich the employers at the expense of the working class.
These groups favored a negotiated peace to bring the war to an
early end on the basis of democratic principles. Then there was
the revolutionary antiwar movement represented by the Socialist
party, which met in special convention the day after America's
entrance into the war to define its position. It adopted a proclamation that the war was launched by the capitalist rulers of the world
for profits and the strengthening of their rule by crushing the
working-class movement under the heel of militarism. The party
affirmed its allegiance to internationalism and called upon the
workers of all countries to refuse support to their governments. It
branded the declaration of war by the United States government
as a crime against the people and pledged itself to continuous
opposition to the war through demonstrations and all other means
within its power.[41]

Gompers grew hysterical in his venom against the socialist
antiwar position, for the strong socialist influence in the labor
movement and the powerful sentiment against war created the
fear that the A.F. of L. would not go along with the declaration
of the union officials on March 12. He had criticized the European
socialists for renouncing their antiwar pledges; he now denounced

the American socialists for adhering to them. To him, socialism had become nothing but a means for German autocracy to control the masses. The European and American socialist parties were merely branches of the German party, carrying out a vast conspiracy to lull the people of the world into a fancied security with their propaganda of internationalism while their Kaiser prepared to conquer the world. The leaders of the American party, he asserted inaccurately, had German names, were German in sympathy, and intended to divide the United States from her allies.[42]

Gompers was greatly concerned, after America's entrance into the war, over the strong antiwar sentiment among the workers of New York, and particularly the Jewish workers on the East Side. The Workmen's Circle, the Jewish Socialist Federation, and a number of unions approved the Socialist party proclamation. Thousands of workers joined the party, and the strength of its influence was revealed in the elections later in the year. Morris Hillquit, running for mayor of New York on an antiwar platform, received twenty-two per cent of the votes, while ten state assemblymen and seven aldermen were elected on the Socialist ticket. These results were duplicated in a dozen other large cities in the East and Midwest.

In May 1917, the People's Council for Democracy and Terms of Peace was formed in New York by a committee that included the president of the I.L.G.W.U., the secretary of the A.C.W., the secretary of the United Hebrew Trades, the president of the Pennsylvania Federation of Labor, Judge Jacob Panken, Hillquit, Rabbi Judah Magnes, and a representative of the Workmen's Circle. The Council's principles were many and generous.* Its sponsors asked Gompers if they could use his name on the call for the founding convention, to which he replied: "I prefer not to ally myself with the conscious or unconscious agents of the Kaiser in America."[43]

The Council soon had 284 affiliates in New York City, includ-

---

*They included: a speedy and universal peace, no indemnities, no forcible annexations, no foreign alliances, international organization after the war, statement of peace terms by the United States government, opposition to conscription, no secret treaties, defense of free speech and free press, opposition to lowering of industrial standards, and heavy taxation of war industries and incomes.

ing 93 labor unions claiming to represent 500,000 workers. It asserted that Gompers was working on the Council of National Defense with notorious antiunion employers to prevent strikes and to foist conscription and exploitation on the workers, while the employers were reaping huge war profits. It accused him of indifference to the suppression of free speech and the right of assembly, and of inactivity in defense of labor's rights and interests in the face of the campaign to destroy standards that had been established by years of struggle. The Council's position was that it was not opposed to the A.F. of L. or the government, but organized to protect American rights which A.F. of L. officials were neglecting to defend. People's Councils were established in other cities and were joined by a number of professors, ministers, and leaders of the Farmers' Non-Partisan League, as well as many socialist and labor leaders.[44]

Gompers, regarding this movement as the result of foreign influences, took steps to counter that influence "so that these people might not have to grope blindly to find the pathway to service." He initiated a campaign for the Americanization of the labor movement and launched it with an address before the Central Federated Union of New York on June 29. Among Jewish workers, "cowed and dominated by radicals," and particularly by the *Forward*, he discerned treasonable tendencies toward the labor movement and the nation. The People's Council was attempting to create confusion and discontent in labor, and it was up to the Federated Union to take the matter in hand and offset their un-American propaganda. The Federated Union appointed a committee to work with Gompers, who also enlisted the services of the National Labor Publicity Organization, the A.F. of L. organizer in New York, and a group of socialist intellectuals who had left the party when it adopted its antiwar resolution.

A number of conferences, including one with the editors of the Jewish newspapers, sought to mobilize support for the war. It established a speakers bureau and chose writers to prepare daily press releases in English and Yiddish and publish leaflets. At the July 29 conference, it adopted the name, American Alliance for Labor and Democracy, and launched a nationwide organization, with headquarters in New York. Gompers was named chairman of the advisory council. He had previously consulted with the Advisory Commission of the Council of National Defense and with George Creel, chief of the government's committee on public information. They approved his plan, and Creel provided funds for office rent and for the costs of the publicity campaign.

On August 15, Gompers issued a circular to all local and international unions and central bodies affiliated with the A.F. of L. It stated that the Alliance had been formed to combat "suspicious bodies in our midst" who were at work trying to undermine the labor movement, "thus giving aid and comfort to the forces of reaction and autocracy." All labor organizations were called upon to organize local branches of the Alliance at once. "Minutes count. The pro-German cause gains by every moment of American delay." They would receive literature for distribution and the complete co-operation of the New York headquarters.[45]

In the summer, the People's Council announced that it would hold a national conference in Minneapolis on September 5. Gompers and Creel received alarming reports about its growing influence and decided to hold the founding convention of the Alliance for Labor and Democracy at the same time and place. Their call for the convention was sent to every central body and local union affiliated with the A.F. of L. While Gompers was attending the convention of the New York State Federation of Labor, he received word that the municipal authorities of Minneapolis had denied the People's Council the right to meet in that city. Gompers protested against the suppression; he would have wished to be seen colliding head-on with the People's Council and vanquishing it. But it was forced to hold its convention in Chicago.

The Alliance went ahead with its plans, working earnestly for three weeks to find delegates to attend the conference. Gompers sent a telegram to all A.F. of L. organizers, at the expense of the Council of National Defense, directing them to devote all their time to securing labor representatives for the conference. A special train, the "Red, White, and Blue Special," was chartered to carry delegates from New York to Minneapolis. The costs of these preparations and of the convention itself were defrayed by the Committee on Public Information, the National Civic Federation, and President Wilson's "secret fund." All press releases of the conference were handled by the Creel committee.

One hundred seventy "delegates" attended the Minneapolis convention, 89 of them trade unionists, the rest an assortment of liberals and ex-socialists. The trade union contingent was composed of representatives from small federal labor unions and officers of the A.F. of L. There was a conspicuous absence of delegates from unions in the important industries.[46]

The convention established a permanent organization with Gompers as president, Morrison secretary, and Woll director. It asserted that the one overshadowing issue was fighting the war to a decisive result, which must end with the defeat of Germany and the destruction of autocracy; a negotiated peace would be shameful servility. The one fundamental need in the crisis was unity of action in support of the government. It denounced the "enemies of the Republic who, falsely assuming to speak in the name of labor and democracy, are now ceaselessly striving to obstruct the operations of the government. In misrepresenting the government's purposes, in traducing the character of the President [Gompers] and his advisors, in stealthily attempting to incite sedition and in openly or impliedly counselling resistance to the enforcement of laws enacted for the national defense, they abuse the rights of free speech, free assemblage and a free press. In the name of liberty they encourage anarchy; in the name of democracy they strive to defeat the will of the majority; and in the name of humanity they render every possible aid and comfort to the brutal Prussian autocracy." It called for the repression of such people by the constituted authorities.

On the other side, the declaration endorsed the defense of unionism and the maintenance of standards established by labor. It called for the conscription of wealth as well as the conscription of men, for cracking down on profiteering, government control of enterprises in which strikes were threatened, labor representation on all war agencies and in the peace commission, and the soldiers' and sailors' insurance bill. Finally, it endorsed the declaration of the trade union conference of March 12.[47]

Gompers wrote out a pledge which was adopted as the only requirement for membership in the Alliance. In it the members affirmed that it was the duty of all to faithfully support the government in carrying on the war to a triumphant conclusion and to uphold every honorable effort for the accomplishment of that purpose, and to support the A.F. of L. and the declaration of March 12. The Alliance established a speakers bureau, printed leaflets and other publicity, and, most important, created a press service which sent out weekly releases to the Yiddish press, labor journals, and some daily papers, eventually reaching some 500 newspapers with an aggregate circulation of 11,000,000. It was, as Gompers said, an unofficial agency through which the Committee on Public Information operated.

Gompers planned the convention of the A.F. of L. in November 1917, known as "Labor's War Convention," as a great demonstration of labor's patriotism. He was particularly anxious to secure overwhelming endorsement of the March 12 declaration and his war policies. He asked Secretary Wilson to convey an invitation to the President to tender a personal message to the convention. Woodrow Wilson accepted and said he wanted to deliver his message in person; it was arranged for him to go to Buffalo where the convention met. This was his first public message since the beginning of the war and the first time he had left Washington. Surrounded by a cordon of soldiers, Wilson made a plea for labor's unstinted co-operation, and in return pledged the administration's support of unionism and maintenance of standards. "I want to express my admiration of [Gompers'] patriotic courage, his large vision, and his statesmanlike sense of what has to be done. I like to lay my mind alongside of a mind that knows how to pull in harness. The horses that kick over the traces will have to be put in a corral."[48]

Gompers' work of "Americanization" had been well done. Helped by the Russian revolution, which removed one of the main causes of Jewish labor's opposition to the Allied cause, and under the influences and pressures of wartime conditions, many of the elements that formed the People's Council had moved into the prowar camp. The only real test of Gompers' position at the Buffalo convention came on a resolution approving his report on the American Alliance and recommending that "full endorsement be given to the patriotic work which has been undertaken" by that organization.

The war spirit was in the air, and Gompers was in no mood to tolerate criticism from "horses that kick over the traces." A number of delegates objected that the resolution was altogether too vague, that the word "patriotism" covered a lot of undefined territory. One wanted to know if the resolution included endorsement of all the principles of the Alliance, and Gompers shot out the challenge: "What is there in that declaration so offensive to you?" The delegate replied that the declaration was not under discussion yet, and until he was informed that that was the issue to be voted on he would retain his criticism. "The delegate will then have to retain his criticism," Gompers shouted. It was plain that he wanted no discussion on the resolution or on the principles of the Alliance—he simply wanted everyone to stand up and be counted for "patriotism."

Other delegates stated that the patriotic crusade was being used as a cover by the worst antilabor employers and politicians to attack unionism, suppress free speech and free assembly, and to profiteer; and some felt that the Alliance's stand on free speech put that organization in the same category. One delegate asked Gompers to define the meaning of the term "conscription of wealth," which was among the principles of the Alliance. Gompers dismissed the question with the remark, "Among the duties prescribed for the President of the American Federation of Labor are not included definitions of terms." Some delegates, while not opposing the Alliance, felt that the whole issue was alien to the purposes of the Federation and was diverting it from its real work. Gompers took the floor and delivered a tirade against the socialists. He stated that anyone who would not sign the membership pledge of the Alliance was a traitor to the government and to the labor movement. The resolution was put to a vote and adopted, 21,602 to 402, with 1,305 abstentions.[49]

On the eve of his war message to Congress, Wilson predicted that war would result in the people going mad with hysteria, stopping thought, and forgetting tolerance. The spirit of ruthless brutality would seize the nation, conformity would be the only virtue, and every man who refused to conform would have to pay the penalty. This turned out to be an exact description of the facts, as the Constitution was suspended and radicals, dissenters, nonconformists, and liberal critics alike fell under the proscription of the government and of extralegal vigilantes. One of their principal targets was the I.W.W., whose leaders were charged with disloyalty and treason for conspiring to obstruct the government.

The real sin of the I.W.W. was its struggle for better working conditions, for actually not a single "Wobbly" was convicted of any crime involving disloyalty or violence, and no connection was ever found between the I.W.W. and German money or agents. As the President's Mediation Commission reported, I.W.W. influence was strongest where the employers most strongly resisted unionism, and I.W.W. strikes were called in self-defense against employers who were using patriotism and prejudice as levers of exploitation. Many labor organizations affiliated with the A.F. of L. had the I.W.W. tag pinned on them in order to disrupt their efforts to maintain labor standards. The Mediation Commission suggested that the way to deal with the I.W.W. was to correct the evils that caused unrest, particularly the autocratic conduct of employers and substandard working conditions, and to treat the workers with understanding.[50]

This advice was not heeded. The I.W.W. was subjected to attacks, suppression, and government prosecution. Immediately after the declaration of war, a sedition act was introduced in Congress. Gompers opposed it as the reflection of the spirit of intolerance that was "totally at variance to the genius and institutions of democracy." There must be discrimination, he asserted, between measures for protection and measures that would destroy the things that gave meaning to the republic of the United States. He believed that the Sedition Bill was instigated by people who wanted to take advantage of the war and the denial of freedom in order to advance their selfish interests.

But when the law was passed, Gompers accepted it without protest. Nor did he protest against the Department of Justice's illegal raids on the I.W.W. and the indictments against its leaders for "denunciation of the war." He even gave his approval, stating that all must abide by the will of the majority and that any man who was unwilling to stand behind the declaration of war was "unworthy to enjoy the guarantees of peace."[51] Bill Haywood stated that he was informed by Robert W. Bruère, who was writing a series of articles on the I.W.W., that Gompers had gone to Secretary of War Baker with a plan to annihilate the I.W.W., and when he failed to take the suggestion seriously, Gompers went to the Justice Department, and that the raids were a result of Gompers' suggestion. Whether this was true or not, it is clear that

Gompers was co-operating with the Justice Department in the prosecution, for an officer of the Department enlisted Gompers' assistance in preventing certain testimony from being offered at the trial.[52]

Gompers was also working with Ralph Easley on a plan to supply the Department of Justice with information on seditious persons in the labor movement. The executive committee of the National Civic Federation organized a Bureau of Information, whose purpose was "to have its members keep their eyes and ears open for every utterance or suspicious action against the interests of this Government." Easley informed the government that Gompers was assisting in the organization of the bureau by selecting in every international union an official "who is known by the labor chief to be absolutely loyal to the interests of this country irrespective of racial or other ties." The man in charge of the organization was also selected by Gompers. "The three most dangerous and criminal groups in the country just now," Easley continued, "are the anarchists, the I.W.W. and the Black Hand. . . . Through the work done by the Civic Federation on strikes and industrial disturbances in the past few years it has been necessary for it to know what these forces were doing and who are their potential members. And it is believed that we can secure information which cannot be secured in any other way. . . ." He had a group of ex-socialists who would supply information on the "inner workings" of the nationality groups, another committee to keep in touch with artists, actors, and other professionals, one for women's organizations, and one for newspapermen.[53]

Congress was soon preparing an amendment to the Sedition Act which would virtually prohibit any public discussion adverse to the war policies of the government. This amendment, later enacted as the Espionage Act, made it a crime to make "false reports or false statements" with intent to interfere with the success of the military forces or the sale of bonds, to incite insubordination in the military forces, to obstruct recruiting, or to utter "any disloyal, scurrilous, or abusive language about the form of government of the United States, or the Constitution of the United States, or the military or naval forces of the United States" or to bring them into contempt or disrepute. Gompers presented his views on this proposed law to the Buffalo convention of the Federation. He made an eloquent defense of the principles of free speech and disputed the contention that compulsion was either necessary or desirable in wartime. He opposed any law which would attempt to define the standards or the limits of permissible expression. But, he went on, the "right-thinking" people must establish their own standards of permissible expression and voluntarily assume the restrictions dictated by those standards. If any citizen failed to so restrict himself voluntarily, if he abused his freedom by speaking or writing treasonable thoughts, then he must be "vigorously dealt with at law."

Similarly with strikes. Gompers opposed legislation which would prohibit strikes, but urged the workers voluntarily to waive the right to strike for the duration of the war. But there was a difference in his attitude on thought control legislation. While he opposed a law to restrict freedom of expression, he advocated the punishment of transgressions on voluntary limitations, using as a standard the undefined term "treasonable." How far he would be willing to go in permitting freedom of speech is indicated by his own definition of treason: the expression of thoughts which would "endanger the perpetuation of our Republic and undermine our free institutions." Gompers had achieved perfection in the art of presenting his real beliefs under an avalanche of words that seemed to mean just the opposite. He opposed compulsion but would "deal vigorously" with any who did not come up to his notions of patriotism. Shortly afterward he asserted that anyone who wanted to argue whether or not the United States should have entered the war was a traitor to his country.[54]

After the Espionage Act was passed by Congress, he then defended the measure as necessary to suppress "reprehensible acts" designed to hamper the prosecution of the war. This was made necessary, it seemed, because of the polyglot character of the American population and the fact that no effort had been made to assimilate the immigrants into American institutions. Those people were subject to propaganda emanating from the German government and spread by its agents in the United States. Interference with freedom of speech and press in time of war was justifiable if not necessary.[55] Stripped of all the verbiage, Gompers' position became clear: he stood for the unqualified freedom of those who agreed with him.

Chapter Twenty-One

STIFFENING EUROPE'S BACKBONE

1. DISRUPTION OF THE WORLD LABOR MOVEMENT

THE INTERNATIONAL FEDERATION OF TRADE UNIONS had hardly been established when its activities were disrupted by the outbreak of war. The Allied labor movements discontinued their dues payments to the International, as did the A.F. of L., in 1914. In order to maintain communication with the national centers of the Allied nations, Legien established a branch office at Amsterdam under the direction of Jan Oudegeest.

The British and French labor organizations were not satisfied with this arrangement and proposed that the headquarters of the I.F.T.U. be moved to Bern, Switzerland, and that the personnel of the International should also be neutrals. Gompers agreed that the plan was practical and in the best interests of the continuity and usefulness of the international movement, and transmitted it with his approval. Legien opposed the suggestion, stating that the future co-operation of world labor depended on the mutual confidence of the national centers and the officers of the International, and the proposal indicated a lack of confidence that would "knock the bottom out" of the I.F.T.U. Furthermore, he contended, such a proposition could be voted on only in a general conference, and he issued a call for a meeting in Amsterdam. All the centers except those of the Central Powers voted against a conference, and most of them voted against the removal of the headquarters. As a result, the future of the I.F.T.U. was extremely precarious, for the British and French spokesmen stated that the extreme animosity toward the Germans would undermine confidence in the International, not only during the war but for many years afterward, if it were to remain in German hands.[1]

In March 1916, Gompers sent to the labor movements of Europe his proposal for a world labor congress to be held at the same time and place as the peace conference at the end of the war. He stated that out of the war must come better conditions and more freedom for the working classes of all countries and a greater participation in the activities of society and government. They must demand that nothing which concerned their life should be decided at the peace conference without their participation and consent. If the workers presented their demands for principles of human welfare and democracy in a representative congress, he believed that the peace conference would be unable to disregard them.[2]

When the British Trade Union Congress rejected this proposal because it would not meet with German unionists while the war was on, Gompers was very disappointed. He wrote to Will Thorne, a Labour Member of Parliament, that the bitterness and vengeance generated by the war should not be allowed to destroy the ideal of fraternity, but should be directed against the interests that brought about the war so that some good might come from it. The old ideals of nationalism and particularism must be abandoned for internationalism, for the economic relations of the world were so closely interwoven that the well-being of the workers of one nation was closely associated with the welfare of the workers of all other countries. "Unless we are big enough and broad enough to subordinate less important matters to the broad, general purposes of the promotion of labor's ideals in the affairs of the world, the ideal of internationalism must be declared impracticable. . . . fighting for the right is one thing and declaring that after the fight is over there shall not be a common ground upon which international fraternity shall be resumed upon a better and firmer fundamental basis, is quite another."[3]

The German trade unions also rejected Gompers' proposal, and he reluctantly abandoned the idea. He then proposed that the A.F. of L. urge the labor movements of the countries that would participate in the peace conference to secure representation in the official commissions of their respective governments.

That was the only other manner in which the workers would be able to influence the deliberation and the decisions of the peace conference.[4]

In July 1916, an Inter-Allied trade union conference was held in Leeds, England. It called for the inclusion of labor clauses in the peace treaty, including guarantees of the right to organize, shorter hours, social insurance, and an international labor organization to gather statistics. In addition, the conference established an international correspondence bureau at Paris, which was virtually a second International Trade Union Federation for the Allied nations. Legien considered this a renunciation of the I.F.T.U. and an attempt to split it, and he proposed an international conference to determine the future of that organization. Gompers appeared sympathetic with Legien's position, expressing the hope that the fraternity of the workers, "as represented by the International Federation of Trade Unions," would not be broken. But due to practical conditions it was impossible to hold a conference at that time.[5]

In March 1917, revolution broke out in Russia. The Tsar was overthrown, a republic established, and soviets of workers' and soldiers' deputies were created in all the large cities. This stimulated the peace sentiment in all countries, which had been growing as a result of war weariness, the military deadlock, discontent with the failure of the governments to carry out reforms, and economic privations suffered by the working masses. The entrance of the United States into the war "to make the world safe for democracy" gave further impetus to the hope for an early and democratic peace. Consequently, an international socialist conference was called to meet in Stockholm in August.[6]

The cry "On to Stockholm" became a stampede in all the belligerent countries, and the governments on both sides were alarmed at the tremendous scope of the antiwar movement, with its revolutionary implications. Although he had nothing to do with the socialist movement, Gompers, with the approval of the United States government, tried to spike the Stockholm meeting. On May 7 he sent cablegrams to the Petrograd Soviet, the French federation of labor, the French Socialist party, and the British Labour party. He told the Russian workers that they could count on the whole-hearted support of the American people in the war against Germany, but warned them against playing into the hands of the "pro-Kaiser socialists." To the British and French labor movements he stated that the Stockholm conference was a result of insidious influences at work to create a pro-Kaiser propaganda and to divide the Allies. It was called by German and pro-German socialists, he said, either to bring about a Kaiser-dictated peace or to deceive the Russian socialists into betraying the Allies by consenting to a separate peace.[7]

Legien decided that the I.F.T.U. should present labor's proposals for the peace treaty to the Stockholm socialist conference. Therefore, at his request, Oudegeest called a meeting of the I.F.T.U. at the same time and place as the socialist gathering; Gompers declined to have the A.F. of L. participate, as he did not see how any good could come from such a congress at that time. The Allied governments refused to give passports to the delegates to either the socialist or the trade union conference. The former was therefore postponed and the latter was held with delegates from the Central Powers and the neutral countries. In view of the limited nature of the meeting, the delegates decided to call another one in Bern on September 17 to discuss labor's demands in connection with the peace terms and the constitution and headquarters of the I.F.T.U. The Executive Council of the A.F. of L. declared that the proposed conference was premature and untimely and could lead to no good purpose. In veiled words it stated that such a conference would be injurious to the Allied war effort and therefore the Federation could not participate in it.[8]

The British Federation of Trade Unions also decided against participation in the Bern conference and decided to hold a meeting of the Allied labor movements in London on September 10. Gompers decided, with the approval of his Executive Council, that the A.F. of L. delegates to the British Trade Union Congress should also attend the Allied conference. The conference affirmed the right of the workingmen to be represented on the government commissions at the peace conference and urged the labor federations to press this demand on their governments.[9]

At the Bern conference were representatives of the same countries that attended the Stockholm conference in June. A program was adopted incorporating most of the Leeds demands

THE WAR, 1914-1919

and a few more. The most important additions were demands that the governments allow union representatives to take part in formulating the economic and social sections of the peace treaty and that the I.F.T.U. be recognized as the spokesman of labor in official proceedings dealing with international labor legislation.[10]

In November 1917, the unrest and war weariness that had been mounting in all countries during the past year erupted in Russia in the most far-reaching revolution in history. Under the leadership of the Bolsheviks and under the banner of "Peace, bread, and land," the people overthrew the government and established the power of the soviets as a dictatorship of the proletariat, which issued decrees for workers' control of industry, division of the land, and nationalization of many industries. The Bolshevik revolution created hysterical alarm among the leaders of the Allied nations, and in Gompers as well. This was due not only to his deep hatred of socialism and the socialists, but because he feared that Russia would make a separate peace and withdraw from the war and that the antiwar and socialist movements in the Allied countries would be stimulated by the revolution.

In order to strengthen Russia's determination to stay in the war after the March revolution and to counteract the growing influence of the Bolsheviks in the soviets, President Wilson decided to send a commission to Russia. He asked Gompers to serve on it. Gompers did not want to leave the country at that critical period and suggested Vice-President James Duncan, who was appointed. "But," Gompers wrote, "all our efforts to prevent the second Russian revolution failed."[11] Nor did they prevent Russia from making peace in January.

In the following months, the Germans launched an all-out offensive to defeat England and France before the United States could send effective help to the front and before the British blockade could starve the Germans into submission. At this time, as Gompers had feared, the movement for an international labor conference to discuss peace terms as a basis for an early end to the war was growing stronger daily. On February 20, 1918, an Inter-Allied Labor and Socialist conference was held in London on the call of the British Labour party and the Trade Union Congress. Its purpose was to consider labor's war aims, the holding of an international labor conference, and arrangements for worker representation at the peace conference. The leading spirit in this movement, as in the previous movement for the Stockholm conference, was Arthur Henderson, secretary of the Labour party and a former member of the British war cabinet. The Executive Council of the A.F. of L. declined to participate in this conference, presumably because of the political character of the meeting.

The conference adopted a detailed declaration of war aims.* But most important, as far as Gompers was concerned, was its declaration that the time was ripe for the convocation of an international labor and socialist congress to remove misunderstandings and to endeavor by mutual agreement to arrange a program of action for "a speedy and democratic peace."[12]

2. THE NEW PAUL REVERE

HAVING SECURED THE DECISIVE ENDORSEMENT OF HIS war policies by the A.F. of L. in November 1917, Gompers now conceived that his principal mission was to perform a similar service on an international scale, and particularly to check the movement for an international labor conference. He believed that Germany was doomed to inevitable defeat unless she could enlist the workers of the Allied countries in support of a negotiated peace at the time when Germany was likely to secure favorable terms. Consequently he would not consider a labor conference until Germany's military power was destroyed. Furthermore, he could see no reason for international labor to discuss war aims and peace terms, as he believed the workers of the world, like himself, needed only to accept Wilson's Fourteen Points. The working classes of the Central Powers could show their good faith only by suing for peace on the basis of those principles. Gompers asserted that the war had exploded working class inter-

---

*These included labor representation at the peace conference, the establishment of the League of Nations, territorial adjustments on the basis of the desires of the people concerned, freedom of the seas, international legislation on factory conditions, a maximum eight-hour day, the prohibition of night work for women and children, and prevention of "sweating" and unhealthy trades.

nationalism and proved that nationalism was and should be a stronger force. The war had taught him that, although the wage earners were a distinct group in society, they were also an integral part of the nation. "The ties that bind workingmen to their national governments are stronger and more intimate than those international ties that unite the workingmen of all countries."[13]

The principal way in which Gompers could combat the rising antiwar sentiment of the Allied workers and the demand for an international labor conference was by making a personal visit to Europe. He conceived of himself as a modern Paul Revere on a mission to warn of danger and rally men to the cause. The governments of Great Britain and France were asking for repayment for their services of the previous year when they had sent their labor leaders to the United States to urge sacrifices and the acceptance of conscription by the American workers. They asked that Gompers come to Europe to bolster the fighting spirit of the workers and win them to the A.F. of L. position of peace by victory rather than by negotiation. The United States government was also anxious for him to go, not only for these reasons, but because Wilson hoped that Gompers would be able to "steer" Henderson away from his antiwar and internationalist position. The continued upsurge of the antiwar movement among the British workers could result in Henderson's becoming Prime Minister and negotiating for peace.

The A.F. of L. authorized Gompers to go to Europe. Gompers cabled to Henderson that if an Inter-Allied labor conference were arranged at the time he would be in England, he would be glad to participate. Such a conference was promptly arranged. The Council named John Frey, Charles Baine of the boot and shoe workers, William J. Bowen of the bricklayers, and Edgar Wallace of the United Mine Workers to serve on the mission with Gompers.

The delegation secured passage on the troopship *Missanabie* sailing August 16 from "an Atlantic to a British port." They were notified to be in New York on the designated day and found that theirs was one of fourteen troopships carrying 40,000 American soldiers. While the ships and convoys assembled, they anchored near the port for thirty-six hours. Each evening all the portholes and doors were closed, sealing the passengers in and oppressing them with the intense summer heat. As they made their zigzag course across the Atlantic, the labor leaders began their experience with war conditions, being assigned to lifeboats, conducting frequent lifeboat tests, and being required to wear or carry life preservers at all times. On the tenth day at sea, the troopships were halted as the convoys dispersed to track down submarines whose presence was suspected. But no attack occurred, and on the following day the fleet put in at Liverpool. On its return trip to the United States, the *Missanabie* was sunk by a submarine with a loss of 64 lives.

Gompers and his party were received by the acting mayor, representatives of the British and American governments, and several representatives of British labor. The American ambassador detailed a staff member to assist the mission, and Captain William Sanders was appointed as the British liaison officer to the delegation. Gompers was deeply impressed with the importance of the occasion and of himself and was evidently disappointed when the newspaper men were not allowed to approach him at the station. After he got into an army car and had gone a little distance, he directed the chauffeur to stop. He got out and talked with the reporters and had pictures taken. He gave out the following statement for publication: "The American Labor Mission has come to Great Britain and expects to go to France and Italy to bring a message of good-will, co-operation, and determination to the workers of the three countries to aid in strengthening the bonds of unity that we may all stand behind our respective democratic governments to win the war for justice, freedom, and democracy."

The party reached London the same day and was lodged at the Savoy Hotel as guests of the British government. Here they were visited by American and British government and military officials and labor leaders to discuss the plans of the mission. Gompers spent some time during his first week in London walking about the city and, as he had done on his two previous visits, went to see his old house in Spitalsfield as well as the Bell Lane School which he had attended as a boy. A reunion was arranged for all the members of the family still in England, about forty people. During the week Gompers also visited the American base hospital, where he addressed the wounded soldiers and went through some of the wards to shake hands and say a word of cheer to each man.

The first public function attended by the mission was a luncheon given by the government at the Carlton Hotel on August 30. Gompers sat between George Barnes, a Labour Member of Parliament and cabinet member, who presided, and Lloyd George, the Prime Minister, who welcomed the delegation to England and praised Gompers for his lifelong fight for democratic progress. Also present were Winston Churchill, General Jan Smuts, Stanley Baldwin, Sir David Shackleton, and other governmental and labor dignitaries. The next night, a dinner was given for the mission by Barnes at the House of Parliament. The following day Gompers attended a dinner given by the Anglo-American League, before whom he exhibited his wartime rhetoric: "They say I am too old to fight. I never regretted so much in my life that I am already 68. I would rather have one day facing the Huns on the field of battle than 20 years of this."[14]

On September 1, the mission went to Derby to attend the British Trade Union Congress. The British liaison officer did not accompany them to the Congress because it was considered indiscreet for them to be attended by a government official. This decision was based on a recognition of British labor's misgivings regarding Gompers' attitude toward the war. Several months earlier, Gompers had sent a labor mission to England, and their attitude was regarded as truculent, warlike, and flamboyant. Many of the British labor leaders, not only socialists but men of the center group, felt that Gompers and his colleagues did not understand or sympathize with the new democratic forces that were stirring in the world. They felt that the American group picked by Gompers, with its expenses paid by the British propaganda department which the British laborites greatly distrusted, was too closely connected with the government and was out of harmony with labor's democratic ideals.[15] This skeptical attitude on the part of British labor was an obstacle to the accomplishment of Gompers' mission but it was just that attitude that he had come to combat.

Gompers attended several public meetings and visited war production plants in Derby. At a luncheon at which he and his colleagues were the guests of the seamen's union to meet the

Prime Minister of Australia, Gompers said that he had been impatient at America's long delay in entering the war, but that Wilson recognized the necessity of first uniting the American people, and the A.F. of L. had helped him to see that the American workers were behind him. When "the psychological hour" came, Wilson asked for the declaration of war. "We were a disorganized lot of people. To transform such a condition into a people who would voluntarily surrender to the Commander-in-Chief of the Army and Navy all that need be surrendered to make the fight effective, was not accomplished by power, but by the workers rising to the occasion and giving the best that was in them." He warned against peace overtures: "I would rather die fighting for the right than not fight at all. I shall then at least retain my self-respect and that of my children."[16]

At the Trade Union Congress, Gompers made an address on American labor's war policy and carefully refrained from criticism or advice on the issues which divided British labor. But he was not always so circumspect. Ray Stannard Baker, former muckraker, now thoroughly committed to war, observed Gompers at his meetings in Europe and wrote later: "He strode full fronted throughout Europe, so sure of himself and his entire equipment of ideas, so conscious of the immense power of American labor behind him, that he scattered to the right and left all peoples of all nations. He told British, French, and Italian labor leaders, quite positively, what they must do to be saved."[17]

At the close of Congress, the mission was invited to attend a joint conference of the Parliamentary Committee and the Executive Committee of the Labour party. Here he exchanged harsh words with Henderson and Jouhaux about whether the forthcoming Allied labor conference was a strictly bona fide labor affair, inasmuch as British labor was to be represented by the Labour party and the French socialists would be there as well as the trade unions. To Jouhaux' insistence that the American socialists should be invited, Gompers replied that there was no such thing as an American Socialist party but only a German adjunct in America of the German Socialist party.

On September 7 the delegation returned to London. On the train, Gompers dictated the proposals which they would submit to the Inter-Allied conference the following week. On the tenth day they left for Scotland on a trip arranged by Admiral William Sowden Sims. They stopped at Rosyth to visit the British and American fleets. After making an inspection of the flagship, they made a cruise along the seventy-five-mile line of warships. That evening they had dinner with the mayor of Edinburgh, following which they addressed a meeting of 3,000 persons called by the Scottish War Aims Committee. There was much more of the same—luncheons, ceremonies, incidents—before the delegation returned to London for the Inter-Allied labor conference which was to begin the seventeenth.[18]

The conference was held in Central Hall, Westminster. On the opening day, credential cards were sent to the delegates to be filled out. Across the top of the cards were the words "Inter-Allied Socialist Conference." The American delegates were indignant and refused to sign the credentials. When they presented themselves at the door, they were refused admittance unless they showed their cards. They asserted that they had credentials from the A.F. of L., which were the only ones they would present. Charles Bowerman, secretary of the Parliamentary Committee of the T.U.C., directed that they be admitted. Henderson apologized for the error and explained that it was due to the fact that the credential cards used in former conferences were sent to the printer and no one had paid any attention to it. But as this was an Inter-Allied Socialist and Labor Conference, the American delegates should be seated with their credentials from the A.F. of L. Gompers commented that the "politicians" regarded labor as of so little consequence that the presence or absence of the name occurred to none of them.

Gompers was appointed to the drafting committee and Frey to the all-important war aims committee, of which he was secretary. Frey came to Gompers for advice and was told: "Fight for the A.F. of L. program, and start fighting from the minute you go in. Give them hell!" Later Frey reported that the chairman of the committee expected to write the report and read it to the conference. Again Gompers advised him that, as secretary, he should insist on his prerogative to write and read the report. Frey followed the advice and won.[19]

On the second morning, the first order of business was the introduction by Gompers of the A.F. of L. resolution, based mainly on declarations of the two previous Federation conventions. His resolution posed the war as a contest between democracy and autocracy and the determination of the workers of the Allied countries to support the military effort of their governments until the enemy forces were defeated and the autocratic governments of the Central Powers destroyed. The resolution endorsed Wilson's Fourteen Points as conditions for the establishment of peace. Finally, it anticipated a world labor congress concurrent with the peace conference with the workers directly represented in the official peace conference delegations from each country.[20] Other resolutions on war aims were introduced.

On the third day the committee on international relations discussed, among other questions, that of Russia. The majority report of the international relations committee expressed sympathy with the labor and socialist organizations of Russia which were continuing the struggle against German imperialism. It warned the workers of the Allied countries against the dangers of Allied intervention in Russia, which would only strengthen reactionary efforts to restore tsarism, and under the pretext of fighting Bolshevism, serve reaction against socialism and democracy: ". . . to such a policy the working classes of the Western democracies would have the elementary duty of offering opposition without stint." The two A.F. of L. delegates on the committee presented a minority report. They favored intervention for the purpose of "counteracting the sinister influence of the Central Powers upon the so-called Bolshevik Government, which has suppressed the utterances and the aspirations of the great majority of the Russian working classes." After a long discussion, a compromise formula was adopted on the question of intervention. In conformity with Wilson's Fourteen Points, the conference would not oppose intervention influenced "only by a genuine desire to preserve liberty and democracy in an ordered and durable world peace in which the beneficent fruits of the Revolution shall be made permanently secure."

Frey presented the report of the committee on war aims. It represented an overwhelming victory for Gompers' policy. It sought to appease the Europeans by presenting the A.F. of L. proposals and the Fourteen Points as confirmations of the policy adopted by the Inter-Allied Socialist Conference. On the issue of an international labor conference, it proposed that the war aims resolutions be submitted to the labor and socialist parties of the Central Powers and if their replies indicated sufficient agreement then a conference would be called. Gompers, of course, accepted the bulk of the report, but proposed a substitute for the last provision which would declare against any conference with labor movements of the Central Powers which were not in open revolt against their governments.[21]

The report of the war aims committee was adopted by an overwhelming majority. Gompers was successful in his mission of defeating the movement for peace by negotiation and an immediate international labor conference. The A.F. of L. policy supplanted that of the British Labour party as the program of the Allied labor movements. Three days after the conference, Ambassador Page told Gompers that the proceedings of the conference had been sent to Germany and Austria, that they proved that the A.F. of L. had broken down the peace movement, and that this would have incalculable effect in convincing the German government and people that there was no longer any hope for a negotiated peace or for a breakdown in the morale of the Allied workers.[22]

On the day following the conference, the American labor mission was received by the King of England at Buckingham Palace. They had a conference for half an hour, in which the King asked Gompers to convey to Wilson the suggestion that the former German island possessions in the Pacific be placed under an American trusteeship. Queen Mary was then introduced to the group. On the 24th they left London for the continent.

In Paris they were met by representatives of the French and American governments, the military, and French labor. Gompers went first to labor headquarters, and attended a fraternal dinner and reception given by the executive committee in the evening. The following day the delegates were entertained by Premier Clemenceau, the foreign minister, and other government officials. They also attended a public meeting held by representatives of the French labor movement. Gompers saw here an opportunity to strengthen the prowar elements in the labor movement against the supporters of an early peace by negotiation. After

Gompers' speech, some of the French socialist leaders spoke. Gompers relates, "I listened to their fantastic and orational proposals as long as I could endure them and then I tersely told them they were traitors to the cause of the people of France. This remark brought the meeting to an abrupt end, for such a verbal tumult followed that speeches were no longer possible."

Gompers and his colleagues went to visit the Chamber of Deputies, quietly taking seats in the gallery. The presiding officer, Paul Deschanel, recognized Gompers, informed the deputies that there were distinguished visitors in the Chamber, and suggested an adjournment so the representatives could meet them. The suggestion was acted upon, and Deschanel escorted the labor mission to the lobby and introduced them to the deputies. Afterwards Gompers addressed the Chamber on his war policy.

Gompers wanted to visit the American front before leaving France. On the morning of September 24, the labor men were taken by André Tardieu to inspect the Citroën munition works. From there they were taken in military autos to the American general headquarters at Chaumont, 185 miles from Paris. The next day they drove to Neufchateau in time to hear the preliminary bombardment preceding the St. Mihiel advance. They covered the ground that had just been crossed by the victorious American troops, passing through Donremy, where they visited the home and the memorial chapel of Joan of Arc, and the United States air service headquarters, where they talked with the commanding general. The first stop was in Flirey, the point from which the American soldiers had entered the valley from the eastern side of the St. Mihiel sector. The town was a heap of ruins, having been devastated by the German bombardments and air raids. The men stopped for a short rest and ate Red Cross doughnuts prepared in the camp kitchens on the roadside. Gompers desired to visit a plot of ground where American soldiers had been buried within the past two days. Walking over to the rows of crosses, the company stood bareheaded and silent for a while. Gompers felt that something appropriate had to be said on the occasion, and asked John Frey to recite "In Flanders' Fields."

As the party was about to enter their car, Gompers spied an

object under some ruins. Scraping away the mud and plaster that encrusted it, he determined that it was a helmet and, removing it from the ground, found that it was very elaborately embellished. Thinking it was undoubtedly the helmet of a high German officer, Gompers cherished it and cleaned it as they drove, constantly spoke about it and boasted of his discovery as though he had captured it himself in the thick of battle. Driving through the devastated battlefields of the valley they returned to Neufchateau at 9:00 in the evening and entered the officers' mess. Just as dinner was being served, the air raid alarm sounded and all the lights were extinguished. While they ate in the dark, with the sound of falling bombs all about, the conversation became animated as the labor leaders and officers joked and laughed to relieve the strain. The talk turned to Gompers' helmet, and the officers began to tease him about it. The rest of the party joined in the bantering, failing to see in the dark that Gompers was becoming livid with humiliation and rage. When the dinner was finished, Gompers came to his associates and expressed disgust. "You have tried to make sport of me when I could not help myself," he admonished. "You have cheapened what would have been an important day. You have tried me almost beyond the point of endurance." He turned and walked away indignantly. Going to the adjoining room, he picked up his treasured helmet and studied it intently. He discerned the word "Pompier" stamped on the front and asked one of the officers what it meant. Feeling that the joke had gone far enough, the officer told him the truth about it—it was the ornamental helmet belonging to the chief of the Flirey fire department, used only on festive occasions. As the situation dawned on him, Gompers struggled between the outraged dignity of the president of the American Federation of Labor and the fun-loving Sam Gompers. Finally the latter won out. He threw the helmet out the window, forgot his official responsibility, and joined in the joke.

During the next three days, the mission toured the British, Belgian, and American fronts, visiting the base hospital, the Belgian general headquarters, where they met King Albert, and the British headquarters, where Gompers was invited to have lunch with General Douglas Haig on the battlefield at Bourlon Wood. They inspected the old Hindenburg Line and underground military headquarters, talked with soldiers eating their lunch in the midst of battle, and witnessed the assault on Cambrai, while artillery shell and airplanes were flying over their heads and bombs were falling all about them, some as close as fifty yards. While at the front they were informed that the Germans had given orders to treat them as prisoners of war if they were captured. Returning to Paris, Gompers addressed a meeting of the minority (prowar) socialist group of the Chamber of Deputies, had a hasty dinner, and rushed to the train for the trip to Italy.

Gompers—and his Italian hosts—regarded his visit to Italy as of special importance, because antiwar sentiment was stronger there than in any of the other Allied nations and the revolutionary antiwar socialists controlled most of the labor movement. In many centers the situation was approaching the stage of revolt against the war and the government, and there was widespread disaffection among the troops, presenting the danger that the military front would collapse, and with it the government.

The labor men went first to Rome, where they were received by representatives of the American ambassador, Signor Bissolati, a former socialist and then member of the cabinet, and representatives of the labor groups. After being briefed on the situation by the Italian division of the American Committee on Public Information, the mission attended a reception given by the Minister of Commerce, a concert, and a dinner given by the American ambassador. On the day of their arrival in Rome, news came of the first German note requesting an armistice and intimating agreement with the Fourteen Points. The mere announcement of the peace move produced strikes and disorders in Milan, Turin, and Florence, and Gompers made it a point to devote part of every speech he made in Italy to warning the people against showing weakness or undue anxiety for peace.[23]

Gompers discussed his plans with the American ambassador, who particularly wanted him to explain how unreservedly American labor was doing its part in support of the war effort and how its effort was strengthening the Allied cause. Gompers' first public address was to be at a mass meeting the following evening arranged by the local unions in the largest auditorium in Rome, the Augusteum. The Italian and American governments regarded this meeting as one of great importance, for it would be the first test of strength between Gompers and Italian "Bolshevism." The correspondents of the international press had gathered to report the meeting, and posters announcing it had been spread on the walls throughout the city. On the morning of the meeting, it was found that the posters had been covered with others announcing that Gompers had not arrived and that the meeting was postponed. A "council of war" was held at the embassy with the labor mission, the ambassador, and the attaché from the American embassy in London who was accompanying them. It was arranged to have all the afternoon newspapers place advertisements of the meeting, at the expense of the American embassy.

Gompers went to his hotel to rest, but soon received an urgent call from the embassy. He was informed that the newspapers, instead of carrying the advertisement ordered by the embassy, printed notices that Gompers had not arrived and that the meeting was abandoned. This had been the work of the printers, nearly all of whom were antiwar socialists. "Mr. Gompers was like a caged lion," wrote Frey. "His enemies had tricked him and brought about a situation which, in addition to being a personal humiliation, would work against the patriotic purpose which had brought him to Italy. . . . [He] paced the conference room. His emotions were so strong that for a while he did not care to speak. Some one suggested that it might be well to postpone the meeting, but the fighting spirit which had made Gompers so strong a character would not consent to this. He was determined to speak, though under the circumstances he dreaded the occasion."

When Gompers was escorted to the stage of the auditorium, instead of seeing the rows of empty seats which he had expected, he saw a packed hall. But it was not packed with workers. The military authorities had been appealed to, and company after company of soldiers and sailors had been marched into the hall, filling the galleries and at least two-thirds of the floor. Gompers was depressed and disheartened, but as he spoke the audience responded with enthusiasm, and he warmed up and delivered a fiery speech. What he did not know was that an Italian officer was standing in a little flag-draped alcove behind the platform giving signals to the audience and directing their applause and cheering. After the speech Gompers was taken to the hotel to celebrate the successful meeting. After he left the hall, a bugle blew and the audience, marching in twos, passed through the exits guarded by sentries and marched back to their barracks.[24]

The mission spent two more days in Rome, attending receptions, dinners, and meetings at the American embassy, the city hall, and the capitol. They were accompanied to the railroad station by members of the cabinet and left for Padua, which was their headquarters during their trips to the front. While they were in Padua, King Victor Emanuel arrived there and invited the labor delegation to his chateau in the forest. They dined with him, and Gompers conveyed to him information that he had received from General Haig to the effect that the Austrian army was very weak and that the Italian army, even though without reserves, could defeat it. The mission visited the American and Italian front lines, witnessed the shelling of the Austrian lines, and were guests of Generals Diaz and Bodilio at dinner. In Venice the labor delegation was invited to visit the poet Gabriel D'Annunzio's aviation camp, where special aircraft displays were arranged for their benefit. They went to Milan, where Gompers spoke at an open air meeting, since all theaters and halls had been closed because of the influenza epidemic, then to Genoa, and finally back to Turin, where they were "boycotted" by the mayor and the labor representatives but received military honors from the authorities.[25]

There was universal agreement that Gompers' mission had been a great success. The American embassy aide who accompanied the delegation on the continent reported that its work had accomplished much in strengthening the hand of the prowar labor and socialist groups, in winning over wavering elements, and in partly neutralizing the antiwar forces. Bissolati expressed his gratification to the mission for having come to Italy at the critical moment when the possibility of peace suddenly came into view and firmness among the Allies was of special importance. Appleton, secretary of the British Federation of Trade Unions, stated that Gompers' visit was worth half a billion dollars, and this view was echoed by the entire British press. And when Lord Balfour, the British Minister for Foreign Affairs, was asked what was America's greatest contribution to the Allied cause, he replied in one word: "Gompers."[26]

Gompers' job was finished, and he desired a rest from the constant strain, tension, and exertion of the trip. But before he could get away from the crowd at his last meeting in Turin, Frey approached him and said he must see him at the hotel at once. When they got there, Frey informed him that as they had entered the banquet hall the American consul had handed him a cablegram which had just been received from Secretary of Labor Wilson. Gompers' only daughter, Sadie, had died from the "flu" that morning. She was the third of his children who had died while he was away from home, as had his mother. This was the greatest blow of all, for Sadie was his youngest daughter, the apple of his eye, and the only one of his six remaining children who still lived at home with him and Mamma. Frey thought her death nearly killed Gompers, and his granddaughter believed that he never recovered from the shock of that blow. He was ill on the train from Turin to Paris and had to receive medical treatment.

When he reached Paris, there were seven letters from Sadie waiting for him. In them she had written of her work entertaining the soldiers in the camps and knitting for them and encouraged her father in the work he was doing for the victory of the Allied cause. Gompers was seriously ill for two days, and his cousin Louis Gompers sent his family physician to attend him. He excused himself from an invitation to dine with President Poincaré. On Sunday evening he went to Brest where he boarded the *Tenadores* for the voyage home. Docking at Hampton Roads, he took the first train to New York, where Sadie's body had been brought. Gompers had his last painful look at her and laid her to rest in the Washington Cemetery with the other departed ones of his family.[27]

Almost immediately after the funeral, Gompers went to Chicago to attend a public meeting that had been arranged by the American Alliance for Labor and Democracy to welcome the labor mission from Europe. Labor men and government officials were there from all over the country, and the meeting took on the appearance of a victory celebration as news of the armistice was imminently expected. Soldiers and sailors, escorted by military bands from nearby camps, paraded through the Loop to the meeting hall. Gompers hardly felt like speaking, much less celebrating, but it could not be avoided. He spoke of America's contributions to the cause, labor's role in the war, and its services in Europe.

"The conditions which we found to exist in our Allied countries was [sic] something to give us all concern," he reported. "Every attempt that we made was combatted by the pro-Germans, by the propagandists, by the pacifists and by the French and Italian bolshiviki. . . . we did try like the mischief and succeeded to some degree in putting some stiffening into the backbone of the people of the countries which we visited to stand behind their countries at least until after the war was won. . . . ."[28]

Chapter Twenty-Two

VERSAILLES

On October 26, 1918, Oudegeest, after consulting with Legien, asked the national trade union centers to appoint delegates to an international conference at the same time and place as the official peace negotiations. The agenda he proposed was the reorganization of the I.F.T.U. and the formulation of labor's peace demands to be submitted to the peace conference. He was, he said, acting in accordance with the expressions of "our friend Gompers" and the Leeds conference of Allied labor, as well as of the Bern conference of the I.F.T.U.: "Considering that the representatives of the capitalist Governments of the belligerent countries will soon sit down together at the same table, I may express the hope that also the representatives of international Labour will come together for the purpose of laying the foundations of a new community of nations, in which liberty, equality, fraternity, and humanity will not be vain and empty words."[1]

The Executive Council declined Oudegeest's invitation, and Gompers wired him that the A.F. of L. would issue a call for such a conference. The reasons given by Gompers for refusing Oudegeest's invitation were entirely irrelevant, for they both proposed the same time and place for the meeting and the same agenda. Gompers' real reason was that he wanted the conference called by the A.F. of L. and not by the I.F.T.U. He aimed to establish a new labor federation rather than to reconstruct the old one, and to present peace demands in accord with Wilson's program rather than based on a condemnation of the "capitalist governments." Before issuing his invitations, Gompers asked Wilson for his approval of the plan. Wilson replied that he had no objection and was sure that Gompers' personal presence in Paris would be of real service.[2]

Three weeks later, Gompers again wired Wilson, complaining

that the French government was debating whether to permit the conference in Paris and that other governments might not give passports to their delegates. The attitude of those governments, he said, was not only unjust but unwise, for it would play into the hands of the radicals who would accuse the governments of denying freedom of assembly and speech and would charge the A.F. of L. with deceiving labor into believing that an opportunity would be afforded them to aid in the solution of labor problems at the peace conference. "Persistence in this course by Allied governments may make impossible American labor coming to Paris and there rendering assistance. Indeed the American Federation of Labor will be humiliated and made the laughing stock of the world. If objection is removed American labor delegates myself included can leave United States soon and remain in Paris until official Peace Conference convenes and be of some service and thereafter meet with the labor conference and help to guide the conference aright."[3]

Gompers' plan was doomed to failure. The French government would not permit a conference in Paris, and Gompers absolutely refused to attend one in a neutral country, for the delegates from the Central Powers would come there as equals and not as representatives of defeated nations. Gompers was determined that they should admit their guilt for inaugurating the war and thus destroy their dominant influence in the international movement. Besides, Oudegeest would not agree to a conference which was not called by the I.F.T.U., and Henderson insisted on a labor and socialist conference rather than a purely trade union meeting, partly because his Labour party was not affiliated with the I.F.T.U. Ultimately three different calls were issued for an international conference: Gompers' meeting at Paris, one by Henderson and the socialist parties at Bern in February, and one by Oudegeest at Amsterdam in March.[4]

The Executive Council designated Gompers and four vice-presidents of the Federation—James Duncan, William Green, John Alpine of the plumbers, and Frank Duffy of the carpenters— as delegates to the Paris labor conference. Gompers named Matthew Woll as acting president of the A.F. of L., and the mission left New York on January 8, 1919. They arrived at Liverpool on the seventeenth, proceeded to London, and spent the next three days conferring with the American ambassador, John Davis, and visiting places of historic interest. On the twentieth a conference was held with the Parliamentary Committee of the British Trade Union Congress. The principal question was the forthcoming Bern conference. The A.F. of L. delegates reiterated their opposition to a conference in which political parties participated or which took place in a neutral country with representatives of the enemy nations. If Gompers could not have an international labor conference in Paris, then he wanted an Inter-Allied conference which could present to the peace congress demands "untainted by enemy influence or propaganda." As Gompers recognized, this would enable the Allied labor movements to force their program on the labor movements of the Central Powers, as any labor clauses of the peace treaty approved by the Allies would be dictated to the defeated nations with the rest of the treaty.[5] The Parliamentary Committee was not moved from its determination to attend the Bern Conference, but it did agree to co-operate later with the A.F. of L. in forming a new trade union international.

From London the American delegates went to Paris, where a meeting had been arranged with the Confédération Général de Travail on January 23. The French were willing to hold an "informal conversation" by the Allied labor heads in Paris, but they would recognize only the Bern conference as the official expression of labor's demands. It was finally agreed that the Inter-Allied meeting should be held in Paris on January 31. The French, Belgian, Canadian, and American trade unions met at the headquarters of the C.G.T., the British having received the invitation too late to attend. No further agreement could be reached in this meeting. So while the Bern conference was being held the first week in February, the American delegation stayed in France, conferring with the American peace commission and President Wilson and visiting the battlefields and other scenes of interest.[6]

Delegates from seventeen Allied, Central, and neutral nations met at the labor and socialist conference in Bern on February 5. The main business was the preparation of demands for international labor legislation to be presented to the peace conference. A proclamation to the workers of the world was issued, declaring for the abolition of wage labor and favoring workers' control of industry in order to prevent exploitation. Meanwhile, the workers should secure protection against the influences of capitalist competition through labor legislation enacted by an international labor parliament comprising a part of a league of nations. The proclamation demanded a labor charter based on the programs of the Leeds and Bern (1917) conferences which would universalize the minimum conditions already established in many countries. Gompers was completely out of harmony with the findings of the Bern conference. It had failed to condemn the Bolsheviks, had not fixed the war guilt on Germany, had declared for "an impossible international super-parliament."[7]

In the meantime, President Wilson, under strong pressure from the A.F. of L. and other sources, finally acceded to the appointment of Gompers as the labor representative on the American delegation to negotiate terms of peace. Gompers had little to offer of a general constructive character. His program of war aims followed the proposals put forth by Wilson, and he was not inclined to go beyond them; as he told reporters: "American labor will be in France to strengthen the hands of our President."[8] His primary purpose was to help prepare and secure the establishment of a labor charter in the peace treaty. He was soon engrossed in that work.

The first document presented to the public by the peace conference was a draft covenant of the League of Nations. Its Article XX stated that the contracting powers would endeavor to secure and maintain fair and humane conditions of labor and establish a permanent labor bureau as part of the League. To give effect to this article, the Supreme Allied Council created a Commission on International Labor Legislation to prepare a labor charter and to devise an agency to supervise its administration. This was the fulfillment of the promises to labor made by several governments during the war, that it would have a voice in determining the peace and that its interests would have consideration in the settlement. Article XX was also a result of the rising industrial unrest and the spread of bolshevism. The European governments were nervous in the face of these developments, and some of the governments represented at the peace conference were in daily danger of being overthrown. They had to offer to labor some definite and formal recognition at the very opening of the conference, both to justify themselves with reference to the war just concluded and to hold forth the hope of a larger measure of justice in the future. The Commission on International Labor Legislation was to meet the challenge of socialism and prove to the workers of the world that the principles of social justice might be established under the capitalist system.[9]

Each of the five great powers was to name two members to the Commission, and five other nations were to appoint one each. As United States commissioners, Wilson appointed Gompers and Edward Hurley, president of the United States Shipping Board.* The first session of the Commission was held on February 1 at the French Ministry of Labor. The Minister of Labor presided over the meeting and outlined its purposes: "The task which we are called upon to perform will assure the establishment of the democratic idea in the economic sphere, and will complete the significance of the Peace Treaty by guaranteeing the dignity and liberty of human labour by means of international conventions." He then proposed Gompers as president of the Commission. "No one appears to be better qualified for this position than the president of the largest and most powerful Trade Union organization in the world, and our choice would, moreover, be an appropriate testimony to one whose life has been devoted to the interests of the workers and to the struggle for social justice." Gompers was unanimously elected. An office was provided for him in the Ministry of Labor. The Commission held meetings four days each week during the next seven weeks.

In serving on the Commission, Gompers had particular difficulties. He was the only representative of organized labor on the Commission. George Barnes was a former labor official and was appointed to the British peace delegation as a labor representative, and Vandervelde was a Belgian socialist leader, but they acted as government rather than labor delegates on the Commission. The other twelve were employers and government officials. Gompers frequently found himself in the minority, and sometimes stood alone on important questions. Also, Gompers' concept of voluntarism in industrial relations was counter to the European idea of dealing with labor problems through legislation. Finally, Gompers had to impress on the Europeans the problems their plan

---

*Hurley was later replaced by Henry Robinson, also of the Shipping Board.

would have due to the federal character of the United States government.

The Commission accepted as a basis of discussion British proposals which would establish two organizations: a General Labor Conference and an International Labor Organization. The Conference was to enact labor laws which the nations would ratify and put into operation; failure to do which would subject them to penalties. The I.L.O. was to be an administrative body which would collect and distribute information and enforce international labor legislation. Each national delegation in the Conference was to be composed of one representative of the government with two votes, one of the employers and one of organized labor.

Gompers had fundamental objections to this plan. He disagreed with the method of representation and voting. He saw no justification in dividing the population into producers, represented by labor and employers, and consumers, represented by the government. There were only two classes in society, the employed and the employers, and they alone had to discuss labor problems. Agreement was seldom possible on major issues between the workers and the employers or between the workers and the government, which was generally on the side of the employers. Consequently, under the British plan, the vote would invariably be three to one against labor.

"I am presumed to be a conservative," he declared, "but save me from such radicalism as would put the workers in such a predicament and in such a minority. . . . How he [Vandervelde] can, in his position, favor the increase of the power of employers and the government as against the representatives of labor, I cannot understand. . . . Labor has enough to contend with in its fight for the just demands it makes upon society, without burdening it with this incubus of power to suppress the voice of labor." The workers would have no interest or confidence in such a body, he asserted, and it would be a mere academic gathering with no possibility of serving the real interests of the masses. "Do not you know," he asked, "that this world is now seething. . . . The unrest and agitation of the masses must not be lost sight of. . . . and if we do not give Labor and the masses of the people that full right and opportunity of expression, they will find another way of expressing themselves." He thought the best arrangement would be to give labor two votes and the employers and the government one vote each, but he would approve the three groups having equal representation and voting power. His proposal was defeated, and finally, although the principle of one vote per delegate was accepted, the advantage to labor was lost when the governments were permitted two delegates.[10]

Gompers also objected to the provision that conventions adopted by the General Labor Conference be immediately ratified and put into effect by the contracting powers. There were matters he wanted withheld from any legislatures, such as hours of labor for adult males. He regarded this as a "socialistic" plan for enhancing the authority of governments instead of strengthening organized labor. Besides, he feared that the legislative authority to be granted the International Labor Conference would enable it to lower some standards already established, particularly in the United States, in an effort to equalize international standards. This objection was removed by the adoption of the principle that the international body should not propose to any country a law, convention, or treaty which contained lower standards than already obtained in that country.

Gompers was also concerned that the plan not fly in the face of the United States Constitution or traditions and suffer rejection by the Senate. As the United States Supreme Court had recently affirmed in the child labor case, many matters of labor legislation were within the sole jurisdiction of the various states. Nor could the President of the United States legislate on such internal questions as labor standards by exercising his treaty powers. The United States Senate would certainly not accept any system of penalties for failing to carry out measures it did not approve. Cogency was added to Gompers' arguments by the action of thirty-seven Senators who signed a statement that they would not vote for the Covenant of the League of Nations. If the Commission on International Labor Legislation were to accomplish anything, it must adopt a convention that would make it easier, not harder, for Wilson to secure ratification by the Senate.

Gompers proposed a number of amendments to the British draft. Any convention of the Labor Conference inconsistent with the constitution of any contracting power would oblige that power only to use its utmost efforts to bring about appropriate legislation.

Gompers' second proposal was more startling: that each of the forty-eight United States be allowed representation in the Conference, inasmuch as they were sovereign as far as labor legislation was concerned. These amendments were defeated, but a British amendment designed to meet his objection was adopted. It provided that in the case of federal states, the national government should communicate conventions to the separate states and each might—it was implied, must—adhere separately.

This was not satisfactory to the American representatives. They proposed to delete the system of penalties for noncompliance with conventions and leave their application to the League of Nations. They proposed, too, that the Conference make recommendations rather than laws, and that contracting powers be required merely to submit those recommendations to their competent national authorities. The British representatives objected vigorously; such provisions would turn the Conference into a mere debating society. After considerable discussion, a subcommittee reported a proposal substantially in accord with the American plan, and it was unanimously adopted.[11]

Finally, the Commission took up the various proposals for a labor charter, "Labor's Bill of Rights," to be included in the peace treaty. The A.F. of L. submitted a list of ten clauses. Three of them, adopted by the Commission, declared that the labor of a human being should not be treated as a commodity or an article of commerce; that all workers had the right to a wage sufficient to maintain a reasonable standard of life; and that women should receive equal wages for equal work. Three of the American clauses were adopted with modifications. The right of free association was recognized, but the A.F. of L. declaration for freedom of speech, press, and assembly was dropped. It was agreed that no commodity should be shipped in international commerce in the production of which children under the age of fourteen had been employed (the A.F. of L. had proposed sixteen years as the minimum). The A.F. of L. proposed that the workday in industry and commerce should not exceed eight hours except in the case of extraordinary emergency; the Commission amended this to read eight hours a day or forty-eight hours a week, and excepted countries in which the workers' industrial efficiency was lower than that in other countries.

Four of the Federation's recommendations for labor clauses were rejected: prohibiting international commerce of commodities produced by convict labor or in private homes; prohibiting involuntary servitude except as punishment for crime; and providing for the right of merchant seamen to leave their vessels when in safe harbor. Three clauses were added to the Labor Charter by the Commission. They provided for a weekly rest, equality of treatment for foreign workmen, and a system of factory inspection in each country.[12]

The Commission concluded its work on March 24 and submitted the draft convention and labor clauses to the Peace Conference, which adopted them with the qualification that the powers should "endeavor to apply" the labor clauses "so far as their specific circumstances will permit." Gompers did not regard the labor clauses of the treaty as the best that labor should have secured. But he was sure they were all it was possible to get and that the official recognition of labor's rights was a great step forward. It opened the way to progress as the thought of the world became more enlightened.[13]

The American labor delegation returned home. Gompers immediately launched a campaign for support of the Versailles Treaty and the League of Nations. His first task was to win the endorsement of the A.F. of L. convention in June, when he defended the treaty as an affirmation of the principles for which the Federation contended. It provided the best machinery yet devised for the prevention of war; it placed human relations on a new basis, endeavoring to enthrone justice in place of strength as arbiter in international relations. The labor clauses recognized the well-being of the wage earners as of supreme international importance.

The main opposition to the treaty was voiced by Andrew Furuseth, who feared that the League was a super-parliament which could fix labor laws and labor standards in every country of the world. He criticized the labor charter because it failed to guarantee free speech and press, prohibit involuntary servitude, and assert the seamen's right to leave their ships, and because it recognized "lawful" association without defining it. "There isn't a solid thing here," he declared, "that leaves any of the American ideals in this document, and then legislation under it is to be enacted by men from all these places who could not understand even the question of involuntary servitude."

Gompers replied that "some people are so constituted that if you were to give them Paradise they would find some fault with it," and intimated that Furuseth was not loyal to the A.F. of L. If the League of Nations were defeated, what barrier would there be against future wars? The treaty was not perfect, but perfection was not to be expected when peoples with different histories, traditions, and interests were involved, especially in the first attempt. But was not any effort better than leaving the world where it was before, when every nation was a law unto itself and national prejudices and aspirations could be checked only by the arbitrament of war? Gompers denied that there was anything in the covenant to prevent American labor from pressing for better conditions; it only tried to bring up the standards of the workers in the backward countries, which would benefit workers everywhere. He appealed to the delegates not to reject this opportunity to establish international relations on a higher plane. The convention endorsed the League by an almost unanimous vote.[14]

The action of the A.F. of L. undoubtedly represented the views of the majority of the American people. But public opinion was beginning to shift away from support of the League under the impact of attacks from Republicans led by Henry Cabot Lodge, who wanted the United States to have a free hand in world affairs; by progressives led by La Follette who objected to the injustices of the treaty and its tendency to perpetuate existing wrongs; and by Irish- and Italian-Americans whose nationalistic sentiments turned them against the treaty and the League. In speech and in writing, Gompers tried to rally support for the President. He dramatized the League as constituting a diplomatic revolution, establishing international relations on a democratic basis, and going far toward making war impossible: the most powerful ally of justice that mankind had ever established. "In the League of Nations is the only safety we know of for the future and the only spiritual recompense we have found for the anguish of the past."[15] During the election of 1920, in which the League was a major issue, Gompers made a final effort to help stem the tide of isolationism. But with the defeat of Wilson's party went the last hopes for his League, and the nation turned to pressing domestic problems.

Part VII

LAST YEARS

1919-1924

Chapter Twenty-Three

RIGHT, LEFT, AND CENTER

WHEN GOMPERS RETURNED FROM THE PEACE CON-
ference in 1919, he was at the height of his power and fame. He
was the president of the largest trade union organization in the
world, the A.F. of L. membership having skyrocketed from two
million to four million during the war years. He had made a
significant contribution to the winning of the war and became an
international figure. He had been lionized by presidents, prime
ministers, kings, and generals, and was on terms of mutual confidence with the President of the United States. He was praised as
second only to Woodrow Wilson in his influence for liberal idealism. He was no longer an agitator but a labor statesman.

In his own organization he was unchallenged. He was
ensconced in a spacious and modern office in the new A.F. of L.
building dedicated during the war by ceremonies in which President Wilson participated. He was provided with a limousine and
chauffeur to bring him to work in the morning and to take him
to the Capitol or the White House. In 1914 his salary had been
increased from $5,000 to $7,500, although he urged the Federation
not to do it because of the effect a large salary would have on the
masses of unorganized workers and the radical labor men of
Europe.

With his increased income he was able to gratify a lifelong
desire—to own a home with four separate walls, "surrounded by
trees and grounds where flowers could grow and where I could
watch the birds and hear them sing." He purchased a large two-
storied corner house on Ordway Street in the fashionable Cleveland Park area. In 1919 his salary was increased to $10,000, and
the following year to $12,000, again over his objections. He bought
some stocks and bonds and a little real estate and was able to
accumulate an estate of about $40,000.

But the enjoyment of his position, his reputation, and his mode of living was tempered by personal misfortune. Gompers was sixty-nine years old and he felt it. He was tired, and his health was declining rapidly under the advances of Bright's disease. For several years he had been under the close supervision of doctors. For months he was unable to sleep more than a couple of hours each night, lying in bed with a book or report in his hands. He was forced to cut down his consumption of cigars to twenty-five a day.

In April 1919, just a few weeks after his return from Paris, Gompers was riding in a taxi in New York when it was struck by a street car. He suffered a lacerated side, two broken ribs, a badly bruised hip and arm, nervous shock, and internal injuries which kept him in pain the rest of his life. He was confined to his room for two weeks, seeing no one but his wife and daughter-in-law, Miss Guard, Matthew Woll, and Lucy Robins. Lucy noted that "from his pallid, withered face his eyes peered out in a strange and disconcerting way." He then confided to her that he was growing blind, as his father had. The accident was not the cause of his failing vision, but from that date practically total blindness closed in on him. When he realized that his eyes had failed him, he was overcome with resentment and depression. The fact that he was an old man was borne in upon him, and fear that he had outlived his usefulness obsessed him. For a week he battled against melancholy and self-pity and the temptation to give up. Then he determined to live with his affliction, to go on as if nothing had happened. Only a few of his most constant and intimate associates knew that he spent the next six years in the shadows. He feared that his opponents would discover his disability; as he said to Lucy, "Your Socialists have always called me blind. What a field day they would have if they knew the truth!"[1]

On several occasions he issued statements to the press, giving assurances of his good health and vigor. On his seventieth birthday he stated that his years did not affect his feelings, his hopes and aspirations, his mental alertness, or his unremitting activity. "We do not grow old except as we permit advancing years to cause us worry. The question of age never occurs to me, nor does it give me worry. Neither does the end of things here. I simply accept the added years as a matter of course. . . . the desire to be helpful to my fellows, to do something worth while for my people and my country is an inspiration that keeps me young both in mind and body."[2]

This was partly concealment and partly self-deception. "I am writing this while attending to important business in my office," his statement said. But he did not write it or anything else during those six years, for he was unable to. Nor did he read a newspaper, a book, or a letter. Every particle of business that went across his desk was done with the help of assistants who read to him the contents of every letter and document. The newspapers were read to him also. After twenty-five years of single-handed editing of the *American Federationist*, he now turned over much of the work to Florence Thorne, his research director, Chester Wright, a labor journalist, and Matthew Woll, A.F. of L. vice-president.

At the Federation conventions an aide always sat by Gompers' side to inform him who was asking for recognition. But when he could hear a delegate's voice he was frequently able to recognize it. Lucy Robins recalled, "There were hundreds of men in the hall, milling around with the brawling vigor of convention democracy, and Gompers ruled them all. He allowed them the greatest laxity, and yet he was as perfectly in control as if they had been an orchestra and he the conductor." Wherever he went, an associate or assistant or a friend was at his elbow. His office and his favorite haunts he knew so well that he needed no sight or guide. But there was no venturing alone in strange places or on the streets.

There would come moments when, in desperation, passing a hand over the almost sightless eyes, Gompers would throw his whole frame into a gesture of resentment at the weakness of his body. But he overcame these moods by a tremendous effort of his iron will. The inferiority complex resulting from his short stature and unattractive appearance was deepened now by his age and his blindness. As a result, he became an exhibitionist, trying to prove that he could do anything better than other men, including drinking. During the 1919 convention he showed off by riding up to the delegates' hotel in a big car with a young woman. After making sure that he was seen, he rode off "like a Don Juan."

He told Lucy that he had done it because he felt the need to impress other men.[3]

Gompers continued to give the impression of fighting determination, if not vigor. One who was not particularly sympathetic with Gompers' work described his "crafty face, strong, lined, stubborn and vindictive as a snapping turtle's; that vital, aggressive body, rugged and dominant, in spite of years and weakness; that impression of the 'little giant,' of force and power bottled up in a container too small and too distorted for normal expression." But he lacked not only vigor but the mental alertness of former years. Some of his close associates and admirers noted that he no longer displayed the quick mental receptivity and elasticity which had always characterized him.[4]

There was sorrow in Gompers' family also. In 1919 his father died in Boston at the age of ninety-two, and his wife, Sophia, suffered a stroke as a result of Sadie's death. She was not well physically or mentally for over a year. Their daughter-in-law Ella came to their home in Washington to look after Mamma and the house. In May 1920, Sophia passed away, and Sam was left alone. But, as he said, it was not in his nature to live in loneliness. Lucy Robins claimed that he proposed marriage to her shortly after Sophia's death, but those who knew him doubted it. However, the next year he married a divorcee, Gertrude Annesley Gleaves Neuscheler, a piano teacher some thirty years younger than himself. Lucy thought he married her only to prove to himself and the world that he was not an old man.

In any case, it is clear that there was little love between them. She apparently married him because she was a social climber and hoped for ingress to the circles of show people, statesmen, and industrialists where he was always welcome. Perhaps she also believed that he had more money than he actually did. She certainly made the last years of his life miserable. She moved into his house with a brother and sister and would not allow his own family to enter. He was often compelled to isolate himself in his home, and even there he found little peace. When he was tired or ill, Miss Guard would bring to his home the correspondence that required attention, but after a while she, too, was kept waiting at the door and often refused admittance. It was said that, in Gompers' absence, his wife's ex-husband sometimes came to visit her.

Fearing disgrace, Gompers swallowed his pride. But finally, in the summer of 1924, he began divorce proceedings and voided his will, leaving all his possessions to his three sons and the daughter of Rose. His wife would get only her dower interest allowed by the law, and that only if he died before the divorce became final. She contested the new will on the ground that he was mentally unfit at the time, but withdrew the case when she saw the list of dignitaries who were to be called as witnesses to his mental alertness. When he died, she stripped the house before his body was brought back to Washington.[5]

From 1919 to 1923, Gompers spent much of his spare time preparing his memoirs. Miss Guard had been urging him to do this for twenty years, and although he never got around to it, she had been gathering documents, preparing memoranda, and building up files of material to be used for that purpose. In 1919 he contracted with E. P. Dutton & Co. for the publication of the work. Miss Thorne did most of the research and much of the writing of the book. She projected her mind into his, learning how he thought and how he expressed himself, so that in the end it was impossible to tell what was her own writing and what had been dictated by him. But every word of the final work was read to him for approval or revision.[6]

After two years of work, Gompers was mightily discouraged. He had spent over $10,000 on the work and found it impossible to continue with it. On his request, the publishers formed a syndicate which provided him with $8,000 to complete the job, and he agreed to transfer to the syndicate all his rights to royalties. He wrote to Matthew Woll, who made these arrangements for him: "I am grateful to you for the trouble and work you are undertaking in this matter, even though it be with reluctance that I consent. If I should consult my own personal wishes in the matter, I am frank to say that I should lay the whole proposition aside and leave it to those who survive me to write what they might desire of my life's work. I did not realize the prodigiousness of the task, or I fear I should have hesitated long before I should have entered upon such a contract with the publishers. However, be that as it may, you and other friends have insisted with every argument you could command that this work should be completed while I am here to direct it and personally supervise it; that justice to the labor movement and to myself demand that this course should be followed; that the history of my life's work should not be left to irresponsible writers to commercialize after I shall have passed over to the other side."[7]

So Gompers worked away at the book for two more years. In November 1923, he brought the story up to date, gave it its title, *Seventy Years of Life and Labor*, and turned the manuscript over to the publishers. He did not live to see it in print, for it appeared in 1925, with an epilogue on his last year written by Miss Thorne.

Nineteen-nineteen found the world, including the United States, in turmoil. Labor was restive, in many parts of the world in open revolt. Workers had been restricted by wartime repressions and prices had soared—now they wanted wage raises and other advances. Governments had led them into Armageddon for what turned out to be not defense of the fatherland, but conquest of territories, markets, and trade advantages, and now many of them wanted an end of imperialism and capitalism. At the same time, reaction everywhere sought to strengthen, or at least retain, its hold. Counter-revolution was organized and despotism established in many countries to suppress the labor movement. Employers determined to check the advance of unionism and reassert their power.

In this worldwide contest between reaction and revolution, Gompers tried to steer labor through the middle while beating off his antagonists on both sides. "The American Federation of Labor is at all times critical of our economic order," he wrote, "seeking always for improvement. . . . But the A.F. of L. stands squarely and unequivocally for the defense and maintenance of the existing order. . . . Therein lies the sharp distinction between the A.F. of L. and the revolutionists. Therein also lies the sharp distinction between the A.F. of L. and the bourbons and reactionaries . . . who believe that all is well with the world and that all change and modification are evil."[8]

But in trying to steer a middle course, Gompers found himself constantly veering closer to the right in order to avoid the left. The attacks of reaction might weaken the trade union movement, but they would also tend to unify it and solidify Gompers' leadership. The attack from the left, however, was primarily an

assault on Gompers' position of leadership in the labor movement and was therefore more dangerous to him. Besides, his
commitment to the maintenance of the existing order made
radicalism, not reaction, appear as his main enemy. All this tended
to make him an ally of the employers in a common fight. In
his desire to gain recognition, respectability, and prestige for
himself and the A.F. of L., he went so far as to condemn even
the mildest liberals as "socialists, pacifists, and revolutionaries."
His continuous attacks on bolshevism proved something of a
boomerang. "His irresponsible exaggeration of the radical menace
intensified the public's fears of social conflict and consequent
demand for forced suppression of strikes."[9]

A more personal factor was involved in Gompers' growing
conservatism. He was tiring of his lifelong struggle. "There
was developing," wrote Miss Thorne, "a gentle remoteness that
shrank from the physical ordeal of contest. The spirit was willing
but the flesh was weak." But, in addition, he had derived great
enjoyment and satisfaction from his wartime role. "All my life
has been a fight and it has so often been my duty to say that
which but few wanted to hear. It was a real comfort for once in
my life to find my purposes understood and appreciated."[10] He
would have liked to retain the confidence of presidents, to sit
on government commissions, to be the labor statesman directing
the hosts of labor in co-operation with business and government,
to solve the nation's reconstruction problems.

Gompers' appraisal of conditions in the United States and
in the world, and of his role in it, led him to revise his social
theory far beyond that which he developed as a leader in the
National Civic Federation twenty years earlier. This revision had
begun during the war, when Gompers and other Federation
leaders had seized the opportunity of wartime national unity to
attempt to establish permanent industrial peace. By collaborating
closely, by being friendly and "reasonable," they had felt they
would draw employers close to them and lay the foundation for
continued co-operation after the war.[11] As he said, in discussing
the organization of world peace: ". . . a program so vast cannot be
established and maintained by one class alone. Urban labor,
agriculture, businessmen of every rank and type must work side
by side in sincere co-operation to secure the world-wide adoption

of those principles which will guarantee the triumph of justice and opportunity for all classes, everywhere."[12]

After America's entrance into the war, Gompers' zeal for national unity led him to more specific rejection of the doctrine of class struggle. He appealed to the employers to take labor into partnership in the constructive work of creating better conditions and relations between men, warning them that the alternative was bolshevism.[13] In the postwar years, Gompers developed these views into a comprehensive program for labor-business co-operation in a system of industrial self-government. Reverting to the old idea of the Knights of Labor which he had repudiated as obsolete forty years earlier, he saw class conflict as no longer between labor and industrial employers, but between industry and finance. Industry was devoted to public service, but finance was interested only in profit: "Wall Street today is a blind fool astride a wild engine of terrific power. There is intelligence in neither."

The problem then was to throw off the control of production by those who merely invested capital and to place it in the hands of those actively engaged in production, who were alone competent to judge production policies and desirous of giving service. The result would benefit the public as a whole, and it would benefit labor. If the incubus of Wall Street could be thrown off, management would no longer resist the trade unions and their demands as an infringement on their profits. They would be able to co-operate with labor in the release of vast creative forces and the production of commodities for use.[14]

Gompers had little to suggest with regard to the means by which industry could purge itself of the domination of high finance. But he did have some ideas about how labor and management could co-operate to eliminate waste and inefficiency, to make it serve the public welfare rather than profits alone, and to evolve a practical industrial democracy. The most important of these was scientific management, Taylorism, which in pre-war years, he had denounced.

The right hand had first been offered by labor. The Commission on Industrial Relations had held hearings on the subject in 1914, and John Lennon, one of the labor members of the Commission, had suggested that labor's opposition to the whole plan might be avoided if the unions were invited to co-operate. Gompers had lent his support to this approach; scientific management might be reformed under the influence of collective bargaining. Through Professor Robert Hoxie, Gompers had offered reciprocal recognition of the unions and scientific management. Frederick Taylor had declined, declaring that unionism and Taylorism were intrinsically inimical.[15]

But a new generation of industrial engineers was developing, and many of them were breaking away from Taylor's hostility to unionism and giving consideration to the human and psychological elements in production. Led by Robert Valentine, they began to recognize the fact that scientific management would never succeed without co-operation, or at least the removal of antagonism, on the part of the workers and urged the possibility and desirability of a rapprochement with labor. These views were strengthened by wartime experiences, when scientific managers entered government service and found themselves co-operating with unionists on production and labor agencies. They discovered that union recognition and collective bargaining were not the danger to efficient production they had imagined. In fact, they began to see it as a valuable asset.

Furthermore, the war brought together Gompers and Morris L. Cooke, who served on various government boards and encouraged a prounion attitude, and a friendship sprang up between the two. After the war, Cooke undertook the job of effecting a broad meeting of the minds between the leaders of scientific management and labor. In 1919 Gompers was assured that neither Cooke nor those he represented were any longer a threat to organized labor. In October he invited Cooke to write an article for the *American Federationist* and asked him to attend the International Labor Conference as his advisor.[16] The literature of scientific management began to lay more stress on industrial psychology, the human element in production, and the relations between efficiency and consent. The old "driver" method of management was being rapidly abandoned.

In January 1920, Gompers appealed for the co-operation of labor and the industrial engineers to promote the production of an adequate supply of the world's needs for use and a higher standard of living. Cooke invited Gompers to collaborate in editing an issue of the *Annals* of the American Academy of Political and Social Science. In September the book appeared under the title, *Labor, Management, and Production*, edited by Cooke, Gompers, and Fred Miller, later president of the American Society of Mechanical Engineers. Some of the leading former antagonists of scientific management among labor leaders and of unionism among the engineers contributed to the volume. In the preface, Gompers wrote: "To the idealism and aggressiveness of the labor movement the technical skill and the inventive genius of the engineer are fitting and needed complements." Cooke did his part by supporting the right of labor to bargain collectively through representatives of their own choosing.[17]

In Gompers' view, scientific management and collective bargaining could be combined to produce industrial democracy.[18] But this could be done only if management used industrial engineering with a mind to securing the workers' good will, if it considered labor as a human factor in production rather than an impersonal factor on a par with machinery. This meant union recognition and collective bargaining and consideration for the health, safety, and morale of the workers. "Once we remove the union's suspicion of the employer and the employer's suspicion of the union [by a fair collective agreement] there is nothing in the world to prevent the most cordial relation. . . . That co-operation develops the finest possible relation in which both sides are not only fair but independent and manly. . . . we are all associates in the same enterprise but approaching [our goal] from somewhat different standpoints." He expressed the hope that the time had passed which required fighting and militant union leaders, and that an era was developing in which constructive labor statesmanship would be able to take its place.[19]

These concepts of union-management co-operation for increased efficiency and productivity were given practical application by a large number of unions, most notably by the "Baltimore and Ohio plan" of the railroad brotherhoods and shop crafts. With these Gompers had little or nothing to do. His job was to formulate, interpret, and publicize the general theoretical foundations of the system. In this task Gompers came to a meeting of the minds with the famous engineer and then Secretary of

Commerce, Herbert Hoover. He reprinted in the *American Federationist*, evidently with his approval, a speech in which Hoover urged the unions to secure a "unity of purpose in constructive increase of production by offering to the employer the full value of the workers' minds and effort as well as hands."[20] Gompers invited him to address the Executive Council on his view of industrial co-operation.

Hoover developed the idea of union-management-engineer co-operation into the concept of "self-governing industry," which he regarded as the great revolution of the near future and almost a panacea for all economic ills. The organization of the voluntary forces of our economic life and the co-operation of economic groups, he prophesied, produce a new economic system based neither on the capitalism of Adam Smith nor the socialism of Karl Marx, but one passing from extremely individualistic action into a period of associational activities. By associational activities, Hoover meant the trade associations which mushroomed in the 1920's. These associations drew together the firms in each trade for the purpose of standardizing products, pooling information, advertising, insurance, traffic, and purchases, and drawing up codes of fair practices. Under the Republican regime of the 1920's, these associations were given immunity from prosecution under the antitrust laws. Since Hoover actively encouraged and promoted their formation, the concentration of industry proceeded unchecked, and with unprecedented rapidity.

Gompers greeted the growth of trade associations with "gratification." He regarded the chief function of these associations to be agreement for the restriction of output in order to prevent over-production. He saw in this activity the "mastering pressure of economic development against a structure of repressive legislation calculated to prevent the doing of that which economic necessity compels." The trade associations, he wrote, were doing in the nontrustified industries what the trusts were doing in the monopolized industries, that is, eliminating unfair and ruinous competition. Since Congress was not sensible enough to repeal the antitrust laws, the trade associations were the next best way of eliminating wasteful competition.[21]

Gompers praised Hoover's conception of industrial self-government as pointing the road toward industrial democracy.

And the idea that industry should cure its own abuses and solve its own problems seemed to Gompers, as to Hoover, the best preventive of communism or state socialism and the surest guarantee for the preservation of free enterprise. Gompers' only criticism of Hoover was that he did not give sufficient attention to the responsibility of labor in this scheme and to the opportunity for labor's greater participation in the impending transformation. He pointed to the Baltimore and Ohio plan as the outstanding example of how labor could play its part in the development of a co-operative, voluntary relationship between workers and management for industrial self-government. But this, said Gompers, was a minor criticism. The important thing was that Hoover had pointed the way to economic efficiency and industrial democracy by a method that would avoid "the death of our civilization under a smothering pall of crushing governmentalism—bureaucracy of the state with all of its incompetence and regimentation, the horror of which must oppress every normal, freedom loving person who contemplates the possibilities."[22]

But Gompers went further than Hoover. Hoover's practice as Secretary of Commerce was to have government and business co-operate in the development of industrial self-government, leaving control of business in the hands of business itself. Gompers wanted industrial self-government worked out co-operatively by labor and management and made virtually an autonomous part of the government. He first presented his idea in rather rough form to the Executive Council in September 1922, introducing it with the thought that there must be opportunity for progressive evolution with industry "or else we must deal with revolution. The constructive method is based upon co-operation to work out better methods, followed by intelligent acceptance of results through mutual agreements." He observed that political government had failed in dealing with economic problems, as in its futile efforts to prevent the growth of monopolies. It was now time to free industry from the control of the state and establish agencies of economic freedom and self-government.[23]

The victory of the Progressives in the congressional elections two months later provided Gompers with an occasion to present these views to the public. In spite of the Progressive gains, it was foolish to hope that existing social evils would be rapidly cured through the enactment of a multitude of laws. "To lead people to believe that the pot of gold is to be found at the foot of a legislative rainbow is to court future disaster." The welfare state philosophy of the Progressives was anathema to Gompers. It represented a bulking bureaucracy, tyranny, the transformation of the workers from citizens of the republic into wards of the state. Economic affairs, he wrote, were not the concern of government, and politicians were incompetent to deal with them. Any attempt to do so would lead to hopeless complication and conflict and to state socialism "which we shall some day, at perhaps great cost, have to destroy." The tendency of industry to develop its own structure of government was the only hope of avoiding state socialism and still guarantee industrial justice.[24]

In April, Gompers discussed his theory further in the *Federationist*. When politicians tried to deal with industrial problems, he wrote, their first idea was to forbid something, to exercise power. But: "Industry is more powerful than politics and it will find a way to be served. . . . Industry goes on, making its laws. Employers make laws and workers make laws. Both, sitting together, make laws, and the laws so made are the laws that today most vitally affect the masses of the people and most surely protect the foundations of civilization. They are the laws that are shaping the future of human life." The enactment of the eight-hour day by the steel industry would be more important than the laws passed by a whole session of Congress. "And the laws that are built as a result of organization are the laws that can be agreed to by those who must live under them. That is important. There may be much crudeness, but in the end it is the way of democracy at work." This was a reality, Gompers said, that would grow and develop. All he asked was that a line be drawn between industrial democracy and political democracy, and that government withdraw from the realm of the former and leave it free to work out its own destiny.[25]

Gompers concluded that it was not the mission of labor and management to clash; that was a manifestation of the birth pangs of an industrial order attempting to find itself and to discover its proper functioning. "The true role of industrial groups, however, is to come together, to legislate in peace, to find the way forward in collaboration, to give of their best for the satisfaction of human needs. There must come to industry the orderly functioning that we have been able to develop in our political life." He suggested that labor and the employers in each industry should elect representatives to a national industrial council to consider the problems of that industry. The council in each industry would in turn elect representatives to a national body comprised of delegates from all the industrial groups. Each industry would submit its recommendations to the national body, which would have legislative power to deal with all matters affecting industry as a whole. This would be, in effect, a third house of Congress, based on economic rather than geographic representation, and having complete authority in its field.[26]

It is not surprising, in view of these theories, that Gompers showed considerable sympathy with the corporate state that was established in Italy in 1922. Gompers denounced Benito Mussolini on several occasions for his antidemocratic views and use of force but seemed to appreciate the fact that Fascism had been able to seize power because of the reaction against the growth of bolshevism, which he regarded as the greater menace.[27] Apparently he knew little about Fascism, however, until the appearance of a book on the subject by an English writer in the fall of 1923. Gompers reviewed this book in the *Federationist*, characterizing it as a balanced judgment. He found that Mussolini was apparently not the thoroughgoing reactionary that he had been thought to be, for the circumstances of his rise to power and his program and philosophy revealed a constructive side of the Fascist movement.

Gompers emphasized that bolshevism probably would have come to power if the Fascists had not seized the government when they did. He was also attracted to the intense nationalism of the Fascist movement and its principle that national unity was essential for the progress of the country. But most important and most exciting to Gompers was the experiment in the corporate state. Gompers learned that the political state and parliamentary institutions were in a deplorable condition of demoralization when the blackshirts made their march on Rome, and that Mussolini was endeavoring to replace them with an industrial state. Mussolini's stated purpose was to establish a parliamentary assembly to deal with general political matters and an industrial council for the solution of economic problems. ". . . the purely political problems which agitated society during the last century are now thrown into the shade," Mussolini declared, "and to a great extent superseded by economic and technical problems which can not well be settled by an interchange of opinion. For their solution, individual knowledge and capacity are needed, not oratory and a crowd. . . . a new road, . . . an improvement in agriculture . . . might be much more important than a whole session of parliament."

The Fascist ideal was a society whose characteristic feature would be the collaboration of the various classes and functions for the common good, principally through the industrial council or vocational parliament. "One can not escape the conviction," Gompers commented, "that if the political franchise is for the moment a somewhat innocuous institution there is in the process of development an industrial franchise which with the promised revival of the political franchise will give the Italian people a voice in the conduct of their daily affairs such as they have never enjoyed before." The dictatorship was a means to the establishment of industrial democracy, and its antipathy to parliamentarism was not actually a tendency toward absolutism but an effort to discover a form of government more suited to modern needs.

"However repugnant may be the idea of dictatorship and the man on horseback," Gompers wrote, "American trade unionists will at least find it possible to have some sympathy with the policies of a man whose dominating purpose is to get something done; to do rather than to theorize; to build a working, producing civilization instead of a disorganized, theorizing aggregation of conflicting groups."

The Fascist state was organizing society on the principle that the various classes were not antagonistic but could exist together, co-ordinated in a functional democracy. It sought to bring the classes into close relation with the state for public ends. This was along the lines that Gompers had been thinking, as was the declaration of Mussolini that "the state ought to resign its economic functions . . . for it can never adequately administer them. I hold that a government which desires speedily to relieve the population from the post-war crisis ought to allow private enterprise free play, and give up all interfering and hampering legislation, which may appease the demagogues of the left, but, as experience is proving, eventually becomes absolutely fatal to general interests and economic development." Gompers noted that these declarations "might easily enough have been taken from the mouths of American trade unionists"—or at least from his own.

Of course, Gompers was concerned for the fate of the trade unions under Fascism. He noted that the labor organizations which existed before the *coup d'état* were being rapidly dissolved and replaced by state-controlled organizations. But evidently this did not disturb him, as the old unions "were honey-combed during the war with the doctrines of pacifism and defeatism and after the war they became most fertile ground for the propaganda of Bolshevism." Compulsory unionism was being established, but that was logical because industrial democracy could not be created without the complete organization of all who were engaged in production. "Legal recognition of the trade unions apparently is intended but it is equally apparent that it is not intended that trade unions shall be anything beyond subordinate parts of the industrial state. The whole concept apparently is that their function must be assistance in production while they must never be permitted to intrude into Italian life the threat of purely class action." Gompers' tone indicated that while he had some misgivings about the shackling of the unions to the state, he was not entirely out of sympathy with the role assigned to them in the corporate system.[28]

Mussolini started his career as a socialist and ended it as a Fascist. Gompers was never one or the other, but he traveled the same circle—he started as a sympathizer and associate of socialists and ended by commending the Fascist system and ideology.

Chapter Twenty-Four

INTERNATIONALISM

1. THE I.F.T.U.

THE MEETING TO REORGANIZE THE INTERNATIONAL Federation of Trade Unions was finally called by Oudegeest to meet in Amsterdam on July 25, 1919. The A.F. of L. elected Gompers as its representative, along with Daniel Tobin and J. J. Hynes. They sailed from New York on July 11 and arrived in Amsterdam on the twenty-fourth. The following day, the old International met to wind up its affairs. Ninety-one delegates were in attendance, representing the trade union centers of fourteen countries with seventeen million members. The main business was the Belgian indictment of the German labor movement for failing to prevent the war, for supporting the German government in the war, and for failing to protest effectively against the violations of Belgian neutrality and the atrocities committed against the Belgians. They demanded that the German delegation admit Germany's war guilt, making this demand a condition for their further participation in the conference. Gompers seconded the demand and added to the Belgian indictment, accusing Legien of refusing to prevail upon the German government to stop the submarine warfare which forced the United States into the war, refusing to support the proposed naval holiday proposed by Great Britain, and failing to support the A.F. of L.'s call for an international labor conference at Paris during the peace congress. The German delegates submitted a statement in reply in which they asserted that the German trade unions had always recognized the wrong of Germany's actions with regard to the Belgians and that they had always condemned the atrocities committed against them. But they had supported the German government in the war because they had been convinced that it was a defensive war.

The Belgian and American complaints and the German declaration were referred to a committee consisting of one delegate from each country. Gompers represented the A.F. of L. on the committee. The German delegates revised their original declaration, somewhat softening the admission of Germany's guilt and adding that the Germans were not so sure about everything the workers in the Allied countries did. Gompers then presented a resolution: the committee was satisfied with the German declaration insofar as they acknowledged the grave injustice suffered by the Belgians, but the Germans had also committed injustices against the people and governments of the Allied countries. It was no excuse to say that they were misled. Everyone knew that Germany was the aggressor. Johann Sassenbach announced that if that resolution was adopted, the German delegation would have to withdraw from the conference. Gompers defended his resolution. The German delegates were defiant and unrepentant; if they would not admit their guilt, then "they would have to stand reprimanded by the heart and conscience of the labor movements of the world."

Edo Fimmen of Holland, the chairman of the committee, appealed for a conciliatory attitude on both sides and urged Gompers to withdraw his resolution. Gompers agreed to do so with the understanding that each delegate reserved the right to take any position he deemed desirable in the conference, depending on the attitude taken by the German delegation. The committee agreed to simply register the declarations of the Germans, and its report was unanimously adopted. Thus the old I.F.T.U. passed into history, on a sour note of "internationalism," to be sure.

On July 28 the conference to form a new International convened. Gompers was appointed to the committee dealing with the international situation, the program of the I.F.T.U., and the Bern resolution on the League of Nations, and was elected chairman by the committee. The American delegation secured the establishment of the International's headquarters in Amsterdam and the rule that it should be composed of the bona fide trade union organizations in each country. The Americans also won agreement that only one national center from each country should be admitted, thus excluding representatives of the socialist and labor parties and dual union organizations.

The first major dispute arose over the report of the committee on the International Labor Organization. It denied that the I.L.O. could be accepted as the full expression of the demands of the world's workers, since the Labor Charter in the Versailles Treaty fell far short of the demands of the Bern conference with regard to child labor and education, the employment of women, the eight-hour day, home work, and other issues. But the report admitted that the Labor Charter might become the basis of a more rational League of Nations and therefore urged co-operation with the first International Labor Conference in Washington, on condition that the trade unions of all countries be admitted and that the delegates appointed by the labor unions be recognized as representative of the workers.

Gompers offered a substitute which declared that the I.F.T.U. did not regard the Labor Charter as the full expression of Labor's demands and urged the labor movements to strive to realize the International's program. He ignored the Bern program and made no mention of the Washington Labor Conference. He appealed for the support of the League of Nations and the Labor Charter, not as perfect instruments, but as the best that could be obtained and a foundation for improvements. But the committee report was adopted, only the American and British delegates voting for Gompers' substitute.

Gompers' committee then reported in condemnation of the Allied blockade against Russia and urged the labor movement in each country to work for its termination; but it opposed a a resolution of the Dutch syndicalists for a general strike against the blockade. The I.F.T.U. approved the report, with only the American and English delegates opposing it. The United States delegation was again in opposition on a resolution calling on the working classes to secure complete trade-union organization as a prelude for socializing the means of production.

Finally, the committee reported on the League of Nations. A Gompers resolution had expressed regret that the League did not wholly realize the aspirations of the workers but admitted that for the first time arbitration and reason were substituting for brute force in an international treaty. After a lengthy discussion,

Gompers was persuaded to withdraw this resolution in favor of another which tacitly recognized the League without endorsing it. It recommended that the League should be a legislative and judicial body elected by the people of the world, considering economic as well as political problems, and it urged that the workers organize internationally so as to control effectively the League and prevent it from becoming a center of reaction. This resolution was adopted, the American delegates abstaining.[1]

On the whole, Gompers was quite satisfied with the results of the congress. In a press release issued at the close of the conference, he characterized it as marking a new stage in the progress of labor and the I.F.T.U. as approximating "the democratic conception of genuine internationalism." Most important to him was the firm stand the conference had taken by defeating the general strike resolution and thus demonstrating that the international labor movement was not to be inveigled into the revolutionary bolshevik movement. "It is true," he conceded, "that the majority of the delegates professed more or less Socialistic doctrines but they finally definitely repudiated the persistent and ceaseless efforts of the Socialist parties to utilize the unions for a revolutionary cataclysm."[2]

The American delegates left Europe immediately after the conclusion of the congress and returned to New York on August 26. By the time of the A.F. of L.'s next convention the following June, Gompers was questioning the wisdom of affiliation with the I.F.T.U. The principal reason for his change of heart was that the Bureau, or executive, of the International was calling for militant action, including an international May Day demonstration, to carry out the resolution that the trade unions should work for the nationalization of the means of production. Gompers neither recommended nor opposed affiliation with the International, and the A.F. of L. authorized the Executive Council to affiliate on the following basis: self-determination on all political matters; the abolition of all authority of the Bureau to act except on instructions of international congresses; abolition of the *Bulletin* and the substitution of a newsletter confining itself to trade union matters; no binding decisions except by unanimous vote; and reduction of the per capita tax.[3]

Shortly after, Poland invaded Russia. The I.F.T.U. Bureau

issued another manifesto condemning war and intervention. It urged all unionists to refuse to transport troops or to manufacture munitions to be used in the war against Russia and if necessary to wage a general strike. Its proclamation concluded: "Comrades! In the year 1914 our organization was much too weak to set itself against war. Today it is a power of *twenty-seven million members*. Above all it is imbued with a pronounced anti-capitalist and anti-militarist spirit. *Today it must of its own accord and within its own ranks, find the power to preserve the world from terror and annihilation.* War against war!"

Gompers characterized this declaration as a design to strengthen the hold of Soviet power in Russia and enable it to dominate neighboring countries, and regarded it as a reversal of the Amsterdam conference's decision on a general strike against the Russian blockade. The manifesto was an appeal for revolutionary violence, and a most unnecessary appeal, for the world was not threatened with "terror and annihilation" unless it was from the Soviets. If the world were to be saved from that danger, it must be by the action of the democratic governments, not by the working classes. He asserted that the action of the I.F.T.U. was doubtless devised in Moscow by the Communist International and was part of an international scheme to bolshevize all of Europe. Therefore, he concluded, the A.F. of L. would not only reject the manifesto but would refrain from joining the I.F.T.U. In March 1921, the Executive Council declared: ". . . we must decline to be a part of a movement which undertakes the destruction of the American labor movement or the overthrow of the democratic government of the United States."[4]

Gompers refused to recognize that the Amsterdam international and its socialist leaders were not bolshevik or sympathetic to bolshevism, but were swept along by tides of unrest among the workers which they could not stem, and their purpose was to divert this unrest from the revolutionary path blazed by the Third International. He raised other objections to the I.F.T.U., arguing that the International's constitution abrogated the principle of autonomy for each national trade union center and made the International's actions binding on all affiliates. It appears that he deliberately misled the A.F. of L., for, as Oudegeest reminded him, he had himself voted for the clause in the International constitution which guaranteed the autonomy of the trade union movement of each country. Gompers also objected to the dues system of the organization as placing an inordinately high burden on the A.F. of L., though he had voted for that, too. He was obviously no more than seeking reasons for not co-operating with the I.F.T.U.

In his reply to the Executive Council, Oudegeest informed the A.F. of L. that if it could not endorse the appeal for action against war, then "we must assume that you have considerably less objection against the provocation and outbreak of a new world war than ourselves, and that as a matter of fact there is an abysmal and incompatible difference between your mentality and that of the workers of Europe. . . . We take the point of view that any war, immaterial as to whether it is commenced by autocratic or democratic governments, must be opposed and prevented by the working class. . . ." Oudegeest also protested that the I.F.T.U. had never referred to or aimed at the overthrow of democratic governments of the world. "We are anxious for the American Federation of Labor to affiliate with the International," Oudegeest concluded. "If you have grievances supported on *real* grounds, which you are able to formulate without false representation of accomplished facts or without attempts at insinuation, we shall be very happy to go into such matters with you." But Gompers would not consider affiliation unless the International, in effect, adopted the views of the A.F. of L. He appealed to European labor to stop wasting its time in "speculative and hysterical ventures in the realm of metaphysics and impossibilities" and to return to sound judgment and sound principles.[5]

Gompers did not give up hope that it would. In the summer of 1924, his discussions with the resident officials of the I.F.T.U. encouraged him to believe reaffiliation might be possible. He said privately: "When I am gone I want someone to do me the justice to let the world know that I was never in entire acord with my colleagues upon withdrawal from the International Federation of Trade Unions. I know they were right in the objections they made against certain acts of the International. I have written as directed but believed we could have met our difficulties in another way—from within."[6] But it was too late, at least for Gompers' time. His dream of a generation, that he might some day form and lead a world trade union federation modeled after the A.F. of L., was lost. But at least he had the satisfaction of fulfilling that dream on a smaller scale in the Pan-American Federation of Labor.

2. PAN-AMERICAN FEDERATION OF LABOR

In 1915 Gompers recommended that the A.F. of L. authorize the Executive Council to enter into correspondence with representatives of organized labor in Latin America to develop a better understanding and closer relationship, with a view to concerted action.[7] The Federation approved the suggestion. The following July, representatives of the Mexican labor movement and the Executive Council called for the establishment of a Pan-American Federation of Labor, and in January a conference committee was formed consisting of Gompers, who was chosen president; John Murray, a crippled printer who was devoted to the Latin American peoples; Carlos Loveira, representing the Yucatan workers; and Santiago Iglesias of the Puerto Rican Federation of Labor. The committee wrote to the labor movements of Latin America urging them to select representatives to join in the preparatory work of organization.

"As is well known," the communication declared, "the capitalists of North America and some European countries are scattering millions of dollars through Latin-America acquiring concessions and business properties which are disposed of to them by Latin-American politicians and speculators without taking into consideration the rights of the masses of the people. . . . it becomes all the more evident that the wage-earners of these countries must also unite for their common protection and betterment. . . . Above all things, the Pan-American Federation of Labor should stand as a guard on watch to protect the Western Hemisphere from being overrun by military domination from any quarter."

A minimum program was outlined for the new organization, calling for better standards of life and work. Favorable responses came in from many countries, and in the meantime the United States entered the war. This gave added impetus to Gompers' desire to complete the organization of the continental labor federation, to secure the co-operation of the Americas in support of the Allies. In May, he sent to Mexico James Lord of the Federation's

Mining Department, and also John Murray of the International Typographical Union; Murray had helped organize the Political Refugees Defense League and sought actively to promote American understanding of the Mexican Revolution. Gompers also persuaded President Wilson that Pan-American labor unity was an important war measure which would help to educate the Mexican people as to the cause of the United States' entrance into the war. Wilson appropriated from special funds several thousand dollars to promote the project, and for several months Murray and Canuto Vargas of the Mine, Mill, and Smelter Workers published a bilingual paper which was shipped into Mexico and which advocated Pan-Americanism.[8]

The Mexican labor syndicates agreed that co-operation with the A.F of L. was desirable to counteract the growth of and oppression by capitalist organizations, but they raised the question of the protection of workers emigrating from one country to another and asked for a system of acceptance and interchange of union cards. As for supporting the Allied cause in the war, it was "very premature and inconvenient, at this moment, to form a labor program which might compromise our efforts and action in the matter relating to international policies."

The following month it was agreed that a conference of the Mexican and United States labor movements be called as soon as possible. The A.F. of L. proposed a program which treated the improvement of conditions for immigrant workers as but one of a number of points emphasizing friendly relations between the two countries. Gompers himself intended to bring up international policies at the ensuing conference. The Mexican labor organizations sought to avoid such discussions and to discuss the protection of migrant workers and their admittance into the trade unions of the country to which they emigrated. They also emphasized the importance of having an equal number of delegates from Mexico and the United States.[9] When Gompers issued the call for the conference, to be held at Laredo, Texas, on November 13, 1918, he listed the A.F. of L. program as the agenda for the meeting, ignoring the Mexican proposals.

He had just returned from his mission to Europe and reached Laredo just in time to hear the news of the armistice. He and the mayor of Nuevo Laredo ceremoniously welcomed the delegates to the convention at the Mexican-United States boundary on the International Bridge. Secretary Wilson, representing President Wilson, and General Garza, representing President Carranza, also expressed appropriate sentiments before the seventy-two delegates from six countries, all but four of whom were from the United States and Mexico. The convention opened with addresses by Ricardo de Leon, representing the workers of Central America, Luis Morones of the Mexican Federation of Labor (Confederacion Regional Obrera Mexicana, or C.R.O.M.), and Gompers.

Gompers was elected chairman of the convention and Morones vice-chairman. The agenda was read by Gompers. Mexican delegates pointed out that there existed obstacles to the friendship of the Mexican and United States workers, principally in discrimination against Mexican workers by the trade unions of the United States and the abuse of the Mexican workers in the border cities by the United States authorities. William Green, chairman of the resolutions committee, tried to shut off discussion on the subject by referring the matter to the Executive Council of the A.F. of L. The delegate of the Mine, Mill, and Smelter Workers Union complained that his organization had been unable to impress on the Mexican workers in the Southwestern states the necessity of organization, with the result that American miners were being completely replaced by Mexican workers and their standards broken down. The Mexicans retorted that if the Mexican workers were dealt with fairly and sincerely, they would respond to appeals for organization. After appeals from both United States and Mexican representatives for closer co-operation and the abandonment of racial prejudices, it was agreed that the A.F. of L. Executive Council, in co-operation with the Mexican labor organizations, should investigate the matter. It was also agreed that the C.R.O.M. should have a resident organizer in the United States to co-operate with the A.F. of L. in organizing the Mexican workers and to watch over their interests.

Three other Mexican proposals were unanimously approved. The A.F. of L. and the C.R.O.M. were to appoint permanent representatives in the border cities to see that workers going from one country to the other received fair treatment, that Mexican workers be allowed to join American trade unions without discrimination, and that the C.R.O.M. be given a larger voice in the preparations for a Pan-American labor congress. The sixth Mexican proposal initiated a discussion that lasted nearly all of the third day. It urged that labor exert itself to secure justice for the I.W.W.'s who were imprisoned on the charge of antiwar propaganda which obstructed the recruitment of soldiers. Green again recommended that the matter be referred to the Executive Council.

Tobin denied that the I.W.W. was a bona fide labor organization. Besides, the Wobblies had received fair trials. The Mexicans pointed out that the war was now over and the spirit of international labor fraternity demanded that all labor organizations have the right to the form of organization and to the principles which they preferred, whether in accord with the A.F. of L. or not. Gompers made a long reply, reciting the gains the A.F. of L. had made for the workers of the United States, Puerto Rico, and Mexico:

"It is all very good for any one to say," he continued, " 'why not give these people, the I.W.W.'s, the opportunity to live and work out their own propaganda as they want to.' But I want to say this to you, my friends, that we have one labor movement, cohesive, militant and determined, in the United States of America, and because we have one labor movement in America we occupy a position of power and influence to bring a better time into the lives of the working people of our country.

"The I.W.W.'s in the United States are exactly what the Bolsheviki are in Russia, and we have seen what the I.W.W. Bolsheviki in Russia have done for the working people of Russia, where the people have no peace, no security, no land and no bread. . . .

"[The A.F. of L.] is going to help you, if you will let us, as best we can. If you place us in the position, as this discussion has developed, of defense, if you in this discussion endeavor to make it appear that you resent our advances, our efforts—well, that is for you to decide. . . . if you will accept our assistance . . . we will gladly do our level best to help you. If, on the other hand, you resent it, cast aspersions upon our motives and our purposes, if you look upon us with suspicion, why, I suppose we shall have to accept the situation. . . ."

Morones replied that the Mexican delegates had not come to accuse the A.F. of L., but in a fraternal spirit to state how the

Mexican workers felt and thought. ". . . you must not feel surprised when in reply to the invitation extended by you the Mexican delegation answers you with absolute frankness." After further attacks on the I.W.W. by Green and Moyer, Green's motion to refer the matter to the Executive Council was adopted.

Finally, the Mexicans asked that the convention exclude all subjects tending to intensify the European war, the breakdown of Mexican neutrality, and intervention in the internal affairs of Mexico by the United States. If this were not agreed to, the Mexican delegation declared that it would have to withdraw from the conference. They explained that the Mexican people were apprehensive about United States efforts to force them into the war. Perhaps they knew of Gompers' efforts to persuade Carranza to join the Allies. Green argued that these matters were not labor problems, but political, and extraneous to the objects of the convention. His recommendation to table the resolution was adopted, but the Mexicans did not withdraw.

Gompers then demanded an endorsement of the peace terms and the labor charter previously adopted by the A.F. of L. for submission to the peace congress. This was, in Gompers' view, the most important thing the convention could do, although it only vaguely related to the agenda. Gompers wanted this additional endorsement to take with him to Paris. Morones agreed with the principles of the labor charter but thought consideration of peace terms should be ruled out for the same reasons that the Mexican resolution on neutrality and intervention had been stricken out. He feared the Mexican people would misconstrue their action as a violation of Mexican neutrality. Gompers' blood boiled at this declaration, and he shouted, "I challenge the delegates from Mexico to vote against the declarations made in this resolution and then defend their position before the Mexican people. . . . I am going to ask this Conference to give our friends and fellow workers of Mexico the chance to vote upon these propositions separately from the others, so that they may vote against them if they choose to do so. I shall not make any arguments."

To this outburst Morones replied that he was not surprised to see that his North American brothers could not understand the Mexican point of view. He begged them not to demand too much

of the Mexicans. The people of Latin America, he said, did not
understand the A.F. of L. and the people of the United States. "All
the knowledge they have of the people of the United States is
through the soldiers' bayonets." The Mexican labor movement
wanted to break down those prejudices against the North Americans, but it could not be done in a day. ". . . if liberty were to be
imposed it would lose the virtue of all the benefits that it intends
to bestow." He could not agree with Gompers' proposal to vote
separately on his resolutions. "Yes, sir; you will," Gompers burst
out, forgetting that he was the chairman and not the dictator of
the conference. Morones went on, unruffled, and declared that
the Mexican delegates would each sign the resolution, but only
in a personal and not a representative capacity. After further discussion, the Mexican delegates agreed to vote for the resolution
subject to the ratification of the Mexican labor movement, and
it was unanimously adopted.

A constitution was adopted, the A.F. of L. was instructed to
organize the Mexican workers in the United States, the Pan-
American Federation of Labor undertook to promote understanding in order to eliminate race prejudice, and the A.F. of L.
was asked to urge the United States government to lift the embargo on exports to Mexico. Gompers was unanimously elected
president of the new federation.[10]

The second congress of the Pan-American Federation of
Labor met in New York City on July 7, 1919, with eight countries
represented. Secretary Canuto Vargas reported on the activities
of the officers since the first congress. A resolution presented by
the A.F. of L. and unanimously adopted demanded that, in
the Pan-American conference called by the United States to discuss
hemispheric financial and economic problems, the labor organizations of the participating countries should be represented. The
A.F. of L. also presented a resolution endorsing the League of
Nations, the International Labor Organization, and the labor
charter of the Versailles Treaty. It was adopted, with an amendment that all nations be entitled to membership and invited to
join the League—an amendment on which Gompers never acted.

The delegate of the Dominican Federation of Labor called
attention to the occupation of his country by American military
forces since 1915, under which freedom of press and political

activities was suppressed and workers denied the right to present grievances or hold meetings; as a result, their condition was deteriorating, while the country's wealth was exploited by American landowners. The resolutions committee recommended that the statement be referred to the A.F. of L. for investigation and whatever action was necessary to secure Dominican rights. The Nicaraguan delegate also called for an investigation of the American military occupation of his country and the possession of its customs houses and public utilities by American capitalists. Both resolutions were approved and the officers directed to use their influence on President Wilson to secure improvement in the conditions of the workers and a free election.

Other urgent resolutions were placed before the congress. The executive committee was directed to assist in organizing trade unions and national labor federations in the Central American countries and in forming a Central American Federation of Labor. It was instructed to continue its efforts to prevent passage of a constitutional amendment in Mexico which would suppress the right to strike.

Several delegates criticized the A.F. of L. for having, just a month before, asked a four-year prohibition on immigration to the United States, including immigration from Mexico. This action violated pledges given at the first Pan-American labor congress, and an explanation was demanded. Gompers explained that the flood of immigration to the United States, reaching one and one-fourth million the year before the war, had become a menace to the standards of the American people. Much of this immigration, he said, was not normal, but stimulated by the corporations and shipping companies. Now there was the added necessity of absorbing four million soldiers and sailors into industry and finding jobs for them. The demand for a moratorium on immigration was simply a matter of self-protection. If the workers of the world were well organized and had established standards approaching those in the United States, or if would-be immigrants were A.F. of L. members, he would welcome them. But "the man who is selfish enough and is ignorant enough to fail or refuse to join the union of his trade wherever he may live, is not a man about which it is necessary to so much concern ourselves." No action was taken by the congress except to agree that each labor

organization should assist union immigrants to secure employment.

Gompers made no report on the imprisoned I.W.W.'s or on
discrimination and mistreatment of Mexican immigrants in the
United States, as he had been charged at the previous convention.
He was unanimously re-elected president.[11]

The following year, President Carranza was assassinated, and
after several months of chaos Alvaro Obregon came to the
presidency. The Mexican revolution swung to the left, as Obregon
called for the nationalization of the land, an anticlerical program,
and heavy taxation of foreign oil holdings. The United States
refused to recognize the Obregon government until assurances
were given regarding compensation for American landowners and
oil interests and on other matters, But the A.F. of L., meeting
with the third Pan-American labor congress in Mexico City,
expressed friendship for the new Obregon government. Receptions and banquets were arranged for the delegates by Obregon,
General Plutarco Calles, the minister for foreign affairs, and
other officials. Gompers endorsed Obregon and his supporters as
men who constituted the closest thing to a workers' government
in history.[12]

At the labor congress, Gompers presented a comprehensive
report by the executive committee. He had, in accordance with
the congress' earlier instructions, written to President Wilson calling attention to the grievances of the Dominican labor organizations and added some of his own. "The description of conditions
existing in the Dominican Republic today," he had told Wilson,
"and with that country under an American military government,
does not conform to the principles of modern civilization; they
are not compatible with the doctrine that men are born free and
must be accorded full opportunities to life, liberty and pursuit of
happiness." Only a few minor reforms having been conceded,
Gompers had written Wilson again, emphasizing that the people
desired above all the reestablishment of their own government.
He hoped that Wilson could give him some tangible promise to
take to the forthcoming Pan-American labor congress.

On December 25, 1920, the Department of State announced
that a commission of Dominican citizens was to be appointed to
draw up revisions to the Dominican constitution and laws in

preparation for the withdrawal of American forces and the re-establishment of a native government. The executive committee had decided that it would be wrong to ask the United States to intervene in the electoral procedure of the country, to insure free elections. The Nicaraguan Federation of Labor wrote to Gompers protesting against the conduct of the elections in Nicaragua, through restrictions on the suffrage and denial of free expression. Gompers was asked to insist that Chamorro be refused recognition and a free election be held, and that there be an investigation of the control of the Nicaraguan economy by North American bankers and other capitalists. Gompers transmitted this protest to the United States government and received "hopeful assurances of a satisfactory solution."[13]

Most of Gompers' report was approved unanimously, but there was an undercurrent of feeling against the A.F. of L. which was expressed in part by the Dominican delegate who repeated that the people of Santo Domingo wanted immediate independence and were not satisfied with Wilson's plan for a gradual restoration of sovereignty. It was the duty of the Pan-American Federation of Labor to prevent the enslaving of nations by imperialism. He asked and the congress agreed that a cablegram be sent immediately to Wilson protesting against the continued occupation of the Republic by armed force and requested the immediate restoration of her sovereignty and independence.

Later the Dominican delegate asked Gompers if he had done so. Gompers stated that he had not, because Wilson had already promised to remove the troops and there was no point in pressing him. He thought the request ought to be changed to ask merely for speeding up evacuation. The Dominican spokesman denounced Wilson's plan for withdrawal as involving conditions which would make Santo Domingo a "repulsive protectorate. . . . American bayonets are supporting American capital in Santo Domingo. The American Government is not actuated by love of liberty, but because the country is a valuable field for American expansion and American capital and because it is valuable for strategic purposes." He and two other Central American delegates threatened to leave the congress unless Gompers sent the telegram immediately, as he had been directed. At the noon recess a compromise was reached which came very close to meeting Gompers' position. He and the Dominican delegate had the congress pledge itself to aid in maintaining the independence of all the American countries, but an appeal made by the San Salvador delegate that Gompers petition Wilson for the immediate ending of the protectorate in Nicaragua was referred to the executive committee for its consideration and action.[14]

Gompers interested himself in trying to obtain recognition of the Obregon government and the withdrawal of American troops from Santo Domingo and Nicaragua, but without notable success. However, in 1923, the C.R.O.M sought the support of the A.F. of L. for Calles as successor to Obregon. But Gompers feared that the Mexicans were planning to ally themselves with the I.F.T.U., as Morones had gone to Europe and invited some European labor leaders to visit Mexico. Consequently, in the fall of 1923, representatives of the A.F. of L. and the C.R.O.M. met at El Paso for a discussion of international labor relations and the political situation in Mexico. Morones assured the Americans that the C.R.O.M. would not join the I.F.T.U. without first consulting them, and under Gompers' inspiration the two delegations announced the "Monroe Doctrine of Labor," jointly declaring their hostility to any efforts on the part of European labor to encroach on the "sovereignty" of labor in the Western Hemisphere. In return, Gompers declared the sympathy of American labor with the Obregon government which was engaged in quelling the revolt of Adolfo de la Huerta. To back up this declaration, Gompers urged Secretary of State Charles Evans Hughes to enforce strictly the law against transporting arms into Mexico. He also asked American unions engaged in transportation work at border posts to assist in the detection of gun-running and the I.F.T.U. for support in stopping the transportation of arms from Europe.

In 1923 the United States recognized the Obregon government when the latter agreed that the 1917 Constitution was not to be construed retroactively. It sent arms to Obregon and placed an embargo on arms to de la Huerta. Gompers, as president of both the American and Pan-American Federations of Labor, did all he could to mobilize public opinion in support of Obregon.[15]

De la Huerta was defeated, and in 1924 General Calles was elected president, with the support of Obregon and the C.R.O.M. The forthcoming congress of the Pan-American Federation of Labor promised to be one of harmony, at least so far as Mexican and United States labor were concerned.

Chapter Twenty-five

THE YEAR OF THE
SCARE

1. POSTWAR STRIKES

WHEN THE UNITED STATES TURNED TO PROBLEMS
of postwar reconstruction in 1918 and 1919, the labor movement was in a critical position. Even before the end of Wilson's
administration, the country had turned from liberalism to reaction, and big business had almost undisputed control of the
government. Alarmed by the worldwide growth of radicalism, the
employers determined to stamp it out at home and to make the
United States at least safe for the profit system. They resolved
to wipe out the wartime gains of labor and to restore the unions
to a status of weakness and semilegality. Above all, they set
themselves to beat back the rising wave of militancy among
the workers. Faced with a rising cost of living and the
threatened annihilation of the trade unions, the workers determined to take advantage of the end of wartime controls to
secure increased wages and improved working and political
conditions.

The year 1919 began auspiciously for labor when a general
strike of some 50,000 clothing workers in New York and a strike
of 120,000 New England textile workers won the eight-hour
day and wage increases. But in February, labor met the first of
a series of defeats. The metal workers in the Seattle shipyards
struck for the 44-hour week and wage increases, and the Central
Labor Committee called a general sympathetic strike of all
workers in the city. Some 60,000 workers responded, and for five
days the industrial life of the city was virtually paralyzed. This
strike was defeated by hostile public opinion whipped up by the
press and Mayor Ole Hanson and by the opposition of the A.F.

of L. and many of the international unions whose locals were participating in the strike.

Several other strikes in the summer and fall, many of them "outlaw" strikes conducted against the orders of their international officers, were partly or completely successful in winning the right of collective bargaining, higher wages, and shorter hours. But industrial spokesmen were mounting a campaign of antiunion propaganda which was arousing a widespread demand for the suppression of strikes in the name of economic and social stability. Based on the hysteria fostered by the "red scare," the antiunion propagandists found grist for their mill in a strike of Boston policemen in September. This strike resulted from the arbitrary firing of nineteen policemen because they had formed a union and affiliated with the A.F. of L. The commissioner deliberately failed to use his reserve volunteers during the first night of the strike and then accused the police of turning the city over

On November 12, Gompers, who had just returned from Europe, urged the strikers to return to their posts and await the outcome of possible mediation. When the police voted to accept this suggestion, he sent a telegram to the Mayor and Governor Calvin Coolidge, requesting that the strikers be reinstated pending arbitration "to honorably adjust a mutually unsatisfactory situation." The police commissioner refused and Coolidge won nationwide fame by replying to Gompers that arbitration was out of the question and that "There is no right to strike against the public safety by anybody, anywhere, any time."

Gompers did not approve of the strike, but he pointed out that it was provoked and practically forced on the policemen by "incapable, negligent or autocratic municipal authorities" who refused to redress bad conditions and refused all attempts to settle the dispute honorably. "If the authorities give no consideration to the human side of the question or to the advice and suggestion which I had the honor to make, then whatever betide is upon the head of the authorities responsible therefor."[1]

The struggles of 1919 reached their culmination in the great strike in the steel industry, that outstanding remnant of open shop tyranny and depressed working conditions. While the corporations were earning unprecedented profits during the war,

President Gary of the United States Steel Corporation acknowledged that the lowest paid workers were receiving only $4.62
in a ten-hour day, the average for unskilled workers being five
dollars and for skilled workers $6.70. About a quarter of the
employees were working twelve hours a day, with the notorious
24-hour stint when passing from the day to the night shift; and
most employees worked 365 days in the year.[2]

The inauguration of an organizing drive in steel was initiated
by William Z. Foster, the representative of the carmen's union
in the Chicago Federation of Labor. In April 1918, he introduced a resolution signed by thirteen metal trades unions, calling
for a national campaign, sponsored by the A.F. of L. and conducted jointly by all the unions having jurisdiction in the industry,
to organize every phase of the industry. The resolution was
adopted unanimously and sent to Gompers, who referred it to
the Amalgamated Association of Iron, Steel and Tin Workers,
now a submissive and almost defunct organization. It evaded the
matter, and the Chicago Federation elected Foster as delegate
to the A.F. of L. convention in June to secure action. It presented
a resolution calling for a meeting during the convention of
delegates from all unions interested in the industry to make plans
for an organizing campaign.

The resolution was adopted, but Gompers neglected to call
the meeting. On inquiry, Secretary Morrison informed Foster
that the conference would be held in about six weeks. Foster
protested that such a delay might be fatal, as it was necessary
to take advantage of the war situation, which might end very soon.
A day or two later, suddenly and without notifying Foster, an
announcement was made just before the noon adjournment that
the meeting would be held during the lunch recess; this, Foster
thought, was "a deliberate attempt to kill the campaign." A few
delegates assembled, called a meeting for the next night, and
invited Gompers to preside. According to Foster, Gompers
became furious and refused, but when shown the list of officials
who were inviting him, he said he might attend. Foster asked
him to announce the meeting, and he answered, "No! You do it!"
That afternoon Foster announced to the convention that on the
request of President Gompers he was authorized to invite all
concerned to the conference, at which Gompers would be present.

"I could see Gompers getting purple as I said this," Foster recalled.[3]

The meeting decided to hold a formal conference in Chicago on August 1 to formulate and launch the organizing drive. Representatives of fifteen unions who attended this conference were designated as the National Committee. Gompers was elected chairman, and Foster secretary-treasurer. Gompers turned to Foster and said, "Well, brother Foster, you have called us together; now what do you propose?" Foster proposed a swift campaign of organization initiated at once and simultaneously in all important steel centers, to be financed by an assessment of twenty-five cents a member by each union, each organization to furnish three or more organizers. The unions would be federated for campaign purposes. Foster estimated that three weeks would be necessary for preparation and three weeks for the campaign, including three meetings in each steel town; then the demands would be placed before the industry with the implied threat of a strike.

"The top A.F. of L. bureaucrats present," wrote Foster, "listened fishy-eyed and with ill-restrained disdain. . . ." They regarded the plan as visionary and proposed instead to concentrate on one locality, or even one mill, to win the confidence of the workers. They brushed aside Foster's assessment proposal and voted for a contribution of only $100 from each union, the campaign to be financed primarily by initiation fees collected from the steel workers whom they would organize. The A.F. of L. contributed nothing. In place of Foster's request for seventy-five to one hundred organizers, six were delegated. "The final defeat of the steel workers 16 months later was directly traceable to rejection of my plan by the Gompers leadership at the Chicago conference." Gompers evidently believed that the War Labor Board would be more instrumental in establishing industrial democracy in the steel industry than would the organizing campaign. But the principle of the federated campaign was adopted and plans were made for setting up local organizing committees.[4]

In spite of everything, the organizing campaign was remarkably successful. Workers attended mass meetings and poured into the unions by the thousands; within one month a majority of the workers in the Chicago district were organized. To head off the campaign, the companies granted four successive wage increases and the basic eight-hour day. Then the war ended, and the employers' counteroffensive was intensified. Organizers were assaulted and arrested, meetings were broken up, union members were discharged by the thousands, and labor spies were planted in the mills. But the greatest handicap was the lack of support from the A.F. of L. leaders. Gompers did not speak to meetings, help to raise money, or secure organizers. He rarely attended meetings of the organizing committee, of which he was chairman. At one time, during a crisis in funds, organizers, and concerted action, Foster wrote a letter urging all union heads to attend the next meeting. Gompers signed it "reluctantly," and when the union leaders called him about it he said it was only a routine meeting; most of them did not attend, not even Gompers himself. On the eve of the strike, Gompers resigned as chairman of the committee and appointed John Fitzpatrick of the Chicago Federation of Labor to replace him. The twenty-four participating unions contributed $100,000, and in return received over half a million dollars in initiation fees and dues from the organizing committee. Six unions outside the industry contributed almost as much as the twenty-four steel unions.[5]

By the summer of 1919, about 100,000 steel workers had been organized. In the meantime, efforts were made to negotiate with the United States Steel Corporation. Gary refused to confer with the Amalgamated Association and did not even answer a request by Gompers that he meet with representatives of the organizing committee. He even refused a request by President Wilson to confer with the union officials in order to avert a strike. On July 24, against the advice of Gompers, a strike vote was ordered, which was all but unanimous in favor of a strike, and the call was issued for the men to walk out on September 22. By this time about 340,000 workers had been organized, representing about two-thirds of the steel workers. The demands of the strike committee were for the right of collective bargaining, reinstatement of all men discharged for union activities, the eight-hour day and six-day week, abolition of the 24-hour shift, a living wage, the check-off system, seniority principles, and the abolition of company unions.[6]

On September 10, President Wilson appealed directly to Gompers for a postponement of the strike until after the industrial

THE YEAR OF THE SCARE

conference which had been called for October 6. The following day Gompers wrote to Fitzpatrick and to the officers of the twenty-four steel industry unions urging them to comply with Wilson's request. Fitzpatrick, Foster, and Tighe, president of the Amalgamated Association, replied that the strike had been ordered only after every other avenue of approach had been closed and that in view of the campaign of terrorism on the part of the steel companies, including the murder of seven organizers and members and the wholesale discharge of men who had joined the unions, a strike was the only way to protect the interests of the workers. They concluded that "any vague, indefinite postponement would mean absolute demoralization and utter ruin for our movement."

Gompers made a final effort to dissuade the strike committee from its plans. He argued that if the committee acceded to his request, Wilson would be more sympathetically inclined to help in bringing about a conference, although he admitted there was no definite assurance that it could be done. But if the President's request was ignored, "I leave it to your own judgment as to the situation which would thus be created. I have never yet run away from or been unduly apprehensive of any situation occurring in the labor movement, but I have not failed to understand that 'discretion is the better part of valor.' . . . I had had authentically communicated to me from two different sources that the big financial and industrial interests of the country had declared that they were 'tired of the domination of labor' and that they planned a campaign to strike a blow at the labor movement; that the U.S. Steel Corporation by reason of its great wealth, ramifications, power and influence, . . . was in the best position to make the fight against labor, and that the U.S.S.C. was really endeavoring to provoke a strike. From several other sources I have received the identical information, and the record of the corporation's action justifies the conviction that the statement conveyed to me was absolutely correct."

A full meeting of the organizing committee was held to consider the matter. It was evident to all present that the workers could not be held in check any longer and that they would walk out on the designated day regardless of any decision by the strike committee. Even some members who had favored postponement were now convinced by the reports of the field organizers that delay would mean disintegration; the only alternative was a disorganized strike without leadership or an organized strike under the leadership of experienced men. It was voted that the strike would go into effect as planned on September 22. The committee wrote Wilson that it had to decline reluctantly his request for delay, since "delay means the surrender of all hope." Gompers again warned against rushing recklessly to destruction, but the die had been cast. Even Gompers came to accept the fact that postponement was impossible and that to attempt it would merely mean a chaotic strike and a loss of confidence in the leadership of the A.F. of L., with the possibility that radical leaders might get control.[7]

On September 22, 275,000 steel workers in fifty cities downed tools and at the end of the first week 365,000, ninety per cent of the workers, were out in the biggest strike in American history up to that time. But the forces against it were too powerful. Corporations and authorities were aggressive and violent. Union meetings were barred or broken up, picket lines forcibly dispersed, twenty-two strikers were killed, hundreds beaten and shot, thousands arrested. Special deputies, labor spies, and strikebreakers were employed by the thousands; in Gary and other places Negro strikebreakers were employed deliberately to arouse racial hatred and provoke violence, which permitted calling in state militia and federal troops. The virtual extinction of the right of assembly, speech, and organization made the conduct of the strike almost impossible.[8]

As effective against the strike was the unbridled use of the "red scare" to discredit it. The press asserted repeatedly that the strike was nothing but an attempt to bolshevize American industry. Because of his record as I.W.W. member and syndicalist, Foster was the chief target of this propaganda. Regardless of his own views, Foster conducted himself as secretary of the organizing committee in accordance with the policies of the A.F. of L. He made no effort to use his position as a means of propagandizing political and social ideas, nor did he counsel violence at any time—on the contrary, he and other strike leaders urged the men to refrain from actions that might be a pretext for retaliatory violence. Gompers himself expressed his complete confidence in

Foster's ability and loyalty, holding that "in view of what Mr. Foster has done in helping to bring about better conditions among the stockyard workers and of the balance of the country, in view of the lawful, honorable methods which he has pursued in this situation under investigation, he is entitled to have something better than a mistaken past thrown not only in his teeth and in his face, but held up to the contumely of the world in order now to make his activities impossible or to neutralize them."[9]

Finally, there was the attitude of the A.F. of L. leaders, which observers and students have described in terms ranging from "half-hearted" to "defeatist" and "treacherous." At least one of the participating unions tried to keep its members at work, and the Amalgamated Association withdrew from the national committee and made a separate agreement with the corporation before the strike was ended. Many of the members of the national committee withheld financial support and tried to curb the movement, apparently not believing in victory or not wanting it. Certainly Gompers made little effort to rally the labor movement behind it. During the year and a half of the organizing campaign, there were only two brief notices about it in the *American Federationist*, and during the strike there was not a single article on the subject.

Gompers' attitude was similar to that of the leaders of the international unions who, according to one historian, "were overawed by the power that they challenged as well as rendered ill at ease by the very depths of the response to the strike call by the several hundreds of thousands of foreign-speaking workers." Gompers recognized, as did Foster, that victory in the steel strike would probably lead to similar organizing campaigns in other basic industries and that this would change the character of the A.F. of L. by shifting the center of gravity to the unskilled workers, lay the basis of industrial unionism, make the labor movement more militant, and threaten the position of the old conservative leadership. Perhaps the most revealing comment on the attitude of Gompers and the other A.F. of L. leaders was made by Attorney General J. Mitchell Palmer when he told a House committee that "through the action of the Department of Justice . . . this strike was terminated with, in reality, a complete victory for the American Federation of Labor."[10]

Even before the grim end of the steel strike, the conflict in the bituminous coal fields was coming to a head. The miners were working under a contract covering the war period. They now demanded an increase in wages to cover the rise in the cost of living since 1917 and a 30-hour week to relieve wide-spread unemployment. The operators refused to consider the demands, blandly arguing that the old contract was still in force because the war had not been declared over, although wartime price restrictions on coal had been lifted by the Federal Fuel Administration. The United Mine Workers called a strike for November 1. On October 31 the Wilson administration secured an injunction from the federal district court in Indianapolis which prohibited any further strike activity by union officials and called upon them to cancel the strike on the ground that it was illegal under the Lever Act. Gompers immediately denounced the government publicly for using war measures to punish those who were forced to protect themselves from the coal barons.

"It is almost inconceivable," he said "that a government which is proud of its participation in a great war to liberate suppressed peoples should now undertake to suppress the legitimate aims, hopes and aspirations of a group of its own people. . . . The injunction against the United Mine Workers bodes for ill. An injunction of this nature will not prevent the strike—it will not fill the empty stomachs of miners—it may restrain sane leadership but it will give added strength to unwise counsel and increase bitterness and friction."

Gompers' prediction that the injunction would not end the strike was fulfilled, for on November 1 some 450,000 miners ceased work. Gompers called a special meeting of the Executive Council for the ninth to consider the situation. The day before the Council met, the court which issued the injunction gave the officers of the U.M.W. seventy-two hours to rescind the strike order. The Council, in turn, denounced the injunction with Gompers' accustomed vigor, and, what was more important, endorsed the strike, pledging the miners "the full support of the American Federation of Labor. . . ."

This was unmistakable advice to the miners to defy the injunction. But the following day the officers of the U.M.W. decided that defiance of the government, with all its civil and military authority arrayed against the miners, would destroy the organization. Acting President John L. Lewis therefore rescinded the strike order, explaining, "We are Americans, we cannot fight our government." Upon receiving this information, the Executive Council issued a brief statement which barely disguised its disgust with the capitulation of the U.M.W.[11]

Large numbers of miners refused to follow Lewis' orders and continued to stay out of the pits. District 14 of Kansas, led by Alexander Howat, was suspended from the U.M.W. for failure to enforce the return-to-work order. Howat and three other officials were also arrested and imprisoned for six months for defying the Kansas Court of Industrial Relations. Twelve hundred more miners struck in protest against this action. Subsequently, over half of the locals in the district were expelled from the U.M.W. Lewis and other mine union officials appeared before the Executive Council on November 14 and asked for assistance in breaking the strike of the Kansas miners. Gompers indicated that he believed the strike justified and that the Federation as well as the U.M.W. should support its fight against the Kansas Court. The U.M.W. leaders asked that the Council at least state that it would not aid the strike. But Gompers was adamant, and the Council decided to remain neutral; it would neither assist the strike nor oppose it. Gompers wrote privately that if he had a free hand he would go to Kansas and help in the fight against the Industrial Court.[12]

The Bituminous Coal Commission finally awarded the miners a wage increase of twenty-seven per cent, nearly half of their demand, but ignored their demand for a 30-hour week. Much more serious, however, was the dangerous precedent of govermment intervention by use of the injunction and the deepening of the antiunion sentiment whipped up by the attacks of the press and public officials. Revealing, too, were the actions of the industrial conference on which Gompers, as well as President Wilson, had pinned much hope for working out a co-operative relationship between labor and capital. This conference that fall of 1919 was to create a new era. It would undermine "bolshevism" in America and anti-A.F. of L. unrest. It would fulfill the promises for which Gompers had sacrificed labor's independence during the War. Fifteen of the conferees were selected by Wilson, fifteen by business organizations, and fifteen by Gompers. Gompers was elected chairman of the labor group and a member of the resolutions committee.

The labor representatives would have had the conference declare in favor of collective bargaining and the time-honored litany of civil rights and humanitarian goals. It also proposed that each group in the conference choose two of its members to serve as an arbitration board to settle the steel strike, pending which the conference should request the workers to return to their jobs and the employers to reinstate them.

The employers also submitted a statement of principles to govern industrial relations. It contained no conciliatory surprises. Though it recognized the desirability of a "satisfactory" standard of living and of "adequate" leisure for workers, these were to be attained through the open shop and the law of supply and demand. Gompers attempted to use the resolution on the steel strike, when it came up, to bring the industrialists to reason. The tension may be imagined when he spoke, perhaps giving a side-wise glance or two to Gary: "... I think that you should hesitate to negative the resolution proposed by this labor group. You may not know us; you may not know our character, the character of our work, the responsibilities which bear upon us, and the effort we try to make to maintain the best possible relations between employers and employees; but just let me impress upon you that this whole world of ours is in a state of unrest, and out of this war from which we have so triumphantly emerged . . . the men and women of America are determined that we shall never again go back to prewar conditions and concepts. . . . We demand a voice in the determination of the conditions under which we will give service; we demand a voice in determining those conditions which make life either fair and worth living or not; we demand that the workers shall have that voice not as supplicants but by right." Gompers warned the employers that if they did not deal with the A.F. of L., which was constructive and stood for the maintenance of agreements and respect for property rights, the I.W.W. would make headway among the workers who had to bear intolerable conditions and tyranny, and the employers would then have to deal with men who would not be arguing or appealing to them as he was.

It was decided to defer action on this resolution until after consideration of the report, due the following day, of the resolutions committee on collective bargaining, which had been recommended unanimously by the labor and public groups and opposed by the employers. The resolution recognized the right of wage earners to organize unions, to bargain collectively through representatives of their own choosing, without limiting the right of any worker to refrain from joining a union or from dealing directly with his employer if he chose. The employers rejected the report on the ground that it would accentuate and make almost intolerable the problems of management and that it endangered the principle of the open shop. They would not consent to bargaining with representatives of their employees who were not employees themselves. The question was discussed for nearly a week, but no progress was made. The labor element had already yielded as much as it could; the employers would yield nothing. When it came to a vote, the labor group voted yes, the employer and public groups no. The same division of votes defeated labor's resolution on the steel strike.

When the conference convened on October 22, there were no resolutions and no committee reports to be presented. The session had ground to a standstill. The members just sat and looked at each other. The chairman then read a letter from President Wilson appealing to them to stay together and strive for some agreement "or until it is revealed that the men who work and the men who manage American industry are so set upon divergent paths that all effort at co-operation is doomed to failure. . . ." The labor group asked for a recess, and upon reconvening Gompers presented a resolution which he hoped would accomplish the President's purpose. It eliminated all mention of the right to join unions, and stated simply that "The right of wage earners to organize without discrimination, to bargain collectively, to be represented by representatives of their own choosing in negotiations and adjustments with employers in respect to wages, hours of labor, and relations and conditions of employment is recognized." But the employers remained adamant. Gompers then rose and offered his swan song. The employers repudiated the right of the workers to organize for real collective bargaining; it was therefore impossible for the labor representatives to remain in the conference. Facing the employers, Gompers defied them: "You have defeated us in our proposition, but you have not broken one line of this movement of ours, nor have you crushed the spirit of that movement, not its men, and you are not likely to do it. You can not do it. It is greater than the stars that the men and women of labor have emerged from immeasurable darkness and shall keep places of equality at least with the whole world, whether they be employers or others." The labor delegation then left the conference room. The following day the conference adjourned.[13]

2. THE RED SCARE

ONE OF THE MOST POTENT WEAPONS IN THE FIGHT against the strikes of 1919 and the attempt to undermine the labor unions was the postwar "red scare" which reached its height in that year. The principal basis for the fear of communism was the Russian revolution, the threat of communism spreading in Europe, and the formation of the Communist International. The Communist party of the United States was formed by the left-wing socialists, and its activities caused some alarm, as did a series of "bomb plots" and "riots" on May Day. But the strength of the communists in the United States was slight. There was no evidence that the bomb plot, the culprits of which were never found, was the work of a wide conspiracy—it might have been perpetrated by provocateurs—while the riots were the result of police interference with parades. The real fear of the conservatives was not of "bolshevism" but of any attack on the *status quo*, any nonconformity, and particularly the challenge of the workers to industrial autocracy. Employers found that the issue of radicalism could be used profitably to fight unionism and the closed shop, politicians found that it could be an excellent political issue, and the press that it could be a good substitute for waning wartime sensationalism.

From propaganda attempting to identify unionism with communism, some organizations, like the Ku Klux Klan and the American Legion, turned to vigilantism to advance their program of "Americanism," and soon agencies of government began to put the seal of approval on red-baiting and to engage themselves in unconstitutional assaults on individual liberties in the name of 100% Americanism." The Overman Committee of the United States Senate and the Lusk Committee of the New York Legislature provided open forums for wild accusations against the loyalty of anyone who did not meet their definition of patriotism, and the latter conducted a series of illegal raids on the Socialist party, the I.W.W., and the Rand School. The Federal Bureau of Investigation also embarked on a search for sedition, culminating in the notorious Palmer raids on New Year's Eve. The state legislatures enacted a raft of "criminal syndicalism" and "anti-sedition" laws which virtually nullified the First Amendment of the Constitution, Congress undertook the consideration of antisubversive legislation, and the courts proved unable or unwilling to act as guardians of civil liberties in the face of the popular hysteria.[14]

In some of the wildest of the anti-bolshevik propaganda, even Gompers was accused of having communistic attitudes or tendencies and of plotting to arm the workers for revolution. More commonly it was recognized that he was not a bolshevik or remotely sympathetic to bolshevism, but it was asserted that he was giving aid and comfort to the red conspiracy by condoning some of its activities, particularly as manifested in strikes. His defense of the Boston police strike and his public protection of Foster as leader of the steel strike, especially, were used by the general press as illustrations of how he was falling into the dangerous path of coddling the revolutionary movement or of being used by it in its effort to sovietize American industry.[15]

Gompers realized that the red scare was being used by the employers to discredit strikes and the labor movement. He constantly denied that the A.F. of L. or any one of its activities was communist-inspired or dominated. But he never met the issue head-on, never struck at the foundation of anti-red hysteria by showing that it was based on the false charge that a widespread revolutionary movement was in progress. On the contrary, he fed the illusion on which that association was based by contributing to the anti-red hysteria:

> Union journals were just as quick as employer magazines to attach any unorthodox labor procedure, such as the general strike, to the Communist philosophy, and they bitterly attacked all such innovations as "monuments of folly" and "revolutionary provoking instruments."

Along with these scathing criticisms, these labor journals also warned union members of the danger of "borers from within" and called upon all local unions to purge these individuals from their membership rolls immediately. The *American Federationist* and the *United Mine Workers Journal* consistently cautioned union workers against those within the movement who wanted to plunge labor into "a sea of turmoil, hatred, and possible bloodshed."[16]

Gompers aided the red scare by helping cultivate the popular belief that bolshevism was a clear and present danger to American institutions. He accused liberal journals like the *Nation, New Republic*, and *Survey* of being revolutionary and asserted that the majority of intellectuals in the United States had attached themselves to the "soviet retinue" and were a major source of communist strength. He tried to convince the employers and the public that the A.F. of L. was a bulwark against bolshevism and that the alternative to recognizing and dealing with the Federation was revolution. Those who obstructed the constructive and conservative efforts of the A.F. of L. were "engaged in a bolshevist manufacturing establishment."[17]

Where Gompers clearly saw that unionism was the real target of so-called anti-communist measures, he took a vigorous stand in opposition. Gompers pointed out that the main purpose of peacetime sedition laws proposed in Congress and enacted in many states was to prevent strikes, and he suggested that they might more properly be entitled bills "to enforce compulsory involuntary servitude, to tie men to their tasks." The particular measure to which he took exception was that which prohibited any publication which advocated or incited the overthrow of the government, resistance to the authority of the government, the overthrow or change of the Constitution by force or violence, or the use of force or violence against persons or property as a means toward the accomplishment of industrial, economic, social, or political change. Gompers observed that the efforts of the unions to achieve economic and political changes through the use of moral force might be brought under the ban by these terms. Other provisions of the law would limit the right of assembly, association, speech, and press if their exercise were interpreted as constituting illegal advocacy of force. Gompers feared that the courts would interpret such a law to hamstring the normal activities of labor unions and believed that was the purpose of the bill. There were already statutes dealing with overt acts involving the use of force and violence. Gompers asserted:

"The right of every citizen of the United States to advocate, by speech or press, changes in the law, or in the Constitution, or in the form of government, should be granted to him unquestionably. . . . now with the war practically closed, during peace times and for peace times, it is proposed to enact and place upon the statute books of our country laws that would place our country in the position of being practically upon the same plane as those forces against which we were contending in the war in which so many sacrifices were made.

"This is not in the order of freedom; it is against freedom. It is not going to stifle discontent; it will increase it. It will make protestants against injustice and unfreedom. . . .

"Nothing is so contributory to a better understanding of the people of the United States, or of any country, of any cause, as publicity—open publicity. And, much as we are disturbed by any so-called radicalism, it is better that it should be permitted and be counteracted by other influences that we can exert than that we should attempt to throttle it. It will not be throttled."

Gompers predicted that such legislation would "spread a reign of terror over the United States, filling the country with spies and special agents of the Department of Justice, filling the land with suspicion, and heresy hunting would quickly become a national industry. American citizens who love liberty and love America can not stand idly by and permit this legislation to be enacted."[18]

One aspect of the fight against red hysteria to which Gompers gave limited support was the campaign for amnesty for political prisoners and for repeal of the wartime sedition and espionage laws. He approved the wartime convictions of those who opposed American participation in the war, and after the war he refused to support amnesty for the I.W.W.'s. But he would assist the movement for release of socialists, pacifists, and conscientious objectors if it were conducted in a quiet, conservative, and "constructive" manner—that is, if it did not resort to mass demonstrations and strikes to accomplish its purpose, if it were not led by extremists, and if it co-operated and worked through the A.F. of

L. Of the many liberal and radical groups which conducted the campaign for amnesty, the one which met Gompers' requirements was that headed by Lucy Robins, the former anarchist who had been converted to "Gompersism."

This organization had its genesis in a little meeting in Emma Goldman's apartment early in 1918, on the eve of Miss Goldman's imprisonment for violation of the draft act. There the League for Amnesty for Political Prisoners was organized, with Miss Robins as chairman. It was decided to induce some other organization to initiate the movement and to secure the co-operation of other groups, particularly in the labor movement. Miss Robins approached some labor leaders, but they either did not approve of the movement or would not take the chance of supporting it while the war was on. President John Fitzpatrick and Secretary Ed Nockels of the Chicago Federation of Labor, however, said they would "go the limit" if she could get Gompers' support, but warned that "patriotic Sam will have nothing to do with Reds."

When Gompers returned from Europe, Miss Robins got an appointment to see him at the Morrison Hotel in Chicago on November 6, 1918, the end of the war only days ahead. When she made her appeal he replied sternly: "My girl, I am not a man hunter. I believe that every man must have his liberty, and that right should be protected above everything else. Yes, I will help you. . . . What do you want me to do?" She said Fitzpatrick wanted a letter from him which he could use as a lever to initiate the movement. Gompers agreed to write one, but only if he received an official written request from the Chicago Federation. She went back to Fitzpatrick and he permitted her to address the reconstruction committee of the Federation. The committee would not support her "wild undertaking" in support of the "slackers."

In June, Miss Robins went to the convention of the A.F. of L. in Atlantic City. She told Gompers of the action of the Chicago Federation. He smiled good humoredly and asked, "Did it discourage you?" She said she was going on with the work and mentioned the three resolutions on amnesty that had been introduced. Gompers assured her that these resolutions were bound to fail because they had been proposed by "radicals." He urged her unsuccessfully to have them withdrawn if the campaign were to accomplish its purpose of freeing the prisoners and not merely to make propaganda.

Gompers told Lucy that if the convention went on record against amnesty it would be very hard to act contrary to its decision. The best course would be to avoid debate and get the resolutions referred to the Executive Council without instructions. John Walker, leader of the Labor Peace Councils, agreed to make such a motion but did not go through with it because he felt there was no chance after seeing the vengeful spirit of the debate: "They are like beasts after the spoils," he explained. The substitute of the resolutions committee, recommending repeal of the laws limiting free speech and press but not recommending amnesty, was adopted.[19] Gompers motioned to Lucy to wait. They walked out of the hall together silently, then he touched her arm and said, "Will you promise me one thing? . . . Do not let them discourage you. Go on with the work. . . . After war comes peace. . . . With peace, perhaps understanding. . . ." He in his turn promised to help her.

A conference of the central labor bodies of New York and vicinity was called to initiate an amnesty campaign in the labor movement. Miss Robins spoke and declared that Gompers was willing to head the movement. Hugh Frayne, the A.F. of L. organizer for New York, did not deny it; evidently he had consulted with Gompers and had his approval to serve on the committee. A permanent committee, which won increased support from labor, was organized with Miss Robins as organizer and secretary, J. P. Coughlin of the central labor union as president, and Frayne as advisor.

But the War Department refused to recognize "political prisoners" as such. Gompers advised Miss Robins to see the Secretary of War. She asked him to arrange a conference, but he hesitated. He was on the spot because of the action of the Atlantic City convention, and because he had received complaints from unions about the activities of the committee. He sat silently, thoughtfully reading the documents of the committee, then suddenly he sat up with a start, asserting that this humane cause was greater than technicalities. He arranged a meeting with Secretary of War Baker for Miss Robins and Frayne in February 1920. Baker promised that military offenders and conscientious objectors would soon be released, but only if they would abide by the labor regulations in their prison barracks. Miss Robins advised the men to do so, even though acceptance of military orders would have amounted to a confession that they were wrong in refusing military service.

For this action, as well as its refusal to support the I.W.W. prisoners, her committee received the condemnation of that organization. Bill Haywood sent out a letter upbraiding "Treacherous labor fakers, like Gompers and his ilk, [who] countenanced the brutal assaults and pernicious persecution upon the membership of the I.W.W., not because they thought we were guilty of the offenses as charged, but because forsooth they regard the I.W.W. as a rival organization. These A.F. of L. officials are contemptible tools of the employing classes."[20] The reactionary press also attacked Gompers, but for supporting the amnesty movement, the New York *Times* accusing him of succumbing to "some sudden, swift, progressive malady of radicalism."

The campaign then focused on the release of violators of the Espionage and Sedition Acts, which were administered by the Department of Justice. The center of that struggle was the campaign for the freedom of Eugene Debs, the most prominent of the prisoners. At the suggestion of the amnesty committee, Gompers appointed a commission to investigate conditions in the Atlanta penitentiary, where Debs was incarcerated, and to confer with him on the amnesty campaign. When Miss Robins showed Debs the amnesty resolution, she told him that Gompers wanted it presented to him as a message of good will and personal greetings. Debs was surprised and immensely pleased. "Is that possible?" he asked. "Tell him that I am grateful and will never forget." Asked about his past conflicts with Gompers, he said: "Comrade, you have opened a wound. Nothing troubles me more than the fratricide in our movement. I will do anything I can to end it. I want to be friends. I wish Sam to know that." The committee reported to Gompers at the convention of the cigarmakers' union. He was delighted, and, as chairman of the convention's resolutions committee, urged the convention to unanimously support Senator Joseph I. France's amnesty bill, which it did.[21]

At the A.F. of L. convention in June 1920, Gompers asserted that the prosecution of the peace advocates was justified during the war but that their continued imprisonment had lost its meaning. Justice had been satisfied, he felt, and it was not democratic to inflict continued punishment for the mere sake of punishing. He urged the release of all those still being held for the expression of opinions. The convention unanimously adopted a resolution endorsing these views.[22]

Gompers then secured a conference with Attorney General Palmer, who warned that Wilson had closed his mind on the subject of amnesty. This led Gompers to comment privately that "the professor of history has lost his historical perspective." Gompers, spokesman for a group consisting of a dozen top A.F. of L. leaders, Congressman Meyer London of New York, and Lucy Robins, urged the necessity of returning to the normal conditions of peace, with opportunity for full and free expression of conflicting opinions on peacetime problems, since "nothing would help more to tranquillizing [*sic*] the people of the United States in the firm conviction that their rights are safeguarded, that they may help in the working out of the destiny of the United States. . . ." Palmer thought a general amnesty was impossible: each prisoner would have to be considered individually on the merits of his case, and that was being done. He promised to present their views to President Wilson, but the group concluded that Palmer could not be trusted, and Gompers wrote a letter directly to Wilson urging him to issue a proclamation of amnesty.[23]

It was impossible for the committee to see Wilson because of his health, but Gompers wrote several more letters to him asking for amnesty. What was taken for an answer was the quiet pardoning of 180 prisoners, Debs not included, in spite of Palmer's specific and public recommendation. Wilson was evidently exercising a personal vindictiveness against the man who had led and symbolized the antiwar sentiment. Miss Robins was utterly disconsolate and convinced that there was no more hope. She went to Gompers' office and expressed her desire to quit. Gompers replied harshly: "Do you mean to say that you are ready to quit this movement, and to deprive every man in prison even of a single ray of hope that anyone is trying to help them? What right have you to do that?"

He gazed at a picture on the wall of Furuseth, who had

fought for thirty years to secure the emancipation of the seamen. He turned to Miss Robins and said, "When labor undertakes a movement and it declares war, labor does it with the knowledge that nine times out of ten the immediate fight is a losing one; but every fight put up by labor brings progress. Of course, progress is so slow that we can scarcely see the immediate gains, but progress in itself is labor's victory. If you were not prepared to meet disappointment and hardship you had no right to undertake this work."

On June 4, Gompers arranged a conference with the new President, Harding, and again headed a delegation of labor leaders to press the demand for amnesty. Harding received them graciously and after an hour's discussion assured them that he would consider their request at an early date and act as favorably as possible. A month later Debs wrote a letter to Miss Robins which Gompers read at the next convention of the A.F. of L. to disprove the allegations from radicals that he was insincere and half-hearted in his efforts. Wrote Debs: "You may say to President Gompers that we are entirely satisfied with the plea he and his associates made and the effort they put forth in our behalf. They did all they could for amnesty, more could not be expected, and their efforts to secure the liberation of the Political Prisoners, I assure you, are fully appreciated." In July, Gompers again spoke to Harding and asked for a definite answer. Harding promised full consideration to the release of the prisoners as soon as official peace was proclaimed.

In September, Gompers went to Atlanta with Lucy to visit Debs in the penitentiary. It was the first time they had met since the Pullman strike twenty-seven years before. When Debs appeared in the warden's office, Gompers jumped to his feet and the long arms of Debs embraced the short arms of Gompers. Gompers said, "It used to be Gene," and Debs replied, "Yes, and always Sam." Having established their relationship on those terms, they reminisced for a while about their younger days and their experience in organizing the miners together in West Virginia. Debs gave his condolences on the death of Sam's wife and daughter. Gompers seemed deeply touched, and after a moment said in a trembling voice: "Gene, I want you to know that whatever I have done for the last couple of years with the hope to free you and the other prisoners, I have done it with my heart, and have done it in the best way that I knew how." After a brief address to the inmates, Gompers assured Debs that he would not rest until they were free. The two embraced again.

On November 14, Harding proclaimed the official end of the war, and on December 23 commuted the sentences of Debs and other political prisoners, to expire on Christmas. Debs immediately went to Washington and conferred with Harding and Attorney General Harry M. Daugherty. He then expressed a wish to see Gompers. Since the A.F. of L. office was closed, Miss Robins called Gompers at home and he and his wife came to Debs' hotel. Following expressions of gratification and appreciation, they gave out a joint press statement that they would continue to work for the release of the remaining prisoners.[24]

Chapter Twenty-Six

YEARS OF REACTION

1. POSTWAR RECONSTRUCTION

IT WAS EVIDENT TO GOMPERS THAT LABOR WOULD face difficult problems of reconstruction. There was a growing unrest and militancy in the labor movement which demanded more positive action by the Federation, particularly in the political arena. Gompers desired both to assure the opposition that the A.F. of L. was meeting its problems energetically, and also to curb its more radical demands. The Executive Council and the representatives of the railroad brotherhoods called a conference of the heads of all national and international unions and the farmers' organizations to give voice to the demands of the masses.[1]

The labor leaders met in the Federation's Council room and adopted a proclamation entitled "Labor, Its Grievances, Protest and Demands." It called for the recognition by industry of the right to organize and bargain collectively and by the government of the right to strike. It denounced government by injunction, urged that the railroads, socialized during the war, be retained under government control for two years in order to make a thorough test of government operation under normal conditions, and advised the immediate ratification of the Versailles Treaty. It called upon workers, farmers, and all liberty-loving citizens to use whatever means were available to carry these measures into effect and to combat reaction.[2]

The year was 1920—an election year. The Federation's National Non-Partisan Political Campaign Committee met to plan labor's part in the congressional and Presidential election. It accused Congress of having taken no action to meet the demands of labor, and of having encouraged policies inimical to labor. It called on national and local labor bodies to prepare to mobilize workers in the primaries to defeat reactionaries and to support those who were sympathetic to labor.[3]

The June convention endorsed the Federation's traditional nonpartisan technique and selected fourteen issues to be presented to the platform committees of the two major parties. Most of these, based on the "Grievances and Protest," sought no advance but only to secure the gains won in the previous decade. The attitude of the Democratic and Republican parties would not really determine whether either was progressive, but which was more reactionary. The Democratic platform appeared slightly less hostile to labor's interests, recognizing the right to organize and bargain collectively and reassuring labor with respect to its established gains. Both parties were ambiguous on the basic issues of anti-injunction legislation and opposition to compulsory arbitration, and neither endorsed labor planks reducing the cost of living, restricting immigration, abolishing judicial review, and providing for the election of federal judges.

Gompers saw in the respective platforms a more basic difference than was justified by the facts. He regarded the Republican party as the "unqualified defender of the enemies of Labor," declaring for "the enslavement of the workers and for an open field to profiteers and those who seek to suppress the aspirations of the great masses of our people." The Democratic platform, on the other hand, seemed to him to mark a measure of progress more nearly approximating labor's demands.[4]

The candidates of the major parties strengthened Gompers' belief that the Presidential campaign represented a clear-cut choice between reaction and progress. He found Harding's voting record as a Senator had been about fifty-fifty, while James M. Cox, as Congressman and Governor of Ohio, had a perfect record on measures of special interest to labor. A comparison of their acceptance speeches also showed Cox to have a fuller understanding of the workers' needs. In the vice-presidential candidates Gompers also saw an unmistakable choice between the Democrat, Franklin D. Roosevelt, who followed a "practical and sympathetic course toward the people," and the Republican, Calvin Coolidge, whom he described as a "police baiter" and *agent provocateur*."[5]

In truth, however, there was little enough difference between the two parties, and the Federation was unable to rally the voters toward progressive goals. The Congress elected in 1920 was the most reactionary in decades, the President the least promising. Labor was faced with a period of bitter struggle to maintain its political and legislative program.

Other than antistrike legislation, Gompers considered the high cost of living and unemployment the most important postwar issues, for they were not only undermining the workers' standard of living but were responsible for much of the unrest among them. In 1919 real wages were less than they had been thirty years before and ten to twenty per cent lower than before the war. Gompers perceived that, under the guise of what Harding called normalcy, the "plutocratic forces of exploitation . . . the non-producers, the middlemen, the gamblers, the brokers, the bankers" were plundering the workers and farmers and amassing enormous profits at their expense.[6]

To meet this situation, Gompers demanded a comprehensive program of governmental action that went far beyond anything he had previously advocated. He proposed the federal licensing of all corporations as a means of securing publicity of business practices and control of profiteering; the regulation of cold storage; the requirement that commodities be marked with the price at which they left the manufacturer or producer; the control of credit capital by public agencies; the purchase of commodities by the government and their distribution through regular retail channels at prices fixed by the government; monthly reports by the Department of Labor on the cost of manufacturing those items which determined the cost of living; continuous government investigation and publicity of profits and prices; the encouragement of the co-operative movement; and a graduated tax on all usable land not cultivated by the owners. During the 1920 election campaign, Gompers published a pamphlet excoriating Congress for its failure to take any action on President Wilson's recommendations for relief from the high cost of living, recommendations which approximated the proposals of the A.F. of L.[7]

In addition to the high cost of living, there was in the years of reconversion a very high proportion of unemployment, and during the depression of 1921 it amounted to about five million in a population of about one hundred million. In August 1921, Secretary of Commerce Herbert Hoover suggested that President Harding call a conference to determine the facts and the needs of the unemployment problem. The President brought together sixty representatives of government, business, and labor as well as economists and statisticians, under the chairmanship of Hoover. Gompers headed the labor delegation. The meetings took place at the Department of Interior. Harding and Hoover opened the conference by expressing convictions that the American economy and social institutions were fundamentally sound but there was a temporary and slight dislocation due to the aftermath of war and the problem of conversion and reorganization. They also advised that conference proposals should be largely confined to those which might be achieved through voluntary private effort rather than through government "paternalism" and "tonic from the public treasury."

Gompers was a member of the committee on manufacturers which unanimously adopted general recommendations for the emergency program. It claimed that the crisis was primarily one for the local communities, responsibility for which should be assumed by the mayors. They should establish efficient public employment agencies, co-ordinate the work of the various charitable institutions, and undertake public construction projects. Congress was urged to make an appropriation for roads. Manufacturers were advised to spread out their work by reducing hours or rotating jobs, to manufacture for stock, to undertake plant construction and repairs, to reduce the work week, and to lower prices.

There was no such unanimity in the committee's recommendations for permanent measures. The business spokesmen theorized that many businesses were operating at a loss but that some selfish groups and individuals were avoiding similar sacrifices which were necessary to revive prosperity. Recovery was being impaired by unwise legislation which artificially restrained economic readjustment. They therefore recommended financial assistance to the railroads by the government, transfer of the functions of the Railroad Labor Board to the Interstate Commerce Commission, repeal of the Adamson Act, and the elimination of waste and inefficiency through reduction of wages.

Gompers and the other two labor members of this committee denounced the majority report as an effort to break down the principle of the eight-hour day and to deprive the railroad workers of the only agency to which they could present their claims for consideration. They agreed that waste ought to be eliminated in industry but resented the assumption that human beings were to be placed in the same category as commodities "to be weighed, measured, bought, and sold in the same manner as commodities or articles of commerce." The emergency declaration adopted by the conference had recommended that the people should buy goods in order to revive business and give work to the unemployed. How could this be done, they asked, unless wages were maintained? On the contrary, sound policy called for the highest possible wage rate in industry and policies to eliminate profiteering, in order to reduce prices and increase purchasing power.

The conference, operating under the rule of unanimity, did not act on either of these reports but was able to agree on such measures for permanent recovery as readjustment of railway rates, reduction of taxes, and definite settlement of tariff legislation.[8] Gompers was in thorough accord with the philosophy and recommendations of the conference. "They endeavor," he wrote, "to meet the needs of the situation without charity and without paternalism. . . . the conference . . . settles definitely for all time the question of social responsibility and of employer and management responsibility for the failure of industry to function in such a manner as to prevent periodical acute unemployment."[9] But the conference was limited by its opposition to any national expenditure or national legislation to meet the problems. Gompers agreed that there should be no federal expenditure for unemployment insurance or for a "dole," but he believed that more than local and voluntary effort was needed. He proposed a large-scale extension of public credit for new public works and other public purposes: "The problem of unemployment can be solved. Seasonal unemployment can be almost eliminated. Cyclical unemployment is a social crime of the highest order and no society which permits it to continue can expect to survive.

"As long as men and women, eager to work, in a country filled with untold riches of materials and land, are denied the opportunity to work and to maintain themselves properly, our society is bankrupt in its most important essential. . . .

"Working people must work to live. To deny the opportunity to work is to enforce death."[10]

An issue related to the problem of unemployment was that of national prohibition of the manufacture and sale of intoxicating liquors. The brewers, the waiters and bartenders, coopers, bottle makers, and teamsters were directly affected, and Gompers waged a continuous fight against prohibition for this reason; but his opposition was based on broader grounds as well.

Immediately after the declaration of war, the General Medical Board of the Council of National Defense adopted two resolutions asking for a wartime prohibition act and the prohibition of alcoholic beverages to soldiers and sailors in and about military camps. The following day Gompers stormed into the meeting room of the Advisory Commission. As soon as the meeting was called to order, he jumped up and leaned over to one of its directors, pointing his finger at him, and demanded: "What have you been doing? Sold out to the so-called 'social hygienists' and prohibition fanatics, long-haired men and short haired women? You shall not make the war an opportunity for these complacent so-called 'reformers' to accomplish their nefarious work! When have fighting men been preached to on the beneficence of continence? The millenium has not arrived, and until it does your pronouncements of yesterday will not be accepted! Real men will be men! And you employ this subtle propaganda in an appeal to the fathers and mothers of young men to foist prohibition upon the men and women of our country without their consent!" As a result of this outburst, the commission dropped the first resolution and substituted the word "control" for "prohibition" in the second. In this form the resolution was subsequently adopted by the Council of National Defense.[11]

In 1918 Congress banned the making or sale of intoxicants as a war measure. In the meantime a constitutional amendment was introduced to prohibit the manufacture and sale of intoxicating liquors, and the House and Senate Judiciary Committees tried to rush it through without hearings. Gompers wrote to the chairmen of those committees, urging that the question be deferred until after the end of the war. He argued that since wartime prohibition was already in effect, the only result of presenting the amendment to the country would be to stir up bitter controversy, arouse the ill will of millions of people, and provide the "anti-American" propaganda with an opportunity to create a feeling of distrust against the government.[12]

Gompers was not as influential, however, as the Anti-Saloon League, which described him as a servile tool of the brewery interests. Congress approved the amendment with little delay and submitted it to the states for ratification. In February 1918, Gompers testified to a joint legislative committee of the New York Legislature in opposition to ratification. He asserted that the Constitution was and should be a charter of rights, not a denial of rights. And liquor drinking was a right, in his opinion, for it was the exercise of the normal activities which should not be prohibited simply because a few people abused that right. He admitted that there was evil in excessive drinking and counted himself an advocate of temperance, declaring that nothing had produced more temperance than the labor movement through its efforts to secure for the workers higher standards of living and more opportunity for the cultivation of the good things of life. This was more effective than any law, which merely drove drinking into clandestine channels. In the states where prohibition laws prevailed, drinking had not been stopped; the law merely made men lawbreakers. He emphasized the danger of creating unrest and dissension at a time when national unity was of the greatest importance.[13]

With unprecedented swiftness and unanimity, forty-six states ratified the amendment and it went into effect in January 1920. As soon as ratification was assured, bills were introduced into Congress to define the term "intoxicating liquors" and to enforce the Eighteenth Amendment. The Volstead Bill defined them as any beverage containing over one half of one per cent of alcohol and provided stringent regulations for the enforcement of prohibition. At the convention of the A.F. of L. in June 1919, a resolution was introduced by over a hundred delegates demanding that the present mild beer of 2¾% alcohol be exempted from the prohibition law. This resolution was passed by a more than six to one majority, and on June 14 virtually the entire convention moved as a body from Atlantic City to Washington to make a public demonstration on the Capitol steps "for the legal right of the workingman to drink a glass of beer after his day's labor." The Senate Judiciary Committee, which was considering the Volstead Bill, held a special session to hear the labor spokesmen.

Gompers, the principal speaker, told the Senators that he was in complete agreement that the elimination of whiskey from the lives of the people had contributed to a better life. But he appealed for the right of the workers to continue "the habit, the necessity" of drinking beer and light wines, which were nonintoxicating and noninjurious, with their dried-out lunches in the factories. Referring to the days when he worked at the cigar bench, he said, "I know what a glass of beer meant to me in the midday, in the factory full of dust, full of foul air. . . . Take the man who works in any industrial establishment for eight or nine hours or more a day; how welcome a glass of beer is to him can not be known except to those who have had the industrial experience." He warned of the great unrest that would be produced among the workers if their beer was cut off and noted that a movement had been inaugurated to quit work if prohibition went into effect, under the slogan, "No beer, no work."

Prohibition would be discriminatory class legislation, he maintained, for while the workers would be unable to get their beer, men of means might have a stock of wines and whiskeys that would last the rest of their lives. The chairman of the committee told Gompers that the president of the Louisiana Federation of Labor believed alcoholic liquors to be the worst curse of the laboring man. "I have heard equally ridiculous statements upon that and other subjects," replied Gompers. "It is the misery of poverty and overwork and undernourishment which has driven men to drink."[14]

After prohibition became law, Gompers fought for repeal or modification of the Volstead Act. He did not live to see it come, but he lived long enough to see poisonous bootleg whiskey sold at exorbitant prices, the development of the bootlegging racket with its subornation of public officials and the crime, graft, and corruption engendered by it, the complacency of the people in the evasion of the law and the resultant indulgence toward all lawbreaking, an increase in drunkenness, and the decline or demise of half a dozen trade unions. These, he observed, were the inevitable results of a prohibition that did not prohibit because people would not take dictation in the exercise of their personal habits and liberties.[15]

To ease the unemployment situation, Gompers also stepped up his efforts to secure permanent immigration restrictions. In 1917 the literacy test had been finally established. But, Gompers stated, employers were clamoring for the repeal of immigration restrictions so that they might again have an unlimited supply of cheap labor and strikebreakers.

It was time to call a halt. He called for the retention of all existing regulations, a prohibition against citizenship as well as immigration for all Orientals, and a complete closing of the doors to all immigrants for a two-year period, which would allow time for re-examination of immigration policy and for observation of the effects of the war on immigration practices.[16]

In 1921, Congress passed an emergency law limiting annual immigration from European countries to three per cent of the number of foreign-born of each nationality present in the United States in 1910. This, like the literacy test, was designed to limit the number of immigrants and to discriminate against those from Southern and Eastern Europe. Gompers, employing old arguments, joined others to make these principles of limitation and national origin quotas a permanent feature of American policy. When the emergency quota act was about to expire in 1924, he advocated a law absolutely forbidding immigration for the next five years. But he knew such a law could not secure enough votes for passage and gave his support to the next best thing, the act of 1924 which limited the total number of immigrants to 150,000 a year and changed the quota basis to two per cent computed on the census of 1890 rather than of 1910.[17] Gompers' fifty-year campaign for immigration restriction and exclusion of "undesirable" immigrants had been won.

2. THE RIGHT TO STRIKE

ALL OTHER LEGISLATIVE ISSUES WERE COMPLETELY overshadowed by the one which Gompers regarded as most menacing: the effort to shackle the labor unions and destroy the right to strike. In addition to the "sedition" bills, thinly concealed efforts to deprive labor of the freedom to carry on normal activities, a number of bills was introduced into Congress in 1919 and 1920 intended to limit the right to strike. While most of these measures were too extreme to command widespread support, legislation motivated by the same spirit had sufficient backing to be enacted. This was the Esch-Cummins Railroad Bill, or Transportation Act of 1920.

It provided for the return of the railroads to private owner-ship, guaranteeing five and one-half to six per cent profits on the book value of the property, including billions of dollars of watered stock and the inflated value of the war years. In addition, it originally declared that any strike by railroad workers was a conspiracy punishable by six months imprisonment and a $500 fine. The Senate committee added a similar penalty for anyone advising or aiding a strike. In hearings on the bill before the Interstate Commerce Committee, Gompers denounced it as violat-ing the Thirteenth Amendment to the Constitution which forbids involuntary servitude. "When the government during the stress of war took over the railroads," he reminded the com-mittee, "the employes were free men. Now you are preparing to turn them back to their owners with the employes handcuffed. . . . I say with all candor, and with a full realization of my responsibility, that American workmen will not surrender the right to stop work when the terms become intolerable. . . . The effect of the [bill] would not be to prevent strikes. It would simply create lawbreakers. I say if this section was passed, I would have no more hesitancy in participating in a strike than I would now."[18]

The bill provided for a Railway Labor Board with power to fix wages, hours, and working conditions for the railroad workers. There was no appeal from its rulings; the workers must accept the terms dictated by it or go to jail. Law or no law, this would not prevent strikes, but encourage them, Gompers warned. He called a meeting of the railroad brotherhoods and shopmen, and they agreed to confine their efforts to the defeat of all labor clauses in the railroad bill and to urge the retention of government ownership for two years. Such a bill was introduced by Senator La Follette, but antilabor sentiment was rampant in Congress and the Esch-Cummins Bill was enacted with modifications that made the labor clauses somewhat less stringent but still establishing compulsory arbitration by a Railway Labor Board. Gompers recommended that labor "boycott" the board by refusing to appoint its three members, but the railroad unions decided to give it a trial. They soon repented of this decision and joined forces with Gompers to secure its repeal.[19]

Perhaps even more dangerous than the antistrike legislation enacted by Congress was the movement to establish compulsory arbitration in the states. Early in 1920, Governor Henry J. Allen of Kansas proposed, and the legislature enacted, a law which made strikes illegal in the public utility, transportation, mining, food, and clothing industries and established a Court of Industrial Relations for the compulsory arbitration of all disputes. Picketing and similar activities were also prohibited. The penalty for disobedience to the court's decisions was $1,000 fine and one year's imprisonment, and double for the officers of striking unions. The court, appointed by the governor, had complete authority to fix wages, hours, working conditions, rules and practices.

In May, Gompers and Governor Allen staged a public debate on the Kansas Court in Carnegie Hall. Gompers told the crowded audience that he would not impute to his opponent the motive of desiring to make the workers subservient to their masters. He assumed that he was merely one of those who, "impatient and tired of the struggle of the human family, wanted to find a royal road to the goal of tranquility and peace. . . . I agree that strikes and cessations of work are uncomfortable, make for inconvenience, but my friends, there are some things worse than strikes . . . and among them is a degraded manhood. A people intelligent, independent and virile with life, activity and aspirations are always the vanguard for progress and civilization." In a supplementary statement published with the report of the debate, Gompers dealt particularly with the alleged rights of the public, which was the justification for the Kansas Industrial Court. He admitted that strikes of magnitude affected the general public, although he denied that they often constituted a real threat to public peace and health, and then it was usually because of the strikebreaking activities of the police, detectives, thugs, and military authorities. Strikes sometimes inconvenienced the public merely because they were effective. When few workers were organized, and when they were weak and ineffective, there was little outcry against strikes.

"The great concern of most newspapers and public officials who propound ready-made remedies is that labor should labor. Stripped of its adornment that is the essence of the outcry against strikes. Workers must work, and while workers work the newspapers and oratorical public officials will be silent about them. . . .

"So far as labor is concerned, the right to strike must and will be maintained, not only as a measure of self-defense and self-advancement, but as a measure necessary to public progress. There is no escaping some inconvenience during strikes, particularly for those who engage in striking. The strike has won its right to a post of honor among the institutions of free civilization and the temporary inconvenience it has caused is but a small price to pay for the permanent benefits it has brought. . . ."[20]

The Kansas Court was taken as a model by employers and antilabor politicians. The legislatures of New Jersey and New York invited both Governor Allen and Gompers to address them, and if the votes of those bodies be taken as evidence, Gompers went off as winner. But in Colorado a compulsory arbitration law was passed and in other states restrictions were placed on the activities of unions. They did not accomplish their purpose, for strikes were not prevented in either Kansas or Colorado, and the Kansas law was virtually nullified by the defiance of the workers and a series of decisions by the United States Supreme Court.

Gompers noted that it was more or less accidental that in this case the Supreme Court took a stand which coincided with the movement for industrial freedom and liberty. For, during the postwar years, it almost invariably exercised its powers to restrict the activities of labor unions and to retard the progress of labor and social legislation. The judges of the country seemed to be in almost unanimous agreement with Supreme Court Justice James Van Siklen of Brooklyn who said, in issuing an injunction, that "The courts must stand at all times as the representatives of capital, of captains of industry," a remark for which Gompers demanded his impeachment.[21]

The injunction menace loomed large again as the courts ignored or swept aside the "Magna Carta" of labor. Even before the war was over, the emasculation of the Clayton Act was begun by the United States Supreme Court in the case of the Hitchman Coal and Coke Company vs. Mitchell. This ruling upheld an injunction which forbade union officers from attempting to organize workers who had signed yellow dog contracts. The court ruled that the right of workers to join unions was overshadowed by the right of employers to run their companies as nonunion establishments. Gompers commented that if employers could exercise their power to force workers to sign a yellow dog contract, then, under the Hitchman doctrine, unions could be barred for all time from trying to organize them, by the simple expedient of obtaining an injunction which would make their efforts an unlawful conspiracy.[22]

In 1921, the first direct test of the labor sections of the Clayton Act was made before the Supreme Court. Fourteen machinists were discharged by the Duplex Printing Machine Company of Battle Creek as the result of a strike. The New York machinists' union instituted a boycott, refusing to install the machinery of that company. An injunction was issued to prohibit the boycott on the ground of interference with interstate commerce. The Supreme Court upheld the injunction in spite of the Clayton Act, ruling that it did not intend to give immunity for conduct in violation of the Sherman Act; that the law gave immunity only to "employees" who were directly party to a dispute, and not to others who were not employees of the company; and that a sympathetic strike in aid of a boycott was not "peaceful and lawful" persuasion. The doctrine of criminal conspiracy was revived with a vengeance as the court sought to perpetuate the very judicial abuses that were supposed to be remedied by the Clayton Act.[23]

The following year, the court surpassed other antilabor decisions in the Coronado Coal Company case. It upheld a suit for damages against the United Mine Workers in Arkansas on the ground that its strike was a conspiracy to deprive the company of its employees by intimidation and violence and held the union responsible for injury to private rights. It was precisely this doctrine, first enunciated in the Danbury hatters' case, that had been presumably overthrown by the Clayton Act. In 1922, ninety-five injunctions against unions were issued in the state and federal courts.

To meet the threat posed by these injunctions and court rulings, the A.F. of L. Executive Council held a special meeting which was attended by the heads of several international unions, the legislative committee, and the Federation's attorneys. It was decided to press for the repeal of all anticonspiracy laws and antitrust laws and for the passage in Congress and each state of a law which would, in unmistakable language, make it lawful for workers to organize unions, to strike, and to boycott, and to prohibit the issuance of injunctions in labor disputes to prevent acts which were legal in the absence of a labor dispute. Gompers continued to advise his old course: that workers ignore injunctions as violations of constitutional rights, even if it meant imprisonment.[24]

The Supreme Court also came to the aid of reaction by nullifying a number of labor laws enacted by Congress. In 1917, Congress had enacted a child labor law which used the power to regulate interstate commerce to forbid the shipment of goods manufactured by children under sixteen. The Supreme Court, to Gompers' dismay, held this act unconstitutional on the ground that it was a violation of state rights. Congress then prohibited child labor by imposing a tax on all products manufactured in factories employing children. The Supreme Court nullified this act too, holding that it was an unconstitutional exercise of the taxing power. Gompers also denounced this decision as a demonstration of the court's class bias: "The Supreme Court deals with childhood exactly as it would deal with pig iron. . . . It observes all the technicalities, weighing the lives of our little ones as so much inert material. . . . Perhaps there is some legal technicality which makes proper and constitutional a tax on colored oleomargarine to keep it off the market, but improper and unconstitutional a tax on child labor to keep child labor products off the market."[25]

The following year the Supreme Court nullified a law establishing minimum wages for women workers in the District of Columbia. Gompers noted with indignation that "in practically every case of importance involving employment relations and the protection of humanity, the court ranges itself on the side of property and against humanity. . . . [This decision] is a logical next step in perfecting the doctrine that those who cannot help themselves shall not be helped."[26]

As a result of such rulings, Gompers undertook a campaign to secure judicial reform that would remove the courts as an obstacle to progress and the will of the people. In 1919 he proposed that the Supreme Court be deprived of the right to nullify acts of Congress and of the states except by a two-thirds vote. Later he recommended that Congress be empowered to re-enact a law over the court's veto by a two-thirds vote. This proposal, adopted by the Progressive party in 1924, became an issue in the Presidential election of that year when President Coolidge attacked it as an effort to destroy the legitimate powers and the independence of the courts and to make Congress the supreme branch of government. He defended his position by asserting that "majorities are notoriously irresponsible" and must be checked by an impartial body in order to protect the rights of individuals and minorities.

Gompers accepted the challenge on those terms and replied that the issue was whether the people were to be responsible to the courts or the courts responsible to the people. He was willing for the courts to be independent—that is, removed from the immediate control of the people—if they were confined to purely judicial functions. But if they were to be allowed to determine the social and political destinies of the country by usurping legislative powers, then their independence became judicial oligarchy and tyranny which would continue to sap away the freedom of the people. This issue typified the struggle being waged between progress and reaction.[27]

3. THE AMERICAN PLAN

THE TURN TOWARD REACTION BY THE EXECUTIVE, legislative, and judicial branches of the government helped to create a climate of opinion in which the employers embarked on the great antiunion campaign of the 1920's. It went far beyond that of two decades before. The National Association of Manufacturers, Chamber of Commerce, Associated Industries, and the National Industrial Conference Board led in the mobilization of the employers, forming national and local branches to co-ordinate the campaign down to every echelon of industry. The basic issue of the employers' campaign was the drive for the establishment throughout industry of the open shop, now dubbed the "American Plan." Gompers spent a good part of his last five years trying to counter the propaganda for the open shop.

This propaganda was based on the alleged freedom of the nonunion worker to secure employment. Gompers denied that open shop employers were interested in the freedom of the individual worker. Out of his rich experience, he could note that the "right" to bargain individually and to sign individual contracts was a relic of the pre-industrial era, and in modern industry it meant nothing more than absolute submission by the individual to the dictates of the employer. In an open letter to Newton D. Baker, now president of the Cleveland Chamber of Commerce, Gompers pointed out that the so-called open shop must in reality be a nonunion shop, for it would remain such only so long as there were sufficient nonunion men to make it so. The employer who was determined not to operate a union shop was bound to see to it that no more than a small minority of union men secured employment in his shop.[28]

All of labor's woes seemed to drop on it when the railway shopmen struck: antagonism by the employers, the compulsory arbitration features of the Esch-Cummins Act, the opposition of the administration, disunity in the labor movement, and the old injunction nemesis. It all began with an order of the Railway Labor Board in June 1921, for a reduction of wages ranging from five to eighteen cents an hour. The railroad labor groups rebelled against this decree and voted to reject it. The Board then revised the national agreement, ending overtime pay for Sunday and holiday work. The evil of contracting out added to the workers' troubles and the railroads refused to abide by the Board's ruling that this practice violated the Transportation Act. Then, in spite of a practically unanimous vote of the workers to have the system federations represent them, the Pennsylvania Railroad ignored them and began negotiations with a company union. When the Labor Board ordered a new vote and summoned the railroad to show cause why it should not be pronounced guilty of violating the law, the company secured an injunction preventing the Board from even publishing its decision, let alone enforcing it. Finally, the Board reduced the wages of the track laborers five cents an hour and ordered a reduction of twelve per cent for the shop crafts to go into effect on July 1, 1922. The unions voted to strike on that date, and ninety per cent of the workers left the shops.[29]

In Gompers' opinion, not only were the workers justified in protesting wage cuts and the lowering of standards in the working rules, but the situation revealed the futility and danger of government boards regulating industrial relations. The Railway Labor Board was not competent to settle these problems because it could not possibly keep up with all the grievances presented to it, it did not have a proper understanding of the industrial problems involved, and the workers' representatives were in a hopeless minority. The only way of settling the dispute was by voluntary and mutual negotiation, and the existence of the Board made that impossible because it turned the employers and employees into litigants and antagonists rather than negotiators and conferees.[30]

When the strike began, the Railway Labor Board branded it as an outlaw movement, declared that the unions participating in it could not again be considered as representatives of the workers before the Board, and urged the roads to form company unions. On July 11, President Harding issued a proclamation enjoining all interference with interstate commerce, asserting that the peaceful settlement of the controversy in accordance with the law and respect for the established agencies of such settlement were essential to the security and well-being of the people. Gompers protested against the implication that the strikers had not proceeded in accordance with the law. The law specifically gave the workers the right to cease work if they could not accept the award of the Board. He pointed out that ninety-two railroads in 104 cases had refused to abide by the awards of the Board and no attempt had been made to coerce them into acceptance. The strike was not against the Labor Board or the government, but against the railroads' effort to cut wages and crush the unions, and could be ended at any moment through joint negotiations between the management and the workers. The workers "have quit work and that is all they have done. . . . The American Federation of Labor, with all of its strength and determination, is back of these men. The American Federation of Labor is proud of their courage and their manhood. It glories in their spirit and in their adherence to the best traditions of our Republic."[31]

The railroad workers were willing to accept Harding's offer to return to work and submit all issues to arbitration, but the companies refused to reinstate the "outlaw" strikers without prejudice to their seniority. This then became the major issue of the strike. Gompers called on organized labor to give financial assistance to the strikers. Then Attorney General Daugherty entered the scene. Characterizing the strike as a "bold challenge to constitutional government," a "mutiny," and defiance of the law which placed the country under an "iron heel of terrorism," he announced that he would use every power at his command to prevent the labor unions from destroying the open shop. He presented to the court 17,000 affidavits allegedly portraying the existence of "anarchy bordering on civil war"—affidavits which Gompers described as being "literally fished out of the sewers among strikebreakers and paid agents of the most desperate character most of whom were perfectly willing to sign anything which they were paid to sign." Daugherty applied for and received the most sweeping injunction ever yet issued in a labor dispute, charging the strikers with unlawful conspiracy under the Sherman Act. It forbade the unions and their members from engaging in activities that even in the remotest degree had any connection with the strike, including the disbursement of union funds, the holding of meetings, and communicating by telephone.[32]

The striking unions declared their determination to continue the strike. Gompers issued a manifesto accusing the Attorney General of violating the law which forbade the expenditure of

Justice Department funds for the prosecution of labor organizations under the antitrust laws. He called upon the workers and their sympathizers to hold mass protest meetings, to pledge support to the strikers, and to demand the impeachment of Daugherty.[33] The injunction failed to stop the strike; if anything, it gained the strikers greater support among organized labor and the public.

The unions now authorized separate settlements on condition that the strikers be restored to their pre-strike status and that grievances be settled by joint commission. By October 15 most of the roads had signed such agreements, saving the unions and the seniority of 225,000 men. The remaining 175,000 eventually had to surrender and submit to company unionism, but the strike had stopped the wage cutting policies of the railroads and virtually eliminated the Labor Board as a factor in railway labor policy.

Chapter Twenty-Seven

RED, WHITE, AND BLACK

1. LABOR RACKETEERING

DURING THE POSTWAR YEARS, THE A.F. of L. suffered a serious decline in membership. After reaching a high point of over four million in 1920, it began to lose large numbers of workers in the war industries where employment had been abnormal and unionism had been encouraged by government protection. The open shop campaign also took its toll, and the depression of 1921 removed many members from the rolls of the unions. By 1924, in spite of business revival, the Federation counted less than three million members. This was still fifty per cent higher than the prewar figure, but decline during a period of prosperity was a new phenomenon in the labor movement. It reflected on Gompers' leadership, and while he was venerated as the grand old chief of the labor movement, many in the A.F. of L., even among his friends, felt that he had little more to contribute, especially in view of his poor health.

These conditions brought about Gompers' only setback in the cigarmakers' union. He had been a perennial representative of his local union since its organization over forty years before, but in 1920 he was defeated by his old antagonist, the socialist secretary of the union, Morris Brown. Out of a total membership of 1,200, Gompers received only 82 votes, while Brown and two other candidates received 420. However, Gompers was permitted to attend the convention as first vice-president of the international union, and was there re-elected to that position.[1]

His post as president of the A.F. of L. was also challenged for the first time in a decade. In 1921, John L. Lewis was nominated in opposition to him. His candidacy was probably induced primarily by Gompers' opposition to the U.M.W.'s position in calling off the 1919 coal strike. In addition, Lewis and the other U.M.W. officials undoubtedly wanted greater influence for their own union and an infusion of "young blood" which they hoped would bring new life to the Federation. Lewis stood for a greater emphasis on political action and favored a program of government ownership of the railroads and mines, government control of the natural resources, and state insurance against sickness, unemployment, and old age. However, Lewis' record was not such as to rally the progressive opposition. While Lewis was more "radical" or progressive than Gompers on political matters, Gompers was more militant than he in economic struggles. Most of the railway union delegates, as well as those from the I.L.G.W.U. and other socialist unions, supported Gompers. Even three of the eight U.M.W. delegates voted for him. Others supported him because of principle, loyalty, tradition, and sentiment—or just because they knew he would win anyhow.[2] Lewis received almost exactly one-third of the votes; it was a strong bid, but Gompers' hold was still too firm to be shaken.

Gompers was being plagued by another issue which he had tried for years to keep from public attention and consideration, the problem of corruption and racketeering in the unions. His unvarying attitude had been: minimize the seriousness of the problem, blame it on the employers, and try to keep it inside the labor movement. Most of the publicity concerning labor corruption involved the building trades, not only because racketeering seemed to be more widespread in that industry but because it had a more direct effect on the public in the form of higher building costs. As far back as the first decade of the twentieth century, widespread graft was revealed in the building trades unions. The boss of the Chicago building trades was "Skinny" Madden, an ally of Gompers in his fight against the socialists and radicals in that city. "Umbrella" Mike Boyle was another Chicago labor racketeer who ran afoul of the law. He was the head of the local electrical workers' union, and in 1911 he secured the closed shop in return for a promise to exclude from the Chicago market all switchboards not made in the city. He had a personal financial interest in one of the local electrical manufacturing companies. He departed from his monopolistic practices only when a contractor first dropped a contribution into Boyle's ever-present umbrella. In 1917, Boyle was fined $5,000 and sentenced to a year in prison for violating the Sherman Act. Gompers interceded in his behalf and persuaded President Wilson to commute his sentence.[3]

The most notorious of the black sheep in the labor family was Robert Brindell. Brindell joined the Independent Dock Union in New York in 1905. Five years later the A.F. of L. revoked its charter as a federal labor union for nonpayment of dues and gave its charter to the Municipal Dock Builders' Union. Brindell gained control of the independent union and in 1914 started a flirtation with the A.F. of L. with the aim of uniting the two dock unions under his control and using that position as a leverage for moving up in labor circles. Gompers' interest in him was probably due to his desire to get an A.F. of L. Building Trades Department in New York, and Brindell was probably recommended to him by the carpenters' union as a coming "strong man" who could force the New York Board of Business Agents into the Building Trades Department. After a conference between Gompers, Brindell, and the executives of the carpenters' union, Brindell's union was given a charter by the carpenters, and Gompers revoked the charter of the Municipal Dock Builders' Union which joined the Bridge and Structural Iron Workers Union.

Brindell gained in power during the war, and began to spread out. With the backing of Hutcheson, of the carpenters, and the employers, who used him as a strike-breaking agency, he became czar of the New York building trades. He converted the Board of Business Agents into a Building Trades Council and received a charter from the Building Trades Department of the A.F. of L. He was elected president of the council for life and ran it with dictatorial efficiency. He was the highest paid labor official in the country and supplemented his salary with strike insurance from the employers.[4]

Brindell's reign came to an end because his lust for graft was surpassed by the employers' greed. Under the protection of the mutually protected monopoly, the contractors raised the cost of construction from one hundred to three hundred per cent during the war, causing a housing shortage. Compelled to take cognizance of the corruption in the industry, the state legislature authorized the Lockwood Committee to investigate the high cost of housing in New York City. The investigation led right to Brindell. In the course of its hearings, Gompers was called to testify. He was questioned by Samuel Untermeyer, counsel for the committee, who sought to elicit from him evidence concerning the nature and extent of corruption and his views on remedial measures. Gompers proved an unco-operative, not to say exasperating, witness. Due to his physical condition, he had to excuse himself from time to time, a circumstance which he exploited to take unnecessarily frequent recesses and to interrupt the questioning. But it was his manner of answering questions, as well as his refusal to admit facts Untermeyer thought were undeniably established, that occasionally brought the latter to the point of desperation. Thus, Untermeyer asked his opinion of a union which fined one of its members because he had made an affidavit in connection with an injunction suit against the union by an employer. Gompers responded that if the affidavit was made to help the employer against the union, he thought it was wrong, even if it contained nothing but the truth. "You don't think he should assist in the administration of justice by telling the truth?" Gompers answered flatly, "I do not think he should assist the employer in a contention with the Union of his trade or calling."[5] Nor would Gompers assist the committee, for in his view the investigation was simply another part of the employers' effort to discredit the labor movement and shackle the unions with government control.

Gompers admitted that there were evils and abuses practiced by some of the building trades unions but he repeatedly insisted that he objected to action by the legislature or the courts to redress those abuses. The only power of review, the only redress should come from the labor organizations themselves. The following colloquy was typical of the two days of testimony:

"Q. In the Plumbers Union these various abuses were agreed to be corrected, Mr. Gompers . . . but . . . they have formally rescinded their resolution to abate these abuses. Under these circumstances, is there anything left for this Committee except to recommend that there should be such regulation as will enforce such reforms as may be found necessary?

"A. Yes, sir.

"Q. What is there?

"A. The recognition of the fact that this is a struggle, a struggle of the working people of our state and of our country for improved conditions. . . .

"Q. . . . you say that you do not think even under those circumstances that this Committee ought to suggest to the Legislature the propriety of finding some way of modifying these abuses, is that right?

"A. By law or by governmental agencies, yes, sir. . . .

"Q. You object to it?

"A. Not only object to it, protest against it. . . .

"Q. What would you do to remedy it, having tried with the Union to remedy it and having failed?

"A. These things will be regulated by the organizations and remedied.

"Q. But don't you see they are not being remedied even after they promised?

"A. The world was not made in a day.

"Q. . . . don't you think the Committee should do anything?

"A. Yes, report the facts.

"Q. Report the facts with recommendations or without them?

"A. Without recommendations of statutory relief or regulations of the character to which you refer. . . ."

The committee recommended a legislative program to deal with the abuses disclosed, but it was defeated by the opposition of organized labor, Tammany Hall, and many liberals. The only result of the investigation was the conviction of a few labor racketeers, including Brindell, who was sentenced to five to ten years in prison on three counts of extortion. Because of his stand before the Lockwood Committee, Gompers was widely accused of tolerating and protecting corruption in the unions. His reply was that in public, or when facing the enemies of labor, he defended the labor movement, even its errors, and if there were no defense he found the best possible excuse for its actions. "But to trade-unionists themselves I am merciless in pointing out foolishness and wrong-doing."[6]

There is little evidence that Gompers was, and certainly he never proposed any reform measures in the A.F. of L. His defense was that as president of the A.F. of L. he had little or no power to enforce discipline or order remedial action by international or local unions. This was partly true but partly an evasion. Gompers and other Federation officials tacitly accepted racketeering and racketeers, and for a number of reasons. They were reluctant to interfere with the independence of the international unions. About half of the voting strength of the A.F. of L. was in the building and transportation unions, where the rackets were most evident. Gompers' strength rested on upholding the rule of autonomous sovereignty, and he found it more convenient to ignore any of their unpleasant activities. At times he not only ignored rackets but supported racketeers when they could be used as allies. In 1918 he joined Brindell in the attempt to oust the radicals from the central body of New York City and to regain control of it for the conservatives.

The racketeers were invariably ultraconservative in their attitude toward labor and social problems, if they had any ideas about them at all. Labor racketeering was, indeed, the fruit of pure and simple unionism. Devoid of idealism or long-range goals, eschewing reforms that might bring more fundamental relief for the needs of the workers, business unionism was not basically out of harmony with the direct-action tactics and goals of the racketeers.[7] At least they did not present a challenge to the leadership of Gompers, as did the radicals.

2. CHALLENGE FROM THE LEFT

AMONG AMERICAN RADICALS, THE TRADITION OF dual unionism had always been strong. Since 1912, William Z. Foster had been its principal opponent among the revolutionists. While he accepted the necessity of organizing the unskilled workers in whom the A.F. of L. showed little interest, he was convinced that as a general policy dual unionism was wrong because it isolated the militant workers from the masses in the established unions and abandoned the unions to the "labor fakers," of whom Gompers was the chief and symbol. Foster determined to work within the A.F. of L., to prod it into mass organizing campaigns, and to win it eventually to a program of class struggle.

Foster's leadership of the packinghouse organizing drive and the steel strike was part of this program. In the postwar period he organized the Trade Union Educational League. Its function was to organize the trade union militants so that they could guide the workers to overthrow the conservative "labor bureaucracy" and "to develop trade unions from their present antiquated and stagnant condition into modern, powerful labor organizations capable of waging successful warfare against Capital."[8]

The program of the T.U.E.L. called for organizing the unorganized, industrial unionism, unemployment insurance, the formation of a labor party, affiliation of the labor movement to the Red International of Labor Unions, support of the Russian revolution and revolutionary goals. This program won wide support in the A.F. of L., and a united front was organized consisting of the leftists (T.U.E.L. and communists) and the progressives or militants led by Fitzpatrick and Nockels, Chicago Federation of Labor officials. In a number of unions the united front opposition became very strong, particularly in the U.M.W., the garment industry, the steel union, and the railroad crafts.[9]

The campaign for amalgamation was initiated in the Chicago Federation of Labor on March 19, 1922. Foster introduced a resolution which declared that the labor movement was suffering defeat from the employers' antiunion drive because the employers were united while the unions were divided on trade lines and unable to offer concerted resistance. It called upon the A.F. of L. to lead the way and proposed as a first step that the international unions confer to amalgamate all the unions in the respective industries into single organizations.[10] This resolution was adopted by a large majority. On April 11, Gompers went to Chicago to spike the amalgamation movement and to "capture the Chicago Federation of Labor from the Reds." He bypassed the Federation itself and called a conference of several hundred union officials in the Morrison Hotel.

"Somehow or other," Gompers declared, "there has grown up in Chicago a spirit which breeds dissension, conflict of views, conflict of plans and of action, estrangement among men so that the great, powerful voice with which organized labor should express the hopes and aspirations as well as the demands of labor is not heard . . . as of yore." He urged the Chicago labor movement to place itself in line with the "united spirit and action" of the toiling masses of the country. Foster and Fitzpatrick spoke in support of the amalgamation resolution. Foster charged that if the unions in the steel industry had been united, the 1919 strike would have been successful, and that there must be one union in each industry or the unions would be destroyed.

Gompers closed the meeting with a long speech in which he called the T.U.E.L. "a monumentally brazen attempt at the dictation of the Labor movement of America." He stated that Foster came back from Russia to work, not for industrial unionism, but for the dictatorship of the proletariat with Foster as dictator. The resolution of the C.F. of L. was an attempt to pull the wool over the eyes of the workers. The A.F. of L. favored amalgamation, but it could not be hurried, and it must not be done as part of a conspiracy to annihilate the A.F. of L.

Gompers was unable to check the amalgamation campaign. During the next year and a half it was endorsed by sixteen international unions, seventeen state federations, scores of central labor councils, and thousands of locals, altogether embracing about half of the organized workers in the United States.[11]

While not so popular as amalgamation, the issue of recognition of and friendly relations with the Soviet government of Russia gained considerable labor support. A number of internationals endorsed recognition, including the miners, locomotive engineers, machinists, clothing workers, painters, and stationary firemen. In 1919 the American Labor Alliance for Trade Relations with Russia was formed, headed by Timothy Healy, president of the firemen's union, William Johnston of the machinists, Sidney Hillman of the clothing workers, and Benjamin Schlesinger of the ladies garment workers. The Alliance presented its position to union meetings throughout the country, thousands of which endorsed it.[12]

In 1921, Gompers, in collaboration with William English Walling, formerly a distinguished socialist, wrote *Out of Their Own Mouths: A Revelation and an Indictment of Sovietism*. In the preface Gompers explained that his purpose was to combat the growing support throughout the world for recognition of the Soviet government and the negotiation of trade agreements. He noted that Lloyd George, advocating recognition in the British

Parliament, contended that the Bolsheviks had become moderates. It was necessary to repudiate this notion and to show that there could be no compromise with Sovietism.

"Labor's interest in putting forth the truth about the Soviets is in part altruistic. Labor's regard for the welfare of the Russian workers is deep and genuine. But it also knows that if an anti-labor despotism may be made to work in one country—however inefficiently—it will encourage the enemies of labor to try the same methods elsewhere. Moreover, if the Soviets are given a certain permanency and success as 'moderates' by the aid of certain governments and financiers they will certainly continue to represent this success to the labor of the world as having come to them from their own efforts as 'ultra-revolutionists.' "[13]

In his report to the Federation convention in 1921, Gompers devoted considerable attention to the issue of recognition and trade, which he noted was being advocated both in the revolutionary press and in "pro-Bolshevik" journals like the *Nation* and *New Republic*. The purpose of the campaign was not only to secure prestige for the Soviet government but to make friends for the international communist movement and to assist in the conspiracy to destroy the trade union movement and the government of the United States. Gompers then presented a lengthy summary of those parts of his book which demonstrated the antipathy of the Soviets to democratic institutions and practices, the enforced labor of the workers, and the lack of freedom for trade unions and the labor and socialist parties. He also reviewed the continued efforts of the Communist International to foment revolution throughout the world and to prepare for this by the development of revolutionary organizations, including the Red International of Labor Unions, which was dedicated to the destruction of the "bourgeois" and "opportunist" leaders of the trade unions.[14]

The convention went on record as opposed to recognition and trade with the Soviet Union so long as its government fostered such evils. The following year the committee on international relations recommended the reaffirmation of that position. A minority report by Max Hayes and Timothy Healy favored recognition and trade in order to relieve unemployment in the United States and to strengthen world peace, which "cannot be established while military or economic pressure is used to deprive peoples of self-determination." In the long debate that ensued, Gompers thundered against Soviet treachery and brutality and appealed to the delegates to exhibit their confidence in his leadership by defeating his critics. His report was sustained by a large majority.[15]

The idea of forming a labor party was, of course, not a new one in the American labor movement; Gompers had been fighting it for fifty years. But after the war it revived because of the obviously reactionary character of the two major parties and the increasing use of government power to regulate labor. In addition to unionists, there was a large number of former progressives and socialists who felt the need for a new party to represent the progressive program that had been abandoned by the Democratic party.

The central labor councils of New York, Chicago, and several other cities had endorsed the idea. Gompers had called a special conference of labor men in New York in December 1918, to express his opposition to the movement. He had argued that in every country of Europe where there was a labor party, that party dominated the labor movement. He had insisted that there was not a single objective of the proposed labor party that was not being fought for by the A.F. of L., and that the organization of a political party would simply divide the activities and allegiance of the labor movement. The nonpartisan policy of the A.F. of L. had proved to be the most effective, he had assured them, and the organization of a labor party would make it impossible for labor to secure any gains through the major parties.[16]

The movement gained momentum, however, as the elections of 1920 approached. In 1919 the Indiana State Federation of Labor held a referendum in which the workers voted overwhelmingly in favor of a labor party. The Federation then called a state convention, at which was formed the Indiana Labor party. Gompers sent Dan Tobin of the A.F. of L. Council to the convention to persuade it to retain the Federation policy of rewarding friends and defeating enemies. The convention repudiated that policy and so informed Gompers by telegram. The workers were fed up with the two old parties, which were dominated by the large corporations, and the convention resented

Gompers' insinuation that they were not good union men because they desired their own party.

Gompers replied that the delegates to the party convention might have been unanimous in their belief that the A.F. of L. policy was not practical, but that belief was based on lack of experience and nothing more substantial than personal opinion and exuberance of spirit, and it was an insult to the labor movement: "It is deplorable that at a time when it is especially necessary that the workers of our country be united in thought and action that there are those who seek to divide them to gratify a desire for experimentation."[17]

The Chicago Federation of Labor also decided to form a labor party after a referendum vote endorsed such a policy, and asked Gompers for his support. His refusal carried a stinging prediction that the only accomplishment of the labor party would be to hamper the success of the Federation's nonpartisan program and result in the election of labor's enemies. He expressed surprise at the Chicago Federation's statement that there were no congressional candidates in that city who were friendly to labor and named six incumbents who had "fair labor records." He offered to compare notes after the election to see whether the A.F. of L. or the Illinois Labor party had the greater success. Secretary Nockels retorted that four of the five "fair" candidates had voted for the Esch-Cummins Act and the other was the acknowledged tool of the meat packers. Nor was he interested in comparing notes after the election, for, unlike Gompers, he was not trying to "pick the winners." He would rather vote for a candidate he wanted and lose than vote for one he didn't want and win.[18]

Later in the year, a Farmer-Labor convention was held in Chicago, sponsored by a committee of left-wing unionists headed by Fitzpatrick and Max Hayes and by leaders of the Non-Partisan League. The new party was a "flop" and was withering away until William Johnston, president of the International Association of Machinists, came forward as the leading champion of a labor party. During late 1921 and early 1922, the sixteen railroad unions, the United Mine Workers, Typographical Union, Amalgamated Clothing Workers, and several smaller international unions, twenty-four state federations, and scores of central labor councils joined with the Farmer-Labor party and the Non-Partisan League in a Conference for Progressive Political Action. But this conference refused to launch a third party, partly because of pressure from Gompers, partly because they would not consent to collaborate with the communists, and partly because the communists refused to accept a liberal program and the candidacy of La Follette. Then in July 1923, Fitzpatrick and his followers also broke with the communists, realizing that, as Foster said, the fight for a labor party at that stage meant the organization of an aggressive rank and file revolt against Gompers and "Gompersism," inevitably culminating in the reorganization of the trade union movement.[19]

The communist and radical element in the labor movement was isolated, its influence all but eliminated. About the same time, the improvement in the economic situation further undermined the effectiveness of the radical program in the labor movement. Finally, the radicals were weakened by the policy of expulsion adopted by many labor unions against communists, members of the T.U.E.L., and others who opposed the administration machines.

Gompers, in spite of his life-long opposition on principle to the expulsion of union members, now went along with it. He ordered the central labor unions of Minneapolis, Cleveland, Seattle, and other cities to expel all communists and members of the T.U.E.L. and conform with the official policies of the A.F. of L., on pain of having their charters revoked. He arbitrarily expelled members of federal labor unions on unproved and vague allegations of "radicalism." At the convention of the Federation in 1923, this policy was dramatized by the unseating of William Dunne, a member of the T.U.E.L. National Committee and the delegate of the Butte Trades Council. Gompers supported his expulsion on the ground that there was no place in an A.F. of L. convention for a person who was opposed to the principles of the trade union movement. The resolutions for amalgamation, recognition of Russia, and a labor party were voted down by overwhelming majorities. The opposition was thoroughly whipped, and Gompers entered his last year in unchallenged control as chief of the labor movement.[20]

Chapter Twenty-Eight

LAST DAYS

On December 24, 1923, Gompers left New York City for the Panama Canal Zone to investigate labor conditions, accompanied by the representative of the Panama Canal employees and the heads of several international unions. He arrived on New Year's Day and spent eight days inspecting conditions on the dredges and locks along the canal. During the week he held seventy-five conferences, delivered a dozen public addresses, and conferred with the governor of the Zone, the President of the Republic of Panama, and the minister and envoy of the United States. He also managed to "escape" into Panama occasionally for a legal glass of beer. He returned to the States on January 17 and subsequently presented to the Secretary of War the recommendations of his committee for improvements in the conditions of the Canal Zone workers. The recommendations were rejected.[1]

On January 27, Gompers "celebrated" his seventy-fourth birthday by putting in a usual day's work. As always, he arose at 7:30 in the morning, reached his office at 9:30 or 10:00, and until 6:00 in the evening was engaged in conferences, press interviews, reading and dictation of correspondence, and preparation of material to present to the Senate Foreign Relations Committee on the recognition of Russia. He stated that he felt as fit as he did at the age of forty and that there was no task he could not accomplish. "I could not keep still if I wanted to. . . . On the boat [to Panama] I could not work and I was never more restless in my life." He recalled that in the past four months he had travelled over 15,000 miles, delivered 210 addresses, presided at 300 conferences, and wrote thousands of letters, circulars, newspaper statements, articles, and editorials.[2]

However, in spite of his continued vigor, he was declining

518 LAST YEARS, 1919-1924

physically to the point where he lost at least half of his effectiveness. The Bright's disease was affecting his heart, he was suffering with diabetes, and he knew that the end was not far away. He was under constant care, being nursed by Miss Guard, who had to force his pills and medicine on him and enforce his diet with cajolery, scolding, or bantering, according to his mood. In May he took a turn for the worse, and, while he continued his daily work, he could no longer walk without the assistance of a cane or a companion's arm.

In May, Gompers inaugurated the A.F. of L. election campaign with the publication of labor's demands, then left Washington for a rest over the long Memorial Day weekend in New York. He went to the Astor Hotel and the following day found it necessary to call in his doctors. They tested his blood and advised him to go to the hospital immediately. He was taken to the Lenox Hill Hospital where, except for brief excursions, he remained for about six weeks. During part of that time, his physicians did not expect him to live more than a few days. He was unable to attend the Republican national convention in Cleveland early in June, but delegated Matthew Woll to present the Federation's platform demands. He listened to the proceedings on his radio. The platform committee gave Woll only a few minutes and rejected his program almost in its entirety.

Gompers' condition became grave. Specialists were called in and cradle baths were administered to induce perspiration in order to carry off the poison in his body. The doctors noted an improvement but stated that it would be only temporary. By the middle of June he was able to sit up and walk around and to take an automobile ride on Riverside Drive. Only then did he let it be known to the public that he had been in the hospital. On June 23, accompanied by a doctor and a nurse, he went to the Astor Hotel and presided over a conference of labor officials to plan their presentation of labor's demands to the Democratic convention which convened in Madison Square Garden the following day. On the twenty-sixth he went with the labor group to the platform committee, of which Bryan was chairman. He presented the Federation's program and made a forty-five minute plea for its endorsement. "If we are disappointed here as we were in Cleveland," he warned, "I leave it to your own judgment where the great masses of the people of the United States will go."[3]

The direction in which Gompers warned that the masses might go was toward the progressive movement. The day after the Democratic convention adjourned, the Federation's National Non-Partisan Political Committee agreed that it had no alternative but to support the candidates of that group. This movement had its origin in five separate groups: the local and state labor parties formed in 1918 and 1919, the Socialist party, the Non-Partisan League, the liberal Committee of Forty-Eight, and the Plumb Plan movement, organized in 1919 by the railroad unions to work for government ownership of the railroads. In 1922 these groups formed the Conference for Progressive Political Action.

After the elections of 1922, a second conference was held in Washington. It was preceded by a gathering of about two hundred progressives at the City Club, including congressmen, labor and farm leaders, and publicists. Among the speakers were Senators La Follette, Norris, and Wheeler, Gompers, Samuel Untermeyer, and Governor John J. Blaine of Wisconsin. The reactionary policies of the administration were assailed and the group went on record as favoring the unity of progressives throughout the country to aid in the advancement of liberal laws and general reconstruction. At the formal meeting of the conference in Cleveland two weeks later, the labor leaders opposed the organization of a third party and defeated a socialist proposal to that end by a small majority. A call was issued for a convention on July 4, 1924, to consider nominations for President and Vice-President of the United States.[4]

This movement was in accord with Gompers' thinking concerning political tactics. He was trying, through the National Labor Non-Partisan Political Committee, to built a bipartisan labor-progressive bloc which would constitute a majority in Congress. And of course he was in complete agreement with the decision not to form a third party, be it labor, progressive, or anything else. He also approved the C.P.P.A.'s denunciation of and disassociation with the communists.

On the eve of the Progressive convention, the national committee of the C.P.P.A. asked La Follette to run for President as an independent candidate; they and La Follette agreed that no new party should be formed, at least until after the election. The convention endorsed his candidacy with Burton K. Wheeler of Montana as his running mate. It also accepted his platform, which stated that the fundamental issue was government for the service of all or for mastery by the few. It dedicated the Progressives to fight against the efforts of organized force and greed to destroy liberty and enslave mankind.*

On the day that the Progressive convention met, Miss Guard was writing to one of Gompers' colleagues and friends that "he is always so eager to give service, so eager to do, his brain is always so aflame with the thoughts of what he wants to do for labor, that it is difficult to curb him to less activities. It is the constant effort of those of us who are daily associated with him to so arrange matters, to so shape and take care of the work, as to spare him every possible thing, and to save him for the big things that no one else can do for him." Four days later Gompers was able to leave the hospital, but not to return to his office. With his nurse and an aide from Federation headquarters, he went to the Shelburne Hotel at Brighton Beach, Coney Island. Miss Guard maintained an auxiliary office at the Continental Hotel to handle work other than routine of the Washington headquarters. Some of it she brought to Gompers each day for his consideration and decision. Gompers wrote to the Executive Council: "It is easy to say, 'Don't do any work; rest; dismiss work from your mind; relax; play.' But to me that is not rest; that is punishment. And so my physicians decided that it is good for me, and that work in a reasonably moderate degree shall not be denied me. . . ."[6]

---

*The platform called for the crushing of private monopoly, public ownership of the nation's water power and strict public control of all natural resources, a liberal revision of Secretary of the Treasury Andrew W. Mellon's tax program, a bonus for veterans, protection of the right to organize and bargain collectively, aid for the farmers and co-operative enterprises, repeal of the Transportation Act and public ownership of the railroads, abolition of the injunction in labor disputes, abolition of the Supreme Court's power to nullify legislation, adoption of the child labor amendment, denunciation of American imperialism, independence for the Philippines, and a foreign policy which would promote treaty agreements with all nations to outlaw war, abolish conscription, reduce armaments, and guarantee public referendums on the declaration of war.[5]

Gompers improved slowly, and at the end of July he, his nurse, and Miss Guard left the beach and moved to the Ambassador Hotel in Atlantic City. Miss Guard established her office in the same hotel. From August 1 to 11 the Executive Council met in Atlantic City and Gompers was able to participate in some of its sessions. On September 11 he returned to the Shelburne and early the following month returned home after an absence of over four months.

At its meeting on August 4, the Executive Council reviewed the platforms and Presidential candidates in the election. There was little difficulty in determining that the Republican platform was intolerable to labor and its candidates unacceptable. The Democratic party, and candidates, too, while not flaunting the desires of labor in the arrogant manner of the Republicans, were evasive or silent on such basic issues as the injunction, the Esch-Cummins Act, and the child labor amendment. On the other hand, La Follette and Wheeler, running as independent Progressives, had throughout their careers "stood steadfast in defense of the rights and interests of the wage earners and the farmers." The committee urged the workers and all who believed in freedom, democracy and progress to co-operate in the support of "the faithful friends and servants of the masses" to defeat " the representatives of reaction and special interests." The endorsement of La Follette and Wheeler was qualified: "Co-operation hereby urged is not a pledge of identification with an independent party movement or a third party, nor can it be construed as support for such a party. . . . We do not accept government as the solution of the problems of life. Major problems of life and labor must be dealt with by voluntary groups and organizations of which trade unions are an essential and integral part."[7]

The organized labor movement was far from unanimous in its support of the Progressives, and many of those who did support them did so with somewhat less than complete enthusiasm. Some union officials gave their endorsement to the traditional parties. Among the Progressives, writes the historian of that movement,

Labor's interest in the La Follette candidacy seems to have been in proportion to La Follette's chances of winning. Conditioned to a campaign strategy by which success was measured by the immediate standard of victory or defeat at the polls, the labor leaders began to fear, before the campaign was completed, that their bargaining power within the old parties would be seriously impaired.

The funds which labor organizations promised failed to materialize, the organizations they planned were never completed, and before the election scores of labor leaders abandoned the ship and switched their endorsement.[8]

However, Gompers' position in the campaign can not be equated with the attitude taken by those who were merely serving their own political and personal interests. It is true that Gompers had serious reservations concerning La Follette's program. In particular, his foreign policy was almost the exact opposite of La Follette's; so was his attitude on antitrust legislation; and he did not agree with his views on government ownership of the railroads and water power. But during the campaign Gompers kept silent on their differences, except for a brief mention of them in the Executive Council's first announcement of support for La Follette. He even stated that La Follette's position during the war was based on honest conviction and that he was ready to forget their differences of opinion at that time; as for the future, he would rather trust America's international relations to La Follette than to either of the other candidates. He disavowed some of the fears he had expressed almost two years before: "Labor is satisfied that it is the purpose of the La Follette platform and of Senator La Follette himself, to bring about that relief [from corporate autocracy] and to do so without plunging the government into a program calculated to lead in the direction of government bureaucracy and state socialism."[9]

Gompers did not campaign for La Follette, but he was still very sick and under a closely supervised regimen of rest. "As the campaign went on," wrote a historian of the Progressive movement,[10] "Gompers did nothing while large unions of the A.F. of L. actually repudiated La Follette or privately knifed his candidacy as part of deals with old-party organizations." It might be asked, What could Gompers do? He had no power to "deliver the labor vote," to compel anyone to support La Follette, or to discipline those who repudiated him. He could only use the influence of persuasion, which he did in all his communications to the labor movement. And when the executive committee of the New York central labor body switched from

La Follette to Davis, Gompers publicly repudiated its action and stated that the original declaration of the organization still stood as the expressed will of the organized workers of New York. If any blame for labor's equivocal and divided stand in the election is to be placed on Gompers' shoulders, it might be ascribed, not to his conduct during the campaign itself, but to his lifelong opposition to the formation of a labor party, which might have been more successful in rallying labor's united support than the nonpartisan policy which left each locality free to determine its own policies and actions.

Lucy Robins related an episode that may fittingly be the last word on the subject. When Gompers was in New York in late September or early October, she went to his hotel and urged him to take a strong stand to spike the rumors that his support for La Follette was halfhearted. He demurred at first, arguing that the Progressives could receive only a small vote and that labor would lose prestige by being too closely identified with it. She replied that that was probably true, but that it was of the greatest importance to him personally to show beyond any question that he was with the Progressives. Otherwise their defeat would be blamed on him, and he would go down in history as a reactionary. "All right," he finally agreed, "I'll play the reckless game, but I know we're going to lose." Shortly after this conversation, La Follette came to New York and told reporters that he planned to visit his sick friend, Sam Gompers. Weak as he was, Gompers decided to go and meet La Follette to "show everyone that I support him." Arrangements were made for the meeting, and in spite of the terrible heat Gompers went over to the Waldorf-Astoria. La Follette rushed up to him, grasped his hand, and exclaimed, "This is the man I wish to serve." And Gompers replied: "I have come to salute President La Follette."[11]

On November 9, Gompers left Washington, accompanied by his nurse, Secretary Morrison, and a party of A.F. of L. employees, to attend the Federation convention in El Paso, Texas. He arrived on the twelfth, weary from the long and trying trip. On the insistence of his nurse, he remained in his hotel during the five days preceding the opening of the convention, holding conferences and meetings and greeting delegates there.

Gompers knew that this would be his last convention, and so did everyone else. He drew on all the resources of his energy, his will, and his sense of drama to make his last days effective and significant, to fill them with meaning and purpose, and to solidify the "Gompers tradition" for posterity. He presided over every session of the convention, although one morning he was physically unable to get to the hall. Vice-presidents Duncan and Frey decided to recess that session rather than hold it without him, but the next day he "gave them hell" for taking that responsibility without consulting him. The whole convention was a personal tribute to his leadership, reflecting the harmony achieved by the defeat and isolation of the left wing and the drawing together of the conservatives, progressives, and socialists. The turbulent era beginning with the war had come to an end, and there was little division of opinion in the A.F. of L. over basic issues. What differences there were were fought out behind closed doors; all that was seen on the floor was "peace and ready agreement; a deliberate softness of tread, a deliberate avoidance of angry controversy. Quiet ruled the convention—a self denial, a reverence and awe."[12]

When the convention opened, there were on the platform, in addition to the Executive Council, fraternal delegates from Great Britain, Canada, Mexico, Germany, and Santo Domingo. The delegates were welcomed by the mayor of El Paso, and by Major General Howze, representing the United States Army. Gompers, for the first time in his life, had prepared a response, which he asked William Green to read for him. It was the message which he wanted to leave with the labor movement as his heritage. After speaking of the early efforts to form a national labor organization, he stated that the A.F. of L. was "an organization that had no power and no authority except of a voluntary character. It was a voluntary coming together of unions with common needs and common aims. That feeling of mutuality has been a stronger bond of union than could be welded by any autocratic authority. Guided by voluntary principles our Federation has grown from a weakling into the strongest, best organized labor movement of all the world. . . .

"Men and women of our American trade union movement, I feel that I have earned the right to talk plainly with you. As the only delegate to that first Pittsburgh convention [in 1881] who has stayed with the problems of our movement through to the present hour, as one who with clean hands and with singleness of purpose has tried to serve the labor movement honorably and in a spirit of consecration to the cause of human liberty—the principles of voluntarism. No lasting gain has ever come from compulsion. If we seek to force, we but tear apart that which, united, is invincible. There is no way whereby our labor movement may be assured sustained progress in determining its policies and its plans other than sincere democratic deliberation until a unanimous decision is reached. This may seem a cumbrous, slow method to the impatient, but the impatient are more concerned for immediate triumph than the education of constructive development. . . .

"Events of recent months made me keenly aware that the time is not far distant when I must lay down my trust for others to carry forward."

As Green read these words, all eyes turned to Gompers sitting behind the rostrum, white, weak, shrunk to a shadow of his former self, obviously shaken. A tremor went through the delegates that put them in a mood for further homage and obeisance. Green continued:

"When one comes to close grips with the eternal things, there comes a new sense of relative values and the less worthy things lose significance. As I review the events of my sixty years of contact with the labor movement and as I survey the problems of today and study the opportunities of the future, I want to say to you, men and women of the American labor movement, do not reject the cornerstone upon which labor's structure has been builded—but base your all upon voluntary principles and illumine your every problem by consecrated devotion to that highest of all purposes—human well being in the fullest, widest, deepest sense.

". . . . As we move upwards to higher levels, a wider vision of service and response will unfold itself. Let us keep the faith. There is no other way."[13]

On the second day of the convention, 1,000 delegates attending the convention of the Mexican Federation of Labor across the river in Juarez marched into the hall as the El Paso municipal band played the national anthems of the two countries. The Mexican unionists came in organized batallions, dressed in their native costumes, some of them fresh from the fields with threadbare clothing. They were led by an army band and carried the flags of the United States, Mexico, and the Mexican Federation of Labor as they sang their revolutionary battle hymns. The American delegates applauded and shouted; some stood on tables and chairs, as boisterous joy and fellowship filled the hall. When quiet was restored, absolute silence filled the hall. Gompers greeted the Mexican delegates, and responses were made by the president and secretary of the Mexican Federation. Juan Rico, the president, declared that the Mexican labor movement had achieved its present strength through the co-operation, experience, and advice of Gompers and the A.F. of L. On Gompers' request, all the foreign fraternal delegates clasped their hands together "in peace and determination to maintain that peace." Again there was a long and enthusiastic demonstration by the delegates.

In the afternoon, the United States delegates returned the visit to Juarez. They were met on the International Bridge, where Rico and Gompers exchanged greetings, pledging eternal comradeship. The delegates were led to the convention hall by a detail of Mexican mounted police, the army band, and a band of boy musicians. The flags of both republics were carried in the middle of the line, and the people of Juarez, including the children from school, greeted them as they passed. Rico introduced Gompers, again praising him for his many services to the Mexican labor movement and the Mexican Republic. Gompers was cheered to the rafters in a standing ovation as he responded. The day ended in feasting and fraternization in Juarez.

On the seventh day of the convention, Morris Sigman of the International Ladies Garment Workers Union asked for the floor on a personal privilege. He announced that his union was celebrating its twenty-fifth anniversary and told of the progress of the organization and the repeated assistance and inspiration given by Gompers. While he talked, two delegates, behind the chair in which Gompers was sitting, unveiled a marble bust of Gompers. The delegates rose to their feet applauding. Gompers, not knowing what it was about, began looking around him. He rose slowly to discover the source of the excitement, then collapsed into his chair, tears rolling down his cheeks. He began to speak hesitantly, finding words with difficulty to express his emotions. As he regained his composure, he continued: "Somehow or other opportunities have been given me which have been given to few men of my time. Whatever I am, whatever I have tried to do, I owe to you, my fellow trade unionists, I owe to the great rank and file of our movement, the men and women who are yearning for a better life and who, many of them, did not know how to accomplish it. . . . I want to live for one thing alone—to leave a better labor movement in America and in the world than I found in it when I entered, as a boy, the field of industrial and humane struggle for the right." Tears fell from the eyes of many strong men who knew that Gompers' desire to live, strong as it was, was succumbing to a greater power.[14]

After the close of the convention, Gompers and the 350 delegates went to Mexico City for the inauguration of General Calles, the first labor President on the North American continent, in whose election Gompers had played an important part. Gompers was examined by a physician before leaving El Paso and was warned not to take the trip, as his heart would not be able to stand it. But he didn't care; in his last days he would play out the drama. Two special trains provided by the Mexican government and the Mexican Federation of Labor came for the delegates. Soldiers rode in iron coal cars, their rifles protruding through holes punched in the sides—an attempt had recently been made to assassinate Morones, and it was feared that counter-revolutionary agents might attack this concentration of labor leaders of two countries.

En route to Mexico City, Gompers was met at Aguascalientes by the governor of the state, representatives of the labor movement, and the press. The trip was a difficult one for Gompers due to the rising altitude and the dust. In the morning he complained that his throat felt dry and parched. The train reached Mexico City at two o'clock Sunday morning, November 30. The delegates remained on the train until ten, when they were received by the officers of the Mexican Federation of Labor and escorted to their hotel.

At 11:00 they were taken to the new stadium, bedecked with flags and banners and filled with 50,000 people, mostly workers and sandaled or barefooted peasants. Gompers was escorted by two friends, his weak, halting steps slowly climbing the stairs to the special platform for the diplomatic and official guests. As he was recognized, he was cheered by the crowd. A few minutes later Secretary of Labor Morones came in and embraced Gompers. The air was filled with red, blue, and green confetti, balloons were released from all parts of the stadium, and airplanes circled overhead, gleaming in the sunlight. In a brief ceremony President Calles took the oath of office, and hundreds of doves were released to inaugurate an era of peace. Everyone was on his feet, singing, cheering, and shouting; bands played, and above all the noise was heard the salute of cannons.

In the evening, Gompers had retired to conserve his strength for the next day. But at 8:00 a Mexican general arrived to bring him to the palace where a diplomatic reception was being held. His doctor tried to stop him, but he arose and went. When he entered the reception hall, President Calles and former president Obregon left the groups with which they were talking and came over to greet him. They escorted him to the Throne Chair and seated themselves on either side. When they went out on the balcony to greet the cheering crowds outside, Gompers was again between the two, and in a dramatic gesture he extended one hand to each, he himself representing the force that had created the constitutional bridge between the two administrations.

The following day Gompers gave himself over to rest. On Tuesday morning he attended a reception given to the A.F. of L. delegates by Calles in the National Palace. At noon they were taken to the Floating Gardens for a luncheon attended by Calles, Obregon, and Morones. After lunch Gompers took a boat ride. In the evening he addressed the University Club. Before he left the Palace a group of barefooted peons approached him, fell on their knees, and embraced him, blessing him for what he had done for them and their country.[15]

At 4:30 p.m. on December 3, President Gompers called to order the fourth congress of the Pan-American Federation of Labor in the amphitheater of the National Preparatory School in Mexico City. He presented, on behalf of the executive committee, a comprehensive report covering the activities of the Federation during the four years since the previous congress.

He reviewed the efforts of the A.F. of L. to secure American recognition of the Obregon government and the support of the Pan-American Federation to his government against the revolt of de la Huerta. The remainder of the report dealt with Santo Domingo and Nicaragua, both still struggling for freedom from American controls.[16]

The report of the executive committee was unanimously approved and its officers were re-elected by acclamation. But Gompers was not present to receive the honor. On December 7 he remained in bed during the day. In the evening he attended the opera with his nurse and Miss Thorne. He returned to the hotel after the performance, and did not leave again until he was taken out on a stretcher three days later. President Calles, Secretary Morones, and a number of other government and labor officials came to the station to say farewell. The trip to San Antonio was a nightmare for him, although the descent to lower altitudes provided temporary relief. He was taken to the St. Anthony Hotel, where two physicians were called in for consultation with his doctor. At 2:00 in the morning on December 13, Gompers said, "Nurse, this is the end. God bless our American institutions. May they grow better day by day." Those were his last words. Twice Vice-President Duncan gave him the Masonic grip, and Gompers responded feebly. At 4:00 he gave the grip for the third time. There was no response.[17]

The casket was placed on a flag-draped military caisson furnished by the War Department and drawn to a black-draped funeral train filled with flowers sent by friends and admirers. Two labor men and a detail of soldiers stood beside the casket as a guard of honor as the train sped eastward. At every station where it was possible, the train stopped to allow the gathered crowds to pass through and pay their last tribute. Six governors, many municipal officials, and thousands of men, women, and children came in the groups along the way. Labor officials joined the train to accompany it to Washington. In the Union Station in the Capital, the President's Room was opened to him. Accompanied by a military escort and by his friends and associates in the labor movement, Gompers was taken to American Federation of Labor headquarters and his casket placed in a room banked with flowers, the American flag which he had taken with him to the annual conventions of the Federation, and the bust presented to him at El Paso. Throughout the day, crowds of people came through labor's headquarters to look once more at the Chief. At night the casket was placed on the funeral train and started on the last trip to New York. On December 17 it was taken by another detail of soldiers to the Elks' Lodge assembly room, and during the day thousands more passed through to offer final tribute.

The following morning a simple funeral was conducted by Rabbi Stephen Wise. Vice-President James Duncan spoke briefly for the A.F. of L., and the service was concluded by the Elks rite. The hall was crowded to overflowing by friends, including the mayor of New York City and Governor Al Smith. At 11:00 the funeral cortege started for Sleepy Hollow at Tarrytown. Gompers could not be buried in the Jewish cemetery where his parents, his first wife, and two of his children were buried, because of his marriage to a Gentile woman. Services at the cemetery were conducted by the Masonic lodge. At the hour of the funeral, the United States Senate paused in its regular business while a number of Senators made eulogies of Gompers' life and labor. The government of Mexico draped the public buildings in mourning, held memorial services and ceased all business for two hours. Observance was also shown in Cuba and the Philippines. In many cities throughout the United States there was a cessation of work so that the workers could pay tribute to their leader. Before the casket was lowered into the grave, James Duncan delivered a message which Gompers had entrusted to him:

"Say to the organized workers of America that as I have kept the faith I expect that they will keep the faith. They must carry on. Say to them that a union man carrying a card is not a good citizen unless he upholds the institutions of our country and a poor citizen of our country if he upholds the institutions of our country and forgets the obligations of his trade association."[18]

NOTES

ABBREVIATIONS USED

AF   *American Federationist,* New York, Indianapolis, and Washington, 1894-1924.

AFL, . . . Conv. American Federation of Labor, *Proceedings of the . . . Annual Convention,* 1881-1924.

CIU   Cigarmakers International Union.

CMOJ   *Cigar Maker's Official Journal,* 1875-1924.

EC   Executive Council, American Federation of Labor.

Life   Samuel Gompers, *Seventy Years of Life and Labor,* N.Y., 1925; 2 vols.

SG   Samuel Gompers.

US, ICCL United States Industrial Commission on the relations and conditions of Capital and Labor, *Report,* Washington, 1901-1902.

US, CIR   United States Commission on Industrial Relations, *Final Report and Testimony,* Washington, 1916. 64C, 1S, Document No. 415.

Letters from Gompers: Unless otherwise indicated, from the Gompers Letterbooks, AFL archives, Washington, D.C. Volume indicated by date.

Letters to Gompers: Unless otherwise indicated, from Incoming Correspondence, AFL archives, Washington, D.C. Volume indicated by box number.

CHAPTER ONE

1. Walter Besant, *East London,* New York, 1901, 11-16; James Grant, *The Great Metropolis,* New York, 1837, I, 293-337; Charles Knight, ed., *London,* London, 1844, II, 386-396; Rowland Hill Harvey, *Samuel Gompers,* Stanford, Calif., 1935, 3ff.

2. H. Lang, "A Few Hours with Samuel Gompers," *Forward* (New York), June 1, 1919.

3. *Life,* I, 1-24.

4. Matthew H. Smith, *Sunshine and Shadow in New York,* Hartford, 1869, 204-206, 365-366; James D. McCabe, *New York by Sunlight and Gaslight,* Philadelphia, 1883; Edward Crapsey, "The Nether Side of New York," *The*

Galaxy, XII, Aug. 1871, 170-178; *Life,* I, 494-495; testimony of SG, in *Report of the Committee of the Senate upon the Relations Between Labor and Capital,* Washington, 1885, I, 273.

5. *Life,* I, 24-41; Florence Thorne to Bernard Mandel, interview, July 7, 1953; Florence Gompers MacKay to Bernard Mandel, Sep. 1, 1953.

6. Felix Adler, *Creed and Deed,* New York, 1877, 1-3, 37-103.

7. *Life,* I, 433; SG to Fred M. Kirby, July 7, 1921; Florence Gompers MacKay to Bernard Mandel, July 5, 1953; John Frey to Bernard Mandel, June 22, 1953.

8. Henry Frank to SG, Jan. 20,

1892; "A Proposed Platform for a Society of Radical Religion and Social Reform," pamphlet in AFL archives, Box 56.

9. SG to William D. Mahon, June 23, 1896; SG, speech in Portland, Oregon, quoted in Portland *Labor Press,* Aug. 7, 1902.

10. SG, "Trade Unions: Their Achievements, Methods, and Aims," paper read before the American Association of Social Science, Sep. 1891, in *Journal of Social Science,* XXVIII, Oct. 1891, 41; SG, debate at meeting of the Presbyterian Ministers' Association, Washington, D.C., in AF, IX, Aug. 1902, 435-436; SG to Thomas I. Kidd, July 26, 1904; SG to Fred M. Kirby, July 27, 1921; Florence Gompers MacKay to Bernard Mandel, July 5, 1953.

11. SG to Rev. H. A. Davis, Aug. 17, 1892; SG to Rev. H. Francis Perry, July 14, 1896; SG to W. H. Whitaker, Feb. 26, 1897.

12. SG to the Evangelical Publishing Co., May 13 and 21, 1890, quoted in Cleveland *Citizen,* Apr. 10, 1891; see also, SG, quoted in Toronto *Telegram,* Nov. 20, 1909; SG to Rev. Henry Stauffer, Apr. 19, 1894; SG to Rev. H. Francis Perry, July 14, 1896.

13. Joseph R. Buchanan, *The Story of a Labor Agitator,* New York, 1903, 133; P.J. Maas to SG, Feb. 21, 1894; Terence V. Powderly, *The Path I Trod,* New York, 1940, 60.

14. SG to David Lubin, Mar. 10, 1894.

15. *Life,* I, 33-67, for this and following information.

16. Philip S. Foner, *History of the Labor Movement in the United States,* New York, 1947, I, 439-445.

17. *Life,* I, 68-75, 90-98, 185 for this and following information.

18. John R. Commons and others, *History of Labour in the United States,* New York, 1918-1935, II, 203-234.

19. *Life,* I, 75, 101-102, 210-212.

20. SG to George Hurst, Jan. 22, 1876, in CMOJ, I, 1st Supplement, Feb. 1876, 4.

21. *Life,* I, 87-88; CMOJ, I, passim.

CHAPTER TWO

1. George E. McNeill, ed., *The Labor Movement,* Boston, 1887, 585-595; Norman J. Ware, *The Labor Movement in the United States, 1860-1895,* New York, 1929, 259-261; New York *Tribune,* July 10, 1877; *Life,* I, 106-108.

2. New York *Tribune,* Feb. 17, 1877; 1st *Annual Report,* of the Ohio Bureau of Labor Statistics, quoted in CMOJ, III, June 1878, 2; testimony of Adolph Strasser before the Hewitt Committee of the House of Representatives, New York, Aug. 5, 1878, quoted in CMOJ, III, Oct. 1878, 1-2.

3. McNeill, *op. cit.,* 585-595; Commons, *op. cit.,* II, 71-74.

4. CMOJ, I, Feb. 1876.

5. *Life,* I, 110-115. The original charter of Local 144 is in the Gompers Memorial Room, AFL, Washington, D.C.

6. CMOJ, I, Jan. 1876, 3.

7. CMOJ, I, Nov. 1875, 2-3; Jan. 1876, 3; *Life,* I, 116-118.

8. SG to George Hurst, Dec. 21, 1875, in CMOJ, I, Jan. 1876, 4; *Life,* I, 136; CMOJ, I, Feb. 1876, 2; Apr. 1876, 1-2; July 1876, 1.

9. *Life,* I, 139-142.

10. CMOJ, III, Oct. 1877, 1; *Life,* I, 142-143; New York *Daily Tribune,* Oct. 15, 1877.

11. Ware, *op. cit.,* 190.

12. CMOJ, III, Oct. 1877, 1.

13. Quoted in CMOJ, III, Nov. 1877, 1.

14. CMOJ, III, Oct. 1877, 2; Feb.

1878, 4.

15. CMOJ, III, Nov. 1877, 3-4; Jan. 1878, 2, 4.

16. SG to the editor, New York *Sun,* Apr. 23, 1878, in CMOJ, III, May 1878, 3; *Life,* I, 149-154.

17. CMOJ, III, Nov. 1877, 1-2; Jan. 1878, 4; *Life,* I, 149-154.

18. Quoted in CMOJ, III, Feb. 1878, 1.

19. New York *Herald,* Jan. 24, 1878; Strasser, "Practical Results," CMOJ, III, July 1878, 1; Strasser, report to Convention, CIU, 1879, in CMOJ, V, Sep. 1879, 2.

20. Alexander Schlesinger, "Samuel Gompers," *American Labor World,* Mar. 1925, 3.

21. *Life,* I, 155-163, 186, 208-209.

22. SG to Thomas I. Kidd, Aug. 3, 1904; SG to P. J. McGuire, Feb. 26, 1889.

23. *Life,* I, 122-123.

24. New York *Tribune,* Nov. 5, 1878.

25. CMOJ, IV, May 1879, 2.

26. *Life,* I, 187; CMOJ, VII, May 1882, 1.

27. Testimony of SG, in *Report of the Committee of the Senate upon the Relations Between Labor and Capital,* I, 271-276; *New Yorker Volkszeitung,* Oct. 31, 1881; *Life,* I, 188.

28. Theodore Roosevelt, *Theodore Roosevelt, An Autobiography,* New York, 1920, 78-80; *Life,* I, 192-193.

29. New York *Tribune,* Dec. 7, 1883.

30. New York *Tribune,* Oct. 9, 1884; *In re Jacobs; Reports of Cases,* Court of Appeals, State of New York, 98 Sickels 110 (1885).

31. *Life,* I, 197.

32. CMOJ, VII, Feb. 1882, 4; Apr. 1882, 3-5.

33. Cigarmakers Progressive Union, "Declaration of Principles," *Progress,* I, Aug. 1882, 1; "Lobbyism," *ibid.,* Sep. 20, 1882; *ibid.,* May 1, May 29, and June 23, 1883.

34. *Life,* I, 191; New York *Herald,* Oct. 9, 1884.

35. CMOJ, III, June 1878, 3; VII, Dec. 1881, 6; Apr. 1882, 3.

36. Proceedings of Convention, CIU, 1883, in CMOJ, VIII, Sep. 1883; *Life,* I, 203.

37. For this and following data: CMOJ, VII, Apr. 1882, 5; VII, June 1882, 4; VII, May 1882, 1; Proceedings of Convention, CIU, 1883, *op. cit.;* CMOJ, VII, June 1882, 4-5; July 1882, 10; Strasser, report to Convention, CIU, 1883, *op.cit.;* CMOJ, VIII, Sept. 1883; Philip Taft, *The A.F. of L. in the Time of Gompers,* New York, 1957, 26-27.

38. *Fourth Annual Report* of the Bureau of Statistics of Labor of the State of New York for the Year 1886, Albany, 1887, 523-529; CMOJ, VII, Aug. 1882, 1.

39. See Robert F. Hoxie, *Trade Unionism in the United States,* New York, 1917, 186.

40. SG, interview, in *Iowa State Register* (Des Moines), May 3, 1899; SG, report to AFL, 13th Conv., 1893, 12; CMOJ, XIII, Sep. 1888, 7-8.

41. For this and following data: CMOJ, III, Oct. 1877, 3-4; CMOJ, VI, Oct. 1880, 5-7; Dec. 1880, 1; VII, Sep. 1881, 5; XIII, July 1888, 7-8; XIV, Nov. 1888, 11; XV, Oct. 1889, 9; Dec. 1889, 11; Proceedings of Convention, CIU, 1889, 17; CMOJ, IV, Apr. 1879, 2; May 1879, 1; Proceedings of Convention, CIU, 1885, in CMOJ, XI, Oct. 1885; V, Oct. 1879, 2-3.

42. SG, address to convention of United Textile Workers, Washington, D.C., Nov. 18, 1901, in AF, VIII, Dec. 1901, 546.

43. CMOJ, I, Sep. 1876, 1; VII, Nov. 1881, 5; SG to the editor, CMOJ, I, Feb. 1877, 4; *Life,* I, 144.

44. Proceedings of Convention, CIU, 1912, in CMOJ, XXXVI, Oct. 1912, 51, 99.

CHAPTER THREE

1. *Life*, I, 126-128.

2. R. B. Donaughey, quoted by "Holland," in the Schuylerville (New York) *Standard*, Jan. 12, 1911.

3. Compare this with the declaration by the IWA in 1874 that "the economic emancipation of workingmen" was the "great end to which the political movement ought to be subordinated as a means." Howard H. Quint, *The Forging of American Socialism*, Columbia, S. C., 1953, 11-12.

4. *Life*, I, 210-212. The letter was dated Sep. 17, 1875.

5. CMOJ, III, June 1878, 1; Strasser, report to Convention, CIU, 1879, *op. cit.;* George A. Tracy, *History of the Typographical Union*, Indianapolis, 1913, 323-325.

6. P. J. McGuire, "The American Federation of Labor," in William Trant, *Trade Unionism*, Washington, 1903, 39; Lyman A. Brant, report to convention of ITU, 1882, in Tracy, *op. cit.*, 337-339.

7. Mark C. Crawford, "Large Oaks From Little Acorns Grow," AF, XXVII, Feb. 1920, 140-149.

8. CMOJ, VII, Oct. 1881, 3f.

9. AFL, 1st Conv., 1881, 10-11; SG to Alfred P. James, Oct. 19, 1922; Crawford, *op. cit.*; Alfred P. James, *The First Convention of the American Federation of Labor*, n.p., 1924 (reprint from the *Western Pennsylvania Historical Magazine*), 16.

10. AFL, 1st Conv., 1881, 4, 15-16; James, *op. cit.*, 44-45.

11. James, *op. cit.*, 6-7. It is not certain that this interview was given by Gompers, but James thought it was, and when asked about it forty years later, Gompers affirmed it. Gompers attested to the fact that he was greatly influenced by the example of the British Trade Union Congress. *Life*, I, 223-224.

12. AFL, 1st Conv., 1881, 3-5, 22-24.

13. Minutes, Legislative Committee of FOTLU, Feb. 19-20, 1881, in AFL archives; *Life*, I, 231.

14. SG, Report on the National Labor Congress, in CMOJ, VII, Dec. 1881, 4-5.

15. AFL, 2nd Conv., 1882, 9-19; P. J. McGuire, "Communicated Suggestion" to FOTLU, in AFL, "History of Trade Unions" file; Hugh McGregor, "American Labor Federation—Its Origins and Progress," AF, VII, June 1900, 156-157.

16. AFL, 3rd Conv., 1883, 15; CMOJ, VIII, Sep. 1883, Supplement.

17. AFL, 4th Conv., 1884, 7f.; 5th Conv., 1885, 17; 6th Conv., 1886, 7.

18. Henry David, *The History of the Haymarket Affair*, New York, 1936, 159-162.

19. AFL, 2nd Conv., 1882, 14-15; Irwin Nack, "The Cigar Makers During the Great Upheaval," unpub. M.A. thesis, Columbia University, 1949, 122-124.

20. AFL, 3rd Conv., 1883, 14; 4th Conv., 1884, 11, 14.

21. AFL, 5th Conv., 1885, 9-14; Minutes, Legislative Committee, Dec. 11, 1885; Ware, *op. cit.*, 252-254.

22. CMOJ, LXIII, July 1939, 9; Strasser, report to Convention, CIU, 1883, *op. cit.;* Proceedings of Convention, CIU, 1885, in CMOJ, XI, Oct. 1885.

23. David, *op. cit.*, 176, 539; Commons, *op. cit.*, II, 384-385.

24. Powderly, *Thirty Years of Labor*, Columbus, 1890, 481-499; Powderly, *The Path I Trod, op. cit.*, 143-160; *Proceedings*, 10th Session of the General Assembly, KL, 1886, 39-40. For variant versions of the operations of the Knights, see Harvey, *op. cit.*, 27ff., and Foner, *op. cit.*, II, 157ff.

25. Ware, *op. cit.*, 254; SG to Florence Kelly Wischnewetzky, Oct. 17, 1888.

26. New York *Herald*, May 2, 1886;

New York *Tribune*, May 2, 1886.
27. David, *op. cit.*, 187-204; Harry Barnard, *Eagle Forgotten*, Indianapolis, 1938, 103-104.
28. David, *op. cit.*, 210-217; SG, testimony before US, ICCL, VII, 623.
29. Barnard, *op. cit.*, 216-235; David, *op. cit.*, 226f.

30. David, *op. cit.*, 408-419.
31. SG to John R. Oglesby, Nov. 7, 1887.
32. Chicago *Tribune*, Nov. 11. 1887; *Life*, II, 178-181.
33. SG to John P. Altgeld, June 27, 1893.

CHAPTER FOUR

1. Powderly, *Thirty Years of Labor*, *op. cit.*, 243-245; Powderly, *The Path I Trod*, *op. cit.*, 47n.; Commons, *op. cit.*, II, 332f; see also Taft, *op. cit.*, 85ff.
2. SG to Antoni Rozanski, June 25, 1889; SG to ?, Feb. ?, 1890; SG to Henry F. Chamberlain, Sept. 8, 1892.
3. SG, "What Does Labor Want?" Paper read before the International Labor Congress, Chicago, Sep. 1893, in *Official Book of the AFL*, 1893; SG, address to Firemen's Convention, Washington, Aug. 1904, in AF, XI, Nov. 1904, 991; address to Omaha unionists, in AF, XII, July 1905, 451-452.
4. For this reference and following, SG, "What Does Labor Want?" *op. cit.*; SG, speech before National Civic Federation, Apr. 25, 1905, in *Samuel Gompers' Credo*, N.Y., 1950, 26; "Labor's Sheet Anchor, Trade Unionism," AF, XX, Dec. 1913, 1032-1033.
5. SG, report to AFL, 30th Conv., 1910, 16-17; ed. in AF, XVIII, July 1911, 532-533; SG to J. H. McWilliams, May 25, 1896; SG to P. J. McGuire, Sept. 14, 1897; SG to A. S. Leitch, Jan. 25, 1892.
6. SG to George W. Perkins, Mar. 22, 1894; report to AFL, 19th Conv., 1889, 15; report to 30th Conv., 1910, 17; SG, "Anent Class Consciousness," AF, IV, Aug. 1897, 116; testimony of SG, in *Report of the Committee of the Senate upon the Relations Between Labor and Capital, op. cit.*, I, 288-289; New York *Leader*, July 25, 1887, quoted in Commons, *op. cit.*, II, 458; SG to A. S. Leitch, Jan. 25, 1892; SG to the Delegates to the

International Labor Congress, Aug. 4, 1891.
7. Wilfred E. Binkley, *American Political Parties*, New York, 1943, 317.
8. SG, testimony before U.S. Strike Commission on the Chicago Strike of June-July, 1894, *Report*, 200.
9. SG, report to AFL, 16th Conv., 1896, 19.
10. SG, report to AFL, 10th Conv., 1890, 13; report to 16th Conv., 1896, 19; SG to John L. Kirchner, Feb. 28, 1889; US, ICCL, VII, 645.
11. SG, "The Eight-Hour Day," AF, IV, June 1897, 70-71.
12. SG to Judge Peter J. Grosscup, Aug. 14, 1894; "Specimens of Journalistic Unfairness," AF, XII, Jan. 1905, 20-22; SG, "The Eight-Hour Work Day," AF, IV, May 1897, 47; "Anent Class-Consciousness," AF, IV, Aug. 1897, 115; interview in Topeka *Journal*, June 12, 1899.
13. SG, report to AFL, 18th Conv., 1898, 12; "Anent Class-Consciousness," *op. cit.*, 116; ed. in AF, VI, Apr. 1900, quoted in SG, *Labor and the Common Welfare*, N.Y., 1919, 30-31.
14. Powderly, *The Path I Trod*, *op. cit.*, 115; Charles A. Madison, *American Labor Leaders*, New York, 1950, 54-57; Commons, *op. cit.*, II, 340-352.
15. SG, testimony before U.S. Strike Commission, *op. cit.*, 195.
16. SG, testimony before US, ICCL, VII, 608; SG to Ambrose McNamara, Apr. 25, 1900; SG to Horace M. Eaton, Aug. 1, 1899; SG to Edward Epperson,

June 22, 1897; ed. in AF, XVIII, Feb. 1911, 121-122.

17. *Proceedings,* 10th Session of the General Assembly, KL, 1886, 265-271; Commons, *op. cit.,* II, 427-429; William C. Birdsall, "The Problem of Structure in the Knights of Labor," *Industrial and Labor Relations Review,* VI, July 1953, 532-546; Powderly, *Thirty Years of Labor, op. cit.,* 640; Ware, *op. cit.,* 155-164, 171f.

18. Ware, *op. cit.,* 66-70.

19. CMOJ, VI, May 1886, 8-9; Commons, *op cit.,* II, 398; Tracy, *op. cit.,* 369-370, 383-387.

20. *Progress,* II, Aug. 24 and Sep. 28, 1883; Ware, *op. cit.,* 265f.; *Progress,* II, July 25, 1884.

21. CMOJ, XI, Nov. 1885, 1, 7-8; Dec. 1885, 7; Jan. 1886, 6.

22. Bureau of Statistics of Labor of the State of New York, *4th Annual Report,* Albany, 1887, 523-539; *Life,* I, 241-253; Ware, *op. cit.,* 265-279; Commons, *op. cit.,* II, 400-401; *Proceedings,* 19th Session of the General Assembly, KL, 1886, 137-138; New York *Tribune,* Aug. 8, 9, 16, 1886.

23. CMOJ, XI, June 1886, 7; CMOJ, XII, Nov. 1886, 6.

24. *Life,* I, 253, 264; AFL, 6th Conv., 1886, 8-10.

25. New York *Tribune,* Jan. 3, 1887.

26. "Twenty-First Annual Convention," unpub. ms. in AFL, "History of Trade Unions" file.

27. Memorandum dictated by George W. Perkins, Jan. 3, 1919, in AFL, "Gompers Biographical" file.

28. "Twenty-First Annual Convention," *op. cit.;* J. M. O'Hanlon, "History of the New York Federation of Labor," unpub. ms. in AFL, "History of Trade Unions" file.

29. *Life,* I, 266-267.

30. *The Union Advocate,* July 1887.

31. SG to Joseph Buchanan, Apr. 4 and 21, 1894; SG to George W. Perkins, Apr. 9, 1894; "Call for a Labor Conference," Mar. 31, 1894. Marden did not attend, but Chris Evans and Frank Foster were added to the AFL delegation.

32. "Official Report of Conference of Labor Representatives, Philadelphia, April 28-29, 1894;" see also AF, I, June 1894, 82-83.

33. AF, I, July 1894, 107-108.

34. SG to Thomas M. Gruelle, June 19, 1894; AFL, 14th Conv., 1894, 57-59; SG, "The Fallacy of It," AF, I, Dec. 1894, 230-231.

35. Powderly to SG, Feb. 18, 1903 (Powderly papers, Catholic University of America).

CHAPTER FIVE

1. *Life,* I, 49, 135-137; Foner, *op cit.,* 475-479; SG to the editor, CMOJ, II, Feb. 1877, 4.

2. Commons, *op. cit.,* II, 240-251; *Life,* II, 75.

3. CMOJ, III, Oct. 1877, 4; Mar. 1878; V, Oct. 1879, 3.

4. For this and following data, Commons, *op. cit.,* II, 446-453; *Life,* I, 311-317.

5. Henry F. Pringle, *Theodore Roosevelt,* New York, 1931, 113-114.

6. AFL, 1st [6th] Conv., 1886, 16.

7. *Life,* I, 317-322; New York *Leader,* July 25, 1887, quoted in Commons, *op. cit.,* II, 458.

8. AFL, 3rd [8th] Conv., 1888, 8-15; SG, report to AFL, 10th Conv., 1890.

9. SG to Harry Glyn, June 25, 1892; SG to George M. Eby, Sep. 24, 1890.

CHAPTER SIX

1. SG to Gabriel Edmonston, Apr. 22, 1887; SG to Dr. Branch Clark, Aug. 6, 1894; SG to William Martin, Dec. 23, 1890.

2. *Life*, I, 271-274, 495; SG, report to AFL, 2nd [7th] Conv., 1887, 11.

3. SG to George N. McNeill, Feb. 15, 1888; SG to P. J. McGuire, Mar. 3, 1887.

4. SG to William Martin, Mar. 22, 1888.

5. *Life*, I, 329-333.

6. SG to Emil Applehagen, Nov. 17, 1888.

7. SG to Daniel McLaughlin, May 23, 1889; SG to Josiah B. Dyer, May 27, 1889.

8. SG to F. S. Whitney, Mar. 6, 1902; testimony before US, CIR, May 21-23, 1914, in AF, XXI, July 1914, 537-539.

9. *Proceedings*, 35th Annual Session, ITU, 1887, 66-67, 112; Tracy, *op. cit.*, 421.

10. AFL, 2nd [7th] Conv., 1887, 22-23; 3rd [8th] Conv., 1888, 9-10, 17, 21; 16th Conv., 1896, 72-73; 18th Conv., 1898, 40-41, 45; 19th Conv., 1899, 10, 136; 21st Conv., 1901, 15, 185-186.

11. AFL, 13th Conv., 1893, 15-16, 66; see also, Taft, *op. cit.*, 185ff.

12. Hermann Schluter, *The Brewing Industry . . . in America*, Cincinnati, 1910, 219-223.

13. SG to J. D. Pierce, Aug. 14, 1899.

14. AFL, 19th Conv., 1899, 126-128; SG to UBW, Aug 4, 1900.

15. Minutes, EC, Apr. 15, 1902, in AF, IX, June 1902, 331-332.

16. AFL, 22nd Conv., 1902, 16-17, 146-147, 208.

17. EC, Report to AFL, 23rd Conv., 1903, 77-79, 218-221; SG to Louis Kemper, Jan. 22, 1904.

18. Minutes, EC, Apr. 1904, in AF, XI, June 1904, 510-511, 521; Louis Kemper to SG, July 6, 1904; SG to John B. Lennon, Oct. 18, 1904

19. SG, address to convention of IBSE, Washington, Aug. 1904, in *Labor and the Common Welfare, op. cit.*, 17-18; address to convention of IBSF, in AFL, "Addresses" file.

20. AFL, 24th Conv., 1904, 217.

21. SG to John B. Lennon, Apr. 29 and May 8, 1907; SG to James Duncan, May 1, 1907, in *Personal Letters*, II, 37-45.

22. AFL, 27th Conv., 1907, 44-45, 275-277; SG to John B. Lennon, Oct. 1, 1907.

23. AFL, 28th Conv., 1908, 71-75, 211-213; 29th Conv., 1909, 300-301; 30th Conv., 1910, 106.

24. *Life*, I, 328, 336; Waldon Fawcett, in the Washington *Sun Star*, Nov. 6, 1908.

25. SG to John F. O'Sullivan, Oct. 12, 1898.

26. *Life*, I, 199.

27. Daniel J. Tobin, "Remembrance of Sam Gompers," *International Teamster*, Jan. 1950, 10-12.

28. SG to P. J. McGuire, May 7, 1896.

29. SG to Joseph A. Bauer, Mar. 9, 1899.

30. E.g., see SG to Charles Foster, June 15, 1891; (?) Hamlin to SG, July 18, 1893; SG to EC, Sep. 27, 1894; SG to Henry W. Blair, Sep. 27, 1894; SG to Henry Wade Rogers, Jan. 18, 1899; SG to John B. Lennon, Dec. 29, 1909.

31. CMOJ, VII, Oct. 1881, 3-11; *Life*, I, 178; AFL, 17th Conv., 1897, 25; 20th Conv., 1900, 127-128.

32. SG to W. D. Mahon, Oct. 3, 1904; *Machinists' Monthly Journal*, XV, July 1903, 546f., and Dec. 1903, 1082; SG to John Mulholland, Oct. 25, 1903; SG to H. F. Sarman, May 15, 1905; AFL, 31st Conv., 1911, 207-208; 32nd Conv., 1912, 162-179, 363-373.

33. CMOJ, XXIX, Mar. 1905, 11-12; Apr. 1905, 6; July 1905, 13; Milwaukee *Journal*, Apr. 7, 1905; SG to Daniel Harris, Apr. 15, 1905; SG to Henry F. Waack, July 5, 1905; SG to Ed Schrumpf, July 14, 1905.

34. SG to Daniel Harris, Feb. 4, 1901,

in *Personal Letters*, II, 181-185; AF, XIX, Nov. 1912, 903-907; *Life*, I, 179-181.

35. 3rd [8th] Conv., 1888, 11; SG to E. Lewis Evans, Aug. 18, 1898; SG to John Mulholland, Oct. 25, 1903.

CHAPTER SEVEN

1. AFL, 3rd [8th] Conv., 1888, 15, 24-30; see also, Taft, *op. cit.*, 142ff.

2. See correspondence of SG from Dec. 1888 to Feb. 1889; SG to George E. McNeill, Mar. 12, 1889; AFL circular, June 26, 1889; SG, report to AFL, 9th Conv., 1889, 14.

3. SG to the Officers and Delegates of the General Assembly, KL, Nov. 9, 1889; Sidney Fine, "The Eight-Hour Day Movement in the United States, 1888-1891," *Mississippi Valley Historical Review*, XL, Dec. 1953, 441-462; Madison, *op. cit.*, 67.

4. AFL, 9th Conv., 1889, 14-15, 32.

5. SG to the Toilers of America, Apr. 28, 1890; SG to August Keufer, May 9, 1890; SG to the editor, *Labor Tribune*, July 27 (?), 1890; SG, quoted in Kansas City *Globe*, Feb. 18, 1891; SG, report to AFL, 10th Conv., 1890, 13.

6. Pat McBryde to Chris Evans, Mar. 27, 1891; J. B. Rae to The Organized Trades and Labor in General, Mar. 31, 1891; Chris Evans to SG, Apr. 1, 1891; EC to the Organized Wage-Workers of America, June 1, 1891; *Life*, I, 306-307.

7. SG to Chris Evans, Apr. 1, 1891.

8. AFL, 15th Conv., 1895, 30, 61-62.

9. AFL, 16th Conv., 1896, 23, 68.

10. AFL, 17th Conv., 1897, 85-86; 18th Conv., 1898, 21, 122; 27th Conv., 1907, 30-31.

11. SG to James McGill, May 3, 1890; SG to August Keufer, May 9, 1890; SG, "May Day," AF, I, May 1894, 51-53.

12. AFL, 2nd [7th] Conv., 1887, 8-12; SG to William Liebknecht, Nov. 22, 1888; AFL, 3rd [8th] Conv., 1888, 8-15.

13. SG to August Keufer, Jan. 10, 1889.

14. AFL, 9th Conv., 1889, 13-17; SG to the Wage-Workers of All Countries, July 2, 1890; AFL, 10th Conv., 1890, 15.

15. For the S.L.P., see Foner, *op. cit.*, 279ff.

16. SG to Ernest Bohm, Nov. 7, 1890; AFL, 10th Conv., 1890, 11-12, 17, 21-26, 38; "An Interesting Discussion at the Tenth Annual Convention of the American Federation of Labor," New York, 1891; David J. Saposs, *Left Wing Unionism*, New York, 1926, 22.

17. SG to Frederick Engels, Jan. 9, 1891; Engels to Hermann Schluter, Dec. 29, 1891, in *Science and Society*, II, Summer 1938, 365-367.

18. SG to P. J. McGuire, Aug. 4, 1891.

19. SG to The Delegates to the International Labor Congress, Aug. 4, 1891.

20. SG to the Delegates to the Trade-Union Congress, Aug. 31, 1891, in SG's clipping book, "International Labor Congress."

CHAPTER EIGHT

1. SG, "Is It to Be Ever Thus?" AF, III, Oct. 1896, 160-161; see also Foner, *op. cit.*, 235ff.

2. SG, "Work, Not Charity," AF, I, Mar. 1894, 11-12.

3. SG and Chris Evans to the Work-

ers of New York, Aug. 11, 1893; SG to Roswell P. Flower, Aug. 24, 1893.

4. *Life*, II, 4-7; *The People*, Feb. 4, 1894.

5. Donald L. McMurray, "The Industrial Armies and the Commonweal," *Mississippi Valley Historical Review*, X, Dec. 1923, 215-222.

6. *Ibid.*, 222-226; *Life*, II, 11; SG, "A Crime Against Freedom," AF, I, June 1894, 76.

7. For this and following data, SG, "What Does Labor Want?" *op. cit.*; SG to August Keufer, Oct. 10, 1893; report to AFL, 13th Conv., 1893, 11-12; SG, "Cause and Effect," AF, I, Apr. 1894, 32; AFL, 16th Conv., 1896, 18-19.

8. E.g., see SG to Fred Swenson, Feb. 27, 1894.

9. Pittsburgh *Post*, Apr. 15, 1891.

10. SG to Samuel Goldwater, June 29, 1892; SG to EC, July 7, 1892; SG to William Weihe, July 11 and 18, 1892; SG to Charles Foster, July 18, 1892; SG to M. Dampf, July 8, 1892. See also, Samuel Yellen, *American Labor Struggles*, New York, 1936, 72ff.

11. Pittsburgh *Leader*, Aug. 14, 1892; SG to EC, June 9, 1893.

12. SG, ed. in AF, I, July 1894, 100; SG to Peter Breen, Mar. 31, 1893.

13. Ray Ginger, *The Bending Cross*, New Brunswick, 1949, 108-112; SG, "Pullman," AF, I, Aug. 1894, 120-121; SG, "The Railway Strike," *ibid.*, 121-122; Yellen, *op. cit.*, 101ff.

14. *Life*, I, 404-406; AF, X, Nov. 1903, 1188.

15. Ginger, *op. cit.*, 83-84, 157-161; Eugene Debs to SG, Oct. 1893, quoted in *Life*, I, 405-406.

16. AFL, 10th Conv., 1890, 20; 11th Conv., 1891, 42; 12th Conv., 1892, 21; *Life*, I, 404; Ray Ginger to Bernard Mandel, Sep. 22, 1952.

17. SG to Eugene Debs, Nov. 20,

1891; Ginger, *op. cit.*, 81; SG to Tom Mann, Sep. 20, 1894.

18. SG to Thomas M. Gruelle, June 19, 1894; SG, "The Railway Strike," *op. cit.*

19. Ginger, *op. cit.*, 114-120.

20. Ray Ginger, "The Pullman Boycott Reconsidered," *Explorations in Entrepreneurial History*, V, May 15, 1953, 225-243; SG, "The Railway Strike of 1894," in John Swinton, *Striking For Life*, Philadelphia, 1894, 299-309.

21. Eugene Debs to SG, June 26, 1894; SG to Debs, June 26, 1894; *Life*, I, 408.

22. Ginger, *The Bending Cross*, *op. cit.*, 128-132; SG, "The Railway Strike," *op. cit.*, 123-124.

23. Ginger, *The Bending Cross*, *op. cit.*, 134-144; SG to Eugene Debs, July 5, 1894; SG, report to AFL, 14th Conv., 1894, 11.

24. SG, testimony before U.S. Strike Commission on the Chicago Strike of June-July, 1894, *Report*, 154-155; SG to Eugene Debs, July 5, 1894.

25. SG, "The Strike and Its Lessons," AF, I, Aug. 1894, 124; SG to M. M. Garland, July 9, 1894; SG to James Linehan, July 19, 1894.

26. AF, I, Aug. 1894, 131-133; Eugene Debs, testimony before U.S. Strike Commission, *op. cit.*, 155.

27. AF, I, Aug. 1894, 133; Debs, testimony before U.S. Strike Commission, *op. cit.*, 146; SG, testimony before *ibid.*, 194; SG to George E. McNeill, July 21, 1894; SG, "The Strike and Its Lessons," *op. cit.*, 124.

28. David Karsner, *Talks With Debs in Terre Haute*, New York, 1922, 60-61; *Life*, I, 414.

29. AF, I, Aug. 1894, 125.

30. "An Appeal For Aid," AF, I, Aug. 1894, 127; SG to Eugene Debs, Aug. 16, 1894.

CHAPTER NINE

1. Henry Demarest Lloyd, *Wealth Against Commonwealth,* New York, 1902, 5; J. Moody, *The Truth About the Trusts,* New York, 1904, 477; Charles A. and Mary R. Beard, *The Rise of American Civilization,* New York, 1942, II, 176; AF, I, June 1894, 69; II, Oct. 1895, 144-145; SG to A. F. Jury, Mar. 28, 1910.

2. SG, "Labor and Antitrust Legislation," Washington, 1914, 3; SG, address at National Wheat Conference, Chicago, June 20, 1923, in AF, XXX, Aug. 1923, 626.

3. SG, ed. in AF, III, Dec. 1896, 217; SG to John F. O'Sullivan, Aug. 30, 1899; "Labor, And Its Attitude Toward Trusts," address before Chicago Conference on Trusts, Oct. 1907, in AF, XIV, Nov. 1907, 880-886; "Attitude of Labor Toward Government Regulation of Industry," *The Annals* of the American Academy of Political and Social Science, XXXII, July 1908, 78-79.

4. SG, report to AFL, 19th Conv., 1899, 15; SG, "Labor, And Its Attitude Toward Trusts," *op. cit.*

5. SG, report to AFL, 19th Conv., 1899, 15; address at conference of National Civic Federation, Jan. 12, 1911, in AF, XVIII, Mar. 1911, 220.

6. SG to Andrew Furuseth, Sep. 18, 1900.

7. SG to John G. Riedel, Dec. 7, 1891; SG to T. Berry, Mar. 12, 1899; see also SG to E.E. Greenawalt, Apr. 11, 1902.

8. Will Herberg, "Jewish Labor Movement in the United States: Early Years to World War I," *Industrial and Labor Relations Review,* V, July 1952, 504-508; SG to George W. Perkins, Apr. 4, 1896, in *Personal Letters,* I, 63; SG to N. F. Brookmeyer, July 3, 1890; SG to W. C. Owen, July 10, 1893; John Frey to Bernard Mandel, June 22, 1953; *Life,*

II, 153.

9. SG to W. L. Rosenburg, May 27, 1896; SG to Matt. Comerford, Jan. 22, 1906; SG to J. W. Wood, Aug. 5, 1903; SG to T. J. Ryan, Aug. 29, 1903; SG to Jere L. Sullivan, June 24, 1904; Taft, *op. cit.,* 302ff.

10. AFL, 3rd Conv., 1883, 17, 19; SG to J. T. Coxgrove, Apr. 10, 1897; SG to D. F. Gahan, June 1, 1893.

11. AFL, 14th Conv., 1894, 25.

12. SG to Frank D. Hamlin, Apr. 31, 1890; SG to Charles W. Murphy, May 16, 1890; SG to Fred J. Carr, Dec. 8, 1891; Foner, *op. cit., passim.*

13. AFL, 10th Conv., 1890, 31-32; 11th Conv., 1891, 12.

14. AFL, 11th Conv., 1891, 40-41; SG to the Convention of the IMU, May 7, 1892; *Monthly Journal* of the IAM, VII, June 1895, 186; John McBride to T. J. Morgan, July 16, 1895.

15. Daniel J. Sullivan to SG, Dec. 7, 1895, in AFL, Box 118; W.E.B. Du Bois, ed., *The Negro Artisan* (Atlanta University Publications, No. 7), Atlanta, 1902, 169-170; SG to Lee Johnson, May 7, 1896.

16. T. J. Morgan to August McCraith, June 3, 1896; W. W. Fenton to SG, Dec. 29, 1896; in AFL, Box 118.

17. SG to John C. Knight, Mar. 6, 1893.

18. SG to H. M. Ives, Nov. 10, 1892; SG to W.H. Luchtenburg, May 9, 1892; SG to Louis F. Klinger, July 18, 1891.

19. Ed J. Donegan to SG, Dec. 5, 1892; SG to Donegan, Dec. 9, 1892; SG to Henry J. Spaeter, Nov. 10, 1893; SG to Julius Friedman, Mar. 31, 1894; SG to David Watkins, July 17, 1893.

20. SG, report to AFL, 3rd [8th] Conv., 1888, 8-15.

21. Lewis L. Lorwin, *The American Federation of Labor,* Washington, 1933, 75.

22. AFL, 13th Conv, 1893, 40, 59-60.

23. AFL, 17th Conv., 1897, 64, 95-96; SG to John Mulholland, Nov. 12, 1900; AFL, 20th Conv., 1900, 19-20, 135.

24. AFL, 19th Conv., 1899, 109-113, 129, 135-136.

CHAPTER TEN

1. John D. Hicks, *The Populist Revolt*, Minneapolis, 1931, 160; Everit Brown and Albert Strauss, *Dictionary of American Politics*, New York, 1907, 522-525; Ray Allen Billington and others, eds., *The Making of American Democracy*, N.Y., 1950, II, 224-227.

2. SG, interview quoted in Cleveland *Citizen*, June 12, 1891; SG to John McBride, Feb. 6, 1893; SG to H. M. Ives, Feb. 23, 1893; SG to O. P. Smith, Feb. 10, 1892; SG to Abe Spring, June 30, 1892.

3. SG, "Organized Labor in the Campaign," *The North American Review*, CLV, July 1892, 91-96.

4. Foner, *op. cit.*, II, 306-309.

5. *Life*, II, 76; AFL, 12th Conv., 1892, 12-13, 43.

6. AFL, 13th Conv., 1893, 12, 37-39, 62-63.

7. SG to Walter MacArthur, Jan. 3, 1894; New York *Herald*, Jan. 7, 1894.

8. SG, editorial in AF, I, Apr. 1894, 31; John M. Snook to SG, May 25, 1893; SG to Snook, May 29, 1893.

9. "The St. Louis Harmony Conference," AF, I, July 1894, 108; Buchanan, *op. cit.*, 435; SG to James Weaver, Sep. 28, 1894.

10. Chester McArthur Destler, "Consummation of a Labor-Populist Alliance in Illinois, 1894," *Mississippi Valley Historical Review*, XXVII, Mar. 1941, 589-602; Destler, *American Radicalism, 1865-1901*, New London, 1946, 175-211.

11. SG, Report to AFL, 14th Conv., 1894, 14; Commons, *op. cit.*, II, 511-513.

12. "A Verbatim Report of the Discussion on the Political Programme, At the Denver Convention of the American Federation of Labor," New York, 1895.

13. SG to Ernest Bohm, Feb. 2, 1895, in *The People*, Feb. 17, 1895.

14. *Life*, I, 361.

15. SG to W. W. De Saville, June 5, 1894; *Life*, I, 510-512.

16. SG to Edward F. McSweeney, Dec. 7, 1894; *Life*, I, 362-365; SG to Charles Reicher, July 1, 1896; New York *Press*, July 21, 1895.

17. *Report of Proceedings, Trades Union Congress*, 1895, 48-49; AFL, 15th Conv., 1895, 47-49.

18. George W. Perkins to SG, Nov. 13, 1895; SG to Perkins, Nov. 16, 1895, in *Personal Letters*, I, 42-44; F. C. Hollister to SG, Nov. 23, 1895.

19. SG to Eva McDonald Valesh, Feb. 28, 1896; SG to Charles F .Reichers, July 14, 1896.

20. SG to W. H. Montgomery, Aug. 20, 1896; SG to F. B. Thurber, July 31, 1896; SG to Ben Tillett, Nov. 4, 1896.

21. AF, III, Aug. 1896, 129-130; *Proceedings,* Convention of the CIU, 1896, 25; see also SG to E. Kurzenknabe, Dec. 5, 1896.

22. Foner, *op. cit.*, II, 337-339.

23. *Life*, II, 76, 88-89; Eric E. Goldman, *Rendezvous with Destiny*, New York, 1952, 65; SG to Mr. Beckley, Sep. 24, 1896, in *Personal Letters*, I, 102.

24. SG to W. J. Webber, Nov. 12, 1896.

CHAPTER ELEVEN

1. AF, VI, June 1899, 84-85.

2. Buffalo *Express*, Jan. 30, 1903; SG to P. J. McGuire, Apr. 16, 1903; SG to Daniel J. Tobin, Jan. 16, 1917.

3. Florence Gompers MacKay to Bernard Mandel, July 5, 1953; Eloise Giles to Mandel, June 24, 1953; Florence Thorne to Mandel, July 7, 1953; John Frey to Mandel, June 22, 1953.

4. SG to Sam Collins, Feb. 4, 1910; Martha Ford to Bernard Mandel, July 7, 1953.

5. Mark Sullivan, "Labor in the New World," *Collier's*, Dec. 21, 1918, 6.

6. Walter Gordon Merritt, *Destination Unknown*, New York, 1951, 10.

7. Washington *Times*, cited in AF, XI, Mar. 1904, 227-228; New York *World*, June 7, 1903, cited in AF, X, July 1903, 579; Benjamin Stolberg, "What Manner of Man was Samuel Gompers?" The *Atlantic Monthly*, March 1925.

8. E. C. Tucker, "Men Who Have Blazed the Way," *Machinists' Monthly Journal*, Dec. 1908, 1082-1083.

9. John Frey, press release in AFL, "Gompers Biographical" file.

10. John Frey to Bernard Mandel, June 22, 1953; Stolberg, *op. cit.*

11. SG to James Brown, Nov. 23, 1899.

12. Memorandum by Rosa Lee Guard, in AFL, SG's personal file; John Frey to Bernard Mandel, June 22, 1953; Guard to A. B. Rawls Reader, June 12, 1908; Guard to Mrs. Ella Rawls Reader, July 16, 1908; Guard to Alton B. Parker, Dec. 24, 1912; in *Personal Letters*, II, 102-103, 113-115, 240-241.

13. SG, report to AFL, 30th Conv., 1910, 46-47; ed. in AF, XXII, Feb. 1915, 113-114.

14. SG, testimony before US, ICCL, VII, 656-657; report to AFL, 17th Conv., 1897, 20; "The Workers and the Eight-Hour Work-day," *op. cit.;*

ed. in AF, XXII, Feb. 1915, 108-114, and May 1915, 353-354.

15. AFL, 19th Conv., 1899, 118-121; *Life*, II, 91-95.

16. Report of J. J. Gardner, Committee on Labor, House of Representatives, Apr. 4, 1898, in AF, V, May 1898, 56-58; *Life*, I, 288-289, 517-518.

17. SG, report to AFL, 5th Conv., 1885; AFL, 14th Conv., 1894, 46; 19th Conv., 1899, 107; 33rd Conv., 1913, 285.

18. SG to Maud Younger, May 17, 1912; AF, XXII, Jan. 1915, 43-46, Mar. 1915, 167-170, 174-176; US, CIR, II, 1499-1502.

19. AFL, 33rd Conv., 1913, 285; US, CIR, II, 1499-1502.

20. AFL, 34th Conv., 1914, 421-443; Commons, *op. cit.*, III, 548-549.

21. SG, ed. in AF, XX, Aug. 1913, 624-627.

22. *Life*, I, 226.

23. SG to Gideon J. Tucker, Aug. 2, 1894.

24. SG to B. Andrus, Apr. 24, 1891.

25. Irene M. Ashby, "Child Life vs. Dividends," AF, IX, May 1902, 215-222.

26. AF, XXI, June 1914, 467.

27. SG, "Industrial Slaughter and the 'Enlightened' Employer," AF, XIV, Aug. 1907, 548-550; address to National Civic Federation, New York, Nov. 22-23, 1909, in AFL, "Addresses" file; report to AFL, 29th Conv., 1909, 27.

28. AFL, 22nd Conv., 1902, 134-135, 140; SG to Thomas Hunt, Mar. 16, 1906.

29. AFL, 27th Conv., 1907, 218-219; 28th Conv., 1908, 99-103, 260; 29th Conv., 1909, 97-99, 330-331.

30. SG, editorial in AF, XXI, Apr. 1914, 311-312; SG to Thomas D. Fitzgerald, Mar. 1, 1916; SG, "Labor vs. its Barnacles," AF, XXIII, Apr. 1916, 268-271.

31. SG, "Voluntary Social Insurance

vs. Compulsion: Shall the Toilers Surrender their Freedom for a Few Crumbs?" AF, XXIII, May 1916, 333f; June 1916, 453f; Aug. 1916, 669f.

32. AFL, 11th Conv., 1891, 15.

33. SG, "Immigration Evils," American Press Association release, Mar. 14, 1893; SG to W. R. Morris, May 28, 1901; SG, "The Chinese Treaty," AF, I, May 1894, 50-51; report to AFL, 14th Conv., 1894, 12; SG, "Wholesale Chinese Immigration Threatened," AF, VIII, Aug. 1901, 305-306.

34. See Arthur Mann, "Gompers and the Irony of Racism," The Antioch Review, XIII, June 1953, 203-214; cf. Taft, op. cit., 318; AFL, 21st Conv., 1901, 21-22. See also, Daniel Levine, "Gompers and Racism: Strategy of Limited Objectives," Mid-America, XLIII, No. 2, offprint, n.p.

35. Life, II, 151-154.

36. SG to Saverio Merlino, Oct. 30, 1896.

37. AFL, 16th Conv., 1896, 81-82.

38. AFL, 17th Conv., 1897, 90-91; 20th Conv., 1900, 120-121; SG, report to AFL, 22nd Conv., 1902, 21-22.

39. SG, "Compulsory Arbitration," AF, I, Sep. 1894, 147-149.

40. AFL, 17th Conv., 1897, 21-22, 88-89.

41. US, ICCL, VII, 600-605, 612-613.

42. Boston Globe, Dec. 5, 1902.

43. SG, "Shades of Jeffries," AF, I, Mar. 1894, 12.

44. SG, "Judge Freedman's Notorious Injunction," AF, VII, June 1900, 162-164.

45. Washington Post and New York Daily News, May 8, 1900; SG "The Happiness Not to Know," AF, VII,

July 1900, 213; see also SG, "Judge Holdom's Injunction Frenzy," AF, XIII, Mar. 1906, 157-158.

46. SG, testimony before Committee on the Judiciary, House of Representatives, Mar. 23, 1900, in Labor and the Common Welfare, op. cit., 61.

47. SG, "Anti-Injunction Legislation," AF, IX, Apr. 1902, 180-181; "Misrepresenting the Anti-Injunction Bill," AF, XI, Mar. 1904, 219-220.

48. SG, "No Property Right in Labor," AF, XIV, Nov. 1907, 835-836.

49. SG, "The Right to Strike," AF, VII, Feb. 1900, 36-37.

50. SG, testimony before Committee on Labor, House of Representatives, Feb. 11, 1904, in Labor and the Common Welfare, op. cit., 63-65.

51. SG, testimony before Committee on the Judiciary, House of Representatives, Mar. 22, 1900, in AF, VII, Apr. 1900, 101-102; ibid., Mar. 14, 1906, 59C., 1S; "The Injunction Mania," AF, IX, May 1904, 397-399; SG to Reuben O. Moon, Mar. 2, 1910; ed. in AF, XVIII, May 1911, 32f.

52. AFL, 17th Conv., 1897, 81.

53. SG, report to AFL, 18th Conv., 1898, 15.

54. AFL, 18th Conv., 1898, 85, 104-110.

55. SG to M. Brown, Aug. 16, 1899; SG to Henry White, Aug. 6, 1899.

56. AFL, 24th Conv., 1904, 237-241.

57. SG, "Direct Legislation," AF, I, June 1894, 77; ed. in AF, XVIII, June 1911, 462-463, and Oct. 1911, 804-806.

58. SG, "Initiative, Referendum, and Recall," AF, XIX, Aug. 1912, 618-622, and Sep. 1912, 694f.

CHAPTER TWELVE

1. Merle Curti and others, An American History, New York, 1950, II, 306-314; Richard Hofstadter, "Manifest Destiny and the Philippines," in Daniel Aaron, ed., America in Crisis, New York, 1952, 173-200; Claude Bowers, Beveridge and the Progressive Era, New York, 1932, 69.

2. The Union Advocate, Oct. 1886; SG, ed. in AF, I, July 1894, 99-100.

3. Foner, *op cit.*, II, 405.
4. SG, "Should Hawaii be Annexed?" AF, IV, Nov. 1897, 215-217.
5. SG to Thomas B. Reed, June 11, 1898.
6. SG to the Cuban Revolutionary Party, Mar. 5, 1896.
7. AFL, 16th Conv., 1896, 50-51.
8. Kansas City *Times*, Apr. 8, 1898.
9. SG, address to Chicago Federation of Labor, Apr. 17, 1898, in the *Inter-Ocean*, Apr. 18, 1898; "American Manhood for Cuba Libre," AF, V, May 1898, 53; Foner, *op. cit.*, II, 414-415; SG to James Duncan, May 14, 1898.
10. New York *Tribune*, Aug. 1, 1898.
11. AF, V, Sep. 1898, 136-140.
12. Chicago *Democrat,* Oct. 18, 1898; Chicago *Tribune*, Oct. 19, 1898; AF, V, Nov. 1898, 179-183; SG to Frank Hall, Feb. 10, 1899.
13. AFL, 18th Conv., 1898, 26-28, 86-91; Henry Healy to SG, Jan. 3, 1899, in AFL, Box 133; SG to Healy, Jan. 17, 1899.
14. SG, report to AFL, 19th Conv., 1899, 16.
15. Foner, *op. cit.*, II, 433.
16. SG, report to AFL, 20th Conv., 1900, 25-26.
17. SG, "A Trip to Cuba," AF, VII, Mar. 1900, 56-62; Edward Rosenberg, report on investigation of Hawaii and the Philippines, AF, X, Oct. 1903, 1021f., and Dec. 1903, 1265-1270.
18. SG, "Imperialism—Despotism; The Flag and the Constitution," AF, VII, Apr. 1900, 98-99.
19. Santiago Iglesias to the editor, *The Bricklayer and Mason*, Aug. 1,

1900, in AFL, Box 2.
20. SG to EC, Nov. 20, 1901; SG to William H. Hunt, Oct. 14, 1901; report to AFL, 21st Conv., 1901, 160.
21. SG to Santiago Iglesias, Nov. 12 and 20, 1901; SG to Sidney McKee and SG to EC, Nov. 20, 1901; SG to William H. Hunt, Dec. 30, 1901.
22. AFL, 22nd Conv., 1902, 16; *Life,* II, 73.
23. SG, address at farewell banquet, San Juan, Mar. 14, 1904, in AFL, "Addresses" file.
24. SG, address to Central Labor Union of Washington, in AF, XI, May 1904, 412-416.
25. SG to Santiago Iglesias, July 27 and Dec. 30, 1904; San Juan *News,* July 7, 1904.
26. Santiago Iglesias to SG, Apr. 28, 1905, in AF, XII, June 1905, 380-381; Washington *Star*, May 7, 1905.
27. SG to Beekman Winthrop, May 5, 1905.
28. SG, "Let Us Have Peace," AF, III, Feb. 1897, 259-260; SG to the New York *World*, Feb. 15, 1897.
29. SG to Adlai E. Stevenson, Feb. 28, 1896.
30. Boston *Globe*, Mar. 20, 1899; Rochester *Herald*, Mar. 22, 1899; SG, report to AFL, 25th Conv., 1905, 20-21.
31. SG, report to AFL, 14th Conv., 1894, 16; 19th Conv., 1899, 16-17; 24th Conv., 1904, 27; see also reports to 20th and 21st Conv., 1900 and 1901.
32. AFL, 15th Conv., 1895, 64-65; SG to EC, Sep. 8, 1896; SG, report to AFL, 16th Conv., 1896, 25.
33. Washington *Post*, Oct. 8, 1905.

CHAPTER THIRTEEN

1. Correspondence between SG, EC, and James A. Cable, Aug. 7 and Nov. 18, 1899.
2. SG to Maurice Mikol, June 20, 1903; Mikol to SG, June 23, 1903; *Life*, I, 373; US, ICCL, VII, 616-618.

3. AF, XXX, Sep. 1923, 718f.; *Life,* I, 182.
4. SG, address to National Civic Federation, New York, Jan. 1903, in SG, *Labor and the Employer*, N.Y., 1920, 171.

5. SG, "Prof. Laughlin's Mare's Nest," AF, XIII, June 1906, 389-391.

6. SG, "The Passing of the Wages-Fund Fallacy," AF, XX, July 1913, 527-530; "Professor Laughlin's Sophistry and Sycophancy," AF, XX, Aug. 1913, 617-619.

7. Commons, op. cit., III, 305-315; Jean Trepp McKelvey, AFL Attitudes toward Production, 1900-1932, Ithaca, 1952, 15; Milton J. Nadworny, Scientific Management and the Unions, Cambridge, 1955, 48-49.

8. SG, ed. in AF, XVIII, Feb. 1911, 117.

9. SG, "The Miracles of 'Efficiency,'" AF, XVIII, Apr. 1911, 273f; SG to Alfred Calvert, Oct. 4, 1905.

10. "Investigation of the Taylor System of Shop Management," Hearings Before the Committee on Labor of the House of Representatives, 62C, 1S, 1911, 22-34.

11. SG to Ralph Easley, Apr. 4, 1911.

12. Commons, op cit., IV, 129-137; Hoxie, op. cit., 191-194.

13. SG, "Labor and Equal Rights," AF, VII, June 1900, 164-165; "More Open Shop Hypocrisy," AF, XI, June 1904, 490-491.

14. SG, "A Word as to Rights," AF, XVII, Oct. 1910, 911-912.

15. Louis Filler, Crusaders for American Liberalism, Yellow Springs, Ohio, 1961 ed.

16. US, ICCL, VII, 644-645; SG, "The Stetson Strike and Profit-Sharing," AF, XXIII, May 1916, 383-385; New York Evening World, July 2, 1919.

17. SG, "Contented Cows," AF, XXX, Sept. 1923, 760-762.

18. SG, "Such Antagonism is Suicidal," AF, X, Mar. 1903, 173-175.

19. SG, "Organized Labor: Its Struggles, Its Enemies and Fool Friends," AF, VIII, Nov. 1901, 479. Emphasis added.

20. SG, interview in Atlanta News, July 4, 1903.

21. US, CIR, II, 1532-1537.

22. Life, I, 166, 399; II, 105-106, 114-115.

23. Sidney Lens, Left, Right & Center, Hinsdale, 1949, 31-49, 115.

24. Herbert Croly, Marcus Alonzo Hanna, New York, 1912, 386f.

25. SG, "Conference on Conciliation and Arbitration," AF, VIII, June 1901, 205-208.

26. Commons, op. cit., IV, 101-104; T. J. Shaffer, report to 27th Annual Session of the AAISTW, 1902, Journal of the Session, 6293f.

27. T. J. Shaffer to SG, Apr. 16, Apr. 30, and May 10, 1901; SG to Shaffer, May 15, 1901; memorandum by SG, in AFL, "AAISTW" file, Box 1. Also, see Life, II, 127.

28. John B. Lennon to SG, Aug. 12, 1901; SG to Lennon, Aug. 14, 1901.

29. Henry White to SG, July 19, 1901, in Ware, op. cit., 322-323; Commons, op. cit., IV, 104-106; Shaffer, report to AAISTW, op. cit.

30. Shaffer, report to AAISTW, op. cit.; memorandum by SG, in AFL, "AAISTW" file.

31. New York Tribune, Aug. 11, 1901.

32. Ware, op. cit., 322-323; T. J. Shaffer to Members of the Amalgamated Association, Sep. 21, 1901, in AF, VIII, Oct. 1901, 415-417.

33. SG and John Mitchell to T. J. Shaffer, Sep. 25, 1901; Shaffer to Mitchell, Sep. 27, 1901, in 27th Annual Session of the AAISTW, op. cit., 6318.

34. SG, "The Steel Strike," AF, VIII, Oct. 1901, 415-431.

35. Selig Perlman and Philip Taft, Labor Movements, vol. IV of Commons, op. cit., 107-109.

36. Michael F. Tighe, testimony before Committee on Education and Labor, U.S. Senate, Investigation of Strike in Steel Industries, 66C, 1S (1919), 341f.

CHAPTER FOURTEEN

1. SG to the Officers and Members of Federal Labor Unions and Local Trade Unions, June 25, 1901; SG to Z. T. Trumbo, May 9 and Oct. 21, 1902; AFL, 22nd Conv., 1902, 10, 49, 105-106, 212-214, 220; 23rd Conv., 1903, 171; SG to C. O. Hill, May 3, 1905.

2. SG, interview in Washington *Star*, Feb. 7, 1905; *Life*, I, 147-148.

3. SG, "Should the Wife Contribute to the Family Support?" *Woman's Home Companion*, Sep. 1905, 16.

4. SG, ed. in AF, XVIII, Oct. 1911, 825-826; "Another Despicable Piece of Union Selfishness," AF, XVIII, Nov. 1911, 896-897.

5. AFL, 17th Conv., 1897, 78-79.

6. SG to W. H. Stokes, Aug. 27, 1896; address at St. Paul, in AF, XII, Sep. 1905, 636; John Roach, "Packingtown Conditions," AF, XIII, Aug. 1906, 534.

7. AF, IV, Feb. 1898, 269-271; SG to Will Winn, Jan. 19, 1898.

8. SG to L. F. McGruder, Oct. 6, 1899; SG to Will Winn, Mar. 9, 1899; SG to James Leonard, June 28, 1900; AF, VI, May 1899, 57; see also Foner, *op. cit.*, 345ff.

9. SG, *Labor and the Employer, op. cit.*, 166-167; "Trade Union Attitude Toward Colored Workers," AF, VIII, Apr. 1901, 118-120; SG to J. H. Powell, Feb. 12, 1901.

10. Du Bois, *op. cit.*, 157; SG, "Unity Drawing Nearer," AF, VII, Feb. 1900, 34-35; Charles Archer to SG, May 25, 1894; SG to Archer, June 1, 1894; AFL, 20th Conv., 1900, 22-23, 112, 129; Sterling D. Spero and Abram L. Harris, *The Black Worker*, New York, 1931, 93-99.

11. New York *Tribune*, Dec. 13, 1901; SG to H. A. Stemburgh, July 20, 1903; SG to L. E. Turley, Sep. 20, 1905; SG to Frank Duffy, Mar. 2, 1906; SG to David Williams, Feb. 16,

1903; Minutes, EC, Sep. 21, 1903, in AF, X, Nov. 1903, 1191; SG to Calmeze E. Henike, Mar. 19, 1902; SG to J. H. Patterson, Mar. 14 and Mar. 23, 1903; SG to L. B. Allen, Mar. 30 and May 8, 1903; SG to James McNair, Nov. 6, 1905; Minutes, EC, Oct. 16-21, 1911, in AF, XVIII, Dec. 1911, 1011; Toledo *News-Bee*, Oct. 27, 1905.

12. SG to C. H. Hogan, Feb. 14, 1910; SG to W. R. Paul, May 31, 1911; SG to W. S. Carter, July 26, 1911.

13. Du Bois, *op. cit.*, 156-158, 177; SG to Du Bois, Jan. 5, 1903; Du Bois to Bernard Mandel, Oct. 3, 1952.

14. Herbert Aptheker, *A Documentary History of the Negro People in the United States*, New York, 1951, 902, 916f; AFL, 30th Conv., 1910, 237; SG, "The Negro in the A. F. of L.," AF, XVIII, Jan. 1911, 34-36.

15. Charles Wesley, *Negro Labor in the United States*, New York, 1927, 275-277; SG, "Trade Union Attitude Toward Colored Workers," *op. cit.*; statement for memorial book of Booker T. Washington, Jan. 24, 1916, in AFL, "Special Articles" file; Florence Thorne to Bernard Mandel, July 7, 1953.

16. AFL, 15th Conv., 1895, 38; Jacksonville *Metropolis*, May 25, 1907; AF, XIV, Feb. 1907, 103.

17. SG to T. J. Shaffer, May 15, 1901; SG, "Organized Labor and the Trusts," *The Independent*, LIII, June 27, 1901, 1487-1488; AFL, 20th Conv., 1900, 147-148, 152.

18. AFL, 21st Conv., 1901, 150, 172, 240; 22nd Conv., 1902, 143.

19. Cincinnati *Enquirer*, Oct. 30, 1902; SG to James Wood, Nov. 2, 1902.

20. EC, report to AFL, 28th Conv., 1908, 69-71.

21. Lorwin, *op. cit.*, 395-396; Marion D. Savage, *Industrial Unionism in America*, New York, 1922, 37-38.

22. *National Conference on Indus-*

trial Conciliation, New York, 1902, 69-72. See also, SG, "The Industrial Conference," AF, IX, Jan. 1902, 23-25.

23. *Ibid.*; SG to Ernest Bohm, Jan. 10, 1902; SG to Ferdinand Laurell, Apr. 12, 1902; address to NCF, Chicago, in AF, X, Dec. 1903, 1296-1300; SG to James Sexton, Mar. 28, 1905.

24. Copy of agreement in AFL, Box 2.

25. Marcus Hanna to SG, July 23, 1903; SG to Thomas Flynn, SG to James McMahon, and SG to Hanna, July 25, 1903.

26. Transcript of conference, in AFL, Box 2.

27. SG to Hanna and SG to Flynn, July 28, 1903; McMahon to SG, July 28, 1903; Flynn to SG, Hanna to SG, and Buffalo Union Furnace Co. to SG, July 29, 1903; SG to Flynn, July 29 and 30, 1903.

28. Flynn to SG, July 31, 1903; Hanna to SG, Aug. 3, 1903; SG to Hanna, Aug. 4, 1903; Hanna to SG and McMahon to SG, Aug. 5, 1903; SG to McMahon, Aug. 18, 1903; McMahon to SG, Aug. 20 and 26, 1903; SG to Flynn and SG to W. J. Clark, Aug. 20, 1903; memorandum by SG, Sep. 4, 1903, in AFL, Box 2.

29. Commons, *op. cit.*, IV, 125-127; *The Motorman and Conductor*, XIII, Jan. 1905, 25, Apr. 1905, 5-6.

30. Harvey, *op. cit.*, 148.

31. AF, XII, May 1905, 294-295; *The Motorman and Conductor*, XIII, Mar. 1905, 13-14; Commons, *op. cit.*, IV, 127-128.

32. *Life*, I, 352-354.

33. SG, address at Baltimore, Mar. 21, 1905, in Atlanta *Journal of Labor*, Mar. 24, 1905.

34. New York *Tribune*, Mar. 27, 1905; SG to Herman Robinson, Mar. 29, 1905; SG to the Committee of the New York CFU, Apr. 28, 1905; New York *Press*, May 8, 1905; New York

Times, June 5, 1905.

35. AFL, 25th Conv., 1905, 181-182.

36. US, ICCL, VII, 655; SG, address at Jacksonville, May 22, 1907, in Jacksonville *Metropolis*, May 25, 1907.

37. AFL, 23rd Conv., 1903, 198.

38. Max Hayes, "The World of Labor," *International Socialist Review*, IV, Jan. 1904, 434-435.

39. Quint, *op. cit.*, 386-387; Daniel Bell, "The Background and Development of Marxian Socialism in the United States," in Donald D. Egbert and Stow Persons, eds., *Socialism and American Life*, Princeton, 1952, I, 277-278; Ira Kipnis, *The American Socialist Movement*, N.Y., 1952, 157-159, 171-172.

40. Commons, *op. cit.*, IV, 215-217; Kipnis, *op. cit.*, 143-145.

41. Commons, *op. cit.*, IV, 192-200; William D. Haywood, *Bill Haywood's Book*, N.Y., 1929, 117f.

42. AFL, 23rd Conv., 1903, 116-117, 157-158.

43 Commons, *op. cit.*, IV, 200-207; Haywood, *op. cit*, 131f.

44. SG to Organized Labor of America, June 20, 1904.

45. SG to EC, July 20, 1904; SG to Chris Evans, July 29, 1904.

46. Baltimore *Herald*, Aug. 3, 1904.

47. Haywood, *op. cit.*, 174-179.

48. SG to the Officers and Members of Affiliated Unions, Mar. 21, 1905, in AF, XII, May 1905, 277; SG, report to AFL, 25th Conv., 1905, 28-29; AFL, Box 6; Boston *American*, Apr. 2, 1905.

49. Haywood, *op. cit.*, 182-189.

50. SG, "The Trade Unions to be Smashed Again," AF, XII, Apr. 1905, 214-215; Pittsburgh *Labor World*, Aug. 10, 1905.

51. Chicago *Record*, Mar. 31, 1906; SG, "Justice Grossly Outraged," AF, XIII, Apr. 1906, 233-235; *Life*, II, 182-183.

52. Ginger, *The Bending Cross, op. cit.*, 251-254; Filler, *op. cit.*, 217f.
53. SG to EC, Dec. 21, 1906.
54. Washington *Evening Star,* Jan. 21, 1907; New York *Evening Journal,* in SG clipping book, vol. 62, p. 87.

55. AF, XIV, May 1907, 334.
56. Atlanta *Journal,* Apr. 17, 1907; Rochester *Union-Advertiser,* Apr. 24, 1907.
57. Haywood, *op. cit.,* 199-217.

CHAPTER FIFTEEN

1. Harry W. Laidler, *Boycotts and the Labor Struggle,* New York, 1913, 137-139; Harvey, *op. cit.,* 155ff.
2. US, 1CCL, VII, 633-636.
3. *The Buck's Stove and Range Co. v. The American Federation of Labor,* Supreme Court of District of Columbia, opinion of Justice Wright, Dec. 23, 1908, App. B; AF, XVI, Feb. 1909, 139-140, May 1909, 429-431; *The Buck's Stove and Range Company v. The American Federation of Labor, et al.,* Supreme Court of District of Columbia, In Equity, No. 27305, 1907, 1-44, 68; Arguments of Thomas C. Snelling for the Defendants, *ibid.;* 35 Wash. Law Rep. 797, 809.
4. SG to EC, Sept. 20, 1907; SG to Andrew Furuseth, Sept. 21, 1907.
5. SG, "Van Cleave Seeks Injunction Against A.F. of L.," AF, XIV, Oct. 1907, 784-785; "Go To——With Your Injunctions," *ibid.,* 791-792; Labor Day speech, in *ibid.,* 789; Elsie Gluck, *John Mitchell,* New York, 1929, 247.
6. SG to Ed. H. Heilman, Dec. 28, 1907.
7. SG, "Free Press and Free Speech Invaded by Injunction against the A.F. of L.," AF, XV, Feb. 1908, 98-105; italics added.
8. Supreme Court, D.C., In Equity, No. 27305, 1907, *op. cit.,* 742f.
9. *American Federation of Labor et al. vs. Buck's Stove and Range Company,* No. 1916, Brief for Appelants, in the Court of Appeals, District of Columbia, Oct. Term 1908.
10. SG, "Van Cleave Hails Us to Court for Contempt," AF, XV, Aug. 1908, 614-615.

11. *Samuel Gompers, John Mitchell, and Frank Morrison vs. The Buck's Stove and Range Company,* Supreme Court of the United States, Oct. Term 1909, On the Writ of Certiorari to the Court of Appeals of the District of Columbia, 23f.
12. *Ibid.,* 269f.
13. SG, "Justice Wright's Denial of Free Speech and Free Press," AF, XVI, Feb. 1909, 130.
14. *The Buck's Stove and Range Company v. The American Federation of Labor et al.,* 36 Wash. Law Rep. 822.
15. AF, XVI, Feb. 1909, 129, 151.
16. J. M. Barnes to SG, Dec. 23, 1908; SG to George Perkins, Dec. 23, 1908; SG to Morris Brown, Feb. 10, 1908.
17. SG, "Justice Wright's Denial of Free Speech and Free Press," AF, XVI, Feb. 1909, 130-147.
18. *American Federation of Labor v. Buck's Stove and Range Company,* 33 App. D.C. 83, Mar. 11, 1909.
19. *The Buck's Stove and Range Company vs. The American Federation of Labor et al.,* No. 27305 Equity, In the Court of Appeals of the District of Columbia, April Term 1909.
20. *Gompers v. Buck's Stove and Range Company,* 33 App. D.C. 562, 579, Nov. 2, 1909.
21. SG, Report to AFL, 29th Conv., 1909, 21-22.
22. Fort Wayne *Labor Times Herald,* Nov. 26, 1909; SG to Fred. W. Gardner, Feb. 25, 1911.
23. AF, XVII, Sep. 1910, 807-812.
24. SG to Joseph F. Valentine, Oct.

10, 1910; SG to C. Legien, Jan. 11, 1911; EC, Report to AFL, 32nd Conv., 1912, 126-130.

25. *Buck's Stove and Range Company v. American Federation of Labor et al.,* 219 U.S. 581.

26. *Samuel Gompers, John Mitchell and Frank Morrison vs. Buck's Stove and Range Company,* In the Supreme Court of the United States, Oct. Term 1909 and Oct. Term 1910.

27. *Ibid.,* 221 U.S. 418, May 15, 1911.

28. SG, "Court of Appeals' Decision," AF, XX, June 1913, 456.

29. *Samuel Gompers, John Mitchell,*

and Frank Morrison vs. United States, in Court of Appeals, District of Columbia, Jan. Term 1913, No. 2477, June 28, 1912.

30. SG, "Guilty of Contempt, Says Justice Wright," AF, XIX, Aug. 1912, 601-611.

31. *Re Gompers,* 40 D.C. App. 313, May 5, 1913.

32. *Samuel Gompers, John Mitchell, and Frank Morrison v. United States,* 233 U.S. 604, May 11, 1914.

33. SG, editorial in AF, XXI, June 1914, 483-486.

CHAPTER SIXTEEN

1. Hearings before Committee on Labor, H.R., 50C 1S, 1900, 428-429.

2. AFL, 25th Conv., 1905, 74-75, 78, 177; Filler, *op. cit., passim.*

3. "Labor's Bill of Grievances," AF, XIII, May 1906, 293-296.

4. *Literary Digest,* Mar. 31, 1906; *Public Opinion,* Mar. 31, 1906.

5. *Life,* II, 243-244.

6. New York *Globe,* July 28, 1906.

7. SG, testimony before House Committee on Labor, May 30, 1906, in AF, XIII, June 1906, 395-396.

8. Dallas *Laborer,* July 21, 1906.

9. Massillon *Independent,* June 22, 1906; *Life,* II, 241-242; SG to Frank K. Foster, Aug. 8, 1906.

10. "A.F. of L. Campaign Program," AF, XIII, Aug. 1906, 529-531.

11. *Current Literature,* XLI, Sep. 1906, 248, 250; *Selections from the Correspondence of Theodore Roosevelt and Henry Cabot Lodge,* New York, 1925, II, 230; *Life,* II, 245-246.

12. In AFL, "Talks on Labor" file.

13. SG, "Labor's First Skirmish," AF, XIII, Oct. 1906, 795-806; "Influence of Labor's Great Campaign Now and for the Future," AF, XIII, Dec. 1906, 970-972.

14. Elias Lieberman, *Unions Before the Bar,* New York, 1950, 56-70.

15. SG, "Labor Organizations Must Not Be Outlawed," AF, XV, Mar. 1908, 180-192.

16. SG to EC, Mar. 3, 1908.

17. "Labor's Protest to Congress," in AFL, 28th Conv., 1908, 81-83.

18. New York *World,* June 19, 1908; Henry F. Pringle, *The Life and Times of William Howard Taft,* New York, 1939, I, 346-355.

19. *Life,* II, 261-265; SG, "Both Parties Have Spoken—Choose Between Them," AF, XV, Aug. 1908, 599-606; Erie *Dispatch* and Buffalo *Evening Times,* July 18, 1908; *Ohio State Journal,* Aug. 8, 1908; Washington *Post,* July 30, 1908; Washington *Times,* Aug. 22, 1908; SG to Daniel Harris, Aug. 28, 1908.

20. SG, address in New York, Nov. 1, 1908, in AFL, "Addresses General" file; SG, "Taft, the Injunction Standard Bearer," 1908; William Howard Taft, *Political Issues and Outlooks,* New York, 1909, 203-224.

21. *Literary Digest,* May 2, 1908; *Life,* II, 269-274.

22. Legislative Committee, Report to AFL, 28th Conv., 1908, 27-35; SG, "The Campaign and Labor's Future," AF, XV, Dec. 1908, 1064-1065; Letters of R. L. Guard, Aug. 8 and 9, 1908,

in SG's copybooks and *Personal Letters*, II.

23. SG, Report to AFL, 30th Conv., 1910, 25-26.

24. *Life*, II, 246-252; New York *Post*, Apr. 10, 1911.

25. AFL, 25th Conv., 1905, 169-171; 26th Conv., 1906, 83, 104-107, 134-135; 27th Conv., 1907, 32-33, 319-320.

26. St. Louis *Globe-Democrat* and St. Louis *Times*, May 3, 1910; SG to EC, May 9, 1910.

27. SG, Report to AFL, 31st Conv., 1911, 56-58; SG, address to Indiana Legislature, Feb. 20, 1911, in AF, XVIII, Apr. 1911, 303-304.

28. SG, "Labor's Political Campaign," AF, XIX, Oct. 1912, 806-807; *Life*, II, 276-282.

29. SG, "The Presidency in the Pending Campaign," AF, XIX, Nov. 1912, 889f.; *Life*, II, 282-283.

30. *Life*, II, 290-295; Arthur S. Link,

Woodrow Wilson and the Progressive Era, 1910-1917, New York, 1954, 55-56; AF, XXI, May 1914, 394.

31. Norman J. Ware, *Labor in Modern Industrial Society*, Boston, 1935, 347-350; Madison, *op. cit.*, 97-98.

32. US, CIR, Final Report, 64; Robert Hunter, *Labor in Politics*, Chicago, 1915, 108-110.

33. SG to Frank P. Walsh, Sep. 15, 1915; Dallas L. Jones, "The Enigma of the Clayton Act," *Industrial and Labor Relations Review*, X, Jan. 1957, 203-221.

34. SG, "The Charter of Industrial Freedom," AF, XXI, Nov. 1914, 957f.

35. Link, *op. cit.*, 224-230.

36. SG, "Promises and Performances," AF, XXIII, July 1916, 537-541; "On Which Side Are You?" AF, XXIII, Nov. 1916, 1067-1068; *Wilson and Labor*, Washington, 1916, 2.

CHAPTER SEVENTEEN

1. SG, "Public Opinion and Labor," AF, XIX, Feb. 1912, 102f.

2. Michael F. Tighe, testimony in *Steel Strike Hearings, op. cit.*, 341f.; Gompers, "Labor and the Steel Trust," AF, XVIII, Jan. 1910, 35-37; Commons, *History, op. cit.*, IV, 138f.

3. SG to George Perkins, Feb. 25, 1910.

4. Levine, *op. cit.*, 144-167; Herberg, *op. cit.*, 512-513; Jack Hardy, *The Clothing Workers*, New York, 1935, 28.

5. SG, "The Struggles in the Garment Trades," AF, XX, Mar. 1913, 192-193.

6. Levine, *op. cit.*, 168-195, 249; Hardy, *op. cit.*, 29-38; SG, *ibid.*, 193-194.

7. Herberg, *op. cit.*, 516-518; Joel Seidman, *The Needle Trades*, New York, 1942, 115-125.

8. *Ibid.; Documentary History of the Amalgamated Clothing Workers of America*, 61-62.

9. *Ibid.*, 134; Charles E. Zaretz, *The Amalgamated Clothing Workers of America*, New York, 1934, 137-138; Seidman, *op. cit.*, 125-130.

10. Melech Epstein, *Jewish Labor in the United States*, New York, 1952, II, 40f.; AFL, 35th Conv., 1915, 144-146, 356-361; J. M. Budish and George Soule, *The New Unionism in the Clothing Industry*, New York, 1920, 89-90; AF, XXIII, June 1916, 470-474.

11. SG, speech at Battle Creek, Michigan, Oct. 5, 1910, quoted in Harvey, *op. cit.*, 119; Taft, *op. cit.*, 272ff.

12. Ira B. Cross, *A History of the Labor Movement in California*, Berkeley, 1935, 282-284; Commons, *History, op. cit.*, IV, 318-320.

13. AF, XVIII, Jan. 1911, 65; June 1911, 433f.

14. Hearings held on House Concurrent Resolution 6, Committee on Rules, H.R., May 27-29, 1911.

15. SG to EC, May 2, 1911.

16. New York *World*, May 8, 1911; Louis Adamic, *Dynamite*, New York, 1934, 189f.

17. In an interview in the New York *World* on June 6, 1903, Gompers had admitted that some unions employed strong-arm methods, but said that was the concern of the police. The unions must not be expected to turn such lawbreakers over to the police, because that would prejudice their case before it went to trial. "The labor union deals with the economic conditions of work; the Government deals with questions of law and order." See also, SG to Seth Low, June 2, 1911; SG to Ralph M. Easley, June 6, 1911.

18. *Life*, II, 187; AF, XIX, Mar. 1912, 204; Report to AFL, 31st Conv., 1911, 71-74.

19. SG, "Brutality in the Industrial Struggle," *United Mine Workers Journal*, XXII, Nov. 9, 1911, 1.

20. Clarence Darrow, *The Story of My Life*, New York, 1934, 179-185; Commons, *History, op. cit.*, IV, 320-325. For the effect of the McNamara Case on the reform movement, Filler, *op. cit.*, 350ff.

21. Adamic, *op. cit.*; Benjamin Stolberg, "What Manner of Man Was Samuel Gompers?" The *Atlantic Monthly*, March 1925.

22. Adamic, *op. cit.*

23. AF, XIX, Jan. 1912, 22-23; EC, Report to AFL, 32nd Conv., 1912, 155.

24. *International Socialist Review*, Jan. 1912; New York *Call*, Dec. 5, 1911; SG, "Socialist Methods vs. Trade Union Methods," AF, XIX, Feb. 1912, 135-141.

25. Adamic, *op. cit.*

26. EC, Report to AFL, 32nd Conv., 1912, 154-155.

27. *Ibid.*, 148-154.

28. The *Bridgemen's Magazine*, XIII, Mar. 1913, 148-152.

29. Lucy Robins Lang, *Tomorrow is Beautiful*, New York, 1948, 197.

30. Commons, *History, op. cit.*, IV, 266-273; Adamic, *op. cit.*, 165-171; AF, XIX, Apr. 1912, 281f; Yellen, *op. cit.*, 171.

31. For this and following data, *The Strike at Lawrence, Massachusetts.* Hearings Before the Committee on Rules, H.R., Mar. 2-7, 1912, 62C 2S, Doc. No. 671, pp. 5, 11f., 31f., 74f., 124f., 261f.; see also editorial in AF, XIX, Apr. 1912, 287-289.

32. SG, editorial in AF, XX, July 1913, 536-537.

33. Miss Neilson to Frank Morrison, May 16, 1910, and Miss Neilson to SG, undated, in AFL, Incoming Correspondence, Box No. 101-A; SG to Marion Webster, Sept. 26, 1910.

CHAPTER EIGHTEEN

1. Ginger, *op. cit.*, 296-298; for this and following data, Kipnis, *op. cit.*, 235-239, 338-345.

2. *United Mine Workers Journal*, XXII, Dec. 14, 1911, 6.

3. AFL, 31st Conv., 1911, 217-258.

4. SG to George Perkins, Dec. 18, 1912, in *Personal Letters*, II, 238-239.

5. SG, "Mr. Hunter's Dilemma Proven," AF, XVII, June 1910, 484-490.

6. SG, "Consistent with Conception and Principle," AF, XIX, Nov. 1912, 913-914.

7. SG, editorial in AF, XXI, Feb. 1914, 126-127; "We are Grateful, with Some Reserves," AF, XVIII, May 1911, 392f.

8. AF, XX, Dec. 1913, 1011; SG to Grace D. Whitnall, July 7, 1915.

9. US, CIR, 1914, II, 1471-1506.

10. SG, "Home Again," AF, XVI, Nov. 1909, 964-965.

11. SG, *Labor in Europe and America*, New York, 1910, 92-104, 128.

12. SG, Report to AFL, 29th Conv.,

1909, 39; AF, XVI, Nov. 1909, 977-978; Washington *Post,* Aug. 31 and Sep. 1, 1909; Lewis L. Lorwin, *Labor and Internationalism,* New York, 1929, 126-128.

13. AFL, 29th Conv., 1909, 39, 318; AF, XVI, Nov. 1909, 978.

14. EC, Report to AFL, 33rd Conv., 1913, 85-86.

15. AFL, 27th Conv., 1907, 178-179, 193; Santiago Iglesias to Theodore Roosevelt, Nov. 29, 1907, in SG's Copybooks, Vol. 146, 895-901; Taft, *op. cit.,* 320ff.

16. SG, Report to AFL, 31st Conv., 1911.

17. SG, "Porto Rico," AF, XXI, May 1914, 386-388.

18. SG to Woodrow Wilson, July 29, 1915; see also SG, "A Plea for Justice for Porto Rico," AF, XXIII, Apr. 1916, 283-285.

19. *Government for Porto Rico,* Hearings before the Committee on Pacific Islands and Porto Rico, U.S. Sen., 64C IS, 1916, part 2, 103-124.

20. SG, editorial in AF, XXIV, Feb. 1917, 127-130, Apr. 1917, 297-298.

21. R. Flores Magon to SG, Mar. 11, 1911.

22. SG to R. Flores Magon, Mar. 18, 1911.

23. R. F. Magon to SG, undated (c. Apr. 3, 1911).

24. SG to EC, Apr. 8, 1911; AF, XVIII, Aug. 1911, 628; AFL, 32nd

Conv., 1912, 256.

25. Link, *op cit.,* 107f.

26. AFL, 33rd Conv., 1913, 364; Remarks of SG on Resolution 163, Nov. 21, 1913, in AFL, "International Peace" file.

27. Thomas A. Bailey, *A Diplomatic History of the American People,* New York, 1947, 604-607; Link, *op. cit.*

28. EC to R. Zubaran, July 25, 1914, in EC, Report to AFL, 34th Conv., 1914, 50-51.

29. SG to Woodrow Wilson, June 14, 1915; Link, *op. cit.*

30. SG to Edmundo E. Martinez, Aug. 23, 1915; SG to Woodrow Wilson, Sep. 22, 1915.

31. SG to Secretary, Casa del Obrero Mundial, May 23, 1916.

32. *International Labor Forum,* New York, 1916, 11-13.

33. SG, "Liberty's Hope is in Thy Keeping, Organized Labor," AF, XXIII, July 1916, 575-577.

34. Memorandum of EC meeting, in AFL, "Mexico" file.

35. Minutes, EC, June 26-July 4, 1916, in AFL, "Mexico" file.

36. SG, "United States—Mexico—Labor—Their Relations," AF, XXIII, Aug. 1916, 633f.

37. Memoranda by SG, Nov. 19, 1916 and Feb. 3, 1917, in AFL, "Mexico" file.

38. Link, *op. cit.*

CHAPTER NINETEEN

1. SG, interview in Washington *Times,* July 29, 1914, in AFL "Press Statements." Compare treatment of subject with Taft, *op. cit.,* 342ff.

2. SG to the Chicago *Examiner,* Aug. 7, 1914.

3. SG, editorial in AF, XXI, Sep. 1914, 726-729; see also speech at Plattsburg, New York, Sep. 7, 1914, in SG, *American Labor and the War,* New York, 1919, 17-30.

4. SG, editorial in AF, XXII, May 1915, 356; speech to League to Enforce Peace, Washington, May 26, 1916, in *Labor and the War,* 69-70.

5. SG, speech at NCF, Washington, Jan. 18, 1916, in *ibid.,* 51-53.

6. SG, speech at Canadian Victory Loan meeting, Toronto, Nov. 28, 1917, in *ibid.,* 142-146.

7. Daniel M. Smith, "Robert Lansing and the Formulation of Ameri-

can Neutrality Policies, 1914-1915," *Mississippi Valley Historical Review,* XLIII, June 1956, 59-81.

8. Florence Thorne to Bernard Mandel, July 7, 1953; SG to Hans Fehlinger, Feb. 8, 1915.

9. SG to Ralph Easley, Sept. 13, 1914; Lorwin, *AFL, op. cit.,* 137-138.

10. AF, XXII, Nov. 1915, 925f.

11. SG to Ernest Bohm, June 18, 1915.

12. Lorwin, *AFL, op. cit.,* 138-141; SG to Frank Buchanan, July 29, 1915; SG to John M. Bogart, Aug. 7, 13, and 16, 1915; SG to Jacob C. Taylor, Aug. 20, 1915; SG to John B. Walker, Sep. 2, 1915.

13. SG to Harry S. Mecartney, July 1, 1915.

14. *Life,* II, 336-349.

15. SG, "Rallying for Defense of the Republic," in *Army and Navy Journal,* April 17, 1915; Gen. John A. Johnston to SG, Apr. 19, 1915.

16. SG, "Preparedness for National Defense," Washington, 1916, Sen. Doc. 311, 64C 1S, 1916.

17. Franklin H. Martin, *Digest of the Proceedings of the Council of National Defense During the World War,* Washington, 1934 (Sen. Doc. No.

193, 72C 2S), 101.

18. SG, interview in New York *Sun,* Dec. 17, 1916.

19. SG, speech at New York State Federation of Labor, Aug. 31, 1917, in *Labor and the War,* 93.

20. SG to Karl Legien, Feb. 4, 1917; Legien to SG, Feb. 11, 1917.

21. SG, speech to National Security League, Chicago, Sep. 14, 1917, in *Labor and the War,* 121.

22. Martin, *op. cit.,* 97-98.

23. Belle Case and Fola La Follette, *Robert M. La Follette,* New York, 1953, I, 603-625.

24. "Conference called by SG, AFL Building, Feb. 27, 1917," in AFL, "Conference of Mar. 12, 1917" file.

25. EC, Report to AFL, 37th Conv., 1917, 59-62; AFL, 39th Conv., 1919, 412; Lorwin, *AFL, op. cit.,* 144-145.

26. SG, address in Padova, Italy, Oct. 12, 1918, in AFL, "Addresses General" file; speech at American Luncheon Club, Paris, Sep. 26, 1918, in *Labor and the War,* 240-241; "Organized Labor and the War of 1917," lecture at Army War College, Washington, Mar. 7, 1922, in AFL, "Army War College Lectures" file.

CHAPTER TWENTY

1. Martin, *op. cit.,* 53-56, 60-62, 81-96.

2. Daniel J. Tobin to SG, Mar. 30, 1917, in AFL, "Scott-Tobin-Dirks" file.

3. *First Annual Report, Council of National Defense,* Washington, 1917, 74-76; SG to Daniel Guggenheim, July 30, 1917.

4. Minutes, meeting of Labor Committee, Washington, Apr. 2, 1917, in AFL, "Council of National Defense" file.

5. SG to J. W. Kline, Apr. 14, 1917.

6. CND, *First Annual Report, op. cit.,* 76-77; Minutes, Executive Committee, Committee on Labor, Apr. 5-16, 1917.

7. SG, speech in Minneapolis, Sep. 7, 1917, in *Labor and the War,* 112-113; *Life,* II, 369.

8. Martin, *op. cit.,* 161; SG to Daniel Willard, Apr. 28, 1917.

9. Report of the War Labor Conference Board, Mar. 29, 1918; Proclamation by the President, Apr. 8, 1918; in U.S. Department of Labor, *National War Labor Program,* 1918.

10. EC, Report to AFL, 38th Conv., 1918, 85-87.

11. SG, speech to National Lecturers' Association, Washington, Apr. 11, 1918,

in *Labor and the War*, 193-194.

12. Martin, *op. cit.*, 227-228; EC to Champ Clark, Apr. 27, 1917.

13. *Life*, II, 369; italics added.

14. Martin, *op. cit.*, 179; *British Labor's War Message to American Labor*, Sen. Doc. No. 84, 64C 1S, 1917.

15. SG, "Organized Labor and the War of 1917," *op. cit.*, 12-23.

16. *Ibid.*; William Howard Taft, address to NCF, New York, Apr. 12, 1919, in AFL, "Addresses General" file; memorandum by R. L. Guard, in AFL, cabinet No. 27.

17. SG, "Preparedness for National Defense," *op. cit.*; EC, Report to AFL, 36th Conv., 1916, 108-109; SG to CND, June 27, 1917; Maxwell C. Raddock, *Portrait of an American Labor Leader*, New York, 1955, 92-93.

18. Commons, *History, op. cit.*, IV, 379-383; EC, Report to AFL, 36th Conv., 1916, 78-80; *Life*, II, 142-144.

19. Commons, *History, op. cit.*, IV, 383-385; *Life*, II, 146-147; CND, *First Annual Report, op. cit.*, 9-10.

20. SG, editorial in AF, XXIV, Apr. 1917, 290-291.

21. Louis B. Wehle, *Hidden Threads of History*, New York, 1953, 18-23.

22. Burton J. Hendrick, "The Leadership of Samuel Gompers," *World's Work*, XXXV, Feb. 1918, 381-387.

23. Robert A. Christie, *Empire in Wood*, Ithaca, 1956, 219-221; Raddock, *op. cit.*, 93-109.

24. Wehle, *op. cit.*, 40-45.

25. SG to Champ Clark, Feb. 4, 1917.

26. EC, Report to AFL, 37th Conv., 1917, 77-78.

27. *British War Labor's Message to American Labor, op. cit.*, 83-84.

28. Memoranda by SG, Mar. 21, Mar. 30, and Apr. 9, 1918, in AFL, "Mooney Case" file.

29. SG, Press Statement, Apr. 12, 1918.

30. Lang, *op. cit.*, 125-128, 131-134.

31. AFL, 38th Conv., 1918, 325-326; 39th Conv., 1919, 334-339.

32. J. G. Brown and E. P. Marsh to SG, Aug. 9, 1917; unless otherwise indicated, the documents on the Northwest lumber situation are located in AFL, "Lumber Situation, Pacific Coast" file.

33. SG to J. G. Brown, Aug. 10, 1917; Brown to SG, Aug. 13 and 14, 1917; SG to Newton D. Baker, Aug. 15 and 22, 1917.

34. C. O. Young to SG, Nov. 13, 1917; Louis Post to Newton D. Baker, Nov. 6, 1917; SG to C.O. Young, Nov. 6, 1917; Brice Disque to SG, Oct. 20, 1917.

35. Raddock, *op. cit.*, 226; C. O. Young to SG, Dec. 15, 1917; C. Covert to SG, Dec. 28, 1917.

36. Brice Disque to SG, Mar. 12, 1918; Bellingham, Washington, *Journal*, Mar. 17 and 25, 1918.

37. SG to Brice Disque, Apr. 12, 1918; Disque to SG, Apr. 20, 1918; John Novland to Frank Morrison, June 13, 1918; EC, Report to AFL, 38th Conv., 1918, 79.

38. Saul Alinski, *John L. Lewis*, New York, 1949, 28.

39. SG, testimony before Sen. Committee on Manufactures, in *Labor, the Courts and the Law*, Washington, 1921, 30-53.

40. Woodrow Wilson, in conference with Sen. Committee on Foreign Relations, Aug. 19, 1918, in La Follette, *op. cit.*, II, 971; Woodrow Wilson, *The Hope of the World*, New York, 1920, 102-103; St. Louis *Post Dispatch*, Sep. 6, 1919; SG, *Labor and the War, op. cit.*, 132, 136, 166, 221, 254-255.

41. "Proclamation and War Program," Socialist Party, St. Louis, Apr. 11, 1917.

42. John P. Frey, "When Labor . . . Turned Down Woodrow Wilson . . .,"

ILNS release, in AFL, "SG Biographical" file; SG, speech to National Lecturers' Association, Washington, Apr. 11, 1918, and speech in Rome, Oct. 8, 1918, in *Labor and the War, op. cit.*, 186-189, 262-263.

43. Louis Lochner and others to SG, May 10, 1917; SG to Lochner, May 10, 1917; Morris U. Schappes, "The Attitude of Jewish Labor to World War I, 1917-1918," *Jewish Life*, IX, Mar. 1955, 21-24.

44. People's Council, press release, in AFL, "American Alliance for Labor and Democracy" file.

45. Minutes of conferences on Americanization and circular letter of Aug. 15, 1917, in *ibid.*; Lorwin, *AFL, op. cit.*, 148; *Life*, II, 379, 381.

46. Lorwin, *AFL, op. cit.*, 148-150; SG to R. L. Guard, Aug. 28, 1917; David A. Shannon, *The Socialist Party of America*, New York, 1955, 117; *Life*, II, 382.

47. EC, Report to AFL, 37th Conv., 1917, 82-83.

48. *Life*, II, 383-385.

49. AFL, 37th Conv., 1917, 283-308, 313-317.

50. John L. Heaton, *Cobb of "The World,"* New York, 1924, 267-270; Madison, *op. cit.*, 278-282; National Civil Liberties Bureau, *The Truth About the I.W.W.*, New York, 1918.

51. SG, "Patriotic but on Guard," AF, XXIV, May 1917, 374; speech to New York State Federation of Labor, Aug. 13, 1917, in *Labor and the War, op. cit.*, 95-96, 100-101.

52. Haywood, *op. cit.*, 299; White E. Gibson to SG, Jan. 15, 1918, in AFL, "IWW" file.

53. Ralph Easley to Gen. Theodore A. Bingham, n.d., in AFL, Cabinet No. 27.

54. EC, Report to AFL, 37th Conv., 1917, 76-77; New York *Times Magazine*, Mar. 24, 1918.

55. EC, Report to AFL, 38th Conv., 1918, 118-119.

CHAPTER TWENTY-ONE

1. IFTU, *Report for the Years 1913 to 1919*, Berlin, 1919, 3-4, 18-38; "Report of the Activities of the Temporary Bureau of the IFTU at Amsterdam from December 1914 to March 1919," 3-6; "Labor's International Relations," AF, XXII, Nov. 1915; EC, Report to AFL, 35th Conv., 1915, 53-55.

2. SG to the Organized Working Class Movement of All Countries, Mar. 26, 1916, in IFTU, *Report*, 1913-1919, 39-41.

3. SG to Will Thorne, Oct. 21, 1916.

4. EC, Report to AFL, 36th Conv., 1916, 55.

5. SG to Karl Legien, Oct. 30, 1916; IFTU, *Report*, 1913-1919, 4-5, 41-44.

6. Lorwin, *Labor and Internationalism, op. cit.*, 157-159.

7. SG to the Petrograd Council of Workmen's and Soldiers' Deputies, and SG to Leon Jouhaux, May 7, 1917.

8. SG to Jan Oudegeest, May 24, 1917; SG to Lindquist, June 27, 1917.

9. Conference of Representatives of National Federations of Trade Unions of the Entente Powers, London, Sep. 10-11, 1917.

10. Lorwin, *Labor and Internationalism, op. cit.*, 184-185.

11. *Life*, II, 398-399.

12. Inter-Allied Labour and Socialist Conference, Westminster, London, Feb. 20-24, 1918.

13. For this and following data, *Life*, II, 404-411; Lang, *op. cit.*, 137; Ray Stannard Baker, *Woodrow Wilson*, New York, 1939, VII, 385-386.

14. William B. Sanders to George Barnes, Sep. 24, 1918, copy in possession of Mrs. Florence Gompers MacKay; London *Daily Mail*, Sep. 2, 1918; *Life*, II, 412-417.

15. Baker, *op. cit.*, VIII, 172-173.

16. Nottingham *Guardian*, Sep. 3, 1918.

17. Quoted in Madison, *op. cit.*, 102.

18. Sanders, *op. cit.*; *Life*, II, 417-425.

19. John Frey to Bernard Mandel, June 22, 1953; *Life*, II, 428-429.

20. "Proposals of AFL Delegates to Inter-Allied Labor Conference, London, Sep. 17-19, 1918."

21. Proceedings of the Inter-Allied Labor and Socialist Conference; *Life*, II, 431.

22. For this and following data, *Life*, II, 435ff.; Sanders, *op. cit.*,; SG, Memorandum, "Description of Luncheon with Marshal Haig," in AFL, "SG Biographical" file.

23. W. H. Buckler to Irwin Laughlin, Oct. 29, 1918, copy in possession of Mrs. MacKay; *Life*, II, 453-456.

24. John Frey, "When Gompers Spoke Before the One Packed Meeting of His Career," in AFL, "SG Biographical" file.

25. *Life*, II, 458-467; David F. Wilbur, "Mr. Samuel Gompers and his Mission to Genoa," copy in possession of Mrs. MacKay.

26. Buckler, *op. cit.*; Grand Rapids *Herald*, Sep. 5, 1918; SG, personal file.

27. John Frey to Bernard Mandel, June 22, 1953; Mrs. Eloise Giles to Mandel, June 23, 1953; Florence Gompers MacKay, "My Grandfather, Samuel Gompers," *Quarterly of the Cleveland Federation of Labor*, XIX, Fall 1950, 25; *Life*, II, 468-472.

28. "The Nation's Tribute to American Labor's Service Abroad," AF, XXV, Dec. 1918, 1073f.

CHAPTER TWENTY-TWO

1. IFTU, *Report*, 1913-1919, 57-58.

2. SG to Jan Oudegeest, Nov. 20, 1918; SG to Woodrow Wilson, Nov. 30, 1918; Wilson to SG, n.d.

3. SG to Woodrow Wilson, Dec. 21, 1918.

4. John W. Davis to Secretary of State, Dec. 20, 24, and 30, 1918, in AFL, "Peace Conference" file; SG to Charles R. Bowerman, Dec. 28, 1918; Report of Temporary Bureau of IFTU, *op. cit.*, 12-14.

5. SG, interview in New York *Tribune*, Feb. 17, 1919; Report of AFL Delegation to the Peace Conference, AFL, 39th Conv., 1919, 13-31; Minutes, AFL Delegation to the Peace Conference, in AFL, "Peace Conference" file.

6. *Ibid.*; James Duncan, *A Few Thoughts Incidental to an American Labor Mission to Europe on the Peace Treaty of 1919*, Quincy, n.d.

7. IFTU, Report of International Conference of Trade-Unions, Bern, Feb. 5-9, 1919; Report of AFL Delegation to Peace Conference, *op. cit.*

8. New York *Evening World*, Feb. 2, 1919; *The Literary Digest*, Feb. 8, 1919.

9. James T. Shotwell, "The International Labor Organization as an Alternative to Violent Revolution," in *The Annals* of the American Academy of Political and Social Science, CLVI, 1933, 18-20.

10. Proceedings of the Commission on International Labor Legislation, in ILO, *Official Bulletin*, I, 1919-1920, Geneva, 1923, 1-49; Remarks of SG at the Commission, Feb. 6-7, 1919, in AFL, "Addresses" file.

11. *Ibid.*, 7-183.

12. *Ibid.*, 158-226; ILO, *Report Presented to the Peace Conference by the Commission on International Labor Legislation*, Geneva, 1920.

13. *Ibid.*, 284-308; SG, address at Philadelphia, Feb. 11, 1921, in AFL, "Addresses General" file.

14. AFL, 39th Conv., 1919, 86, 399-416.

15. SG, "Why the Peace Treaty Should be Ratified," Washington, 1919.

CHAPTER TWENTY-THREE

1. Lang, *op. cit.*, 144-148; "Six Years in the Shadow," AF, XXXII, Jan. 1925, 39-41.

2. SG, Press Statement, Jan. 27, 1920.

3. Lang, *op. cit.*; "Six Years in the Shadow," *op. cit.*

4. *The Independent*, CXIII, Dec. 27, 1924, 558; John Spargo, "The Passing of Gompers and the Future of Organized Labor," *The North American Review*, CCXXI, Mar. 1925, 412.

5. *Life*, I, 509; John Frey to Bernard Mandel, June 22, 1953; Lang, *op cit.*, 196, 221; Florence Gompers MacKay to Mandel, July 5, 1953; New York *Times*, Dec. 21, 1924, Mar. 22 and 23, 1925.

6. Florence Thorne to Bernard Mandel, July 7, 1953.

7. SG to Matthew Woll, Sep. 15, 1921, in *Personal Letters*, II, 348-349.

8. SG, editorial in AF, XXXI, June 1924, 481.

9. Francis Tyson, "Why Mr. Gompers Is Afraid," *The New Republic*, XXXVI, Sep. 5, 1923, 40-42; Foster Rhea Dulles, *Labor in America*, New York, 1955, 230.

10. *Life*, II, 513, 533.

11. Lens, *op. cit.*, 163.

12. New York *Sun*, Dec. 17, 1916.

13. New York *Times Magazine*, Mar. 24, 1918; SG, address at Council of Foreign Relations, New York, Dec. 10, 1918, in AF, XXVI, Feb. 1919, 158f.; address to Chamber of Commerce, Jan. 8, 1920, in AF, XXVII, Feb. 1920, 134.

14. SG, "The Fundamental Issue," New York *Times*, July 23, 1922; "The Wall Street Incubus on Industry," Aug. 19, 1922, in AFL, "Wheeler Syndicate" file.

15. SG to Robert Hoxie, Sept. 17, 1914; Nadworny, *op. cit.*, 73-74, 89.

16. SG to Morris L. Cooke, Sep. 6 and Oct. 2, 1919; McKelvey, *op. cit.*, 77; Nadworny, *op. cit.*, 104-121.

17. SG to Morris Cooke, Jan. 19, 1920; *Annals* of the American Academy of Political and Social Science, XCI, 1920.

18. Nadworny, *op. cit.*, 144-151.

19. SG, address to Associated Advertising Clubs, New Orleans, Sep. 22, 1919, in *Labor and the Employer*, *op. cit.*, 55-57; "If I Were an Employer," *System*, XXXVII, Apr. 1920.

20. AF, XXVIII, Jan. 1921.

21. SG, "Let Us All Know," AF, XXIX, May 1922, 351-352; *Life*, II, 25-26.

22. SG, "The Road to Industrial Democracy," AF, XXXI, June 1924, 481-485.

23. SG, remarks to EC, Sep. 16, 1922, in AFL, "Addresses General" file.

24. SG, "The Coming Congress," Jan. or Feb. 1923, in AFL, "Wheeler Syndicate" file.

25. SG, "From Politics to Industry," AF, XXX, May 1923, 396-399.

26. SG, "Industry Must be its Own Doctor," Sep. 20, 1923, in AFL, "Wheeler Syndicate" file; Edward F. Roberts, "Proposes Third House of Congress," Feb. 1924, in AFL, "Press Statement" file; EC, Report to AFL, 43rd Conv., 1923, 31-34.

27. SG, "What Means the Red Dragnet in America?" Oct. 12, 1923, in AFL, "Wheeler Syndicate" file; speech at cigarmakers' convention, Aug. 24, 1923, in AF, XXX, Oct. 1923, 810-811.

28. "An Analysis of Fascism," AF, XXX, Nov. 1923, 927-933; SG, "Significant Movements in Europe," AF, XXXI, July 1924, 565-569.

CHAPTER TWENTY-FOUR

1. Delegates' Report, Amsterdam Congress, IFTU, 1919, to AFL, in AF, XXVI, Oct. 1919, 92lf.

2. SG, press statement, Amsterdam, Aug. 26, 1919, in AFL, "IFTU" file. Either the city or the date is wrong, probably the date; Aug. 16 is likely correct.

3. AFL, 40th Conv., 1920.

4. SG and Matthew Woll, "European Brainstorm," AF, XXVII, Oct. 1920, 919-928; EC to Oudegeest, Mar. 5, 1921, in AF, XXVIII, Apr. 1921, 328-330.

5. Oudegeest to EC, Apr. 12, 1921, in AF, XXVIIII, July 1921, 592-594; SG, "Labor in Europe and America," AF, XXX, June 1923, 461-467.

6. Life, II, 543.

7. EC, Report to AFL, 35th Conv., 1915, 56-59.

8. Pan-AFL Conference Committee to the Workers of Latin America, Feb. 9, 1917, in AF, XXIV, Mar. 1917, 196-197; Memorandum by SG, May 8, 1918, in AFL, "Mexico" file.

9. AF, XXV, Nov. 1918, 986.

10. Proceedings, 1st Conv., Pan-AFL, 1918, in Pan-American Labor Press, Dec. 4, 1918.

11. Proceedings, 2nd Congress, Pan-AFL, 1919.

12. Lorwin, Labor and Internationalism, op. cit., 296.

13. Proceedings, 3rd Cong., Pan-AFL, 1921, 16-63.

14. New York Times, Jan. 18, 1921, 17; Proceedings, 3rd Cong., Pan-AFL, 1921, 86-93, 132-133; Lorwin, Labor and Internationalism, op. cit., 297.

15. Lorwin, Labor and Internationalism, op. cit., 298-301; SG, "Foreign Labor," op. cit.

CHAPTER TWENTY-FIVE

1. American Alliance for Labor and Democracy, press release, Sep. 17, 1919; SG, address to Boston Chamber of Commerce, Jan. 18, 1920, in AF, XXVII, Feb. 1920, 134-137.

2. Steel Strike Hearings, op. cit., 117-118, 156; see also Yellen, op. cit., 251ff.

3. William Z. Foster, From Bryan to Stalin, New York, 1937, 103-108.

4. Ibid., 108-112; SG, "Steps Toward Democracy," AF, XXV, Sep. 1918, 805-808.

5. Ibid., 112-116.

6. Steel Strike Hearings, 16-18, 30, 80-81, 97-98, 161, 177, 224-225, 368.

7. SG to EC, Sep. 19, 1919; SG to John Fitzpatrick, Sep. 11, 1919; Fitzpatrick to SG, Sep. 12, 1919; SG to M. F. Tighe, Sep. 16, 1919; Fitzpatrick to Woodrow Wilson, Sep. 18, 1919; Steel Strike Hearings, 4-8, 106-110; SG, address, Oct. 28, 1919, in Labor and the Employer, op. cit., 200-201.

8. Robert K. Murray, "Communism and the Great Steel Strike of 1919," Mississippi Valley Historical Review, XXXVIII, Dec. 1951, 445-466; Steel Strike Hearings, 31-34.

9. Steel Strike Hearings, 110-117, 380-429.

10. Commons, History, op. cit., IV, 468; Murray, op. cit., 452; Horace B. Davis, Labor and Steel, New York, 1933, 250-251; William Z. Foster, Misleaders of Labor, n.p., 1927, 145; Foster, From Bryan to Stalin, op. cit., 122f; Hearings, Rules Committee of the H.R., 66C 2S, 1920, 156-157, 171-173, quoted in Robert W. Dunn, ed., The Palmer Raids, New York, 1948, 23.

11. EC, Report to AFL, 40th Conv., 1920, 182-193; EC, press statement, Nov. 9, 1919.

12. Minutes, EC, Nov. 14, 1919; SG to James Duncan, Dec. 23, 1921 (?), in SG, Personal Letters, II, 345-

346.

13. *Proceedings of the First Industrial Conference,* Oct. 6-23, 1919, Washington, 1920.

14. Robert K. Murray, *Red Scare,* Minneapolis, 1955, 67-82, 223-238.

15. Matthew Josephson, *Union House, Union Bar,* New York, 1956, 147-148; New York *Times,* Nov. 1919, *passim.*

16. Murray, *Red Scare, op. cit.,* 108-109; AF, XXVI, Mar. 1919, 237, April 1919, 316-318, Nov. 1919, 1050-1055, Dec. 1919, 1131.

17. SG, "What Means the Red Dragnet in America?" *op. cit.*; SG, "The Safety of Trade Unionism," AF, XXVI, May 1919, 398-400; address to N.J. legislature, Mar. 22, 1920, in AF, XXVII, May 1920, 432; editorial, AF,

XXVII, June 1920, 547-548.

18. *Hearings before the Committee on the Judiciary,* H.R., 66C 2S, Feb. 4 and 6, 1920, 231-252; SG, "The Graham-Rice 'Sedition Bill' Would Manufacture Law-Breakers," AF, XXVII, Feb. 1920, 138-139; EC, Report to AFL, 40th Conv., 1920, 101-102.

19. AFL, 39th Conv., 1919, 391-396.

20. Lucy Robins, *War Shadows,* New York, 1922, 1-97.

21. Lang, *op. cit.,* 160-170.

22. AFL, 40th Conv., 1920, 212-213.

23. Conference between Attorney-General and representatives of AFL, Sept. 14, 1920, in SG Conference Book No. 1; Lang, *op. cit.,* 178-181; SG to Woodrow Wilson, Oct. 15, 1920.

24. Robins, *op. cit.,* 271-273, 318f.

CHAPTER TWENTY-SIX

1. SG to International Unions, Oct. 28, 1919; John Frey to SG, Nov. 26, 1919; SG to Frey, Dec. 1, 1919.

2. "Labor, Its Grievances, Protest and Demands," Washington, 1920.

3. SG to All Organized Labor, Feb. 12, 1920, in AF, XXVII, Mar. 1920, 233-236.

4. SG, editorial in AF, XXVII, July 1920, 656f.; SG, "Read! Think! Choose!" *ibid.,* Aug. 1920, 729f.; William English Walling, *American Labor and American Democracy,* New York, 1926, I, 57-60.

5. Report of Labor Non-Partisan Political Campaign Committee, AF, XXVII, Sep. 1920, 810f.; SG, "How Calvin Coolidge Became a 'Great' National Figure," Washington, 1919.

6. Matthew Woll, "Labor Seeking Light on Wages," *Forbes Magazine,* 1922, quoted in David J. Saposs, *Readings in Trade Unionism,* New York, 1926, 267; SG, editorial in AF, XXVII, Mar. 1920, 246f., and XXVIII, Sep. 1921, 784-787.

7. SG, "Labor's Protest Against a

Rampant Tragedy," Washington, 1920; Walling, *op. cit.,* I, 170-189.

8. "Report of the President's Conference on Unemployment," Sep. 26-Oct. 13, 1921, 1-30, 135-141; *Life,* II, 16-17.

9. SG, editorial in AF, XXVIII, Nov. 1921, 959-960.

10. SG, "Abolish Unemployment," AF, XXIX, Jan. 1922, 13f.

11. Martin, *op. cit.,* 149-153.

12. SG to Edwin Y. Webb, Dec. 6, 1917; SG to Woodrow Wilson, Dec. 14, 1917.

13. SG, *Address before Joint Legislative Committee Hearing, Albany, New York, Feb. 26, 1918.*

14. *Hearings before the subcommittee of the Committee on the Judiciary,* U.S. Sen., 66C 1S, on the Bills to Prohibit the Liquor Traffic, Wash., 1919, I, 5-25.

15. SG to J. de Lagerberg, June 29, 1922; The *Bulletin* of the Association Against the Prohibition Amendment, Feb. 26, 1924.

16. SG, editorial in AF, XXV, Jan. 1918, 58-60; EC, Report to AFL, 39th

Conv., 1919.

17. SG, "America Must Not be Overwhelmed," AF, XXXI, Apr. 1924, 313-314.

18. EC, Report to AFL, 40th Conv., 1920, 97-98; New York Times, Sep. 24, 1919, 27.

19. SG, "Era of Slavery is Passed," AF, XXVI, Nov. 1919, 1046-1047; EC, Report to AFL, 40th Conv., 1920, 98-100.

20. Debate Between Samuel Gompers and Henry J. Allen, May 28, 1920, New York, 1920, 1-16, 66, 77-84.

21. SG, editorial in AF, XXVIII, July 1921, 580-581.

22. SG, editorial in AF, XXV, Jan. 1918, 52-54; "The Open Shop," address before the Empire Club, Toronto, Apr. 19, 1921, in Empire Club of Canada: Addresses . . .,Toronto, 1923, 164-179.

23. Lieberman, op. cit., 99-107; Charles O. Gregory, Labor and the Law, New York, 1946, 165-168.

24. EC, Report to AFL, 41st Conv., 1921; SG to EC, Feb. 8, 1922.

25. SG, "Let's Save our Children,"

AF, XXIV, Oct. 1917, 860; "Child Life Must be Conserved," AF, XXV, Aug. 1918, 692.

26. SG, editorial in AF, XXIX, June 1922, 413-414; AFL, Press Statement, Apr. 10, 1923.

27. SG, "The Coolidge Challenge Accepted," Chicago Daily News, Sep. 26, 1924.

28. SG, " 'Open Shop' Hypocrisy Exposed," AF, XXVIII, Feb. 1921, 110-114; SG to Newton D. Baker, Oct. 2, 1922, in AF, XXIX, Nov. 1922, 834-836.

29. Commons, History, op. cit., IV, 516-524.

30. SG, "The Railroad Crisis," AF, XXVIII, Nov. 1921, 964-966.

31. AFL, Press Statements, July 13, 14, and 17, 1922.

32. AFL, Press Statement, Aug. 1, 1922; SG to All Organized Labor, Aug. 19, 1922, in AF, XXIX, Sep. 1922, 663-664; AFL, Press Statement, Oct. 23, 1922; Lens, op. cit., 170; Commons, History, op. cit., IV, 516-524.

33. SG to All Organized Labor, Sep. 18, 1922, in AF, XXIX, Oct. 1922, 769.

CHAPTER TWENTY-SEVEN

1. New York Times, Jan. 27, 1920, 12.

2. William English Walling, "Labor at Cross-Ways," New York Times, July 3, 1921, VI, 5.

3. Harold Seidman, Labor Czars, New York, 1938, 58-60.

4. Christie, op. cit., 200-216; Seidman, op. cit., 70-74, 81-82; Lens, op. cit., 73, 102; Madison, op. cit., 146-147.

5. New York State, Joint Legislative Committee on Housing, Hearings on New York City Housing, Annual Session of the Legislature, 1922, 6714-6889.

6. Life, II, 18; Lang, op. cit., 146-147.

7. C. Wright Mills, The New Men of Power, New York, 1948, 129-131;

Seidman, op. cit., 53-55.

8. William Z. Foster, "The Principles and Program of the Trade Union Educational League," The Labor Herald, I, Mar. 1922, 3-7.

9. Foster, From Bryan to Stalin, op. cit., 164-165; "Twenty Years of Communist Trade Union Policy," The Communist, XVIII, Sep. 1939, 804-809.

10. The Labor Herald, I, Apr. 1922, 12.

11. "Conference of representative labor men of Chicago, Apr. 12, 1922," in AFL, "TUEL" file; see also SG, "Another Attempt at Soviet Dictatorship Unmasked," AF, XXIX, May 1922, 337-340; Lens, op. cit., 177.

12. Alexander Trachtenberg, "The

Soviet Union and the American People," *The Communist*, XVIII, Sep. 1939, 873-874.

13. SG and William English Walling, *Out of Their Own Mouths*, New York, 1921, v-vii.

14. EC, Report to AFL, 41st Conv., 1921, 90-102.

15. AFL, 42nd Conv., 1922, 420-459.

16. SG, "Should a Political Party Be Formed," address to a Labor Conference, New York, Dec. 9, 1918, Washington, 1919; AF, XXVI, Jan. 1919, 33f.

17. William Mitch to SG, Feb. 23, 1920; SG to Mitch, Mar. 8, 1920; AF, XXVII, Apr. 1920, 332-334.

18. Ed. Nockels to SG, Mar. 10, 1920; SG to Nockels, Mar. 16, 1920; Nockels to SG, Mar. 25, 1920; in AF, XXVII, May 1920, 438-442.

19. William Z. Foster, "The Federated Farmer-Labor Party," *The Labor Herald*, II, Aug. 1923, 3-7; Saposs, *Left Wing Unionism, op. cit.*, 75.

20. SG, statement at EC meeting, Feb. 14-20, 1922, in AFL, "Addresses General" file; New York *Times*, July 11 and 12, 1922; Foster, *From Bryan to Stalin, op. cit.*, 175-184; AFL, 43rd Conv., 1923.

CHAPTER TWENTY-EIGHT

1. EC, Report to AFL, 44th Conv., 1924, 54-56; AF, XXXI, Mar. 1924, 209-221, Apr. 1924, 343-349.

2. AFL, Press Statement, Jan. 28, 1924.

3. "Memo regarding the activities of President Samuel Gompers immediately upon his return to headquarters after his months of illness in New York and Atlantic City," in AFL, "SG Biographical" file, hereafter cited as "Activities of SG"; W. C. Roberts, "Brief Memorandum of the last six months of Samuel Gompers' life," in AFL, "SG Biographical" file; Memorandum, June 24, 1924, and Report of Meeting of Subcommittee of Committee on Platform and Resolutions, June 25, 1924, in AFL, "Addresses General" file.

4. Kenneth Campbell MacKay, *The Progressive Movement of 1924*, New York, 1947, 54-91.

5. Kirk H. Porter, Comp., *National Party Platforms*, New York, 1924, 516-522.

6. SG to EC, July 8, 1924.

7. AFL, Press Statement, Aug. 4, 1924, AF, XXXI, Sep. 1924, 708-711.

8. MacKay, *op. cit.*, 199-204.

9. New York *Times*, Sep. 23, 1924.

10. Goldman, *op. cit.*, 295-296.

11. Lang, *op. cit.*, 224-225.

12. Frank Tannenbaum, "Samuel Gompers' Last Convention," *The Survey*, LIII, Jan. 1, 1925, 391-394.

13. AFL, 44th Conv., 1924, 5-6; Tannenbaum, *op. cit.*

14. *Ibid.*, 277-281.

15. "Activities of SG"; *Life*, II, 546-549.

16. Report of the Proceedings of the 4th Congress of the Pan-AFL, Dec. 3-9, 1924, 27-104.

17. "Activities of SG."

18. Roberts, *op. cit.*; *Life*, II, 550-557; *In Memorium*, Washington, 1925.

INDEX

Note: Unions are entered under trade or industry. E.g., the United Mine Workers is listed under "Miners."